The Sportsman's Almanac

THE
Sportsman's Almanac

A Guide to Hunting and Fishing in the
50 American States and National Forests
and Their Principal Game—
Mammals, Birds, and Fishes

by
CARLEY FARQUHAR

Illustrated by
Matthew Kalmenoff

Harper & Row, Publishers
New York, Evanston, and London

FIRST EDITION

LIBRARY OF CONGRESS CATALOG CARD NUMBER: 64-25143

B-P

Contents

Foreword

It took courage and vision to outline the *Sportsman's Almanac* and a vast amount of work to put it together.

The result of this effort is an attractive and well-illustrated volume that contains an amazing amount of useful information, carefully arranged, and well presented.

It will be useful to any outdoorsman whether hunter, fisherman, canoe artist, or one who just likes to hike in unfamiliar territory. It will be almost indispensable to those who are planning hunting and fishing trips to states in which they are not residents.

The book is packed with information on each of the 50 states, giving major geographical features, license requirements for both resident and nonresident hunters, fishermen, and trappers. It lists for each state the principal game birds, mammals, and fish, and gives the major hunting, fishing, and trapping laws.

Where public facilities are available, it provides information on state fishing lakes, public hunting areas, state parks and forests, and access points to waters for anyone seeking unposted hunting, fishing, or camping areas. It lists guides and outfitting centers in areas where these are necessary, and also contains much material on salt water fishing in coastal states. In other sections are state listings of national forests, wilderness, primitive and wild areas, wildlife refuges, even ski slopes. There are also selections on canoe and wilderness trips and many other items useful to today's out-of-door man.

One interesting feature is the well-selected lists of the common names of game birds, mammals, and fish, together with cross references which make it possible to follow these local names through to the more widely used scientific designations.

With America turning more and more to the open country for recreation, it is easy to see the value of this book not only to the hunters, fishermen, and outdoor enthusiasts for whom it is primarily designed, but also to those planning automobile trips or vacations. Turning the pages of this book for a few moments will give any reader ideas of new and delightful vacation spots.

The author has skillfully assembled a vast number of facts and tabulated them in an easy-to-follow, tightly organized book. Because of the varied information it contains, *Sportsman's Almanac* should be a standard reference on the shelf of every outdoorsman regardless of his or her special interest.

Coming when state after state is providing increased outdoor facilities and when a vast national recreational program is just being launched, it could not be more timely.

IRA N. GABRIELSON
President, Wildlife Management Institute

Introduction

Each state issues regulations for fishing, hunting, and trapping designated mammals, birds, and fish, including license requirements, open and closed seasons, daily or season bag and possession limits, fishing gear and firearms permitted or prohibited, and methods of transporting game. Mammals, birds, and fish should not be taken unless listed as game or unprotected species. Special permits are usually issued for regulated fishing and hunting in wildlife management units and federal or state recreational areas. State regulations for taking waterfowl and other migratory game birds are within the framework of annual regulations established by the Fish and Wildlife Service, U.S. Department of the Interior. All hunters of waterfowl and other migratory game birds should check state regulations, and if 16 or more years of age, purchase the annual "Duck" stamp at a post office.*

Naturally seasons and license costs vary over the years. Yet in this book exact dates and prices are included to show the sportsman the relative costs of various types of licenses and tags, how the federal and state governments regulate firearms, and the regular seasons for each game animal. Before the hunter or fisherman sets out on a trip, he should contact the appropriate state department of fish and game, local U.S. Forest Service, or other authorized agent for current regulations. Addresses of these officials and other local information are listed for each state in Part I of this book.

In all states, resident and nonresident fishermen, hunters, and trappers must be prepared to show their licenses, permits, tags, firearms and equipment if requested to do so by a game warden or any authorized agent of the state. Servicemen on active duty at military installations are entitled to purchase resident licenses, and some states issue free permits to servicemen during their return home on

* The ban on shooting Canvasback and Redhead Ducks was lifted in the fall of 1964. The law now limits the hunter to a total of two birds of the following three species: Canvasback, Redhead, Woodduck; but not more than one of each species.

official leaves or furloughs. Resident owners (or renters) may fish, hunt, and trap on their lands without purchasing licenses, but some states restrict such privileges to lands used only for agricultural purposes.

It is *unlawful* in all states to fish, hunt, or trap on private property without permission granted by the landowner (preferably in writing); to fish, hunt, or trap on land other than his own residence without the required licenses, permits, tags, and/or stamps in possession; to change, mutilate, borrow, or transfer any license, stamp, or tag; fail to fill out and attach required stamps and tags to licenses or permits; carry or transport loaded guns or longbows ready for action except in hunting areas; shoot any firearms (including bow and arrow) from, or upon, a public highway; shoot game mammals, birds, and freshwater fish from any type of aircraft, sailboat, land or water motor vehicles; use a crossbow unless specifically permitted by law; carry firearms during special archery seasons; discharge any type of firearms within a limited distance of a dwelling, or any building used in connection with such dwelling (owner or renter excepted); use explosives or poison to take mammals, birds, or fish; hunt while under the influence of intoxicating liquor; fail to report an accident or death. Violations are punishable by fines and/or imprisonment plus loss of licenses, which are usually not reissued to convicted persons for one or more years.

If an unexpired license is lost, duplicates can usually be obtained for a small fee by filing an affidavit with an authorized agent of a state fish and game department, and providing proof of the loss or destruction, date of issue, and number of the original license. Full original fees are paid for lost game tags, which are generally issued at headquarters of state departments. Nonresidents may purchase licenses from the proper state department by forwarding a written request with the following information: the applicant's name, address, place of birth, citizenship if foreign born, age, sex, personal description (height, weight, color of eyes and hair), and a certified check or money order covering total cost of licenses and tags, plus 35 cents for the return of licenses and tags by certified or registered mail. A nonresident should send for his license at least two weeks before it is needed, or obtain the necessary licenses and tags after arriving in the state.

Licenses are required to take unprotected wildlife (including predators) in all states except California, Illinois, Kansas, Louisiana, Mississippi, Montana, Nebraska, Nevada, North Dakota, Utah, and Wyoming. In Florida a license is required only during the general hunting season. Only nonresidents must possess licenses to hunt unprotected wildlife in Maryland, Minnesota, and New Mexico. Nonresidents must purchase hunting licenses in all states except Arizona, Connecticut, Massachusetts, Nevada, New York, and Washington to hunt on private licensed shooting preserves, which usually provide excellent hunting of pen-raised game birds from September 1–March 31.

The American Forest Products Industries have generously permitted fishing, hunting, and trapping on most of their private lands in spite of fire hazards, broken gates and locks, garbage litter, theft, and vandalism. Regular state licenses are required, and according to recent surveys by Chief Forester J. C. McClellan, hunters now have access to 53,654,702 acres, trappers to 46, 992, 548 acres, and 2,375,992 acres are game refuges or game management areas. There are 56,646,-326 acres open to fishermen, including 2,436 natural lakes, 370 artificial lakes, 37,255 miles of streams, and 2,500 miles of shoreline. Sportsmen should not trespass without permission from owners, who may charge fees in some places. For detailed information, write to the Chief Forester, American Forest Products Industries, Inc., 1816 N Street, N.W., Washington 6, D.C.

The Bureau of Land Management, U. S. Department of the Interior, administers approximately 177 million acres in 27 states (mainly western) and 300 million acres in Alaska. Some wilderness tracts are adjacent to federal or state forests, parks, recreation areas, and wildlife refuges. Under the Recreation and Public Purposes Act of 1954, the Secretary of the Interior was authorized to sell or lease public domain lands for recreation, education, health, and other purposes. State and local governments, nonprofit associations and corporations, civic and service groups, and sportsmen's associations are qualified applicants, provided that substantial financial investments in facilities are proposed or that the tract will complement a program on adjoining lands. Millions of persons use such public lands for camping, fishing, and hunting in remote areas, and the Bureau of Land Management (BLM) cooperates with other government agencies in the development of public recreation facilities. The pamphlet *Community Recreation and the Public Domain* containing the Recreation and Public Purposes Act and related laws may be purchased for 25 cents from the Superintendent of Documents, U. S. Government Printing Office, Washington 25, D.C.

Open seasons and regulations may be changed because of local conditions, and sportsmen should request the latest information when applying for licenses, permits, and tags.

The information about the states was derived from material sent to me by officials of various departments. The following persons were particularly helpful in tracking down facts: Bert R. Coleman of the Arizona Development Board; Vernon Craig of the Montana Department of Fish and Game; R. A. Hodgins of the South Dakota Department of Game, Fish, and Parks; Rosser Malone of the Georgia State Game and Fish Commission; George C. Moore of the Kansas Forestry, Fish, and Game Commission; Frank Phipps of the Kentucky Department of Fish and Wildlife Resources; and Charles R. Shaw of the Louisiana Wild Life and Fisheries Commission.

The advice and scientific knowledge of W. I. Follett, Curator of Fishes at the California Academy of Sciences in San Francisco was my good fortune. Dr. A. H. Miller of the University of California at Berkeley, and Charles S. Thaeler, Assistant Curator of Birds and Mammals at the Museum of Vertebrate Zoology were kind enough to check my lists of birds and mammals.

The helpful suggestions and important information received from the following persons were greatly appreciated in my research: Steward M. Brandborg, Associate Executive Director of the Wilderness Society; David Brower, Executive Director of the Sierra Club; William K. Carpenter, President of the International Game Fish Association; Leonard L. Davis, Jr., Executive Secretary of the National Rifle Association of America; Malcolm Davis of the Division of Conservation, National Wildlife Federation; Ira N. Gabrielson, President of the Wildlife Management Institute; Wes Hunnicut, Chief of the Bowhunting Division of the National Field Archery Association of the United States; Tim Kelley, editor and publisher of the *Official Colorado Fishing and Hunting Guide*; J. C. McClellan, Chief Forester of the American Forest Products Industries; and F. A. Williams, Acting Chief, Branch of Management and Enforcement, Bureau of Sport Fisheries and Wildlife, U.S. Department of the Interior.

Forest supervisors of the U.S. Department of Agriculture Forest Service promptly answered all queries and sent information and pictures that gave me a better insight into their service to the people. I am most grateful to George Brown and Loren S. Woerpel of the North Central Region; Howard C. Cook of the Wayne and Hoosier National Forests; T. C. Fearnow and L. K. Kelley of the Eastern Region; E. Arnold Hanson of the Northern Region; R. E. Hedland and L. P. Neff of the Superior National Forest; J. N. Hessel of the Rocky Mountain Region; Lyle M. Klubben of the California Region; John Mattoon of the Intermountain Region; Chandler P. St. John and J. Morgan Smith of the Southwestern Region; John Sieker, Director of the Division of Recreation and Land Uses; A. E. Smith of the Winema National Forest; J. K. Vessey of the Southern Region; J. H. Wood and J. Kreimeyer of the Pacific Northwest Region.

The encouragement and interest of Nancy Frost McCarthy and the assistance of Teddie Galvan of Gilroy aided in the completion of this book.

C. F.

Gilroy, California
September 1964

PART I

ALABAMA

Area: 51,998 square miles (land area—51,060 square miles); rank in nation–28
Bird: Yellowhammer (*colaptes auratus lateus*), adopted 1927
Capital city: Montgomery on the Alabama River in Montgomery County; population (1960)–134,393; rank in state–3
Counties: 67
Elevations: Highest, Cheaha Mountain (2,407 ft.) in Clay and Talladega counties; lowest, Mobile Bay (sea level)
Fish: Tarpon (*Tarpon atlanticus*), adopted 1955
Flower: Camellia, adopted 1959
Geographic center: 12 miles southwest of Clanton, Chilton County
Nicknames: Cotton State, Cradle of the Confederacy, Heart of Dixie, Lizard State, Yellowhammer State
Population (1960): 3,266,740; rank in nation–19
Tidal shoreline: 607 miles (including islands, bays, and streams to a point where tidal waters narrow to 100 ft. wide)
Tree: Southern Pine (*Pinus palastris*), adopted 1949

Alabama is a Deep South state with a northern boundary line between Tennessee extending along the 35th parallel from Georgia on the east to Mississippi on the west. The great Appalachian Range terminates in the rugged northeastern highlands of Lookout and Raccoon mountains between the Piedmont Plateau ending in Chambers, Clay, Randolph, and Tallapoosa counties, and the Cumberland Plateau stretching across northern Alabama. Fertile foothills gradually slope southward into rolling plains and coastal lowlands at Mobile Bay on the Gulf of Mexico.

Major rivers among among the network of large and small streams include the Chattahoochee River on the Georgia boundary; the Perdido River flowing into the Gulf of Mexico between Baldwin County and the state of Florida; the Coosa and Tallapoosa rivers rolling down from the northeast, and the Cahaba River in central Alabama. All their waters flow into the Alabama River. The western Black Warrior River merges with the Tombigbee River at Demopolis and at the southern tip of Clarke County, the Alabama and Tombigbee pour their waters together. The Mobile River flows through Mobile County to reach Mobile Bay; and a tributary, the Tensaw River, runs through Baldwin County to empty in the Gulf of Mexico. The city of Mobile (1960 population—

3

202,779) at the head of the deep 30-mile Mobile Bay is a famous fishing and shipping port.

The mighty Tennessee River penetrates the northeastern corner of the state at Long Island in Jackson County, and harnessed by dams, it winds through the Cumberland Plateau and at the northwest tip of Alabama, re-enters the state of Tennessee at Pickwick Lake (67 square miles) near Waterloo in Lauderdale County. Other large reservoirs forming a chain of lakes on the Tennessee River are Guntersville Lake (108 square miles) in Jackson and Marshall counties; Wheeler Lake (105 square miles) between Colbert, Lauderdale, Lawrence, Madison, and Morgan counties; and Wilson Lake (25 square miles) in the Muscle Shoals area near the tri-cities of Florence in Lauderdale County, Sheffield, and Tuscumbia in Colbert County. Impounded waters on the Coosa River include Lay Dam Reservoir and Mitchell Lake between Chilton and Coosa counties, and Jordan Lake north of Wetumpke in Elmore County. Bartletts Ferry Lake, created by a dam on the Chattahoochee River, is near Blanton in Lee County, and Lake Martin (62 square miles) on the Tallapoosa River is west of Dadeville in Tallapoosa County. The smaller Choctawhatchee, Conecuh, Escambia, and Pea rivers with many tributaries are in southeastern Alabama.

LICENSES

Resident licenses to fish and hunt are issued to persons between the ages of 16–65 who have been residents for at least 6 months prior to an application for any license. A resident under the age of 16 may fish without a license, but must have a permit to hunt upon lands other than his own residence, or be accompanied by a person at least 21 years of age who is authorized to hunt on such areas. Residents 65 or more years of age may obtain free permits (issue fee 15 cents) to hunt and fish without licenses. Fishing with an ordinary hook and line in the county of a person's legal residence, and for saltwater fish in tidal waters does not require a license.

Sport spearing of commercial and nongame fish in fresh and salt water is lawful provided that the fisherman is completely submerged while in the act of spearing. The possession of a spear, spear gun, or spearing device in a boat, on or in the water, is considered to be prima facie evidence that the person in possession of such equipment is engaged in spear fishing. Such person must possess a spear fishing license in addition to his fishing license.

No person may obtain a license to take, attempt to take, catch or kill furbearing animals unless he has lived continuously in Alabama for at least one year prior to the opening date of the furbearing animal season. Fur dealers are required to live continuously for one year prior to October 1 before applying for a resident license. Licenses to breed game for commercial purposes are issued to any properly accredited person, firm, association, or corporation but Quail offered for sale must not be killed by shooting with firearms. All persons 16 or more years of age must purchase a federal "Duck" stamp to hunt migratory game birds. State license period: Oct. 1–Sept. 30.

*Resident license fees:** Hook and line fishing outside of county of residence, $1.00; rod and reel fishing, (or) use of artificial bait, fly, or lure (includes right to fish by hook and line, $2.00; spear fishing (in addition to fishing license), $5.00; statewide hunting (includes archery), $3.00; county hunting (including archery), $1.00; trapping furbearing animals, $5.00; fur dealer (minimum fee), $25.00; game breeder (game animals and birds, fur-bearers), $10.00; commercial Quail breeder, $25.00; animal and bird collector (scientific purposes only), $1.00; federal "Duck" stamp, $3.00; permit for "Coon-on-the-Log" contest (date of show only), $1.50.

*Nonresident license fees:** Annual fishing, $5.00; fishing 7 consecutive days, $2.00; annual spear fishing, $7.50; spear fishing 7 consecutive days, $2.50; annual hunting, $25.00; hunting 7 consecutive days, $10.00; hunting preserve shooting, $10.25; fur dealer, $300.00; federal "Duck" stamp, $3.00.

HUNTING AND TRAPPING

Game animals: Alligator, Bear, Beaver, Deer, Fox, Opossum, Rabbit, Raccoon, Squirrel. OPEN SEASONS: Deer—Nov. 1–Jan. 1, including archery only during first 9 or more days. Opossum, Rabbit, Raccoon—mid-October to mid-February. Squirrels—mid-October to mid-January. There are special days for use of bow and arrow, guns, dogs, and stalk hunting of Deer and other game during controlled hunts lasting 1–30 or more days in Wildlife Management areas. Free permits for such hunts are issued during open seasons. SEASON BAG LIMITS: Buck Deer with antlers visible above the natural hairline—3. Rabbits, 6 per day. Squirrels, 10 per day. Opossum and Raccoon, no limits.

Furbearing animals: Bear, Beaver, Civet Cat, Fox, Mink, Muskrat, Opossum, Otter, Raccoon, Skunk, Weasel. OPEN TRAPPING SEASONS: Civet Cat, Fox, Mink, Muskrat, Opossum, Otter, Raccoon, Skunk, Weasel—mid-November to mid-February. Opossum and Raccoon may be killed or captured with the use of a light, and/or dog, but without guns between sunset and daylight during open season in about 20 counties. Raccoon for "Coon-on-the-Log" contests may be captured only during open seasons. Not more than 10 Raccoons may be kept in cap-

---

* Plus issue fee of 15 cents.

tivity by a sportsmen's association, which should be incorporated as a nonprofit organization with a paid-up membership of not less than 25 members. FULLY PROTECTED: Alligator, Bear—no open seasons. NOT PROTECTED: Beaver, Bobcat, Fox (except trapping), and Nutria may be taken at any time. There are no bag limits on any furbearing animals.

Game birds: Brant, Coot (commonly called Poule d'Eaux or Mud Hen), Dove, Ducks (except Canvasback and Redhead), Gallinule, Geese, Merganser, Bob White Quail, Rails, Sora, Wild Turkey Gobbler, Wilson's Snipe (Jacksnipe), Woodcock. OPEN SEASONS*: Coot, Ducks, Merganser—3 weeks in December. Dove—split seasons of about 6 weeks after Oct. 1 and from mid-December into January. Gallinule, Rails, Sora—Oct. 1 to mid-November. Brant, Geese—mid-November to early January. Quail—mid-November to mid-February. Wilson's Snipe— mid-December to mid-January. Turkey Gobbler—Nov. 1–Jan. 1 and mid-March to mid-April. Woodcock—mid-December to mid-January. Hunting preserve shooting—at any time. FULLY PROTECTED: Canvasback and Redhead ducks, Turkey Hens, Ring-neck Pheasant or "other exotic bird" not designated as a game bird or unprotected species. NOT PROTECTED: Blue Darters, Buzzards, Crows, Chicken Hawks, Cooper's Hawk, Sharp-shinned Hawk, Great Horned Owl, English Sparrows, and Starlings may be taken at any time.

FIREARMS

Game animals and birds may be taken with shotguns not larger than 10 gauge, and capable of holding not more than 3 shells in the magazine and chamber combined. If originally capable of holding more than 3 shells, magazines should be plugged with one-piece metal or wooden fillers incapable of removal through the loading end. If any person has in his possession during open seasons on the waters, in the fields or forests, any automatic loading or hand-operated repeating shotgun not reduced to lawful capacity, it is considered to be prima facie evidence that the possessor is hunting with an unplugged gun.

Deer may be hunted with rifles of .240 caliber or larger, but in the Covington County Management area, only shotguns using buckshot are legal. In Colbert County, only rifled slugs may be used in shotguns to take Deer. Rifles may be used to take other game except migratory game birds. There are no special regulations for the use of bow and arrows.

Shooting hours: Resident game, daylight to sunset. Exceptions are Opossum and Racoon, sunset to daylight; Fox, day or night; Gobbler Turkey, daylight until 12 o'clock noon. Opossum and Raccoon may be taken

---

* Check current state regulations.

in 47 counties between sunset and daylight with the use of a light and/or shotgun not larger than no. 8. Migratory game birds, sunrise to sunset. Exceptions are Dove, 12 o'clock noon until sunset; 12 o'clock noon on the opening day of the Duck season, otherwise sunrise to sunset.

FISHING

Game fish: Largemouth and Smallmouth Bass (commonly called Trout or Green Trout), Rock Bass (Goggle Eye), Calico Bass, White Lake Bass (commonly called Striped Bass), Yellow Bass, Bream, Crappie, Perch and Pickerel families including Jack Pickerel, Wall-eyed Pike (Jack Salmon), and all members of the Sunfish family including Bluegill, Coppernosed, and Red Belly. Saltwater Striped Bass and Rockfish are considered game when taken in fresh water. OPEN SEASONS:* All year and no size limits.

Game fish may be caught only with an ordinary hook and line, fly, troll, or spinner. Trolling from any boat or other floating device is prohibited in Bay Delvan, Bay Grass, Bay Minette, Big Bateau, Big Bay John, Chuckfey, Chocolata Bay, D'Olive Bay, Grand Bay, Gustang Bay, John's Bend, Little Bateau, Little Bay John, and Polecat Bay. The use of a fyke, gill, hoop, or trammel nets and slat boxes are prohibited in Chilton, Colbert, Coosa, Jackson, Lauderdale, Lawrence, Limestone, Macon, and Morgan counties. The use of a gig, spear, or any similar device, or grabbing in an attempt to take freshwater fish in public waters is prohibited, except that a gig may be used between sunrise and sunset to take nongame fish in the Guntersville, Pickwick, Wheeler, and Wilson reservoirs.

The following commercial and nongame fish may be taken by bow and arrow or spears—Buffalo, Carp, Channel Cat, and other Catfish, Drum, Gar, Spoonbill, Spotted Sucker, and all members of the Sucker family including Black Horse and Red Horse. Spearing is limited to the use of a spear or similar instrument that is held in the hand and propels a projectile attached to a line, rope, or cord. The Department of Conservation must be notified at least one week prior to the date set for any spear fishing contest.

Popular annual fishing contests include the Fishing Rodeo in May at Demopolis Lake (10,000 acres) in Marengo County; the 3-day Alabama Deep Sea Rodeo at Mobile in late July or early August; and the Alabama Speckled Trout Rodeo at Foley during Thanksgiving week.

STATE FISHING LAKES

Barbour County (250 acres, 80 acres of water, near Clayton; *Butler County* (289 acres with 12-acre and 30-acre lakes) near Greenville;

* See current state regulations.

Clay County (417 acres with 120-acre and 38-acre lakes) near Delta: Coffee County (203 acres, 80 acres of water) near Elba; Crenshaw County (240 acres, 53 acres of water) near Luverne; Cullman County (160 acres, 32 acres of water) near Cullman; Dallas County (307 acres, 100-acre lake) near Selma; Fayette County (255 acres, 80 acres of water) near Fayette; Geneva County (388 acres with 28-acre and 34-acre lakes) near Coffee Springs; Lamar County (195 acres, 60-acre lake) near Vernon; Marengo County (290 acres, 50-acre lake) near Linden; Marion County (380 acres, 45-acre lake) near Guin; Pike County (407 acres, 45-acre lake) near Troy; Tuskegee Lake (200 acres, 100-acre lake) near Tuskegee, Macon County; Tuscaloosa County (1,614 acres, 250 acres of water) near Tuscaloosa; Walker County (460 acres, 162-acre lake) near Jasper.

STATE FORESTS

Geneva (7,210 acres) in Geneva County; Little River (2,120 acres) in Escambia and Monroe counties; Weogufka (240 acres) on Flag Mountain in Coosa County.

STATE PARKS

Bladon Springs (358 acres) east of Silas—Choctaw County; Chattahoochee (596 acres, 80-acre lake) south of Gordon—Houston County; Cheaha (2,719 acres) northeast of Talladega—Clay, Cleburne, and Talladega counties; Chewacle (877 acres, 26-acre lake) southeast of Auburn—Lee County; Chickasaw (560 acres) north of Linden—Marengo County; De Soto (4,825 acres) on Lookout Mountain near Hammondsville—De Kalb County; Gulf (5,678 acres, 3 lakes total 1,500 acres) on Gulf of Mexico south of Foley—Baldwin County; Joe Wheeler (2,200 acres) at Wheeler Lake and Wilson Reservoir north of Town Creek—Lauderdale and Lawrence counties; Little Mountain (4,000 acres) at Lake Guntersville—Marshall County; Monte Sano (2,042 acres) east of Huntsville—Madison County; Oak Mountain (9,940 acres 18-acre and 85-acre lakes) near Pelham—Shelby County; Valley Creek (1,080 acres, 960 acre lake) about 20 miles north of Selma—Dallas County.

Hunting and trapping any protected animals and birds in state forests and parks, the Forest Fire Tower area, or any state or federal game sanctuary are prohibited except in the Geneva State Forest, Choccolocco Corridor, and Lawrence Fire Tower. State lakes are well stocked, and persons 16 or more years of age pay a fishing fee of 50 cents per day.

WILDLIFE MANAGEMENT AREAS

Barbour County; Black Warrior in the Bankhead National Forest; Blue Spring in the Conecuh National Forest; Brown Creek in Marshall

County; *Butler County*; *Choccolocco* in the Talladega National Forest; *Coosa County*; *Covington County* in Covington and Geneva counties, where a state license is required to hunt on both sides of the yellow-painted county line separating the area; *Crow Creek, Mud Creek, Raccoon Creek,* and *Skyline* in Jackson County; *Fox Creek* in Lawrence and Morgan counties; *Hollins* in Clay and Talladega counties; *Lauderdale* and *Seven Mile Island* in Lauderdale County; *Mallard Creek* in Lawrence County; *Oakmulgee* in Bibb, Hale, and Perry counties; *Rob Boykin* in Mobile and Washington counties; *Scotch* in Clark County; *Swan Creek* in Limestone County; *Thomas* in Colbert and Franklin counties; *Wolf Creek* in Fayette and Walker counties.

Licenses, permits, regulations, and information about current seasons, bag and possession limits can be obtained from the Director, Alabama Department of Conservation, Montgomery 4; and the Chief, Division of Game and Fish; the Chief, Division of Forestry; Judges of Probate, and local authorized agents throughout the state. The U.S. Forest Service, Post Office Building, Montgomery, issues information about camping, fishing, and hunting in national forests.

ALASKA

Area: 586,400 square miles (land area—571,065, square miles); rank in nation–1
Bird: Willow Ptarmigan (*Lagopus alascensis*), adopted 1959
Capital city: Juneau guarded by Mount Juneau and Mount Roberts on the Gastineau Channel is on the Inside Passage of southeastern Alaska; population (1960)—6,797; rank in state–3
Counties: none; boroughs to be organized
Elevations: highest, Mount McKinley (20,329 ft.—southern summit; 19,470 ft.—northern summit) is called Denali, "the high one, home of the sun" by Indians; Lowest, Pacific Ocean (set level)
Flower: Forget-me-not (*Myosotis alpestri*), adopted 1931
Geographic center (including islands): 10 miles southwest of Lake Minchumina at 63° 46′ N. latitude, 152° 20′ W. longitude
Nicknames: Land of Midnight Sun, Last Frontier, Walrussia
Population (1960): 226,167; rank in nation–50
Shoreline: 33,904 miles including more than 18,000 miles in southeastern Alaska. Tides vary from a few inches or none at all in the Arctic Ocean; 15–23 feet in southeastern Alaska; 42 feet in Turn-Again-Arm near Anchorage
Tree: Sitka Spruce (*Picea sitchensis*)

Alaska is an enormous peninsula surrounded by ocean waters except on the east. The Canadian border starts at the southern tips of Dall and Prince of Wales islands and continues through the Portland Canal up to Mount Lewis Cass (6,864 ft.) and Devils Thumb (9,074 ft.) in the Coast Range, Chilkoot Pass leading to the Klondike above Skagway on the Lynn Canal, veers westward to Mount Fairweather (15,300 ft.) and northward to Mount Hubbard (14,950 ft.), zigzags at Mount Vancouver (15,700 ft.), Mount Cook (13,760 ft.), Mount Augusta (14,070 ft.) and Mount St. Elias (18,008 ft.) to follow the 141st meridian to the Arctic Ocean.

The Panhandle of southeastern Alaska consists of a Coast Range mainland about 350 miles long and 30 miles wide framing a submerged mountain system of more than 1,000 islands. Deep fiords and an intricate maze of channels provide many ports, and steamships follow the Inside Passage to the "Salmon Capital of the World" at Ketchikan on Revillagigedo Island, Wrangell, a port of entry to the Stikine River, Petersburg at the north end of Wrangell Narrow, Juneau on Gastineau Channel, and up Lynn Canal to Haines–Port Chilkoot, and Skagway. The Fairweather Range extends from Glacier Bay to Yakutat Bay, and this region contains large rivers of ice such as the Milaspina Glacier (1,500 square miles) spreading from snowfields on the international boundary to Icy and Yakutat bays, and the Muir Glacier (350 square miles) fed by 26 tributaries pushing masses of ice over a 200-foot cliff into Glacier Bay. Other portions of the Panhandle have comparatively mild climate, and rainfall varies from 25–155 inches among dense forests of cedar, hemlock, and Sitka spruce.

South central Alaska from Icy Bay below Mount St. Elias to Cook Inlet and Shelikof Strait on the Gulf of Alaska is dominated by the Alaska Range, containing Mount McKinley, the highest peak in North America and perpetually blanketed with snow. Mount Foraker (17,395 ft.) is also in Mount McKinley National Park (1,939,493 acres) where a fishing license is not required to catch Grayling in the streams and large Mackinaw in Wonder Lake. The Wrangell Range glistens with glaciers on Mount Blackburn (16,523 ft.), Mount Sanford (16,208 ft.), and Mount Wrangell (14,005 ft.), and the Tanana River starts on a northwest course to join the Yukon River at Tanana. On the Gulf of Alaska, Prince William Sound and numerous islands west of Copper River Flats are within sight of Mount Marcus Baker (13,250 ft.) and lower summits. The Copper River was blocked by a portion of the Allen Glacier during the 1963 earthquake, and a new lake was formed a few miles upstream from the mouth of this river known for annual Salmon runs. The Kenai Peninsula with ice fields on the eastern coast, and Trout streams, Lake Skilak, and Lake Tustumena on the Cook Inlet side, is a big game region. On Shelikof Strait, the Afognak Island portion of the Chugach National Forest is north of Kodiak Island, famous for enormous Kodiak Bears.

The Alaska Peninsula in the southwest between Cook Inlet, Shelikof Strait, and the Bering Sea has almost treeless, rolling and mountainous grasslands. The Katmai National Monument (2,697,590 acres) below lovely Lake Iliamna (1,057 square miles) contains the volcanic Valley of Ten Thousand Smokes, Mount Denison (7,606 ft.), Snowy Mountain (7,244 ft.), Brooks, Colville, Grosvenor, and Naknek lakes with camps for sportsmen. The bleak, rocky Aleutian Islands including Unimak Island (70 miles long, 20 miles wide) form a 1,000-mile chain of partially submerged volcanic mountains placed in such a wide arc that tiny Attu Island on the western tip is almost due north of New Zealand.

The Bering Sea region from Bristol Bay to the Arctic Circle line at the northern end of the Seward Peninsula is a rolling tundra plain interlaced with lakes, streams, and mountains, rising 3,000–4,500 feet. Large isolated islands include Nunivak Island between Bristol Bay and Norton Sound; St. Matthew Island, and the Pribilof Islands where fur seals congregate annually from May to August. St. Lawrence Island is south of Bering Strait where the Soviet Union's Big Diomede (Ostrov Ratmanov) is only 2.4 miles from the American Little Diomede. Generously doused with fog, rain, wind, and snow, this region is inhabited mostly by Eskimos.

Point Barrow on the Arctic Ocean is the most northern tip of land and strong winds pack ice floes into bluffs and ridges. The sun continuously circles the sky from early June until August and is not seen from late November until late January. The Arctic treeless tundra is perpetually frozen below the surface, but lakes and streams provide good fishing. The Brooks Range, Baird, Waring, De Long, Endicott, Smith, and Davidson mountains are in the Arctic Circle.

Central Alaska between the Arctic Circle mountains and the southern Alaska Range contains tundra lowlands, forested plateaus, isolated mountains, lakes, and numerous streams. Large streams fed by many tributaries include the Kuskokwim River wandering 500 miles from its source on the western slope of the Alaska Range to carve a broad valley through the Kuskokwim Mountains northeast of the Kilbuck Mountains on the way to Bethel and Kuskokwim Bay on the Bering Sea. The great Yukon River leaving Canada east of Eagle flows by Circle, Fort Yukon, Rampart, Tanana, Koyukuk, and Anvik for about 1,200 miles before draining through deltas into Norton Sound. The Yukon River is open for navigation from late May to October. More than $100,000 may be paid annually in the Ice Pool at Nenana for guessing the exact minute of the spring ice breakup on the Nenana River, a tributary of the Yukon River.

The largest streams rising in the Arctic Circle are the Noatak River, flowing westward 350 miles from the Brooks Range to Kotzebue Sound on the Chukchi Sea, and the Koyukuk River, moving southward to join the Yukon River at Koyukuk.

Time zones of Alaska compared to 12:00 o'clock noon at Washington, D.C.: Pacific Standard Time (9:00 A.M.) at Juneau and the Panhandle, except a portion between Cape Fairweather and Icy Cape: Yukon Standard Time (8:00 A.M.); Central Alaska has Alaska Standard Time (7:00 A.M.); Bering Standard Time (6:00 A.M.) divided by a line running north from Coal Harbor on Unga Island through the Alaska Peninsula to Osviak, and along the 165th meridian to the Arctic Sea. Kuskokwim Bay, Norton Sound, Seward Peninsula, the Chukchi Sea coast, and Bering Sea islands are in the Bering Standard Time zone. The International Date Line west of the Aleutian Islands cuts through Bering Strait to the Arctic Circle.

LICENSES

Resident licenses to fish, hunt, and trap are issued to any citizen 16 or more years of age who has maintained a voting residence and a permanent place of abode within the state for 12 consecutive months, including members of military services and their dependents. Resident privileges are granted to any association, corporation, partnership, joint stock company, or trust which has maintained its main office or headquarters in Alaska. An alien must maintain a permanent place of abode within the state for 3 consecutive years to obtain resident licenses. It is not necessary for a resident under the age of 16 to have a hunting or trapping license, but juveniles less than 11 years of age may not take Beaver. All persons 16 or more years of age must purchase a federal "Duck" stamp to take migratory game birds. Nonresidents may not take big game without previously purchasing appropriate tags in addition to valid hunting licenses. Numbered nontransferable tags must be affixed and locked to a big game animal immediately after taking it. Any tags not used for the animal specified may be utilized during the calendar year of issue on any species of game, if the tag fee is of equal or less valuation.

A sport fishing license is required for taking Razor Clams, fresh water, marine, or anadromous fish not for sale or barter. A sport fishing, hunting, and trapping license may be obtained by the head of a family, or by any person solely dependent for support on himself, upon proof by the applicant that he is receiving, or has obtained during the preceding 6 months, "assistance under any State or Federal welfare program to aid the indigent [Workmen's Compensation is not considered to be welfare]; or has an annual family gross income of less than $3,600 for the year immediately preceding application; or has historically been dependent on fish and game for subsistence," and the fee is only 25 cents.

Resident license fees: Sport fishing, $5.00; hunting, $7.00; trapping, $3.00; hunting and trapping, $10.00; hunting and sport fishing, $12.00; hunting, trapping, and sport fishing, $15.00; registered guide, $50.00; assistant guide, $25.00; fur dealer and taxidermy, $20.00; fish, fur, or game farming, 5.00; federal "Duck" stamp, $3.00.

Nonresident license fees: Sport fishing, $10.00; visitor 10 consecutive days fishing, $5.00; hunting, $10.00; hunting and sport fishing, $20.00; hunting and trapping, $100.00; fur dealer, $100.00; federal "Duck" stamp, $3.00. *Tags* (in addition to hunting license): Black Bear, Deer (each), $10.00; Brown Bear, Grizzly Bear (each), $75.00; Polar Bear (each), $150.00; Bison, Moose, Mountain Sheep (each), $50.00; Caribou, Elk, Mountain Goat (each), $25.00; Walrus (each), $100.00.

HUNTING AND TRAPPING

Big game: Black Bear (including blue and cinnamon color phases), Brown Bear, Grizzly Bear, Polar Bear, Bison, Caribou, Deer, Elk, Mountain Goat, Moose, Musk Ox, Mountain Sheep, Wolf, Wolverine. Alaska is divided into 26 game management units, and portions may be closed to hunting, but many areas are open all year. Dates of open seasons may include shorter periods in some units, but show when such species may be taken somewhere in Alaska. OPEN SEASONS:* Black Bear—mid-August to June 30, and open all year in some units. Brown and Grizzly Bears— September 1–June 30. Polar Bear—mid-October to mid-May in 4 units (Kuskokwim–Yukon Delta, Seward Peninsula, Kotzebue Sound, Arctic Sea), and residents may take Polar Bear for food at any time. Deer— Aug. 1–Dec. 31 in designated units. Elk—Aug. 1–Dec. 31 in Unit 8 (Afognak, Chirikof, Kodiak, Semidi, and adjacent offshore islands). Mountain Goat and Moose—Aug. 1–Dec. 31. Mountain Sheep—mid- August to mid-September. Wolf—no open season in 4 units and no closed season in other units. Wolverine—Nov. 1–April 15, and no open season in most of southeastern Alaska. ANNUAL BAG LIMITS:* Black Bear —3 including not more than 1 Blue or Glacier Bear. Brown Bear—1. Grizzly Bear—1. Polar Bear—1. Caribou—3 and no limit in the Arctic Circle area. Deer—2 or 4 in designated units. Elk—1. Mountain Goat —2. Moose—1 bull in designated units and 1 antlerless Moose by registration only. Mountain Sheep—1 Ram with ¾ curl horn (or larger) in designated units.

Furbearing animals: Beaver, Coyote, Fox, Lynx, Marmot, Marten,

---

* Check current state regulations.

Mink, Muskrat, Land and Sea Otter, Raccoon, Squirrels (Ground, Flying), Weasel. OPEN SEASONS:* Beaver—Jan. 1–May 15, and no open season in 2 units. Coyote—no closed seasons except in 2 units. Blue and White Foxes—Dec. 1–April 15, and no closed season in the Aleutian Islands. Other Foxes, Marten, Mink, Weasel—Nov. 1–Jan. 31 in designated units. Lynx and Land Otter—Nov. 1–March 31 in some units. Muskrat —Nov. 1 to mid-June. Marmot, Raccoon, and Squirrels—no closed season.

Small game: Brant, Coot, Ducks (except Canvasback and Redhead), Little Brown Crane, Eider, Geese, Jacksnipe, all species of Grouse and Ptarmigan, Merganser, Scoter, Arctic Hare and Snowshoe Rabbit, Marmot, Raccoon, and Red Squirrel. OPEN SEASONS:* Brant, Coot, Ducks, Eider, Geese, Scoter, Merganser—Oct. 15–Jan. 15 in the Aleutian and Pribilof islands, and September 1 to mid-December in remainder of Alaska. Grouse—Aug. 1–April 30. Little Brown Crane—Sept. 1–30. Arctic Hare and Snowshoe Rabbit—Sept. 1–April 30 in 5 units, and all year in the remaining units. Ptarmigan—Aug. 1–April 30. Marmot, Raccoon, Red Squirrel—all year.

Marine mammals: Beluga Whale, Porpoise, Sea Lion, Seals (Bearded, Harbor, Ribbon, Ringed), Walrus. OPEN SEASONS:* Beluga Whale, Porpoise, Sea Lions, Seals—all year, except a special permit must be obtained to take Sea Lions for commercial purposes. Walrus—no closed season in units open for taking Polar Bear. ANNUAL BAG LIMIT: Walrus—1 adult bull per nonresident; 5 cows or subadults of either sex, and no limit of bulls for residents. No limits for other mammals. FULLY PROTECTED: Cub Bears and female Bears accompanied by cubs, Canvasback and Redhead Ducks, Musk Ox, Sea Otter—no open seasons. Bison in the Delta herd (Delta-Clearwater area about 100 miles southeast of Fairbanks) may be transferred to persons and associations for breeding or raising as domestic stock for commercial, educational, and scientific purposes. A few Bison may be hunted to control the herd size, and applications for free hunting permits should be directed to the Commissioner of Fish and Game. NOT PROTECTED: Bats, Crow, Magpie, Mice, Marmot, Porcupine, Raccoon, Rats, Shrews, Flying, Ground, and Red Squirrels may be taken at any time. Unclassified game are continuously protected by closed seasons, but at any time Eskimos and Indians may take and transport Auklets, Auks, Guillemots, Murres, Puffins, and their eggs for personal use but not for sale. Any person may take game (except migratory game birds) for food during closed seasons in case of dire emergency or in defense of life or property. If game is killed for the latter reason, the Department of Fish and Game must be notified in a written report within 15 days. The use of game as food for dogs, fur animals, or as bait is prohibited except:

---

* Check current state regulations.

(a) bones, hide, skin, viscera; (b) skinned carcasses of Bears and fur animals; (c) marine mammals; (d) Hares and Rabbits. It is unlawful to shoot from, or use, any aircraft, motor-powered vehicle, or watercraft for the purpose of driving, herding, or molesting game except that a motor-powered watercraft may be used in taking marine mammals. Coyotes and Wolves may be taken by use of an aircraft only under terms of a special permit issued by the Department of Fish and Game.

FIREARMS

Big game may be taken with pistols and rifles using centerfire cartridges, and shotguns not larger than 10 gauge or capable of holding more than 3 shells in the magazine and chamber combined. The use of rimfire cartridges, a machine gun or submachine, or set gun to take game is prohibited. Marine mammals may be taken by use of a pistol, rifle, shotgun, harpoon, or net. There are no restrictions on bows and arrows but a special permit should be obtained from the commissioner to take Seals by bow and arrow. See FEDERAL REGULATIONS FOR MIGRATORY GAME BIRDS.

Shooting hours: Migratory game birds; one-half hour before sunrise until sunset. No hours specified for other game.

FISHING

Game fish: Arctic Char, Grayling, Northern Pike, Salmon (Chum, King, Pink, Red, Silver), Steelhead, Trout (Brook, Dolly Varden, Mackinaw, Rainbow). OPEN SEASONS:* All year, except some areas are closed to Salmon fishing. King Salmon may not be taken from any freshwater drainages of southeastern Alaska from the Dixon Entrance of the Portland Canal to Cape Suckling west of Icy Cape. The general King Salmon season in designated freshwater areas of the Kenai Peninsula, May 7–July 8 or July 31; in the Susitna River drainage, May 7–July 8. Dolly Varden and Lake Trout may be taken without limit for subsistence by means of fyke and gill nets, or a seine in the waters of Iliamna, Becharof and Ugashik Lakes and their outlet streams, Dec. 1–April 30. Northern Pike may be taken at any time without limit by use of fyke and gill nets, seine, and spear in all waters except portions of the Tanana River. Taking Grayling by any means other than hook and line is prohibited.

Anglers should use only a closely attended single line held in the hand or attached to a rod, and not more than 1 plug, spoon, spinner or series of spinners, or 2 flies, or 2 hooks. Char, Salmon, and Trout may not be taken in freshwater by sport fishermen using (a) fixed or weighted

---

* Check current state regulations.

hooks and lures (except of standard manufacture) or multiple hooks to which a weight is attached in such a manner that the weight follows the hook when retrieved by the angler; (b) any multiple hook with gap between point and shank larger than one-quarter inch when not attached to a plug, spoon, spinner, or artificial lure; (c) any plug, spoon, spinner, or artificial lure having multiple hook(s) with a gap between point and shank larger than one-half inch; (d) an arrow or a spear except when person is completely submerged. It is unlawful to take Salmon in saltwater by means of treble hooks in southeastern Alaska.

Southeastern Alaska: Abalone—50 per day; minimum width of shell, 3 inches. Dungeness Crab—30 per day; minimum width of shell, 7 inches. These Crabs are easily caught in shallow water and can have an 8-inch shell. Geoducks—6 daily. Razor Clams may be taken only by manually operated guns, shovels, and forks, Jan. 1–June 30, and Sept. 1–Dec. 31; and in the Cook Inlet area, Jan. 1–July 9, Sept. 1–Dec. 31; No limit.

GAME REFUGES AND SANCTUARIES

Hunting is prohibited on the Bering Sea islands of Hall, Pinnacle, and St. Matthew; Bogoslof Islands; Chamisso Island; Forrester Island (except Sea Lions for commercial purposes under special permit); Krigegagand Nunivakehak Islands in Hazen Bay; Hazy Islands in southeastern Alaska (except Sea Lions for commercial purposes); St. Lazaria Island at the entrance of Sitka Sound; the Semidi Island Group, Chisik, Egg, and other small islands in Tuxedni Harbor, Cook Inlet; the Walrus Island State Game Sanctuary including Crooked, High, Round, and Summit islands, The Twins, and Black Rock in Bristol Bay closed to the taking of Walrus only.

The Aleutian Islands are closed except that Adak, Attu, Great Sitkin, and Shemya Islands are open to Ptarmigan and waterfowl hunting. Akun, Akutan, Atka, Sanak, Tigalda, Umnak, Unalaska, and Unimak Islands are open to hunting and trapping. The Kenai National Moose Range on Kenai Peninsula, the Kodiak National Wildlife Refuge on Kodiak Island, and Nunivak Island in the Bering Sea are open to hunters and trappers. Permits may be issued for taking game in closed areas.

GUIDE AND OUTFITTING CENTERS

Anchorage (1960 pop.—44,237) on Knik Arm of Cook Inlet; Alaska Big Game Trophy Club awards in late April or early May; Trophy Sheep Contest awards early in October. *Cordova* (1960 pop.—1,128) at Boswell Bay on Gulf of Alaska. *Fairbanks* (1960 pop.—13,311) the "Golden Heart of Alaska" on the Chena River in Tenana Valley; May

30–31 boat marathon on the Yukon River, 700-mile round trip to Ruby. *Haines–Port Chilkoot* (1960.—512) on Lynn Canal. *Homer* (1960 pop.—1,247) at Katchemak Bay on Kenai Peninsula; Halibut Derby July 4 to August. *Juneau* (capital city) Golden North Salmon Derby 3 days in early August. *Ketchikan* (1960 pop.—6,483) on island of Revillagigedo; King Salmon Derby late April or early May for 3 months with weekly prizes and season grand prize. *Kodiak* (1960 pop.—2,628) at St. Paul Harbor on Kodiak Island; Halibut Derby 6 days in July and King Crab Festival in August. *Nome* (1960 pop.—2,316) on Seward Peninsula; aircraft facilities at Mark Field, steamships June–October. *Palmer* (1960 pop.—1,181) in Matanuska Valley between Talkeetna and Chugach Mountains. *Petersburg* (1960 pop.—1,502) on Mitkof Island at head of Wrangell Narrows; Deer Derby Aug. 1–Nov. 30. *Seward* (1960 pop.—1,891) at Resurrection Bay on Kenai Peninsula; July 4 annual foot race from center of Seward to top of Mount Marathon (3,008 ft.); Silver Salmon Derby in mid-August. *Skagway* (1960 pop.—659) at head of Lynn Canal. *Valdez* (1960 pop.—555) the "Switzerland of Alaska" at Valdez Arm of Prince William Sound; Silver Salmon Derby Aug. 1 to Labor Day. *Wrangell* (1960 pop.—1,315) at mouth of Stikine River in southeastern Alaska; King Salmon Derby during June and July. *Kotzebue* (1960 pop.—1,290) on Kotzebue Sound of the Chukchi Sea. This Eskimo village is headquarters for Polar Bear, Wolf, and Walrus hunting, and Beluga Whales are caught from mid-May to mid-June.

Licenses and tags can be obtained from local authorized agents, or by mail from the Licensing Section, Alaska Department of Revenue, 156 South Franklin, Juneau. Free permits, regulations, and information about current seasons, bag, and possession limits are issued by the Commissioner, Alaska Department of Fish and Game, Subport Building, Juneau. There are local representatives at Anchorage, Aniak, College, Cordova, Craig, Dillingham, Fairbanks, Clenallen, Homer, Ketchikan, King Salmon, Kodiak, Nome, Palmer, Petersburg, Sand Point, Seldovia, Seward, Sitka, Tok, Wrangell, and Yukutat. Alaska Travel Division, Box 2391, Juneau. *Alaska Hunting and Fishing Guide*, P.O. Box 2102, Anchorage—$1 (guides and outfitters).

ARIZONA

Area: 113,956 square miles (land area—113,575 square miles); rank in nation–6
Bird: Cactus Wren (*Heleodytes brunneicapillus*), adopted 1931
Capital city: Phoenix on the Salt River in Maricopa County; population (1960)—439,170; rank in state–1
Counties: 14

Elevation: Highest, Humphreys Peak (12,611 ft.) in Coconino County; lowest, Colorado River near Yuma (137 ft.)
Flower: Saguaro Cactus (*Cereus giganteus*), adopted 1931
Geographic center: 55 miles southeast of Prescott, Yavapai County
Nicknames: Apache State, Grand Canyon State, Land of Adventure, Sunshine State, Valentine State
Population (1960): 1,320.161; rank in nation–35
Tree: Palo Verde (*Cercidium floridium; Cercidium microphyllum*)

Arizona shares the eastern border with the state of New Mexico, and a southern international boundary with the Republic of Mexico. The Colorado River flowing from the north is impounded by the Glen Canyon Dam to create Lake Powell (254 square miles) on the Arizona-Utah border. This remarkable river swerves across northwestern Arizona and through magnificent Grand Canyon to Lake Mead (247 square miles) formed by Hoover Dam, and Lake Mohave (45 square miles) at Davis Dam on the Nevada border, and continues on the southerly course with California on the western side. Parker Dam created Hasasu Lake (46 square miles); and downstream the Imperial and Laguna Dams impound the Colorado near Yuma. North of the Lake Mead Recreational Area, a straight line through the Virgin Mountains to Utah separates Nevada from the northwestern corner of Arizona. A portion of the Kaibab National Forest and huge mesas named Vermillion Cliffs north of the Grand Canyon are in a wilderness region known as the Arizona Strip. Most of the northeastern plateau is high and dry. A granite marker pinpoints a desolate bluff at Four Corners where 4 states share a common corner—Arizona, Colorado, New Mexico, and Utah.

Among many spectacular gorges is the world famous Grand Canyon in northern Arizona (217 miles long, 4–13 miles wide, 3,000–6,000 ft. deep); the smaller but beautiful Oak Creek Canyon in the Sedona red cliff region of Coconino and Yavapai Counties. The Little Colorado River (Colorado Chiquito) wanders from the highlands of Apache National Forest and runs on a northwesterly course through the Painted Desert to join the great Colorado River in the Grand Canyon National Park. North of Flagstaff, snow-covered Humphreys Peak dominates the wooded San Francisco Range containing Agassiz Peak (12,340 ft.), Fremont Peak (11,940 ft.), San Francisco Mountain (12,000 ft.), and Core Ridge (10,500 ft.) near Fremont Saddle (10,800 ft.).

Extending diagonally from rolling hills, mountains, and desert plains in southeastern Arizona to the northwestern plateau region are green-forested mountains and valleys including Santa Catalina Mountains near Tucson, the Pinaleno Mountains southwest of Safford, the eastern White Mountains in Apache County, and the Mogollon (Mo-go-YOWN)

Plateau in Coconino County. Timbers area elevation are from 6,000–9,000 feet. The majestic Mogollon Rim rises 2,000 feet high to divide desert from mountain regions, and is nearly 250 miles long; this escarpment has a precipitous portion known as the Tonto Rim. Streams flow northward on the Mogollon Plateau, and waters drain toward the south below the rim.

In the virgin Pine forests of the White Mountains are Baldy Peak (11,590 ft.), Greens Peak (10,115 ft.), and the Black River leaving the Apache National Forest to rush through remote canyons for more than 150 miles through Fort Apache and the San Carlos Indian Reservations. The low southwestern desert region is broken by craggy mountains rising abruptly to about 3,000 feet.

Major streams crossing the Mexican boundary in the southeast are the San Pedro River flowing from the Huachuca (WAH-choo-KAH) Mountains to Benson, Mammoth, and at Winkleman merging with the Gila (HEE-lyah) River. The Santa Cruz River goes through Tucson and veers on a northwesterly course to join the Gila River near Komatke. Waters of the Black and White rivers form the Salt River which flows through spectacular Salt River Canyon and fed by many streams is impounded by dams to form a chain of lakes. From the Prescott National Forest, the Hassayampa River runs southward through Wickenburg to enter the Gila River near Buckeye. The Gila continues on a southwesterly course to empty into the Colorado River at Yuma. The Big Sandy and Santa Maria rivers of western Arizona form the Bill Williams River, which marks a boundary between Mohave and Yuma counties before reaching Havasu Lake.

Large impounded waters include San Carlos Lake (34 square miles) at Coolidge Dam southeast of Globe; Roosevelt Lake (27 square miles) connected by the Salt River with Apache Lake at Horse Mesa Dam, Canyon Lake at Mormon Flat Dam, and Saguaro Lake at Stewart Mountain Dam. Lake Bartlett on the Verde River is northeast of Phoenix, and Lake Pleasant on the Agua Fria River is near Castle Hot Springs and New River.

LICENSES

Resident licenses to fish and hunt are issued to persons 14 or more years of age who have been bona fide residents of Arizona for at least one year, and to members of the U.S. Armed Forces on active duty in the state for 30 or more days. All persons hunting wildlife must possess a combination hunting and fishing license (Class F) or a general hunting license (Class G). Hunters 16 or more years of age should also purchase a federal "Duck" stamp to take migratory game birds. A Pioneer complimentary license entitles the holder to hunt and fish during his lifetime with the same privileges as the holder of a Class F license. A trapping license is issued if furbearing animals are to be taken only by the use of traps. A valid hunting license allows the use of firearms and traps to take furbearing animals, except that a special permit must be obtained to take Beaver with firearms.

The Shooting Preserve License is required for any commercial or private preserve established by an individual, club, or association on private property not exceeding 1,000 acres to be used for the propagation or shooting of pen-raised upland game birds. No license is necessary to hunt on licensed shooting preserves, but birds taken away must be tagged.

No hunter may purchase more than one Antelope permit and one Elk permit annually, nor take more than one Antelope and one Elk during any 3-year period. Only one Buffalo and one Bighorn Sheep may be taken during a hunter's lifetime. Tags are issued with the permits. Drawings are held for special big game hunts, and if a unit is not filled after a second drawing, the remaining permits are issued on a first-come basis at the Phoenix office. Only 2 hunters may apply as a group for Bighorn Sheep hunts, and 4 persons as a group for other controlled hunts. Buffalo hunting is limited to residents of Arizona. The head, hide, and one quarter of a Buffalo may be retained by the successful hunter, and all the remaining parts of the animal are sold to the public.

Blind residents and juveniles under the age of 14 may fish without licenses, but they are entitled to only one-half the legal bag limit for Trout. The Trout stamp validates an A or B Class fishing license and is required to take Trout, but no Trout stamp is required for Class D, E, and F fishing licenses. A valid Arizona fishing license and a tribal permit are necessary to fish on the Fort Apache, Navajo, and San Carlos Indian reservations. Special Use permits are required to fish on the Colorado River boundary waters from a boat or other floating device. A California–Colorado River special use stamp attached to an Arizona fishing license is valid from July 1–June 30 to coincide with the Arizona license period. Arizona Special Use permits are valid with California angling licenses from Jan. 1–Dec. 31. Any person fishing on the waters of Lake Mead, Lake Mohave, and the Colorado River where it forms a mutual boundary between Arizona and Nevada must possess an appropriate Arizona or Nevada fishing license. The Arizona Special Use permits with Nevada fishing licenses, and Nevada Special Use stamps attached to Arizona licenses are valid from July 1–June 30. A similar agreement with Utah for Lake Powell and the waters of the Colorado River below the lake to the Marble Canyon Dam require Arizona or Utah Special Use permits, except that juveniles under the age of 14 are allowed to fish without licenses and permits.

Resident license fees: General fishing except Trout (Class A), $3.00; one-day fishing for all fish except Colorado River (Class D), $2.00; combination hunting and fishing (Class F), $9.00; general hunting (Class G), $5.00. *Stamps* (in addition to licenses): Federal "Duck" stamp, $3.00; special use permit to fish on Colorado River boundary waters, $2.00; Trout (validates Class A fishing license), $2.00. *Tags* issued with permits (in addition to licenses): Archery, $1.00; Antelope, $10.00; Black Bear, $1.00; Deer, $1.00; Kaibab North Deer Hunt, $5.00; Buffalo, $25.00; Elk, $15.00; Javelina, $1.00; Bighorn Sheep, $25.00; Wild Turkey, $1.00; shooting preserve, $25.00; shooting preserve game tags (each), 10 cents.

Nonresident license fees: General fishing except Trout (Class A), $9.00; fishing 5 consecutive days except Trout (Class B), $3.00; one-day fishing for all fish except on Colorado River (Class D), $2.00; Colorado River fishing for all fish (Class E), $10.00; general hunting (Class G), $20.00; combination general hunting and fishing (Class F), $25.00; archery hunting only, $15.00; predator hunting only, $5.00. *Stamps* (in addition to licenses): federal "duck" stamp, $3.00; special use permit to fish on Colorado River boundary waters: California or Nevada residents and nonresidents—$2.00, Utah residents—$2.00, Utah nonresident license holders—$3.00; Trout (validates Class A fishing license), $6.00; Trout (validates Class B fishing license), $2.00. *Tags* issued with permits (in addition to licenses): Archery, $1.00; Antelope, $35.00; Bear, $10.00; Deer, $25.00; Elk, $55.00; Javelina, $1.00; Bighorn Sheep, $125.00; Wild Turkey, $1.00.

HUNTING AND TRAPPING

Big game: Antelope, Black Bear (several color phases), Buffalo, Deer (Coues, Mule, white-tailed), Elk, Javelina, Bighorn Sheep. OPEN SEASONS:* Antelope—a few days in September. Black Bear—September through February. Buffalo (residents only)—a few days in October. Deer (archery only, either sex)—3 weeks in September; firearms (including bow and arrow)—October and November and special permits are not required for many areas; Kaibab North Deer Hunt in November; permits for Fort Huachuca Deer Hunt issued only to personnel. Elk—about 5 days in late September or early October plus a few days in mid-November. Javelina—Jan. 1–31 (archery only) and about 2 weeks in late February or early March with firearms. Bighorn Sheep—3 weeks in December. SEASON BAG LIMIT:* Antelope and Elk—1 each per hunter every 3 years. Bear—1. Deer—1 on archery tag, 1 on firearms tag, 2 in controlled hunts. Buffalo and Bighorn Sheep—1 each during a hunter's lifetime. Javelina—1. A legal Buck Deer should have antlers forked at the tip, not including brow tine or eye guard.

* Check current state regulations.

Furbearing animals: Badger, Beaver, Coati-mundi, Mink, Muskrat, Opossum, Otter, Raccoon, Ring-tailed Cat. OPEN SEASONS: All year and no bag limits, but hunters and trappers should carefully check regulations.

Small game: Coot, Dove (Mourning, White-winged), Ducks (except Canvasback and Redhead), Gallinule, Geese, Merganser, Quail (Gambel's, Mearn's, Scaled), Wilson's Snipe, Wild Turkey, Cottontail Rabbit, Tree Squirrels including Abert Squirrel. OPEN SEASONS: Coot, Ducks, Gallinule, Geese, Merganser—second week in October to first week in January. Doves—about 3 weeks in September and 3 weeks in December throughout state, except in a few Wildlife areas. Gambel's and Scaled Quail— about 3 weeks in October and from second week in December through January, except in a few designated areas. Mearn's Quail—3 weeks in December. Wilson's Snipe—about 5 weeks from late November to early January. Wild Turkey—about 10 days in October. Cottontail Rabbit— July 1–June 30 throughout state except at Kaibab North, Tucson Mountain, and Santa Rita Wildlife areas, or in Antelope, Elk, and Bighorn Sheep areas during controlled hunts. Squirrels—archery only, 3 weeks in September; firearms, from early October to mid-November in designated areas. Upland game birds on shooting preserves—Sept. 1–March 31. FULLY PROTECTED: Black Brant, Canvasback, and Redhead Ducks—no open seasons. PREDATORS: Bobcat, Coyote, Fox, Jaguar, Mountain Lion, Ocelot, Porcupine, Skunk, Weasel, Wolf, and wild house cats may be taken at any time by holders of valid hunting licenses. The $75 bounty for a Mountain Lion is paid only to residents of Arizona. Golden Eagle, Goshawk, Cooper's and Sharp-shinned Hawks, Osprey, Great Horned Owl, Gopher, Prairie Dog, and Jack Rabbit may be taken at any time.

FIREARMS

Prohibited: (a) Automatic firearms and tracer, full metal-jacketed or altered metal-jacketed bullets; (b) shotguns larger than 10 gauge, or capable of holding more than 2 shells in magazine and chamber combined for taking Dove, Quail, and Wilson's Snipe, or holding more than 3 shells for taking waterfowl; (c) semiautomatic firearms of .23 caliber or larger with a magazine capacity of more than 5 shells; (d) possession of any contrivance designed to silence, muffle or minimize the report of a firearm during hunts.

Other small game, furbearers, nongame, and predatory mammals may be taken with any firearms not prohibited under items a, b, and c. No game birds, except Turkey, may be taken with rifled firearms. Only rifles of .23 caliber or larger are permitted for taking big game, except the .22 caliber rimfire magnum rifle firing magnum ammunition; and any centerfire rifle may be used to take Javelina. The .357 magnum and .44

magnum pistols using magnum cartridges may be used to take big game. Any shotgun not prohibited in item b may be used to take Turkey.

A longbow having a pull of not less than 40 pounds, and an arrow with a sharp-blade broadhead not less than seven-eighths of an inch in width may be used to hunt Antelope, Bear, Deer, Javelina, and Wild Turkey. Any longbow and arrow may be used to take small game, furbearers, nongame, and predatory animals, rough fish, and frogs. The use of a crossbow, or any bow drawn, held, or released by mechanical means, and arrows with explosive or poisoned tips are prohibited in Arizona.

Shooting hours: Daylight hours for all game except migratory game birds and Raccoon. Migratory game birds—one-half hour before sunrise to sunset, except that shooting starts at 12:00 o'clock noon on the opening day of a season for Coot, Ducks, Gallinule, Geese, and Merganser. Raccoons may be hunted at night with the aid of artificial lights and dogs.

FISHING

Game fish: Black Bass (Largemouth, Smallmouth), Striped Bass, Yellow Bass (commonly called Stripies), Catfish (Channel, Forktail), Crappie, Kokanee Salmon, Trout (Brown, Brook, Rainbow). OPEN SEASONS:* all year, at any time of day or night throughout the state.

Rough fish such as Buffalo, Carp, Mullet, and Suckers may be taken by snares, spears, bow and arrow, but not within one-half mile of a boat dock or swimming area.

Frogs: OPEN SEASON: June 1–Nov. 30. BAG AND POSSESSION LIMIT: 12. A fishing license is required to take Bullfrogs, day or night, by hook and line, bow and arrow, gig, and spears.

The Colorado River Valley is a natural flyway for waterfowl. The Glen Canyon National Recreation Area (1,429,007 acres including 96,163 acres in Arizona) near Page, the Lake Mead National Recreation Area (1,951,928 acres including 1,209,901 acres in Arizona), Lake Mohave, Topock Swamp, Havasu Lake, and smaller reservoirs downstream have convenient airfields at Bullhead City, Kingman, Parker, and Yuma in Arizona; Needles, California, and Boulder City, Nevada. Airfields serve north central Arizona sportsmen at Camp Verde, Clarkdale, Flagstaff, Littlefield, Prescott, Sedona and Williams. In the White Mountains region are airfields at Show Low, St. John's, Springerville, and Winslow; and southeastern Arizona at Clifton, Globe, Nogales, Safford and Tucson.

There is superlative fishing for Largemouth Black Bass, Rainbow Trout, Crappie, Channel Catfish, and panfish in Lake Mead; and Havasu Lake also has Striped Bass; Kokanee Salmon has been added to Lake Mohave. Major Trout streams are in National Forests. Other favored

---

* Check current state regulations.

waters are the Lyman Reservoir near St. John's, Show Low Lake in the White Mountains, and Ashurst Lake southeast of Flagstaff (Kokanee Salmon, Rainbow Trout); Apache, Canyon, Saguaro, and Roosevelt lakes impounded by the Salt River dams; Bartlett and Horseshoe lakes on the Verde River east of Cave Creek, and Lake Pleasant north of Sun City.

Licenses, permits, regulations, and information about current seasons, bag and possession limits can be obtained from the Director, Arizona Game and Fish Department, 105 State Building, Phoenix 7. Applications for Buffalo meat should be made not later than September 15 by mail or at the counter. Write for maps and the attractive detailed booklets *Arizona Fishin' Holes* prepared by the Arizona Game and Fish Department, and *Camping and Camp Grounds in Amazing Arizona* published by the Arizona Development Board, 1500 West Jefferson St., Phoenix 7. The *Arizona Highways* published monthly by the Arizona Highways Department, is a beautifully illustrated magazine with good articles about the state. Subscription $4 annually; address: 2039 West Lewis Ave., Phoenix.

ARKANSAS

Area: 53,225 square miles (land area—52,499 square miles); rank in nation–27
Bird: Mocking Bird *(Mimus polyglottus)*, adopted 1929
Capital city: Little Rock on the Arkansas River in Pulaski County; population (1960)—107,813; rank in state–1.
Counties: 75
Elevations: Highest, Magazine Mountain (2,823 ft.) in Logan County; lowest, Ouachita River (55 ft.) in Ashley and Union counties.
Flower: Apple Blossom *(Pyrus malus)*, adopted 1901
Geographic center: 12 miles north of west of Little Rock
Nicknames: Land of Opportunity, Bowie State, Hot Water State, Wonder State.
Population (1960): 1,786,272; rank in nation–31
Tree: Shortleaf Pine *(Pinus echinata)*, adopted 1939

Arkansas is a south central state with the Mississippi etching an eastern shoreline from Missouri on the northern boundary to Louisiana across the southern border. Oklahoma is on the west except where Texas juts into the southwestern corner of the state.

The west and northwest highlands slope down to a Gulf Coastal Plain which fills the eastern and southern portion of the state, and lowland elevations vary from about 70 feet in the south to 700 feet on northeastern Crowley's Ridge. The thickly wooded Ozarks in the northwest fringed by scenic Boston Mountains are separated from the Ouachita* (wash-i-taw) Range by a broad Arkansas River Valley. Boat Mountain (2,220 ft.) and Sherman Mountain (2,250 ft) are among 9 summits rising above 2,000 feet in the Boston and Ozark mountains. The long ridges and wide flat valleys of the Ouachitas extend from Oklahoma to central Arkansas near Little Rock and also contain summits above 2,000 feet including Blue Mountain (2,750 ft.). Mount Magazine and Petit Jean Mountain (1,100 ft.) with its sparkling 75-foot Cedar Creek Canyon Falls are landmarks in the Arkansas River Valley. Pine trees predominate in the Ouachita Mountains and the eastern Gulf Coastal Plain, and hardwoods are in other areas.

Among 9,700 miles of streams, major rivers drain south and southeast except the Red River flowing across the southwestern corner of the state. The great Arkansas River and tributaries cross the state from Oklahoma at Fort Smith and join the Mississippi River at Desha County. The Black River and Little Red River in the north are tributaries of the remarkable White River. In Fulton County on the Missouri border, Mammoth Springs (18 acres) pours 36 million gallons of water per hour, and the impounded waters overflow into Spring River which merges with Eleven Point River before increasing the flow of the Black River. East of Crowley's Ridge, the St. Francis River meanders southward to the Mississippi River north of Helena. The Ouachita River, rising in Polk County, is impounded by dams before meeting the Saline River in southeastern Arkansas to flow into Louisiana.

The "Great Lakes of the Ozarks" extending across the Missouri border are formed by dams, and include Norfolk Lake (48 square miles) on Norfolk River between Gamaliel and Norfolk; the Beaver Reservoir (47 square miles) north of Eureka Springs, and Bull Shoals Lake (111 square miles) north of Flippen and Yellville on the White River. The Mountain View Recreation Area is between Bull Shoals and Norfolk Lakes. Lake Ouachita (75 square miles) impounded by the Blakely Mountain Dam in the Ouachita National Forest, Lake Catherine at Remmel Dam, and Lake Hamilton, formed by Carpenters Dam, are on the Ouachita River near Hot Springs. Blue Mountain Lake on Petit Jean Creek east of Booneville, Nimrod Lake on Fourche La Favre River at Fourche Junction, and Lake Greeson at the Narrows Dam on Little Missouri River north of Murfreesboro are in western Arkansas. Lake Conway (6,700 acres) near Conway, and Harris Brake south of Houston are in central Arkansas. Lake Chicot (10,880 acres) at Lake View in southeastern Chicot County is the largest natural lake in the state. Bear Creek and Stony Creek lakes

---

* Ouachita is derived from French spelling of an Indian expression meaning "good hunting grounds."

between Helena and Marianna, Seven Devils Lake east of McGehee, and Peckerwood Lake north of Stuttgart are among the numerous popular lakes in the state.

LICENSES

Resident licenses to fish and hunt are issued to any person 16 or more years of age who has been a bonafide resident for at least 60 days, and declares his intention of becoming a citizen of Arkansas. Members of the U.S. Armed Forces officially stationed in Arkansas may obtain resident licenses to hunt and fish immediately after arrival in the state. No license is required to fish from a bank with a handpole or rod if using worms as bait.

All nonresidents of any age and residents 16 or more years of age must possess valid licenses to hunt wildlife including predators. Hunting and trapping furbearing animals for commercial purposes requires a trapper's license in addition to a hunting license. Dogs used to chase, hunt, or take wild animals or birds must be licensed and wear a license tag on a collar with the name and address of the owner; or such information may be tattooed in the dog's ear. Bird dog trainer's licenses are not valid from May 15–Aug. 15. Special hunting licenses issued by county clerks are required in Chico and Desha counties in addition to valid state licenses.

Resident license fees: Fishing, $2.50; hunting, $2.50; trapping, $5.00; fishing guide, $5.00; combination fishing and hunting guide, $10.00; Hunting dog, $1.50; Amateur bird-dog trainer, $5.00; professional bird-dog trainer, $25.00; professional bird-dog trainer's helper, $10.00; federal "Duck" stamp for taking migratory game birds, $3.00; wild pet permit, $2.50; game breeders permit to raise legally acquired furbearing animals, birds, Trout, and Frogs for sale, $25.00; permit to raise same species for scientific and restocking purposes only, $2.50.

Nonresident license fees: Annual fishing, $5.00; fishing trip for 14 days, $2.50; hunting (except Deer and Turkey), $15.00; hunting all game, $25.00; archery permit to hunt Deer, $5.00; hunting or trapping furbearing animals for commercial purposes, $50.00; federal "Duck" stamp for taking migratory game birds, $3.00; hunting preserve shooting, daily –$2), annual–$5.00; permit to take Turtles or Turtle eggs, $200.00.

If an archer does not have an all-game hunting license ($25) and a Deer is taken, the archery permit must be surrendered and the difference of $20 paid for an all-game hunting license.

HUNTING AND TRAPPING

Game animals: Deer, Rabbit, Squirrel. OPEN SEASONS: Deer (archery only)—Oct. 1–Dec. 31; (firearms)—about 5 days in November and 10

days in December. Rabbits and Squirrels—Sept. 15–Dec. 31 in North
Zone; Rabbits—Oct. 1–Jan. 31; and Squirrels—Oct. 1–Jan. 15 in South
Zone. BAG LIMITS: Deer—2 per year. Rabbits and Squirrels—8 each
per day.

Furbearing animals: Beaver, Fox, Muskrat, Otter, Raccoon, Skunk.
OPEN SEASONS:* mid-November to mid-January, and extended to March
31 for Beaver, Muskrat, and Otter. Fox, Rabbit, and Raccoon may be
chased for pleasure all year, except during a closed season for Raccoon—
April 1–July 31. No bag or possession limits. Deer, Opossum, Rabbit,
Raccoon, Skunk, Squirrels, and Quail must be captured with hands only,
if taken for pets. NOT PROTECTED: Bobcat, Coyote, and Wolves may be
taken at any time.

Game birds: Coot, Mourning Dove, Ducks (except Canvasback and
Redhead), Gallinule, Geese, Merganser, Quail, Rails, Scaup, Wilson's
Snipe, Wild Turkey, Woodcock. OPEN SEASONS:* Coot, Duck, Merganser,
Scaup—about 3 weeks in December. Dove—1 week in September and
about 3 weeks in late December into January. Geese—month of October,
Gallinule, Rails—September and about 3 weeks in October. Quail and
Woodcock—December 1 into January. Wilson's Snipe—mid-December
to mid-January. Turkey—designated days in April. Game birds on licensed
shooting preserves—Oct. 1–March 31. FULLY PROTECTED: Canvasback
and Redhead Ducks—no open season. NOT PROTECTED: Crows, all
Hawks, and Owls may be taken at any time.

A legal Buck is a male Deer with antlers at least 4 inches long.
Resident hunters under the age of 16 must report to a warden for tagging
a Deer. The North and South zones are divided by Highway 64 from
Fort Smith to West Memphis.

FIREARMS

Migratory game birds and Quail may be taken with shotguns not
larger than 10 gauge, and capable of holding only 3 shells in the magazine
and chamber combined. It is unlawful to use or possess in the field any
buckshot or rifled slugs except during the open gun season on Deer and
Turkey. Deer hunters must use rifles larger than .22 caliber, and shotguns
not less than 20 gauge with ball shot, rifle slugs, or buckshot not smaller
than no. 4. All rifles of less than .22 caliber, or rifles using rimfire
cartridges, and shotguns of 410 gauge or smaller are prohibited. The
possession of firearms in fields, forests, along streams, or in any location known to be game cover, is considered to be prima facie evidence
that the possessor is hunting. There are no restrictions on longbow and
arrows.

---

* Check current state regulations.

The crossbow season (1 week in October) for Deer is held in the northern part of Franklin County and southern part of Madison County in the Ozark National Forest.

Shooting hours: Daylight hours. Exceptions: migratory game birds, sunrise to sunset; and the opening day of the Duck season (including split seasons) starts at 12 o'clock Noon. If the opening day for Brant, Coot, Geese, or Wilson's Snipe is concurrent, shooting hours for all species start at Noon. Hunting, or any attempt to take wild animals or birds, furbearers, and Frogs during hours of darkness are prohibited.

FISHING

Game fish: Black Bass, White Bass, Bream, Catfish (other than Bullhead), Goggle-Eye, Perch, Pickerel, Walleyed Pike, and Trout. OPEN SEASONS:* All year with local exceptions. White River National Wildlife Refuge (116,390 acres)—March 15–Oct. 31. Trout may not be taken by artificial bait between Nov. 1–March 1 in the Norfolk and White rivers below Bull Shoals and Norfolk dams to Lock no. 1. On the state capitol grounds, a pond stocked with Bass, Bream, Catfish, and Crappie is open every day (except Sunday) during daylight hours, only to anglers under 15 years of age.

Not more than 1 pole, or rod and line with a single hook or 1 legal artificial lure is permitted within 100 yards below any dam or similar areas on running streams. Gaffing and gigging game fish are prohibited, but rough-scaled fish may be gigged during December and January for personal use. Buffalo, Carp, Cat, Drum, and Suckers may be grabbed with the hands for personal use from Aug. 1–Oct. 31. Shooting Alligator Gar with longbow and arrow is permitted during daylight hours. Rough-scaled fish may be taken by bow and arrow, gig, spear, and underwater spear guns between sunrise and sunset in the following lakes only: Blue Mountain, Bull Shoals, Catherine, Conway, Greeson, Hamilton, Nimrod, Norfolk, Ouachita Lakes, and Harris Brake.

Frogs: OPEN SEASON: April 16–Dec. 31. DAILY BAG LIMIT: 12. A fishing license is required to take Bullfrog by hook and line, gig, hand nets, spears, or by use of hands.

Anglers find superb Rainbow Trout fishing in the tailwaters of Bull Shoals Dam downstream for about 100 miles of the White River. The Bull Shoal and Norfolk Lake region, and Lake Ouachita are tops for Bass, Catfish, and Walleye fishing. Single or group float trips of 1–10 days are popular on many streams, particularly on the Buffalo, Norfolk, and White rivers. Waterfowl flock down the Mississippi River Flyway, and the rice fields of the Grand Prairie region and Bayou Meto (31,000 acres)

---

* Check current state regulations.

also attract hunters. The World Championship Duck Calling Contest is held annually at Stuttgart in December. There is good fishing and hunting in national forests, but fishing only is available in state parks.

STATE PARKS

Buffalo River (1,948 acres) 12 miles south of Yellville, Marion County; *Bull Shoals* (994 acres) on southern shore of Bull Shoals Lake north of Flippen and Yellville, Marion County; *Daisy* (272 acres) at Lake Greeson near Murfreesboro, Pike County; *Lake Catherine* (2,179 acres) north of Malvern, Hot Springs County; *Lake Chicot* (45 acres) near Lake Village, Chicot County; *Lake Ouachita* (290 acres) near Mountain Pine, Garland County; *Petit Jean* (4,100 acres) on Petit Jean Mountain west of Oppello, Conway County.

Licenses, permits, regulations, and information about current seasons, bag and possession limits can be obtained from the Director, Arkansas Game and Fish Commission, State Capitol Grounds, Little Rock; or from county clerks and authorized agents. Special permits to hunt in the White River National Wildlife Refuge are issued by the manager at St. Charles. Camping and tourist information is available from the Arkansas Publicity and Parks Commission, State Capitol, Little Rock.

CALIFORNIA

Area: 158,297 square miles (land area—156,573 square miles); rank in nation—3
Animal: Grizzly Bear (*Ursus horribilis*), adopted 1953
Bird: California Valley Quail (*Lophortyx californica*), adopted 1931
Capital city: Sacramento on the Sacramento River in the Great Central Valley; population (1960)–191,667; rank in state–8
Counties: 58
Elevations: Highest, Mount Whitney (14,496 ft.). Inyo and Tulare Counties; lowest, Death Valley (282 ft. below sea level), Inyo County
Fish: Golden Trout (*Salmo aqua-bonita*), adopted 1947
Flower: Golden Poppy (*Eschscholtzia californica*), adopted 1903
Geographic center: 35 miles northeast of Madera in Madera County
Nicknames: Bear State, Golden State, Land of Sunshine, Poppy State
Population (1960): 15,717,204; rank in nation–2*
Tidal shoreline: 3,427 miles (including offshore islands, and to a point where tidal waters narrow to 100 feet wide)

---

* The U.S. Bureau of Census reported in 1963 that the population rose to 17,590,000, thereby competing with New York for first place.

Tree: California Redwoods (*Sequoia gigantea; Sequoia sempervirens*), adopted 1937. General Sherman Tree (*Sequoia gigantea*) in Sequoia National Park is 272 ft. tall with a base circumference of 101½ ft. and a diameter of 18½ ft. at 100 ft. above ground. Founders Tree (*Sequoia sempervirens*) in Coast Range is 364 ft. tall.

California faces the Pacific Ocean from Oregon on the northern boundary to the Republic of Mexico on the southern border. The eastern slope of the Sierra Nevada Range and the Mojave Desert are shared with Nevada down to the Colorado River, which divides Arizona from southeastern California. Off the coast of southern California are famous fishing waters around the Channel Islands—Anacapa, San Clemente, San Miguel, San Nicolas (76 miles from Los Angeles harbor), Santa Barbara, Santa Catalina, Santa Cruz, and Santa Rosa.

The great Central Valley contains the northern Sacramento Valley, 160 miles long and 60 miles wide at the southern end, and adjacent to the 250-mile long San Joaquin (Wah-KEEN) Valley. The Sacramento River rising in northern California wanders 382 miles before reaching Suisun Bay. The San Joaquin River from the southern Sierra Nevada foothills meanders for 350 miles to Suisun Bay and joins the Sacramento River to flow through San Pablo Bay and the Golden Gate of San Francisco Bay to the Pacific Ocean.

Shasta Lake (46 square miles) at the confluence of the McCloud, Pit and Sacramento Rivers is a key unit in an intricate system of canals, reservoirs and streams known as the Central Valley Project. The southern Salton Sea Basin with a 40-mile long lake was a desert area 235 feet below sea level until about 50 years ago.

The massive Sierra Nevada Range extends for about 430 miles north of Tehachapi Pass in Kern County to the Mount Lassen (10,435 ft.) volcanic region. The average elevation is 6,000-7,000 feet at the northern and southern ends, but there are 10 peaks above 14,000 feet in Fresno, Inyo, Mono and Tulare Counties including Mount Whitney and Mount Williamson (14,384 ft.). Precipitous canyons characterize the central portion of the Sierra Nevada although the western slope is broad and gentle. Glacial bodies of water vary from small pools to beautiful Lake Tahoe; and this natural "Lake of the Skies" at an elevation of 6,225 feet, extends for 23 miles along the California-Nevada boundary.

The rugged Klamath Range crosses the California-Oregon line west of the Cascade Range, and Thompson Peak (8,936 ft.) in Trinity County is the highest point. The sparkling white cone of Mount Shasta (14,162 ft.) in Siskiyou County crowns the northern tip of the Central Valley, and marks the southern end of the wooded and snowy Cascade Range which extends through Oregon and Washington.

The Coast Range for about 400 miles between the Pacific Ocean and Central Valley consists of numerous indistinct chains of broken ridges, spurs, plateaus, and small valleys among forests. The east-west Transverse Ranges of southern California include the Santa Inez, Santa Monica, San Gabriel, and San Bernardino Mountains.

The Santa Inez highlands rise to approximately 6,000 feet in the Ventura district about 70 miles northwest of Los Angeles. The highest point in the San Bernardino Mountains is San Gorgonio Peak (11,485 ft.), and in the San Gabriel Mountains, Mount San Antonio or Old Baldy rises to 10,080 feet. The Peninsular Range in the southwestern corner of California contains Mount San Jacinto (10,508 ft.) near Palm Springs, and Santa Rosa Mountain (8,046 ft.) to the southwest.

LICENSES

Resident licenses to fish and hunt are issued to persons 16 or more years of age who have lived in California for at least 6 months prior to the date of an application for a license, and to persons on active duty with the U.S. Armed Forces and any auxiliary branch. A sport fishing license is required for persons 16 or more years of age to take fish, amphibians, crustaceans, and mollusks in California waters. No license is necessary to fish from public piers in waters of the Pacific Ocean, if such piers are in the open sea adjacent to the coast and islands of California, or in the waters of open or closed bays contiguous to the ocean. One license stamp is required to take all fish from inland waters except Trout, but including Steelhead. Two stamps are necessary to take all species of Trout and other fish.

A Colorado River Special Use Stamp must be purchased in addition to a valid fishing license to fish from a boat or other floating device on the boundary waters of the Colorado River between Arizona and California. The angler should possess either an Arizona Special Use Stamp affixed to a California license, or a California Special Use Stamp with an Arizona license. Such a stamp is required even though the angler holds both an Arizona and a California license. To fish on the boundary waters of Lake Tahoe and Topaz Lake from the shore of either state or in any part of the lakes requires possession of either a valid California sport fishing license with appropriate stamps or a valid Nevada fishing license. A sport fishing license does not permit the holder to barter, exchange, or sell fish and frogs. State licenses are required to fish in national parks.

Persons under 18 years of age may trap furbearing animals without a license. Hunting licenses are granted to juveniles under the age of 18 upon presentation of a license from a prior year, or a certificate showing completion of a state-approved hunter safety training course. Special Deer hunt permits, and Deer or Bear tags are not issued to juveniles under 12 years of age. Applications for Special Deer hunt permits are attached to regular Deer tags. Any person possessing a hunting license and a Deer tag may file one application and designate his first and second choice of more than 20 Special Deer hunts held annually. After names have been drawn, hunters are notified by mail to send fees for their permits. All persons 16 or more years of age must purchase a federal "Duck" stamp at a post office to hunt migratory game birds. A hunting license is not required to take nonprotected animals and birds. Fees for hunting on military reservations are in addition to licenses and special Deer hunt permits.

State license period: fishing—Jan. 1–Dec. 31; hunting—July 1–June 30.

Resident license fees: Sport fishing, $3.00; citizen special 3-day fishing in Pacific Ocean, $1.00; hunting including archery (18 or more years of age), $4.00; hunting including archery (under 18 years of age), $1.00; trapping (18 or more years of age), $1.00. *Permits* (in addition to valid licenses): Special Deer hunts, $5.00; deer hunting on Camp Joseph Pendleton (per week end), $2.00; deer hunting on Hunter Liggett and Camp Roberts (per day), $2.00. *Stamps* (in addition to licenses): Federal "Duck" stamp, $3.00; sport fishing (each stamp) 2 for Trout and all fish, $1.00; Colorado River Special Use, $2.00. *Tags* (in addition to licenses): Bear, $1.00; Deer, $2.00; Pheasant, $2.00.

Nonresident license fees: Annual sport fishing, $10.00; fishing 10 consecutive days, $3.00; citizen special 3-day fishing in Pacific Ocean, $1.00; annual hunting (including archery), $25.00; hunting on licensed shooting preserves, $5.00. *Permits* (in addition to licenses): Special Deer hunts, $5.00; Deer hunting on Camp Joseph Pendleton (per week end), $2.00; Deer hunting on Hunter Liggett and Camp Roberts (per day), $2.00. *Stamps* (in addition to licenses): Sport fishing, each stamp (2 for Trout), $1.00; Colorado River Special Use, $2.00; federal "Duck" stamp for taking migratory game birds, $3.00. *Tags* (in addition to licenses): Bear, $1.00; Deer, $10.00; Pheasant, $2.00.

HUNTING AND TRAPPING

Big game: Pronghorn Antelope, Black Bear (including brown and cinnamon color phases), Mule Deer (California, Columbian, Rocky Mountain), Elk (Rocky Mountain, Roosevelt, Tule), European Wild Pig, Bighorn Sheep. OPEN SEASONS:* Bear—archery only during first 2 weeks of September in northeastern and late Deer season areas; firearms (including bow and arrow), mid-September to January. Buck Deer— archery only during 2 weeks in late July in designated areas, and during

---

* Check current state regulations.

the Bear archery season. Archery hunting in Los Angeles County generally extends from September through December or until 200 Deer have been taken. Firearms (including bow and arrow) in designated areas from the first week in August to November; special hunts for antlerless Deer of either sex in designated areas from late September through October. Wild Pig—Oct. 1–March 31 in Monterey County, and no closed season in remainder of California. SEASON BAG LIMITS: Bear—2; Buck Deer, 2 in designated areas, 1 antlerless Deer in special hunts, and 1 Buck in remainder of state. Wild Pig—1 per day in Monterey County, and no limit in remainder of state.

During the regular Deer season, a hunter may use one dog to take Bear and Deer, but the use of dogs is prohibited during an archery season. Three dogs per person or hunting party may be used to hunt Wild Pigs during an open season.

A legal forked-horn Buck is "a male Deer having a branched antler on either side with the branch in the upper two-thirds of the antler. Eye guards or other bony projections on the lower one-third of the antler shall not be considered as points or branches." Antlerless Deer include female Deer, fawn of either sex (other than spotted fawn), and male Deer with unbranched antlers not more than 3 inches in length on both sides.

Furbearing animals: Badger, Beaver, Fisher, Fox (Gray, Kit, Silver), Marten, Mink, Muskrat, Raccoon, Ring-tailed Cat, River Otter, Wolverine. OPEN SEASONS:* Badger, Fox, Mink, Ring-tailed Cat—mid-November through February. Muskrat—mid-November through March in 20 counties, all year in remainder of state. SEASON BAG LIMITS: None. Badger, Beaver, Ring-tailed Cat, Fox, Mink, Muskrat, and Raccoon may also be taken by bow and arrow. FULLY PROTECTED: Fisher, Sea Elephants, Sea Lions, Seals, Marten, River and Sea Otter, Bighorn Sheep, Wolverine—no open seasons. Antelope and Elk hunts are rare and usually spaced many years apart. The last Antelope hunts were in 1951, 1959, and Elk hunts in 1955, 1961. NOT PROTECTED: Bobcat, Cougar, Coyote, Gopher, Moles, Opossum, Porcupine, Jack Rabbits, Raccoons, Rodents including Ground Squirrels, Skunks, and Weasels may be taken at any time.

Small game: Brant, Coot, Dove (Chinese Spotted, Mourning, Ringed Turtledove), Ducks (except Canvasback and Redhead), Gallinule, Geese, Grouse (Ruffed, Sage, Sierra), Merganser, Chukar Partridge, Pheasant, Band-tailed Pigeon, Quail (Gambel, Mountain, Valley), Wilson's Snipe, Rabbit and Hare (Brush, Cottontail, Pigmy, Snowshoe), Tree Squirrels. OPEN SEASONS:* Brant—late November through January. Coot, Ducks, Geese, Gallinule, Merganser—October to January. Doves— usually month of September. Grouse—a few days in September or early

---

* Check current state regulations.

October in about 30 counties. Partridge—early November to mid-December in Lassen, Plumas, and Sierra counties, and to New Year's Day in 20 or more counties. Pheasant—last week in November and first week of December throughout state. Band-tailed Pigeons—during October in about 13 northern counties, and from mid-December in remainder of state. Wilson's Snipe—late November to first week in January. Shooting preserve seasons vary throughout state. Rabbits—September 1 to mid-December in 5 northeastern counties, and to New Year's Day in remainder of state. Tree Squirrels—November and December in 30 counties, but only to mid-December in Plumas, and parts of Shasta and Siskiyou counties. FULLY PROTECTED: Condor, Canvasback and Redhead Ducks, Bald Eagle, White-tailed Kite, Trumpet Swan—no open seasons. NOT PROTECTED: Crows, English Sparrow, California or Scrub Jay, Crested or Stellar's Jay, Magpie, and Starlings may be taken at any time.

FIREARMS

It is unlawful to take big game with a pistol, revolver, rifle using rim-fire cartridges, or bullets with full metal jackets, air gun, or shot shell in a shotgun. Game birds may not be taken with a pistol, revolver, air gun, pellet gun, rifle, or slug in a shotgun. The use of pistols or rifles to take Rabbit in Los Angeles County is prohibited. Automatic loading or hand-operated repeating shotguns, shotguns larger than 10 gauge, and holding more than 3 shells may not be used to take game animals and birds. If a shotgun is capable of holding more than 3 shells, the magazine must be plugged with a one-piece metal or wooden filler which cannot be removed through the loading end. The possession of a machine gun, silencer, shotgun with a barrel less than 18 inches in length, or rifle with a barrel less than 16 inches in length is prohibited. Pistols and revolvers up to and including .45 caliber, or shotguns with BB-sized shot or smaller, are the only firearms permitted during night hunting of Raccoon.

Any longbow used to take big game must cast a legal hunting arrow a horizontal distance of 130 yards, and the arrow should have a broadhead-type blade which will not pass through a hole seven-eighths of an inch in diameter. Other type arrows may be used for other purposes, but explosive heads are prohibited. No crossbow, autoloading crossbow, or any device consisting of a bow affixed to a stock may be used for taking game birds or mammals.

Shooting hours: One-half hour before sunrise to one-half hour after sunset for all game except migratory game birds and Raccoon. Dove, Wilson's Snipe, and waterfowl—one-half hour before sunrise to sunset. Shooting on the first day of the open Duck season starts at 12:00 o'clock noon. Raccoon may be hunted at night, and the use of lights (6-cell, 9-volt flashlights or smaller) are permitted if hand-held or worn on the head.

FISHING

Freshwater game fish: Black Bass (Largemouth, Smallmouth), Spotted Bass, Striped Bass, Bluegill, Catfish, Crappie, Sacramento Perch, Salmon (King, Kokanee, Silver), Steelhead, Sturgeon, Trout (Brown, Eastern Brook, Golden, Rainbow), Walleye, Mountain Whitefish. OPEN SEASONS:* All year except in designated waters where Salmon and Trout seasons extend from May through October. The special Steelhead season in tidewaters of Del Norte, Humboldt, Marin, Mendocino, Monterey, Napa, San Luis Obispo, San Mateo, Santa Cruz, and Sonoma Counties— Nov. 1 through February. Mountain Whitefish may only be taken in Trout waters. All freshwater fish, Salmon and Trout in ocean waters, and fish migrating into freshwater including Striped Bass, may be taken only between one hour before sunrise to one hour after sunset. Exceptions: Trout and Mountain Whitefish in Lake Tahoe may be caught until 2 hours after sunset; all species of fish in Millerton Lake in Fresno and Madera counties, Success Lake and Terminus (Kaweah) lakes in Tulare County until 10 P.M.; day or night in the Colorado River–Salton Sea Area, Coachella Valley, Bass Lake in Madera County, and Pine Flat Lake in Fresno County. Trout may be taken day or night from Bucks Lake in Plumas County during the open season. Lights may be used during night fishing if part of the fishing tackle.

Only one rod and line with not more than 3 single or multiple hooks, or not more than 2 plugs or similar lines, irrespective of the number of attached hooks or attractor blades, may be used by an angler in Lake Tahoe or Topaz Lake. In the Colorado River–Salton Sea Area, a fisherman may use only one line held in the hand or attached to a rod, with not more than 2 hooks; or one line and one artificial lure, or 2 flies. Otherwise, all freshwater fish and fish migrating into freshwater, including Striped Bass, Salmon, Sturgeon, and Trout in ocean waters, may be taken only by angling with one closely attended rod and line, and not more than 3 hooks attached to the line. The use of any multiple hook with the shortest distance between points greater than 1¼ inches, or shank longer than 2 inches; and any weight exceeding one-half ounce attached to a multiple hook, or to a line within 18 inches of a multiple hook (either directly or indirectly) are prohibited. Not more than 2 attractor blades (excluding terminal gear) may be used to take any fish from inland waters.

Candlefish (Eulachon) and Lamprey Eels may be taken with hand dip nets at any time, day or night, in the mainstream of the Klamath River and the main Trinity River from its mouth to the Humboldt–Trinity County line; Daily bag limit—25.

---

* Check current state regulations.

Chumming is prohibited in all inland waters except at Carquinez Straits, San Francisco, San Pablo, and Suisun Bays, the Sacramento River and tidewater of tributaries up to Capitol Avenue Bridge between Sacramento and West Sacramento; the San Joaquin River and tidewaters of tributaries to the Highway 50 bridge near Tracy, and the Colorado River–Salton Sea Area.

Carp may be taken with an underwater spear or bow and arrow in the Colorado River–Salton Sea Area, but not within one-half mile of any boat dock, swimming area, or other place where people congregate. There are designated waters where persons floating or swimming may use underwater spears to take Carp, Squawfish, and Suckers.

Saltwater game fish: Albacore, Barracuda, Bass (Kelp, Sand, Spotted), Bonito, Cabezon, Lingcod, Corbina, Croaker (Spotfin, Yellowfin), Halibut, Marlin, Opaleye, Rockfish, Salmon, Saltwater Perch, Sea Bass, Skipjack, Smelt, Sturgeon, Swordfish, Trout, Tuna (Bluefin, Yellowfin), and Yellowtail. OPEN SEASONS: All year, except Salmon may be taken from the Saturday nearest February 15 through the Sunday nearest November 15 south of Tomales Point including all bays, except San Francisco, San Pablo, and Richardson bays between Carquinez Bridge and Golden Gate —no closed season. North of Tomales Point including Tomales Bay and other bays—no closed season. Salmon may not be taken during August and September in ocean waters at the mouth of Eel River within 2 nautical miles north and south of a line drawn due west for 2 nautical miles from the center of the river's mouth, or within 3 nautical miles from the center of the mouths of the Klamath and Smith rivers.

Between May and September, surf casters enjoy the annual Bass blitz when thousands of Striped Bass are heralded by Cormorants circling overhead along the coast near San Francisco.

Crustaceans and mollusks: Crab, Spiny Lobster, Abalone, and Clams. OPEN SEASONS: Abalone—March 16–Jan. 14. Clams—at any time, except Gaper and Washington clams in Bodega Bay, Tomales Bay south of Sand Point, and Bolinas Lagoon, Oct. 1–June 30. Pismo Clams— Sept. 1–April 30 in Monterey and Santa Cruz counties. Razor Clams—all year, except only in odd or even-numbered years in some areas. Crab— Dec. 15–July 15 in Del Norte, Humboldt, and Mendocino counties, except in tidal waters of Eel River, Dec. 15–Aug. 30, and from the second Tuesday in November to June 30 in other counties. Spiny Lobster—first Wednesday of October through first Wednesday after March 15.

Any person wearing a self-contained underwater breathing device, goggles, face plates, and using spears when completely submerged may take any fish except Salmon, Striped Bass, Trout, Crustaceans, or Mollusks in ocean waters. No person may possess or use a spear within 100 yards of the mouth of any stream in ocean waters northerly of Ventura County.

Swordfish may be harpooned, and bow and arrow fishing tackle, harpoons, and spears may be used to take all species of rays, skates, and sharks except Soupfin Shark.

Elusive Grunion, found only on the coast of southern California from the Morro Bay area to Ensenada, Baja California, sweep in on extremely high tides to deposit eggs on sandy beaches during nights following a new or full moon. No holes may be dug, or appliances of any kind used to entrap these thousands of Grunions except a person's hands. Open season—June 1–March 31. Bag limits—none.

Frogs: The American Bullfrog and California Redlegged Frog of any size may be taken day or night by the use of hands, hook and line, bow and arrow fishing tackle, dip nets, paddles, and spears. OPEN SEASONS: central and northern California, March 1–Nov. 30; Colorado River–Salton Sea Area, Imperial, Los Angeles, Orange, Riverside, San Bernardino and San Diego Counties, June 1–Nov. 30. DAILY BAG LIMITS: central and northern California—24; remainder of state—12.

Excellent fishing and waterfowl hunting are found in national forests, and regions near the Lower Klamath and Tulelake National Wildlife refuges near the Oregon line. Popular impounded waters include Lake Alamor (44 square miles) on the North Fork of Feather River; Lake Berryessa (32 square miles) at Monticello Dam on Putah Creek; Folsom Reservoir (185 square miles) on American River; Millerton Lake (12,769 acres) at Friant Dam on the San Joaquin River; Pine Flat Reservoir (9 square miles) on Kings River; Shasta Lake (46 square miles) at confluence of McCloud, Pit, and Sacramento rivers; Trinity Reservoir (26 square miles) on the Trinity River. Steelhead and Trout anglers converge on the American, Eel, Feather, Klamath, Russian, Trinity, and Tuolumne rivers, and Kings Canyon, Sequoia, and Yosemite national parks in the Sierra Nevada. Rare Golden Trout lurk in the meadow region of the Upper Kern River watershed.

The state has developed a network of lakes and streams for freshwater fishing, and public beaches where sportsmen try surf casting and offshore deep sea fishing. There are public piers and jetties for saltwater fishing at Eureka (jetties) and Trinidad—*Humboldt County;* Long Beach, Malibu, Manhattan Beach, Playa Del Rey (jetties), Redondo Beach, San Pedro (breakwater), and Santa Monica—*Los Angeles County;* Bolinas and Point Reyes—*Marin County;* Monterey—*Monterey County;* Balboa, Capistrano Beach, Huntington Beach, Newport Beach (pier and jetties), San Clemente, and Seal Beach—*Orange County;* Mission Bay (jetties), Ocean Beach, Oceanside, Pacific Beach—*San Diego County;* Avila, Cayucos, and Pismo Beach—*San Luis Obispo County;* Princeton—*San Mateo County;* Gaviota, Goleta, and Santa Barbara—*Santa Barbara*

County; Avalon—*Santa Catalina Island;* Aptos, Capitola, Moss Landing, and Santa Cruz—*Santa Cruz County;* Port Hueneme (Wye-NEE-me) and Ventura—*Ventura County.*

Hunting is prohibited in national parks, game refuges, state beaches, parks, and other such public places except in Wildlife Management Areas.

POPULAR STATE PARKS

Freshwater fishing: *Big Basin Redwoods* (11,029 acres)—Santa Cruz County; *D. L. Bliss* (1,237 acres)—El Dorado County; *Brannan Island* (224 acres)—Sacramento County; *Calaveras Big Trees* (5,437 acres)—Calaveras and Tuolumne counties; *Castle Crags* (5,311 acres)—Shasta County; *Caswell Memorial* (258 acres)—San Joaquin County; *Clear Lake* (559 acres)—Lake County; *Colusa–Sacramento River* (9.6 acres)—Colusa County; *Henry Cowell Redwoods* (1,737 acres)—Santa Cruz County; *Curry–Bidwell Bar* (21 acres)—Butte County; *Cuyamaca Rancho* (20,819 acres)—San Diego County; *Del Norte Redwoods* (5,852 acres)—Del Norte County; *Donner Memorial* (353 acres)—Nevada and Placer counties; *Emerald Bay* (590 acres) at Lake Tahoe—El Dorado County; *Folsom Lake* (15,693 acres) on American River—El Dorado, Placer, and Sacramento counties; *Fremont Ford* (114 acres)—Merced County; *Gold Discovery Site* (92 acres) at Coloma—El Dorado County; *Grizzly Creek Redwoods* (150 acres)—Humboldt County; *George J. Hatfield* (47 acres)—Merced County; *Humboldt Redwoods* (22,531 acres in 4 segments—Burlington, Dyerville-Bull Creek, Stephens Grove, Williams Grove)—Humboldt County; *Kern River* (978 acres)—Kern County; *McArthur–Burney Falls Memorial* (485 acres)—Shasta County; *McConnell* (56 acres)—Merced County; *Mount San Jacinto* (12,708 acres)—Riverside County; *Pfeiffer–Big Sur* (803 acres)—Monterey County; *Portola* (1,665 acres)—San Mateo County; *Prairie Creek Redwoods* (9,568 acres)—Del Norte and Humboldt counties; *Richardson Grove* (591 acres)—Humboldt County; *Salton Sea* (8,123 acres)—Imperial and Riverside counties; *Jedediah Smith Redwoods* (9,540 acres)—Del Norte County; *Standish and Hickey* (555 acres)—Mendocino County; *Tahoe* (13.37 acres)—Placer County; *Samuel P. Taylor* (2,332 acres)—Marin County; Turlock Lake (228 acres)—Stanislaus County.

Saltwater fishing: *Alamitos Beach* (10.5 acres)—Los Angeles County; *Arroyo Burro Beach* (6.48 acres)—Santa Barbara County; *Asilomar Beach* (95.5 acres)—Monterey County; *Avila Beach* (10 acres)—San Luis Obispo County; *Capitola Beach* (5.66 acres)—Santa Cruz County; *Cardiff Beach* (8.37 acres) and *Carlsbad Beach* (10 acres)—San Diego County; *Carmel River Beach* (105.5 acres)—Monterey County; *Carpenteria Beach* (36.21 acres)—Santa Barbara County; *Carrillo Beach* (1,577.95 acres)—Los Angeles County; *Cayucos Beach* (15.6

acres) San Luis Obispo County; *Corona Del Mar Beach* (28.35 acres) and *Doheny Beach* (46.23 acres)—Orange County; *Dry Lagoon Beach* (926.74 acres)—Humboldt County; *El Capitan Beach* (111.22 acres), *Gaviota Beach* (8.8 acres), and *Goleta Beach* (22.91 acres)—Santa Barbara County; *Huntington Beach* (78.48 acres)—Orange County; *La Costa Beach* (14.2 acres)—San Diego County; *Little River Beach* (111.63 acres)—Humboldt County; *MacKerricher Beach* (263.18 acres) and *Manchester Beach* (261.43 acres)—Mendocino County; *Malibu Lagoon Beach* (37 acres) and *Manhattan Beach* (41.43 acres)—Los Angeles County; *Manresa Beach* (20.9 acres)—Santa Cruz County; *Moonlight Beach* (10 acres)—San Diego County; *Morro Bay* (1,476.69 acres) and *Morro Strand Beach* (33.69 acres)—San Luis Obispo County; *Natural Bridges Beach* (34.75 acres) and *New Brighton Beach* (49.32 acres)—Santa Cruz County; *Patrick's Point* (425.18 acres)—Humboldt County; *J. D. Phelan Beach* (6 acres)—San Francisco City-County; *Pismo Beach* (555 acres)—San Luis Obispo County; *Point Lobos Reserve* (355 acres)—Monterey County; *Point Sal Beach* (48.93 acres)—Santa Barbara County; *Ponto Beach* (10.6 acres) San Diego County; *Redondo Beach* (26.29 acres)—Los Angeles County; *Refugio Beach* (35.76 acres)—Santa Barbara County; *Russian Gulch* (1,115 acres)—Mendocino County; *San Buenaventura Beach* (113 acres)—Ventura County; *San Clemente Beach* (114 acres)—Orange County; *San Simeon Beach* (34 acres)—San Luis Obispo County; *Santa Monica Beach* (32.42 acres)—Los Angeles County; *Seacliff Beach* (80 acres)—Santa Cruz County; *Silver Strand Beach* (428 acres)—San Diego County; *Sonoma Coast* (697 acres)—Sonoma County; *Stinson Beach* (30.58 acres)—Marin County; *Sunset Beach* (169 acres)—Santa Cruz County; *Thornton Beach* (49.7 acres)—San Mateo County; *Tomales Bay* (936 acres)—Marin County; *Torrey Pines Beach* (61 acres)—San Diego County; *Trinidad Beach* (20 acres)—Humboldt County; *Van Damme Beach* (1,776 acres)—Mendocino County; *Will Rogers Beach* (186.5 acres)—Los Angeles County; *Zmudowski Beach* (144 acres)—Monterey County.

Licenses, permits, stamps, and tags can be obtained from the California Department of Fish and Game, License Office, 1325A–"K" St., Sacramento. Information about open seasons, bag limits, and regulations are available from the Director, Department of Fish and Game, 722 Capitol Mall, Sacramento; and regional offices at 1312 Blackstone Ave., Fresno; 724 S. Spring St., Los Angeles; 627 Cypress St., Redding; Ferry Building, San Francisco. Other information: Division of Beaches and Parks, California Department of Natural Resources, 1125 Tenth St., Sacramento. California Department of Fish and Game issues the *Quarterly* (annual subscription, $2); *Outdoor California* (annual subscription,

$1); a new series of ocean-fishing maps (free); and excellent booklets for nominal sums. Sporting goods stores also carry free copies of current regulations.

COLORADO

Area: 104,247 square miles (land area—103,922 square miles); rank in nation–8
Animal: Rocky Mountain Bighorn Sheep (*Ovis canadensis*)
Bird: Lark Bunting (*Calamospiza melanocorys*), adopted 1931
Capital city: Denver on Cherry Creek and South Platte River at Front Range of the Rocky Mountains overlooking the High Plains. Population (1960)–493,887; rank in state–1
Counties: 63
Elevations: Highest, Mount Elbert (14,431 ft.) in Lake County; lowest, Arkansas River (3,350 ft.) in Prowers County
Flower: Rocky Mountain Columbine (*Aquilegia coerulea*), adopted 1889
Geographic center: Near Lake George in Park County
Nicknames: Centennial State, Rocky Mountain State, Switzerland of America
Population (1960): 1,753,947; rank in nation–33
Tree: Blue Spruce (*Picea pungens*), adopted 1939

Colorado extends from the eastern boundary shared by Kansas and Nebraska to Utah on the west, and from Nebraska and Wyoming on the northern border to New Mexico and Oklahoma on the southern line. Four Corners is the only place in the United States which 4 states share —Arizona, Colorado, New Mexico, and Utah.

The entire state is interlaced with lakes, reservoirs, and streams including the eastern portion known as the High Plains; and the remainder of the state contains the magnificent Rocky Mountain System. The crest of the Continental Divide follows peaks of the northern Park Range in the Routt National Forest down through Rabbit Ears Pass (9,680 ft.) in an easterly direction to Longs Peak (14,256 ft.) in Rocky Mountain National Park, and zigzags southwesterly through the Gore Range in Gunnison National Forest to the San Juan Mountains and swings southeast of Chromo into New Mexico. There are high plateaus, glaciers, gorges, alpine lakes and streams, wide fertile valleys, and 54 snow-covered mountains rising above 14,000 feet plus about 800 peaks over 11,000 feet above sea level.

The Front, or Snowy, Range, including Longs Peak, is northwest of Denver and contains the beautiful Rocky Mountain National Park (260,018 acres). The Ramparts rise abruptly from the High Plains to

Pikes Peak (14,110 ft.) near Colorado Springs, and the green-forested and cloud-crowned Sangre de Cristo Range guarding San Luis Valley has 7 summits above 14,000 feet including Blanca Peak (14,317 ft.) south of the Great Sand Dunes National Monument (36,740 acres). The massive San Juan Range framing the western portion of San Luis Valley contains 15 peaks above 14,000 feet including Mount Wilson (14,246 ft.) southwest of Telluride. Castle Peak (14,259 ft.) and Moroon Peak (14,158 ft.) with lovely Lake Moroon are near Aspen in the White River National Forest; and Mount Elbert towers above Twin Lakes near 15 summits rising above 14,000 feet in the impressive Sawatch Range.

There are 27 mountain passes varying in elevations from Raton Pass (7,834 ft.) at the New Mexico border south of Trinidad, to Trail Ridge High Point (12,183 ft.) in the Rocky Mountain National Park. The only passes closed to winter travel are Cumbres Pass (10,022 ft.) and La Manga Pass (10,230 ft.), southwest of Conejos near the New Mexico boundary; Independence Pass (12,095 ft.), southeast of Aspen; Lizard Head Pass (10,222 ft.), between Dolores and Telluride; Trail Ridge High Point and Milner Pass (10,759 ft.), in the Rocky Mountain National Park. The Grand Mesa Plateau north of Delta on the Gunnison River has more than 200 lakes and reservoirs among scenic canyons and cataracts. The Uncompahgre Plateau, creased by many streams between the Dolores and Gunnison rivers, contains Columbia Pass (8,500 ft.) on the road between Delta and Nucia.

The Arkansas River ripples down from Turquoise Lake near Leadville east of the Continental Divide, and cuts through the Royal Gorge (2,600 ft. deep, 8 miles long) west of Canon City to roll by Pueblo and across the southeastern High Plains to Kansas on a long journey to the Mississippi River. The South Platte River runs swiftly northward from Eleven Mile Reservoir, and falls 4,830 feet in 140 miles before crossing the High Plains in northeastern Colorado to Nebraska. The Colorado River rising in the Rocky Mountain National Park plunges down western slopes of the Continental Divide, passing Hot Sulphur Springs, Glenwood Springs, and Grand Junction before entering Utah eventually to reach the Gulf of California. The East and Taylor rivers mingle waters at Almont to continue as the Gunnison River. The 9,180-acre lake created by the Blue Mesa Dam near the Black Canyon of the Gunnison National Monument (13,547 acres) should draw more anglers to this famous Trout stream, which joins the Colorado River at Grand Junction. The Rio Grande del Norte, fed by the Conejos River and other tributaries, flows through the San Luis Valley for about 130 miles to New Mexico. In northwestern Colorado, the White River leaves Trappers Lake in the Flattops region to pass Meeker before reaching Utah. The Yampa River rising above Steamboat Springs in the Park Range ripples by Craig to join the Little Snake River before merging with the Green River in the Dinosaur National Monument (204,136 acres) on the Utah border. From Jackson County, the North Platte River formed by Grizzly and Little Grizzly creeks runs north across the Wyoming boundary. Martin Reservoir (180 acres) on the Arkansas River is in Huajatilla Park near Walsenburg in southeastern Colorado.

LICENSES

Resident licenses to fish and hunt are issued to persons 15 or more years of age who have maintained a permanent abode in the state for at least 6 months; to personnel of the U.S. Armed Forces, and other nations allied with the United States; and to personnel of the diplomatic service of any nation recognized by the United States who are stationed on permanent duty in Colorado. Any active member of the U.S. Armed Forces who is a resident patient at any Veterans Administration hospital, Armed Forces hospital, or convalescent station may obtain a free fishing license during his stay in Colorado. Big game hunting is restricted to persons 18 or more years of age. Juveniles 14–18 years of age may hunt after obtaining appropriate licenses, and must be accompanied by licensed adults. Any person under the age of 15 without a license may take only one-half the legal bag and possession limits.

A bow and arrow license is required for special archery seasons, and a big game license to hunt with bow and arrow during regular and special firearm seasons. Deer hunting on a Southern Ute Indian Reservation requires a Colorado big game license and a special permit issued by the Southern Ute Tribal Council. A Bear license is valid only during the special Bear season, but possession of a first Deer license, or an Elk license entitles the holder to take Bear during the big game seasons. Hunter's Choice Permits are granted by public drawings for choice of bull, cow, or calf during the special Elk season. Applications are available July 1 at local authorized dealers for residents, and at the Colorado Game and Fish Department in Denver for nonresidents. The nonresident application accompanied by a certified check or postal money order for $50 should be received in Denver not later than August 20. Antelope, Bighorn Sheep, and Wild Turkey hunting is open to residents only. A small game hunting license is required to take unprotected game, except that any person (or members of his immediate family and employees) may hunt, trap, and kill predatory animals and birds on his lands, or as a member of a group organized for such purposes.

Juveniles under the age of 15 may fish without a license, but are permitted to take only one-half the legal bag limits. State fishing licenses are required in national forests and parks. All persons 16 or more years of age must purchase a federal "Duck" stamp to take migratory game birds. *Resident license fee:* Fishing, $4.00; small game hunting, $2.00; combination fishing and hunting small game, $5.00; archery Deer hunting, $5.00; first, or original Deer hunting (firearms), $7.50; second Deer hunting (firearms), $5.00; Antelope hunting, $10.00; Bear hunting, $5.00; Elk hunting, $10.00; Bighorn Sheep hunting, $25.00; Wild Turkey, $5.00; federal "Duck" stamp, $3.00.

Nonresident license fees: Annual fishing, $10.00; fishing 5 consecutive days, $3.50; small game hunting, $10.00; Bear hunting, $10.00; first or original Deer hunting, $40.00; second Deer hunting, $7.50; archery Deer hunting, $10.00; Elk hunting, $50.00; federal "Duck" stamp, $3.00; hunting on shooting preserves, $5.00.

HUNTING AND TRAPPING

Big game: Antelope, Bear, Mule Deer, Elk, Moose, Mountain Goat, Rocky Mountain Bighorn Sheep. OPEN SEASONS:* The regular big game season usually opens on the third Saturday of October on the western slope of the Continental Divide and in San Luis Valley; and on the fourth Saturday in October on the eastern slope of the Divide; and runs about 2 weeks. A special archery season from mid-August to mid-September in the Rock Creek Area of Rio Grande County permits the use of bow and arrow only to take Bear, Deer, and Elk. Antelope—varies by region from a few days in September in Moffat County and South Park to November on the High Plains. Bear—April 1–September 15, and during Deer and Elk seasons with proper licenses, but not at any time in the San Juan–Rio Grande Bear Management Area. Deer—mid-August to mid-December with about 10 preseasons and postseasons in Game Management Units. Elk—about 3 weeks from mid-October into November. Bighorn Sheep— about 2 weeks in September. ANNUAL BAG LIMITS:* Antelope—1. Bear— 3 (one each with a Bear, Deer, and Elk license). Deer—3 (one each on first and second Deer licenses, and one on the Deer tag issued without cost on the second Deer license). Bighorn Sheep—1 Ram. Dogs may be used to hunt Bear until September 1, and any hunter using more than one dog must be accompanied by a licensed guide. FULLY PROTECTED: Buffalo, Black-footed Ferret, Fisher, Mountain Goat, Moose, Otter, Abert Squirrel, Wolverine—no open seasons. Designated areas and bag limits for taking Beaver are set under special permits. NOT PROTECTED: Badger, Bobcat, Canada Lynx, Cougar (Mountain Lion), Coyote, Fox, Gopher, Porcupine, Prairie Dog, Jack Rabbit, Raccoon, Skunk, Squirrels (except Abert), Wolves, unlicensed domestic cats and dogs not claimed or under human

---

* Check current state regulations.

control and running at large on game cover and trails may be taken at any time. Bounty for Mountain Lion—$50.

In any area bounded by a mountain ridge, licensed hunters may cross the ridge and take antlered Deer and Bighorn Sheep on the farthermost slope down to the timberline. A legal antlered buck is a male Deer with hard antler material protruding through the skin. Antlered Elk should have antlers at least 10 inches in length measured on the outside curve of the antler from burr to tip. Bear, Cougar, and Deer only may be taken with tribal permission on a Southern Ute Indian Reservation. Guides are not required by law, but are recommended for their expert knowledge of rugged regions, and hunters are advised to wear red or flame-orange clothing.

Small game: Coot, Mourning Dove, Ducks (except Canvasback and Redhead), Geese, Grouse (Blue, Sage, Sharp-tailed), Merganser, Chukar Partridge, Quail (Bob White, Gambel's, Scaled), Ring-necked Pheasant, Ptarmigan, Turkey, Cottontail and Snowshoe Rabbits. OPEN SEASONS:* Coot, Ducks, Merganser—early October to January west of the Continental Divide, and mid-November to mid-December east of the Divide, except a special San Luis Valley season of about 2 weeks in October. Dove—Sept. 1–Oct. 30. Geese—concurrent with Duck season west of the Divide; early November to mid-January east of the Divide; and a special season of about 7 weeks after the first of November in a portion of Larimer County. Grouse, Ptarmigan—1 week in September and 1 week in November. Pheasant, Quail—1 week in November throughout the state, and longer in designated areas. Rabbits—mid-October through February. Turkey—1 week in October and 1 week in late November. Hunting on shooting preserves—Oct. 1–March 31. FULLY PROTECTED: Canvasback and Redhead Ducks, Prairie Chickens, Swans, and Woodcock —no open seasons. NOT PROTECTED: Crow, English or European Sparrow, Blue Jay, Pinyon Jay, Cooper's Hawk, Duck Hawk, Goshawk, Sharp-shinned Hawk, Magpie, and Great Horned Owl may be taken at any time.

FIREARMS

Migratory game birds may be taken with shotguns not larger than 10 gauge, and capable of holding only 3 shells in the magazine and chamber combined. Chukar Partridge, Pheasant, and Quail may be taken only with shotguns. Blue Grouse and Ptarmigan may be taken only with shotguns, and .22 caliber rimfiring weapons. Turkey—only shotguns not larger than 10 gauge or smaller than 20 gauge. Cottontail and Snowshoe

---

* Check current state regulations.

Rabbits—shotguns, handguns, and rifles of all calibers, and longbows, but trapping by any means is prohibited. Big game—shotguns not smaller than 20 gauge and firing a single slug; muzzle-loading rifles of 40 caliber or larger; hand-operated and semiautomatic rifles holding not more than 6 rounds in the magazine and chamber combined; and using centerfire ammunition and cartridges having soft-nosed bullets of more than 70 grains in weight, and with a rated impact energy 100 yards from the muzzle of more than 1,000 foot pounds. Archers may use nonmechanical (longbow) bows capable of casting the hunting arrow a minimum distance of 130 yards to take Blue Grouse, Ptarmigan, Turkey, and big game. The possession of any firearms with cartridges in the magazine, or of a strung bow in any vehicle while using a spotlight, is unlawful. The entire state is closed to rifle hunting 3 days prior to the opening of the general Deer and Elk season, except those areas in which a preseason extends to the opening date of the Deer and Elk season.

Shooting hours: Dove, Chukar, Grouse, Pheasant, Quail, and Turkey —sunrise to sunset. Waterfowl—sunrise to sunset east of the Continental Divide; one-half hour before sunrise to sunset in the Pacific Flyway; shooting for all species starts at 12:00 o'clock noon on the opening day of the Duck season. Big game—one-half hour before sunrise until one-half hour after sunset. Cottontail and Snowshoe Rabbits—same as big game, except in areas open for taking upland birds and waterfowl, where shooting coincides with the most restrictive hours.

FISHING

Game fish: Black Bass (Largemouth, Smallmouth), White Bass, Catfish (Bullhead, Channel), Crappie, Drum, Yellow Perch, Northern Pike, Kokanee Salmon, Trout (Brook, Brown, Mackinaw, Rainbow), Walleye (Pike-perch), Whitefish. OPEN SEASONS:* all year, except closures in designated areas for fall-winter or winter-spring periods. American Crystal Sugar Lake (Otero County), April 1–Sept. 30. Parvin Lake (Larimer County), from third Saturday in May to Sept. 30. Two Buttes Reservoir (Baca County), April 1 through the day before opening of the migratory waterfowl season. Waters open to angling all year except during the migratory waterfowl season: Burchfield Reservoir (Baca County); Adobe Creek or Blue Lake, John Martin and Scotchfield reservoirs (Bent County); Boulder City Reservoir (Boulder County); Smith Reservoir (Costilla County); Meredith Reservoir (Crowley County); Eads Lake or Queens Reservoir (Kiowa County); Boyd Lake (Larimer County); Julesburg or Jumbo Reservoir (Logan and Sedgwick counties); Jackson Reser-

---

* Check current state regulations.

voir (Morgan County); Prewitt Reservoir (Washington County); Bonny Reservoir (Yuma County).

Fishing hours in streams, Beaver ponds, and Parvin Lake—4:00 A.M.–9:00 P.M.; except in all streams east of U.S. Highway 87 and portions of the Colorado, Green, White, and Yampa rivers west of Highway 13, and all lakes (except Parvin) and reservoirs—day and night fishing is permitted during open seasons.

Legal angling is a personally attended line, or rod and line with not more than 3 hooks attached; and a double or treble hook with one common shaft is considered as one hook.

Kokanee Salmon may be taken by angling, archery, or snagging from Nov. 1–Dec. 31, except during a closed season in the Shadow Mountain Spillway on the North Fork of the Colorado River: Nov. 15–Dec. 15. Carp, Minnow, Squawfish, and Suckers may be taken for bait by seines and traps.

Frogs: Bullfrogs may be taken during August and September. Daily bag limit—10. A fishing license is required, and the use of nets, seines, traps, firearms, poisons, or any stupefying substances are prohibited.

Beautiful Grand Lake (500 acres) is adjacent to the Shadow Mountain National Recreation Area (18,240 acres) at the west entrance of the Rocky Mountain National Park. Lake Granby (72,056 acres), and Shadow Mountain Reservoir (1,800 acres) are also good Kokanee Salmon and Trout waters. There are 2,400 lakes and 11,300 miles of streams to tempt novice and expert anglers.

PUBLIC RECREATION AREAS

Lathrop State Park (720 acres of land, 180-acre Martin Lake) 2 miles west of Walsenburg—Huerfano County; *Antero Reservoir** (290 acres of land, 2571 acres water) west of Hartsel near Trout Creek Pass—Park County; *Bonny Dam Reservoir* (3,600 acres land, 2,400 acres water) southeast of Idalia—Yuma County; *Cherry Creek Reservoir* (3,765 acres land, 904 acres water) 12 miles southeast of Denver; *Crawford Reservoir* (355 acres land, 397 acres water) at Crawford—Delta County; *Eleven Mile Reservoir** (1,742 acres land, 3,169 acres water) west of Lake George—Park County; *Golden Gate Canyon* (2,471 acres) near Central City—Gilpin County; *Green Mountain Reservoir* (1,438 acres land, 2,125 acres water) between Dillin and Kremmling—Summit County; *Gross Reservoir** (1600 acres land, 421 acres water), west of Eldorado Springs —Boulder County; *Lester Creek Reservoir* (222 acres land, 167 acres

* Leased from Denver, and maintained by the Colorado Game, Fish, and Parks Department.

water) near Clark–Routt County; *Paonia Reservoir* (1,110 acres land, 309 acres water) at Paonia—Delta County; *Ramah Reservoir* (400 acres land, 150 acres water) at Ramah—El Paso County; *Sweitzer Lake* (17 acres land, 160 acres water) 2 miles south of Delta—Delta County; *Sylvan Lake* (113 acres land, 42 acres water) at Eagle—Eagle County; *Vega Reservoir* (1,830 acres land, 900 acres water) 10 miles east of Colbran—Mesa County; *Williams Fork Reservoir* (2,000 acres land, 1,630 acres water) 4 miles south of Parshall—Grand County; *Willow Creek Reservoir* (800 acres land, 303 acres water) north of Granby—Grand County.

Licenses, permits, regulations, and information about current seasons, bag and possession limits can be obtained from the Colorado Game, Fish, and Parks Department, 6060 Broadway (P.O. Box 720), Denver 1. Regional offices: Southeast—1904 North Circle Drive, Colorado Springs; Northeast—317 West Prospect, Fort Collins; Northwest—215 Petroleum Building, Grand Junction; Southeast—209 North Townsend, Montrose. The department also publishes an illustrated and interesting bimonthly magazine *Colorado Outdoors* ($1.00 annually).

State and county maps: Colorado State Highway Department, 4201 East Arkansas Ave., Denver 22. National Forest maps: Forest Supervisor of each national forest; and Regional Forester, U.S. Forest Service, Building 85, Denver Federal Center, Denver 25. *Colorado Camp Grounds, Colorado Guide List,* and *Ranch Accommodations For Big Game* are issued by the Colorado Department of Public Relations, Capitol Building, Denver 2. General Tourist information: Colorado Visitors Bureau, 225 West Colfax, Denver. The *Official Colorado Fishing and Hunting Guide,* revised annually, is a valuable source of information for sportsmen, and includes a Wyoming supplement. Published by Tim L. Kelley, 774-15th, Boulder ($2.00).

CONNECTICUT

Area: 4,965 square miles (land area—4,899 square miles); rank in nation —48
Bird: Robin (*Turdus migratorius*), adopted 1943
Capital city: Hartford on the Connecticut River; population (1960)—162,178; rank in state—1
Counties: no organized counties
Elevations: Highest, Bear Mountain (2,355 ft.) north of Salisbury; lowest, sea level on Long Island Sound
Flower: Mountain Laurel (*Kalmia latifolia*), adopted 1907
Geographic center: at East Berlin

Nicknames: Constitution State, Charter Oak State, Nutmeg State
Population (1960): 2,535,234; rank in nation–25
Tidal shoreline: 618 miles (including islands, bays, and streams to a point where tidal waters narrow to 100 ft.)
Tree: White Oak (*Quercus alba*), adopted 1947

Connecticut is bordered by New York on the west, Rhode Island on the east partially divided by Pawcatuck River below Clark Falls, Massachusetts across the northern boundary, and the deeply indented southern shoreline on the Long Island Sound of the Atlantic Ocean.

There are countless lakes, ponds, reservoirs, and streams among forests, rolling hills, and sheltered valleys east and west of the broad Connecticut River flowing from Massachusetts near Thompsonville southward to Long Island Sound. The river is enlarged by many tributaries including Farmington River merging southeast of Windsor, the Salmon River above East Haddam, and Eight Mile River at Hamburg Cove northeast of Essex. The largest stream in western Connecticut is the Housatonic River rising in the Berkshire Hills of Massachusetts, and before reaching Long Island Sound, it receives waters from the Aspetuck, Still, and Shepaug rivers above and below New Milford, and the Naugatuck River near Derby. The French and Quinebaug rivers enter the northeastern corner of the state and combine waters near Mechanicsville, and fed by many streams including the Pachaug and Shetucket rivers, join the Yantic at Norwich to form the Thames River which flows between Groton and New London to Long Island Sound. Among other tidewater streams are the Mianus River near Greenwich running from the Mianus Reservoir on the New York border; the Noroton and Rippowan rivers at Stamford; the Norwalk, Saugatuck, and Poquonock rivers west of the Housatonic; the Quinnipiac River at New Haven; and the Mystic River at Noank and Mason Island.

LICENSES

Resident licenses to fish, hunt, and trap are issued to persons 16 or more years of age who are bona fide residents of the state. A nonresident landowner, spouse, and lineal descendants, or any nonresident lineal descendant of a Connecticut resident who owns improved real estate assessed for taxation purposes in the amount of at least $1,000, may procure a resident license from the town clerk where the property is located. A valid fishing license is required to take fish (including marine species) in tidal waters within the inland district of the state. Free fishing licenses are issued to blind persons. No hunting license will be issued to any person unless he has held a license to hunt with firearms in any state or country within 10 years prior to the date of application, or can present to the town clerk a certificate proving completion of a course in the safe handling and use of firearms. A juvenile between 12–16 years of age with a certificate issued by an instructor in the safe handling and use of firearms may hunt if accompanied by a licensed hunter at least 21 years of age. Juveniles under the age of 12 are not permitted to hunt in Connecticut.

Any person 16 or more years of age with a valid hunting license may procure a special archery license to hunt Deer. Trapping licenses are issued only to residents, and special permits are required to trap on lands owned or leased by the state. Any resident 65 or more years of age who has held valid licenses for at least 5 times to hunt, trap, and fish (or any combination) may obtain a permanent license of the same type for $5.35, or an annual license for $1.35. Not more than 5 Deer hunting permits are issued to one person, and only 2 Deer may be taken annually regardless of the number of permits held by a sportsman. Special licenses are not required to hunt on private shooting preserves. Hunting is prohibited on Sundays, and possession of any weapon in the open is considered as a violation of that law.

Resident license fees: Annual fishing, $4.35; fishing 3 consecutive days,* $1.35; hunting, $4.35; archery Deer hunting (in addition to regular license), $5.35; hunting and fishing, $6.35; hunting and trapping, $6.35; hunting, trapping, and fishing, $8.35; trapping (16 or more years of age), $3.35; trapping (under age of 16), $1.35; Deer hunting permits (issued to licensed hunters), $5.00; federal "Duck" stamp for taking migratory game birds, $3.00.

Nonresident license fees: Annual fishing, $6.35; fishing 3 consecutive days,* $1.85; hunting, $11.35; hunting and fishing, $15.35; archery Deer hunting (in addition to regular license), $5.35; Deer hunting permits (issued to licensed hunters), $5.00; federal "Duck" stamp for taking migratory game birds, $3.00.

HUNTING AND TRAPPING

Game animals: Deer, Moose, Rabbit (Cottontail, Snowshoe), Raccoon, Gray Squirrels. OPEN SEASONS:** Deer—Nov. 1–Dec. 31 by bow and arrow on private and public lands; Dec. 1–Jan. 31 by shotgun or bow and arrow on private lands. Cottontail Rabbit and Gray Squirrel—mid-October to first week in January. Snowshoe Rabbit—December 1 to early January. Raccoon—October to early January. SEASON BAG LIMITS: Deer—2. Cottontail Rabbits—25; Snowshoe Rabbits—10. Raccoon—40. Squirrels—40. FULLY PROTECTED: Moose—no open season.

Furbearing animals: Bear, Beaver, Bobcat, Fox (Gray, Red), Canada

---

* Issued only between July 1–Dec. 31.
** Check current state regulations.

Lynx, Mink, Muskrat, Opossum, Otter, Raccoon, Skunk, Weasel. OPEN TRAPPING SEASONS:* Beaver—Nov. 1–March 15 in Fairfield, Hartford, and Litchfield townships. Mink, Muskrat, Otter, Raccoon, Skunk—Nov. 1– March 15 statewide. Beaver, Mink, Muskrat, and Skunk may not be hunted with firearms or bow and arrows, and trapping Gray Squirrels, Cottontail and Snowshoe Rabbits is prohibited. NOT PROTECTED: Black Bear, Bobcat, Fox, Canada Lynx, Belgium or European Hare, Opossum, Otter, Panther, Porcupine, Red Squirrel, Weasel, and Woodchuck may be hunted at any time. Bounties: Bobcat and Canada Lynx—$5 each.

Game birds: Brant, Coot, Mourning Dove, Ducks (except Canvasback and Redhead), Eider, Gallinule, Geese (except Snow Goose), Ruffed Grouse, Merganser, Partridge (Chukar, Hungarian), Pheasant, Quail, Rails, Scota, Sora, Wilson's Snipe, Turkey, Woodcock. OPEN SEASONS:* Brant, Geese, Wilson's Snipe—mid-October to mid-November. Coot, Ducks, Merganser—about 2 weeks in October. Eider, Old Squaw, Scota—Oct. 1–Jan. 15 in coastal waters lying seaward from the first upstream bridge, but same as Duck season in other areas. Gallinule, Rails, Sora—September and October. Grouse—mid-October to early January. Quail—mid-October for about 2 weeks. Woodcock—mid-October to late November. Game birds on private shooting preserves—Sept. 15–March 15. FULLY PROTECTED: Mourning Dove, Hungarian Partridge, Snow Goose, Canvasback and Redhead Ducks, Turkey—no open seasons. NOT PROTECTED: Crows. Hawks may be killed in the act of destroying property.

FIREARMS

Rifles using ammunition larger or heavier than .22 caliber rimfire long-rifle cartridges, and shotgun ammunition of loads larger or heavier than no. 2 shot may not be used in state forests or on any state-owned lands.

Rifles and shotgun ammunition of loads larger or heavier than no. 2 shot may not be possessed during the open season for upland game on state leased lands or hunting areas requiring permits, except by landowners, lessees, their spouses, lineal descendants, and regular employees on their lands. Rifles of any caliber, and shotgun ammunition of any load (except rifled slug and ball shot) may be used to take unprotected wildlife during upland game closed season. Migratory game birds may not be taken with shotguns larger than 10 gauge or capable of holding more than 3 shells in the magazine and chamber combined.

Deer may be taken by a longbow capable of propelling an arrow of not less than 400 grains for at least 150 yards free flight on level ground.

---

* Check current state regulations.

The arrowhead should have 2 or more blades measuring not less than seven-eighths of an inch at the widest point. Only shotguns and longbows may be used to hunt Deer under special Deer hunting permits. During the archery Deer season, archers are not permitted to carry firearms, and all arrows must be marked with the full name and address of the owner.

Shooting hours: Hunting is prohibited on Sunday. Migratory game birds—sunrise to sunset. Other game—one-half hour before sunrise to one-half hour after sunset; except that Fox and Raccoon may be hunted after sunset on state-owned lands open to hunting, and on private lands with owner's permission.

FISHING

Game fish: Alewives, Black Bass, Striped Bass, Bullhead, Catfish, Chain Pickerel, Perch (White, Yellow), Great Northern Pike, Pike-perch (Walleye), Sockeye Salmon, Shad, Smelt, Sturgeon, Sunfish, Trout (Brook, Brown, Cutthroat, Lake, Rainbow). OPEN SEASONS:* Bass, Carp, Eels, Panfish, Northern Pike, Smelt, and Sturgeon may be taken all year in the Connecticut River and coves, Farmington River (downstream from Route 75 at Poquonock), French River, Housatonic (except in towns of Cornwall and Sharon), Pachaug River (downstream from Sawmill Dam) Quinebaug River (except between South Canterbury railroad crossing and dam on Wauregon Pond), Quinnipiac River (certain downstream stretches, below Hanover Dam), Shetucket River (except between dam at Windham downstream to Route 97, Baltic), Thames River and coves (except portion closed to fishing Oct. 31). Other inland waters generally open mid-April. There are more than 300 streams and many lakes and ponds stocked with Trout; and portions of some streams, and ponds free from ice have been set aside for anglers under 16 years of age.

Anglers may not use more than 2 personally attended lines (with or without rods), and each line is limited to not more than one artificial lure, or 3 flies, or 2 baited hooks. Sport fishing includes angling, bobbing, ice fishing, spearing, scoop netting, and use of bow and arrow.

Ice fishing is open from the first ice to mid-April. Juveniles under the age of 16 may not fish through ice unless accompanied by a licensed fisherman. Not more than 6 tip-ups, floats, hand-held jigs, or any combination of such devices may be used at one time. Juveniles under the age of 16 may use only 2 such devices and combined catch of a juvenile and licensed fisherman may not exceed the creel limit for one fisherman. Not more than 2 hand-held jigs may be used by an ice fisherman after the last Sunday in February.

---

* Check current state regulations.

Carp, Eel, Lamprey, and Suckers may be taken with bow and arrow from mid-April through May 31 in the Housatonic River and impoundments below Shepaug Dam, Candlewood Lake, Lake Zoar, Lake Housatonic, Connecticut River (including coves and pools formed by flood waters) and all other areas open to commercial fishing. They may also be speared in streams not stocked with Trout, but spearing is prohibited in lakes and ponds. No spear guns of any type are permitted, and underwater spearing is unlawful in all inland districts.

Popular public waters stocked with fish are in state forests and parks, Candlewood Lake (5,420 acres) between Danbury and Sherman, Gardner Lake (487 acres) north of Oakdale, Highland Lake (444 acres) near Winstead, Lake Lillinonah (1,900 acres) on the Housatonic River near Brookfield Center, Lake Waramaug (680 acres) north of New Preston, Quaddick Reservoir (467 acres) east of Thompson, and Stafford Reservoir (165 acres) at Staffordville. Either New York or Connecticut fishing licenses are legal on the entire Indian Pond north of Sharon; and Rhode Island or Connecticut licenses permit fishing on Beach Pond near Voluntown, Keatch Pond near Thompson, and Killingsly Pond at Killingsly. Only fishing is permitted in the following state parks, but state forests and other public areas are open to hunting and fishing.

STATE FORESTS

Algonquin (1,806 acres) at Colebrook; *American Legion* (783 acres) at Barkhamsted; *Cockaponset* (14,957 acres) at Chester; *Housatonic* (9,153 acres) at Sharon; *Mattatuck* (4,365 acres) near Northfield and Waterbury; *Meshomasic* (7,488 acres) at Portland; *Nassahegan* (1,226 acres) at Burlington; *Natchaug* (10,566 acres) near Phoenixville; *Naugatuck* (3,264 acres) at Beacon Falls; *Nehantic* (3,247 acres) at East Lyme; *Nepaug* (1,198 acres) at New Hartford; *Nipmuck* (7,864 acres) at Union; *Nye Holman* (718 acres) at Tolland; *Pachaug* (22,389 acres) at Voluntown; *Paugnut* (1,479 acres) at Torrington; *Paugusset* (1,044 acres) at Newtown; *Peoples* (2,954 acres) at Barkhamsted; *Pootatuck* (1,042 acres) at New Fairfield; *Quaddick* (496 acres) at Thompson; *Salmon River* (6,102 acres) at East Hampton; *Shenipsit* (6,144 acres) at Somers; *Tunxis* (8,071 acres) at Hartland; *Wyantenock* (3,178 acres) at Kent.

STATE PARKS

Beaver Brook* (401 acres) near North Windham; *Bigelow Hollow** (513 acres) at Mashapaug Lake near Union; *Black Rock* (451 acres) on West Branch of Naugatuck River near Reynolds Bridge; *Burr Pond** (437

---

* Public boat launching ramps.

acres) at Burrville; *Campbell Falls* (102 acres) north of Norfolk; *Chatfield Hollow* (345 acres) near Killingworth; *Day Pond* (180 acres) near Westchester; *Devils Hopyard* (860 acres) on Eight Mile River at Millington; *Gay City* (1,542 acres) on Blackledge River near Gilead; *Haddam Meadows** (158 acres) on Connecticut River near Haddam; *Hammonasset Beach** (1,015 acres) on Hammonasset River and Long Island Sound between Clinton and Madison; *Haystack Mountain* (287 acres) north of Norfolk; *Harkness Memorial* (231 acres) on Long Island Sound west of Ocean Beach; *Higganum Reservoir* (152 acres) at Higganum; *Hopeville Pond** (316 acres) at Hopeville; *Housatonic Meadows* (440 acres) on Housatonic River at Cornwall Bridge; *Hurd* (698 acres) on Connecticut River south of Middle Haddam; *Indian Well** (152 acres) on Housatonic River near Shelton; *Kent Falls* (275 acres) on Housatonic River near North Kent; *Kettleton* (485 acres) on Housatonic River south of Southbury; *Lake Waramaug* (95 acres) between East Kent and New Preston; *Macedonia Brook* (1,845 acres) north of Macedonia; *Mansfield Hollow** (110 acres) at Willimantic Reservoir near Mansfield Center; *Mashamoquet Brook* (628 acres) east of Abington; *Mount Tom* (223 acres) on Bantam River southeast of Woodville; *Old Furnace* (101 acres) southeast of Danielson; *Putnam Memorial* (220 acres) on Little River north of Redding Ridge; *Quaddick** (118 acres) at Quaddick Reservoir near Thompson; *Rocky Neck* (561 acres) on Long Island Sound near South Lyme; *Sherwood Island* (203 acres) on Long Island Sound east of Saugatuck; *Sleeping Giant* (1,216 acres) on Mill River at Mount Carmel north of New Haven; *Squantz Pond** (175 acres) on Candlewood Lake North of New Fairfield; *Stratton Brook* (145 acres) west of Simsbury; *Wadsworth* (285 acres) at Rockfall; *Wharton Brook* (106 acres) near Quinnipiac.

REGULATED HUNTING AREAS

Permits are not required to hunt on state-owned or leased areas, but permission must be obtained on other regulated sections of private lands.

DISTRICT 1. *Fairfield-Litchfield Area.* Permits required: Brookfield Sportsmen's Club (1,530 acres); Canaan Landowners (2,095 acres); Goshen Rod & Gun Club (1,392 acres); Naugatuck Fish & Game Club (1,253 acres); New Milford Sportsmen's Association (2,628 acres); Newtown Fish & Game Club (2,196 acres); Seymour Fish & Game Club (2,722 acres); Thomaston Fish & Game Club (2,466 acres); Torrington Fish & Game Club (7,021 acres); Woodbury-Southbury Rod & Game Club (5,966 acres). State-owned or leased (no permits required): East Swamp (87 acres) at Bethel; Bridgeport Hydraulic Shooting Area (1,075

---

* Public boat launching ramps.

acres) at Monroe, Shelton, and Trumbull; Monroe Shooting Grounds (2,932 acres); Charles E. Wheeler Wildlife Area (62 acres) on Housatonic River at Stratford.

DISTRICT 2. *Hartford—New Haven Area.* Permits required: Branford Rod & Gun Club (1,285 acres); Bristol Fish & Game Club (1,250 acres); Deep River Sportsmen's Club (2,007 acres); Hamden Fish & Game Association (3,684 acres); Higganum-Haddam Rod & Gun Club (1,326 acres); Madison Rod & Gun Club (1,667 acres); Meriden Rod & Gun Club and Meriden Farmers (5,134 acres); Middlefield Fish & Game Club (2,066 acres); Middletown Sportsmen's Club (1,916 acres); Old Saybrook Rod & Gun Club (2,078 acres); Pataconk Fish & Game Association (2,872 acres); Suffield Sportsmen's Association (3,720 acres); Wallingford Rod & Gun Club (5,678 acres); Westfield (2,004 acres). State-owned or leased (no permits required): Cromwell Meadows (496 acres); Durham Meadows (556 acres); Farmington Shooting Grounds (998 acres); Great Harbor (188 acres); Hammonasset Beach State Park (966 acres); Metropolitan District Shooting Grounds (4,559 acres) at Colebrook and New Hartford; Ragged Rock Creek (160 acres) near Old Saybrook; Charles E. Wheeler Wildlife Area (750 acres) on Housatonic River at Milford and Orange.

DISTRICT 3. *Tolland-Middlesex Area.* Permits required: Belltown Sportsmen's Club (3,848 acres); East Windsor-Enfield Farmers (6,746 acres); Glastonbury Sportsmen's Association (1,860 acres); Manchester Sportsmen's Association (1,321 acres); Nathan Hale State Forest Management Area (700 acres). State-owned or leased (no permits required): Great Island (488 acres) at mouth of Connecticut River near Old Lyme; Holbrook Pond (70 acres) near Hebron; Lord's Cove (245 acres) at Lyme; Mansfield Shooting Grounds (2,500 acres); Pelton's Pasture (261 acres) at East Windsor; Seldon's Neck State Park (527 acres) at Lyme; Sheffield Scientific School (465 acres) at East Lyme; South Windsor Shooting Grounds (2,977 acres) at South and East Windsor; Stone Ranch (2,000 acres) at Lyme; Tolland Shooting Grounds (17,768 acres) at East Windsor, Ellington, Enfield, Somers, Vernon; Waterford Shooting Grounds (1,520 acres) at East Lyme and Waterford.

DISTRICT 4. *Windham—New London Area.* Permits required: Eastern Connecticut Sportsmen's Association (1,000 acres) at Ashford; Groton Sportsmen's Club (2,315) at Ladyard; Norwich Fish and Game Club and Wawecus Hill Farmers (3,021 acres); Sprague Rod & Gun Club (3,400 acres); Woodstock Landowners (6,953 acres); Yale Forest (1,700 acres) at Eastford. State-owned or leased (no permits required); Assekonk Swamp (694 acres) at North Stonington; Barn Island (557 acres) near Stonington; Brooklyn-Pomfret Shooting Grounds (3,021 acres); Franklin Swamp (301 acres) at North Franklin; Lebanon-Franklin Shooting

Grounds (11,796 acres); Pease Brook (207 acres) at Lebanon; Tetreault Pond (60 acres) at Killingly.

Licenses, permits, regulations, and information about current seasons, bag and possession limits, demarcation lines between marine and inland districts, and lists of lakes, ponds, and reservoirs open to public pleasures can be obtained from town clerks, or the Director, Connecticut Board of Fisheries and Game, State Office Building, Hartford 15. Write to Subscription Supervisor for subscription to the interesting bimonthly *Connecticut Wildlife Conservation Bulletin* (50 cents per year). For Marine District information write to the Connecticut Shell Fish Commission, State Dock, Milford.

DELAWARE

Area: 2,399.2 square miles (land area—1,961.7 square miles); rank in nation–49
Bird: Blue Hen Chicken, adopted 1939
Capital city: Dover on Silver Lake and St. Jones Creek in Kent County; population (1960)—7,250; rank in state–4.
Counties: 3
Elevations: Highest, Centerville (440 ft.) in New Castle County; lowest, sea level.
Flower: Peach Blossom (*Prunus persica*)
Geographic center: 11 miles south of Dover in Kent County
Nicknames: First State, Diamond State, Blue Hen State
Population (1960): 446,292; rank in nation–46
Tidal shoreline: 381 miles (including islands, bays, and streams to a point where tidal waters narrow to 100 ft.)
Tree: American Holly (*Ilex opaca*), adopted 1939

Delaware on the Atlantic Ocean and Delaware Bay and River shares the "Eastern Shore" of the Delmarva Peninsula with Maryland on the southern and western border. Pennsylvania is north of an arched area of rolling hills; and the Delaware Memorial Bridge south of Wilmington connects the state with New Jersey east of the Delaware River.

Between Delaware City and Port Penn, the Chesapeake and Delaware Canal serves as an intracoastal waterway for 13 miles between the Delaware River and Maryland's Elk River flowing into Chesapeake Bay. There are numerous small streams, tidal estuaries, coves, and marshlands on Delaware Bay and sandy shores of the Atlantic Ocean. The largest port is Wilmington on Brandywine Creek and the Christina River in northern Delaware. The Nanticoke River in southwestern Delaware links

Seaford with Chesapeake Bay. In the southeastern corner of the state, Little Assawoman, Indian River, and Rehoboth bays are Atlantic tidal waters.

LICENSES

Resident licenses are issued to persons who have lived in Delaware for at least one year immediately preceding an application for a license. Resident males over 16 years of age, and nonresident males over 15 years of age must possess licenses to fish in ponds and nontidal streams. No license is required to fish where the tide regularly ebbs and flows, including the Chesapeake and Delaware Canal. Female anglers are not required to have a license if they are accompanied by a licensed fisherman, or anyone lawfully fishing. A trout stamp is required to fish in designated Trout waters.

A resident and the immediate members of his family who live on a farm containing 20 or more acres may fish, hunt, and trap on the farm without licenses. Otherwise, all residents and nonresidents over 15 years of age should obtain a license to hunt and trap. Residents, and nonresidents other than aliens who are under the age of 15, may hunt without a license when accompanied by a person with the lawful right to hunt. Nonresidents other than aliens should obtain a special license to hunt on regulated shooting preserves. A federal "Duck" stamp to hunt migratory game birds must be purchased by all persons 16 or more years of age. Frogs may be taken by the holder of a fishing or a hunting license. Annual license period: July 1–June 30.

Resident license fees: Annual fishing, $2.20; hunting and trapping, $3.20; Trout stamp (in addition to license), $2.10; federal "Duck" stamp (in addition to hunting license), $3.00.

Nonresident license fees: Fishing, $7.50; hunting and trapping, $20.00; hunting on regulated shooting preserves, $3.00; Trout stamp (in addition to fishing license), $2.10; federal "Duck" stamp (in addition to hunting license), $3.00.

HUNTING AND TRAPPING

Upland game: Deer, Red Fox, Opossum, Pheasant, Quail, Raccoon, Gray Squirrels. OPEN SEASONS:* Deer—archery, about 4 days in early October; shotguns, about 4 days in early November. Cock Pheasant and Rabbits—mid-November to first week in January. Quail—mid-November through January. Squirrels—mid-September through October. Opossum and Raccoon—Nov. 1–Jan. 31, except that Raccoon may be taken at any time in Kent and New Castle counties east of routes 13 and 113

---

* Check current state regulations.

from Washington to Mispillion River. Red Fox may be chased from Oct. 1–April 30, except during the shotgun season for Deer. Hunting on regulated shooting preserves—Oct. 15–March 31. SEASON BAG LIMITS:* Deer—1. Cock Pheasant—2. Quail—8. Rabbit—4. Squirrel—4. Opossum and Raccoon—no limit.

Migratory game birds: Brant, Coot, Ducks (except Canvasback and Redhead), Mourning Dove, Eider, Gallinule, Geese (except Snow Geese), Merganser, Old Squaw Duck, Rails, Scaup, Scota, Sora, Wilson's Snipe, Woodcock. OPEN SEASONS:* Coot, Ducks, Merganser, Scaup, Scota—3 weeks in November and 3 weeks in December. Brant, Geese—opens same day as Duck season and extends through December. Mourning Dove—Mid-September to mid-October, 3 weeks from mid-November into December, and 2 weeks from late December into January. Gallinule, Rails, Sora—early September to mid-November. Wilson's Snipe—mid-November through December. Woodcock—about 6 weeks from mid-November into January.

Furbearing animals: Mink, Muskrat, Otter. OPEN SEASONS:* Mink, Otter—Dec. 1 to mid-March. Muskrat—Dec. 1 to mid-March in New Castle County and extended an extra 10 days on embanked meadows; Kent and Sussex counties, mid-December to mid-March. SEASON BAG LIMITS: none. FULLY PROTECTED: Canvasback and Redhead Ducks, Snow Geese and Osprey—no open seasons. NOT PROTECTED: Crows, Hawks, Owls, Gray Fox, Skunk, Weasel, and Groundhog may be taken at any time.

FIREARMS

Groundhogs and Squirrels may be taken with rifles. Upland game and migratory game birds may be taken only with shotguns using not larger than no. 2 shot, and the gun must be plugged to hold only 3 shells in the magazine and chamber combined. It is unlawful to carry buckshot, rifle slugs, or pumpkin balls except when hunting Deer with a shotgun no smaller than 20 gauge during the gun Deer season, and using only the above ammunition. Archery Deer hunters may use long-bows and arrows with sharpened broadheads not less than seven-eighths of an inch in width.

Shooting hours: Deer, Pheasant, Quail, Rabbit, Squirrel—one hour before sunrise to one hour after sunset. Dove—12:00 o'clock noon to sunset. Waterfowl, Snipe, Woodcock—sunrise to sunset, except that on the opening day of the Brant, Coot, Duck, and Geese season, shooting starts at 12:00 o'clock noon. Frogs, Muskrat, Raccoon, Opossum, Mink, Otter, and Fox may be hunted at night. Sunday hunting is prohibited, except for Groundhog and Red Fox.

* Check current state regulations.

FISHING

Game fish: Bass, Trout (Brook, Brown, Rainbow). OPEN SEASONS: Trout—from the second Friday in April to second Saturday in November. All year for other fish. Hours for Trout fishing—one-half hour before sunrise to one-half hour after sunset.

All freshwater fish should be caught with hook and line. Only Carp may be taken with hook and line, bow and arrow, spear, or by special permit, seined from nontidal waters.

Frogs: OPEN SEASON: May 1–Dec. 31. SEASON BAG LIMITS: 10 (fishing license) or 24 (hunting license).

Surf casting and offshort deepwater fishing in chartered "head" boats are popular at Big Stone Beach, Bowers Beach at Murderkill River, Broadkill Beach, Fowler Beach, Kitts Hummock, Lewes, Mispillion Light, Primehook Beach, and Woodland Beach on Delaware Bay; Bethany Beach, Oak Orchard on Indian River Inlet, Rehoboth Beach, and other public beaches on the Atlantic Ocean.

PUBLIC FISHING AREAS

Kent County: Little Creek Wildlife Area* (2,468 acres) on Delaware Bay east of Dover; Moore's Lake (48 acres) south of Dover; Silver Lake at Dover; Coursey Pond (60 acres) and McCauley's Pond (55 acres) near Frederica; Blair's Pond (73 acres), Griffith Lake (35 acres), Haven Lake (76 acres), Silver Lake (34 acres), and Tub Mill near Milford; Garrison Pond* (100 acres) and Lake Como south of Smyrna; Woodland Beach Wildlife Area (3,341 acres) on Delaware Bay east of Smyrna; Derby Pond (20 acres) near Woodside. *New Castle County:* Augustine Beach Recreational Area (96 acres) and Reedy Island* (50 acres) on the Delaware River near Port Penn; Beck's Pond (37 acres) near Glasgow; Canal Wildlife Area* (4,999 acres) bordering the Chesapeake and Delaware Canal. *Sussex County:* Assawoman Wildlife Area* (1,459 acres) on Little Assawoman Bay southeast of Dagsboro; Burton's Pond on Herring Creek near Angola; Hoxsey's Pond (61 acres), Raccoon Pond (15 acres), Records Pond (100 acres), Trap Pond, and Trussum Pond near Laurel; Ingram Pond (35 acres) near Millsboro; Primehook Wildlife Area* (635 acres) northeast of Milton.

Public hunting areas also include the Appoquinimink Wildlife Area (35 acres) near Odessa in New Castle County; on the Atlantic Coast from Dewey Beach to Fenwick (2,650 acres); and the Owens Tract (170 acres) east of Greenwood in Sussex County; and state forests.

---

* Also hunting during open seasons.

STATE FORESTS

Blackbird (676 acres) south of Middleton in New Castle County; *Ellendale* (993 acres) and *Redden* (2,820 acres) south of Ellendale in Sussex County.

Licenses, regulations, and information about current seasons, bag and possession limits can be obtained from the Director, Delaware Board of Game and Fish Commissioners, Dover. For information relating to motorboats, write to the Delaware Commission of Shell Fisheries, Small Boat Safety Division, P.O. Box 48, Rehoboth Beach. Charts and maps are available from the U.S. Coast and Geodetic Survey, Department of Commerce Building, Constitution Avenue at 15 St., Washington, D.C.

FLORIDA

Area: 58,560 square miles (land area—54,252 square miles); rank in nation–26
Bird: Mocking Bird (*Mimus polyglottus*), adopted 1927
Capital city: Tallahassee among lakes and wooded hills of Leon County; population (1960)—48,174; rank in state–11
Counties: 67
Elevations: Highest, Iron Mountain (325 ft.) in Polk County; lowest, Atlantic Ocean (sea level)
Flower: Orange Blossom (*Citrus trifoliata*), adopted 1909
Geographic center: 12 miles west of north of Brooksville in Citrus County
Nicknames: Everglades State, Land of Flowers, Orange State, Peninsula State, Sunshine State
Population (1960): 4,951,560; rank in nation–10
Tidal shoreline: 8,426 miles (including islands, bays, and streams to a point where tidal waters narrow to 100 ft.)
Tree: Sabal Palm (*Sabal palmetto*), adopted 1953

South of Alabama and Georgia, Florida is a pistol-shaped peninsula thickly fringed with barrier keys (islands), bays, lagoons, sandy beaches, and marshes on the Atlantic Ocean and Gulf of Mexico. For more than 100 miles, bridges of the Overseas Highway link Miami on the mainland with Key West, one of the dangling chain of keys varying in size from shreds of coral limestone to 30-mile long Key Largo. Northern Florida extends more than 400 miles from the Perdido River forming the western Alabama-Florida border, to Amelia Island in the Atlantic Ocean at the mouth of the twisting St. Marys River on the Georgia boundary.

The broad and beautiful St. Johns River rising from a swampy area west of Melbourne wanders northward for about 200 miles parallel to the northeast coast in a series of natural lakes ranging in size from little Lake Helen Blazes at the source, larger Lake Harney, and 11-mile Lake George before turning at the deep water port of Jacksonville to flow eastward through a 20-mile estuary of the Atlantic Ocean. The Indian River consists of 150 miles of lagoons and sounds protected by narrow islands on the northeastern coast near Smyrna Beach south to Stuart. It is known as the Halifax River at Daytona Beach, and called Lake Worth at Palm Beach. The "Venice of America" between Palm Beach and Miami, Fort Lauderdale, has 200 miles of waterways, and one of the largest marinas in the nation at Bahia-Mar Yacht Basin. The Intracoastal Waterway from Fernandia Beach at the northern end of Amelia Island to Miami on Biscayne Bay and Key West is a favorite route of many sportsmen.

On the Gulf of Mexico, Pensacola Beach on Santa Rosa Island is connected by a bridge with the City of Pensacola in the northwestern corner of the state. The Gulf coast is bordered by primeval growth south of Port Joe and around the region known as the Great Bend. On the southwestern coast are large sheltered ports such as Charlotte Harbor behind Boca Grande, a famous Tarpon fishing area, and the great Tampa Bay flanked by Boca Ciega, Old Tampa, Hillsborough, and Sarasota bays.

A central ridge bisecting the peninsula from north to south for about 200 miles is covered with coniferous woods, and the highlands of northern Florida are laced with lakes, streams, pine, and oak forests. Hardwood and palm tree hammocks stand out among lakes and swamps of central Florida, and the Highlands Hammock State Park (3,800 acres) near Sebring is a dense jungle wilderness accessible by marked trails and gravel roads. Sportsmen flock to Lake Apopka, Tsala Apopka Lake, Tohopekaliga Lake, Lake Kissimmee, and Lake Istokpoga among other inland waters. The Everglades is a shallow sea of grass with hammocks of tropical trees, prairies, and extensive water areas. Lake Okeechobee (730 square miles) drains the central ridge through the Kissimmee River system, and the volume of water flowing to the sea is controlled by canals. The Cross State Canal is a small boat channel extending from the eastern terminis at Stuart via St. Lucie Canal, Lake Okeechobee, Caloosahatchee River to San Carlos Bay west of Fort Myers. Big Cypress Swamp is between Lake Okeechobee and the mangrove-covered Ten Thousand Islands on the Gulf. The Everglades National Park (1,400,533 acres) is on the southern tip of the Florida peninsula.

Major streams flowing into the Gulf of Mexico are the Choctawatchee River between Pensacola and Panama City; the Apalachicola River impounded at the southwest corner of Georgia to form the Jim Woodruff Reservoir at Chattahoochee; the Ochlockonee River from Lake Talquin west of Tallahassee; the Suwannee wandering from Okefenokee

Swamp in the northeast to a marshy delta near Cedar Key; the With-lacoochee River leaving Tsala Apopka Lake at Floral City to reach Tampa Bay; and Peace River, which flows from the Lakeland region into Charlotte Harbor. The Tamiami Trail from Miami is a modern highway through the Everglades to Nogales, turning northward to Fort Myers, Sarasota, and Tampa.

LICENSES

Resident licenses for fishing, hunting, and trapping are issued to citizens 15 through 64 years of age who have been bona fide residents of the state for at least 6 months and to members of the U.S. Armed Forces on active duty in Florida. Licenses are not required for saltwater fishing, or to fish in freshwater with not more than 3 cane poles in the county of the angler's legal residence. All persons 15 through 64 years of age must possess valid fishing licenses to use any rod and reel or artificial lures in freshwater. Any person fishing outside his home county should obtain a state fishing license. Nonresidents except juveniles under the age of 15 are required to possess valid fishing licenses to fish by any method in freshwater and to hunt wildlife throughout the state. Non-resident owners paying taxes on at least 3,000 acres of land may purchase special licenses to hunt in the county where the property is located. Alien hunting licenses are issued only by the Game and Fresh Water Fish Commission in Tallahassee.

Hunting licenses are required to take furbearing animals with guns and dogs for noncommercial purposes, but licenses or permits are not necessary to kill unprotected furbearing animals if they are damaging personal property. Persons holding valid trapping licenses and any person exempted from possessing a license for reason of age may take furbearing animals commercially by use of guns, snares, traps, and dogs. Trapping is prohibited in all Wildlife Management Areas unless authorized by area regulations. Hunting on such areas usually requires a public hunting permit in addition to a regular hunting license. Party permits (not to exceed 17 persons) may be purchased for 3-day managed Bear hunts in the Apalachicola and Osceola national forests. Special permits are also required for Deer and Quail hunts in Citrus County, and on the Elgin Air Force Base. All persons 16 or more years of age must purchase a federal "Duck" stamp to take migratory game birds.

Resident license fees: Fishing (statewide), $2.00; game hunting in county of residence, $2.00; game hunting in other counties (statewide), $7.50; game hunting in a county other than county of residence, $4.50; hunting on licensed private preserves only, $5.50; trapping in county of residence, $3.25; trapping in counties other than place of residence, $10.50; statewide trapping, $25.50; alien hunting license, $50.00; federal

"Duck" stamp (in addition to hunting license), $3.00; hunting guide, $10.00. *Permits* (in addition to regular hunting license): Wildlife Management Area hunting, $5.00; Elgin Air Force Area hunting, $4.00; Elgin Air Force Area hunting and fishing, $5.00; Cecil M. Webb Area hunting (per day), $5.00; Citrus County archery Deer Hunt, $5.00; Citrus County Quail hunt (per day), $2.00; Bear hunting in Apalachicola and Osceola national forests, $50.00 (party).

Nonresident license fees: Statewide fishing (annual), $8.00; fishing 14 consecutive days, $3.25; fishing 5 consecutive days, $2.25; statewide hunting (annual), $26.50; hunting 10 consecutive days, $11.50; county hunting only by taxpayer, $11.50; county trapping only, $25.50; statewide trapping, $100.50; alien hunting license, $50.00; hunting on private shooting preserves, $5.25; federal "Duck" stamp, $3.00. Permits for managed hunts cost the same as for residents.

HUNTING AND TRAPPING

Game animals: Black Bear, White-tailed Deer, Wild Hog, Cottontail and Swamp Rabbits, Fox and Gray Squirrels. OPEN SEASONS:* The general hunting season opens on the third Saturday in November and extends into January, and Squirrels may also be taken through February. Seasons usually include Sundays to allow week-end hunting, and if Christmas or New Year's Day falls on Sunday, the following Monday is open. There is no closed season for Rabbits. Days of the week may be designated for hunts in Wildlife Management Areas. The Apalachicola and Osceola Bear hunts are held from the last week in September to mid-November, and the date of a party hunt is determined by drawings, but there is no hunting on Sunday. A hunt supervisor accompanies each group (not to exceed 17 persons) during each 3-day hunt. SEASON BAG LIMITS: Deer—2. Wild Hog—2 except on the Camp Blanding Management Area—4. Bear, Rabbits and Squirrels—no limit except only 2 Fox and 10 Gray Squirrels per day. A legal buck is a male Deer with antlers not less than 5 inches long.

Furbearing animals: Beaver, Bobcat, Civet Cat, Fox (Gray, Red), Mink, Nutria, Opossum, Otter, Raccoon, Skunk, Weasel. OPEN SEASONS:* Beaver, Mink (except Everglades Mink), Otter—Dec. 1–March 1. BAG LIMITS: none. FULLY PROTECTED: Alligator, Crocodile, Club Bear, Axis Deer, Key Deer, fawn Deer, Everglades Mink, Panther, Florida Weasel—no open seasons. NOT PROTECTED: Armadillo, Bobcat, Civet Cat, Gray and Red Fox, Mice, Moles, Nutria, Opossum, Raccoon, Rats, Shrews, Skunk, Flying Squirrels, amphibians and reptiles may be taken at any time (local exceptions).

Game birds: Coot, Mourning Dove, Ducks (except Canvasback and

* Check current state regulations.

Redhead), Gallinule, Geese (except Ross's and Snow), Merganser, Pheasant, Quail, Rails, Scaup, Sora, Gobbler Turkey, Wilson's Snipe, Woodcock. OPEN SEASONS:* Coot, Ducks, Geese, Merganser, Scaup—Late November through December. Dove—season usually divided into 3 parts during October through December. Gallinule, Rails, Sora—mid-September to mid-November. Pheasant, Quail, and other nonnative upland game birds —mid-November to late February. Wilson's Snipe—mid-November through December. Turkey—mid-November to January plus 2 weeks in April. Woodcock—mid-November to January. Game birds on licensed hunting preserves—Oct. 1–March 31. FULLY PROTECTED: Brant, Canvasback and Redhead Ducks, Eagles, Ross's and Snow Geese, Hawks, Owls, Swans no open seasons. NOT PROTECTED: Crow, English Sparrow, Starling, Black and Turkey Vultures may be taken at any time.

FIREARMS

Game birds may be taken with shotguns not larger than 10 gauge and capable of holding only 3 shells in the magazine and chamber combined. Rifles and pistols may not be used to take game birds, and it is unlawful to use full-jacketed bullets or .22-caliber rimfire cartridges for taking Bear and Deer. Only rifles using centerfire cartridges, or shotguns 16 gauge or larger may be used in the Apalachicola and Osceola Bear hunts. The longbow used to take Bear, Deer, and game birds must be capable of casting a one-ounce arrow 150 yards. A crossbow, fully automatic firearms, set guns, nets, snares, traps, live decoys, and the possession of any gun when using artificial lights at night in woods or on waters are prohibited. It is unlawful to carry firearms (including bow and arrow) during closed seasons or without a hunting license during open seasons in national forests and in state-controlled Wildlife Management Areas. A gun is defined as an airgun, blowgun, gas gun, shotgun, pistol, revolver, rifle, bow and arrow, or any device mechanically propelling a projectile. Falcons may be used to take game, but the use of dogs to hunt Turkey is prohibited.

Shooting hours: Resident game: one-half hour before sunrise to one-half hour after sunset. Exception during spring season for Turkey —one-half hour before sunrise until 12:00 o'clock noon daily. Migratory game birds: Dove—12:00 o'clock noon until sunset daily; other birds— sunrise to sunset except that opening day of the Duck season shooting starts at 12:00 o'clock noon.

FISHING

Game fish (freshwater): Largemouth Black Bass (commonly called Trout); Rock Bass; Bream (also called Bluegill, Copperhead, Sunfish);

* Check current state regulations.

Bowfin (Blackfish, Dogfish, Grindle, Mudfish); Channel, Speckled, White and Yellow Catfish; Black Crappie (Calico Bass, Speckled Perch); Flier (Panfish); Alligator, Longnosed and Shortnosed Gar; Chain Pickerel (Jackfish, Pike); Redbreast; Gizzard (Stink) and Threadfin Shad, Shellcracker (Red-ear); Stumpknocker (Black-spotted, Blue-spotted, Redspotted Sunfish); Sucker; Warmouth (Goggle Eye, Warmouth Bass, Warmouth Perch). OPEN SEASONS: All year.

There are about 30,000 named freshwater lakes, more than 900 fishing camps and charter-boat operators, and approximately 600 species of fresh- and saltwater fish in and around Florida and the nearby Bahamas. The St. Johns River and lakes are famous Largemouth Bass waters. The Florida Keys extending more than 100 miles from the peninsula to Key West are connected by a chain of bridges which have sturdy fishing catwalks protected by safety rails. Islamorada, or Marathon are bluewater and reef fishing headquarters for taking Amberjack, Barracuda, Bluefish, Bonefish, Flounder, Grouper, Grunt, Hogfish, Jack, Jewfish, Ladyfish, King Mackerel, Marlin, Mullet, Pompano, Redfish, Spotted Trout, Sharks, Snapper, Snook, and Tarpon circulating around the Keys.

Competition is keen during the annual Deep Sea Rodeo at Destin between Pensacola and Panama City; the National Freshwater Bass Tournament from January through April at Leesburg; the Miami Winter Fishing Tournament from mid-December to mid-April and the Summer Tournament from July 4 to early September; the International Tarpon Tournament from mid-May to August at Sarasota; the St. Petersburg Tarpon Round-Up May 1–July 31, and the Kingfish Derby during March and April; the Tarpon Tournament at Tampa July 1–August 31; and the Silver Sailfish Derby at West Palm Beach in late January and early February.

The Blackwater River State Forest (182,000 acres) is northeast of Milton.

STATE PARKS

Anastasia (1,035 acres) south of St. Augustine; *Bahia Honda* (13 acres) south of Marathon; *Hugh Taylor Birch* (180 acres) north of Fort Lauderdale; *Jonathan Dickinson* (8,923 acres) on the Loxahatchee River, north of Jupiter; *Fort Clinch* (1,105 acres) near Fernandia Beach on Amelia Island; *Fort Pickens* (1,659 acres) on Santa Rosa Island near Pensacola; *Gold Head Branch* (1,614 acres) east of Gainesville near Keystone Heights; *Hillsborough River* (2,637 acres) near Zephryhills; *Little Talbot Island* (2,500 acres) on Atlantic Ocean 18 miles northeast of Jacksonville; *Manatee Springs* (1,799 acres) on the Suwannee River near Chiefland; *Myakka River* (26,898 acres) 17 miles east of Sarasota; *O'Leno* (1,387 acres) on Santa Fe River near High Springs; *St. Andrews*

(1,022 acres) southwest of Panama City; *Suwannee River* (1,703 acres) between Madison and Live Oak; *Tomoka* (834 acres) at confluence of the Halifax and Tomoka rivers near Ormond Beach; *Torreya* (1,038 acres) on the Apalachicola River northeast of Bristol.

WILDLIFE MANAGEMENT AREAS

Aerojet (40,000 acres)—Dade County; *Apalachee** (6,000 acres) at Jim Woodruff Reservoir—Jackson County; *Aucilla* (110,000 acres)—Jefferson, Taylor, and Wakulla counties; *Avon Park** (108,000 acres)—Highlands and Polk counties; *Blackwater** (85,000 acres)—Okaloosa and Santa Rosa counties; *Camp Blanding* (56,000 acres)—Clay County; *J. W. Corbett* (90,000 acres)—Palm Beach County; *Croom* (17,000 acres)—Hernando and Sumter Counties; *Devils Garden** (40,000 acres)—Hendry County; *Elgin Field** (39,000 acres)—Elgin Air Force Base in Santa Rosa, Okaloosa, and Walton counties; *Everglades* (720,000 acres)—Broward, Dade, and Palm Beach counties; *Farmton** (50,000 acres)—Brevard and Volusia counties; *Roy S. Gaskin* (118,300 acres)—Bay, Calhoun, and Gulf counties; *Fisheating Creek* (100,000 acres)—Glades County; Guano River (10,000 acres)—St. Johns County; *Gulf Hammock* (100,000 acres)—Levy County; *Lake Butler* (96,000 acres)—Baker, Columbia, and Union counties; *Lee** (40,000 acres)—Lee County; *Leon-Wakulla* (67,000 acres)—Leon-Wakulla counties; *Liberty* (133,120 acres)—Liberty County in Apalachicola National Forest; *Ocala* (203,680 acres)—Marion and Putnam counties in Ocala National Forest; *Okechobee** (16,000 acres)—Okechobee County; *Osceola* (92,000 acres)—Baker and Columbia counties in Osceola National Forest; *Richloam* (60,000 acres)—Hernando, Pasco, and Sumter counties; *Steinhatchee* (225,000 acres)—Dixie and Lafayette counties; *Tomoka* (100,000 acres)—Flagler and Volusia counties; *Cecil M. Webb* (625,000 acres)—Charlotte County.

Licenses, regulations, current dates of open seasons, bag and possession limits can be obtained from the office of a county judge and the Director of the Game and Fresh Water Fish Commission, 646 West Tennessee Ave., Tallahassee. Regional offices: Lake City, Lakeland, Ocala, Panama City, West Palm Beach. The Alien Hunting License and the Guide Hunting License are issued only at the Tallahassee office of the commission. The special party permit to hunt Bear should be obtained from the Regional Manager, P.O. Box 576, Panama City (Apalachicola Bear Hunt), or Regional Manager, P.O. Box 908, Lake City (Osceola Bear Hunt) and applications should be sent with the $50 fee in time

---

* Use of rifles prohibited.

to be received by the managers before Aug. 30. Archery hunt permits for the Elgin Air Force Area are issued by the Air Force Forestry Section, Jackson Guard Station, Niceville. Information about saltwater fishing can be obtained from the State Board of Conservation, Tallahassee, and specific information about charter boats is generally available from local chambers of commerce.

There are many interesting free leaflets and pamphlets about Florida wildlife published by the Florida Game and Fresh Water Commission which also publishes the very attractive *Florida Wildlife* magazine monthly for 25 cents a single copy and $2 per year.

GEORGIA

Area: 59,265 square miles (land area—58,274 square miles); rank in nation–21
Bird: Brown Thrasher *(Toxostoma rufum)*
Capital city: Atlanta in the foothills of the Blue Ridge Mountains in Fulton County; population (1960)—487,455; rank in state–1
Counties: 159
Elevations: Highest, Brasstown Bald (4,768 ft.) in Towns and Union counties; lowest, Atlantic Ocean (sea level)
Flower: Cherokee Rose *(Rosa sinica)*, adopted 1916
Geographic center: 18 miles southeast of Macon, Twiggs County
Nicknames: Empire State, Peach State, Cracker State, Goober State
Population (1960): 3,943,116; rank in nation–16
Tidal shoreline: 2,344 miles (including islands, bays, and streams to a point where tidal waters narrow to 100 ft.)
Tree: Live Oak *(Quercus virginianus)*, adopted 1937

Georgia is a southeastern state on the Atlantic Ocean with Florida on the south partially separated by St. Marys River flowing into the sea from Okefenoke Swamp. Alabama is west of the Chattahoochee River, and the stateline from Miller's Bend runs straight to the northern border shared by Tennessee and North Carolina, with South Carolina on the northeast boundary formed by the Tugaloo and Savannah rivers. The Ossabaw, St. Catharines, Blackbeard, Sapelo, St. Simons, Sea, Jekyll, and Cumberland islands are close to the mainland.

Marshlands, palms, pine forests, and moss-draped oak trees are on the islands and Atlantic Plain below the picturesque Piedmont Plateau of central Georgia. In the extreme north, summits of the Appalachian System include Brasstown Bald east of Blairsville, and Rabun Bald (4,663 ft.) northeast of Clayton. The scenic Blue Ridge escarpment varies in height from 500–2,000 feet. Rounded ridges of the wooded Piedmont

Plateau average 1,000 feet elevation; and Stone Mountain (1,668 ft.) east of Atlanta is a granite dome with a 7-mile base circumference. Mount Oglethorpe is the southern terminus of the 2,054 miles of the Appalachian Trail for hikers to Mount Katahdin, Maine.

Clear mountain streams rush down to fall lines on the Piedmont Plateau, and wander through forests and marshes of the coastal lowlands. From the confluence of the Seneca and Tugaloo rivers, the Savannah River descends more than 300 miles to the beautiful port of Savannah. Dams on the river created Hartwell Reservoir (97 square miles) and Clark Lake (122 square miles) north of Augusta. The Chattahoochee River was impounded to form Lake Sydney Lanier (71 square miles) near Gainesville, and Bartletts Ferry Lake on the Alabama border north of Columbus. The Flint River flows southward by Albany to be impounded with the Chattahoochee River in the southwest corner of the state to form the Jim Woodruff Reservoir (37,500 acres) on the Florida boundary. The Etowah and Oostanaula rivers merge near Rome to continue westward as the Coosa River in Alabama. The Oconee River flows by Athens, and is impounded to create Lake Sinclair, which has a 500-mile shoreline near Milledgeville. The Ocmulgee River forms Jackson Lake south of Covington, and flows by Macon to join the Oconee and continue as the Altamah River to the Atlantic Ocean north of St. Simon's Island. The Satilla River in southeastern Georgia empties into St. Andrews Sound between the Cumberland and Jekyll islands. From headwaters in Green County, the Ogeechee River moves slowly through swamps and pine forests for 250 miles to reach Ossabaw Sound. From the wilderness of Okefenokee Swamp (660 square miles), the Suwannee River flows into Florida. The Tallulah River in the northeast has a spectacular 1,000-foot gorge, Hurricane Falls (91 ft.), and Tempesta Falls (76 ft.). The Burton, Lloyd Shoals, Nacoochee, Tugaloo, and Yonah reservoirs are clustered in this region. The Allatoona Lake Recreation Area on the Etowah River is near Centersville, and Nottley Reservoir (4,180 acres) is northwest of Blairsville. Lake Taccoa (3,290 acres) formed by Blue Ridge Dam on the Taccoa River, is near Morgantown.

LICENSES

Resident licenses are issued to persons who have lived in Georgia for at least 6 months prior to an application for a license. There is no waiting period for members of the U.S. Armed Forces officially stationed in the state, and their immediate families are also entitled to resident privileges. Residents 65 or more years of age may obtain licenses without cost. Residents and nonresidents 16 or more years of age must possess valid licenses to fish, hunt, and trap; and a federal "Duck" stamp is required also to take migratory game birds. Rangers issue daily permits to fish for Trout in designated waters of management areas, but permits are not required to fish the outside streams. Permits for small game managed hunts are issued at checking stations. Only residents may obtain permits to take Alligators. Nonresidents are not required to possess Georgia hunting licenses when competing in regulated field trials. Annual license period: April 1–March 31.

Resident license fees: Sport fishing, $1.25; spear fishing, $2.25; Shad fishing, $1.00; archery hunting, $2.25; gun hunting, $2.25; fishing and hunting, $3.25; trapping, $3.00; federal "Duck" stamp, $3.00; private hunting preserve operator, $10.00; public hunting preserve operator, $25.00; fur dealer, $100.00; fur dealer's agent, $5.00. *Permits* (in addition to licenses): Trout fishing in Management Areas (per day), $1.00; Alligator hunting, $50.00; managed Deer hunts (1 buck), $5.00; managed Deer hunts (1 Deer of either sex by archery), $5.00; small game managed hunt (per day or night), $2.00.

Nonresident license fees: Annual sport fishing, $6.25; fishing 3 consecutive days, $1,25; spear fishing (annual), $3.25; spear fishing 3 consecutive days, $1.25; Shad fishing, $10.00; hunting small game, $10.25; archery combination big and small game hunting, $20.25; gun combination big and small game hunting, $20.25; trapping, $25.00; federal "Duck" stamp, $3.00; fur dealer, $200.00. *Permits* (in addition to licenses): Trout fishing in Management Areas (per day), $1.00; hunting on licensed shooting preserves, $5.25. Managed hunt fees are same as for residents.

HUNTING AND TRAPPING

Big game: Alligator (residents only), Bear, Deer. OPEN SEASONS:* Alligator—June 1–Jan. 31 in Bryan Camden, Chatham, Glynn, Liberty, and McIntosh Counties. Bear—Nov. 1 to January in counties open for taking Alligator, and the counties of Brantley, Charlton, Clinch, Echols, Long, Ware, and Wayne. Deer—bow and arrow during month of October, except closed season in 24 counties; firearms, mid-October to January in designated areas. Managed Deer hunts are generally limited to 5-day archery periods, and 1–2 days with guns. Deer hunting on the Fort Benning Military Reservation, November and December; Fort Stewart Military Reservation, mid-October to January, but the commanding generals may close seasons after a total of 1,000 Deer have been taken at Fort Benning, and 1,500 Deer at Fort Stewart. ANNUAL BAG LIMIT: Alligators and Bears—no limits. Deer—2. A legal Buck is a male Deer with visible antlers.

Furbearing animals: Beaver, Fox, Mink, Muskrat, Opossum, Otter,

---

* Check current state regulations.

Raccoon, Skunk. OPEN TRAPPING SEASON:* Mid-November to Jan. 31 in the counties of Butts, Cowetta, Hancock, Heard, Jasper, McDuffie, Putnam, Richmond, Spalding, Warren; and counties north of these areas; mid-November through February in all other counties.

Small game: Brant, Coot, Mourning Dove, Ducks (except Canvasback and Redhead), Gallinule, Geese (except Snow Geese), Ruffer Grouse, Merganser, Bobwhite, Quail, Rails, Scaup, Sora, Wilson's Snipe, Wild Turkey, Woodcock, Opossum, Rabbit, Raccoon, Squirrels. OPEN SEASONS:* Brant, Geese—early November to mid-January. Coot, Ducks, Merganser, Scaup—late November to January. Mourning Dove—mid-September to mid-October and mid-December to mid-January. Gallinule, Rails, Sora—September to mid-November. Ruffed Grouse—mid-October to early January. Quail—mid-November through February. Wilson's Snipe—December to mid-January. Woodcock—late November to mid-January. Wild Turkey—Nov. 1 to early January in Chattahoochee, Marion, Muscogee, and Stewart counties; mid-November through February in 10 counties; Dec. 1 to early January in 17 counties; late March to mid-April in 39 counties; and about 6 days in April within the Chattahoochee, Chestate, Clark Hill, and Johns Mountain management areas. Opossum—October through February in designated areas. Rabbit—mid-November through February. Raccoon—mid-October through February in designated areas. Squirrel—mid-October to early January with shorter period in some counties. Game birds on licensed shooting preserves—Oct. 1–March 31. FULLY PROTECTED: Canvasback and Redhead Ducks, Snow Geese—no open seasons. NOT PROTECTED: Beaver, Bobcat, Fox, Skunk, and Weasel may be taken at any time.

FIREARMS

Deer hunters are limited to .20 gauge shotguns or larger, loaded with slugs, or no. 1 buckshot (or larger); and rifles using any centerfire cartridges .22 caliber or above with the following exceptions: .25–.20, .32–.20, .30 Army carbine, .22 Hornet, or .218 Bee. Archers must use a longbow with a minimum pull of 40 pounds to take deer. Opossum, Rabbits, Raccoons, and Squirrels may be hunted with .22 rimfire rifles and shotguns using no. 4 shot or smaller. Bow and arrow or shotguns with shot not larger than no. 2 may be used in the spring Turkey hunts. All shotguns must be plugged to limit their capacity to 3 shells in the magazine and chamber combined, and migratory game birds may be taken only with shotguns not larger than 10 gauge.

Shooting hours: Sunrise to sunset; except that the opening day of the Duck season starts at 12:00 o'clock noon.

---

* Check current state regulations.

FISHING

Game fish: Black Bass (Largemouth, Smallmouth), Coosae or Redeye Bass, Kentucky Bass, White Bass, Yellow Bass, Rockfish or Striped Bass, Channel Catfish, Crappie, Eastern Pickerel or Jackfish, Muskellunge, Yellow Perch, Walleye Pike, Sauger, Shad, Trout (Brook, Brown, Rainbow). OPEN SEASONS:* All year, except April 15–Sept. 15 for Trout streams outside management areas in the mountain counties of Dawson, Fannin, Gilmer, Habersham, Lumpkin, Murray, Pickens, Rabun, Towns, Union, White; and the Chattahoochee River from Buford Dam to Roswell Bridge on Highway 19 between Roswell and Sandy Springs, including all backwaters in streams between those points. Trout streams in management areas—May through Labor Day on designated days including Sundays. There is no closed season on taking Shad with a fly rod, rod and reel, or pole and line, but the use of nets is prohibited from sundown on Friday of each week until sunrise on the following Monday. Dockery Lake in the Chestatee Management Area is open for Trout fishing by juveniles only under the age of 16, on about 7 Saturdays from 1–6 P.M. in June, July, and August.

Trout permits are required in the following management areas: Blue Ridge, Chestatee, and Lake Burton near Dahlonega; Chattahoochee near Robertson; and Warwoman near Clayton. No permit is necessary to take Bass, Salmon, or Trout from the Conasauga and Jacks Rivers in the Cohutta Management Area. There is excellent waterfowl hunting, surf and deep sea fishing along the coast, and freshwater angling in national forests, state parks, and well-stocked lakes and streams.

STATE PARKS

Amicalola Falls (239 acres) at Juno—Dawson County; *Bainbridge* (7 acres) on the Flint River—Decatur County; *Bobby Brown* (632 acres) at Clark Hill Reservoir—Elbert County; *Crooked River* (592 acres) 12 miles northeast of Kingsland—Camden County; *Fort Mountain* (2,526 acres) near Chatsworth—Murray County; *Stephen C. Foster* (80 acres) on southwestern edge of Okefenokee Swamp—Clinch County; *Georgia Veterans Memorial* (1,300 acres) on Lake Blackshear, west of Cordele —Crisp County; *Hard Labor Creek* (5,850 acres) north of Rutledge— Morgan and Walton counties; *Indian Springs* (250 acres) south of Jackson—Butts County; *Kolomoki Mounds* (1,283 acres, 75-acre lake) north of Blakely—Early County; *Jekyll Island* (11,000 acres) near Brunswick— Glynn County; *Little Ocmulgee* (1,397 acres, 300-acre lake north of McRae—Telefair and Wheeler counties; *Magnolia Springs* (1,106 acres) north of Millen—Harris County; *Red Top Mountain* (1,457 acres) at

* Check current state regulations.

Allatoona Lake on the Etowah River, near Cartersville—Bartow County; *F. D. Roosevelt* (2,063 acres) south of Pine Mountain—Harris County; *Seminole* (295 acres) at Jim Woodruff Reservoir, south of Donaldsville—Seminole County; *A. H. Stephens Memorial* (1,175 acres) near Crawfordville—Taliaferro County; *Unicoi* (1,800 acres) north of Helen—White County; *Vogel* (229 acres, 40-acre Lake Trahlyta) south of Blairsville—Union County; *L. S. Walker* (160 acres) east of Waycross—Ware County.

Licenses, regulations, and information about current seasons, bag and possession limits can be obtained from the Director, Georgia Game and Fish Commission, 401 State Capitol, Atlanta 3; and authorized agents throughout the state. Fort Benning is southeast of Columbus, and Fort Stewart in Bryan and Liberty counties has a main gate near Hinesville. Hunt permits are issued by the Game and Fish Club on each military reservation. For information about fishing in Okefenokee Swamp, write to the Refuge Manager, P.O. Box 117, Waycross.

HAWAII*

Area: 6,421 square miles; rank in nation—47
Bird: Nene *(Branta sandwicensis)* or Hawaiian Goose, adopted 1957
Capital city: Honolulu on leeward coast of the island of Oahu; population (1960)—294,194; rank in state—1
Counties: 5
Elevations: Highest, Mauna Kea (13,796 ft.) on island of Hawaii; lowest, Pacific Ocean
Flower: Pua Aloalo *(Hibiscus hibiscus)*, adopted 1923
Nicknames: Aloha State, Crossroads of the Pacific, Paradise of the Pacific
Population (1960): 632,772; rank in nation—43 (Caucasian, 202,230; Japanese, 203,455; Filipino, 69,070; Chinese, 38,197; Negro, 4,943; all other, 114,877)
Tidal shoreline: 1,052 miles (including islands, bays, and streams to a point where tidal waters narrow to 100 ft.)
Tree: Kukui *(Aleurites moluccana)* or Candlenut Tree, adopted 1959

The islands are portions of a great volcanic mountain system forming an archipelago in the Pacific Ocean. The port of Honolulu, 2,091 nautical miles from San Francisco in California, is the principal gateway to all other islands.

* Names: There are only 12 letters in the Hawaiian alphabet—5 vowels *a, e, i, o, u;* and 7 consonants *h, k, l, m, n, p, w.* Each vowel in a word is pronounced: *a* as in "ah," *e* as in "they," *i* as in "ee," *o* is in "foe," *u* as in "oo." Hawaii may be pronounced as "Hah-vy-ee" or "Hah-wy-ee."

Island of Oahu: 595 square miles (44 miles long, 30 miles wide)—deep green valleys, numerous streams and waterfalls, sandy beaches lined with palm trees; sheer cliffs including famous Nuuanu Pali; Mount Kaala (4,025 ft.) in northwestern Waianae Mountains; the rugged Koolau Range on windward side; crescent-shaped Waikiki Beach between Diamond Head and the Ala Wai Yacht Harbor; 45 public parks along the coast; pineapple and sugar cane plantations; airfields, military and naval installations; charter boat operators at Kewalo Basin for trophy fishing off the Wainae Coast. *"Big Island" of Hawaii*: 4,030 square miles (93 miles long, 76 miles wide)—rain forests and tropical vegetation; dormant volcano Mauna Kea north of active volcanoes Kilauea (4,090 ft.) and Mauna Loa (13,680 ft.) in the Hawaii Volcanoes National Park (22,345 acres); Hereford cattle on Parker Ranch (265,000 acres) in the Waimea Plateau region; public hunting grounds on slopes and Saddle (6,650 ft.) of Mauna Kea and Mauna Loa; Kailua on Kona Coast, port of charter boats for superb Marlin fishing; county seat and orchid capital Hilo and Kawaihae are regular ports of call. *"Garden Island" of Kauai*: 551 square miles (33 miles long, 25 miles wide)—forested mountains, picturesque valleys, streams and waterfalls; navigable Wailua River; pineapple and sugar cane plantations; Mount Waialeale (5,080 ft.) with annual rainfall 472 inches and nearby areas with less than 20 inches a year; the vast Alakai Swamp; steep Na Pali coast; spectacular Waimea Canyon (2,857 ft. deep) in Kokee Plateau; county seat Lihue near port Nawiliwili and airfield. *"Pineapple Island" of Lanai*: 141 square miles (18 miles long, 13 miles wide)—developed as a single plantation; Maunalei Game Reserve; winding road conects Lanai City with the port of Kaumalapau about 1,600 feet below although only 8 miles away. *"Valley Isle" of Maui*: 728 square miles (48 miles long, 26 miles wide)—cattle ranches, pineapple and sugar cane plantations; mountain streams, tropical flowers and forests; Puu Kukui rising 5,788 feet above lovely Iao Valley; Haleakala Crater (circumference 21 miles) of a volcano (10,023 feet high) in the Haleakala National Park (26,403 acres); county seat Wailuku at entrance of Iao Valley is 3 miles from Port of Kahului. *"Friendly Island" of Molokai*: 259 square miles (38 miles long, 10 miles wide)—cattle ranches and pineapple plantations; Kamakou (4,970 ft.) and other mountains; game management areas on leeward side of island; Kalaupapa, the Hansen's disease community on a peninsula cut off by a 2,000-foot cliff; the largest port is Kaunkakai, about 8 miles from the airport. *"Aloof Island" of Niihau*: 72 square miles; has been privately owned for generations, and strangers are not permitted to visit or live there. Kahoolawe Island has been nibbled bare by wild goats, and is used as a target by U.S. Armed Forces. *The Leeward Islands* about 1,000 miles from Honolulu include the Brooks Shoals (14 miles long), French Frigate Shoal (12 miles long) Dowsett Reef (9 miles long), Gardner Pinnacles (170 ft. high, 1 mile long), Laysan Island (3 miles long), Lisianski or Lassien Island (1½ miles long), Nihoa Island or Moku Manu (155 acres of volcanic ash rising to 895 ft.), Hermes and Pearl Reef (8 miles long).

LICENSES

Resident licenses may be obtained by any person who has lived in the state of Hawaii for at least one year prior to an application for a license and by military personnel officially stationed on the islands. Licenses are not required for saltwater fishing, but all persons 9 or more years of age should obtain a license to fish in freshwater. Juveniles under the age of 9 without licenses must be accompanied by a licensed adult, and the daily bag limit for the adult includes game fish taken by the child. Regardless of age, all residents and nonresidents must possess valid licenses to hunt wildlife. A hunter is not allowed to enter a game management area without a license and a permit. Free permits may be issued for one day, 6 months, or a season. Guide service is required for hunting on the Mauna Kea Game Management Area and Public Shooting Ground (island of Hawaii), except in the Pohakuloa portion. Reservations for guided hunting parties should be made prior to the chosen date with a division officer in Hilo. Bookings are made by authorized guides who have complete charge, and must be paid before a hunt. Permits to fish in the Ku Tree Reservoir on the Schofield Military Reservation near Wahiawa (island of Oahu) are issued without cost by the provost marshal's office. Annual license period: July 1–June 30.

Resident license fees: Freshwater game fishing (persons 15 or more years of age), $2.50; freshwater game fishing (9–15 years of age), $1.00; hunting (archery or firearms), $5.00; game bird farming, $1.00; Leeward Islands fishing permit, $1.00.

Nonresident license fees: Annual freshwater game fishing, $5.00; tourist 30 consecutive days fishing, $2.50; hunting (archery or firearms), $10.00; Leeward Islands fishing permit, $1.00.

Guide fees are 8 hours at $18 for up to 4 persons in a party; $21 for 5 persons; $24 for 6 persons; time over 8 hours per day—$2.25 an hour. Guide service for less than 4 hours is one-half of the 8-hour rates. Round trip transportation from Pohakuloa—$25 for the first day, plus $10 for each additional day. Cabins equipped for 4 persons—$2 per person each night.

HUNTING

Big game: Axis Deer, Wild Goat, Wild Pig, Wild Sheep. OPEN ARCHERY SEASONS: Island of Hawaii: Kaohe, Horse Pasture, Mauna Loa, Pohakuloa, and Puuanahula Game Management Areas—all year for Wild

Goats, Pigs, and Sheep; daily bag limit: 2 each. Island of Lanai: daily hunts 4:00–6:30 P.M., except Sundays and state holidays 6:00 A.M.–6:30 P.M. in designated areas; bag limit: 1 Deer of either sex and 2 Wild Goats per permit. OPEN GUN SEASONS:* Island of Hawaii Mauna Kea Game Management Area—all year for Wild Goats, Pigs, and Sheep. Daily bag limits: Wild Goat and Wild Pig—2 each; Wild Sheep—1 Ram. Island of Kauai: designated areas of Puu Ka Pele and Na Pali Kona Forest Reserve —July and August for Wild Goats and Pigs. Bag limits: Wild Goats—2 per season; Wild Pigs—1 per day. Island of Lanai: Lanai Game Management Area—Deer on Sundays only during September and October; Wild Goats—2 weeks in March. Bag limit: Deer—1 of either sex; Wild Goats —2 males, or 1 male and 1 female. Island of Molokai: Molokai Game Management Area—Deer on Saturdays and Sundays only during August and September; bag limit: 1 Deer of either sex per season. Island of Oahu: Mokuleia Game Management Area—all year for Wild Goats and Pigs; Daily bag limit: 1 each. FULLY PROTECTED: Pronghorn Antelope, Black-tailed Deer, Mouflon Sheep—no open seasons. NOT PROTECTED: Mongoose may be taken at any time.

Game birds: Dove (Barred, Lace-necked), Chukar Partridge, Pheasant (Japanese Blue, Ring-necked), Quail (California Valley, Japanese), Wild Pigeon. OPEN SEASONS:* Barred Dove—first Saturday in July to second Sunday in January on islands of Hawaii, Kauai, Maui, Oahu; first Saturday in July to last Sunday in June on island of Molokai. Other game birds—first Saturday in November to second Sunday in January; except Chukar Partridge—no open seasons on island of Kauai, Lanai, Molokai, and Oahu. California Valley Quail may be taken on islands of Hawaii and Molokai, but not on islands of Lanai and Oahu. Japanese Quail—no open season on island of Oahu. Wild Pigeon—no open season on islands of Kauai, Lanai, Maui, Molokai, and Oahu. During open seasons, game birds may be taken only on Saturdays, Sundays, and state holidays between sunrise and sunset. FULLY PROTECTED: Migratory birds and waterfowl, Nene, Bamboo Partridge, Gambel Quail—no open seasons.

Open seasons do not apply to private and commercial shooting preserves, or to field trials held by organized clubs where only farm-raised birds are used under permits issued by the Board of Land and Natural Resources.

There are special flights for hunters during open seasons in addition to regular schedules of airlines. Flight distances from Honolulu to island of Hawaii: Hilo on northeast coast—214 miles, and Kona on west coast—170 miles; island of Kauai: Lihue on east coast—102 miles; island of Lanai —74 miles; island of Maui: Kahulua on northern coast—100 miles, and Hana on eastern coast—128 miles; island of Molokai—54 miles.

---

* Check current state regulations.

FIREARMS

Game mammals may be taken with rifles using cartridges that supply a muzzle energy of at least 1,200 foot-pounds; and shotguns using cartridges that supply a muzzle energy of 1,200 foot-pounds using multiple ball loads not less than size oo, or rifled slugs. Bullets with full metal jackets, incendiary or tracer bullets are unlawful. The use of slingshots, air guns, pellet guns, crossbow, longbow, spears, snares, or traps to take game birds is prohibited except on the island of Lanai where longbows and arrows are legal. The longbow for hunting big game should have a minimum weight of 45 pounds, and the archer must use broadhead arrows with 2 blades not less than seven-eighths of an inch or more than 1¼ inches wide.

FISHING

Freshwater game fish: Black Bass (Largemouth, Smallmouth), Channel Catfish, Bluegill Sunfish, Tilapia, Rainbow Trout. OPEN SEASONS:* Trout—on island of Kauai from the first Saturday in August for 16 consecutive days, and only on Saturdays, Sundays, and state holidays for the remainder of August and month of September. Other fish—all year throughout the state. FULLY PROTECTED: Oscar and Tucanare—no open seasons.

There are 6 State Public Freshwater fishing areas. Free seasonal permits are issued with regulations governing each area. Island of Hawaii— Kohala Public Fishing Area (5 reservoirs) south of the town of Hawaii, and Waiakea Public Fishing Area (26-acre pond) in Hilo; Island of Kauai —Kokanee Public Fishing Area (13 miles of streams, 15-acre reservoir, 2 miles of fishable ditches) in Kokee Park and Waimea Canyon region, and Wailua Public Fishing Area (30 acres) about 4 miles from town of Wailua; Island of Maui—Wailuku Public Fishing Area (1 reservoir in Puunene and 1 in Wailuku); Island of Oahu—Wahiawa Public Fishing Area (300 acres of water) at town of Wahiawa. Fishing is also available at private reservoirs on plantations with permission of owners, at the Kahama Trout Farm, and the Shoestring Ranch in Waiahole Valley.

Surf casting from reefs, rocks, and sandy shores, pole fishing, spear fishing, bottom fishing in outrigger canoes, and trolling offshore are enjoyed by old and young sportsmen.

Hawaiian names for fish were derived from many nationalities, and the Bishop Museum (1355 Kalihi St., Honolulu) has an exceptional collection of local fish molds done in color and labeled with their Latin and local names.

---

* Check current state regulations.

Licenses, regulations, lists of authorized private guides, current open seasons, bag limits, and other information can be obtained from the Director, Division of Fish and Game, Department of Land and Natural Resources, 400 South Beretania St., Honolulu, Oahu, and at regional offices —Lanai City, island of Lanai; Hilo, island of Hawaii; Lihue, island of Kauai; Kahului, island of Maui; Kaunakakai, island of Molokai. Information about guides, hotels, transportation facilities, recreational activities, and special events is available at the Hawaii Visitors Bureau, 2051 Kalakaua Ave., Honolulu, Oahu; and at mainland offices: 400 North Michigan Ave., Chicago, Illinois; 609 Fifth Ave., New York, New York; 212 Stockton St., San Francisco, California. The Honolulu Department of Parks and Recreation, 1455 South Beretania St., Honolulu, has charge of beach parks on the island of Oahu; There is also a Diamond Head Archery Club, 3118 Williams St., Honolulu, Oahu; and a Hawaiian Trail and Mountain Club, P. O. Box 2238, Honolulu, Oahu.

IDAHO

Area: 83,557 square miles (land area—82,708 square miles); rank in nation–12
Bird: Mountain Bluebird (*Sialis currucoides*), adopted 1931
Capital city: Boise on the Boise River in Ada County; population (1960) —34,481; rank in state–1
Counties: 44
Elevations: Highest, Borah Peak (12,655 ft.) in Lost River Range, Custer County; lowest, Snake River (720 ft.) near Lewiston in Nez Perce County
Flower: Syringa (*Philadelphus lewisii*), adopted 1931
Geographic center: 24 miles west of Challis, Custer County
Nicknames: Gem State, Gem of the Mountains
Population (1960): 667,191; rank in nation–42
Tree: White Pine (*Pinus monticolae*), adopted 1937

Idaho is a northwestern state with British Columbia on the northern Canadian boundary, Nevada and Utah across the southern border, and Wyoming on the southeastern line up to Yellowstone Park where the Continental Divide traces an uneven course through the magnificent Bitterroot Range on the northeastern border between Montana and the Idaho panhandle; Oregon on the southwestern boundary shares the Snake River for about 250 miles; and Washington is on the northwestern border of the panhandle.

There are broad plains, timber-fringed plateaus, virgin White Pine forests, snow-mantled mountains, numerous racing white water streams, large reservoirs, and more than 1,800 natural lakes. The turbulent Snake

River plunges through canyons, crosses southern plains to veer northward through Hells Canyon (100 miles long, nearly 8,000 ft. deep in the main chasm) and at Lewiston, elbows westward into Washington. The American Falls Reservoir (88 square miles), and picturesque Idaho Falls, Shoshone Falls, and Twin Falls are among many cascades on the Snake River. Henry's Lake near Targhee Pass (7,078 ft.) is a famous game area west of Yellowstone National Park. Big and Little Lost Rivers vanish in the Lost Rivers Sinks perhaps to emerge 150 miles away as the Thousand Springs in Hagerman Valley, west of Jerome. The Boise, Payette, and Weiser rivers flow into the Snake River south of the rugged Seven Devils Mountains towering over Hells Canyon. The Salmon "River of No Return," rising in the Sawtooth Mountains, rushes through the colorful Upper Salmon River Gorge to the Bitterroot Range and swerves westward at North Fork to Riggins near He Devil Mountain (9,387 ft.), and turns north into scenic Lower Salmon River Canyon finally to join the Snake River near White Bird. The Clearwater River fed by many tributaries, merges with the Snake River near Lewiston. Among evergreen forests in the northern panhandle are beautiful Coeur d'Alene and St. Maries Rivers, and the highest navigable stream in the nation, the "Shadowy" St. Joe River flowing through Benewah, Chatcolet, and Coeur d'Alene lakes. The Kootenai, Moyie, and Priest rivers cross the Canadian boundary, and the Pend Oreille (POND-o-ray) River joins the Priest River east of Albeni Falls Dam to run into Washington.

Smith Peak (7,650 ft.) looms above the Priest Recreational Area near Ordman, and Upper Priest Lake is accessible only by watercraft. Lake Pend Oreille (147 square miles, 1,100 ft. deep) is the famous "Big Pond" between Clark Fork, Granite, Hope, and Sandpoint. The popular Payette Lakes Recreational Area is near McCall, and a Trail Creek Summit Route leads to Sun Valley and the Hyndman Peak (12,078 ft.) region south of the Stanley Basin Recreational Area.

LICENSES

Resident fishing licenses are issued to persons 14 or more years of age who have been bona fide residents of Idaho for at least 6 months. Nonresident juveniles under the age of 14 may fish without a license, but must be accompanied by the holder of a valid fishing license, and all game fish caught by the juvenile are counted in the creel limit of the licensed fisherman. Members of the U.S. Armed Forces may purchase resident licenses immediately after reaching their permanent stations, but members of their families must wait for 6 months. Nonresident military personnel and National Guardsmen assigned to Idaho for temporary duty or training may purchase resident fishing and hunting licenses which expire on the last day of their assignment. Residents of Idaho assigned to military duty with the U.S. Armed Forces outside the state may purchase regular resident licenses during visits to their homes, or obtain free furlough permits valid only during the period specified in their official orders.

Any person 12 or more years of age may obtain a license to hunt. All persons carrying uncased guns in fields and forests must possess hunting licenses. Permits for controlled hunts are issued after drawings held in Boise during August and September. No permits or tags are required to take Bear. All persons 16 or more years of age must possess a federal "Duck" stamp to take migratory game birds.

The holder of an Idaho fishing license may take fish from the eastern side of the Snake River main channel between Idaho and Washington, and from the entire waters of the Snake River between Oregon and Idaho, except the shoreline, sloughs, and tributaries on the Oregon side. The holder of an Idaho or Utah license may fish anywhere on Bear Lake except in areas closed to all fishing by the states. Idaho anglers fishing in boundary waters are limited to the Idaho creel limit although they may possess additional licenses from adjoining states.

Resident license fees: Fishing, $4.00; hunting (guns or bow and arrow), $4.00; combination fishing and hunting, $6.00; federal "Duck" stamp (in addition to hunting license), $3.00. *Tags* (in addition to hunting license): Antelope, Deer (each), $1.00; Elk, $2.00; Mountain Goat, Moose, Bighorn Sheep (each), $10.00. *Permits for controlled hunts* (in addition to license): Antelope, Deer (each), $3.00; Elk, $5.00; Mountain Goat, Moose, Bighorn Sheep (each), $25.00.

Nonresident license fees: Annual fishing, $15.00; tourist fishing 7 consecutive days, $5.00; Daily fishing—first day, $2; each additional day, $1.00; bird hunting, $25.00; combination game animals and bird hunting, fishing, $75.00; federal "Duck" stamp (in addition to hunting license), $3.00. *Permits for controlled hunts* and *tags*: same as resident fees.

HUNTING

Game animals: Antelope, Black Bear (color phases vary to light brown), Buffalo, Deer (Mule, White-tailed), Elk, Mountain Goat, Moose, Bighorn Sheep, Cottontail Rabbit, Tree Squirrels. OPEN ARCHERY SEASONS:* Antelope—first 2 weeks in September plus 1 week in December. Bear—mid-September to mid-November. Deer—Sept. 1–Dec. 31. Elk—Sept. 1 to mid-October plus 1 week in November. Mountain Goat—Sept. 1–30. Controlled archery hunts: Elk—1 week in September and 1 week in October. Mountain Goat—3 weeks in September. Archers may hunt only on Saturdays and Sundays during open season in Farragut Wildlife Area. OPEN GUN SEASONS: Bear—all year; except in Benewah, Bonner, Boundary,

---

* Check current state regulations.

Kootenai, and Shoshone counties, Sept. 1–Nov. 30; and only during the general Deer season in Clark and Fremont counties. Deer and Elk—mid-September to mid-December. Mountain Goat—late August and early September. Bighorn Sheep—late August to mid-September. Cottontail Rabbit—September through February. Controlled hunts: Antelope—a few days in September. Deer and Elk—early October to mid-November. Mountain Goat—late August through November. Moose—mid-September to early November (about 5 weeks). Bighorn Sheep—last 2 weeks in September. ANNUAL BAG LIMITS: Antelope, Bear, Elk, Mountain Goat, Moose, Bighorn Sheep (Ram with three-quarters curled horn)—1 each. Deer—1 on regular tag, 2 or 3 in designated units with special tags, but not more than 5 Deer during a calendar year. Hunters may take only one Antelope during 2 successive years. Cottontail Rabbits—5 daily during open season. FULLY PROTECTED: Grizzly Bear, Buffalo, Caribou, and Tree Squirrels—no open seasons. NOT PROTECTED: Badger, Bobcat, Chipmunk, Cougar (Mountain Lion), Coyote, Canada Lynx, Porcupine, Prairie Dog, Rabbits (except Cottontail), Raccoon, Skunk, Ground Squirrels, Weasel, Woodchuck, and other burrowing rodents may be taken at any time.

There are about 85 big game management units with general and special seasons. Hunting big game is prohibited in the following areas: Atomic Energy Reactor Station site in Bingham, Bonneville, Butte, Clark, and Jefferson counties; Craters of the Moon National Monument (53,545 acres) in Blaine and Butte counties; David Thompson Game Preserve in Bonner County; Duck Valley Indian Reservation in Owyhee County; Farragut Wildlife Management Area (except Bear and Deer archery season); Fort Hill Indian Reservation in Bannock, Bingham, Caribou, and Power counties; Heyburn State Park in Benewah County; Minidoka Wildlife Refuge in Blaine, Cassia, and Minidoka Counties; Sand Creek Wildlife Management Area; and Yellowstone National Park (31,488 acres in Idaho).

Game birds: Coot, Mourning Dove, Ducks (except Canvasback and Redhead), Geese, Grouse (Blue, Franklin, Ruffed, Sage, Sharp-tailed), Merganser, Partridge (Chukar, Hungarian), Pheasants (Chinese, Mongolian, and mutant), Quail (Bobwhite, Gambel's, Mountain, Valley), Wilson's Snipe, Wild Turkey. OPEN SEASONS:* Coot, Ducks, Geese, Merganser—early October to early January. Dove—first 2 weeks in September. Grouse (Blue, Franklin, Ruffed)—early September to early December; Sage Grouse—a few days in September. Partridge and Quail—mid-September through December. Pheasant—early October to early December. Grouse, Partridge, Pheasant, and Quail are hunted only in designated areas. FULLY PROTECTED: Brant, Canvasback and Redhead Ducks, Swan, and

---

* Check current state regulations.

Wild Turkey—no open seasons. NOT PROTECTED: Cormorant, Crow, Kingfisher, Magpie, Pelican, Raven, English Sparrow, and Starlings may be taken at any time.

Upland game birds may be hunted in the following game preserves during open seasons for the region: Payette River, South Fork Preserve—Boise County; Pocatello Game Preserve—Bannock and Power counties; Sawtooth State Bird Sanctuary*—Cassia, Oneida, Power, and Twin Falls counties; Heyburn Park Game Preserve (Pheasant only)—Benewah County. Migratory waterfowl may also be hunted during open season in the Pocatello Game Preserve and the Sawtooth State Bird Sanctuary.

FIREARMS

Pistols, rifles, and shotguns may be used to hunt Blue, Franklin, and Ruffed Grouse. Migratory game birds may be taken with shotguns not larger than 10 gauge and capable of holding not more than 3 shells in magazine and chamber combined. If originally capable of holding more than 3 shells, the shotgun must be plugged with a filler incapable of being removed through the loading end. It is unlawful to hunt game birds with shotgun shells longer than 3½ inches; or with any pistol or rifle (including air rifles) except to take Blue, Franklin, and Ruffed Grouse. There are no restrictions on guns, longbow and arrows to take big game, except that the use of rimfire cartridges in a .22 caliber gun is prohibited. Juveniles under 12 years of age may not carry any gun in fields, forests, or motor vehicles. It is unlawful to hunt with the use of any artificial lights.

Shooting hours: One-half hour before sunrise until sunset, except that shooting on the opening day of a Duck season starts at 12:00 o'clock noon.

FISHING

Game fish: Black Bass (Largemouth, Smallmouth), Catfish (Bullhead, Channel, Flathead), Cisco, Crappie, Grayling, Perch, Salmon (Chinook, Kokanee, Sockeye), Steelhead, Sturgeon, Sunfish (Bluegill, Pumpkinseed), Trout (Brook, Cutthroat, Dolly Varden, Golden, Kamloop, Mackinaw, Rainbow), Whitefish. OPEN SEASONS:** General fishing—first week in June to Oct. 31. Pend Oreille and Priest lakes, May 1–Nov. 30. Idaho is divided into 6 areas and open seasons vary in designated waters, although numerous lakes and streams are open all year. Fishing hours—4:00 A.M.–10:00 P.M., and night fishing is permitted in waters open to year-round fishing for all species.

---

* Formerly called Minidoka Forest State Bird Sanctuary.
** Check current state regulations.

Salmon and Steelhead less than 20 inches in length are classed as Trout. Only Sturgeon 36–72 inches may be taken in Idaho. The use of more than one hand line, or one rod (or pole) with line and hook (or hooks) to take fish is prohibited. A gaff hook may not be used except to land fish from a boat. It is unlawful to fish for Salmon, Trout, or Bullfrog with the aid of artificial lights. Carp, Chub, Minnows, Squawfish, and Suckers or other nongame fish may be taken by hook and line, underwater spears, bow and arrows.

Bonners Ferry on the Kootenai River, Clark Fork at Pend Oreille Lake, Coeur d'Alene on north shore of beautiful Coeur d'Alene Lake, St. Maries on the St. Joe River, and Lewiston at the confluence of Clearwater and Snake rivers are gateways to fabulous fishing and hunting in the panhandle of Idaho. Fishing is available in state parks.

STATE PARKS

Heyburn (7,838 acres, 2,333 acres of water) near mouth of St. Joe River, about 10 miles west of St. Maries—Benewah County; *Lawyers Canyon* (30 acres) in Payete Lakes region near McCall—Valley County; *Spaulding Memorial* (15 acres) on Clearwater River, near Lewiston—Nez Perce County.

Licenses, permits, maps, and information about current seasons, bag and possession limits can be obtained from the Director, Idaho Fish and Game Department, 518 First St., Boise. Detailed regulations with maps for fishing are available in March annually. Big game regulations with maps, and a list of licensed guides can be obtained in July. Write before June 1 for application and information about controlled hunts. Temporary licenses and free furlough permits are issued to military personnel by the Fish and Game Department in Boise, and by conservation officers. The Idaho Department of Commerce and Development, Capitol Building, Boise, has information about pack trips into wilderness areas.

ILLINOIS

Area: 56,665 square miles (land area—55,930 square miles); rank in nation–24
Bird: Cardinal (*Richmondena cardinalis*), adopted 1929
Capital city: Springfield at lovely Lake Springfield Park (9,000 acres) in Sangamon County; population (1960)—83,271; rank in state–4
Counties: 102
Elevations: Highest, Charles Mount (1,241 ft.) in Jo Daviess County; Lowest, Alexander County (279 ft.) at junction of Ohio and Mississippi rivers

Flower: Native violet *(Viola)*, adopted 1908
Geographic center: Logan County, 28 miles northeast of Springfield
Nicknames: Land of Lincoln, Prairie State, Corn State
Population (1960): 10,081,158; rank in nation–4
Tree: Burr Oak *(Quercus macrocarpa)*, adopted 1908

Illinois on lower Lake Michigan is a north central state with Wisconsin on the northern boundary, and Kentucky on the southern bank of the Ohio River. Indiana on the eastern border is partially separated by the Wabash River which flows into the Ohio River at Gallatin County. The Mississippi River serves as an irregular boundary with Iowa and Missouri on western shores until joined by the Ohio River below Cairo in Alexander County.

The entire state has fertile plains and valleys, rolling hills in the northern counties, numerous large and small streams. The Illinois River, formed by the Des Plaines and Kankakee rivers in northeastern Grundy County, is fed by many tributaries including the Fox, Vermillion, Spoon, and Sangamon rivers, and moves on a southwesterly course for about 270 miles before reaching the Mississippi River between Calhoun and Jersey counties. The 100-mile Illinois-Michigan Canal connects Lake Michigan with the navigable waters of the Illinois River at La Salle. The great city of Chicago on Lake Michigan has marinas, parks, and parkways along a 30-mile shoreline. The Cach, Embarrass, Little Wabash, and Saline rivers empty their waters into the Ohio and Wabash rivers. The Kaskaskia rises west of Urbana and flows on a southwesterly course for about 300 miles to the Mississippi River, and in northwestern Illinois, the Rock River enters the Mississippi River at Moline. Lake Peoria, formed by silt deposits, is an expansion of the Illinois River at Peoria. Large man-made lakes include Lake Springfield (4,000 acres), Crab Orchard Lake (6,695 acres) east of Carbondale, and Carlyle Reservoir (26,000 acres) on the Kaskaskia River near the town of Carlyle.

LICENSES

Resident licenses to fish and hunt are issued to persons 16 or more years of age who verify that they have lived for at least 6 months in the state prior to an application for a license, and to members of the U.S. Armed Forces on active duty in Illinois. Any juvenile under the age of 16 may fish without a license if using only a hook and line. The use of any bow and arrow device, gig, pitchfork, or spear requires a hook and line license. This license must be in the possession of any person 16 or more years of age who uses a pole and line, bank pole and line, throw line, and other legal devices not exceeding 50 hooks in the aggregate (except trotline), or if taking frogs and mussels by any means in the state, or in that part of Lake Michigan under the jurisdiction of Illinois. Any person possessing an Illinois license may fish in the Mississippi River from shore to shore, but nonresident Kentucky licenses are required on the Ohio River as this stream belongs to Kentucky up to the shore of Illinois. Nonresidents pay the same fees for hunting licenses that a resident of Illinois would have to pay in the nonresident's home state. All persons 16 or more years of age must purchase a federal "Duck" stamp to take migratory game birds.

Resident license fees: Fishing with hook and line devices not exceeding 50 hooks, $2.00; fishing with hook and line for blind persons, 50 cents; fishing with hook and line for service-connected disabled veterans, 50 cents; fishing with hook and line for persons 65 years or older, 50 cents; Trotline, each 100 hooks, $2.00; hunting, $3.00; Deer permit, $5.00; federal "Duck" stamp, $3.00.

Nonresident license fees: Fishing with hook and line (not exceeding 50 hooks) annual, $4.00; fishing 10 days with hook and line devices, $2.00; Trotline, each 100 hooks, $4.00; hunting, reciprocal with home State fees but not less than a minimum fee of $15.00; hunting on private shooting preserves, $5.00; federal "Duck" stamp, $3.00.

HUNTING AND TRAPPING

Game animals: White-tailed Deer, Rabbits, Squirrels (Black, Fox, Gray). OPEN SEASONS:* Deer—archery for about 5 weeks during November and December; shotgun for about 6 days between archery periods. Rabbit —mid-November through January. Squirrels—August and September in Southern Zone; September and October in Northern Zone. BAG LIMITS: Deer—1. Rabbits—5 per day. Squirrels—5 per day.

Furbearing animals: Beaver, Fox (Gray, Red), Mink, Muskrat, Opossum, Raccoon, Skunk, Weasel. OPEN HUNTING SEASONS:* Opossum, Raccoon, Skunk,Weasel—Northern Zone, November through January; Southern Zone, mid-November to January. OPEN TRAPPING SEASONS: Beaver —mid-November to March. Mink, Muskrat, Opossum, Raccoon, Skunk, Weasel—Northern Zone, mid-November through December; Southern Zone, December 1 to January. No bag or possession limits. Ground hog— Sept. 1–Oct. 15 in 29 northern counties, and at any time in all other counties. No bag or possession limits. NOT PROTECTED: Bobcat, Coyote, Fox, Gopher, Marten, Porcupine, and Prairie Dog may be taken at any time.

Game birds: Coot, Mourning Dove, Ducks (except Canvasback and Redhead), Geese, Ruffed Grouse, Partridge (Chukar, Hungarian), Merganser, Prairie Chicken, Cock Pheasant, Quail, Wilson's Snipe, Wild Turkey, Woodcock. OPEN SEASONS:* Dove—September 1 to mid-Novem-

---

* Check current state regulations.

ber. Coot, Ducks, Merganser—November to first week in December. Geese—mid-October to late December or early January. Hungarian Partridge and Cock Pheasant—mid-November to mid-December. Quail and Woodcock—mid-November through December. Wilson's Snipe—early November to early December. Wild Turkey—about one week in November. FULLY PROTECTED: Canvasback and Redhead Ducks, Ruffed Grouse, Chukar Partridge, Prairie Chicken—no open seasons. NOT PROTECTED: Crows may be taken at any time.

Southern Zone: Counties of Alexander, Bond, Calhoun, Clay, Clinton, Crawford, Edwards, Effingham, Fayette, Franklin, Gallatin, Hamilton, Hardin, Jackson, Jasper, Jefferson, Jersey, Johnson, Lawrence, Madison, Marion, Massac, Monroe, Perry Pope, Pulaski, Randolph, Richland, St. Clair, Saline, Union, Wabash, Washington, Wayne, White, Williamson. Northern Zone: all other counties.

FIREARMS

Game animals and birds may be taken only with a shotgun not larger than 10 gauge, and capable of holding not more than 3 shots in the magazine and chamber combined. If originally capable of holding more shells, the gun must be plugged with a filler which cannot be removed from the loading end without taking the gun apart. Deer may be taken only by a shotgun loaded with rifled slugs or by a bow and arrow. The longbow used to hunt Deer must have a 40-pound pull. Deer hunters should wear flame orange, red, or yellow caps and coats. It is unlawful to use a shotgun loaded with rifled slugs except to take Deer, or to use a shotgun load larger than BB to take any species of wild game. The use of an airgun, pistol, or rifle to take game birds, or of any device to muffle the sound of a gun being fired at wild game, is prohibited.

Shooting hours: Sunrise to sunset; the opening day of all hunting and trapping seasons starts at 12:00 o'clock noon. Exceptions: Mourning Dove—12:00 o'clock noon to sunset daily; Deer—archery season: one-half hour before sunrise to 4:00 P.M., shotgun season: 6:30 A.M.–4:00 P.M. Furbearing animals may be taken at night.

FISHING

Game fish: Black Bass (Largemouth, Smallmouth), Kentucky (Spotted) Bass, Pickerel, Northern and Walleyed Pike, Sauger, Trout (except Lake). OPEN SEASONS: Pickerel, Northern Pike—May 1–Nov. 30. Walleyed Pike, Sauger—May 1–Feb. 15, except in the Mississippi River, all year. No closed season for other fish.

It is unlawful to use a gill net except in Lake Michigan and the Mississippi River. Not more than 2 poles and lines with 2 hooks attached to each line may be used to fish through any ice hole. All portable fishing shelters must be removed from the ice at the end of each fishing day after March 1. Buffalo, Carp, Gar, Dogfish, and Suckers may be taken by gig, pitchfork, spear, or bow and arrow during the spearing season March 15–Oct. 15.

Bullfrogs: OPEN SEASON: June 15–Aug. 31. DAILY BAG AND POSSESSION LIMIT: 8. No airguns or any firearms may be used in frogging.

Migratory waterfowl flock to the Fox Chain-O-Lakes region and along the Illinois River Valley to the Chautauqua National Wildlife Refuge (4,470 acres) near Havana, and the Crab Orchard National Wildlife Refuge (43,003 acres) near Carbondale. Geese congregate in the Horseshoe Lake Conservation region near Cairo at the confluence of the Mississippi and Ohio rivers. Posted areas are open to public hunting, and Carlyle Reservoir will be open to waterfowl hunting. There are approximately 9,350 miles of fishable streams, and numerous public lakes in addition to federal waters—Crab Orchard (6,695 acres), Devil's Kitchen, and Little Grassy Lakes near Carbondale; Lake Chautauqua and Spring Lake near Savanna; 26 water areas in the Forest Preserve District of Cook County; and state parks. Fox Chain-O-Lakes comprises Bluff Lake (65 acres), Catherine Lake (145 acres), Channel Lake (320 acres), Grass Lake (1,360 acres), Marie Lake (455 acres) near Antioch in Lake County, Fox Lake (1,670 acres), Nippersink Lake (450 acres), Petite Lake (155 acres), Pistakee Lake (1,550 acres) near Fox Lake—Lake County.

STATE PARKS AND PUBLIC FISHING LAKES

Anderson Lake (2,007 acres, lake 1,364 acres) near Marbletown—Fulton County; *Apple River Canyon* (157 acres) on Apple River, west of Warren—Jo Daviess County; *Argyle Lake* (1,052 acres, lake 95 acres) near Colchester—McDonough County; *Beaver Dam* (737 acres, lake 59 acres) south of Carlinville—Macoupin County; *Black Hawk* (207 acres) on Rock River at Rock Island—Rock Island County; *Buffalo Rock* (43 acres) on Illinois River near Ottawa—LaSalle County; *Cave-in-Rock* (64.5 acres) on Ohio River at Cave-in-Rock—Hardin County; *Dolan Lake* (510 acres, lake 76 acres) near McLeansboro—Hamilton County; *Fern Clyffe Lake* (1,026 acres, lake 12 acres) west of Goreville—Johnson County; *Stephen A. Forbes Lake* (2,520 acres, lake 585 acres) near Omega—Marion County; *Fort Kaskaskia* (201 acres) on Mississippi River north of Chester—Randolph County; *Fort Massac* (840 acres) on Ohio River, east of Metropolis—Massac County; *Fox Ridge* (752 acres) on Embarrass River, south of Charleston—Coles County; *Gebhard Woods* (30 acres) on Nettle Creek and the Illinois-Michigan Canal, west of Morris—Grundy County; *Giant City* (1,675 acres) at Little Grassy Lake, south of Carbondale—Jackson and Union counties; *Grand Marais* (1,125 acres, 3 lakes— 197 acres) near East St. Louis—St. Clair County; *Gladstone Lake* (84 acres, lake 27 acres) at Gladstone—Henderson County; *Horseshoe Lake* (8,679 acres, lake 2,400 acres) near Cairo—Alexander County; *Illini* (406 acres) on Illinois River opposite Marseilles—LaSalle County; *Illinois Beach* (1,651 acres) on Lake Michigan between Zion and Waukegon—Lake County; *Johnson Sauk Trail Lake* (395 acres, lake 64 acres) north of Kewanee—Henry County; *Kankakee River* (2,074 acres) northwest of Kankakee—Kankakee County; *Kickapoo Lakes* (1,578 acres, water 170 acres) near Oakwood—Vermillion County; *Le-Aqua-Na Lake* (615 acres, lake 47 acres) north of Lena—Stephenson County; *Lincoln Trail* (914 acres, lake 158 acres) south of Marshall—Clark County; *Lowden Memorial* (208 acres) on Rock River near Oregon—Ogle County; *Marshall County Area* (2,600 acres, water 1,875 acres) near Lacon; McClean County Lake (733 acres, lake 158 acres) near LeRoy; *Mermet Lake Conservation Area* (2,461 acres, lake 690 acres) near Mermet—Massac County; *Murphysboro Lake* (946 acres, lake 142 acres) at Murphysboro—Jackson County; *Mississippi Palisades* (1,293 acres) on Mississippi River, north of Savanna—Carroll County; *Nauvoo* (150 acres) on Mississippi River at Nauvoo—Hancock County; *New Salem* (328 acres) on Sangamon River, south of Petersburg—Menard County; *Pere Marquette* (5,180 acres) on Illinois River Lakes near Grafton—Jersey County; *Ramsey Lake* (815 acres, lake 45 acres) near Ramsey—Fayette County; *Randolph County Lake* (684 acres, lake 85 acres) near Chester; *Red Hills Lake* (1,150 acres, lake 40 acres) near Sumner—Lawrence County; *Rice Lake* (2,530 acres, lake 1,385 acres) near Banner—Fulton County; *Rock Cut* (708 acres, Pierce Lake 162 acres) near Rockford—Winnebago County; *Saline County Lake* (525 acres, lake 105 acres) near Equality; *Sanganois-Knapp Island Area* (6,634 acres, water 4,100 acres) near Browning—Schuyler County; *Siloam Springs* (3,026 acres, lake 68 acres) near Kellerville—Adams County; *Spring Lake* (1,557 acres, lake 1,285 acres) northwest of Manito —Tazewell County; *Starved Rock* (1,437 acres) on Illinois River between La Salle and Ottawa—LaSalle County; *Washington County Lake* (1,358 acres, lake 335 acres) near Nashville; *Wayne County Lake* (940 acres, lake 194 acres) near Johnsonville; *Weldon Springs* (120 acres, lake 28 acres) near Clinton—DeWitt County; White Pines Forest (385 acres) on Pine Creek, southwest of Oregon—Ogle County; *Wolf Lake* (580 acres, lake 442 acres) near Chicago—Cook County; *Woodford County Area* (2,900 acres, water 2,790 acres) near Spring Bay.

Licenses, permits, regulations, and information about current seasons, bag and possession limits can be obtained from the Director, Illinois

Department of Conservation, State Office Building, 400 South Spring St., Springfield; Chicago office: 160 North LaSalle St.; and authorized agents throughout the state.

INDIANA

Area: 36,354 square miles (land area—36,185 square miles); rank in nation–38
Bird: Cardinal *(Richmondena cardinalis)*, adopted 1933
Capital city: Indianapolis on the White River and Fall Creek in Marion County; population (1960)—476,258; rank in state–1
Elevations: Highest, Franklin Township (1,257 ft.) in Wayne County; lowest, Ohio River (316 ft.) in Vandenburg County
Flower: Peony *(Paeonia)*, adopted 1957
Geographic center: 14 miles west of north of Indianapolis in Boone County
Nickname: Hoosier State
Population (1960): 4,662,498; rank in nation–11
Tree: Tulip Tree *(Liriodendron tulipfera)*, adopted 1931

Indiana at the lower end of Lake Michigan is a north central State with Michigan above the northern border, Ohio across the eastern line, and Kentucky on the southern shore of the Ohio River; Illinois shares a western boundary partially formed by the Wabash River flowing from the Terre Haute region to the Ohio River.

The Lake Michigan shore is lined with sandy beaches and dunes piled high by winds. Hundreds of lakes are scattered across the northern plain including the largest waters: Wawasee Lake (3,600 acres) in northeastern Kosciusko County, Lake Maxinkuckee (1,854 acres) at Culver in Marshall County, Freeman Lake (1,800 acres) between Carroll and White Counties, and Lake James (1,318 acres) in Steuben County. South of the fertile prairie region are rocky hills known as knobs, the Knobstone escarpment rising to 500 feet in places along the Ohio River; deep valleys, streams, mineral springs, numerous sink holes, and limestone caverns.

The Wabash River fed by the Salamonie, and the Mississinewa, Wild Cat, Tippecanoe, and White rivers flow for more than 400 miles on a southwesterly course to the Ohio River. The largest tributary is the White River, and the East Fork and West Fork drain central and southern Indiana. The Kanakee River in northwestern Indiana forms a boundary between Lake and Newton counties before entering Illinois. The St. Joseph and St. Mary's rivers merge at Fort Wayne to continue on as the Maumee River moving from northwestern Indiana to Ohio.

LICENSES

Resident fishing licenses are issued to bona fide residents 18 or more years of age, and to members of the U.S. Armed Forces on active duty in the state. Regardless of age, all persons must possess valid licenses to hunt and trap, except owners or tenants and their immediate families living on farm lands who may fish, hunt, and trap on their farms without licenses. Special Deer permits are required in addition to state licenses to participate in controlled hunts on the following military reservations: Camp Atterbury (Bartholomew, Brown, and Johnson counties), Crane U.S. Naval Ammunition Depot (Greene and Martin counties), and Jefferson Proving Ground (Jefferson, Jennings, and Ripley counties). Permits are issued at each area. All persons 16 or more years of age should purchase a federal "Duck" stamp to take migratory game birds. A hunting license is required to take Frogs. A Trout stamp affixed to a fishing license is necessary to take any species of Trout.

Resident license fees: Fishing (to females only), $1.50; general combination fishing, hunting, and trapping, $2.50; D-net fishing in Wabash River only, $1.10; D-net fishing in areas of Wabash and White Rivers, $3.00; cisco gill net, $2.00; Mussel permit, $2.00; Trout stamp, $2.00; Deer hunting (in addition to combination license), $5.50; Deer hunting permit on military reservation, $5.50; federal "Duck" stamp, $3.00; fur buyer, $10.00; game breeder, $5.00; private shooting area, $100.00; taking game for scientific purposes, $1.00; Wabash River boundary seine (100 yards), $10.00.

Nonresident license fees: Annual fishing, $3.50; fishing 14 consecutive days, $2.50; combination fishing, hunting, and trapping, $16.00; D-net fishing in areas of Wabash and White rivers, $15.00; Trout stamp, $2.00; federal "Duck" stamp, $3.00; hunting game birds on private shooting preserves, $2.50; fur buyer, $25.00; fur jobber, $2.00.

HUNTING AND TRAPPING

Game animals: Deer, Fox (Gray, Red), Mink, Muskrat, Opossum, Rabbit, Raccoon, Skunk, Squirrel. OPEN HUNTING SEASONS:* Deer— archery, late October to late November; firearms, about 10 days from late November to early December with some areas restricted to one or more days of shooting. Rabbit—mid-November to mid-January. Squirrel—mid-August to mid-October. BAG LIMITS: Deer—1 Buck in general hunting; one of either sex in designated areas; or 2 of either sex on military reservations (1 on Deer permit and 1 on special permit). Rabbits—5 per day. Squirrels —5 per day. Raccoon—2 per day. OPEN TRAPPING SEASONS: Nov. 15–Jan.

---

* Check current state regulations.

31 for Fox, Mink, Muskrat, Opossum, Raccoon, Skunk. No bag limits. FULLY PROTECTED: Badger, Otter, Black and Flying Squirrels—no open seasons. NOT PROTECTED: Coyote, Fox, Gopher, Weasel, and Woodchuck may be taken at any time.

A legal Buck is a male Deer with at least one forked antler.

Game birds: Coot, Mourning Dove, Ducks (except Canvasback and Redhead), Gallinule, Geese, Ruffed Grouse, Merganser, Chukar Partridge, Pheasant, Prairie Chicken, Quail, Rails, Sora, Wilson's Snipe, Wild Turkey, Woodcock. OPEN SEASONS:* Coot, Ducks, Merganser—about 3 weeks in November plus a week in December. Gallinule, Rails, Sora—September 1 to mid-October. Geese—mid-October to January 1 split by a short closed season. Hungarian Partridge, Pheasant, Quail—mid-November to mid-December. Wilson's Snipe—mid-October to mid-November. Woodcock —mid-October through November. Private shooting preserves—Oct. 1– March 31. FULLY PROTECTED: Dove, Canvasback and Redhead Ducks, Ruffed Grouse, Chukar Partridge, Prairie Chicken, Wild Turkey—no open seasons unless increase permits a season. NOT PROTECTED: Crow, English Sparrow, and Starling may be killed at any time.

FIREARMS

It is unlawful to use or possess any firearms except a shotgun not larger than 10 gauge and plugged to hold only 3 shells in the magazine and chamber combined when hunting migratory game birds. Deer may be hunted only with a 12, 16, or 20 gauge shotgun loaded with rifled slugs; or a flintlock or percussion cap muzzle-loading rifle of 45 caliber (or larger) without scopes and loaded with ball-shaped bullets. Longbows must have a pull of 35 or more pounds. The possession of sidearms, or the use of dogs, domestic animals, or mechanical conveyances to hunt Deer are prohibited. The yellow license number should clearly be displayed on a hunter's back.

Shooting hours: Hunting on Sunday is prohibited. Sunrise to sunset except that shooting starts at 12:00 o'clock noon on the opening day of Duck season. Rabbits, Squirrels, and furbearing animals—opens 12:00 o'clock noon and closes at 12:00 o'clock noon on the last day. Raccoon— 6:00 P.M.–6:00 A.M. Night hunters on property other than their own (with owners permission) must carry a continuously burning light which is visible for 500 feet in all directions.

FISHING

Game fish: Black Bass (Largemouth, Smallmouth), Kentucky Bass, Rock Bass (Goggle-eye), Silver Bass, Striped Bass, White Bass, Bluegill,

---

* Check current state regulations.

Bream, Channel Catfish, Crappie, Pickerel or Pike, Pike-perch or Walleye, Yellow Perch, Red-eared Sunfish, Trout (any species). OPEN SEASONS: All year, except Trout in streams—May 1–Aug. 31. D-nets in Wabash and White Rivers—mid-April through May.

Only 3 poles or handlines may be used by an angler at one time, or not more than one trotline per fisherman in any lake or stream, except in the Illinois-Indiana boundary waters of the Wabash River. Each person fishing through ice is limited to only 2 holes (maximum diameter 12 inches), and one line with one hook for each hole. Rough fish may be taken by a gig, spear, bow and arrow, or snares at any time. It is unlawful to operate a motorboat in a circle around a fisherman.

Frogs: OPEN SEASON: April 1–30 and mid-June through October. DAILY BAG LIMIT: 25.

More than 300 lakes and 500 streams are stocked with game fish including the famous Black Bass waters, Wawasee Lake and Tippecanoe River. Game preserves in the state fish and game areas, national and state forests provide good hunting and fishing, but hunting is prohibited in state parks.

PUBLIC FISHING SITES

Bartholomew County—Azalia, City of Columbia, Lowell Bridge; *Decatur County*—Greensburg Public Fishing Area; *De Kalb County*— Story Lake; *Elkhart County*—Fish Lake, Simonton Lake, Yellow Creek Lake, St. Joseph River; *Fulton County*—Manitou Lake, Nyona Lake; *Jennings County*—Brush Creek Lake; *Kosciusko County*—Carr Lake, Chapman Lake, Grassy Creek, Palestine Lake, Beaver Dam Lake, Tippecanoe River; *LaGrange County*—Adams Lake, Appleman Lake, Emma Lake, Fish Lake, Little Turkey Lake, Oilver Lake, Pretty Lake, Wall Lake, Westler Lake; *LaPorte County*—Hog Lake; *Lawrence County*— White River, William's Dam; *Marshall County*—Maxinkuckee Lake, Mill Pond Lake, Lake of the Woods, Lawrence Lake; *Martin County*—White River, Hindostan Falls; *Noble County*—Cree Lake, Crooked Lake, Knapp Lake, Sylvan Lake, Loon Lake, Sparta Lake, Little Long Lake; *Perry County*—Anderson River, Tell City; *Posey County*—Wabash River, New Harmony, and Dogtown; *Ripley County*—Batesville Reservoir; *Steuben County*—Ball Lake, Beaver Dam Lake, Big Turkey Lake, Clear Lake, Fawn River, Fish Lake, Golden Lake, Lime Lake, Little Turkey Lake, Otter Lake, Pigeon Lake, Loon Lake, Big Bower; *St. Joseph County*—St. Joseph River, Pleasant Lake; *Vigo County*—Terre Haute; *Wabash County* —Eel River (3 sites); *Washington County*—White River; *Whitely County*—Old Lake; *Vermillion County*—Montezuma.

PUBLIC HUNTING PRESERVES (fishing and hunting)*

Crosley (3,309 acres) 15 miles northeast of Seymour—Jennings County; *Hovey Lake* (900 acres including 600-acre lake) south of Mount Vernon—Posey County; *Jasper Pulaski* (7,199 acres) southwest of North Judson—Jasper and Pulaski counties; *Kankakee* (2,300 acres) on Kankakee River northwest of Knox—Starke County; *Tri-County* (2,733 acres) near North Webster—Kosciusko County; *Willow Slough* (8,360 acres) west of Enos—Newton County.

STATE FORESTS (fishing and hunting)*

Clark (18,800 acres) about 10 miles south of Scottsburg—Clark County; *Ferdinand* (7,594 acres, 52-acre lake) 6 miles east of Ferdinand —DuBois County; Greene-Sullivan (4,139 acres) north of Pleasantville— Greene and Sullivan counties; *Harrison County* (20,018 acres) on Big Blue River and Indian Creek, west of Corydon; *Jackson County* (10,372 acres) near Brownstown; *Martin County* (3,580 acres) northeast of Shoals; *Morgan-Monroe* (21,515 acres) about 15 miles south of Martinsville— Monroe and Morgan counties; *Pike County* (2,785 acres) east of Winslow; *Salamonie River* (805 acres) east of Wabash—Wabash County; *Selmier* (350 acres) north of Vernon—Jackson County; *Francis Slocum* (1,085 acres) on Mississinewa River, southwest of Peru—Miami County; *Yellowwood* (21,564 acres) contains Ault Lake (17 acres), Bear Creek Lake (11 acres), Yellowwood Lake (147 acres) southwest of Nashville— Brown County.

STATE PARKS

Bass Lake Beach (21 acres) at Bass Lake, 7 miles south of Knox— Starke County; *Brown County* (15,332 acres) south of Nashville; *Chain O' Lakes* (1,920 acres) southeast of Albion—Noble County; *Clifty Falls* (668 acres) on Big Clift Creek, near Madison—Jefferson County; *Kankakee River* (1,793 acres) near Schneider—Lake County; *Lieber* (8,248 acres) southwest of Cloverdale at Cataract Lake (1,500 acres) between Owen and Putnam counties; McCormicks Creek (1,225 acres) at White River, near Spencer—Owen County; *Mounds* (254 acres) on White River, east of Anderson—Madison County; *Muscatatuck* (260 acres) at North Vernon—Jennings County; *Pokagon* (956 acres) at Lake James, north of Angola—Steuben County; *Raccoon Lake* (3,938 acres) at the 2,100-acre reservoir, south of Hollandsburg—Parke County; *Scales Lake Beach* (477 acres) northeast of Bonnville—Warwick County; *Shades* (2,571 acres) 12

---

* Check current state regulations.

miles southwest of Crawfordsville—Montgomery County; *Shakamak* (1,016 acres) northwest of Jasonville—Greene County; *Spring Mill* (1,209 acres) east of Mitchell—Lawrence County; *Tippecanoe River* (2,744 acres) north of Winamac—Pulaski County; *Turkey Run* (1,741 acres) north of Marshall—Parke County; *Versaille* (5,856 acres) northeast of Versailles—Ripley County; *Whitewater* (1,515 acres, 200-acre lake) south of Liberty—Union County.

Licenses, regulations, and information about current seasons, bag and possession limits may be obtained from county clerks, and the Director, Department of Conservation, Division of Fish and Game, State Office. Building, Room 605, Indianapolis 4. Lake contour maps may be purchased from the Division of Water Resources, 100 North Senate Ave., Indianapolis 4. Maps 8½ × 11 inches, 30 cents each; 17 × 22 inches, 60 cents each.

IOWA

Area: 56,147 square miles (land area—56,032 square miles); rank in nation—23
Bird: Eastern Goldfinch *(Spinus tristis),* adopted 1933
Capital city: Des Moines at the confluence of the Des Moines and Raccoon rivers in Polk County; population (1960)—208,982; rank in state—1
Counties: 99
Elevations: Highest, Ocheyedan Mound (1,675 ft.) in Osceola County; lowest, at Keokuk (477 ft.) in Lee County on the Mississippi River
Flower: Wild Rose *(Rosa virginianus),* adopted 1897
Nicknames: Hawkeye State, Land of the Rolling Prairie.
Population (1960): 2,757,537; rank in nation—24

Iowa is a prairie state with Minnesota on the north, Missouri across the southern boundary; the eastern shores of the Mississippi River are shared by Wisconsin and Illinois. On the western border, the Missouri River separates Iowa from Nebraska, and the Big Sioux River etches the Iowa–South Dakota line.

There are approximately 100 lakes, 900 miles of inland streams, and 600 miles of boundary rivers. Major inland rivers are the eastern Iowa River merging with the Cedar River in Louisa County, the Wapsipinicon River, and the Skunk River all flowing into the Mississippi River; the Des Moines River with many forks and tributaries draining central Iowa from the northern lakes region to the Mississippi River in the southeastern corner of the state; the Rock River in northwestern Iowa joins the Big Sioux River in Sioux County; and the Floyd River, Little Sioux River, and many small streams flow southwesterly to the picturesque bluffs of the Missouri River.

LICENSES

Resident licenses to fish, hunt, and trap are issued to persons 16 or more years of age who have lived for at least 30 days in the state. Legal residents on active duty as members of the U.S. Armed Forces during a period when the United States of America is at war may fish and hunt without licenses. Inmates of county homes or any resident receiving old age assistance under Chapter 249 are not required to possess licenses. Residents under 16 years of age, nonresidents less than 14 years of age, and minors who are pupils in state schools for the blind and deaf, or minors who are inmates of other state institutions, except inmates of the men's reformatory at Animosa and the women's reformatory at Rockwell City, may fish without licenses. A resident under the age of 16 may hunt without a license if he is accompanied by his parent, guardian, or other competent adult with a valid hunting license. Each hunter under 16 years of age must be accompanied by one licensed adult. Owners or tenants and their children may hunt, fish, and trap on their own lands, and may also shoot Ground Squirrels, Gophers, and Woodchucks upon adjacent roads without possessing licenses.

Aliens must obtain nonresident licenses unless they are residents who have applied for naturalization papers. Nonresidents are charged the same fees for licenses that a resident of Iowa would have to pay in the nonresident's home state. No trapping licenses are issued to nonresidents from states that do not extend a similar privilege to residents of Iowa. Any person licensed by the authorities of Illinois, Minnesota, Missouri, Nebraska, South Dakota, and Wisconsin to take fish, mussels, game animals and birds, or furbearing animals from, or in, waters forming a boundary between these states and Iowa, may take such wildlife from the portion of waters within Iowa without an Iowa license, providing that a similar privilege is extended to residents of Iowa by the other State. Licenses to hunt Deer are issued only to residents of Iowa. Permits are required to trap on state game management areas and federal wildlife refuges. All persons 16 or more years of age must purchase a federal "Duck" stamp to take migratory game birds. Trout stamps are necessary to take Trout in designated waters in addition to a fishing license. Frogs may be taken by holders of a valid fishing license.

Resident license fees: Fishing, $2.50; hunting, $2.50; combination hunting and fishing, $4.50; bow and arrow Deer hunting, $10.00; shotgun Deer hunting, $10.00; trapping (16 or more years of age), $3.00; trapping (under age of 16), $1.00; federal "Duck" stamp (affix to hunting license), $3.00; Trout stamp (affix to fishing license), $2.00; trotline—not more than 100 hooks (in addition to fishing license), $1.10; bait dealer, $5.00; fur dealer, $10.00.

Alien and nonresident license fees: Annual fishing (reciprocal), see home state nonresident fee; fishing 6 consecutive days (reciprocal*) not less than, $3.00; hunting (reciprocal*) not less than, $5.00; trapping (reciprocal*) not less than, $10.00; fur dealer (reciprocal*) not less than, $50.00; federal "Duck" stamp (affix to hunting license), $3.00; Trout stamp (affix to fishing license), $2.00; hunting on private shooting preserves, $5.00.

HUNTING AND TRAPPING

Game animals: Deer, Rabbits (Cottontail, Jack), Raccoon, Squirrels (Gray, Fox). OPEN HUNTING SEASON:** Deer—bow and arrow, mid-October through November; shotgun, a few days in mid-December. Rabbits—mid-September to mid-February. Raccoon—mid-October through February. Squirrels—mid-September to mid-December. BAG LIMITS: Deer (any age or sex)—1. Rabbits—10 per day. Raccoons—no limit. Squirrels —6 per day.

Furbearing animals: Badger, Beaver, Coyote, Fox (Gray, Red), Ground Hog, Mink, Muskrat, Opossum, Otter, Raccoon, Skunk, Spotted Skunk (Civet Cat), Weasel, Wolf. OPEN TRAPPING SEASON:** Mink— mid-November to mid-December. Badger, Beaver, Muskrat, Opossum, Raccoon, Skunk, Spotted Skunk—mid-November through February. BAG LIMITS—none. NOT PROTECTED: Coyote, Fox, Gopher, Ground Hog, Weasel, and Wolf may be taken at any time.

Game birds: Coot or Mud Hen, Ducks (except Canvasback and Redhead), Geese (except Ross's Goose), Merganser, Hungarian Partridge, Ring-necked Pheasant, Quail, Wilson's or Jack Snipe. OPEN SEASONS:** Coot, Ducks, Merganser—early October to mid-November. Geese—early October to mid-December. Partridge, Quail—November and December. Wilson's Snipe—one week in October. FULLY PROTECTED: Mourning Dove, Gallinule, Grebe, Ross's Goose, Rails, Swan, and Woodcock—no open seasons. NOT PROTECTED: Blackbird, Crow, Cooper's Hawk, Sharp-shinned Hawk, Great Horned Owl, English or House Sparrow, and Starling may be taken at any time.

Bird dogs may not be trained on game in the wild between March 15—July 15.

FIREARMS

Hunters may only use 10, 12, 16, and 20 gauge shotguns with rifled slugs, or longbows with 40-pound pull (or more) and broadhead arrows

---

* See home state for nonresident fee.
** Check current state regulations.

to take Deer. Firearms commonly shot from the shoulder or hand may be used in hunting, but guns larger than 10 gauge, and swivel guns are prohibited. A gun is defined as including all types of guns except a pistol or revolver. See FEDERAL REGULATIONS FOR MIGRATORY GAME BIRDS. It is unlawful to kill Beaver, Mink, Muskrat, and Otter with a shotgun or spear.

Shooting hours: Deer—archery, one-half hour before sunrise to one-half hour after sunset; shotguns, 8:00 A.M.–4:00 P.M. Partridge, Pheasant, Quail—8:30 A.M.–5:00 P.M. Waterfowl—sunrise to sunset except that on opening day of Duck season shooting starts at 12:00 o'clock noon. Rabbit—6:00 A.M.–6:00 P.M. Raccoon, and trapping fur-bearing animals: 12:00 o'clock noon on opening day until mid-night on last day.

FISHING

Game fish: Black Bass (Largemouth, Smallmouth), Rock Bass, Silver Bass, Catfish, Crappie, Muskellunge, Paddlefish, Perch, Northern Pike (Pickerel), Sauger, Sturgeon, Walleye. OPEN SEASONS:* Black Bass —late May to February 15. Northern Pike—mid-May to February 15. Sauger, Walleye—mid-May to February 15 north of U.S. Highway 30 and all year south of highway. Continuous open season for other fish, except in a few lakes: Black Bass—from Saturday before May 30 to November 30; Catfish—from Saturday before May 15 to February 15. Muskellunge and Rock Sturgeon—no open season.

Trotlines may be used only in the Big Sioux, Missouri, and Mississippi rivers, and all streams south of U.S. Highway 30. It is unlawful to use artificial light, a grab hook, snag hook, net seine or trap, except gaff hooks and landing nets to assist in landing fish. Spears or longbow and arrows may be used to take Buffalo, Carp, Dogfish, Gar, Quillback, Redhorse, Gizzard Shad, and Suckers if the fisherman is not hidden from view within an enclosure.

Frogs: OPEN SEASON: Mid-May to November 30. DAILY BAG LIMIT: Bullfrogs, 12; other frogs, 48.

Catfish, Crappie, Northern Pike, and Sauger may be caught in the Missouri River, and Largemouth Black Bass, Bluegill, Catfish, Crappie, Northern Pike, Perch, Sheepshead, and Walleye in the Mississippi River. There are about 200 state-owned access sites to good fishing, and outboard motor boats with motors not to exceed 6 horsepower are permitted upon state-owned artificial lakes of 100 acres or more in size. Hunting is allowed in state forests but not in state parks, although public hunting areas may be adjacent to state parks.

* Check current state regulations.

STATE PARKS

Backbone (1,411 acres, lake 125 acres*) on Maquoketa River near Strawberry Point—Delaware County; *Beaver Meadows* (74 acres) at Beaver Creek near Parkersburg—Butler County; *Beeds Lake* (291 acres, lake 130 acres*) northwest of Hampton—Franklin County; *Bellevue* (148 acres) south of Bellevue—Jackson County; *Black Hawk* (267 acres) at Lakeview—Sac County; *Bob White* (380 acres, lake 115 acres*) west of Allerton—Wayne County; *Browns Lake* (23 acres) at 784-acre lake near Salix—Woodbury County; *A. A. Call* (130 acres) on East Fork of Des Moines River, at Algona—Kussuth County; *T. F. Clark* (24 acres) on Wolf Creek, northeast of Traer—Tama County; *Clear Lake* (70 acres) at 3,643-acre lake, west of Mason City—Cerro Gordo County; *Cold Springs* (104 acres) south of Lewis—Cass County; *Dolliver Memorial* (613 acres) on Des Moines River near Lehigh—Webster County; *Eagle Lake* (21 acres) at 906 acre lake near Britt—Hancock County; *Five Island Lake* (945 acres) at Emmetsburg—Palo Alto County; *Geode* (1,573 acres, lake 205 acres*) near Danville—Henry County; *Frank Gotch* (57 acres) at junction of Des Moines River East and West forks, near Dakota City —Humboldt County; *Green Valley* (966 acres, lake 390 acres*) near Creston—Union County; *Gull Point* (59 acres) at West Okoboji Lake, northwest of Milford—Dickinson County; *Heery Woods* (384 acres) on Shell Rock River south of Clarksville—Butler County; *Lacey-Keosauqua* (1,613 acres) on Des Moines River at Keosauqua—Van Buren County; *Lake Ahquabi* (770 acres, lake 130 acres*) south of Indianola—Warren County; *Lake Darling* (1,425 acres, lake 302 acres*) near Brighton— Washington County; *Lake Keomah* (366 acres, lake 82 acres) east of Oskaloosa—Mahaska County; *Lake MacBride* (744 acres) at 950-acre lake,* west of Solon—Johnson County; *Lake Manawa* (919 acres) near Council Bluffs—Pottawattamie County; *Lake Of Three Fires* (386 acres, lake 125 acres*) near Bedford—Taylor County; *Lake Wapello* (1,143 acres, lake 287 acres*) west of Drakesville—Davis County; *Ledges* (896 acres) on Des Moines River, south of Boone—Boone County; *Lennon Mills* (21 acres) access to Raccoon River at Panora—Guthrie County; *Lewis and Clark* (315 acres) at Blue Lake, west of Onawa—Monona County; *Lost Island* (32 acres) at 1,260-acre lake north of Ruthven— Palo Alto County; *McIntosh Woods* (60 acres) at Clear Lake east of Ventura—Cerro Gordo County; *Mill Creek* (158 acres) near Paulina— O'Brien County; *Mini-Wakan* (28 acres) at Spirit Lake, northeast of Orleans—Dickinson County; *Nine Eagles* (1,135 acres, lake 57 acres) southeast of Davis City—Decatur County; *Oak Grove* (102 acres) on Big Sioux River, northwest of Hawarden—Sioux County; *Oakland Mills*

* Artificial lake.

(112 acres) on Skunk River, near Mount Pleasant—Henry County; *Okamanpedan* (19 acres) at Tuttle Lake, near Dolliver—Emmet County; *Palisades-Keplar* (689 acres) on Cedar River, west of Mount Vernon—Linn County; *Pammel* (289 acres) on Middle River, near Winterset—Madison County; *Pikes Point* (6 acres) on West Okoboji Lake at Okoboji—Dickinson County; *Pine Lake* (584 acres, lake 101 acres*) on Iowa River at Eldora—Hardin County; *Pioneer* (14 acres) on Little Cedar River at Brownsville—Mitchell County; *Prairie Rose Lake** (210 acres) southeast of Harlan—Shelby County; *Red Haw Hill* (420 acres) near Chariton—Lucas County; *Rice Lake* (47 acres) at 612-acre lake, near Lake Mills—Winnebago County; *Rock Creek* (1,220 acres, 640-acre lake*) near Kellogg—Jasper County; *Rush Lake* (62 acres) at 460-acre lake, west of Mallard—Palo Alto County; *Silver Lake* (52 acres) near Delhi—Delaware County; *Springbrook* (640 acres) 7 miles north of Guthrie Center—Guthrie County; *Spring Lake* (240 acres) northwest of Grand Junction—Greene County; *Steamboat Rock* (5 acres) on Iowa River at Steamboat Rock—Hardin County; *Stone* (875 acres) on Big Sioux River at Sioux City—Woodbury County; *Storm Lake* (55 acres) at 3,097-acre lake—Buena Vista County; *Swan Lake** (130 acres) near Carroll—Carroll County; *Trappers Bay* (58 acres) at 1,058-acre Silver Lake, south of Lake Park—Dickinson County; *Twin Lakes* (15 acres) at North (596 acres) and South (600 acres) Twin Lakes, north of Rockwell City—Calhoun County; *Union Grove* (270 acres, lake 110 acres*) near Gladbrook—Tama County; *Viking Lake* (1,000 acres, lake 150 acres*) near Stanton—Montgomery County; *Walnut Woods* (260 acres) on Raccoon River, near Des Moines—Polk County; *Wanata* (160 acres) on Little Sioux River at Peterson—Clay County; *Wapsipinicon* (248 acres) on Wapsipinicon River at Anamosa—Jones County; *George Wyth Memorial* (352 acres) on Cedar River at Cedar Falls—Black Hawk County.

STATE FORESTS

Holst (334 acres), at Fraser, and *Pilot Mound* (333 acres), at Pilot Mound—Boone County; *Shimek* (3,975 acres) east of Farmington—Lee and Van Buren counties; *Stephens* (4,302 acres) near Lucas—Lucas and Monroe counties; *White Pine Hollow* (650 acres) near Luxemburg—Dubuque County; *Yellow River* (5,250 acres) near Waukon Junction—Allamakee County.

PUBLIC HUNTING AREAS

State-owned public hunting areas (113,954 acres) are in all counties including the following largest areas: *Benton County*—Dudgeon Lake

---

* Artificial lake.

(1,171 acres) north of Vinton; *Bremer County*—Sweet Marsh (1,648 acres) east of Tripoli; *Cerro Gordo County*—Clear Lake (3,643 acres) and Ventura Marsh (630 acres) at end of lake; *Buena Vista County*— Storm Lake* (3,097 acres); *Butler County*—Big Marsh (2,760 acres) north of Parkersburg; *Clay County*—Barringer Slough (1,071 acres), Trumbull Lake (1,229 acres) near Ruthven; *Dickinson County*—East Okoboji* (1,875 acres at Okoboji), West Okoboji* (3,939 acres) at Arnolds Park, Silver Lake* (1,058 acres) at Lake Park, Spirit Lake* (5,684 acres) near Orleans; *Emmet County*—East Swan Lake (788 acres) near Maple Hill, Ingham Lake* (939 acres) near Wallingford, Tuttle Lake* (981 acres) near Dolliver, West Swan Lake (1,043 acres) near Gruver; *Fremont County*—Fourneys Lake* (1,069 acres) near Thurman, Riverton Area* (941 acres) near Riverton; *Jackson County*—Green Island (2,722 acres) at Sabula; *Johnson County*—Hawkeye Wildlife Area* (3,500 acres) south of Swisher; *Louisa County*—Lake Odessa (3,200 acres) east of Wapello, Muscatine Slough (1,813 acres) near Muscatine; *Monona County*—Blue Lake (987 acres) west of Onawa; *Muscatine County*—Weise Slough (1,180 acres) near Atalissa; *Palo Alto County*— Five Island Lake* (1,110 acres) near Emmetsburg, Lost Island* (1,260 acres) near Ruthven; *Pottawatamie County*—Lake Manawa* (919 acres) near Council Bluffs; *Ringgold County*—Mount Ayr (1,158 acres) south of Mount Ayr; *Sac County*—Black Hawk Lake* (957 acres) at Lakeview; *Tama County*—Otter Creek Marsh (2,112 acres) near Chelsea; *Winnebago County*—Rice Lake* (1,831 acres) near Lake Mills; *Worth County* —Elk Creek Marsh (1,529 acres) north of Joice; *Wright County*—Big Wall Lake (978 acres) north of Blairsburg.

Licenses, regulations, information about current seasons, maps and lists of public fishing and hunting areas can be obtained from the Director, Iowa State Conservation Commission, East Seventh and Court, Des Moines 8. *Iowa Conservationist*, $1.00 for 24 issues.

KANSAS

Area: 82,276 square miles (land area—82,048 square miles); rank in nation–13
Animal: American Buffalo (*Bison bison*), adopted 1955
Bird: Western Meadowlark (*Sturnella neglecta*), adopted 1937
Capital city: Topeka on the Kansas (Kaw) River in Shawnee County; population (1960)—119,484; rank in state–3
Counties: 105

---

* Open water or partial refuge; no hunting on posted areas.

Elevations: Highest, Wallace County (4,135 ft.) at the Colorado border; lowest, Montgomery County (725 ft.) where the Verdigris River crosses the Oklahoma boundary
Flower: Sunflower *(Helianthus annus)*, adopted 1903
Geographic center: 15 miles northeast of Great Bend, Barton County
Nicknames: Sunflower State, Jayhawker State, Cyclone State
Population (1960): 2,178,611; rank in nation—28
Tree: Eastern Cottonwood *(Populus deltoides)*, adopted 1937

Kansas in central United States is bordered by Nebraska on the north, Oklahoma on the south, Colorado on the west, and Missouri on the east with the Missouri River forming an uneven boundary in the northeastern corner of the state.

The land slopes eastward to the Osage Plains and the rolling Flint Hills between El Dorado, Eureka, Cottonwood Falls, and Manhattan. The Blue Hills Uplands are west of the Smoky Hills Uplands and north of the Great Bend Prairie which was named for the great bend of the Arkansas River from Dodge City to Wichita. In the southwest, there are Red Hills and the escarpments of the Cimarron Breaks formed by tributaries of the Cimarron and Medicine Lodge rivers. The High Plains of western Kansas are vast treeless fields of grain. The Arkansas River flowing from Hamilton County on the Colorado border through southern Kansas is increased by many streams including the Pawnee, Little Arkansas, Ninescah, and Walnut rivers, and crosses into Oklahoma at Cowley County. The Smoky Hill River moves from Wallace County on the Colorado line through central Kansas to be fed by the northern Saline and Solomon rivers before joining the Republican River in Geary County, and continuing 169 miles as the Kansas (Kaw) River to its confluence with the Missouri River at Kansas City. The Delaware and Blue rivers are also tributaries of the Kansas River in northeastern Kansas. The Cottonwood River merges with the Neosho River, and the Verdigris River fed by the Elk and Fall rivers flows through southeastern Kansas into Oklahoma.

LICENSES

Resident licenses to fish, hunt, and trap are issued to persons 16–70 years of age who have lived in the state for at least 60 days before applying for a license, and to members of the U.S. Armed Forces on active duty in Kansas. Regardless of age, nonresidents must obtain licenses to fish and hunt, and only residents are permitted to trap wild animals. A fishing license is required to take rough fish by bow and arrow, or Bullfrogs by hands, hand dip net, or hook and line. Regular hunting licenses permit archers to take game by bow and arrow during firearms hunting seasons. All persons 16 or more years of age must purchase a federal "Duck" stamp in addition to a hunting license to take migratory game birds. Owners or tenants on land used for agricultural purposes, and their immediate families, may fish, hunt, and trap on their property without licenses, but not on adjacent land owned or controlled by other persons. Free permits are issued to any person, municipal corporation, or educational institution maintaining a zoological collection and desiring to add protected wild animals, birds, eggs, and nests for scientific or exhibition purposes.

Licenses for private game preserves may be obtained by a person owning or controlling by lease or otherwise any contiguous tract of land not less than 320 acres or more than 1,280 acres for at least 5 years. A game preserve may be less than 320 acres if the game-breeding and controlled-shooting area is to be used exclusively for the propagation and shooting of hand-reared Mallard Ducks. The applicant must file with the Forestry, Fish, and Game Commission a $2,000 bond executed by a Kansas insurance company.

License periods: Jan. 1–Dec. 31; except Mussels—July 1–June 30, and private game preserve—March 16–March 15.

Resident license fees: Fishing, $3.00; hunting, $3.00; combination fishing and hunting, $6.00; trapping, $1.50; Mussel fishing in Missouri River, $5.00; upland game bird stamp (affix to hunting license), $1.00; federal "Duck" stamp (affix to hunting license), $3.00; game breeding, $2.00; private game preserve, $200.00.

Nonresident license fees: Annual fishing, $5.00; fishing 10 consecutive days, $3.00; hunting on private shooting preserves only, $3.00; upland game bird stamp (affix to hunting license), $1.00; federal "Duck" stamp (affix to hunting license), $3.00; Mussel fishing in Missouri River, $50.00.

HUNTING AND TRAPPING

Game animals: Antelope, Deer, Hare and Rabbit, Tree Squirrels (Black, Fox, Gray). OPEN SEASONS: Hare and Rabbit—Dec. 15–Oct. 15 and during Pheasant, Prairie Chicken, and Quail seasons. Squirrels—Sept. 15–Dec. 15. DAILY BAG LIMITS: Hare and Rabbit—10. Squirrels—5.

Furbearing animals: Badger, Beaver, Bobcat, Civet Cat, Fox (Gray, Red, Prairie, or Swift), Marten, Mink, Muskrat, Opossum, Otter, Raccoon, Skunk, Weasel. OPEN SEASONS: Beaver—January and February. Bobcat, Civet Cat, Marten, Mink, Muskrat, Opossum, Weasel—December and January. Raccoon and Skunk may be hunted at any time, but trapped only during December and January. BAG LIMITS: none. FULLY PROTECTED: Antelope, Deer, Otter, Prairie or Swift Fox—no open seasons. NOT PROTECTED: Badger, Coyote, Fox, Gopher, Moles, and Wolves may be taken at any time.

Game birds: Coot, Mourning Dove, Ducks (except Canvasback and

Redhead), Gallinule, Geese, Merganser, Cock Pheasant, Prairie Chicken, Quail (Bobwhite, Scaled), Rails, Sora, Wilson's Snipe, Woodcock. OPEN SEASONS: Coot, Ducks, Merganser—late October to late November. Dove —September and October. Gallinule, Rails, Sora—Sept. 1 to late October. Geese—early October to mid-December. Prairie Chicken—opens first Saturday in November, Pheasant—opens second Saturday in November, and Quail—opens third Saturday in November for a number of days or weeks in designated counties. Wilson's Snipe and Woodcock—October to mid-November. Private shooting preserves—Oct. 1–March 31. FULLY PROTECTED: Canvasback and Redhead Ducks—no open seasons. NOT PROTECTED: Blackbirds, Blue Jays, Crows, Goshawks, Cooper's Hawks, Sharp-shinned Hawks, Great Horned Owls, English or European Sparrows, and Starlings may be taken at any time.

FIREARMS

Wild game may not be hunted with any gun larger than 10 gauge, and shotguns used to take migratory game birds must be plugged to hold not more than 3 shells in the magazine and chamber combined. Plugs may be used in automatic and repeating shotguns if they can be removed only by taking the gun apart. There are no restrictions on longbows and arrows except for taking fish, and longbows should have a minimum weight of 25 pounds to shoot rough fish with arrows not longer than 30 inches with a barbed head and attached to the bow with a line. The possession of any firearms (including bow and arrows) in a state park is prohibited.

Shooting hours: One-half hour before sunrise to sunset for upland game and Dove; sunrise to sunset for migratory game birds, except that on the opening day of the Coot, Duck, and Merganser season, shooting does not start until 12:00 o'clock noon.

FISHING

Game fish: Black Bass (Largemouth, Smallmouth), Kentucky (Spotted) Bass, Rock Bass, White Bass, Catfish (Blue, Bullhead, Channel, Flathead), Crappie (Black, White), Drum, American Perch, Sauger, Sturgeon, Sunfish (Bluegill, Green, Long-eared, Orange-spotted), Walleye, Warmouth. OPEN SEASON: all year, and no size limit on any fish.

An angler may use 2 rods and lines with not more than 2 single baited hooks on a rod or pole line, or one multiple hook of not more than 3 baited hooks attached to one shank with hooks limited to 1-12 in size. A fisherman may also operate one trotline with not more than 25 hooks, or set 8 bank lines with not more than 2 hooks per line. Ice fishing is permitted in ponds and lakes, but not in streams. Rough fish (Buffalo, Carp, Drum, Gar) may be taken with bow and arrow only during daylight hours and not within 100 yards of a boat dock, picnic and swimming areas, or any place where people are congregated. It is unlawful to use a fish gig, fish spear, fish trap, hoop net, trammel net, seine, or other device to take fish and frogs.

Bullfrogs: OPEN SEASON: July 1–Sept. 30. DAILY BAG LIMIT: 8.

Countless lakes, ponds, reservoirs, and streams offer a wide variety of fishing, including strip mine pits in southeastern Kansas, state lakes, parks, public hunting and wildlife management areas. Public hunting areas are scattered, and sportsmen should contact managers of reservoirs to determine areas open for taking waterfowl and other game.

STATE LAKES AND PARKS

Atchison County (248 acres, lake 70 acres) northwest of Atchison; *Barber County* (197 acres, lake 77 acres) at Medicine Lodge; *Bourbon County* (394 acres, lake 103 acres) east of Elsmore; *Brown County* (189 acres, lake 62 acres) 8 miles east of Hiawatha; *Butler County* (351 acres, Lake Clymer 124 acres) near Latham, and *Park* (568 acres, lake 232 acres) west of Augusta; *Chase County* (469 acres, lake 109 acres) in Flint Hills west of Cottonwood Falls; *Clark County* (1,243 acres, lake 337 acres) at Bluff Creek Canyon, 10 miles south of Kingsdown; *Cowley* (197 acres, lake 80 acres) 13 miles northeast of Arkansas City; *Crawford County no.* 1 (418 acres, strip mine small lakes total 50 acres) 4 miles north of Pittsburg, and *no.* 2 (460 acres, lake 150 acres) northeast of Farlington; *Decatur County no.* 1 (92 acres, lake 47 acres), and *no.* 2 (481 acres, lake 160 acres) north of Oberlin; *Finney County* (852 acres, lake 324 acres) west of Kalvester; *Geary County* (451 acres, lake 96 acres) south of Junction City; *Grant County* (224 acres, lake 44 acres) east of Ulysses; *Hamilton County* (432 acres, lake 94 acres) northwest of Syracuse; *Hodgeman County* (333 acres, lake 85 acres) southeast of Jetmore; *Jewell County* (165 acres, lake 57 acres) west of Mankato; *Kanopolis* (800 acres at Kanapolis Reservoir (3,550 acres) on Smoky Hill River, 10 miles northwest of Marquette in McPherson County; *Kingman County* (1,562 acres, lake 180 acres) 8 miles west of Kingman; *Leavenworth County* (506 acres, lake 175 acres) near Tonganoxie; *Logan County* (271 acres, lake 75 acres) near Russell Springs; *Lyon County* (582 acres, lake 135 acres) west of Reading; *Meade County* (1,240 acres, lake 100 acres) southwest of Meade; *Miami County* (277 acres, lake 90 acres) 12 miles southeast of Paola; *Montgomery County* (408 acres, lake 105 acres) south of Independence; *Nemaha County* (705 acres, lake 356 acres) 4 miles from Seneca; *Neosho County* (216 acres, lake 92 acres) northeast of Parsons; *Osage County* (506 acres, lake 140 acres) near Carbondale; *Ottawa County* (711 acres, lake 138 acres) 6 miles from Bennington; *Pottawatomie County no.* 1 (100 acres, lake 24 acres) 5 miles north of Westmoreland, and *no.* 2 (215 acres, lake 75 acres) 4 miles from Manhattan; *Republic County* (1,064 acres, lake 765 acres) northwest of Jamestown; *Rooks County* (222 acres, lake 67 acres) southwest of Stockton; *Scott County* (1,280 acres, lake 155 acres) 13 miles north of Scott City; *Shawnee County* (608 acres, lake 135 acres) northeast of Silver Lake; *Sheridan County* (343 acres, lake 87 acres) west of Studley; *Trego County–Cedar Bluff* (1,450 acres) at Cedar Bluff Reservoir (6,600 acres) 13 miles southwest of Ogallah; *Washington County* (463 acres, lake 111 acres) 10 miles northwest of Washington; *Wilson County* (281 acres, lake 119 acres) near Buffalo; *Woodson County* (445 acres, lake 179 acres) east of Toronto.

PUBLIC FISHING AND HUNTING AREAS

Cedar Bluff Reservoir (6,600 acres) 13 miles southwest of Ogallah—Trego County; *Cheyenne Bottoms* (19,790 acres including 12,000 acres of water) northwest of Great Bend—Barton County; *Cimarron National Grassland* (106,000 acres) north of Elkhart—Morton County; *Fall River Reservoir* (10,892 acres, water 2,600 surface acres) 20 miles northwest of Fredonia—Greenwood County; *Kanopolis Reservoir* (5,000 acres, surface water 3,550 acres) 10 miles northwest of Marquette—Ellsworth County; *Kearny County State Lake* (3,000 acres) also called Lake McKinney, 2 miles east of Lakin; *Kirwin Reservoir* (1,890 acres, water 5,000 acres) near Kirwin—Phillips County; *Lovewell Reservoir* (1,960 acres, water 3,000 acres) west of Lovewell—Jewell County; *Marais des Cygnes Waterfowl Management Area* (6,343 acres including 3 lakes totaling 1,525 acres) north of Pleasanton—Linn County; *Maxwell State Game Management Area* (2,560 acres including McPherson County Lake) northwest of Canton; *Republic Waterfowl Management Unit* (2,244 acres) on Republic River, south of Scandia—Republic County; *Sheridan Wildlife Management Area* (436 acres, lake 124 acres) northeast of Quinter—Sheridan County; *Strip Pit Areas* (approximately 3,000 acres in scattered tracts)—Crawford County; *Toronto Reservoir* (4,369 acres) at Toronto—Greenwood and Woodson counties; *Tuttle Creek* (1,780 acres at reservoir, 16,000 acres) on Big Blue River, north of Manhattan—Pottawatomie and Riley counties; *Webster Reservoir* (2,089 acres at reservoir, 4,000 acres) and Woodston Unit of *Webster Wildlife Management Area* (210 acres) on South Fork of Solomon River, near Stockton—Rooks County.

Licenses, regulations, and information about current seasons, bag and possession limits can be obtained from the Director, Kansas Forestry, Fish, and Game Department, Pratt. Write to Information Division for attractive detailed publications such as *Where to Fish in Kansas*, and *What Have I Caught?*

KENTUCKY

Area: 40,598 square miles (land area—39,863 square miles); rank in nation—36
Bird: Cardinal *(Richmondena cardinalis)*
Capital city: Frankfort on the Kentucky River, Franklin County in the Blue Grass region; population (1960)—18,365; rank in state—10
Counties: 120
Elevations: Highest, Big Black Mountain (4,150 ft.) in Harlan County; lowest, Mississippi River (257 ft.) in Fulton County
Flower: Goldenrod *(Solidago patula)*
Geographic center: 3 miles west of north of Lebanon, Marion County
Nicknames: Blue Grass State, Corncracker State, Tobacco State
Population (1960): 3,038,156; rank in nation—22
Tree: Tulip Tree *(Liriodendron tulipifera)*

The navigable Ohio River forms an irregular boundary for 640 miles with Illinois, Indiana, and Ohio on the northern shoreline, and a tributary, the Tug Fork of the Big Sandy River, traces an eastern line between West Virginia and Kentucky. The Mississippi River from the confluence of the Ohio River runs a twisting course for about 80 miles along the western Kentucky-Missouri border. On the southern boundary, Tennessee extends from the Mississippi River to the Cumberland Gap National Historical Park (20,193 acres) where Virginia starts to share a southeastern line through the Allegheny Plateau region. The southeastern thickly forested Cumberland Mountains (average elevation 2,000 ft.) have parallel ridges with deep narrow valleys, scenic gorges, and numerous streams. The Cumberland National Forest extends along the highlands, and the remainder of Kentucky is a series of plateaus, gradually sloping to the Ohio and Mississippi rivers. There are countless streams, fertile valleys, rolling hills, saline-incrusted marshy areas known as salt licks, and limestone caverns. Mammoth Cave National Park (51,354 acres) contains 150 miles of explored underground passages.

The Tennessee River flowing into the Ohio River at Paducah is impounded at Gilbertsville to create Kentucky Lake (407 square miles) which spreads into Tennessee. The Cumberland River rising in the Alleghenies is impounded by Wolf Creek Dam to form Lake Cumberland (99 square miles), and continues west of Tompkinsville into Tennessee only to veer northward to Kentucky near Linton. The river is impounded by Barkley Dam to form a 150-square-mile lake near Kentucky Lake, and finally empty into the Ohio River at Smithland. The Tennessee Valley Authority is developing 170,000 acres between Barkley Lake and Kentucky Lake for fishing, hunting, camping, and wildlife management. Other major streams flowing into the Ohio River are the Green and Treadwater rivers in western Kentucky, and the Kentucky River and Lick River with many tributaries in the central and eastern portion of the commonwealth. Breaks Interstate Park (1,250 acres) south of Elkhorn City on the Russell Fork of the Big Sandy River contains a spectacular gorge (1500 ft. deep) on the Virginia boundary known as the "Breaks of the Cumberland" or "Breaks of the Sandy."

Other large impounded waters are the Barren Reservoir (10,000 acres) on Barren River near Glasgow and Scottsville; Buckhorn Lake (1,230 acres) on the Middle Fork of the Kentucky River between Buckhorn and Hazard; Dale Hollow Reservoir (48 square miles) spreading into Tennessee on Obey River, south of Albany and Burkesville; Herrington Lake (3,600 acres) on the Dix River, northeast of Danville; Nolin Reservoir (5,000 acres) on Nolin River between Leitchfield and Munfordville; Rough River Reservoir (4,860 acres) on Rough River, north of Leitchfield.

LICENSES

Resident licenses are issued to bona fide residents 16 to 65 years of age, and any person 65 or more years of age may fish and hunt without a license if he carries proof of his age and residence in Kentucky. A fishing license authorizes the holder to fish by angling (including trotline), gigging, tickling, bow and arrow, underwater spear, and to take a maximum of 500 crayfish, 500 minnows, 30 salamanders, 30 tadpoles, 30 frogs, and/or 500 other aquatic invertebrates with a legal seine. A hunting license is necessary to take frogs with a gun or bow and arrow. An Ohio River fishing license may be purchased only by residents of Illinois, Indiana, and Ohio who may perform the same acts in the Ohio River that regulations permit any holder of a Kentucky resident fishing license.

No person may hunt wildlife without a hunting license, and a permit to take Deer is issued only to holders of a valid hunting license. Deer permits are not issued to nonresidents if their home states do not extend the privilege of hunting Deer to residents of Kentucky. All persons under the age of 18 must be accompanied by an adult when hunting Deer. Migratory game birds may not be taken by persons 16 or more years of age without a federal "Duck" stamp affixed to a hunting license. A trapping license is required to take wild animals by a trapper on his own or on other lands, and each trap must be tagged with the name of the person using it.

Resident license fees: Statewide fishing, $3.25; seine tag (each 100 feet or less of a seine), $2.25; statewide hunting (16 to 65 years of age), $3.25; hunting (under 16 years of age), $1.15; Deer hunting (in addition to hunting license), $10.50; federal "Duck" stamp (in addition to hunting license), $3.00; trapping, $3.25; fur buyer, $5.00; fur processor, $100.00; commercial guide, $5.00; taxidermist, $3.00; game propagation permit (pet permit), $2.00; propagation farm permit, $2.00; commercial shooting preserve, $25.00.

Nonresident license fees: Statewide fishing, $5.50; fishing 10 consecutive days, $2.25; Ohio River fishing only, $3.25; seine tag (each 100 feet of seine or less), $4.25; hunting, $5.50; Deer hunting (in addition to hunting license), $10.50; hunting on shooting preserve (valid for preserve issued), $5.00; federal "Duck" stamp (in addition to hunting license), $3.00; trapping, $15.50; fur buyer, $75.00; commercial guide, $10.00.

HUNTING AND TRAPPING

Game animals: Deer, Rabbit, Squirrel. OPEN SEASONS:* Deer—archery, Oct. 15–Nov. 15 in about 48 counties and Camp Breckridge (portion in Union County), Dewey Lake Refuge (Floyd County), Ford Management Area (Clay and Leslie counties), Fort Campbell Management Area, Fort Knox Management Area, Knobs State Forest (Nelson County), Pine Mountain Refuge (Letcher County), Robinson Forest Management Area (Breathitt, Knott and Perry Counties) and a few 2-day periods in October and early November at the Blue Grass Army Depot (Madison County) and Kentucky Woodlands National Wildlife Refuge (Lyon and Trigg Counties); guns, one to 5 days in late November in about 48 counties and the above archery hunting areas, except Fort Campbell Management Area—8 days divided into 2-day seasons in late October to mid-November. Rabbit—mid-November to mid-January. Squirrel—September, October, mid-November to mid-December in the Eastern Zone; mid-August through October and about 10 days in late November in the Western Zone; and in the Ballard County, Central Kentucky, and Western Kentucky Management Areas, Aug. 15–Oct. 15. BAG LIMITS: Deer—1. Rabbits—8 per day. Squirrels—6 per day.

Other types of game may not be taken on management areas or wildlife refuges during the gun season for hunting Deer. All Deer hunters must wear some visible red or yellow clothing. The use of ferrets in hunting, or dogs to hunt Deer are prohibited.

Furbearing animals: Bobcat, Coyote, Fox (Gray, Red), Mink, Muskrat, Opossum, Raccoon, Skunk, Weasel. OPEN SEASONS: Red Fox, Mink, Muskrat, Opossum, Raccoon, Skunk—mid-November to mid-January. Opossum and Raccoon—training season, Sept. 1 to mid-October, mid-January through February; shakeout season, mid-October to mid-November. BAG LIMITS: none. NOT PROTECTED: Bobcat, Gray Fox, Ground Hog, and Weasel may be taken at any time.

---

* Check current state regulations.

Game birds: Coot, Mourning Dove, Ducks (except Canvasback and Redhead), Gallinule, Geese, Ruffed Grouse, Merganser, Chukar Partridge, Quail, Rails, Sora, Wilson's Snipe, Wild Turkey, Woodcock. OPEN SEASONS:* Coot, Ducks, Merganser—Dec. 1 to early January. Dove—Sept. 1 to mid-October plus 3 weeks in December. Gallinule, Rails, Sora, Wilson's Snipe, Woodcock—late November into January. Geese—early November to mid-January. Grouse—December and January. Turkey—a few days in early November and mid-April in Breathitt, Clay, Jackson, Knott, Laurel, McCreary, Perry, Powell, Pulaski, Whitley, and Wolf counties. Commercial shooting preserves: Ducks (more than 2 generations removed from the wild), Partridge, Pheasant, Quail—Oct. 1–March 31. NOT PROTECTED: Crow, Cooper's Hawk, Sharp-shinned Hawk, Great Horned Owl, English Sparrow, and Starlings may be taken at any time. If crops are being damaged by protected wild animals and birds, a farmer should notify his conservation officer before killing such wildlife.

FIREARMS

Deer may be taken with shotguns not larger than 10 gauge or smaller than 20 guage with shells carrying a single slug, and plugged to hold not more than 3 shells in the magazine and chamber combined; centerfire rifles .243 caliber or larger; muzzle-loading rifles of .38 caliber or larger; and semiautomatic rifles. All rifles to take Deer are prohibited on the Blue Grass Army Depot and the Fort Knox Management Area. Fully automatic rifles, Army M-1 30-caliber carbines, tracer bullets, full-jacketed (military type) ammunition, buckshot, or any type of shot shells may not be used to take Deer. The only restriction on longbows and hunting arrows is that only barbless arrows with broadhead points at least seven-eighths of an inch wide may be used during archery Deer and Wild Turkey seasons. Archers are not permitted to carry firearms during archery seasons. Hunting Squirrel with rifles of .243 caliber or larger (except muzzle-loading rifles) or shotguns with buckshot or slugs are prohibited. See FEDERAL REGULATIONS FOR MIGRATORY GAME BIRDS.

Shooting hours: Daylight hours, except that Opossum and Raccoon may be hunted at night. Some counties prohibit hunting on Sunday by enforcement of their old civil "blue laws."

FISHING

Game fish: Black Bass (Largemouth, Smallmouth), Rock Bass (Goggle Eye), White (Striped) Bass, Crappie, Muskie, Northern Pike, Sauger (Sand Pike), Walleye Pike, Rainbow Trout. OPEN SEASONS:* Angling—all year.

---

* Check current state regulations.

Rough fish may be taken by bow and arrow all year in lakes and streams open to commercial fishing, and from March 1–April 30, June 1–Sept. 15 in streams not open to commercial fishing. No fish may be taken by bow and arrow, or gigging within 200 yards of any dam, 700 yards of the Kentucky Dam, or one mile below Wolf Creek Dam. Gigging and snagging rough fish on foot only—March 1 to mid-May in all except a few designated streams, and all lakes except Buckhorn Reservoir and its tributaries. Noodling and tickling by bare hands only—mid-June to mid-July in overflow waters of Ballard, Carlisle, Fulton, and Hickman counties.

Frogs: OPEN SEASON: May 15–Oct. 31. BAG LIMIT: 15 each noon to noon period.

There is unsurpassed fishing for Bass, Catfish, Muskies, Pike, and Trout in numerous streams, and anglers flock to runs of Walleye in mid-February and of White Bass weeks later in the Lake Cumberland region; White Bass during mid-April in the Dix River headwaters of Herrington Lake; and the Crappie run in early April at Kentucky Lake. Superb Bass fishing is also found in Barren Reservoir, Buckhorn Lake, Dale Hollow Reservoir plus Rainbow Trout below the dam, Nolin Reservoir, Rough River Reservoir, Dewey Lake (860 acres) near Prestonburg, Falmouth Lake (225 acres) west of Falmouth, Greenbo Lake (225 acres) near Greenup, Guist Lake (325 acres) east of Shelbyville, Lake Beshear (857 acres) in Pennyrile Forest near Dawson Springs; Lake Malone (826 acres) near Dunmore; and lakes of Bernheim Forest (14,500 acres) south of Shepherdsville. The Kentucky Lake Fall Fishing Derby: Aug. 15–Nov. 1.

STATE PARKS (fishing and camping)

Audubon (590 acres) north of Henderson—Henderson County; *Buckhorn Lake* (4,903 acres) east of Buckhorn—Perry County; *Carter Caves* (1,000 acres) of Olive Hill—Carter County; *Cherokee* (360 acres) at Kentucky Lake, east of Hardin—Marshall County; *Cumberland Falls* (1,098 acres) in Cumberland National Forest, near Corbin—McCreary County; *Falmouth Lake* (700 acres) at Falmouth—Pendleton County; *General Butler* (809 acres) southwest of Carrollton—Carroll County; *Greenbo Lake* (3,330 acres) near Greenup—Greenup County; *Jenny Wiley* (1,940 acres) at Dewey Lake, east of Prestonburg—Floyd County; *Kentucky Dam Village* (1,200 acres) at Kentucky Lake, and *Kentucky Lake* (1,414 acres) east of Hardin—Marshall County; *Lake Cumberland* (3,000 acres) southeast of Jamestown—Russell County; *Lake Malone* (307 acres) west of Dunmore—Muhlenberg County; *Natural Bridge* (1,337 acres) in Cumberland National Forest, east of Stanton—Powell County; *Pennyrile Forest* (14,000 acres) south of Dawson Springs—Hopkins County; *Pine Mountain* (2,500 acres) at Pineville—Bell County;

Rough River (9,234 acres) on Rough River Reservoir at Falls of the Rough—Grayson County.

Licenses, permits, regulations, and information about current seasons, bag and possession limits can be obtained from the Commissioner, Department of Fish and Wildlife Resources, State Office Building Annex, Frankfort. Regulations are also on file in the offices of county court clerks. Write to Travel Division, Department of Public Information, Capitol Annex Building, Frankfort, for the illustrated manual *Fishing in Kentucky*, the park rate and information booklet *Kentucky Vacation Parks*, and the attractive *Official Highway Map* prepared by the Kentucky Department of Highways.

LOUISIANA

Area: 48,506 square miles (land area—45,106 square miles); rank in nation–32
Bird: Eastern Brown Pelican (*Pelicanus occidentalis*)
Capital city: Baton Rouge in East Baton Parish is a deep water port on the Mississippi River; population (1960)—152,419; rank in state–3
Counties: see Parishes
Elevations: Highest, Driskill Mountain (535 ft.) in Bienville Parish; lowest, New Orleans (5 ft. below sea level) on the Mississippi River in Orleans Parish
Flower: Magnolia Tree blossom (*Magnolia grandiflora*), adopted 1900
Geographic center: 3 miles southeast of Marksville in Avoyelles Parish
Parishes: 64
Population (1960): 3,257,022; rank in nation–20
Tidal shoreline: 7,721 miles (including islands, bays, and streams to a point where tidal waters narrow to 100 ft. wide)
Tree: Magnolia tree (*Magnolia grandiflora*)

Louisiana in the Deep South on the Gulf of Mexico is separated from Texas on the west by Sabine Lake and River to the Logansport area where the Sabine River intersects the 32° parallel, and the line continues north through Caddo Lake to Arkansas. The northern Arkansas-Louisiana boundary follows the 33° parallel to the Mississippi River which loops southward, with the state of Mississippi on the east bank; and at the 31° parallel, the Louisiana-Mississippi line cuts eastward to the Pearl River flowing south into the Gulf of Mexico.

There are about 4,800 miles of navigable rivers, lakes, and bayous through Louisiana; and the most important artery is the Mississippi River, twisting through flood plains protected by levees and the southern delta region to the Pass-a-Loutre Game Fish Preserve on the Gulf of

Mexico. The largest deep water port New Orleans is also on Lake Pontchartrain (625 square miles) which is connected by channels with Lake Maurepas on the west, and eastern Lake Borgne on the Mississippi Sound of the Gulf of Mexico; and all waters rise and fall with tides. The Intracoastal Waterway from Lafourche Parish winds westward through lowlands to Morgan City on Lower Atchafalaya River (alternate route to Baton Rouge), Intracoastal City, Grand Lake, Calcasieu River, and the Sabine River. Lake Charles is a deep water port known as the "Gateway to the Southwest" via the Calcasieu River and Lake course to the Gulf of Mexico. Shreveport in the northwest is at the head of navigation on the Red River which meanders across the state, fed by many tributaries, including the Ouachita River from the northeast and the southern Atchafalaya River, before joining the Mississippi River east of Symmesport.

There are many large and small lakes scattered throughout the state. Marshes and flood plains extend from narrow belts to broad level land 50 miles wide protected by levees as high as 50 feet in some places. Fishermen, hunters, and trappers find an abundance of wildlife in and around the intricate network of interior freshwater bayous and saltwater coastal bays, lagoons, marshes, and islands on the Gulf of Mexico.

LICENSES

Resident licenses to fish and hunt are issued to persons 16–60 years of age who are bona fide residents of the state, and to members of the U.S. Armed Forces on active duty in Louisiana. No fishing license is required if a resident uses only a hook and line, rod, or fishing pole without a reel or artificial bait. Any person 60 or more years of age who has been a resident of the state for at least 2 years may receive free permits to fish and hunt. If a nonresident owns, or leases, a resort cottage on an annual basis, and occupies it for 30 or more days during the year, he may obtain a resident basic hunting license. A nonresident owner of property with an assessed value of at least $500, and if adjacent to a well-known lake or hunting club, may procure resident fishing and basic hunting licenses. This privilege does not apply to property held in the name of a club, company, or corporation. Free daily permits may be obtained at entrances to scheduled hunts in game management areas except for specified Deer hunts, for which nontransferable permits are issued by mail. Deer hunting permits for the Zemurray Game Management Area are issued by mail only to residents after a public drawing held in New Orleans. Permits and tags for Deer are issued upon request by persons under 16 years of age. No hunting license is required to take animals and birds listed as not protected. All persons over 16 years of age must purchase a federal "Duck" stamp to take migratory game birds.

The Pass-a-Loutre Waterfowl Management Area at the mouth of the Mississippi River offers exceptional Duck hunting. The Louisiana Wild Life and Fisheries Commission issues permits for 2-day hunts and provides public camps with beds, cooking gear, decoys, duck boats, and boat transportation from and to Venice for $5. Free permits for 4-day hunts on other portions of the area are issued to hunters who provide their own equipment, facilities, and transportation.

Annual license period: July 1–June 30.

Resident license fees: Annual sport fishing, $1.00; annual basic hunting, $2.00; big game hunting (in addition to basic hunting), $2.00; trapping, $2.00; federal "Duck" stamp (in addition to basic hunting), $3.00; hunting club, $5.00; fur buyer, $25.00; fur dealer, $100.00; commercial hunting preserve for pen-raised birds, $200.00.

Nonresident license fees: Annual sport fishing, $5.00; fishing 7 consecutive days, $2.00; annual basic hunting, $25.00; basic hunting 2 consecutive days, $5.00; big game hunting (in addition to basic hunting), $2.00; federal "Duck" stamp (in addition to basic hunting), $3.00; fur buyer, $100.00; fur dealer (plus a $1,000 deposit), $150.00; hunting on private shooting preserve, $5.00.

The hunting preserve license is good for 4 consecutive days, but a basic hunting license may be used instead of the special hunting preserve license.

HUNTING AND TRAPPING

Game animals: Alligator, Bear, Deer, Rabbit, Squirrel. OPEN SEASONS:* Alligators (over 5 feet long)—April 15–June 15 in a few southwestern parishes. Bear—a few days in late December in designated areas of East Carroll, Iberia, Madison, St. Mary, and Vermillion parishes. Deer—archery, during first 2 weeks of October; firearms (including bow and arrow), from late November into January, and various hunting periods of 3–30 or more days in game management areas and about 8–40 days in designated portions of parishes. Rabbits—early October to mid-February. Squirrels—early October to early January. SEASON BAG LIMITS: Bear—1. Deer—2. Rabbits and Squirrels—8 each per day. Only legal Buck may be taken by firearms, and in controlled hunts. A legal Buck is a male Deer with antlers 3 or more inches in length. The use of dogs to hunt Deer is prohibited in many areas.

Furbearing animals: Beaver, Bobcat, Civet Cat, Cougar, Fox, Mink, Muskrat, Nutria (Coypu), Opossum, Otter, Raccoon, Skunk, and Wolf. OPEN TRAPPING SEASON: Beaver—January and February in the parishes of East Baton Rouge, East Feliciana, Livingston, St. Helena, St. Tammany,

---

* Check current state regulations.

Tangipahoa, and Washington. Mink—mid-November to mid-January. Muskrat—Dec. 1 to late February. Opossum, Otter, Raccoon, Skunk—Nov. 15–Feb. 15. Nutria—Nov. 15–Feb. 15 except in 17 parishes, no closed seasons. *Bag limits*: none. FULLY PROTECTED: Alligators under 5 feet in length, Cub Bears, and spotted fawn Deer—no open seasons. NOT PROTECTED: Cougar (Panther), Fox, Wildcats (Bobcat or Catamount), and Wolves may be taken at any time.

Game birds: Coot, Mourning Dove, Ducks (except Canvasback and Redhead), Gallinule, Geese (except Canada and subspecies), Merganser, Bobwhite Quail, Rails, Scaup, Sora, Wilson's Snipe, Gobbler Turkey, Woodcock. OPEN SEASONS:* Coot, Ducks, Merganser, Scaup—late November to early January. Dove—2 weeks in early September, mid-October to early November, and early December to January. Gallinule, Rails, Sora—early October to late November. Geese—early November to mid-January, except east of the Mississippi River, mid-October to mid-November, and early December to mid-January. Quail—late November to late February. Wilson's Snipe—mid-December to mid-January. Gobbler Turkey—2 weeks in April. Woodcock—early December to mid-January. Pen-raised birds on shooting preserves—Oct. 1–March 31. FULLY PROTECTED: Sandhill and Whooping Cranes, Canvasback and Redhead Ducks, Canada Geese and subspecies, Herons, Kildeer, Papabotte, Black Bellied and Golden Plover, Prairie Chicken, Swan, and shorebirds not named as game—no open seasons. NOT PROTECTED: Bobo-link (True Rice Birds) and Grackles (Chocks) when destructive to crops, Red-winged Blackbirds (Rice Birds), Cormorants (Nigger Geese), Crows, Cooper's Hawk (Blue Darter), Duck Hawk, Sharp-shinned Hawk, Great Horned Owl, English Sparrow, Starling, and Vultures may be taken at any time.

FIREARMS

Deer hunters may use rifles of .22 caliber or more, and shotguns not less than 10 gauge, with no restrictions on ammunition. Only shotguns not larger than 10 gauge, and capable of holding only 3 shells in the magazine and chamber combined may be used to take migratory game birds. Any shotgun capable of holding more than 3 shells must be plugged with one-piece metal fillers which cannot be removed without taking the gun apart. Archers hunting Deer must use a longbow having a pull of at least 30 pounds, and hunting arrows with sharpened metal broadhead blades not less than seven-eighths of an inch or more than 1½ inches in width. There are no restrictions on ammunition, or size of rifles and shotguns to take upland game.

Shooting hours: One-half hour before sunrise to sunset. Exceptions:

---

* Check current state regulations.

Doves—12:00 o'clock noon to sunset; migratory game birds—sunrise to sunset, except that opening day of Coot and Duck season, shooting starts at 12:00 o'clock noon. Frogs—day or night.

FISHING

Freshwater game fish: Black Bass (Green Trout), White Bass (Bar fish), Yellow Bass (Striped Bass), Crappie (Sac-a-lait, Speckled, or White Perch), Sunfish (Bluegill, Bream, Goggle-eye, Perch). OPEN SEASON: all year; freshwater commercial fish—Buffalofish, Catfish, Gaspergou, Paddlefish—may be taken at any time.

Game fish may be taken only with a rod or fishing pole, hook and line, handline, troll line, and a bait-casting or fly-casting apparatus. Bow and arrow, guns, spears, and traps may be used to take Gar. Bait seines (30 feet or less), dip nets, and minnow traps may be used in freshwater only to take Minnow, Shrimp, and other legal bait.

Frogs: OPEN SEASON: throughout the year except during April and May. BAG LIMITS: none. American and Southern Bullfrogs may be taken with the aid of artificial light, but not by the use of spears or any devices that puncture the skin or redden the meat of a frog. It is unlawful to carry or possess rifles, shotguns, or any firearms while hunting Frogs during the night.

Annual fishing rodeos: Empire Charterboat Captain's Association at Empire (Plaquemines Parish)—one day in May and 3 days in August; Grand Isle Tarpon Rodeo—3 days in mid-July; Cameron Rodeo—June 28–30; Southwest Louisiana Fishing Club of Lake Charles deep sea and inland fishing rodeo—June 28–30; New Orleans Skindiving Tourney (New Orleans–Grand Isle): June 28–30.

In addition to game management areas leased or owned by the Louisiana Wild Life and Fisheries Commission, there are 34,000 acres of hardwood timber land in the Bayou Lafourche bottom, 40,000 acres of Red River overflow bottom land, and 170,000 acres of artificial impoundments open to public hunting and fishing. Through an agreement with the U.S. Army Corps of Engineers, the commission is developing a fine game management area on the Bodcau Flood Control Project which extends along Bayou Bodcau from the Arkansas stateline to Bellevue in Bossier and Webster parishes.

GAME MANAGEMENT AREAS*

Bodcau (32,471 acres) along Bodcau Bayou—Bossier and Webster parishes; *Caldwell* (12,203 acres) near Columbia—Caldwell Parish;

---

* Deer and small game.

Catahoula (40,000 acres) near Packton—Grant and Winn parishes—Kisatchie National Forest; *Chicago Mills* (102,000 acres)—Franklin, Madison, and Tensas parishes; *East Carroll* (9,640 acres)—southern part of East Carroll Parish; *Evangeline* (15,000 acres) near Alexandria—Rapides Parish–Kasatchie National Forest; *Fort Polk* (52,000 acres) near Leesville—Vernon Parish; *Jackson-Bienville* (22,000 acres) between Jonesboro and Ruston—Bienville Parish; *Lutcher Moore* (54,000 acres) at Burr Ferry—Vernon Parish; *Red Dirt* (40,000 acres) near Derry—Natchitoches Parish–Kisatchie National Forest; *Russel Sage* (15,000 acres) east of Monroe in LaFourch Swamp—Morehouse, Ouachita, and Richland parishes; *Sabine* (12,000 acres) near Fisher—Sabine Parish; *Thistlewaite* (11,280 acres) near Washington—St. Landry Parish; *Union* (10,000 acres) near Farmville and Marion—Union Parish; *West Bay* (58,000 acres) near Oakdale—Allen Parish; *Zemurray* (5,295 acres) south of Husser—Tangipahoa Parish. Special permits are not required to hunt Dove, Quail, and Rabbit at the *Bonnet Carré* Game Management Area (3,324 acres) between Lake Pontchartrain and the Mississippi River —St. Charles Parish; and *DeRidder Airport* Public Hunting Area (800 acres)—Beauregard Parish.

PUBLIC SHOOTING AREAS (waterfowl)

Biloxi Marshlands (39,728 acres) at Lakes Borgne and Eugene, Bayous Loutre and Marron—St. Bernard Parish; *Finch Bayou* (600 acres) 4 miles east of Haile—Union Parish; *Fisher Creek* (500 acres) 3 miles west of Sondheimer—East Carroll Parish; *Grassy Lake* (25,000 acres) near Borderlonville—Avoyelles Parish; *Lafourche* (1,875 acres) 10 miles west of Rayville—Richland Parish; Pass-a-Loutre (66,000 acres) at mouth of Mississippi River south of Venice—Plaquemines Parish; *Shilo Creek* (1,200 acres) 5 miles west of Vaughn—Morehouse Parish; *Soda Lake* (525 acres) 15 miles north of Shreveport—Caddo Parish; *Wisner* (30,000 acres) south of Leesville—LaFourche Parish.

STATE PARKS (fishing)

Bogue Falaya (13 acres) on Bogue Falaya River, near Covington—St. Tammany Parish; *Chemin-a-Haut* (550 acres) on Bayou Bartholomew, north of Bastrop—Morehouse Parish; *Chicot* (6,479 acres, lake 2,000 acres) north of Ville Platte—Evangeline Parish; *Fontainbleu* (2,600 acres) on Lake Pontchartrain, east of Mandeville—St. Tammany Parish; *Fort Pike* (125 acres) on Rigolets Pass between Lake Borgne and Lake Ponchartrain—Orleans Parish; *Lake Bistineau* (950 acres) south of Doyline—Webster Parish; *Sam Houston* (1,068 acres) on Indian

Bayou and west fork of Calcasieu River, north of Westlake and Lake Charles—Calcasieu Parish.

WILDLIFE REFUGES (fishing and trapping)

Coulee (3,300 acres) near Coulee—Morehouse Parish; *Marsh Island* (79,000 acres) in Gulf of Mexico—south of Iberia Parish; *Rockefeller* (86,000 acres) on Gulf of Mexico—Cameron and Vermillion parishes (no fishing between Oct. 1–March1); *State* (13,000 acres) coastal marsh south of Intracoastal City—Vermillion Parish; *Terzia* (46,000 acres) northwest of Bastrop—Morehouse Parish.

Licenses, regulations, and information about current seasons, bag and possession limits can be obtained from the Louisiana Wild Life and Fisheries Commission, 400 Royal Street, Wild Life and Fisheries Building, New Orleans 16. Season permits for all game management areas (unless otherwise specified) are available at district offices: P.O. Box 1041, Alexandria; 6350 Perkins Road, or P.O. Box 14526, Southeast Station, Baton Rouge; DeRidder Airport, P.O. Box 405, DeRidder; P.O. Box 426, Ferriday; 117 Pearl St., or P.O. Box 224, Minden; P.O. Box 4004, Ouachita Station, Monroe; 225 North Union St., or P.O. Box 585, Opelousas. Permits for Fort Polk Game Management Area issued at Alexandria or DeRidder. An excellent map showing hunting and fishing areas is issued by the Louisiana Department of Highways, Baton Rouge 4.

MAINE

Area: 33,040 square miles (land area—31,012 square miles); rank in nation–39
Bird: Chicadee *(Penthestes artricapillus)*, adopted 1927
Capital city: Augusta on the Kennebec River in Kennebec County at the head of navigation about 45 miles from the sea; population (1960)—21,680; rank in state–6
Counties: 16
Elevations: Highest, Mount Katahdin (5,267 ft.) in Piscataquis County; lowest, Atlantic Ocean (sea level)
Flower: Pine cone and tassel *(Pinus strobus)*, adopted 1895
Geographic center: 18 miles north of Dover in Piscataquis County
Nicknames: Pine Tree State, Border State, Polar Star State
Population (1960): 969,265; rank in nation–36

Tidal shoreline: 3,478 miles (including islands, bays, and streams to a point where tidal waters narrow to 100 ft. wide)
Tree: Eastern White Pine *(Pinus strobus)*, adopted 1895

Maine is a New England State on the Atlantic Ocean bordered by New Hampshire on the west, and the Canadian Provinces of Quebec on the northwest and New Brunswick on the northeast.

There are more than 2,200 lakes and ponds at the source or formed by over 5,000 streams including large navigable rivers. The Penobscot River, rising near the Quebec boundary, flows through Seboomook Lake; as the West Branch Penobscot River it continues on to Chesuncook Lake and others, to Pemadumcook Lake, and near East Millinocket merges with the East Branch Penobscot River to be impounded by dams before reaching Bangor at the head of deep water navigation, and gradually widen southward between forested hills to beautiful island-dotted Penobscot Bay after a 350-mile journey to the Atlantic Ocean. From the East Outlet of Moosehead Lake and Indian Pond, the Kennebec River, fed by the Dead River and other streams, forms Wyman Lake near Bingham, and wanders southward by Skohegan, Waterville, Augusta, Gardiner, and at Merrymeeting Bay mingles waters with the Androscoggin River and empties into the Atlantic Ocean south of Bath.

Headwaters of the Allagash River include several ponds, lakes, and streams including the Allagash, Eagle, Churchill, Chemquasabanticook (Ross), Umsaskis, Long, and Musquacook lakes before the Allamagash River rushes over rapids to join the St. Johns River in northwestern Maine. Rising near Seboomook Lake, the St. Johns River flows northward to merge with the St. Francis River on the Quebec border and etch the Canadian line eastward to pass Fort Kent, Madewaska, and Van Buren, and enter New Brunswick near Grand Falls. A watercourse separating New Brunswick from eastern Maine begins at Monument Stream about 20 miles south of Holton, and with the North, Grand, and Spednik lakes forms the 75-mile St. Croix River flowing through Passamaquoddy Bay and Quoddy Roads at Lubec to the Atlantic Ocean. In southwestern Maine, the Saco River ripples down from the White Mountains of New Hampshire to empty into the Atlantic Ocean near Biddeford. The Presumpscot River impounded by several dams is a waterway between Sebage Lake and Portland on Casco Bay.

Rocky headlands, deep indentations, and protected harbors are among hundreds of islands and evergreen hills fringing the coast of Maine. There are numerous mountains with wooded sloping summits, and nearly 100 rise above 3,000 feet. Mount Katahdin in Baxter State Park is the northern terminus of the Appalachian Trail to Georgia. North Brother Mountain (4,143 ft.) and Hamlin Peak (4,751 ft.) are among other mountains in the state park. Mount Kinco (1,806 ft.) is a landmark on the eastern shore of Moosehead Lake (120 square miles, 25 miles long, 2–10 miles wide) a gateway to a remarkable canoeing, fishing, and hunting region north of Guilford on the Piscataquis River. Old Spec (4,250 ft.) and Bald Mountain (3,996 ft.) form Grafton Notch in the Mahoosuc Range on the New Hampshire border. Saddleback Mountain (4,116 ft.), Deer Mountain (3,445 ft.), Beaver Mountain (3,160 ft.), Bemis Mountain (3,138 ft.), Old Blue Mountain, (3,600 ft.) and Elephant Mountain (3,774 ft.) overlook lovely Rangeley Lake linked with Cupsuptic, Mooselookmeguntic, Upper and Lower Richardson lakes, and Umbagog Lake shared with New Hampshire. Chains of lakes and streams in Kennebec County include beautiful Belgrades, China, and Winthrop regions. The Moosehorn National Wildlife Refuge (22,566 acres) on the St. Croix River near Woodland is southeast of many linked lakes and streams including Grand Falls Lake at Princeton, and the Big, Grand, Horseshoe, Upper, and Lower Sysladobsis lakes.

LICENSES

Resident licenses to fish and hunt are issued to citizens 16 or more years of age who have been bona fide residents of Maine, and to members of the U.S. Armed Forces officially stationed in the state, and to members of the Canadian Armed Forces at military installations within Maine. An alien may obtain a resident license after living continuously in the state for 2 or more years, and paying taxes on assessed real estate in his home municipality. Citizen civilian employees of the U.S. Armed Forces must live at a military or naval installation for at least 3 months before applying for a resident license. All employees of the Veterans Administration at the Togus Facility classify as residents. Free fishing permits are issued to groups of mental patients undergoing rehabilitation training in the Veterans Center at Togus.

Fishing, hunting, and trapping licenses are issued without charge or fee to Indians over 16 years of age who present a certificate from the Commissioner of Health and Welfare, stating that the Indian is a member of either the Passamaquoddy or Penobscot tribes. The governor may issue complimentary fishing and hunting licenses to members of the Canadian Immigration Customs Forces serving on the Maine border and to persons holding a Congressional Medal of Honor. Not more than 500 complimentary licenses are issued to visiting dignitaries of national or international importance, and to writers, photographers, and others who assist in publicizing the state of Maine. The qualifications of such persons are determined by a committee composed of the commissioner of inland fisheries and game, commissioner of economic development, and a representative of the governor. Residents under the age of 16 may trap any wild animals except Beaver without a license in municipalities, but licenses are required to trap in unorganized townships.

Residents 10 or more years of age, and nonresidents 12 or more years of age may purchase archery hunting licenses. No resident under the age of 10 or nonresident under the age of 12 may hunt with bow and arrow. Junior licenses to hunt birds and animals (except Deer) with guns are issued to nonresidents 12–16 years of age if the application is accompanied by the written consent of a parent or guardian. A resident 10–16 years of age may use firearms to hunt without a license if accompanied at all times by a parent, guardian, or an adult approved by the parent or guardian. Residents and members of their families over 16 years of age may hunt without a license on their own property if the land is used for agricultural purposes. An archery license allows game to be taken during the archery season, but a regular hunting license is required to hunt with bow and arrow during a gun season.

Crabs may be taken for home consumption without a license if caught with bare hands, hook and line along the shore, under rocks, or in pools left by receding tides. No license is required by a resident or a riparian owner of shores or flats to dig clams and quahogs to feed his family.

A regular guide license may be granted by the commissioner to any person 18 or more years of age upon proof of his competency. Guide certificates are issued to persons 14–21 years of age by the Junior Guides Examining Board, but junior guides may not receive remuneration for their services or compete with regular guides. Any person who guides without a license may be fined not less than $25, and each day of guiding constitutes a separate offense. Counselors at children's licensed summer camps may perform the usual duties of a camp counselor without a guide license.

Resident license fees: Sport fishing, $2.75; archery hunting, $4.25; gun hunting, $2.75; combination sport fishing and gun hunting, $5.25; federal "Duck" stamp to take migratory game birds, $3.00; trapping Beaver, $10.00; trapping furbearing animals except Beaver, $10.00; trapping furbearing animals except Beaver in municipalities, $5.00; citizen taxidermist, $5.00; alien taxidermist, $25.00; dealer in Deer heads and skins, $25.00; fur dealer, $25.00; breeding game birds, furbearing or other wild animals, $10.00 regular guide, $8.50; junior guide, 50 cents; sporting camp, $5.00; Beaver tags (each), $1.00; Fisher tags (each), 50 cents; Deer tag, $2.00; permit to take sea moss, $2.00.

Nonresident license fees: Annual sport fishing, $8.75; fishing 15 consecutive days,* $5.75; fishing 3 consecutive days,* $3.75; annual junior

---

* Fee may be credited on annual license during same year.

fishing (10–15 years of age), $2.25; hunting except Deer, $10.25; hunting including Deer, $25.25; junior hunting except Deer (12–15 years), $5.25; archery hunting including Deer, $10.25; trapping, $200.00; regular guide, $50.00; fur dealer, $50.00; permit to take sea moss, $15.00.

HUNTING AND TRAPPING

Game animals: White-tailed Deer, Hare or Rabbit, Gray Squirrel. OPEN SEASONS:* Deer—archery, Oct. 1–31; firearms, 4–6 weeks between mid-October and early December in designated areas. Hare or Rabbit—October 1 through February, and extended through March in Aroostook, Franklin, Hancock, Kennebec, Knox, Lincoln, Oxford, Penobscot, Piscataquis, Somerset, and Washington counties. Gray Squirrel—October 1–November 15. BAG LIMIT: Deer—1 per season; Hare or Rabbit—4 per day. Squirrel—4 per day. It is unlawful to use a dog when hunting Deer.

Furbearing animals: Bear, Beaver, Bobcat, Fisher, Fox, Loupcervier, Canada Lynx, Marten (Sable), Mink, Muskrat, Otter, Raccoon, Skunk. OPEN SEASONS:* Beaver—January and February with closed or shorter periods in designated areas; firearms including bow and arrow may not be used to take Beaver. Fisher, Mink—Nov. 1–30. Muskrat—Nov. 1–30 except in Aroostook and Washington counties, April 1–30; Oxford County, November 1 to late April; York County, mid-March to mid-April; Tribal Indians may also trap Muskrat on lands and islands belonging to the Penobscot Tribe, March 1–May 1. Otter—during November, January, and February. Raccoon—Aug. 15–Dec. 15. Skunk—Sept. 1–Dec. 15. BAG LIMITS: none; but each Beaver and Fisher skin must be tagged by a game warden. Traps (except Beaver sets) in organized or incorporated places must be visited at least once every 24 hours including Sundays. Seals—It is unlawful to hunt, shoot at, or kill any Seals within 2 miles of any part of Green Island in the Western Bay in Hancock County from May 15 to October 15; or during June, July, and August in Casco Bay, and waters between Branch River in the town of Kennebunk and the easterly end of Goose Rock Beach in the town of Kennebunkport. FULLY PROTECTED: Caribou, Elk, Moose, Marten—no open seasons. NOT PROTECTED: Bear, Bobcat, Canada Lynx, Fox, Hedgehog, Loupcervier, and Woodchuck may be taken at any time. Any owner or occupant of land where substantial damage is done to his growing crops, orchard, poultry, or property may take or kill any animals (except Beaver) caught in the act. Bounty for Bobcat, $15.

Game birds: Brant, Coot, Ducks (except Canvasback and Redhead), Eider, Gallinule, Geese (except Snow Geese), Ruffed Grouse (Birch Partridge), Merganser, Old Squaw, Pheasant, Rails, Scoter, Snipe, Sora,

---

* Check current state regulations.

Woodcock. OPEN SEASONS:* Brant, Geese—early October to mid-December. Coot, Ducks, Merganser—about 3 weeks in October and from mid-November to mid-December. Eider, Old Squaw, Scoter—Oct. 1–Jan. 15 in coastal waters and all rivers lying seaward from the first upstream bridge, and in other areas during regular open Duck season. Gallinule, Rails, Sora—early September to early November. Ruffed Grouse, Pheasant, Snipe, Woodcock—October 1 to mid-November. FULLY PROTECTED: Canvasback and Redhead Ducks, Snow Geese—no open seasons. NOT PROTECTED: Cormorants (Shag), Crows, Kingfishers, Great Horned Owls, English or European House Sparrows, and Starlings may be taken at any time. Owners or occupants of land may kill any Hawks or Owls caught in the act of destroying poultry.

FIREARMS

No hunter may use or have in his possession at any time in the fields and forests, or on the waters of Maine any automatic firearm, or any firearm converted to an automatic type, or which has built-in mechanical adjustments permitting it to function as an automatic arm. Autoloading firearms having a magazine capacity of more than 5 cartridges must be altered to reduce the capacity to 5 cartridges. The use of any gun larger than 10 gauge to hunt or kill any game animals or bird is prohibited, and shotguns for taking migratory game birds must be capable of holding not more than 3 shells in the magazine and chamber combined. It is unlawful to use or possess any firearms except a .22 caliber pistol while hunting Raccoon and Skunk at night. Only an electric flashlight of not more than 3 cells may be used to locate and take a Raccoon treed by a dog. Cartridges containing explosives, or tracer bullets, and arrows with poisonous tips, or the use of crossbows are prohibited. Archers may only hunt Deer with a longbow capable of propelling an arrow at least 150 yards, and the arrowhead must be not less than seven-eighths of an inch in width.

Shooting hours: Hunting on Sunday is prohibited, and possession of firearms (including bow and arrow) in fields or forests, and on waters or ice is considered as prima facie evidence of hunting, unless the firearms are completely wrapped, or disassembled and carried in separate pieces. Shooting hours: one-half hour before sunrise to one-half hour after sunset except migratory game birds, sunrise to sunset. Raccoons and Skunks may be hunted during night hours. Shooting starts at 12:00 o'clock noon on the opening day of the Duck season.

FISHING

Game fish: Black Bass, Striped or Sea Bass, White Perch, Pickerel, Atlantic or Sea Run Salmon, Lake Salmon, Togue, Trout (Brook, Brown,

---

* Check current state regulations.

Rainbow). OPEN SEASONS:* In lakes and ponds naturally free from ice, all fish except Black Bass, and Trout in streams of Oxford and York counties —April 1–Sept. 30. Local exceptions including Moosehead Lake and principal tributaries, Moose River, East and West Outlets, and several southern Maine waters—May 1–Sept. 30. Black Bass—mid-June to mid-August in brooks and streams, and extended to mid-September above tidewaters in rivers, and to September 30 in lakes and ponds. If bag limits for Black Bass are removed in special waters, the season is the same as for Salmon and Trout. All fish (except Black Bass) in brooks and streams free from ice—April 1–August 15, and extended to September 15 in rivers above tidewaters. Cumberland County fishing in brooks and streams—last Saturday of April to Aug. 15. Atlantic Salmon—July 16–September 15 by rod and reel only in all tidal waters. Smelt—March 15–June 15 in tidal waters by angling with hook and line, or by hand dip net used by a single person. Fish may be caught with a single-baited hook and line, artificial flies, artificial insects and minnows, spinners, and spoon hooks. Striped Bass may be taken only by hook and line or rod and reel, and Tuna by hook and line or harpoon in tidal waters of rivers. It is unlawful to jig for fish, and use or possess gill nets on any inland waters. ICE FISHING: A fisherman may use not more than 5 lines (set or otherwise) under his immediate supervision. Lines set for taking Cusk during night hours in waters open to Salmon and Trout fishing must be visited at least once every hour by the fisherman. Shacks or temporary structures with owner's name painted on the outside (2-inch letters) must be removed within 3 days after the waters are closed to fishing. Penalties for failing to remove structures are fines of not more than $300 and costs, or imprisonment for not more than 90 days, or both.

There are about 1,200 lakes and ponds containing game fish including Moosehead Lake noted for Lake Salmon, Togue, and Trout. The upper Kennebec River system, Allagash, Moose, Narraguagus, and St. Johns rivers are top fishing waters. Schools of Striped Bass swarm into coastal bays and Bluefin Tuna are caught offshore. Hunting is prohibited in state parks and the Arcadia National Park (27,860 acres) on Mount Desert Island and Schoodic Point. There are 43 game preserves and sanctuaries to protect wild animals and birds, but trapping furbearers may be permitted in the Bangor (Penobscot County), Fairfield (Somerset County), Limington, Hollis, and Waterloo (York County), Narragansett (Cumberland County), Wells and York (York County) game preserves. Bobcat, Canada Lynx, and Fox are hunted from the end of the Deer season until closed season on Fox in the Rangeley Game Preserve in Franklin County. Upland game and waterfowl may be hunted in the following game management areas during regular open seasons.

---

* Check current state regulations.

GAME MANAGEMENT AREAS

Brownfield (2,839 acres) at Brownfield, Denmark, and Fryburg in Oxford County—waterfowl; *Chesterville* (466 acres) at Chesterville in Franklin County—waterfowl; *Fahi Pond* (297 acres) at Embden in Somerset County—waterfowl; *Frye Mountain* (5,031 acres) at Montville in Waldo County—upland game; *Great Works* (640 acres) at Edmunds in Washington County—waterfowl; *Hodgdon* (400 acres) at Hodgdon in Aroostook County—waterfowl; *Jonesboro* (713 acres) at Jonesboro in Washington County—upland game; *Madawaska* (295 acres) at Palmyra in Somerset County—waterfowl; *Newfield* (2,154 acres) at Newfield in York County—upland game; *Ruffingham* (610 acres) at Montville and Searsmont in Waldo County—upland game and waterfowl; *Sandy Point* (540 acres) at Stockton Springs in Waldo County—waterfowl; *Scammon* (1,813 acres) at Eastbrook and Franklin in Hancock County—upland game and waterfowl; *Swan Island* (1,600 acres) at Perkins Township in Sagadahoc County—upland game and waterfowl.

STATE PARKS

Aroostook (577 acres) southwest of Presque Isle—Aroostook County; *Baxter* (193,254 acres) northwest of Millinocket—Penobscot and Piscataquis counties; *Camden Hills* (4,966 acres) north of Camden—Waldo County; *Lake St. George* (360 acres) near Liberty—Waldo County; *Lamoine* (55 acres) on Frenchman Bay, southeast of Ellsworth—Hancock County; *Lily Bay* (576 acres) on eastern shore of Moosehead Lake, north of Greenville—Piscataquis County; *Moose Point* (178 acres) at Searsport on Penobscot River—Waldo County; *Mount Blue* (1,273 acres) near Weld and Lake Webb—Franklin County; *Quoddy Head* (400 acres) south of Lubec, at entrance to Quoddy Bay on Atlantic Ocean—Washington County; *Reid* (792 acres) east of Georgetown at entrance to Boothbay Harbor on Atlantic Ocean—Sagadahoc County; *Sebago Lake* (1,296 acres) west of Casco—Cumberland County; *Two Lights* (40 acres) the Cape Elizabeth Lights south of South Portland on Atlantic Ocean—Cumberland County.

Licenses, permits, regulations, and information about current seasons, bag and possession limits may be obtained from town clerks, or the Commission, Department of Inland Fisheries and Game; and the Commissioner, Department of Sea and Shore Fisheries, State House, Augusta. Although not primarily a sportsman's magazine, there is a monthly section on "Outdoor Maine" in *Down East* and excellent articles and illustrations about the state; Subscription: 1 year (10 issues), $4.25—Down East Magazine, Camden.

MARYLAND

Area: 12,327 square miles (land area—9,874 square miles); rank in nation–42
Bird: Baltimore Oriole (*Icterus galbula*), adopted 1882
Capital city: Annapolis near the mouth of Severen River on Chesapeake Bay in Anne Arundel County; population (1960)—34,385; rank in state–5
Counties: 23
Elevations: Highest, Backbone Mountain (3,360 ft.) in Garrett County; lowest, Atlantic Ocean (sea level)
Flower: Black-eyed Susan (*Rudbeckia hirta*), adopted 1918
Geographic center: 3 miles east of Collington, Anne Arundel County
Nicknames: Old Line State, Cockade State, Oyster State, Queen State
Population (1960): 3,100,689; rank in nation–21
Tidal shoreline: 3,190 miles (including islands, bays, and streams to a point where tidal waters narrow to 100 ft. wide)
Tree: White Oak (*Quercus alba*), adopted 1941

Maryland is bordered by the District of Columbia, Virginia, and West Virginia on the south and east, Pennsylvania on the north, Delaware sharing Delmarva Peninsula on the northeast, and the Atlantic Ocean on the southeast.

Chesapeake Bay (10–40 miles wide) divides the low coastal plain region into the Eastern Shore of Delmarva Peninsula and a Western Shore which rises to broad rolling hills, the Piedmont Plateau, and western forests, ridges, and narrow valleys of the Appalachian Mountains. Among 11,175 miles of streams, there are 30 navigable rivers, and ocean vessels dock at Baltimore on the Western Shore and Patapsco River. The Potomac River flows from western Maryland along the West Virginia and Virginia boundaries and through the nation's capital, Washington, D.C., to reach lower Chesapeake Bay. Other large rivers flowing into Chesapeake Bay are the Susquehanna River from Pennsylvania, Patuxent River on the Western Shore, the Elk, Sassafras, Chester, Choptank, Nanticoke, Wicomico, and Pocomake rivers of the Eastern Shore. The Chesapeake Bay Bridge (7¼ miles long) connects Stevensville on the Eastern Shore with Skidmore at Sandy Point on the Western Shore.

The Intercoastal Waterway from Delaware Bay follows the Delaware and Chesapeake Canal to Elk River in upper Chesapeake Bay. There are 350 marinas and marine facilities, 375 small boat launching ramps, 60 yachting centers; and Annapolis is a focal point for the 473-mile yacht race to Newport, R. I. Chesapeake Bay is noted for crabs, oysters, clams, and other seafood, and Ocean City at Sinepuxent Bay sheltered by Assateague Island is a famous port for offshore fishing known as the "White Marlin Capital of the World."

LICENSES

Resident fishing licenses are issued to persons 16 or more years of age who have lived in Maryland for at least 6 months preceding applications for licenses. Any person owning property assessed at not less than $500 in Garrett County may obtain resident licenses for himself and family to fish in Deep Creek Lake. Regardless of age, all persons must possess a license to hunt and trap, except landowners or tenants on their own lands, but they are required to have a permit to hunt for antlerless Deer. A landowner or his tenant has the exclusive right to trap Muskrat to the mean low water mark on marsh land adjacent to his land. Riparian owners have first rights to procure licenses for Duck blinds opposite their shores, and the annual application should be made prior to October 10. Any person who had a licensed blind on the waters of Anne Arundel County prior to Jan. 1, 1927, retains the privilege of filing for a renewal of that license during the month of June. All body booting rigs must possess a bushwacking rig or sneak boat license. It is unlawful for a nonresident to shoot from a body booting rig on the Susquehanna Flats unless the legal holder or resident co-owner of the license accompanies the rig.

All persons 16 or more years of age must purchase a federal "Duck" stamp to take migratory game birds. Permits for a special antlerless Deer hunt in November are issued one per hunter only to landowners and residents of Dorchester, St. Marys, Somerset, Wicomico, and Worcester counties. Permits for a similar hunt in December are issued first to residents of Calvert, Caroline, Cecil, Charles, Dorchester, Kent, Queen Anne's, Somerset, Talbot, Wicomico, and Worcester counties, and remaining permits are issued on a "first come" basis. Each hunter must apply in person and present his hunting license with a Deer stamp.

Every member of a party on a Raccoon or Opossum hunt is required to have a hunting license in his possession. A club or organization of 20 or more citizens in Maryland may obtain a permit for a special dog training area of not less than 100 acres or more than 250 acres under certain conditions and restrictions.

The special Potomac River angler's license permits residents of Virginia and West Virginia to fish by wading or boat and from the shores of their states, but not on Maryland shores. Any resident of the District of Columbia holding a Potomac River license may fish in the river and from Maryland shores.

Resident license fees: Sport fishing, $3.00; statewide hunting and trapping, $5.25; county hunting and trapping, $1.75; Duck blind, $5.50;

sneak boat, body booter, or bushwack rig, $5.50; federal "Duck" stamp, $3.00; special archery Deer stamp, $3.00; special firearms Deer stamp, $2.00; Fur dealer, $2.00; fish breeder, $5.00; game breeder, $5.00; taxidermist and tanner, $5.00; scientific collecting permit, $1.00; permit to purchase or possess live wild animals, $2.00; dog training area permit, $10.00; regulated shooting area permit, $25.00.

Nonresident license fees: Annual fishing, $10.00; tourist fishing 3 consecutive days, $3.00; Potomac River fishing, $3.00; fishing pond fee, $3.00; fishing lake fee, $25.00; fish breeder, $5.00; hunting and trapping, $20.00; hunting on regulated shooting area, $3.00; fur dealer, $25.00; federal "Duck" stamp, $3.00; special archery Deer stamp, $3.00; special firearms Deer stamp, $2.00.

HUNTING AND TRAPPING

Game animals: Deer, Hare or Rabbit, Squirrels (Black, Fox, Gray, Red). OPEN SEASONS:* Deer—archery (either sex), mid-October to mid-November with periods of 2 or 3 weeks in designated areas; firearms (including bow and arrow), about 1 week in early December for Buck, and a 3-day special hunting period for antlerless Deer in November, and a similar 3-day period in late December in designated counties. Hare or Rabbit—Nov. 15 to early January. Squirrels—about 3 weeks in October. BAG LIMITS: Deer—1 per year. Hare or Rabbit—4 per day. Squirrels—6 per day, except Red Squirrel—no limit.

A legal Buck is a male Deer with 2 or more points to one antler, and a Spike Buck's antler must be at least 3 inches. It is unlawful to kill White Fallow Deer in Talbot County at any time, or Sika Deer in Dorchester County with a bow and arrow. The use of artificial lights, nets, snares, pitfalls, and dogs to hunt Deer are prohibited.

Furbearing animals: Beaver, Bobcat, Fox (Gray, Red), Mink, Muskrat, Opossum, Otter, Raccoon, Skunk. OPEN SEASONS:* Beaver—mid-January through February. Mink, Muskrat—Jan. 1–March 15, except Allegany, Carroll, Frederick, Garrett, Howard, Montgomery, and Washington counties, Dec. 15–March 1. Otter—Jan. 1–March 15. Opossum, Raccoon—mid-September to March 1 except Cecil County, November 1 through February. FULLY PROTECTED: Bear—no open season. NOT PROTECTED: Bobcat, Fox (local exceptions), Skunk, and Woodchuck may be taken at any time.

Game birds: Brant, Coot, Mourning Dove, Ducks (except Canvasback and Redhead), Eider, Gallinule, Geese (except Snow Geese), Ruffed Grouse, Merganser, Old Squaw, Cock Pheasant, Bobwhite Quail (Partridge), Rails, Scaup, Scota, Sora, Wilson's Snipe, Wild Turkey,

---

* Check current state regulations.

Woodcock. OPEN SEASONS:* Brant, Geese—early November to mid-January. Coot, Ducks, Eider, Merganser, Old Squaw, Scaup, Scoter—mid-November through December. Dove—mid-September through October and late December to mid-January. Ruffed Grouse—mid-November to early January. Cock Pheasant—mid-November to early January except no open season in about 12 counties. Quail—mid-November through January. Wilson's Snipe—mid-November to late December. Turkey—about 3 weeks in October in Allegany, Garrett, Somerset, Washington, and Worcester counties. Woodcock—mid-November to early January. Regulated shooting preserves (Mallard Duck, Chukar Partridge, Pheasant, Bobwhite and Coturnix Quail, Turkey)—Oct. 1–March 31 (except Sundays). FULLY PROTECTED: Canvasback and Redhead Ducks, Snow Geese —no open seasons. NOT PROTECTED: Crows may be killed at any time. Hawks and Owls may be shot only in counties paying a bounty, but landowners or agents may kill them at any time to protect property.

It is unlawful to use any bushwack rig or sneak boat within 500 yards of a licensed blind in Cecil, Harford, and Worcester counties. A body booter may be used only on Susquehanna Flats. Bushwack rigs and sneak boats may be used on the waters of the Isle of Wight, Assawoman Bay, Chincoteague Bay, Sinepuxent Bay, and their tributaries in Worcester County. Sneak boats are permitted on Susquehanna Flats and waters of the Elk and Sassafras rivers in Cecil County, the Monocasy River in Carroll and Frederick counties, and the Potomac River in Allegany, Frederick, Montgomery, and Washington counties. It is unlawful to cross boundary lines with sneak boats before 3:15 A.M. on open days.

FIREARMS

The use of pistols, rifles, automatic firearms, or shotguns larger than 10 gauge or capable of holding more than 3 shells in the magazine and chamber combined for hunting waterfowl are prohibited. Upland game except Deer) may be hunted with a .22 caliber rifle. Deer may be hunted with unplugged shotguns loaded with rifled slugs, or rifles using a cartridge giving a muzzle energy of 1,200 pounds or better, but not with shot or buckshot, full-jacketed, incendiary, or tracer bullets, fully automatic firearms, or crossbows. Hunting Deer with rifles is prohibited in Anne Arundel, Calvert, Caroline, Charles, Harford, Howard, Kent, Prince George's, Queen Anne's, St. Mary's, and Talbot Counties. Archers may take Deer with a longbow having a full draw and pull of not less than 30 pounds, and arrows with sharpened broadhead metal points at least seven-eighths of an inch in width.

* Check current state regulations.

Shooting hours: Hunting on Sunday is prohibited. Sunrise to sunset, except Dove, 12:00 o'clock noon to sunset; Opossum and Raccoon, sunset to sunrise.

Using only starter pistols loaded with blank cartridges, dogs may be trained to hunt game birds, hares, or rabbits between September and March.

FISHING

Game fish: Black Bass (Largemouth, Smallmouth), Striped Bass (Rockfish), Muskellunge, Pike or Pickerel, Great Northern Pike, Trout (Brook, Brown, Rainbow), Walleyes. OPEN SEASONS:* Trout—April 15–March 14; except in the Savage River and tributaries only in Garrett County, April 15–Sept. 15, but regular season in New Germany Lake and Savage River Reservoir. Walleye—April 1–Nov. 15. No closed seasons for all other fish. Three rods and lines with not more than 2 hooks to each line may be used to fish, and artificial lures, or plugs with multiple or gang hooks are considered as one unit. A licensed fisherman may use a trotline for all species of fish except Black Bass in nontidal waters of the Potomac River (tributaries excepted) but not during April, May, and June. Not more than 25 single hooks may be used on a nonmetallic trotline not exceeding 100 feet in length. It is unlawful to anchor a trotline from one shore to another at any time. Only bona fide residents of Maryland may use nets of any kind, and no person may practice snagging. Carp and Eels may be taken by gigging July 1–March 31 in Washington County in the Potomac River, Conocheague Creek, Licking Creek, and Big Antietam Creek only from Route 40 east of Hagerstown to the Potomac River and in the Potomac River, and the Monocacy River in Frederick County, and in the waters of Allegany County (except designated Trout streams) but not in tributaries of the above streams. Every person in a gigging party must possess an angler's license. Licensed fishermen may take Carp by bow and arrow in nontidal waters except in Trout streams or state-controlled lakes and ponds. Six tip-ups, bobs, or hand lines with not more than one hook per line, and under the immediate control of one fisherman may be used to fish through ice. Offshore fishing for Albacore, Bluefish, Channel Bass, Flounder, Marlin, Sea Bass, Sea Trout, and Tuna begins in May and lasts through September. Chesapeake Bay offers a wide variety of freshwater and saltwater fish, and Tidewater Maryland is a nationally known wildfowl region. Good hunting and fishing is found in state forests, but only fishing is permitted in state parks.

---

* Check current state regulations.

PUBLIC FISHING LAKES*

Atkisson Reservoir (91 acres) near Emorinton; *Big Mills Pond* (10 acres) at Pocomoke City; *Big Pool* (90 acres) near Indian Springs; *Conowingo Reservoir* (5,000 acres) at Conowingo; *Deep Creek Lake* (3,900 acres) near Salisbury; *Frazer Lake* (40 acres) near Cecilton; *Garland Lake* (45 acres) near Denton; *Herrington Lake* (44 acres) near Oakland; *Johnson Lake* (108 acres) near Salisbury; *Lake Roland* (80 acres) near Baltimore; *Leonard's Lake* (30 acres) near Salisbury; *Liberty Reservoir* (3,100 acres) near Finksburg; *Linchester Lake* (25 acres) near Preston; *Little Pool* (31 acres) near Hancock; *Loch Raven Reservoir* (2,400 acres) near Towson; *Mixon Pond* (33 acres) near Oldtown; *Piney Reservoir* (18 acres) near Finzel; *Pleasant Valley Lake* (18 acres) near Bittinger; *Prettyboy Reservoir* (1,500 acres) near Parkton; *Rocky Gorge Reservoir* (300 acres) near Laurel; *Savage Reservoir* (350 acres) near Bloomington; *St. Paul's Lake* (30 acres) near Fairlee; *Schumaker Lake* (35 acres) near Salisbury; *Smithville Lake* (40 acres) at Smithville; *Triadelphia Reservoir* (800 acres) near Unity; *Urieville Lake* (35 acres) near Chestertown; *Wye Mills Lake* (50 acres) at Wye Mills; *York Reservoir* (800 acres) near Friendsville.

STATE FORESTS

Cedarville (3,520 acres) east of Waldorf—Charles and Prince George counties; *Doncaster* (1,461 acres) east of Doncaster—Charles County; *Elk Neck* (2,742 acres) near North East—Cecil County; *Green Ridge* (25,631 acres) west of Hancock—Allegany County; *Pocomoke* (12,250 acres) on Pocomoke River between Pocomoke City and Snow Hill—Worcester County; *Potomac* (12,052 acres) on North Branch Potomac River and Backbone Mountain (3,360 ft.) near Deer Park—Garrett County; *Savage River* (5,250 acres) on Casselman River, near Frostburg—Garrett County; *Swallow Falls* (7,453 acres) on Youghiogheny River, north of Oakland—Garrett County.

STATE PARKS

Cunningham Falls (4,446 acres) in Catoctin Mountains, south of Thurmont—Frederick County; *Deep Creek Lake* (1,773 acres) on north side of lake near McHenry—Garrett County; *Elk Neck* (657 acres) on Elk and Northeast rivers south of North East—Cecil County; *Fort Frederick* (279 acres) south of Clear Springs—Washington County; *Gambrill* (1,134 acres) northwest of Frederick—Frederick County; *Patapasco* (6,062 acres) on Patapasco River near Ellicott City—Howard County;

---

* Among more than 60 public lakes stocked with game fish.

Rocks (203 acres) on Deer Creek northwest of Bel Air—Harford County; *Sandy Point* (725 acres) north of Revell Highway at western terminus of Chesapeake Bay Bridge—Anne Arundel County; *Seneca Creek* (340 acres) west of Gaithersburg—Montgomery County. Beautiful *Catoctin Mountain Park* (5,747 acres) adjoins Cunningham Falls State Park and is under the National Capital Parks.

Licenses, permits, regulations, and information about current seasons, bag and possession limits may be obtained from the Director, Maryland Game and Inland Fish Commission, State Office Building, Annapolis; and from a clerk of the circuit courts, clerk of the court of common pleas in Baltimore City, and authorized agents. The commission also publishes the interesting *Maryland Conservationist* at $1.00 per year for 6 issues.

MASSACHUSETTS

Area: 8,266 square miles (land area—7,867 square miles); rank in nation–45
Bird: Chickadee (*Penthestes artricapillus*), adopted 1941
Capital city: Boston in Suffolk County on Massachusetts Bay; population (1960)—697,197; rank in state–1
Counties: 14
Elevations: Highest, Mount Greylock (3,491 ft.) in Berkshire County; lowest, Atlantic Ocean
Flower: Mayflower (*Epigaea repens*), also called Trailing Arbutus and Ground Laurel, adopted 1918
Geographic center: City of Worcester, Worcester County
Nicknames: Bay State, Codfish State, Old Colony, Puritan State
Population (1960): 5,148,578; rank in nation–9
Tidal shoreline: 1,519 miles (including islands, bays, and streams to a point where tidal waters narrow to 100 ft. wide)
Tree: American Elm (*Ulmus americana*), adopted 1941

Massachusetts facing the Atlantic Ocean is a New England State bordered by New Hampshire and Vermont on the north, Connecticut, Rhode Island, and the Atlantic Ocean on the south, and New York on the west.

Interlaced with lakes, ponds, and streams, the state gradually slopes from western wooded Berkshire Hills to Boston between the rocky North Shore and sandy South Shore of the enormous Massachusetts Bay marked by Rockport and Gloucester on northeastern Cape Ann, and Provinceton on the tip of a beckoning finger of sand, sheltered inlets, ponds, and woodlands known as Cape Cod. The Bourne and Sagamore bridges over the

Cape Cod Canal between Buzzards Bay on Rhode Island Sound and Cape Cod Bay link Cape Cod to the mainland. The Housatonic River flows through the Hoosac Hills and Taconic Range of the Berkshires from Vermont to Connecticut. The highest summits in the state include Mount Greylock, Saddle Ball (3,300 ft.), Mount Fitch (3,140 ft.), and Mount Williams (2,951 ft.) on the Appalachian Trail in the Hoosac Range, Mount Everett (2,624 ft.) and Alexander Mountain (2,243 ft.) in the southwestern Taconic Range.

The Connecticut River leaves the New Hampshire–Vermont boundary to cross broad Pioneer Valley on a southward journey through Springfield to Connecticut. The largest lake in Massachusetts is Quabbin Reservoir (39 square miles) on Swift River northwest of Ware. The Merrimack River from New Hampshire wanders through northeastern Massachusetts to Newburyport and Plum Island on the Atlantic Ocean. The meandering Charles River and shorter Mystic River from Mystic Lakes flow into Boston Harbor on Massachusetts Bay. The Elizabeth Islands between Buzzards Bay and Vineyard Sound are west of Woods Hole on Cape Cod. Muskeget Channel from Nantucket Sound to the Atlantic Ocean separates the island of Martha's Vineyard (20 miles long) from Nantucket Island (14 miles long) south of Cape Cod. These islands are accessible by aircraft, watercraft, and ferry steamers from New Bedford on Buzzards Bay, Woods Hole and Hyannis on Cape Cod. Boston, Gloucester, and New Bedford are famous fishing ports, Marblehead on the North Shore a noted racing point, and among other fine harbors are more than 65 yacht clubs and countless marinas.

LICENSES

Licenses to fish, hunt, and trap are required for all persons 15 or more years of age, except legal residents and their immediate families on leased or owned land used exclusively for agricultural, forestry, or woodlot purposes. Resident licenses are issued to citizens who have lived in the state for at least 6 months, and to members of the U.S. Armed Forces officially stationed in Massachusetts, and to nonresident citizens who own real estate assessed for not less than $1,000, and to associations or clubs incorporated for the purpose of fishing, hunting, or trapping on land equal in value to $1,000 for each member. An alien must obtain a permit from the Division of Fisheries and Game to hunt, trap, or possess wild birds or mammals, and own or have any firearms in possession or under his control.

The written consent of a parent or guardian is required before a minor 15–17 years of age (inclusive) may receive a hunting license. The juvenile must also present one of the following: (a) a written statement that he shall at all times be accompanied by an adult 21 years of age or older while hunting or target practicing anywhere except on a recognized shooting range; (b) show proof that a hunting or sporting license was issued to him during a prior year; (c) present a certificate of competency with firearms as provided by the Division of Law Enforcement. Each juvenile 12–14 years of age (inclusive) may accompany one licensed adult with only one firearm to be used during the joint hunt, and any game taken is counted as a single bag limit. All persons 16 or more years of age must procure a federal "Duck" stamp to take migratory game birds.

Blind persons and paraplegics of any age, and recipients of old age assistance may obtain fishing licenses without cost, and free sporting licenses are issued to any person 70 or more years of age. Nonresidents holding valid licenses issued by adjacent states may fish in interstate lakes, ponds, or streams. No license is required to fish in coastal waters.

Resident license fees: Fishing (males), $4.25; fishing (females), $3.25; fishing (15–17 years of age), $2.25; hunting, $4.25; sporting (fishing and hunting), $7.25; trapping, $7.75; trapping (15–17 years of age), $2.25; archery Deer hunting stamp, $1.10; federal "Duck" stamp, $3.00.

Nonresident license fees: Fishing, $8.75; fishing 7 consecutive days, $4.25; hunting, $15.25; archery Deer hunting stamp, $1.10; federal "Duck" stamp, $3.00.

HUNTING AND TRAPPING

Game animals: Black Bear, Deer, Snowshoe Hare, Opossum, Rabbits (Cottontail, Jack), Raccoon, Gray Squirrel. OPEN SEASONS:* Bear—mid-October through December. Deer—archery, about 10 days in mid-November; firearms (including bow and arrow), about 5 days in early December. Snowshoe Hare—mid-October to early February, except in Dukes and Nantucket counties, mid-November to early February. Opossum, Raccoon—mid-September through December. Cotttontail Rabbit—mid-October through February except in Dukes and Nantucket counties, mid-November through February. Jack Rabbit—mid-October to early February and no open season in Dukes County. Gray Squirrel—mid-October to late November. BAG LIMITS: Bear—1 per year. Deer—1 per year. Snowshoe Hare—2 per day. Cottontail Rabbit—5 per day. Jack Rabbit—no limit. Squirrel—5 per day. Opossum—no limit. Raccoon—3 from sunset to sunset by one person, or 6 by two or more persons hunting as a group.

Furbearing animals: Beaver, Fox, Mink, Muskrat, Opossum, Otter, Raccoon, Skunk, Weasel, Wildcat (Bobcat). OPEN TRAPPING SEASON:* Beaver—Dec. 16–March 31. Mink, Otter—Nov. 1–Jan. 31. Muskrat—

---

* Check current state regulations.

Nov. 1–Dec. 15. Other furbearers—Nov. 1–March 31. NOT PROTECTED: Chipmunk, Fox, Porcupine, Skunk, Flying and Red Squirrels, Weasel, Wildcat, and Woodchuck may be taken at any time. Bounty: Wildcat, $10.

Game birds: Brant, Coot (Mud Hen), Ducks (except Canvasback and Redhead), Eider, Gallinule, Geese (except Snow Geese), Ruffed Grouse, Merganser, Old Squaw, Cock Pheasant, Quail, Rails, Scaup, Scoter, Sora, Wilson's Snipe (Jacksnipe), Woodcock. OPEN SEASON:* Brant, Geese—mid-October to late December. Coot, Ducks, Merganser —about 2 weeks in late October and 4 weeks from late November into December. Eider, Old Squaw, Scoter—Oct. 1–Jan. 15. Gallinule, Rails, Sora—Sept. 1 to early November. Ruffed Grouse, Cock Pheasant, Woodcock—mid-October to late November. Quail—mid-October to late November in Barnstable, Bristol, Dukes (Martha's Vineyard), Nantucket, and Plymouth counties. Wilson's Snipe—Sept. 1–Oct. 15. Except during Duck open season, Eider, Old Squaw and Scoter may be hunted only on coastal waters, rivers, and streams lying seaward from the first bridge upstream, but not within 300 yards of any bathing, picnic, or residential beach, or any land except uninhabited points, rocks, or islands. FULLY PROTECTED: Canvasback and Redhead Ducks, and Snow Geese—no open seasons. NOT PROTECTED: Crow, Grackle, Jay, English Sparrow, and Starling may be taken at any time.

FIREARMS

Deer and migratory game birds may be taken with shotguns not larger than 10 gauge, or with bow and arrow. The possession of any shotgun shells loaded with a single ball or shot larger than no. 1 is prohibited where birds or mammals might be found, except during the Deer season. Rifles, pistols, and revolvers may not be used on state-operated public shooting grounds during the upland game season, or on any field, woodland, or highway during an open season for Deer. Pistols and revolvers larger than .38 caliber, and rifles chambered to take larger than .22 caliber long rifle ammunition are prohibited between one-half hour after sunset and one-half hour before sunrise. Archers hunting Deer may not possess firearms on their person, in any motor vehicle, or use dogs.

An archer hunting Bear and Deer may use a long bow with at least 40 pounds pull at 28-inch draw, and arrows with sharpened steel broadhead blades not less than seven-eighths inch or more than 1½ inches in width. Arrows must be marked with the owner's name and address, and they may not be released within 150 feet of a state or paved highway.

---

* Check current state regulations.

The use of bows drawn, held, or released by mechanical means and of arrows with explosive or poisoned tips is prohibited.

Dogs may be used for waterfowl hunting on coastal waters during the open season for Deer, but not to hunt Deer. All Deer hunters must wear at least 200 square inches of daylight fluorescent orange or red clothing or material on the head, chest, and back, or on the chest and back. Dogs may be trained to hunt at any time except during an open season for Deer, but only pistols and revolvers loaded with blank cartridges are permitted as firearms.

Shooting hours: Hunting on Sunday is prohibited. Migratory game birds, sunrise to sunset, except that on opening day of Duck season, shooting starts at 12:00 o'clock noon. Deer, 6:30 A.M.–5:00 P.M. Grouse, Pheasant, Quail, Rabbit, Squirrel, one-half hour before sunrise to sunset except on public shooting grounds during upland game season, sunrise to sunset. Opossum and Raccoon, a 24-hour day reckoned as from sunset to sunset when counting bag limit. All traps must be visited daily 4:00 A.M.–8:00 P.M. No traps may be set before 6:00 A.M. on Nov. 1.

FISHING

Game fish: Black Bass, Pickerel, Northern Pike, Pike-perch, Salmon, Shad, Trout (Brook, Brown, Lake, Rainbow). OPEN SEASONS:* Salmon and Trout—third Saturday in April (1 hour before sunrise) to third Saturday of October in lakes and ponds; last Saturday in April (1 hour before sunrise) to third Saturday of October in streams; Trout may also be taken in ponds and lakes not reclaimed for Trout from the third Sunday in October through February. Other game fish—third Saturday in April (1 hour before sunrise) through February in lakes and ponds; last Saturday in April (1 hour before sunrise) through February in streams, except Black Bass may be taken in Wallum Lake only from July 1–Oct. 31.

A license is not required to take Trout in coastal waters (salters), but anglers must adhere to other regulations. Freshwater fish may be taken with not more than 2 hooks or 2 flies (2 lines with one hook or one line with 2 hooks), and a total of 5 hooks may be used to fish through ice.

All persons fishing in the following interstate waters must adhere to regulations applied to Massachusetts waters: Bent Pond near Warwick, Lake Monomonac near Winchendon, Tuxbury Pond near Amesbury, Long Pond near Dracut, and Tyngsboro on the New Hampshire boundary; and Lake Wallum near Douglas on Rhode Island border.

There is excellent offshore fishing; and Striped Bass, Bonito, Sword-

---

* Check current state regulations.

fish, Tuna, and White Marlin are among sought after saltwater fish. The Vineyard Striped Bass Derby, Sept. 15–Oct. 15, draws sportsmen to the rips and shoals near the Elizabeth Islands, Martha's Vineyard, and Nantucket Island. State beaches, forests, parks, and reservations provide good fishing, and hunting is also permitted in wildlife management areas.

STATE FORESTS

Bash Bish Falls (390 acres) southwest of Egremont—Berkshire County; *Beartown* (8,000 acres) contains Beartown Mountain (1,865 ft.), Livermore Peak (1,863 ft.), Sky Peak (1,947 ft.), Mount Wilcox (2,155 ft.) and Appalachian Trail, northeast of Great Barrington—Berkshire County; *Brimfield* (3,058 acres) near Brimfield—Hampden County; *Chester-Blandford* (2,328 acres) contains 100-foot Sanderson Brook Falls, north of Blandford—Hampden County; *D.A.R.* (1,000 acres) north of Goshen —Hampshire County; *Douglas* (3,468 acres) including Wallum Lake, southwest of Douglas—Worcester County; *Erving* (5,681 acres) near Erving and West Orange—Franklin County; *Granville* (2,233 acres) on Hubbard River near West Granville—Hampden County; *Leominster* (3,673 acres) southwest of Leominster—Worcester County; *Mohawk Trail* (6,080 acres) west of Charlemont—Franklin County; *Monroe* (4,237 acres) in the Hoosac Range near Monroe Bridge, north of Charlemont—Franklin County; *Mount Grace* (1,100 acres) contains 1,617-foot summit and ski trails, near Warwick—Franklin County; *Myles Standish* (11,578 acres) south of Plymouth—Plymouth County; *Roland C. Nickerson* (1,777 acres) at East Brewster on Cape Cod—Barnstable County; *October Mountain* (11,589 acres) on the Appalachian Trail west of Beckett—Berkshire County; *Otis* (3,800 acres) near West Otis—Berkshire County; *Otter River* (830 acres) northwest of Baldwinville—Worcester County; *Harold Parker* (2,906 acres) northwest of Middleton— Essex County; *Peru* (2,185 acres) south of Peru—Berkshire County; *Pittsfield* (7,093 acres) west of Pittsfield—Berkshire County; *Sandisfield* (3,923 acres) near Sandisfield—Berkshire County; *Savoy Mountain* (10,766 acres) in the Hoosac Range, southeast of North Adams—Berkshire County; *Shawme-Crowell* (5,917 acres) near Sagamore on Cape Cod—Barnstable County; *Spencer* (776 acres) south of Spencer—Worcester County; *Tolland* (2,940 acres) between Farmington River and Otis Reservoir near New Boston—Berkshire County; *Willard Brook* (2,042 acres) north of Fitchburg—Worcester County; *Windsor* (1,616 acres) north of West Cummington—Berkshire County.

STATE PARKS

Ames Nowell (611 acres) in Abington—Plymouth County; *Ashland* (320 acres) west of Ashland—Middlesex County; *Clarksburg* (364 acres) between North Adams and Vermont border—Berkshire County; *Cochituate* (1,032 acres) east of Framingham—Middlesex County; *John C. Robinson* (1,086 acres) on Westfield River near Springfield—Hampden County; *Joseph A. Skinner* (375 acres) on Mount Holyoke (954 ft.) in Pioneer Valley, south of Hadley—Hampshire County; *Rutland* (1,400 acres) at West Rutland—Worcester County.

STATE RESERVATIONS

Fort Phoenix Beach (27 acres) at Fairhaven on Buzzards Bay—Bristol County; *Horseneck Beach* at Westport Point on Buzzards Bay, southwest of Dartmouth—Bristol County; *Mount Everett* (1,000 acres) in Taconic Range, summit 2,624 feet, west of Sheffield—Berkshire County; *Misery Island* (98 acres) in harbor of Salem—Essex County; *Mount Greylock* (8,660 acres) containing 100-foot Massachusetts War Memorial Beacon on the 3,491-foot summit, near North Adams—Berkshire County; *Mount Tom* (1,800 acres) with 1,214-foot summit, south of Northampton—Hampshire County; *Salisbury Beach* (520 acres) at Salisbury, north of Newburyport—Essex County; *Scusset Beach* (380 acres) near Sandwich at the eastern entrance of Cape Cod Canal—Barnstable County; *Wachusett Mountain* (1,600 acres) with 2,108-foot summit, south of Westminster—Worcester County; *Walden Pond* (150 acres) south of Concord—Middlesex County.

WILDLIFE MANAGEMENT AREAS

Barre Falls (15,000 acres including 1,000 acres managed by Division of Fisheries and Game) near Barre, Hubbardston, Oakham, and Rutland —Worcester County; *Birch Hill* (4,277 acres) near Royalston, Templeton, and Winchendon—Worcester County; *Crane* (1,400 acres) near Falmouth—Barnstable County; *Fort Devens* (2,000 acres) near Ayer, Lancaster, and Shirley—Middlesex and Worcester counties; *Hubbardston* (2,200 acres) at Hubbardston—Worcester; *Knightsville* (500 acres) at Huntington—Berkshire County; *Myles Standish* (11,578 acres including 2,000 acres managed by Fisheries and Game Division) near Plymouth—Plymouth County; *Northeast* (3,500 acres) at Georgetown, Groveland, and Newburyport—Essex County; *Harold Parker State Forest* (2,906 acres) near Middleton—Essex County; *Pantry Brook* (377 acres) between Concord and Sudbury—Middlesex County; *Peru State Forest* (2,185 acres) south of Peru—Berkshire County; *Phillipston* (822 acres) near Barre and Hubbardston—Worcester County; *Westboro* (175 acres) east of Worcester—Worcester County; West Meadows (387 acres) near West Bridgewater—Plymouth County; *Williamstown* (2,000 acres) near Williamstown—Berkshire County.

Licenses and regulations, or information about current seasons, bag and possession limits may be obtained from the Director, Division of Fisheries and Game, 73 Tremont St., Boston. Trout waters and public hunting guides are available from the Chief, Information and Education, Division of Fisheries and Game, Field Headquarters, Westboro. The official bimonthly magazine *Massachusetts Wildlife* is free to any person requesting it from the Field Headquarters. Information about recreation areas is issued by the Chief of Recreation, Department of Natural Resources, Division of Forests and Parks, 15 Ashburton Place, Boston 8.

MICHIGAN

Area: 57,980 square miles (land area—57,019 square miles); rank in nation–22
Bird: Robin (*Turdus migratorius*)
Capital city: Lansing on the Cedar and Grand rivers of Ingham County in the south central portion of the Lower Peninsula; population (1960)—107,807; rank in state–5
Counties: 83
Elevations: Highest, a peak in the Porcupine Mountains (2,203 ft.) of Ontonagon County; lowest, Lake Erie shore (572 ft.)
Flower: Apple Blossom (*Pyrus coronaria*), adopted 1897
Geographic center: 5 miles west of north of Cadillac, Wexford County
Nicknames: Lady of the Lakes, Water Wonderland, Wolverine State
Population (1960): 7,823,194; rank in nation–7
Shoreline on the Great Lakes: approximately 2,500 miles
Tree: White Pine (*Pinus monticolae*), adopted 1955

Two huge peninsulas divided by the Strait of Mackinac contain approximately 11,000 inland lakes and 36,000 miles of streams flowing into the surrounding Great Lakes. The Lower Peninsula, shaped like a mittened hand with a thumb indentation at Saginaw Bay, is north of Indiana and Ohio, bordered by Lake Michigan on the west and Lake Huron on the northeast, the St. Clair River (66 miles), Lake St. Clair (460 square miles), and the Detroit River (54 miles) flowing into Lake Erie on the southeast to form an international waterway between Michigan and Ontario Province, Canada. Ambassador Bridge and the Windsor Tunnel are between Detroit, Michigan, and Windsor, Canada. There are high sand dunes on Lake Michigan shores, and the largest portion of the Lower Peninsula is level or gently rolling with elevations 1,000–1,200 feet above sea level; and a broad eastern ridge extends from the southern border to the St. Clair River region. Streams generally drain east and west into the Great Lakes. The Burt-Mullet chain of lakes in

Cheboygan County are accessible from Lake Huron through a 14-foot lock on the Cheboygan River, the Indian River to Burt and Mullet lakes, and from Burt Lake into Crooked and Hay lakes via the Crooked River. A chain of lakes in Antrim and Grand Traverse counties on Lake Michigan are connected by the Torch River and navigable channels with Elk, Round, Torch, and several other lakes.

Wisconsin and the Green Bay of Lake Michigan west of the Strait of Mackinac are along the southern border of the Upper Peninsula. Lake Huron narrows northward around Drummond Island into Munuscong Lake, and the waterway continues through Lake George and Lake Nicolet east of the Soo Locks on St. Marys River (87 miles) into Whitefish Bay on Lake Superior between the northern sandy shores of the Upper Peninsula and Ontario, Canada. A toll bridge over the Strait of Mackinac connects Mackinaw City on the Lower Peninsula with St. Ignace on the Upper Peninsula. International Bridge over St. Mary's River links Sault Ste. Marie, Michigan, with Sault Ste. Marie, Ontario. There are several chains of lakes in the rugged Upper Peninsula where frosts may occur throughout the year, and snow covers the ground for 5 months. Elevations of the western tablelands are about 1,600–1,800 feet above sea level. The most western county on the Upper Peninsula contains 488 lakes and 1,200 miles of streams in a wilderness area containing the Cisco Chain of Lakes near the Wisconsin border, and the largest lake in the state, Lake Gogebic. The Chippewa Indian name Gogebic means "where trout rising make rings on the water." The largest county is Marquette with about 835 inland lakes, 1,906 miles of streams, and a Lake Superior 68-mile shoreline.

LICENSES

Resident licenses are issued to persons who have lived in the state for at least 6 consecutive months prior to an application for a license; and to members of the U.S. Armed Forces officially stationed in Michigan; and to military personnel who were legal residents at the time of their enlistment or induction into service and return home on leave or furlough. Property owners not living in Michigan are not entitled to purchase resident licenses. Nonresidents may not hunt Raccoon, or obtain licenses to trap any animals. All persons 17 or more years of age must possess licenses to fish inland waters except on their private lands. A resident's wife may obtain a free identification license to fish, and is not required to purchase a Trout stamp if one is affixed to her husband's license. A Cisco net license is required to take Cisco from mid-November to mid-December in designated inland lakes.

Regardless of age, all persons must possess licenses to hunt on land other than their own farm properties. A juvenile under the age of 17 may procure a hunting license only by an application of a parent or legal guardian, and must be accompanied by an older person chosen by a parent or guardian while hunting on land other than his own residence. Licenses to hunt Deer with firearms are issued to persons 14 or more years of age, but juveniles under 14 may hunt Deer only with bow and arrow. Archery Deer hunting licenses are not valid during firearms seasons, and an archer must obtain a regular Deer hunting license to hunt with bow and arrow during a gun season. Bear may be taken under a Deer license, or with a Bear stamp affixed to a small game license. It is unlawful to possess a live Bear taken in Michigan, and a special permit is required to trap Bears. Residents living on enclosed farm lands may hunt or trap there without licenses except to take Deer, Beaver, and Otter. All persons 16 or more years of age must purchase a federal "Duck" stamp to take migratory game birds.

Resident license fees: Annual fishing (except Trout), $2.00; small game hunting, $3.00; regular Deer hunting, $5.00; archery Deer hunting, $5.00; trapping Beaver and Otter, $2.00; trapping other furbearers, $3.00; camp permit for Deer hunting, $10.00; bear stamp, $2.00; federal "Duck" stamp, $3.00; trout stamp, $2.00; Cisco net stamp, $1.00.

Nonresident license fees: Annual fishing (except Trout), $5.00; fishing 15 consecutive days (except Trout), $4.00; small game hunting, $20.00; regular Deer hunting, $35.00; archery Deer hunting, $15.00; hunting on private shooting preserves, $5.00; Bear stamp, $2.00; federal "Duck" stamp, $3.00; Trout stamp, $2.00.

HUNTING AND TRAPPING

Game animals: Bear, Deer, Cottontail Rabbit, Snowshoe Rabbit (Varying Hare), Mink, Raccoon, Squirrels (Black, Gray), Woodchuck. OPEN HUNTING SEASONS:* Bear—archery, October to early November except in Keweenah County; firearms, first 2 weeks in September and during month of October in Zone 1 except in Keweenah County, and first week of October in Zone 2, from opening date of the waterfowl or small game season to early November in Zone 3, and in all zones during the regular Deer hunting season. Deer of either sex may be taken in 46 designated areas during special seasons. Deer—archery, October 1 to early November except in Allegan County, where the season extends to mid-December; firearms, 2 weeks during November. Mink—Nov. 1– Dec. 31 in Zone 1, and extended to Jan. 31 in Zones 2 and 3. Rabbits —Oct. 1 through February, except that the season does not open until late October in Zone 3. Raccoon—Oct. 1–Dec. 15 in Zone 1, and from late October through December in Zone 2 and 3. Squirrels—about 6

---

* Check current state regulations.

weeks in October and November. Woodchuck—no closed season in Zone 1, Oct. 1–Jan. 31 in Zone 2, and late October to January in Zone 3. Nonresidents may not hunt Raccoon. BAG LIMITS: Bear—1 per year. Deer —1 except under a special camp permit, parties of 4 or more licensed Deer hunters may take one extra Buck for camp use. Rabbits—5 per day and 50 per season in the aggregate. Squirrels—5 per day and 50 per season in the aggregate. Mink, Raccoon, and Woodchuck—no limits.

Furbearing animals: Badger, Beaver, Bobcat, Coyote, Fisher, Fox, Canada Lynx, Marten, Mink, Muskrat, Opossum, Otter, Raccoon, Skunk, Weasel, Wolf. OPEN TRAPPING SEASONS:* Badger—Nov. 1–Jan. 31. Beaver and Otter—spring season set annually. Bobcat, Lynx—Zone 1, no closed season; Zone 2, Dec. 15–Feb. 15; Zone 3, no open season. Bobcats may not be trapped in Zone 2, or hunted south of State Highway 55 on the Lower Peninsula, in Crawford County or Oscoda County lying west of State Highway 33. Mink, Muskrat—late October through December in Zone 1, mid-November to mid-January in Zone 2, late November through January in Zone 3 except that on Crow Island State Game area (Saginaw County), the season extends to April 1. Raccoon— late October to mid-December in Zone 1, mid-November to mid-December in Zone 2, late November through December in Zone 3. No bag or possession limits. Traps may not be set out or staked until 12:00 o'clock noon on the opening day. FULLY PROTECTED: Caribou, Elk, Moose, Fox Squirrels, Fisher, Marten—no open seasons. NOT PROTECTED: Coyote, Fox, Opossum, Skunk, Red Squirrel, Weasel, and Wolf may be taken at any time. Bounties: Bobcat, $5.00 (Upper Peninsula only); male Coyote, $15.00, and female Coyote, $20.00; Red Fox, $5.00. It is unlawful to possess a wild live Skunk.

A legal Buck is a male Deer with antlers not less than 3 inches above the skull. Dogs may be used to hunt Bear, Fox, Opossum, Raccoon, and game birds, but any dog running or tracking Deer may be killed by an officer.

Game birds: Coot, Ducks (except Canvasback and Redhead), Gallinule, Geese (except Ross's), Ruffed Grouse (Partridge), Sharp-tailed Grouse, Merganser, Ring-necked Pheasant, Prairie Chicken, Rails, Sora, Wilson's Snipe, Woodcock. OPEN SEASONS:* Coot, Ducks, Gallinule, Merganser, Rails, Sora, Wilson's Snipe—early October to early November. Geese—early October to mid-December. Grouse—about 6 weeks during October and November including shorter seasons in designated areas. Pheasant—about 10 days to 3 weeks in designated areas during October and November. Prairie Chicken—about 6 weeks after October 1 except in designated areas of Zone 1, and no open seasons in Zones

---

* Check current state regulations.

2 and 3. Woodcock—about 6 weeks after October 1 in Zones 1 and 2, and from late October to mid-November in Zone 3. Shooting preserves —Sept 15–March 31. FULLY PROTECTED: Canvasback and Redhead Ducks, Ross's Goose—no open seasons. NOT PROTECTED: Crow, English Sparrow, and Starling may be taken at any time. Landowners and farmers may kill Hawks and Owls when they are doing actual damage to domestic animals or poultry.

FIREARMS

The use of any firearms other than a shotgun not larger than 10 gauge, or any automatic, or hand-operated shotgun capable of holding more than 3 shells in the magazine and barrel combined is prohibited. A regular Deer hunting license is required during Deer firearms season to carry or transport any rifle other than a .22 caliber rimfire, or a shotgun with bucket shot, ball load, or cut shells. Transporting firearms, slingshots, bows and arrows during closed seasons is prohibited unless the person has a valid hunting license in his possession, and is traveling to a hunting camp during 5 days preceding the opening date of a season. Hunting with a pistol or revolver requires a hunting license in addition to a concealed weapon permit. No license is required to transport bows and arrows, or firearms (except pistols and revolvers) from or to a target range, trap or skeet shooting grounds, providing that such weapons are enclosed in a case, or within the trunk of a motor vehicle.

Only blank cartridges may be used in pistols or revolvers while training hunting dogs during the training season, July 15–April 1.

Shooting hours: Sunday hunting is prohibited in Branch, Hillsdale, Lenawee, Livingston, and Macomb counties, and landowners may grant permission in Jackson County; not on another person's land in Lapeer, Shiawassee, Tuscalo, and Washtenaw counties; or in Monroe County except for migratory waterfowl in Lake Erie marshes, and in Huron, Sanilae, and St. Clair counties for migratory waterfowl upon the waters of Lake Huron, Lake St. Clair, Saginaw Bay, and St. Clair River. Shooting hours: sunrise to sunset except that between March 1–Sept. 1, hours are from 6:00 A.M.–7:00 P.M. The opening day of the waterfowl season starts at 12:00 noon.

FISHING

Game fish: Black Bass (Largemouth, Smallmouth), Speckled or Strawberry Bass, Bluegill, Crappie (Calico or Strawberry Bass), Grayling, Muskellunge, Yellow Perch, Northern Pike, Pike-perch (Walleyed Pike), landlocked Salmon, Sturgeon, Common or Pumpkinseed Sunfish, Trout (Brook, Brown, Lake or Mackinaw, Rainbow), Whitefish. OPEN SEASONS:*

* Check current state regulations.

Black Bass—June 1 to mid-September in all Trout lakes and streams; mid-June to Dec. 31 in Lake St. Clair, Detroit, and St. Clair Rivers; June 1–Dec. 31 in the Great Lakes, St. Marys River, and other lakes and streams. Muskellunge, Northern Pike, Pike-perch—late April to mid-September except in Saginaw Bay, mid-April to early March; Lakes Huron, Michigan, and Superior, late May to March 31; and at any time in Betsie Lake (Benzie County), Charlevoix and Round lakes (Charlevoix County), Bar Lake at Arcadia, Manistee and Portage lakes (Manistee County), Pere Marquette Lake (Mason County), Muskegon, Spring, and White lakes (Muskegon County), Macatowa and Spring lakes (Ottawa County), Muskegon River downstream from Rogers Dam (Mecosta County), Lake Erie, Lake St. Clair, Detroit, St. Clair, and St. Marys rivers. Brook, Brown, and Rainbow Trout—late April to mid-September. Lake or Mackinaw Trout—late April to mid-September in Trout lakes and Trout streams; Nov. 1–Sept. 30 in Lake Huron, Lake St. Clair, Detroit, St. Clair, and St. Marys rivers; mid-November to mid-October in Lake Michigan; early November to early October in Lake Superior; at any time in other lakes and non-Trout streams. Rainbow or Steelhead Trout—June 1–Nov. 30 from the Soo Rapids, U.S. Power Canal and tailrace, North and South Canals, locks and approaches, between the International Railway bridge and a line drawn from the ferry dock immediately below St. Marys Falls in Sault Ste. Marie, Ontario, but not including the Michigan Northern Power Canal. Sturgeon—no open seasons in Trout lakes and Trout streams; no closed seasons in the Great Lakes, Lake St. Clair, Detroit, St. Clair, and St. Marys rivers, but only during the month of February in all other lakes and streams. Other game fish—late April to mid-September in Trout lakes and Trout streams; at any time in other waters. INLAND WATERS: All waters in Michigan except the Great Lakes, Lake St. Clair, Detroit, Saginaw, St. Clair, and St. Marys rivers are classified as inland waters including tributaries to the above lakes and rivers.

A sport fisherman may use only 2 lines under his immediate control and a total of not more than 4 hooks baited with natural or artificial bait for still fishing, casting, trolling, or ice fishing, except Smelt may be taken with any number of hooks on one line. It is unlawful to use a single hook more than three-eighths of an inch between the point of hook and shank to fish in a Trout stream except from June 1 to Labor Day. Dip nets may be used April 1–May 31 on the Lower Peninsula, and during the month of May on the Upper Peninsula to catch Carp, Dogfish, Gar, Mullet, Smelt, and Suckers in non-Trout streams (except Muskegon River) and designated Trout streams. Hoop nets may be used to take Burbot in designated streams from Dec. 15 through February. Carp, Dogfish, and Gar may be taken from designated inland waters with artificial lights, spears, bow and arrows May 1–Aug. 15. Artificial lights, spears, bow and arrows may be used to take nongame fish at any time from the Great Lakes not otherwise closed to spearing except during closed seasons provided by commercial fishing laws.

Ice fishing: Carp, Catfish, Cisco, Dogfish, Gar, Lake Trout, Mullet, Muskellunge, Northern Pike, Pilotfish or Menominee Whitefish, Redhorse Sheepshead, Smelt, and Suckers may be speared through ice during January and February in designated areas. Sturgeon may be speared in designated waters only during the month of February. Spears, bows and arrows may be used on Lake St. Clair, Detroit, St. Clair, and St. Marys rivers to take Bullhead, Carp, Catfish, Dogfish, Gar, Herring, Lake Trout, Mullet, Muskellunge, Perch, Pike-perch, Northern Pike, Pilotfish, Redhorse, Shad, Sheepshead, Smelt, Sturgeon, Sucker, Trout, and Whitefish, Pike-perch may be speared through ice on Lake Huron at any time for personal use. All shelters and structures on ice must be identified on the outside with the name and address of the owner in letters (not less than 2 inches high) of insoluble material. Unless structures are removed before the ice becomes unsafe, they will be removed and destroyed or stored and costs assessed against owners in addition to other penalties.

The Au Sable, Boardman, and Platte rivers on the Lower Peninsula, and the Carp, Huron, and Two Hearted rivers on the Upper Peninsula are famous Trout streams. Lake St. Clair, known not only as one of the best Muskellunge waters in the country, also offers excellent Black Bass, Northern Pike, and Walleye fishing. The Raber Bay area of St. Mary's River, Green Bay between Escanaba and Sturgeon Bay, the Drummond Island area of Lake Huron, and Isle Royale National Park are exceptional pike waters.

Good fishing is available in state parks, national and state forests. There are more than 500 public fishing sites on lakes plus about 235 on streams throughout Michigan. Boat launching ramps have been provided at most public fishing sites, and no fees are charged for their use. Hunting and trapping are prohibited in all state parks except the following: Porcupine Mountains, Tahquamenon Falls, and posted areas of the Algonac, Benzie, Cheboygan, Detour, Hartwick Pines, P. H. Hoeft (no trapping), Hoffmaster, Indian Lake, Ludington (Bear and Deer only), Palms Book, Petoskey, Silver Lake, Sleeper, Sterling (no hunting), Tawas Point, Van Riper, Warren Dunes (no trapping) J. W. Wells, and Wilderness state parks.

MICHIGAN STATE FORESTS

Upper Peninsula: Escanaba River (163,682 acres) near Gwinn in Marquette County; *Grand Sable* (202,390 acres) near Shingleton and containing Kingston Lake in Alger County, Ross and Twin lakes in Schoolcraft County; *Lake Superior* (224,949 acres) near Newberry and extending to Lake Superior includes the Two Hearted River, Bodi, Culhane, Holland, Muskellunge, Perch, Pike, and Pratt lakes in Luce County; *Mackinac* (308,939 acres) near Newberry, and extending to Lake Michigan includes the Black River, Garnet, Little Brevort, and Milakookia rivers in Mackinac County; *Manistique River* (163,873 acres) near Manistique in Schoolcraft County; *Munuscong* (116,866 acres) near Sault Ste. Marie, includes Duke's Lake in Chippewa County; *Sturgeon River* (215,802 acres) near Iron Mountain in Dickinson County.

Lower Peninsula: Allegan (32,416 acres) on Kalamazoo River at Allegan in Allegan County; *Alpena* (74,510 acres) near Alpena and Oscoda, with Thunder Bay River in Alpena County and Van Etten Lake in Iosco County; *Au Sable* (290,432 acres) on Au Sable and Manistee rivers with Guernsey, Higgins, and Jones lakes near Grayling in Crawford County; *Black Lake* (145,906 acres) includes Black and Twin lakes, near Onaway in Cheboygan County; *Chippewa River* (60,698 acres) includes Tubbs Lake, near Midland in Mecosta County and Black Creek in Midland County; *Fife Lake* (188,939 acres) near Traverse City, with Grass Lake, Lake Ann, and Platte River in Benzie County, Boardman River, Arbutus, Fife, Spider and Spring lakes in Grand Traverse County, Healy Lake in Manistee County, and Long Lake in Wexford County; *Hardwood* (188,484 acres) contains Pigeon River and Weber Lake near Indian River in Cheboygan County; *Houghton Lake* (325,492 acres) with Pike Lake in Clare County, Goose and Long lakes in Missaukee County, Muskegon River, Houghton and Twin lakes in Roscommon County; *Ogemaw* (181,882 acres) near West Branch with the Tittabawassee River, Hoister and House lakes in Gladwin County, Ambrose Lake and Rifle River in Ogemaw County; *Pere Marquette* (59,724 acres) near Baldwin with Little Leverents Lake, Bray and Silver creeks in Lake County; *Pigeon River* (176,157 acres) near Gaylord with Beaver Island in Charlevoix County, Chub Creek, Bear, Marjory, Pickerel, and Round lakes in Otsego County; *Thunder Bay River* (189,438 acres) near Atlanta with Avery, Clear, Ess, Fifteen, Little Wolf, and McCormick lakes in Montmorency County, Big Creek and Muskrat Lake in Oscoda County.

STATE PARKS

Algonac (980 acres) on St. Clair River, north of Algonac in St. Clair County; *Aloha* (66 acres) south of Cheboygan, on Mullet Lake in Cheboygan County; *Baraga* (41 acres) on Keweenaw Bay in Baraga County; *Bay City* (196 acres) on Saginaw Bay, north of Bay City in Bay County; *Benzie* (180 acres) on Platte River and Lake Michigan in Benzie County; *Brimley* (105 acres) on Whitefish Bay of Lake Superior, 12 miles southwest of Sault Ste. Marie in Chippewa County; *Burt Lake* (407 acres) near

Indian River village in Cheboygan County; *D. H. Day* (32 acres) on Sleeping Bear Lake, Lake Michigan, in Leelanau County; *Dodge Brothers* (no. 4) 78 acres on Cass Lake, southwest of Pontiac in Oakland County; *East Tawas* (16 acres) on Tawas Bay, Lake Huron, in Iosco County; *Fort Wilkins* (106 acres) between Lake Fanny Hooe and Lake Superior on tip of Keweenaw Peninsula northeast of Copper Harbor in Keweenaw County; *Gladwin* (17 acres) on the Cedar River in city of Gladwin in Gladwin County; *Gogebic Lake* (361 acres) 12 miles northeast of Marenisco in Gogebic County; *Grand Haven* (44 acres) at mouth of Grand River near Grand Haven in Ottawa County; *Harrisville* (77 acres) on Lake Huron at Harrisville in Alcona County; *Hartwick Pines* (8,942 acres) on East Branch Au Sable River, 7 miles northeast of Grayling in Crawford County; *W. J. Hayes* (677 acres) on Round Lake (90 acres) and Wamplers Lake west of Clinton in Jackson, Lenawee, and Washtenaw counties; *Higgins Lake* (312 acres) southwest of Roscommon in Roscommon County; *P. H. Hoeft* (300 acres) on Lake Huron northwest of Rogers City; *Holland* (43 acres) on Lake Michigan, west of Holland in Ottawa County; *Interlochen* (186 acres) on Duck and Green lakes, 15 miles southwest of Traverse City in Grand Traverse County; *Lakeport* (374 acres) on Lake Huron, 10 miles north of Port Huron in St. Clair County; *Ludington* (3,597 acres) contains Hamlin and Lost lakes, Sable River, 8 miles north of Ludington in Mason County; *Mackinac Island* (2,180 acres) in Strait of Mackinac with access by ferry from Mackinaw City and St. Ignace; *M. J. McLain* (338 acres) on Lake Superior and Bear Lake, west of Calumet in Houghton County; *Michilimackinac* (27 acres) in Strait of Mackinac near Mackinaw City, in Cheboygan and Emmet Counties; *William Mitchell* (26 acres) on Cadillac and Mitchell lakes, west of Cadillac in Wexford County; *Muskegon* (1,357 acres) on Muskegon Lake and Channel, and Lake Michigan, west of North Muskegon in Muskegon County; *Onaway* (158 acres) on Black Lake north of Onaway in Presque Isle County; *Orchard Beach* (211 acres) on Lake Michigan, north of Manistee in Manistee County; *Otsego Lake* (67 acres) south of Gaylord in Otsego County; *Palms Book* (308 acres) 12 miles northwest of Manistique in Schoolcraft County; *Porcupine Mountains* (58,170 acres) on Big Carp and Little Carp rivers, Lake of the Clouds, Mirror Lake, and Lake Superior, 20 miles west of Ontonagan in Godebic and Ontonagon counties; *Silver Lake* (1,754 acres) on Lake Michigan and Silver Lake, southwest of Hart in Oceana County; *A. E. Sleeper* (921 acres) near tip of the "Thumb" on Saginaw Bay, Lake Huron, northeast of Caseville in Huron County; *Sterling Monroe* (586 acres) on Lake Erie at Monroe in Monroe County; *Straits* (41 acres) on the Strait of Mackinac at St. Ignace in Mackinac County; *Tahquamenon Falls* (18,563 acres) on Tahquamenon River with the Big Falls (Upper, 40 ft.; Lower, series of cascades) northeast of Newberry in Chippewa and Luce counties; Traverse (38 acres) on Grand Traverse Bay, Lake Michigan, east of Traverse City in Grand Traverse County; *Van Riper* (886 acres) on Lake Michigamme, 21 miles west of Ishpeming in Marquette County; *J. M. Wells* (931 acres) on Green Bay, 2 miles south of Cedar River in Menominee County; *White Cloud* (90 acres) at White Cloud village near lakes and streams in Newaygo County; *Wilderness* (8,035 acres) on Strait of Mackinac, 8 miles west of Mackinaw City in Emmet County; *Wilson* (32 acres) on Budd Lake north of Harrison in Clare County; *Young* (563 acres) on Lake Charlevoix north of Boyne City in Charlevoix County.

STATE RECREATION AREAS

Excellent fishing waters, hunting, winter sports, hiking and bridle trails, and other forms of recreation within 60 miles of Detroit. *Bald Mountain* (2,500 acres) with small lakes and Trout streams, 7 miles north of Pontiac in Oakland County; *Brighton* (4,501 acres) contains Appleton, Bishop and other lakes southwest of Brighton in Livingston County; *Highland* (5,407 acres) contains Haven Hill, Teeple, and several lakes, Teeple Hill Winter Sports Area, 17 miles west of Pontiac in Oakland County; *Holly* (6,082 acres) contains Valley and Wildwood lakes, 12 miles north of Pontiac in Oakland County; *Island Lake* (2,979 acres) on the Huron River east of Brighton in Livingston County; *Metamora* (683 acres) on Minnewanna Lake near village of Metamora in Lapeer County; *Ortonville* (3,771 acres) with several lakes and skiing in season in Oakland and Lapeer counties; *Pinckney* (9,500 acres) contains numerous lakes including Silver Lake, east of Gregory in Livingston and Washtenaw counties; *Pontiac Lake* (3,600 acres) 7 miles west of Pontiac in Oakland County; *Proud Lake* (3,000 acres) contains Commerce, Proud, Reed, and other lakes near Milford in Oakland County; *Rochester-Utica* (822 acres) on Clinton River and historic Kalamazoo Canal near Rochester and Utica in Macomb and Oakland counties; *Waterloo* (14,578 acres) contains Big Portage Lake, several fishing lakes, and 2 Trout ponds set aside solely for fly fishermen, between Jackson and Chelsea in Jackson and Washtenaw counties; *Yankee Springs* contains Gun Lake and other lakes near the Barry County Game Area (13,000 acres) south of Middleville in Barry County.

Licenses, permits, regulations, and information about current seasons, bag and possession limits, and camping may be obtained from the Director, Michigan Department of Conservation, Lansing, 48926; and field offces at Baldwin, Baraga, Crystal Falls, Detroit, Escanaba, Gaylord, Gladwin, Imlay City, Jackson, Marquette, Mio, Newberry, Roscommon, Plainwell, Sault Ste. Marie, Traverse City, and Wakefield. Write to the Michigan

Tourist Council, Lansing, 48926, for the *Boat Launching Guide to Michigan Water Wonderland*, and *Michigan Calendar of Events*.

MINNESOTA

Area: 84,682 square miles (land area—80,009 square miles); rank in nation—14
Bird: Loon (*Gavia immer*)
Capital city: St. Paul below St. Anthony Falls on the Mississippi River, in Ramsey County; population (1960)—313,411; rank in state—2
Counties: 87
Elevation: Highest, Misquah Hills (2,230 ft.) in Cook County; lowest, Lake Superior (602 ft.)
Flower: Lady Slipper (*Cypripedium reginae*), adopted 1902
Geographic center: 10 miles southwest of Brainerd in Crow Wing County
Nicknames: Gopher State, Land of the Sky Blue Waters, North Star State, Wheat State, Bread and Butter State
Population (1960): 3,413,864; rank in nation—18
Tree: Red Pine (*Pinus resinosa*), also called Norway Pine, adopted 1953

Minnesota is bordered by Lake Superior and Wisconsin on the east, Iowa on the south, North and South Dakota on the west, and the Canadian provinces of Manitoba and Ontario on the north.

The north central highlands covered with evergreen forests, thousands of lakes among a maze of streams form a watershed for the Mississippi River and Red River of the North systems. The "Big Woods" area in a portion of the hardwood belt is in central and southeastern Minnesota. The remainder of the state is a rolling treeless plain broken in the southwest by the Coteau des Prairies. There are several muskeg marshes and swamps in the north, and the remote Northwest Angle between Manitoba and Lake of the Woods is accessible only by air, watercraft, and dogsled. A shallow small stream leaves Lake Itasca in the highlands to meander southward as the Mississippi River before reaching the Twin Cities of Minneapolis and St. Paul at the head of navigation. The Red River of the North flows northward from Lake Traverse to cross the international boundary below Winnipeg in Manitoba Province. The St. Louis River also leaves the highlands on an eastward course to Lake Superior. The St. Croix River known as the "Rhine of America," on the Wisconsin border and the Minnesota River from the southwest pour their waters into the Mississippi River.

There are about 11,000 lakes of 25 or more acres in this "Land of 10,000 Lakes" and the fabulous Boundary Waters Canoe Area is a chain of lakes and streams in the Superior National Forest contiguous with the

Quetico Provincial Park in Canada. The Minnesota-Canada boundary is an inland waterway from Pigeon Bay on Lake Superior to Lake of the Woods. This historic canoe route of fur traders and *voyageurs* includes the Pigeon River, North and South Fork lakes, Granite River, Gunflint and Little Gunflint lakes, Lily, Magnetic, Maraboeuf, Moose, and Mountain lakes, Pine Lake and River, Rat, Rose, Round, Saganaga, South, and Watab lakes in Cook County; Basswood Lake and River, Birch, Carp, Cypress, Knife, and Little Knife lakes, Knife River, Melon, Seed, Sucker, and Swamp lakes in Lake County; Crooked Lake in Lake and St. Louis counties; Bottle and Iron lakes, Lac la Croix, Loon Lake and River, Namakan, Sand Point, and Little Vermillion lakes in St. Louis County; Rainy Lake and River in Koochiching, Lake of the Woods, and St. Louis counties; and Lake of the Woods in Lake of the Woods and Roseau counties.

Other boundary waters are the Bois de Sioux River and Red River of the North on the North Dakota border; Big Stone and Mud Lakes, Lake Hendrick, Lake Traverse, and the Bois de Sioux River shared with South Dakota; Little Spirit Lake (Jackson County), Iowa Lake (Jackson and Nobles counties), Iowa, Okampeedan or Tuttle, and Swag lakes (Martin County) on the Iowa line; the Mississippi and St. Croix rivers forming the Wisconsin boundary except for a few miles south of Duluth.

Among large lakes outside of national forests are Rainy Lake (345 square miles) and Lake of the Woods (with 14,000 islands) west of International Falls on the Canadian boundary; Red Lake (451 square miles) on Red River in the northwestern wilderness; Kabetogama Lake on Ash River and linked to Namakan Lake; Pelican Lake near the Lake Indian Reservation; and Vermillion Lakes adjacent to the Superior National Forest. Mille Lacs Lake east of Brainerd has a 150-mile shoreline, and Lake Pepin (20 miles long) on the Mississippi River is below Red Wing. There are dozens of lakes with identical names such as Clear, Long, Muddy, Round, and Twin lakes. On beautiful North Shore Drive (u.s. 61) along Lake Superior from Duluth to the Pigeon River are several state parks, the Grand Portage, Caribou, Gunflint, and Sawbill trails to boundary waters, and connecting lakes and streams in the Superior National Forest.

LICENSES

Resident licenses are issued to any citizen who has maintained a legal residence in the state for at least 6 months immediately preceding an application for a license; to any domestic or foreign corporation which has conducted a licensed business for 10 or more years at an established place in Minnesota; and to full-time students from other states while they attend a private or public educational institution in Minnesota; and to military personnel of the U.S. Armed Forces stationed within the state. Any resident who is a member of the U.S. Armed Forces stationed outside of Minnesota, and returns on leave or furlough, may hunt and fish without regular licenses provided that he carries his official leave or furlough papers. All regular coupons, seals, and tags required by law are given to him without charge. Free identification cards instead of licenses may be issued to any citizen receiving old age assistance, and to his wife and minor children living with him.

An alien living in Minnesota must purchase nonresident licenses unless he has made a declaration to become a citizen in accordance with U.S. statutes. An alien spouse of a citizen resident is granted resident privileges to take, buy, sell, transport, or possess wild animals.

Free fishing licenses are issued to blind persons, and to any citizen of a foreign country while he attends a public, private, or parochial school. Special permits are issued without charge to licensed hunters allowing them to hunt or shoot from a standing vehicle if they are paraplegics or otherwise physically unable to walk. Courtesy nonresident fish and game licenses may be issued without charge by the State Conservation commissioner to any person officially employed in a federal or state fish and game or conservation department who is in Minnesota to consult or cooperate with the commissioner, and to officials of other states, the federal government, foreign countries, and officers or representatives of conservation organizations and publications while they are in Minnesota as guests of the governor or commissioner. Municipal corporations and educational institutions maintaining zoological collections may procure special permits without charge to collect specimens of eggs, nests, or wild animals for scientific or exhibition purposes. Free permits are issued to take any protected wild animals damaging private or public property.

Residents under the age of 16 may fish and may trap furbearing animals (except Beaver and Otter) without licenses. Small game may be taken by residents 12–16 years of age without licenses providing that they possess valid firearms safety certificates. No juvenile under the age of 14 may have in his possession or under his control any firearms or airguns of any kind for hunting, target practicing, or any other purpose unless accompanied or under the immediate control of his parent or guardian, unless such juvenile is on land owned or occupied as the usual residence of himself, parent, or guardian. The guardian may be a legal guardian, or a person over the age of 21 who has been selected by the parent or legal guardian to supervise the juvenile. Only small game may be taken without a license by residents under 12 years of age. All persons 16 or more years of age must procure a federal "Duck" stamp to take migratory game birds.

A nonresident under the age of 16 may fish without a license if his parent or guardian has a valid nonresident fishing license, and any fish caught by the juvenile must be counted in the bag limits of the parent or guardian.

Reciprocal agreements permit fishing in boundary waters of states provided that the residents and nonresidents hold valid licenses issued by Minnesota or the state sharing the lakes and rivers, but fishermen must comply with the regulations of the state which issued the license. Commercial fishing is permitted in Lake-of-the-Woods, Rainy Lake, Lake Superior, Namakan and Sand Point lakes, Upper and Lower Red lakes, the Minnesota River from Mankato to the Mississippi River, and from the St. Croix River junction to St. Anthony Falls on the Mississippi River.

Resident license fees: Individual angling, $2.25; combination angling (husband and wife), $2.75; dark or fish house used for ice fishing, $1.00; dark house spearing (additional to angling license), $1.00; whitefish netting per 100 feet (additional to angling license), $1.00; hunting small game, $3.00; archery Deer hunting, $5.00; firearms Deer hunting, $5.00; Moose hunting, $3.50; federal "Duck" stamp, $3.00; trapping furbearing animals except Beaver (additional to hunting license), $3.00; trapping Beaver (additional to hunting license), $2.50; fur dealer, $20.00; fur and game farm (including Deer), $5.00; Muskrat farm, $2.50; private fish hatchery, $5.00; dressing or tanning raw fur, $2.00; taxidermist, $2.00; annual vehicle permit for state parks, $2.00.

Nonresident license fees: Individual angling, $5.25; combination angling, $8.25; hunting small game and unprotected animals by firearms including bow and arrow, $26.00; hunting Deer and unprotected animals by firearms including bow and arrow, $50.25; hunting Deer and unprotected animals by bow and arrow only, $10.25; Moose hunting in Northwest Angle, $50.25; federal "Duck" stamp (additional to small game license), $3.00; dealer in raw fur, $200.00.

HUNTING AND TRAPPING

Big game animals: Caribou, Deer, Elk, Moose. OPEN SEASONS:* Deer —bow and arrow, during October statewide, and 3 weeks of December in designated areas; firearms including bow and arrow, about one week in November divided into several shorter shooting periods in designated areas. Camp Riley in Morrison County may hold archery Deer hunting on October week ends subject to regulations by military authorities. Moose— about 10 days in October, in the Northwest Angle. BAG LIMITS: Deer—1 (either sex) per year. Antlered Moose—1 per year.

Small game animals: Rabbits (Cottontail, Jack Snowshoe), Raccoon, Squirrel (Fox, Gray). OPEN SEASONS:* Rabbits—October through March.

---

* Check current state regulations.

Raccoon—October through December. Squirrels—mid-September through December.

Furbearing animals: Badger, Beaver, Fisher, Marten, Mink, Muskrat, Otter, Raccoon. OPEN TRAPPING SEASONS: Badger, Mink, Muskrat, Raccoon—for about 6 weeks after November 1. Beaver—set annually, and does not exceed 45 days between November 1 and May 31. Otter—set annually, and does not exceed 15 days between Nov. 1 and April 30. Unprotected animals may be trapped in Ramsey and Rochester counties—Nov. 2–March 1. BAG LIMITS: Beaver—10 per year. Badger, Mink, Muskrat, Raccoon—no limits. FULLY PROTECTED: Caribou, Elk, Fisher, Marten. NOT PROTECTED: Bear (except in Cook, Lake, and St. Louis counties during firearms Deer season), Bobcat, Civet Cat, Coyote, Fox, Gopher, Groundhog, Canada Lynx, Porcupine, Skunk, Weasel, and Wolf may be taken at any time. Bounties: Bear, $10; Cub Bear, $5; Bobcat, Canada Lynx, $15 each (regardless of age); Coyote (Brush Wolf), $25; Cub Timber Wolf, $25; Adult Timber Wolf, $35; Common Gopher or Ground Squirrel, 3 cents; Pocket Gopher, 20 cents; Groundhog, 15 cents; Rattlesnake, $1.

Game birds: Coot, Ducks (except Canvasback and Redhead), Gallinule, Geese (except Ross's Goose), Grouse (Ruffed, Sharp-tailed or White-fronted), Merganser, Partridge (Chukar, Hungarian), Pheasant, Prairie Chicken (Pinnated Grouse), Quail, Rails, Scaup, Sora, Wilson's Snipe, Woodcock. OPEN SEASONS:* Coot, Ducks, Merganser, Scaup—early October to early November. Gallinule, Rails, Sora—mid-September to early November. Geese—early October to mid-December. Ruffed Grouse, Wilson's Snipe, Woodcock—mid-September to early November. Sharp-tailed Grouse—mid-September to mid-October. Hungarian Partridge, Pheasant—late October through November. FULLY PROTECTED: Crane, Canvasback and Redhead Ducks, Mourning Dove, Ross's Goose, Canada Spruce and Pinnated Grouse, Chukar Partridge, Upland Plover, Quail, Swan, Wild Turkey—no open seasons. NOT PROTECTED: Blackbirds, Cormorants, Crows, Magpies, Great Horned Owls, English Sparrows, and Starlings may be killed at any time.

FIREARMS

Deer may not be taken with a rifle of smaller caliber than 23; or with cartridges less than 1¾ inches in length, unless the gun is of 25 caliber or larger. All cartridges must contain a soft point or expanding bullet. Single slugs may be used in shotguns to take Deer, but buckshot or fine shot are prohibited. Big game may be hunted with longbows having a pull of not less than 40 pounds at full draw, and steel barbless arrows with bicarbon

* Check current state regulations.

steel heads having the blade or blades not less than a 3-inch circumference for 3 or more blades (not less than 1 inch wide for a single 2-inch blade) with a minimum weight of all types 110 grain.

No shotgun larger than 10 gauge, or capable of holding more than 3 shells in the magazine and chamber combined may be used to take migratory game birds. It is unlawful to use a pistol or revolver for killing unprotected animals.

Shooting hours: Sunrise to sunset, except Deer—archery, 5:30 A.M.– 6:00 P.M.; firearms, 6:30 A.M.–5:00 P.M. Hungarian Partridge, Pheasant; Ducks—opening day 12:00 o'clock noon to sunset; other days 10:00 A.M. to sunset. Shooting starts at 12:00 o'clock noon on the open day of a Duck season.

A hunting or trapping license may be revoked for one year from the date of violation if the visible portion of a hunter's or trapper's cap and outer coat are not bright red or blaze orange (or covered with such colors) in any region open to taking Deer with firearms. Any dog pursuing or killing Caribou, Deer, or Moose may be shot by a game warden.

FISHING

Game fish: Black Bass (Largemouth, Smallmouth), Rock Bass, White Bass, Bluegill or Sunfish, Catfish, Crappie, Muskellunge, Pickerel, Great Northern Pike, Sauger (Sand Pike), Walleyed Pike, Trout (Brook, Brown, Lake, Rainbow, or Steelhead). OPEN SEASONS: Black Bass—June 1– Feb. 15 in all waters east and north of U.S. Highway 53 from Duluth to International Falls, and opens a week earlier in other waters. Muskellunge, Great Northern Pike, Pickerel, Walleyed Pike, Sauger—mid-May to Feb. 15. Trout (except Lake)—early May to mid-September, except in Cook, Lake, and St. Louis counties, March 30–Nov. 30. Lake Trout—January until September; Lake Superior Trout (only under special permit)—all year except about 4 weeks in October. Other fish—no closed seasons. Grayling and Splake—no open seasons except under special regulations.

It is unlawful to fish in any waters except boundary waters of the states of Iowa, Minnesota, Wisconsin, North and South Dakotas by angling with more than one line and one hook, or 3 artificial flies for Black Bass, Rock Bass, Crappie, Sunfish, and Trout, but a single artificial bait or trolling spoon may contain more than one hook. Northern Pike or Pickerel, Catfish, Whitefish, and all rough fish may be taken by spearing through ice from Dec. 1 to Feb. 15. Structures upon ice must be removed on the last day of February, except that in the Canada-Minnesota boundary waters structures may remain until March 31. The name and address of the owner and the house license number must be painted on the exterior in letters at least 3 inches in height.

Dip nets, harpoons, spears, bows and arrows may be used to take the following rough fish in all inland waters: Buffalo Fish, Carp, Dogfish, Eel-pout, Gar, Goldeyes, Perch, Sheepshead, Sucker and Tullibee—6 weeks after May 1; and Bullhead, Redhorse, Sucker—6 weeks after May 1 and Dec. 1–Feb. 15.

Frogs: OPEN SEASON: May 15–April 1. POSSESSION LIMIT: 150. A fishing license is required to take Frogs for bait.

There are many famous Bass and Pike lakes, Trout streams, and more than 1,250,000 Trout are stocked in Minnesota waters each year. Ely and Grand Marais are excellent outfitting points for sportsmen. There are ice fishing contests and other winter sports at the St. Paul Winter Carnival, which is usually held in early February for 10 days. Special permits are issued for hunting and trapping in many wildlife refuges.

STATE PARKS

Baptism River (706 acres) on North Shore Drive of Lake Superior, near Illgen City—Lake County; *Bear Head Lake* (4,417 acres) near Tower—St. Louis County; *Beaver Creek Valley* (325 acres) northwest of Caledonia—Houston County; *Camden* (470 acres) in Red River Valley, southwest of Marshall—Lyon County; *Caribou Falls* (88 acres) at mouth of Caribou River on North Shore Drive of Lake Superior, north of Little Marais—Lake County; *James Carley* (211 acres) on North Branch Whitewater River, south of Plainview—Wabasha County; *Cascade River* (1,895 acres) between Lutzen and Grand Marais on North Shore Drive of Lake Superior—Cook County; *Crow Wing* (476 acres) 10 miles south-west of Brainerd—Crow Wing County; *Father Hennepin* (198 acres) on southeastern shore of Mille Lacs Lake at village of Isle—Mille Lacs County; Flandrau (836 acres, lake 209 acres) at New Ulm—Brown County; *Frontenac* (950 acres) at Frontenac on Lake Pepin—Good-hue County; *Gooseberry Falls* (638 acres) at mouth of Gooseberry River on Lake Superior North Shore Drive, 12 miles northeast of Two Harbors—Lake County; *Helmer Myre* (117 acres) at Albert Lea Lake southeast of Albert Lea—Freeborn County; *Interstate** (167 acres) on St. Croix River at Taylors Falls—Chisago County; *Itasca* (31,976 acres) containing more than 150 lakes including Lake Itasca, between Bemidji and Park Rapids—Becker, Clearwater, and Hubbard counties; *Jay Cook* (8,367 acres) on St. Louis River between the village of Thomson in Carlton County and village of Fond de Lac in St. Louis County; *Kaplan Woods* (180 acres) on Straight River, south of Owatonna—Steele County; *Kilen Woods* (172 acres) on Des Moines River, northwest of Jackson—Jackson County; *Lac Qui Parle* (457 acres) on Chippewa and Lac Qui Parle rivers, north-

* Plus 508 acres in Wisconsin.

west of Montevideo—Chippewa and Lac Qui Parle counties; *Kadunce River* (128 acres) on Lake Superior North Shore Drive between Grand Marais and Hoveland—Cook County; *Lake Bemidji* (205 acres) northeast of Bemidji—Beltrami County; *Lake Bronson* (746 acres) east of the town of Bronson—Kittson County; *Lake Carlos* (404 acres) 10 miles north of Alexandria—Kittson County; *Lake Shetek* (263 acres) north of Currie—Murray County; *John A. Latsch* (350 acres) along limestone bluffs Faith, Hope, and Charity on Mississippi River near Whitman Dam, 14 miles north of Winona—Winona County; *Charles A. Lindbergh* (110 acres) on Mississippi River, south of Little Falls—Morrison County; *McCarthy Beach* (135 acres) between Side and Sturgeon lakes, 20 miles northwest of Hibbing—St. Louis County; *Mille Lacs Kathio* (6,826 acres) on Rum River, west of Onamia—Mille Lacs County; *Monson Lake* (199 acres) southwest of Sunberg—Swift County; *Nerstrand Woods* (468 acres) on Prairie Creek near Nerstrand—Rice County; *William O'Brien* (180 acres) on St. Croix River, north of Marine-on-St. Croix—Washington County; *Old Crossing* (111 acres) along north bank of Red Lake River, 10 miles northeast of Crookston—Red Lake County; *Old Mill* (285 acres) 10 miles east of Argyle—Marshall County; *Oronoco* (105 acres) at Shady Lake, adjacent to village of Oronoco—Olmsted County; *Pine Tree* (32 acres) at Black Duck Lake, west of Black Duck—Beltrami County; *St. Croix* (30,557 acres) on St. Croix River, east of Hinckley—Pine County; *Savanna Portage* (10,571 acres) north of McGregor—Aitkin County; *Scenic* (2,121 acres) on a peninsula between Coon and Sandwich lakes, 6 miles southeast of Bigfork—Itasca County; *Sibley* (379 acres) on Lake Andrew, 7 miles west of New London—Kandiyohi County; *Split Rock Creek* (228 acres) south of Ihlen—Pipestone County; *Temperance River Falls* (128 acres) on Lake Superior North Shore Drive, near Schroeder—Cook County; *Whitewater* (688 acres) on Whitewater River, between Winona and Rochester—Winona County.

WILDLIFE REFUGES (hunting and fishing)

Aitkin County, Carlton County, Chippewa County, Cloquet Valley (St. Louis County), Floodwood (Aitkins County), Hiawatha (Pipestone County), Kandiyohi County, Le Sauk (Stearns County), McGrath County, Mille Lacs County, Minnesda Lake (Blue Earth County), Mad Goose (Cass County), Monongalia, except in Sibley State Park (Kandiyohi County), Okabena (Nobles County), Owens Lake (Itasca County), and Pine Island (Koochiching County). Only trapping is permitted in Bellwood (Dakota County), Blooming Grove (Waseca County), Brooklyn Center West River Road (Hennepin County), Henley Falls (Yellow Medicine County), Minnesota River (Hennepin County), Ocheda Lake (Nobles County), and Spectacle Lake (Isanti County).

Licenses, regulations, and information about current seasons, bag and possession limits may be obtained from the Commissioner, Department of Conservation, State Office Building, St. Paul.

MISSISSIPPI

Area: 47,223 square miles (land area—46,362 square miles); rank in nation–31
Bird: Mocking Bird (*Mimus polyglottus*), adopted 1944
Capital city: Jackson on the Pearl River in Hinds County; population (1960)—144,422; rank in state–1
Counties: 82
Elevations: Highest, near Iuka, Knob triangulation station in Tishomingo County (806 ft.); lowest, Gulf of Mexico (sea level)
Flower: Magnolia Blossom (*Magnolia grandiflora*), adopted 1952
Geographic center: 9 miles north of west of Carthage, Leake County
Nicknames: Magnolia State, Bayou State, Eagle State, Mudcat State
Population (1960): 2,178,141; rank in nation–29
Tidal shoreline: 359 miles (including islands, bays, and streams to a point where tidal waters narrow to 100 ft. wide)
Tree: Magnolia (*Magnolia grandiflora*), adopted 1938

Mississippi is a Deep South state on the Gulf of Mexico with Alabama on the east, Tennessee on the north, and the Mississippi River cutting an irregular border between Arkansas on the northwest and Louisiana on the southwest. Slender sandy islands along the coast create Mississippi Sound in the Gulf of Mexico.

There are coastal marshlands, a broad prairie region in the east, fertile bottomlands bordering the Mississippi River, and the broad Pontotoc Ridge with narrow valleys in north central Mississippi. The Tombigbee River starts from the northeastern hills on a long journey into Alabama. The Coldwater, Sunflower, and Tallahatchee rivers rise in the north and and their waters to the Yazoo River flowing into the Mississippi River north of Vicksburg. The Big Black River and the Homochitto River join the Mississippi River south of Vicksburg. The southern portion of the Pearl River flows along the Louisiana border in the southwest and empties into Mississippi Sound. The Chickasawhuy and Leaf rivers merge to form the Pascagoula or Singing River flowing into eastern Mississippi Sound at Pascagoula Bay.

LICENSES

Resident licenses are issued to citizens 16 or more years of age who have lived in the state for at least 6 months immediately preceding any application for a license, and to military personnel of the U.S. Armed Forces. Citizens 65 or more years of age may fish and hunt without a license, but must possess a certificate from a circuit clerk or sheriff showing proof of his age and residence. Persons of any age may fish in the county of their residence without a license if not using artificial bait. Nonresident juveniles under 14 years of age are not required to possess fishing licenses or tourist permits. If a nonresident's home state does not issue hunting licenses to residents of Mississippi, or does not have a reciprocity agreement with the Mississippi Game and Fish Commission, such a nonresident is not permitted to purchase a small game, all-game, or 3-day hunting license.

Deer and Turkey licenses and tags are issued only to holders of the basic hunting license. Reciprocity agreements permit the use of Mississippi resident licenses to fish in the state line waters of Pickwick Lake, the Mississippi River, and the Pearl River along the Louisiana border. Any person fishing with more than 2 trotlines and/or 100 hooks, or with nets and seines for nongame gross fish for personal use, is required to obtain a commercial fishing license.

Resident hunting licenses issued by Mississippi, Arkansas, and Louisiana permit the holders to hunt waterfowl on specified common boundary waters of the Mississippi and Pearl rivers. A reciprocal agreement between Mississippi and Louisiana also allows hunting other game along the Mississippi River. All persons must procure a federal "Duck" stamp, in addition to a basic hunting license, to take migratory waterfowl. It is unlawful for any person to hunt, catch, or kill Frogs and Turtles for commercial purposes without a resident hunting and fishing license, or a special permit issued by the State Game and Fish Commission.

*Resident license fees:** combination hunting and fishing, $3.00; archery Deer hunting, $2.00; Deer tag (addition to license), $2.00; Wild Turkey tag (in addition to license), $2.00; federal "Duck" stamp, $3.00.

Nonresident license fees: Annual fishing, $6.00; tourist 3 consecutive days' fishing, $1.00; annual hunting small game (except Turkey and Deer), $15.00; tourist 3 days' hunting small game (except Turkey and Deer), $5.00; annual hunting all game, $25.00; archery Deer hunting (archery season only), $5.00; federal "Duck" stamp, $3.00; hunting on licensed shooting preserves, $3.00; trapping, $200.00; commercial Frog and Turtle special permit, $200.00.

HUNTING AND TRAPPING

Game animals: Deer, Opossum, Rabbit, Raccoon, Squirrel. OPEN SEASONS:** Deer—archery, from mid-October to mid-November; firearms,

---

* Plus 25 cents issue fee.
** Check current state regulations.

about 10 days in late December and 14 days from late December into January in designated areas, and special hunts in game management areas. Opossum, Raccoon—October 1 to mid-November without a gun, for food; from mid-November to January 31 with guns; run with dogs throughout the year. Rabbit—Oct. 1 to mid-February, and open seasons vary in designated areas. Squirrel—October 1 to mid-January, and open seasons vary in designated areas. BAG LIMITS: Deer—archery season, 1 of either sex; gun season, 1 Buck; and not more than 2 per year. Opossum and Raccoons—no limits. Rabbits—5 per day. Squirrels—5 per day.

A legal Buck is a male Deer with antlers 4 or more inches long.

Furbearing animals: Bear, Beaver, Fox, Mink, Muskrat, Opossum, Otter, Raccoon, Skunk, Weasel. OPEN TRAPPING SEASONS: Mink, Opossum, Otter, Raccoon, Skunk, Weasel—Dec. 1–Jan. 31. Muskrat—mid-December to March 1. BAG LIMITS: none. Muskrats and Raccoons may be sold for food during open hunting and trapping seasons. FULLY PROTECTED: Bear—no open season. NOT PROTECTED: Beaver, Bobcat, and Fox may be taken at any time.

Game birds: Coot, Mourning Dove, Ducks (except Canvasback and Redhead), Gallinule, Geese (except Canada Geese and subspecies), Merganser, Bobwhite Quail, Rails, Sora, Wilson's Snipe, Wild Turkey, Woodcock. OPEN SEASONS:* Coot, Ducks, Merganser—early December to early January. Dove—about 2 weeks in late September, 2 weeks from late October to mid November, and from mid-December to mid-January. Gallinule, Rails, Sora—about 6 weeks from October 1. Geese—mid-October to mid-November, early December to mid-January; except the land and waters lying westerly of the center line of the Mississippi River main navigable channel to latitude 31° North, early November to mid-January. Quail—early December to mid-February, except that the season ends January 31 in Benton, DeSoto, Marshall, Tippah, and Tunica counties. Wilson's Snipe—early December to mid-January. Wild Turkey—various periods in April for designated areas. Woodcock—late November to mid-January. Licensed shooting preserves—Sept. 1–March 31. FULLY PROTECTED: Canvasback and Redhead Ducks, and all species of Canada Geese—no open seasons. NOT PROTECTED: Crows, Cooper's Hawks, Duck Hawks, Sharp-shinned Hawks, and Great Horned Owls may be taken at any time.

Baiting, feeding, and hunting Wild Turkeys with dogs or live decoys, electrically or mechanicaly operated calling or sound-reproducing devices are prohibited. Deer may be hunted with dogs in designated areas, but not during archery season.

---

* Check current state regulations.

FIREARMS

No automatic or hand-operated repeating shotguns capable of holding more than 3 shells in the magazine and chamber combined may be used to hunt game animals and birds, except Deer, Opossum, Rabbit, and Raccoon. There are no specific restrictions on guns to hunt Deer, but migratory game birds may be taken only with shotguns not larger than 10 gauge. Crossbows, sidearms, and all firearms are prohibited while hunting Deer during an archery season.

Shooting hours: Sunday hunting in game management areas is prohibited. Sunrise to sunset for migratory birds except Dove 12:00 o'clock until sunset. Shooting starts at 12:00 o'clock noon on the opening day of a Duck season. Hunting Deer at night with the aid of light is prohibited, and the penalty is a fine of $150 with all equipment including vehicles subject to confiscation.

FISHING

Game fish: Black Bass, Goggle-eye or Warmouth Bass, Striped Bass, White Bass, Yellow Bass, Bream, Blue Catfish (in lakes and non-navigable streams), Crappie, Perch family, Walleyed Pike, Sauger or Sand Pike, Jack Salmon, and the Sunfish family. OPEN SEASONS: all year, and no size limits.

Game fish may be taken only by hook and line with one or more hooks (including rod and reel with artificial bait) or a trotline, trolling, and dip net. Taking fish of any species by gigging, shooting, slat or wire baskets, and use of poisons, explosives, or electrical devices of any kind is prohibited.

Longbow and arrow may be used to take Buffalo, Carp, Gar, and Gunnell at any time. Catfish and nongame fish may be taken by hand grabbling May 1–July 31 except in 22 counties.

There is excellent fishing on the Mississippi Sound and in the Gulf of Mexico for such saltwater fish as Bonito, Cavalla, Dolphin, King and Spanish Mackerel, Mullet, Pompano, Red Snappers, Speckled Sea Trout, and Tarpon. The Biloxi Fishing Rodeo is held in June (1 week), and the Mississippi Deep Sea Rodeo July 4–7 is at Gulfport. The following state parks are well stocked with fish.

STATE PARKS

Carver Point* (750 acres) on Grenada Reservoir—Grenada County; *Clarkco* (795 acres, 65-acre lake) 6 miles north of Quitman—Clark

---

* Constructed for Negroes.

County; *J. P. Coleman* (1,468 acres) at Pickwick Lake (67 square miles) on the state line near Inka—Tishomingo County; *Holmes County* (463 acres, 55-acre lake) south of Durant—Holmes County; *Leroy Percy* (2,442 acres) on the Mississippi Delta near Hollandale—Washington County; *Percy Quinn* (2,221 acres, 621-acre lake) near McComb—Pike County; *Roosevelt* (562 acres, 125-acre lake) south of Morton—Scott County; *Sardis Lake* (740 acres) at Sardis Reservoir (91 square miles) on Little Tallahatchie River, near Batesville—Panola County; *Shelby* (820 acres, 400-acre lake) south of Hattiesburg—Forrest County; *Tombigbee* (822 acres, 100-acre lake) southeast of Tupelo—Lee County; *Wall Doxey* (855 acres, 60-acre lake) south of Holly Springs—Marshall County; *Hugh White* (745 acres) at Grenada Reservoir (101 square miles) on the Yalobusha River near Grenada—Grenada County.

Licenses, regulations, information about current seasons, bag and possession limits can be obtained from the Executive Director, State Game and Fish Commission, Box 451, Jackson. Licenses are also issued from the sheriff's office at county court houses, authorized agents, and state game wardens in each county. Commercial fishing licenses are sold only by state game wardens, but commercial Frog, Turtle, and Minnow dealers' licenses, shooting preserve and Quail breeders' licenses are issued only by the State Game and Fish Commission.

MISSOURI

Area: 69,420 square miles (land area—69,138 square miles); rank in nation–18
Bird: Bluebird (*Sialia sialis*), adopted 1927
Capital city: Jefferson City on the Missouri River in Cole County; population (1960)—28,228; rank in state–12
Counties: 114
Elevations: Highest, Taum Sauk Mountain (1,772 ft.) in Iron County; lowest, St. Francis River (230 ft.) in Dunklin County
Flower: Hawthorne (*Crataegus*), adopted 1923
Geographic center: In Miller County, 20 miles southwest of Jefferson City
Nicknames: Iron State, Lead State, Ozark State, Show Me State
Population (1960): 4,319,813; rank in nation–13
Tree: Dogwood (*Cornus florida*), adopted 1955

Missouri is a central state between Arkansas on the south and Iowa on the north, and Kansas shares the western border with Oklahoma in the southwest and Nebraska in the northwest. Across the eastern boundary formed by the Mississippi River are Illinois, Kentucky, and Tennessee.

The Missouri River outlines the northwestern border and swerves eastward at Kansas City to join the Mississippi River north of St. Louis.

There are rolling hills in northern Missouri, prairies in the northeast and southwest, rugged forested hills with deep valleys in the southern Ozark region. Among many streams flowing into flat bottom lands of the Missouri River are the Nodaway and Tarkio Rivers in the northwestern corner of the state, and the Platte River, and One Hundred and Two River between St. Joseph and Kansas City, and the Chariton and Grand rivers draining the northern counties. The Osage River from Oklahoma is impounded by Bagnell Dam to form a Lake of the Ozarks (64,000 acres, shoreline 1,372 miles), and it continues eastward to merge with the Missouri River in Osage County. In the southeast are Lake Wappapello (6,000 acres) on the St. Francis River, Clearwater Lake (1,700 acres) on the Black River, and Little River flowing through the fertile "Boot Heel" region into Arkansas. The Current and Eleven Point rivers also follow a southward course east of Lake Norfolk (48 square miles) on the North Fork White River. Lake Taneycomo with a shoreline 100 miles long, Table Rock Lake (82 square miles), and Bull Shoals Lake (111 square miles) extending into Arkansas, are reservoirs on the White River's jaunt into southwestern Missouri.

There are several great caverns, and tremendous springs form clear cold streams in the Ozark region. Big Spring near Van Buren daily pours 864 million gallons of water through a limestone cliff opening and short channel into beautiful Current River.

LICENSES

Resident permits to fish, hunt, and trap are issued to citizens who have maintained a legal residence in Missouri for at least 3 months prior to an application for a license; to legal residents employed in the District of Columbia by the federal government or serving in the U.S. Armed Forces; and to all members of the armed forces stationed and residing in Missouri. Any person under 17 years of age may fish without a permit, but all fishermen must possess a permit to take Trout except in areas where a daily fishing tag is required. Special fishing permits are issued without cost to patients in veterans hospitals. Fishermen holding valid Illinois licenses may fish with hook and line in the flowing part of the Mississippi River forming the Illinois-Missouri boundary, and anglers with valid Kansas licenses have similar privileges in the flowing part of the Missouri River on the Kansas-Missouri boundary, but a Missouri license is required to fish in tributaries, backwaters, and bayous of these rivers.

Permits to trap furbearing animals are issued only to residents. All persons 16 or more years of age are required to procure a federal "Duck" stamp to take migratory game birds. An authorized representative of an educational institution, municipality, wildlife society, state or federal agency may obtain a scientific collector's permit to possess and preserve wildlife for scientific purposes. A permit to hold one Squirrel or a fur-bearing animal in captivity may be granted if the animal was taken legally. The wildlife hobby Permit authorizes the possession and propagation of not more than 50 Chukar Partridges, Pheasants, and Quails for personal use and not for sale. A permit to operate a commercial shooting preserve requires a bird shooting area in a single tract of not less than 160 acres or more than 640 acres at least 5 miles from any Conservation Commission game management release areas; a preserve for hoofed animals must have not less than 320 acres or more than 1,280 acres fenced to exclude all hoofed wildlife from becoming a part of the commercial enterprise.

*Resident permit fees:** Fishing, $3.00; Trout, $2.00; combination fishing and hunting (except Deer and Turkey), $6.00; hunting (except Deer and Turkey), $3.00; archery Deer hunting (archery season only), $5.00; firearms Deer hunting, $5.00; Wild Turkey hunting, $5.00; federal "Duck" stamp (affix to hunting license), $3.00; trapping, $3.00; fur buyer, $25.00; fur dealer, $125.00; wildlife breeder, $20.00; wildlife hobby, $5.00; taxidermy and tanning, $10.00; guide, $3.00; commercial shooting area, $100.00.

*Nonresident permit fees:** Annual fishing, $5.00; fishing 14 consecutive days, $3.00; Trout, $2.00; hunting small game (except Deer, Turkey, Beaver, Mink, Muskrat), $20.00; archery hunting during archery season (except Turkey, Beaver, Mink, Muskrat), $10.00; firearms Deer hunting, $20.00; federal "Duck" stamp, $3.00; commercial shooting preserve (3 days), $3.00.

HUNTING AND TRAPPING

Game animals: Deer, Rabbit, Squirrels. OPEN SEASONS:** Deer—archery from October 1 and firearms from November 15 to closing dates established annually. Rabbit—May 30 to last day of February. Squirrels—May 30–Dec. 31. BAG LIMITS: Deer—2 (1, archery, 1, gun) per year. Rabbits—10 per day. Squirrels—6 per day.

Furbearing animals: Badger, Beaver, Bobcat, Fox (Gray, Red), Mink, Muskrat, Nutria, Opossum, Raccoon, Spotted Skunk (Civet Cat), Striped Skunk, Weasel. OPEN HUNTING SEASON:** Badger, Opossum, Raccoon, Skunk, Weasel—mid-November to mid-January. OPEN TRAPPING SEASON: Beaver—Dec. 1–March 15; Badger, Bobcat, Fox, Opossum, Raccoon, Skunks, Weasel—Dec. 1–Jan. 15. BAG LIMITS: None. NOT PROTECTED:

---

* Plus 25 cents issue fee.
** Check current state regulations.

Bobcat, Coyote, Fox (except trapping), Groundhog, Nutria, and Weasel may be taken at any time.

Game birds: Coot, Mourning Dove, Ducks (except Canvasback and Redhead), Gallinule, Geese, Merganser, Pheasant, Quail, Rails, Sora, Wilson's Snipe, Wild Turkey, Woodcock. OPEN SEASONS: Coot, Ducks, Merganser—late October to late November. Dove—September 1 to mid-October, and about 2 weeks in November. Gallinule, Rails, Sora—September 1 to mid-October. Geese—in Swan Lake area, from mid-October to mid-November; remainder of state, late October to January. Pheasant—about 2 weeks in November west of U.S. Highway 36, and no open season in remainder of state. Quail—from mid-November to date set annually. Wilson's Snipe, Woodcock—October 1 to mid-November. Wild Turkey —spring season usually announced in January. Commercial shooting preserve—Oct. 1–March 31. FULLY PROTECTED: Canvasback and Redhead Ducks—no open season. NOT PROTECTED: Crows, English Sparrows, and Starlings may be taken at any time.

FIREARMS

Deer may be taken with a muzzle-loading rifle not smaller than .28 caliber; or with a rifle firing only centerfire ammunition propelling one projectile weighing not less than 60 grains; or with a gun not smaller than 20 gauge or larger than 10 gauge, propelling one projectile at a single discharge; or with a longbow or crossbow. Only shotguns not larger than 10 gauge, and having a capacity of not more than 3 shells in the magazine and chamber combined may be used for hunting all game birds except Wild Turkey. Pistols, revolvers, and rifles propelling a single projectile at one discharge, and shotguns not larger than 10 gauge may be used to hunt other wildlife (except fish) during open seasons.

Shooting hours: Sunrise to sunset; except Deer—archery season, 5:30 A.M.–6:00 P.M.; firearms season, 6:30 A.M.–5:00 P.M. Dove—one-half hour before sunrise to sunset. Shooting is not permitted until 12:00 o'clock noon on the opening day of a Duck season. Furbearers may not be hunted with firearms from a boat at night.

FISHING

Game fish: Black Bass (Largemouth, Smallmouth), Kentucky or Spotted Bass, Rock Bass (Goggle-eye, Redeye), Silver Bass, Striped Bass, Catfish, Crappie (Calico or Strawberry Bass), Sauger (Sand Pike), Wall-eyed Pike (Jack Salmon, Pike-perch), Trout. OPEN SEASONS: All year, except Black Bass and Spotted Bass in all streams, May 29 to last day of February.

Game fish may be caught by use of poles and lines, bank lines, block or jig lines, limb lines, throw lines, trotlines, artificial lures, and by Falcons.

Rainbow Trout fishing in the Bennett Springs, Maramec, Montauk, and Roaring River state parks requires a daily Trout tag ($1).

Nongame fish: May be taken by bow and arrow, gigging, grabbling, snagging, snaring, and spearfishing. OPEN SEASONS: Oct. 1 (12 noon) to Dec. 31 (midnight) by gig or longbow; and from impounded waters north of the Missouri River, March 1 to August 31; except that Gar may be taken by longbow at any time. Buffalo, Carp, Drum, Gar, Redhorse, Shad, and Sucker may be taken by gig, crossbow, longbow, or underwater spearing, January 1 to September 30 (sunrise–sunset) from Lake of the Ozarks, Bull Shoals, Clearwater, Norfolk, Pomme de Terre, Table Rock, and Wappapello lakes. Grabbling, snagging, and snaring are permitted from March 15 to May 15, and October 31 to December 31. Paddlefish may be snagged from March 15 to May 15, and October 1 to December 31. In Lake of the Ozarks and upstream in the Osage and South Grand rivers, all species of nongame fishing may be snagged from March 15 to April 30.

Frogs: OPEN SEASON: July 1–Nov. 30. BAG LIMIT: 8 per day. Bullfrogs may be taken under a fishing license with the use of hands, hand net, hook and line, gig, and longbow; and under a hunting license with the use of hands, hand net, longbow, pellet gun, pistol, or a .22 rimfire rifle.

Float fishing from an expertly guided "john" boat for Bass and other fish is extremely popular in about 25 streams in the Ozark region. There is excellent fishing in state parks and trout management areas, and also hunting in state forests and wildlife areas.

STATE FORESTS

Daniel Boone, south of Pendleton—Warren County; *Deer Run,* south of Ellington—Reynolds County; *Huckleberry Ridge,* east of Pineville—McDonald County; *Huzzah,* east of Leesburg—Crawford County; *Indian Trail,* at Sligo—Dent County; *Maramec,* north of Potosi—Washington County; *Reifsnider,* south of Truesdale—Warren County; *George O. White,* south of Sherril—Texas County.

STATE PARKS

Alley Spring (407 acres) west of Eminence—Shannon County; *Sam A. Baker* (7,178 acres) on Big Creek and St. Francis River, north of Patterson—Wayne County; *Bennett Spring* (730 acres) on Niangua River, 12 miles west of Lebanon—Dallas County; *Big Lake* (111 acres) southwest of Bigelow—Holt County; *Big Spring* (5,836 acres) south of Van Buren—Carter County; *Confederate Memorial* (95 acres) near Higginsville—Lafayette County; *Crowder* (640 acres) west of Trenton—Grundy County; *Cuivre River* (5,822 acres) east of Troy—Lincoln

County; *Johnson Shut-ins* (2,478 acres) on Black River, north of Lesterville—Reynolds County; *Knob Noster* (3,441 acres) at Knob Noster—Johnson County; *Lake of the Ozarks* (16,335 acres) on the eastern shore of the lake at Kaiser—Miller County; *Lake Wappapello* (1,854 acres) at lake about 10 miles north of Poplar Bluff—Stoddard County; *Lewis and Clark* (61 acres) on Sugar Lake, south of Rushville—Buchanan County; *Mark Twain* (1,192 acres) near Florida—Monroe County; *Maramec* (7,153 acres) on Maramec River, east of Sullivan—Franklin County; *Montauk* (846 acres) at headwaters of the Current River, southeast of Licking—Dent County; *Pershing* (1,836 acres) west of Laclede—Linn County; *Pomme de Terre* (496 acres) at Pomme de Terre Lake (7,800 acres) south of Hermitage—Hickory County; *Roaring River* (2,988 acres) south of Cassville—Barry County; *Round Spring* (75 acres) at Round Spring—Shannon County; *Table Rock* (552 acres) at Table Rock Lake, west of Branson—Taney County; *Thousand Hills* (3,152 acres, 703-acre lake) west of Kirskville—Adair County; *Wallace* (160 acres) south of Cameron—Clinton County; *Washington* (1,101 acres) south of DeSoto—Washington County.

TROUT MANAGEMENT AREAS

Capps Creek between Granby (Newton County) and Monett—Barry County; *Dry Creek* near Cherryville—Crawford County; *Eleven Point River* north of Alton—Oregon County; *Maramec Spring* near Steelville—Crawford County; *Roubidoux Creek* near Waynesville—Pulaski County.

WILDLIFE AREAS (fishing)

Hunnewell Lake east of Shelbina—Shelby County; *Lake Paho* near Princeton—Mercer County; *Henry Sever,* north of Newark—Knox County; *Squaw Creek,* southwest of Mound City—Holt County.

WILDLIFE AREAS (hunting)

Atlanta west of Atlanta—Macon County; *Dean Davis* southeast of Willow Springs—Howell County; *Honey Creek* on Nodaway River, east of Oregon—Andrew County; *Hungry Mother* east of Glasgow—Howard County; *Mincy* south of Kirby—Taney County; *Neeper* at Neeper—Clark County; *Pleasant Hope* east of Brighton—Polk County; *Richter Memorial* near Berryman—Crawford County.

WILDLIFE AREAS (hunting and fishing)

August A. Busch, south of Wentzville—St. Charles County; *Deer Ridge,* northwest of Monticello—Lewis County; *Marshall I. Diggs,* west of Wellsville—Montgomery County; *Duck Creek,* near Kinder—Stoddard County; *Fountain Grove,* east of Bedford—Livingston County; *Montrose,*

north of Montrose—Henry County; *Haysler A. Pogue*, near Clinton—
Henry County; *James A. Reed*, southeast of Kansas City—Jackson County;
Schell-Osage, near Schell City—Vernon County; *Swan Lake*, near Mendon
—Chariton County; *Trimble*, east of Tremble—Clinton County; *Upper
Mississippi*, southeast of Elsberry—Lincoln County.

Permits, regulations, and information about current seasons, bag and
possession limits may be obtained from the Director, Missouri State
Conservation Commission, Farm Bureau Building, Jefferson City; and
offices at 1535 Grand Ave., Kansas 8; and at 8206 Delmar Boulevard, St.
Louis 24; or from county clerks. The State Highway Commission publishes
road and contour maps; and for information about recreation areas write
to the State Park Board and Missouri Boat Commission in Jefferson City.

MONTANA

Area: 146,997 square miles (land area—145,736 square miles); rank in
nation–4
Bird: Meadowlark (*Sturnella neglecta*), adopted 1931
Capital city: Helena overlooking Prickly Pear Valley in Lewis and Clark
County; population (1960)—20,227; rank in state–5
Counties: 56
Elevation: Highest, Granite Peak (12,850 ft.) in Park County; lowest,
Kootenai River (1800 ft.) in Flathead County
Flower: Bitterroot (*Lewisia rediviva*), adopted 1895
Geographic center: 12 miles west of Lewistown, Fergus County
Nicknames: Treasure State, Bonanza State, Land of the Shining Mountain
Population (1960): 674,767; rank in nation–41
Tree: Ponderosa Pine (*Pinus ponderosa*), adopted 1949

Montana is a northwestern state bordered by North Dakota and
South Dakota on the east, Wyoming on the south, Idaho on the west,
sharing the Bitterroot Range, and British Columbia, Alberta, and Saskatchewan provinces of Canada on the north.

There are 10 national forests among the majestic mountains, great
canyons, and basins of the Rocky Mountain Range in western Montana.
The Continental Divide follows along the Bitterroot Range to Lost Trail
Pass (6,951 ft.) on the Idaho border, and swerves eastward along the
steep crests of Mount Evans (10,635 ft.), Mount Haggin (10,598 ft.),
Mount Howe (10,475 ft.), and Short Peak (10,240 ft.) within sight of
Anaconda, and near Butte turns northward to the Waterton-Glacier
International Peace Park on the Canadian boundary. Two-thirds of Mon-
tana consists of the Great Plains covered with bunch grass, sage brush,

wheatlands, bluffs, and groves of cottonwood and willow trees along streams, buttes, and isolated groups of mountains.

The Missouri River, formed by the Gallatin, Madison, and Jefferson rivers merging at Three Forks in southwestern Montana, travels an erratic course northward through the Gates of the Mountains near Helena, to be joined by the Sun River rushing down from the Continental Divide to Great Falls near a series of cataracts, and dropping 512 feet in 10 miles, and in Choteau County, moves eastward to be fed by the Teton and Marias rivers north of Fort Benton; impounded by the Fort Peck Dam southeast of Glasgow, it forms a reservoir spreading over 382 square miles in the northeast, and increased by the northern Milk and Poplar rivers continues on into North Dakota. Large southern tributaries include the Smith River joining the Missouri at Ulm, the Judith River in Choteau County, Musselshell River at the Fort Peck Reservoir, and the Redwater River at Poplar. Four miles from Great Falls, the phenomenal Great Springs pours 388,800,000 gallons of clear water into the Missouri River every 24 hours.

The Yellowstone River rising in Wyoming flows through Yellowstone National Park to be increased by the Sweetgrass River east of Big Timber, the Clark River near Billings, Big Horn River at Bighorn, Tongue River at Miles City, Powder River near Terry; and at the North Dakota border, the Yellowstone joins the Missouri River.

Major streams west of the Continental Divide include the Flathead River impounded by Kerr Dam to create Hungry Horse Reservoir (22,500 acres) near Columbia Falls; the Swan River connecting several lakes in the Mission Range; the Yaak and Kootenai rivers in the northwestern corner of Montana; the Clark Fork of the Columbia River joined by the Bitterroot and Big Blackfoot rivers near Missoula. The Big Hole River from the eastern slopes of the Bitterroot Range joins the Beaverhead and Ruby rivers to form the Jefferson River near Twin Bridges in southwestern Montana. At Lewistown, the Big Springs send 62,700 gallons of cold clear water per minute into a creek well stocked with Trout.

Flathead Lake (191 square miles, maximum depth 300 ft.) on the Flathead River north of Polson is the largest natural lake in the state. In addition to beautiful natural lakes such as Whitefish Lakes (7 miles long) at Whitefish, large impounded waters include Canyon Ferry Reservoir (55 square miles) east of Helena and the Tiber Reservoir (35 square miles) on the Marias River southeast of Shelby.

LICENSES

Resident licenses are issued to bona fide residents, and to members of the U.S. Armed Forces officially assigned to duty and stationed in Montana for at least 30 days prior to an application for a license. Juveniles under the age of 15 are not required to possess licenses for fishing or to hunt any game birds except Wild Turkey. Residents 12–14 years of age must have a certificate of competency in handling firearms, and residents 15–17 years of age should present evidence of having held a prior Montana big game license or a certificate of competency when applying for a big game hunting license. Nonresident juveniles are not required to show evidence of training in the handling of firearms. Juveniles under 12 years of age are not permitted to purchase big game licenses or hunt big game. All persons hunting big game must have valid big game licenses including persons 70 or more years of age.

The holder of a nonresident big game license is entitled to fish, and to hunt upland game birds, Bear, Deer, Elk, and apply for special permits to take Antelope, Mountain Goat, Moose, and Bighorn Sheep. All persons must have a current big game license before their applications are entered in drawings for special permits. If a hunter is successful in taking a Moose, or a Bighorn Sheep, he may not obtain permits for taking such animals during the next 7 years. Less fortunate hunters may apply annually for Moose and Sheep hunts if their unused tags are returned with their applications for new permits. There is no fee for the Antelope coupon, which should be detached from a big game license and sent with an official Antelope application to be entered in the regular drawing for hunting in a designated district. Six persons may apply as a group, and the first name listed represents the other applicants. If the first name is drawn, special licenses are also issued to all members of the group. Districts preferred by hunters should be designated on application forms for all limited drawings, and sent to the Montana Fish and Game Department postmarked on or before July 15. Applications for the $20 Antelope licenses are not entered in the regular drawing, and may be postmarked not later than August 15. This special license is issued to nonresidents only if district quotas for taking Antelope are not taken by residents. Applicants may designate districts in order of preference, but only one Antelope license is issued to a hunter.

Holders of big game licenses may hunt with bow and arrow during a gun season without an archery stamp. The possession and use of any firearms by a hunter is prohibited during archery seasons.

Resident license fees: Bird and fish (Class A), $3.00; big game hunting (must possess Class A), $3.00; bow and arrow hunting, $2.00; trapping (must possess Class A), $10.00; trapping on own land, $1.00; fur dealer, $10.00; fur dealer's agent, $10.00; taxidermist, $15.00; federal "Duck" stamp (must possess Class A), $3.00; Wild Turkey tag, $2.00. Special districts hunting: Mountain Goat, $5.00; Moose, $25.00; Bighorn Sheep, $15.00.

Nonresident license fees: Annual fishing, $10.00; tourist fishing 6 consecutive days, $3.00; hunting upland game birds, $25.00; general hunting and fishing (Bear, Deer, Elk, small game), $100.00; Wild Turkey tag (must hold upland game bird or general hunting license), $2.00; archery stamp (additional to special or big game license), $2.00; federal "Duck" stamp (in addition to hunting license), $3.00. Special districts hunting: Antelope, $20.00; Deer, $20.00; Mountain Goat, $5.00; Moose, $25.00; Bighorn Sheep, $15.00.

HUNTING AND TRAPPING

Big game animals: Antelope, Black Bear (various color phases), Grizzly Bear, Deer (Mule, White-tail), Mountain Goat, Moose, Bighorn Sheep. OPEN SEASONS:* Antelope—early September to late November, and seasons vary from short periods to 8 weeks in special areas. Black Bear—mid-March to late November, and female Black Bears and cubs may be hunted from September 15 to end of season in areas open to Black Bear hunting. Grizzly Bear—season coincides with Deer and Elk seasons. Deer—September 15 to late November in 4 districts, and from mid-October to late November in other areas. Elk, Mountain Goat, Bighorn Sheep—September 15 to late November including shorter periods in designated areas. ANNUAL BAG LIMITS: Antelope—1. Bear—1. Deer—2 of either sex, but only 1 Deer on a nonresident special district license; holders of big game licenses may take 2 Deer. Elk—1. Mountain Goat —1. Moose—1 during a 7-year period. Bighorn Sheep—1 Ram with three-quarter curl horn during a 7-year period.

Furbearing animals: Badger, Beaver, Bobcat, Fisher, Fox, Canada Lynx, Marten, Mink, Muskrat, Otter, Rabbit, Raccoon, Skunk, Weasel, Wolf, Wolverine. FULLY PROTECTED: Fisher, Lynx— no open seasons. NOT PROTECTED: Badger, Beaver, Coyote, Fox, Gopher, Porcupine, Prairie Dog, Rabbit, Raccoon, Skunk, Weasel, Wolverine, and Woodchuck may be killed at any time.

Game birds: Coot, Ducks (except Canvasback and Redhead), Geese, Mountain Grouse (Blue, Franklin's), Prairie Grouse (Sage, Sharptailed), Merganser, Chukar and Hungarian Partridge, Ptarmigan, Ringnecked Pheasant, Wild Turkey. OPEN SEASONS:* Coot, Ducks, Merganser—mid-October to mid-November east of the Continental Divide, and extended to late December west of the divide. Geese—early October to mid-December east of the divide, and extended to late December west of the divide. Grouse—starts in mid-September. Partridge and Pheasant usually opens in late October. Other game birds—seasons not set until August or September annually. FULLY PROTECTED: Canvasback and Redhead Ducks, Blue, Ross's, and Snow Geese in Beaverhead, Gallatin,

---

* Check current state regulations.

and Madison counties—no open seasons. NOT PROTECTED: Crows, Hawks, and Owls may be taken at any time.

Big game hunters must wear bright orange, red, or yellow caps, hats, shirts, jackets, coats, or sweaters as external garments. Guides are not required by law, but hunters planning to go into remote areas need them. Only tribal Indians may hunt on Indian reservations.

FIREARMS

Pistols and revolvers may be carried (if not concealed) during open firearms seasons, and there are no caliber restrictions on big game rifles, although hunting may be restricted in some areas to shotguns. Fully automatic firearms are prohibited, and migratory game birds may be taken only with shotguns not larger than 10 gauge and capable of holding not more than 3 cartridges in the magazine and chamber combined.

Shooting hours: One-half hour before sunrise to one-half hour after sunset; except migratory game birds, sunrise to sunset east of the Continental Divide and one-half hour before sunrise to sunset west of the divide.

FISHING

Game fish: Bass (all species of genus *Micropterus*), Grayling (all species of family Thymallidae), Muskellunge, Pickerel, and Pike (all species of genus *Esox*), Walleye Pike, Sandpike, or Sauger (all species of genus *Stizostedion*), Salmon and Trout (all species of family Salmonidae), Whitefish (all species of family Coregonidae). OPEN SEASONS:*
All year in some waters. Seasons may open on last Sunday in May, or last Sunday in June and extend to November 30. Whitefish may be taken in designated waters from December 1 to March 31. The season for snagging Kokanee Salmon is generally Oct. 1–Dec. 15.

All game fish (except Kokanee Salmon special season) may be caught only with a single pole and/or single line. It is unlawful to use a fish spear, or shoot fish with a rifle, gun, or bow and arrow, except that Carp may be shot with bow and arrow.

Montana is divided into 8 drainage areas with special regulations for numerous lakes and streams. The Madison and Sun rivers, Georgetown Lake near Anaconda, Whitefish Lake, Fort Peck and Tiber reservoirs are exceptional Grayling and Trout waters. The Missouri and Yellowstone rivers provide prime Trout fishing in their headwaters, and Pike, Catfish, and Crappie in the lower stretches. The following state parks and recreation areas offer fishing and boating.

---

* Check current state regulations.

Bitterroot Lake (30 acres) north of Marion—Flathead County; *Canyon Ferry* (1,800 acres) east of Helena—Lewis and Clark County; *Flathead Lake* (65 acres) on the west shore, north of Polson—Lake County; *Hell Creek* (200 acres) at Fort Peck Reservoir, 26 miles north of Jordan—Garfield County; *James Kipp* (400 acres) on the Missouri River, 65 miles north of Lewistown—Fergus County; *Nelson Reservoir* 25 miles northeast of Malta—Phillips County; *Missouri River Headwaters* near Three Forks—Gallatin County; *Rock Creek* (200 acres) on eastern side of Fort Peck Reservoir, 35 miles south of the Fort Peck spillway—Mc-Cone County; *Thompson Falls* (25 acres) west of Thompson Falls—Sanders County; *Tiber Dam* (1,500 acres) near Chester—Liberty County; *West Shore* (68 acres) South of Somers on Flathead Lake—Lake County; *Yellow Bay* (15 acres) on eastern shore of Flathead Lake, south of Bigfork—Lake County.

The National Fresh Water Trout Derby is held at Livingston in August, and the annual Trout Derby at Great Falls in September.

Licenses, permits, regulations, and information about current open seasons, bag and possession limits may be obtained from the Director, State Fish and Game Department, Helena; and authorized agents throughout the state. Applications for Antelope, Mountain Goat, Moose, and Bighorn Sheep must be made on forms available from offices of the Fish and Game Department or license agents, and mailed to Helena postmarked on or before July 15. For an excellent map of the state showing location of national forests, write to the State Highway Commission of Montana, Helena.

NEBRASKA

Area: 77,520 square miles (land area—76,612 square miles); rank in nation—15
Bird: Western Meadowlark (*Sturnella neglecta*), adopted 1929
Capital city: Lincoln on Salt Creek in Lancaster County; population (1960)—128,521; rank in state—2
Counties: 93
Elevation: Highest, southwestern part of Banner County (5,340 ft.) lowest, southeastern corner of state (825 ft.)
Flower: Goldenrod (*Solidago serotina*), adopted 1895
Geographic center: 10 miles northwest of Broken Bow, Custer County
Nicknames: Antelope State, Cornhuskers State, Treeplanters State

Population (1960): 1,411,330; rank in nation—34
Tree: American Elm (*Ulmus americana*), adopted 1937

Nebraska on the Great Plains is a north central state bordered by South Dakota in the north, Iowa and Missouri on the eastern banks of the Missouri River, Kansas on the south, Wyoming on the west, and Colorado projecting into the southwestern region.

The prairie slopes gradually from western elevations of 4,000–5,000 feet to less than 1,000 feet at the Missouri River in the east. The Niobrara River leaves Wyoming to flow through the Sand Hills and continue eastward to join the Missouri River at Niobrara. The wide North Platte River from Wyoming and the South Platte River from Colorado unite in Lincoln County and on the eastward course are joined by the Loup and Elkhorn rivers before merging with the Missouri River at Plattsmouth. The Calamus, Cedar, North Loup, Middle Loup, and South Loup rivers flow on parallel courses from northern Nebraska to form and increase the Loup River. From Kansas, the Republican River enters near Benkelman and moves along southern Nebraska fed by many creeks, only to return to Kansas near Superior. Several tributaries of the Big Blue and Little Blue rivers flow through southeastern Nebraska.

There are 11,000 miles of streams, and among 3,350 lakes are chains of reservoirs on the Missouri, Platte, and Republican rivers including the 33-mile-long Lewis and Clark Lake on the Missouri River north of Crofton; Lake McConaughy (55 square miles) on the North Platte River between Ogallalah and Oshkosh, and 13-mile-long Harlan County Reservoir on the Republican River at Alma. Fertile farmlands cover Nebraska except where cattle roam over grasslands in the Sand Hills which extend westward from the Great Plains for about 24,000 square miles south of the Niobrara River. Unique landmarks are the Chimney Rock towering 150 feet above a reddish sandstone base near Bayard, the 700-foot Scotts Bluff on the Old Oregon Trail, and the forested bluffs of the Pine Ridge in the northwestern corner of the state. In the Bad Lands near Crawford, the Agate Springs Fossil Quarries have yielded the remains of several prehistoric creatures.

LICENSES

Resident permits to fish and hunt are issued to persons 16 or more years of age who have lived in the state for at least 90 days immediately preceding an application for a permit. Any member of the U.S. Armed Forces officially stationed in Nebraska for 30 or more days may obtain resident permits upon satisfactory proof that he has been actually present on duty. Every nonresident must obtain a permit to hunt game animals and birds, but may fish without a permit if under the age of 16 and if accompanied by a parent or guardian possessing a valid nonresident fishing permit. Any person fishing in the boundary waters of the Missouri River or Lewis and Clark Lake must carry a valid license issued by the state from which he enters and returns from such waters. All persons 16 or more years of age must possess an upland game bird stamp to hunt Grouse, Pheasant, and Quail, and a federal "Duck" stamp to take migratory waterfowl. Permits to trap animals are required for all trappers regardless of age.

Resident permit fees: Sport fishing, $2.00; hunting small game, $2.50; combination fishing and hunting small game, $4.00; Antelope hunting, $10.00; Deer hunting (archery), $10.00; Deer hunting (rifle), $10.00; Wild Turkey hunting, $5.00; trapping, $2.50; upland game birds stamp (affix to hunting permit), $1.00; federal "Duck" stamp (affix to hunting permit), $3.00.

Nonresident permit fees: Annual sport fishing, $5.00; fishing 5 consecutive days, $2.00; hunting small game, $15.00; Antelope hunting, $25.00; Deer hunting (archery), $25.00; Deer hunting (rifle), $25.00; Wild Turkey hunting, $15.00; trapping (1,000 or fewer furbearing animals), $100.00, plus $5.00 for each additional 100 or less; upland game bird stamp, $1.00; federal "Duck" stamp, $3.00.

HUNTING AND TRAPPING

Game animals: Antelope, Deer (Mule, Whitetail), Cottontail Rabbits, Gray Squirrels. OPEN SEASONS:* Antelope—a few days in September in designated areas. Deer—archery Sept. 15–Dec. 31 except during the firearms period; rifle, about 10 days in mid-November in designated areas. Cottontail Rabbit—June 1–Dec. 31. Gray Squirrel—Sept. 1–Jan. 15. BAG LIMITS: Antelope—1 per year. Deer—1 per year. Cottontail Rabbits —8 per day. Gray Squirrels—5 per day.

Furbearing animals: Badger, Beaver, Bobcat, Fox, Mink, Muskrat, Opossum, Raccoon, Skunk, Weasel. OPEN SEASONS: Beaver, Muskrat— Nov. 15 (noon) to March 15. Mink—Nov. 15 (noon) to January 15. NOT PROTECTED: Badger, Bobcat, Coyote, Fox, Gopher, Opossum, Porcupine, Prairie Dog, Raccoon, Skunk, Weasel, Woodchuck may be taken at any time.

Game birds: Coot, Ducks (except Canvasback and Redhead), Gallinule, Geese, Sharptailed Grouse, Merganser, Ring-necked Pheasant, Prairie Chicken (Pinnated Grouse), Bobwhite Quail, Rails, Scaup, Sora, Wilson's Snipe, Wild Turkey. OPEN SEASONS:* Coot, Ducks, Merganser, Scaup—mid-October (noon) to mid-November. Gallinule, Rails, Sora—

---

* Check current state regulations.

early October to late November. Geese—October 1 to mid-December. Grouse, Prairie Chicken—about 4 weeks after the first Saturday in October. Cock Pheasant—from fourth Saturday in October to mid-January. Bobwhite Quail—from fourth Saturday in October or first Saturday in November to December in the Northern Area, and extended to late December in the Southern Area. Wilson's Snipe—early October to early November. Wild Turkey—8 or 10 days in November. FULLY PROTECTED: Canvasback and Redhead Ducks—no open season. NOT PROTECTED: Crow, Cooper's Hawk, Goshawk, Sharp-shinned Hawk, and Great Horned Owls may be killed at any time.

Northern Area: North of U.S. Highway 30 from the Iowa-Nebraska border westward to U.S. Highway 138, then south and along the same highway to the Colorado-Nebraska boundary line. Southern Area: Remainder of the state.

FIREARMS

Deer hunters should use rifles with at least 900 foot-pounds of energy at 100 yards, and muzzle loaders must be .40 caliber or larger. Longbows with a 40-pound pull for a 28-inch draw are legal. It is unlawful to hunt game birds with a pistol, revolver, rifle, or shotgun larger than 10 gauge and capable of holding more than 3 shells in the magazine and chamber combined. A magazine may be cut off or plugged with a piece of metal or wood filler which cannot be removed without disassembling the shotgun.

Shooting hours: Sunrise to sunset; except Antelope, Deer, and Wild Turkey—one-half hour before sunrise to one-half hour after sunset. Shooting migratory game birds starts at 12:00 o'clock noon on the opening day for Ducks.

FISHING

Game fish: Black Bass (Largemouth, Smallmouth), Catfish (Blue, Channel, Flathead), Paddlefish, Northern Pike, Sauger, Trout (Brook, Brown, Rainbow), Walleye. OPEN SEASONS:* All year by hook and line or snagging (local exceptions). Archery (game and nongame fish), April 1–Dec. 1. Spearing (nongame fish), April 1–Dec. 1 in designated waters.

Bullfrogs: A fishing permit is required to take Bullfrogs by hand, hand net, gig, hook and line, and a hunting permit if taken by hand, hand net, bow and arrow. Bag limit, 12 daily.

Not more than 2 lines with 2 hooks each are permitted in any lake, pond, or reservoir, or for one-half mile in their outlets, inlets, and canals.

---

* Check current state regulations.

It is unlawful to use more than 5 hooks on a line, or more than 15 hooks on all lines while fishing in streams or through ice. Bow and arrow fishing, gigging, snagging, or snaring are prohibited in Trout streams, Twin Rivers, and other special areas.

STATE PARKS, RECREATION, AND SPECIAL-USE AREAS

Fishing: Chadron (1,525 acres) in Pine Ridge region south of Chadron—Dawes County; *Cottonmill* (98 acres) near Kearney—Buffalo County; *Fort Robinson* on the 36,000-acre military reserve, west of Crawford—Dawes County; *Niobrara* (450 acres) on a forested island in the Niobrara River at the junction with the Missouri River—Knox County; *Otter Creek* on north shore of McConaughy Lake, near Lemoyne —Keith County; *Ponca* (495 acres) overlooking the Missouri River north of Ponca—Dixon County; *Victoria Springs* (60 acres) north of Merna— Custer County; *Walgren Lake* (130 acres) southeast of Hay Springs— Sheridan County; *Willow Lake* 20 miles south of Valentine—Cherry County.

Hunting and fishing: Alexandria Lakes (440 acres) east of Alexandria—Thayer County; *Arnold Lake* (40 acres) south of Arnold—Custer County; *Atkinson Lake* (50 acres) west of Atkinson—Holt County; *Big Alkali Lake* about 15 miles southwest of Valentine—Cherry County; *Blue River* (14 acres) north of Dorchester—Saline County; *Bowman Lake* (46 acres) west of Loup City—Sherman County; *Box Elder Canyon* near Maxwell—Lincoln County; *Bridgeport* at Bridgeport—Morrill County; *Champion Lake* (11 acres) on Frenchman River at Champion—Chase County; *Cottonwood Canyon* 6 miles south of Maxwell—Lincoln County; *Box Butte* at 3,900-acre reservoir north of Hemingford—Box Butte County; *Crystal Lake* (55 acres) north of Ayr—Adams County; *Dead Timber* (200 acres) southeast of Crowell—Dodge County; *Duke Alexis* (100 acres) on Red Willow Creek, 12 miles northeast of Hayes Center— Hayes County; *Enders Reservoir* on Frenchman River, 8 miles southeast of Imperial—Chase County; *Fremont Lakes* (800 acres) west of Fremont —Dodge County; *Gallagher Canyon* on South Platte River, 9 miles south of Cozad—Dawson County; *Gavins Point* at Lewis and Clark Lake— Knox County; *Gilbert Baker* north of Harrison—Sioux County; *Goose Lake* (350 acres) near Bliss—Holt County; *Grove Lake,* north of Royal —Antelope County; *Harland County Reservoir* south of Alma on Republican River; *Hord Lake* near Central City—Merrick County; *Hull Lake* south of Butte—Boyd County; *Johnson Reservoir* on Platte River between Lexington in Dawes County and Elwood in Gasper County; *Long Lake* (80 acres), 25 miles southwest of Ainsworth—Brown County; *Louisville Lakes* (192 acres) on the Platte River at Louisville—Cass County; *Maloney Lake* 8 miles south of North Platte—Lincoln County; *Mc-*

Conaughy Reservoir 8 miles north of Ogallala—Keith County; *Medicine Creek Reservoir* (Strunk Lake) north of Cambridge—Furnas County; *Memphis* (233 acres) at Memphis—Saunders County; *Midway* 5 miles west of Cozad—Dawson County; *Milburn Dam* on the Middle Loup River at Milburn—Custer County; *Pibel Lake* (65 acres) south of Cumminsville—Wheeler County; *Plum Creek* 15 miles south of Cozad—Dawson County; *Pressy* (80 acres) on the South Loup River, 5 miles north of Ocono—Custer County; *Rat* and *Beaver lakes* (245 acres) at edge of Valentine Migratory Waterfowl Refuge—Cherry County; *Ravenna* (81 acres) near Ravenna—Buffalo County; *Rock Creek Lake* (100 acres) north of Parks—Dundy County; *Shell Lake* (640 acres) near Irwin—Cherry County; *Smith Lake* (640 acres) 23 miles south of Rushville—Sheridan County; *Swanson Reservoir* on the Republican River, west of Trenton—Hitchcock County; *Two Rivers* south of Waterloo—Douglas County; *Verdon Lake* (75 acres) west of Verdon—Richardson County; *Wellfleet Lake* (164 acres) at Wellfleet—Lincoln County.

Other special-use hunting areas include *Ballards Marsh* (1,583 acres) 20 miles south of Valentine—Cherry County; *Jeffrey Canyon* 5 miles southwest of Brady—Lincoln County; *Sioux Strip* 3 miles southeast of Randolph—Cedar County. *Wildcat Hills Big Game Refuge* (852 acres) 9 miles south of Gering—Scotts Bluff County.

Permits, regulations, information about current seasons, bag and possession limits may be obtained from the Executive Secretary, Game, Forestation, and Parks Commission, State Capitol, Lincoln, 9. Approximately 97 per cent of Nebraska is under private ownership, and permission to hunt or trap must be obtained from the landowner or his agents. The commission and any local chamber of commerce have lists of landowners in hunting areas. The very attractive *Outdoor Nebraska* is published monthly ($2 annually) by the commission.

NEVADA

Area: 110,690 square miles (land area—109,788 square miles); rank in nation—7
Bird: Mountain Bluebird (*Sialia currucoides*)
Capital city: Carson City in the Eagle Valley of Grimsby County; population (1960)—5,163; rank in state—7
Counties: 17
Elevation: Highest, Boundary Peak (13,145 ft.) in the Sierra Nevada in Esmeralda County; lowest, Colorado River (470 ft.) in Clark County
Flower: Sagebrush (*Artemisia tridentata*), adopted 1917

175 *Nevada*

Geographic center: 23 miles southeast of Austin, Lander County
Nicknames: Battle Born State, Sagebrush State, Silver State
Population (1960): 285,278; rank in nation–49
Tree: Single-leaf Pine or Pinyon (*Pinus monophylla*)

Nevada is bordered by Idaho and Oregon on the north; Utah on the east; and Arizona in the southeast separated by a short line through the Virgin Mountains, the Colorado River, Lake Mead, and Lake Mohave; and shares with California the Sierra Nevada Range in the west and Mojave Desert in the southwest.

The state is in a great basin of broad sagebrush valleys between a series of north and south parallel mountains. The highest peak entirely in Nevada is Mount Wheeler (13,001 ft.) towering above the Lehman Caves National Monument west of Baker near the Utah line. The Humboldt River, fed by several creeks and Mary's River in northeastern Elko County, by the Little Humboldt River from Paradise Valley in Humboldt County, and by the Reese River near Battle Mountain in Lander County, is impounded to form the Rye Patch Reservoir north of Lovelock. From the eastern slopes of the Sierra Nevada, the Carson and Truckee rivers, impounded by Lahontan Dam near Fallon, move on to disappear in the Carson Sink below the Stillwater Range. The East Walker and West Walker rivers from the California High Sierras merge to flow through Yerington and the Walker River Indian Reservation to Walker Lake north of Hawthorne. Lovely Lake Tahoe, extending for 23 miles along the Nevada-California border, is 14 miles west of Carson City. The blue waters of Pyramid Lake (182 square miles) sparkle among the desert sands and sage-covered hills of the Pyramid Lake Indian Reservation north of Reno in the Washoe County. Topaz Lake on West Walker River is on the California line southwest of Wellington. The Lake Mead National Recreational Area contains Lake Mead (247 square miles) impounded by Hoover Dam on the Colorado River near Boulder City, and Lake Mohave (45 square miles) formed by the Davis Dam southeast of Searchlight. The Virgin River flows into Lake Mead near Overton. Mount Charleston (11,919 ft.) in the Spring Mountains northwest of Las Vegas is in the southern triangle. The vast Tonopah Bombing and Gunnery Range in Southern Nevada contains the Belted, Cactus, Desert, and Pintwater ranges between Tonopah and Las Vegas. Beatty on Amargosa River is the gateway to the Death Valley National Monument.

The Mount Rose (10,800 ft.) winter sports area is 17 miles southwest of Reno, and the Reno Ski Bowl on Slide Mountain is 22 miles away. There is a Pilot Peak (10,704 ft.) in the Toana Range of Elko County and another Pilot Peak (9,207 ft.) east of Mina in Mineral County.

LICENSES

Resident licenses to fish, hunt, and trap are issued to citizens 16 or more years of age who have lived in the state for at least 6 months immediately prior to an application for a license; and to members of the U.S. Armed Forces after their arrival for permanent duty in Nevada. Free licenses are granted to resident Indians; to Nevada servicemen home on leave; and to persons 60 or more years of age who have lived in the state for at least 10 years prior to a request for an exempt license. All aliens (noncitizens) must obtain nonresident licenses. Persons under the age of 12 may not hunt big game, and juveniles 12–14 years of age (inclusive) must be accompanied by a licensed adult. Nonresidents and noncitizens regardless of age are required to possess nonresident licenses, permits, and tags to hunt or trap game animals and birds. Upland game bird permits are required of noncitizens and nonresidents in addition to regular hunting licenses for taking Chukar Partridge in Eureka, Humboldt, and Pershing counties; to take Chukar Partridge and Quail in Elko, Lander, and Nye counties; to take Pheasants and Quail in Clark County; and to take Blue Grouse, Chukar Partridge, Pheasant, and Quail in Douglas and Grimsby counties.

Only residents of Nevada may hunt Antelope, Elk, and Bighorn Sheep, except that a few permits have been issued to nonresidents for Bighorn Rams in Clark County. A buck or a Deer of either sex may be taken during a regular Deer season in designated areas, and the antlerless quota tag entitles a sportsman to take an additional Deer. The archery Deer tag is valid only during a regular archery season, and hunters holding an archery tag are not eligible for the antlerless quota tag. No hunting license is required to kill predatory or unprotected animals and birds. Dogs may be used for tracking or trailing wounded Deer if permission is obtained from a county game management board to have a dog in a Deer hunting camp. No hunting license is required for taking game birds on private shooting preserves. All persons 16 or more years of age must purchase a federal "Duck" Stamp to take migratory game birds.

A special "use" stamp is required in addition to a valid fishing license for all residents 16 or more years of age and nonresidents 14 or more years of age to fish in boundary waters. An Arizona special use stamp with an Arizona license entitles the holder to fish from a boat or other floating device on Lake Mead, Lake Mohave, and the Colorado River. A Lake Tahoe or Lake Topaz fisherman must possess a California special use stamp affixed to his Nevada license or a Nevada stamp on a California sport fishing license. A special Indian reservation permit is required in addition to a fishing license for all persons 16 or more years of age to take trout in Pyramid Lake. Annual fishing license period, July 1–June 30.

Resident license fees: fishing, $5.00; hunting, $5.00; trapping, $1.00. *Tags* (in addition to license): Antelope, $10.00; archery Deer, $2.50; regular Deer season, $2.50; quota antlerless Deer, $2.50; Elk, $10.00; Bighorn Sheep, $10.00; special use stamp (affix to fishing license), $2.00; Pyramid Lake Indian Reservation season permit, $3.00; fishing one day on Pyramid Lake permit, $1.00; federal "Duck" stamp, $3.00.

Nonresident license fees: Fishing, $10.00; fishing 5 consecutive days, $3.50; archery season hunting, $20.00; hunting (firearms, including bow and arrow), $25.00; trapping, $10.00. *Tags* (in addition to license): archery Deer, $10.00; regular season Deer, $25.00; quota antlerless Deer, $10.00; Bighorn Deer, $15.00; upland game bird permit, $5.00; federal "Duck" stamp, $3.00; special use stamp, $2.00; Pyramid Lake Indian Reservation season permit, $3.00; fishing one day on Pyramid Lake permit, $1.00.

HUNTING AND TRAPPING

Game animals: Antelope, Deer, Elk, Bighorn Sheep, Cottontail and Pygmy Rabbits. OPEN SEASONS:* Antelope—usually last week of August in quota units. Deer—archery only, first 3 weeks of September; regular firearms (including bow and arrow), early October to mid-November, and opens one week earlier in the Jarbidge unit in Elko County at the Idaho border. Elk—mid-October to mid-November. Bighorn Sheep—late November to late December. Rabbits: Sept. 1–Dec. 31. BAG LIMITS: Antelope—1 per year. Deer—2 per year (1, archery or regular season; 1, antlerless quota). Bull Elk—1 per year. Bighorn Sheep—1 Ram with three-quarter curl horn per year. Rabbits—10 per day.

A legal buck Deer or buck Elk must have a branched antler. An antlerless Deer may be a Spike Buck or any Deer with less than one branched antler. Except in one area, Antelopes should have horns longer than their ears.

Furbearing animals: Badger, Beaver, Fox (Gray, Red, Silver, Swift), Otter, Raccoon, Skunk, Weasel. OPEN SEASONS:* Beaver, Otter—Oct. 1–March 15 in Elko County, Nov. 1–Feb. 15 in all other counties. Red, Silver, and Swift Foxes—Nov. 1–March 15. NOT PROTECTED: Badger, Beaver, Bobcat, Coyote, Gray Fox, Gopher, Mountain Lion, Porcupine, Prairie Dog, Raccoon, Skunk, Weasel, and Woodchuck may be killed at any time.

Game birds: Coot, Dove (Mourning, Whitewinged), Ducks (except Canvasback, Redhead), Gallinule, Geese, Grouse (Blue, Sage), Jacksnipe, Merganser, Partridge (Chukar, Hungarian), Pheasant, Quail (Gambel, Mountain, Valley). OPEN SEASONS:* Coot, Ducks, Gallinule, Geese,

---

* Check current state regulations.

Merganser—mid-October to early January. Dove—about 6 weeks from September 1 to early October. Grouse—during September in designated areas with periods varying from 1 to 30 days, and in O'Neil Basin of Elko County, about 1 week in late August. Jacksnipe—about 6 weeks from November into December. Partridge—late September to early December in Douglas, Esmeralda, Eureka, Lyon, Mineral, Nye, Ormsby, Washoe, and White Pine counties; ˋand extended to December 31 in Churchill, Elko, Humboldt, Lander, Pershing, and Washoe counties. Pheasant—late October and early November in Churchill, Clark, Douglas, Humboldt, Lyon, Ormsby, Pershing, Storey, and Washoe counties. Quail —from about October 1 to December 31 in designated areas of counties open to Partridge and Pheasant hunting with periods varying from 1 week to the entire season. FULLY PROTECTED: Brant, Canvasback and Redhead Ducks, Swans—no open season. NOT PROTECTED: Cormorant, Crow, Blue Darter, Prairie Falcon, Goshawk, Cooper's Hawk, Duck Hawk, Pigeon Hawk, Sharp-shinned Hawk, Magpie, Great Horned Owl, Raven.

FIREARMS

Migratory game birds may be taken only with shotguns not larger than 10 gauge, and having a capacity of not more than 3 shells in the magazine and chamber combined. The shotgun must be fired from the shoulder; and if originally capable of holding more than 3 shells, it must be plugged with a filler in such a manner as to make removal impossible without taking the gun apart.

Big game hunting rifles should exert at least 1,000 foot-pounds of energy at 100 yards. Under this standard, the following guns do not qualify: all .22 caliber rimfires, .218 Bee, .219 Zipper, .22 Hornet, .22 Savage; .25-20, .25-35, .32-20, .32 Winchester self-loading; .32-40, .35 Winchester self-loading; .351 Winchester self-loading; .38-40, .38-55, .44-40, .351 Winchester self-loading. It is unlawful to hunt big game with a pistol, revolver, shotgun, or any firearm capable of firing two or more rounds with one continuous pull of the trigger, or with any full steel, full steel core, full metal jacket, tracer, or incendiary bullet. An archery Deer hunter must use a long bow capable of throwing a 400-grain arrow 150 yards over level terrain, and the arrows should have hunting type tips at least three-quarters of an inch.

Shooting hours: Sunrise to sunset. Exceptions: migratory game birds, one-half hour before sunrise to sunset, and on first day of Duck season, shooting starts at 12:00 o'clock noon; Quail, 8:00 A.M. to sunset in all except Clark and Lincoln counties. No artificial light of any kind may be used to take game animals or birds.

FISHING

Game fish: Black Bass (Largemouth, Smallmouth), Calico Bass, Bluegill, Catfish, Crappie, Perch (Sacramento, Yellow), Kokanee Salmon, Steelhead and other Trout, Whitefish, and all varieties of Sunfish. OPEN SEASONS:* all year with local exceptions.

It is unlawful to take game fish with any net, seine, spear, setline, snagline, trotline, grab hooks, set hooks or by any manner of snagging. Except for the Lake Mead National Recreational Area, not more than 3 baited hooks, or 3 fly hooks, or more than 2 plugs or similar lures (regardless of the number of attached hooks or attractor blades) may be attached to one line. In Lake Mead, Lake Mohave, and the Colorado River, not more than 2 bait or fly hooks, not more than 2 artificial lures may be used on one line attached to a rod, held in the hand, or closely attended by a fisherman. Chumming and spear fishing are prohibited in Lake Tahoe and Lake Topaz, but nongame fish and Bullfrogs may be taken with spear and/or bow and arrow during open season in other waters, except within one-half mile of a dock or swimming area.

Bullfrogs: All year, except in Lyon County, June 15–Aug. 31; in Pyramid Lake Indian Reservation, July 1–Dec. 31. No open season in Elko, Esmeralda, and White Pine counties.

There is prime fishing for Black Bass, Rainbow Trout, Channel Catfish, and Crappie in Lake Mead and Lake Mohave, which is also stocked with Kokanee Salmon; and the Truckee River is an excellent Trout stream. The following state parks are good fishing, hunting, and camping areas.

STATE PARKS

Beaver Dam (1,713 acres) 35 miles east of Caliente near the Utah border, Lincoln County; *Cathedral Gorge* (1,570 acres) north of Caliente near the town of Panaca; *Snyder Meadows* at Clear Creek in the High Sierra, south of Carson City; *Ward Charcoal Ovens* (40 acres) at base of Ward Mountain (10,936 ft.) south of Ely-White Pine County.

Licenses, permits, regulations, and information about current seasons, bag and possession limits, guides, and packers may be obtained from the Directors, Nevada Game and Fish Department, 1100 Valley Road (P.O. Box 678) Reno; and authorized agents throughout the state, including sporting goods stores. Permits for Clark County upland game bird hunting are issued at the Charleston District Office of the Fish and Game Commission, Room 107, State Office Building, Las Vegas.

---

* Check current state regulations.

NEW HAMPSHIRE

Area: 9,341 square miles (land area—9,014 square miles); rank in nation—44
Bird: Purple Finch (*Carpodacus purpureus*), adopted 1957
Capital city: Concord on the Merrimack River in Merrimack County; population (1960)—28,991; rank in state—3
Elevations: Highest, Mount Washington (6,288 ft.) in Coos County; lowest, Atlantic Ocean
Flower: Purple Lilac (*Syringa vulgaris*), adopted 1919
Geographic center: 3 miles east of Ashland, Belknap County
Nicknames: Granite State, Mother of Rivers, Old Man of the Mountain State, White Mountain State
Population (1960): 606,921; rank in nation—45
Tidal shoreline: 131 miles
Tree: White Birch (*Betula papyrifera*), also called Paper Birch; adopted 1947

New Hampshire is a New England state bordered by Maine on the east; Massachusetts on the south, Vermont on the west bank of the Connecticut River, and the Canadian province of Quebec on the north and northwest.

The Connecticut River rises near the Quebec border below Salmon Mountain (3,364 ft.) and Deer Mountain (3,005 ft.) to flow from Third Lake, Moose Falls, and Second Lake at Idlewild to the First Connecticut Lake, and Lake Francis at Pittsburg, and from Stewartstown starts to form the boundary line between New Hampshire and Vermont. The Dead Diamond River from the northern Magalloway Mountain (3,360 ft.) merges with the Swift Diamond River near Mount Dustan to flow into Umbagog Lake, the source of the Androscoggin River which flows southward to Gorham and then swerves eastward into Maine. Several streams in Coos County form the Ammonossuc River, a tributary of the Connecticut River. The Pemigewasset River, increased by many streams in the White Mountain National Forest, is impounded north of Franklin to create the Franklin Falls Reservoir and then merge with the Winnipesaukee River to become the Merrimack River flowing southward through Concord, Manchester, and Nashua to Massachusetts. From a series of ponds on the southeastern border, the Salmon River joins the Piscataqua River from Maine to continue southward between Portsmouth and Kittery into the Atlantic Ocean.

The Ossipee Mountains overlook Lake Winnipesaukee (72 square miles) northeast of Laconia. There are about 275 habitable islands on this lovely lake called the "Smile of the Great Spirit" by Indians. Squam

Lake near Ashland, Ossipee Lake near Effingham Falls on the Ossipee River, Squam Lake at Holderness, and Winnisquam Lake at Laconia are among several popular lakes in this region. West of Lake Sunapee, the Sugar River flows between the Croydon Mountains and Sunapee Mountains near Claremont and Newport.

The Franconia Notch State Reservation (6,000 acres) in the White Mountains north of Woodstock contains a remarkable 40-foot Great Stone Face formed by 5 mountain ledges 1,200 feet above Profile Lake, a craggy landmark also known as The Profile and the Old Man of the Mountain. Flume Brook drops 25 feet over Avalanche Falls to race through Flume Gorge, and adding to the scenic attractions of Franconia Notch are Echo Lake below Mount Lafayette (5,249 ft.), Mount Lincoln (5,108 ft.), Mount Liberty (4,468 ft.), Cannon Mountain (4,200 ft.), and Mount Flume (4,327 ft.). Crawford Notch on the Saco River north of Bartlett is called a "Gateway to the North" and contains Arethusa Falls more than 200 feet high, the Silver Cascades, and Crawford Pond within sight of Mount Webster (3,875 ft.) and Mount Willey (4,261 ft.). Dixville Notch on the Colebrook-Errol Highway, is a magnificent gorge between Dixville Peak (3,482 ft.) and Rice Mountain (3,370 ft.) near several lakes and streams including Lake Abeniki and the Mohawk River. Pinkham Notch north of Jackson is a spectacular gap in the White Mountain National Forest leading to the lofty Presidential Range, Tuckerman Ravine, and the Carter Mountains.

LICENSES

Resident licenses are issued to citizens who have lived in the state for at least 6 months prior to an application for a license and have not claimed residence in another state for any purpose; and to members of the U.S. Armed Forces and their dependents stationed at military bases in New Hampshire. Any alien who has lived continuously in the state for not less than one year may obtain resident licenses by submitting evidence of his military service and honorable discharge from the armed forces of the United States. Military personnel stationed outside New Hampshire who were legal residents prior to entry into the armed forces may apply for a free residential serviceman's license by submitting satisfactory evidence of residence and a copy of his leave or furlough papers. Totally and permanently disabled veterans of any war in which the United States has been engaged may apply annually for free licenses to fish and hunt. A disabled veteran suffering from paraplegia or from the loss of both lower extremities and who holds a current hunting license may obtain from the Director of the Fish and Game Department a special permit to use a motor vehicle while hunting, but not an aircraft or boat with an attached motor. Special daily fishing permits may be issued in the veterans hospitals at Manchester (N.H.) and White River Junction (Vt.) to patients if such recreation could be of therapeutic value. Residents 65 or more years of age receiving public aid, and blind persons may obtain free fishing licenses.

Juveniles under the age of 16 are not required to possess fishing and hunting licenses, but they must be accompanied while hunting by a licensed hunter 21 or more years of age. No resident or nonresident between 16 and 19 years of age may obtain a hunting license unless the minor presents evidence of possessing a license issued to him during a prior year; or a certificate of competency in the safe handling of firearms; or proof of existing or previous membership in a branch of the U.S. Armed Forces, including any women's auxiliary unit. A nonresident student over 18 years of age who is attending an educational institution may purchase a student hunting license for one-half of the nonresident hunting license fee, if he submits evidence that he attended and passed the National Rifle Association's Hunter Safety Training program.

A bow and arrow license to hunt Deer is valid for 31 days immediately prior to the open season in the Bear Brook Reservation, and for 20 days before a firearms Deer season in other areas. The nonresident Coos County small game license is valid only during the month of October for taking any game animal except Bear and Deer. Vermont and New Hampshire resident fishing licenses are valid for the Connecticut River, but holders of Vermont licenses may not fish beyond the ordinary low water mark on the Vermont side of the river. Honorary licenses (50 hunting, 75 fishing) may be issued annually without charge to such nonresidents as the President and the Vice President of the United States, governors, game officials, conservationists, and sports writers. All persons 16 or more years of age must have a federal "Duck" stamp to take migratory game birds.

Resident license fees: Fishing, $3.50; regular hunting, $3.50; combination fishing and hunting, $5.00; federal "Duck" stamp (in addition to hunting license), $3.00; bow and arrow (valid with regular hunting license), $3.00; trapping (over 16 years of age), $5.00; trapping (under 16 years of age), $1.00; guide (fishing and hunting), $3.00; fur buyer (one county only), $5.00; fur buyer (Statewide), $35.00; taxidermist, $1.00; fish breeder, $2.00; game breeder (including birds), $2.00.

Nonresident license fees: Fishing, $8.25; fishing 15 consecutive days, $5.25; fishing 3 consecutive days, $3.75; hunting, $25.25; Coos County small game hunting, $10.25; student hunting (18 or more years of age), $12.75; bow and arrow hunting (valid with regular hunting license), $4.00; special bow and arrow Deer hunting (no other license necessary), $10.00; trapping, $200.00; guide (fishing and hunting), $30.00.

HUNTING AND TRAPPING

Game animals: Black Bear, Caribou, Deer, Elk, Moose, Hare and Cottontail Rabbit, Gray Squirrel. OPEN SEASONS:* Bear—October 1 to mid-December, and during May, September, and October with dogs by permit. Deer—archery, Oct. 1–31 in Bear Brook Reservation, and 20 days prior to regular Deer season elsewhere; firearms, November 1 to mid-December in designated areas. Hares and Rabbits—Oct. 1–March 31. Squirrels: Oct. 1–Nov. 1. BAG LIMIT: Bear—no limit. Deer—1 per year. Hares and Rabbits—5 per day (in the aggregate). Squirrels—5 per day.

Furbearing animals: Beaver, Fisher, Canada Lynx, Marten, Mink, Muskrat, Otter, Raccoon, Sable, Skunk. OPEN SEASON:* Beaver—Nov. 1–April 15. Fisher–Nov. 1–30 in Rockingham and Strafford counties only. Mink, Muskrat, Otter, Skunk—mid-October to February 1 in Carroll, Coos, and Grafton counties; Nov. 1–March 31 in all other counties. Raccoon—Sept. 1–Dec. 1. FULLY PROTECTED: Caribou, Elk, Fisher (except in Rockingham and Strafford counties), Marten, and Sable—no open seasons. NOT PROTECTED: Bobcat, Fox, Canada Lynx, Porcupine, Weasel, Prairie or Timber Wolves, and Woodchucks may be taken at any time. Any animal doing substantial damage to poultry may be killed by the owner or occupant of the land.

Game birds: Brant, Coot, Ducks (except Canvasback and Redhead), Gallinule, Geese (except Snow Geese), Ruffed Grouse or Partridge, Spruce Grouse commonly called Spruce Partridge, Merganser, Chukar Partridge, European Partridge, Pheasant, Plover (all species), Bobwhite Quail, Rails, Scaup, Sora, Wilson's Snipe, Woodchuck, and all shore birds. OPEN SEASONS:* Brant, Geese—mid-October to mid-December. Coot, Ducks, Merganser, Scaup: mid-October to late November. Gallinule, Rails, Sora—September 1 to early November. Ruffed Grouse— Oct. 1–Dec. 1. Pheasant: Oct. 1–Nov. 1. Wilson's Snipe, Woodcock —October 1 to mid-November. FULLY PROTECTED: Doves, Canvasback and Redhead Ducks, Snow Geese, Spruce Grouse, Chukar and European Partridge, Upland Plover, Bobwhite Quail—no open season. NOT PROTECTED: Crows, English Sparrows, and European Starlings may be taken at any time.

FIREARMS

Deer may not be taken with a .22 caliber rimfire firearm at any time, or with a shotgun loaded with a single ball or loose buckshot in the municipalities of Amherst, Bedford, Brookline, Goffstown, Hollis, Hudson, Litchfield, Manchester, Merrimack, Nashua, and Pelham in Hillsborough

---

* Check current state regulations.

County, and about 30 towns in Rockingham County. A longbow used for hunting Deer must have a pull of at least 40 pounds, and the broad metal head of the arrow should be not less than seven-eighths of an inch nor more than 1½ inches in width. The name and address of the hunter must be clearly printed on each arrow. The use of a pistol, revolver, or rifle larger than .22, or shotgun shells carrying shot larger than no. 4, or a light other than a kerosene lantern (exclusive of pressure type), or a flashlight with more than 7 cells to hunt Raccoon at night are prohibited.

Shooting hours: One-half hour before sunrise to one-half hour after sunset; except migratory game birds—sunrise to sunset; and on opening day of the Duck season, shooting starts at 12:00 o'clock noon. Raccoons —season opens at 12:00 o'clock noon and closes at 12:00 o'clock noon.

Traps set through ice for Beaver should be checked at least once in each 72 hours, but other traps must be visited daily between regular hours for hunting upland game.

FISHING

Game fish: Black Bass (Largemouth, Smallmouth), Perch (White, Yellow), Pickerel, Pike-perch, Horned Pout, Salmon, Shad, Trout (Aureolus or Golden, Brook, Brown, Lake, Rainbow), Whitefish. OPEN SEASON (local exceptions):* Black Bass: June 1–Oct. 31. Pickerel— fourth Saturday in April to October 31. Salmon—April 1–Sept. 30. Shad, Whitefish—Jan. 1–Aug. 31. Golden Trout—April 1 to Labor Day, and artificial fly fishing only from the day after Labor Day to September 30. Lake Trout—Jan. 1–Sept. 30. Brook, Brown, and Rainbow Trout—fourth Saturday in April to Labor Day, and artificial fly fishing only from day after Labor Day to October 15. A fisherman may troll with bait or artificial flies for either Salmon or Lake Trout April 1–Sept. 30.

Freshwater Smelt may be taken for food or bait by a hand-held dip net not over 18 inches in diameter, but not at any time from a boat propelled by mechanical power. Carp may be taken by bow and arrow (with cord attached) from Mascoma Lake (Grafton County) and the Connecticut River.

Ice fishing (local exceptions): Jan. 1–March 31 in all Lake Trout and Salmon Lakes. A single hook either for bait or attached to artificial lures may be used with a line. Any quantity of Cusk may be taken by the use of 6 lines. A person holding a New Hampshire fishing license may drive a motor vehicle over ice on Grant Bay (near Portsmouth) at a speed of 10 or fewer miles per hour, provided that he does not drive or park his vehicle any closer than 300 feet to an occupied bob house,

---

* Check current state regulations.

fishing shanty, or fishing hole other than his own structure. Only 2 fishing devices may be used to fish through ice in the following lakes: *Merrymeeting Lake* at New Durham in Strafford County; *Newfoundland Lake* at Alexandria, Bristol, and Hebron in Grafton County; *Opechee Lake* at Laconia in Belknap County; *Ossipee Lake* at Freedom and Ossipee; *Silver Lake* at Madison in Carroll County; *Big Squam Lake* at Center Harbor in Belknap County, at Moultonbore and Sandwich in Carroll County, and at Holderness in Grafton County; *Waukewan Lake* at Center Harbor, Meredith, and New Hampton in Belknap County; *Winnipesaukee Lake* (including Paugus Bay and The Basin in Tuftsboro) at Alton, Center Harbor, Gilford, Laconia, and Meredith in Belknap County, and at Moultonboro, Tuftonboro, and Wolfeboro in Carroll County; *Winnisquam Lake* at Belmont, Laconia, Meredith, Sanfornton, and Tilton in Belknap County.

STATE PARKS

Bear Brook (7,303 acres) around Bear Hill (800 ft.) at Allenstown —Merrimack County; *Crawford Notch* (5,950 acres) north of Bartlett— Carroll County; *Forest Lake* (420 acres) south of Whitefield—Coos County; *Franconia Notch* (6,592 acres) at Echo Lake between the Franconia and Kinsman ranges, near North Woodstock—Grafton County; *Hampton Beach* (50 acres) south of Portsmouth—Rockingham County; *Kingston* (44 acres) at Great Pond in Kingston—Rockingham County; *Moose Brook* (755 acres) west of Gorham—Coos County; *Mount Sunapee* (1,787 acres) at southern end of Lake Sunapee, east of Newport— Sullivan County; *Pillsbury* (3,702 acres) contains 5 ponds, north of Washington—Sullivan County; *Rye Harbor* (160 acres) south of Portsmouth —Rockingham County; *Wadleigh* (52 acres) at Kezar Lake, North Sutton—Merrimack County; *Wellington* (105 acres) north of Bristol— Grafton County; *Wentworth* (17 acres) at Lake Wentworth, east of Wolfeboro—Carroll County; *White Lake* (603 acres) north of West Ossipee—Carroll County.

Licenses, regulations, and information about current seasons, bag and possession limits may be obtained from the Director, New Hampshire Fish and Game Department, Concord; and from town clerks and some sporting goods and general stores.

NEW JERSEY

Area: 8,224 square miles (land area—7,521 square miles); rank in nation –46
Bird: Eastern Goldfinch (*Spinus tristis*), adopted 1935

Capital city: Trenton on Assunpink Creek and the eastern bank of the Delaware River in Mercer County; population (1960)—114,167; rank in state–5
Counties: 21
Elevations: Highest, High Point (1,801 ft.) in northern Sussex County; lowest, Atlantic Ocean
Flower: Purple Violet (*Viola*), adopted 1913
Geographic center: 5 miles southeast of the state capitol at Trenton in Mercer County
Nicknames: Garden State, Clam State, Mosquito State
Population (1960): 6,066,782; rank in nation–8
Tidal shoreline: 1,792 miles (including islands, bays, and streams to a point where tidal waters narrow to 100 ft. wide)
Tree: Red Oak (*Quercus rubra*), adopted 1950

New Jersey is a huge peninsula south of New York, bordered by the Hudson River and Atlantic Ocean on the east, and separated from Delaware on the southwest by Delaware Bay, and from Pennsylvania on the west by the Delaware River.

The lower half of the state is a coastal plain with isolated hills, sand dunes, tidal salt marshes, and shallow lagoons protected by long narrow sandy beaches. The Great Egg Harbor River flows into the ocean near Atlantic City, and Maurice River empties into Delaware Bay between Egg Island Point and Cape May on the southern tip of New Jersey. The Delaware River flows through the Kittatinny Range from Port Jervis in the north to Water Gap where the sides of this opening rise abruptly to about 1,200 feet, and continues southward to Delaware Bay. The Delaware-Raritan Canal connects Trenton on the Delaware River with Perth Amboy at the mouth of the Raritan River which flows into Lower New York Bay. The picturesque Palisade Ridge on the Hudson River, and the nearby Hackensack River, following nearly parallel courses, extend from New York into northeastern New Jersey. The Passaic River from the highlands meanders for about 100 miles, and drops 70 feet at Paterson on a course to Newark Bay only about 15 miles in a straight line from its source. Among the lakes and forested hills of northern New Jersey, Lake Hopatcong (2,443 acres) is the largest lake in the state. Lake Greenwood at Awosting in Passaic County extends into New York.

LICENSES

Resident licenses are issued to citizens of the United States who have lived in the state for at least one year immediately preceding an application for a license, and to nonresident members of any branch of the U.S. Armed Forces officially stationed in New Jersey. A bona fide resident on active duty with the armed forces may fish and hunt without licenses. Juveniles under the age of 14 may fish without licenses, and any blind person may obtain a free license to fish. No resident 10 or more years of age or any nonresident of any age may hunt and trap game or unprotected animals and birds without a license, except on his own farm lands.

A parent or legal guardian must apply for any license issued to a juvenile 10–13 years of age (inclusive) who may hunt only when accompanied by a licensed adult 21 or more years of age. Any person 14–21 years of age who applies for a trapping and firearms hunting license must present either a similar license issued to him in a previous year, or a certificate showing that the applicant has satisfactorily completed a recognized course in the safe handling of firearms. A juvenile hunting license will not be accepted, and a minor 14 or more years of age must take a firearms safety course. The bow and arrow hunting license will not be issued to any person who does not have a certificate showing satisfactory completion of a course in archery safety and proficiency. Any person causing the injury or death of a person by negligent use of a gun or bow and arrow may have his license revoked for a period of 5 years, and pay a fine of not more than $500.

A group of 4 persons holding trapping and firearms hunting licenses may apply for a party permit to take Deer of either sex in a designated area. Each member of the group must send the descriptive part of his license in the same envelope, which should also contain an application for one area and the fee ($2) for the entire party. Applications may not be made in person, and must be postmarked from October 1 to not later than October 15 to be accepted at the Division of Fish and Game. Members of the party are not required to hunt as a group, but the Deer may be taken only by a member in possession of the party deer tag.

All aliens must obtain nonresident licenses to fish, hunt, or trap. A federal "Duck" stamp is required of all persons 16 or more years of age to take migratory game birds. Woodcock may be taken without the special Woodcock license during that portion of a prescribed season extending into the upland game season. Fishing licenses from either state are recognized on the waters of the Delaware River, and nonresidents may fish without a license in Delaware Bay, and bays or waters of the Atlantic Ocean, but a license is required to fish in all tidal rivers, except Shark River and Manasquan River below Allenwood Bridge.

Resident license fees: Fishing, $4.15; trapping and firearms hunting, $5.15; bow and arrow hunting, $5.15; juvenile hunting (10 through 13 years of age), $1.00; Woodcock hunting (in addition to regular license), $2.00; federal "Duck" stamp, $3.00; Trout stamp (affix to fishing license), $2.00.

Nonresident license fees: Fishing, $7.15; vacation fishing 3 consecutive days (after June 1), $3.65; trapping and firearms hunting, $15.15; bow and arrow hunting, $15.15; juvenile hunting (10 through 13 years of age), $1.00; Woodcock hunting (in addition to regular license), $2.00; federal "Duck" stamp, $3.00; special one-day hunting on private shooting preserves, $2.15; Trout stamp (affix to fishing license), $5.00.

HUNTING AND TRAPPING

Game animals: Bear, Deer, Fox, Hares and Rabbits, Raccoons, Gray Squirrel, Woodchuck. OPEN SEASONS:* Bear—archery, early October to early November; firearms (including bow and arrow), about one week in December. Deer—archery, early October to early November; firearms (including bow and arrow), about one week in December. Fox—early November to February 1 in Atlantic, Burlington, Camden, Cape May, Cumberland, Gloucester, and Salem counties; and extended to April 30 in the remainder of the state. Hares and Rabbits—early November to December 31 except during the firearms Deer season. Raccoon—from about October 1 to March 15. Gray Squirrel—early November to early December and Dec. 16–Feb. 1. Woodchuck—March 15–Oct. 1, and during upland game seasons. BAG LIMITS: Bear—1 per year. Deer—1 antlered Buck, and 1 of either sex on archery or party permit. Squirrels—5 per day. Hares and Rabbits—4 in the aggregate per day. Fox, Raccoon, and Woodchuck—no limits.

A legal Buck is a male Deer with antlers at least 3 inches long.

Furbearing animals: Beaver, Mink, Muskrat, Opossum, Otter, Raccoon, Skunk. OPEN SEASONS:* Mink, Muskrat, Otter, Raccoon—Nov. 30–March 15. On state public shooting grounds—Jan. 1–March 15, except Raccoons may be trapped only on tidal meadows and impoundments. FULLY PROTECTED: Beaver—no open season. NOT PROTECTED: Bobcat, Opossum, Porcupine, Skunk, Red Squirrel, and Weasel may be taken at any time. Fox may be trapped at any time if destroying crops, poultry, or property.

Game birds: Brant, Coot, Ducks (except Canvasback and Redhead), Eider, Gallinule, Geese (except Snow Geese), Ruffed Grouse, Merganser, Old Squaw, Pheasants, Bobwhite Quail, Rails, Scaup, Scoter, Sora, Wilson's Snipe (Jacksnipe), Wild Turkey, Woodcock. OPEN SEASONS:* Brant, Geese—late October to early January. Coot, Ducks, Eider, Merganser, Old Squaw, Scaup, Scoter—late October to mid-November and mid-December to early January. Gallinule, Rails, Sora—early September to early November. Ruffed Grouse, Quail—early November to February 1 except for a closed season of about one week in mid-December. Pheasant

---

* Check current state regulations.

—opens with Quail season and closes after about 4 weeks. Wilson's Snipe —late October to early December. Woodcock—mid-October through November. Game birds on shooting preserves—Sept. 1–March 15. FULLY PROTECTED: Doves, Canvasback and Redhead Ducks, Snow Geese, Swans, and Wild Turkey—no open seasons. NOT PROTECTED: Crows, English Sparrows, and Starlings may be killed at any time.

FIREARMS

Shotguns for hunting game animals or birds must be not larger than 10 gauge or capable of holding more than 3 shot shells in the magazine and chamber combined. Any shotgun originally capable of holding more than 3 shells must be plugged to reduce the capacity. Possession of any shotgun missile larger than no. 4 fine shot is prohibited, except that hunters may use no. 2 or smaller fine shot when shooting waterfowl in tidal waters and tidewater marshes. It is illegal to use a rifle or any firearm of a caliber smaller than 12 gauge, or possess any firearm missile except buckshot to hunt Deer. The buckshot may not be cut, strung, waxed, or joined in any manner. Archery Deer hunters must use a longbow with at least a minimum draw pull weight of 35 pounds, which is capable of propelling an arrow at least 125 yards over level terrain. The arrowhead should be sharpened metal not less than three-quarters of an inch and not more than 1½ inches in width. Special permits must be obtained to hunt Woodchuck with a rifle, except on an owner's or occupant's farm property.

Shooting hours: Hunting on Sunday is prohibited except on licensed shooting preserves and private farmlands, but Raccoons may be taken between midnight Saturday and sunrise Sunday. Migratory game birds— sunrise to sunset except that on opening day of Duck season, shooting starts at 12:00 o'clock noon. Other game—one-half hour before sunrise to one-half hour after sunset, except during the firearms Deer season, 7:00 A.M.–5:00 P.M.

FISHING

Game fish: Black Bass (Smallmouth, Oswego, or Largemouth), Calico Bass, Rock Bass, Striped Bass, White Bass, Catfish, Perch (White, Yellow), Pickerel (Chain or Eastern), Pike-perch (Walleyed Pike), Land-locked Salmon, Sturgeon (Shortnosed, Atlantic, or Sea), Sunfish, Trout (Brook, Brown, Rainbow). OPEN SEASONS: Striped Bass—March 1–Dec. 31 with hook and line. Salmon and Trout—all year except during March. All fishing is prohibited during March in waters stocked with Trout by the state. Delaware River between New Jersey and Pennsylvania: Striped Bass—May 1–Dec. 31; Trout—April 15–Sept. 30; all other fish at any time.

Any species of fish except Black Bass, Pickerel, Pike-perch, Salmon, and Trout may be taken at any time by longbow and arrow with attached line if the archer holds a fishing license. Only Bullheads, Carp, Eels, Herring, and Sucker may be taken by bow and arrow in Greenwood Lake. Spears not mechanically propelled or bows and arrows may be used to take Bullheads, Carp, Eels, Herring, Shad, and Suckers in the Delaware River except within 50 rods (825 feet) of an eel weir.

Ice fishing: Only one handline or rod and reel may be used to fish through ice except during January, when 10 tip-ups are permitted if each tip-up is attached to only 1 hook. Five tip-ups, or a combination of 5 devices that include not more than 2 handlines or 2 rods and lines, are legal in the Delaware River.

Red Bank on Navesink River, and Atlantic City, Beach Haven on Long Beach Island, Cape May, Long Branch, Ocean City at Great Egg Harbor, Stone Harbor, and Wildwood on the Atlantic Ocean are favorite fishing centers for sportsmen. Good fishing and hunting is provided in the following public areas, except that hunting is not permitted in state parks.

PUBLIC HUNTING AND FISHING GROUNDS

Berkshire Valley (1,140 acres) north of Dover—Morris County; *Cadwalader* (2,678 acres) on Maurice River and Delaware Bay, near Heislerville and Leesburg—Cumberland County; *Colliers Mills* (9,556 acres) west of Jackson—Ocean County; *Dennis Creek* (1,162 acres) on Delaware Bay near Dennisville—Cape May County; *Dix* (913 acres) on Delaware River, near Greenwich—Cumberland County; *Egg Island* (6,247 acres) on Delaware Bay, south of Cedarville—Cumberland County; *Flat Brook* and *Roy* (2,235 acres) adjacent to Stokes State Forest, near Layton—Sussex County; *Glassboro* (2,337 acres) east of Glassboro —Gloucester County; *Greenwood Forest* (7,663 acres) south of Whiting —Ocean County; *Hainesville* (282 acres) south of Montague—Sussex County; *Hamsburg* (3,469 acres) near McAfee—Sussex County; *Mad Horse* (3,139 acres) on the Delaware River, near Canton—Salem County; *Manahawkin* (965 acres) south of Barnegat—Ocean County; *Manchester* (2,300 acres) northwest of Whiting—Ocean County; *Marmora* (850 acres) on the Intracoastal Waterway near Marmora—Cape May County; *Medford* (214 acres) north of Medford—Burlington County; *Millville* (11,796 acres) south of Millville—Cumberland County; *Pasadena* (2,300 acres) adjacent to Greenwood and Lebanon state forests—Ocean County; *Peaslee* (9,538 acres) on Tuckahoe River, east of Millville—Cumberland County; *Tuckahoe* (2,800 acres) on Great Egg Harbor River—Atlantic County; *Wenaque* (1,400 acres) north of Wenaque Reservoir—Passaic County; *Wharton* (94,756 acres) near Washington—Burlington County;

Whiting (1,190 acres) southwest of Lakehurst—Ocean County; Winslow (1,882 acres) on Great Egg Harbor River, west of Winslow—Camden County.

STATE FORESTS

Bass River (9,270 acres) north of New Gretna—Burlington and Ocean counties; Belleplain (6,792 acres including Lake Nummy) near Woodbine—Cape May and Cumberland counties; Green Bank (1,833 acres) on Mullica River near village of Green Back—Atlantic and Burlington counties: A. S. Hewitt (1,890 acres) in Bearfoot Mountains, north of West Milford—Passaic County; Jackson (43 acres) at Jackson—Ocean County; Jenny Jump (967 acres) south of Hope—Warren County; Lebanon (22,216 acres) in the Pine Belt north of Chatsworth—Burlington County; Norvin Green (2,260 acres) at Wenaque Reservoir, north of Bloomingdale—Passaic County; Penn (2,958 acres) at Lake Oswego, southeast of Chatsworth—Burlington County; Stokes (12,429 acres) including Lake Ocquittunk, near Branchville—Sussex County; Wharton (95,106 acres) near Green Bank—Burlington County; Worthington (6,200 acres) north of Hainesburg—Warren County.

STATE PARKS

Barnegat Lighthouse (32 acres) on Long Beach Island—Ocean County; Cheesquake (975 acres) north of Matawan—Middlesex County; Cranberry Lake (199 acres) near Netcong—Sussex County; Fort Mott (104 acres) at Finns Point on the Delaware River, northwest of Salem—Salem County; Hacklebarney (193 acres) on Black River, south of Milltown—Morris County; High Point (10,935 acres) along Kittatinny Ridge, near Cloesville—Sussex County; Hopatcong (9,107 acres) at Lake Hopatcong near Landing—Sussex County; Island Beach (2,200 acres) east of Barnegat—Ocean County; Musconetcong (343 acres at 315-acre lake) near Netcong—Sussex County; Parvin (1,025 acres) near Vineland—Salem County; Ringwood Manor (579 acres) on Ringwood River—Passaic County; Saxton Falls (9 acres) and Stephens Park (222 acres) on Musconetcong River near Hackettstown—Warren County; Swartswood (704 acres including 519-acre lake) west of Newton—Sussex County.

Hunting is permitted in the following state parks: Farny (803 acres) near Marcella—Morris County; and Voorhees (429 acres) north of Hainesburg—Warren County.

Licenses, permits, regulations, and information about current seasons, bag and possession limits may be obtained from the Commission, Department of Conservation and Economic Development, Division of Fish and Game, 230 West State St. (P.O. Box 1809), Trenton 25. New Jersey

Outdoors, published by the Division of Fish and Game for $1.00 per year, is a very interesting magazine.

NEW MEXICO

Area: 122,634 square miles (land area—121,510 square miles); rank in nation–5
Bird: Road Runner (*Geococcyx californianus*), adopted 1949
Capital city: Santa Fe on the Santa Fe River in Santa Fe County; population (1960)—34,676; rank in state–3
Counties: 32
Elevations: Highest, North Truchas Peak (13,306 ft.) in Rio Arriba County; lowest, Red Bluff (2,876 ft.) in Eddy County
Fish: Cutthroat Trout (*Salmo clarki*), adopted 1955
Flower: Yucca (*Yucca*), also called Spanish Bayonet, adopted 1927
Geographic center: 12 miles west of south of Willard, Torrance County
Nicknames: Land of Enchantment, Cactus State, Land of Opportunity, Sunshine State
Population (1960): 951,023; rank in nation–37
Tree: Piñon Pine (*Pinus edulis*), adopted 1949

New Mexico in the southwest is bordered by Arizona on the west, the Republic of Mexico on the south, Texas on the south and east with Oklahoma on the northeastern corner, and Colorado across the northern boundary. Four Corners in the Navajo Indian Reservation is the only point in the United States common to 4 states—Arizona, Colorado, New Mexico, and Utah.

The Continental Divide in western New Mexico follows an irregular line from the Mexican boundary northward between the Animas and Peloncillo mountains in Hidalgo County, along the crest of the Burro Mountains, Black Range, Pelona Mountain (9,204 ft.), Coyote Peak (8,382 ft.), Datil Mountains, and across the Lava Beds in Valencia County to the Zuni Mountains, Cejita Blanca, and to Colorado west of Cumbres Pass (10,022 feet). Rivers from the western slopes of the divide include the Animas, Chaco, and San Juan rivers in San Juan County; Rio Puerco of the West near Gallup; and the Gila River rising north of Silver City.

The Rio Grande from Colorado flows through central New Mexico to be increased by the Rio Chama, Rio Puerco, Rio Salado; and north of Truth and Consequences, it is impounded to form the Elephant Butte Lake (57 sq. miles) and Cabello Reservoir and continues on a course to El Paso in Texas. Conchas Lake in the northeastern part of the state is formed by a dam at the junction of the Canadian and Conchas rivers northwest of Tucumcari. The Alamogordo Reservoir on the Pecos River north of Fort Sumner, Lake McMillan (5,120 acres) downstream near Artesia, and Avalon Reservoir near Carlsbad are in eastern New Mexico.

The great plateau region is broken by parallel ranges such as the Sand Hills and Mescallero Ridge east of the Pecos River. The Organ, Sierra Cabello, San Andres, Muerto Pinos, Oscura, and Manzano mountains are along the eastern slopes of the Rio Grande Valley. The Gallinas and San Mateo mountains overlook the Plains of San Augustine northwest of Truth and Consequences. The White Sands National Monument (146,535 acres) near Alamogordo contains shining white gypsum sand dunes 10–45 feet high and wildlife of unusual camouflage colorings.

LICENSES

Resident licenses are issued to landowners and to persons who have lived in the state for 6 or more months immediately preceding an application for a license; and to students in educational institutions who have attended at least one full term prior to applying for a license; and to members of the U.S. Armed Forces who submit a certificate signed by a commanding officer proving permanent assignment to a military installation in New Mexico. All persons 14 or more years of age must possess a license to fish by angling, set line, trotline, gig, spear, longbow and arrows. Guests of landowners hunting Antelope or Elk may purchase landowner licenses in the Cimarron and Elk Nest units from license vendors at Amalia, Cimarron, Eagle Nest, Questa, and Vermejo Park. The authorization application forms for landowners in other areas must be completed and sent to the Department of Fish and Game at Santa Fe before the opening day of a hunt. One application form may be used by a party of 4 hunters. Entry permits may be required in special areas, and a landowner's permission must be obtained for access over private property to public lands.

Special permits should be obtained from tribal headquarters to hunt on Indian Reservations, and hunters must also possess a state license to hunt. The Navajo have closed the reservation to hunting by non-Indians, and the Jicarillo Apache Tribe does not issue permits to hunt Bear, Elk, and Turkey to non-Indians. Permits may be issued by the Mescalero Apache Tribe to nonmembers for hunting Bear and Deer.

Juveniles under the age of 14 may take furbearing animals (except Beaver) without a trapper's license. Regardless of his age, a person must have a tag for each pelt and a trapper's license to take Beaver. Residents may kill unprotected wild animals and birds without a license, but all nonresidents must possess a big game or special nongame hunting license. All persons 16 or more years of age must possess a federal "Duck" stamp to take migratory game birds. A trapping license expires on March 31 each year.

Resident license fees: Fishing, $3.50; general hunting (animals and birds), $6.50; general hunting and fishing, $9.00; big game hunting, $5.00; bird hunting (upland game birds), $4.00; Antelope hunting, $10.00; Barbary Sheep, $20.00; Bighorn Sheep, $20.00; Elk hunting, $15.00; special Deer season tag (in addition to big game license), $2.00; bow hunting Deer tag (in addition to big game license), $2.00; trapping, $1.10; Beaver tags (per pelt), $1.00; federal "Duck" stamp, $3.00; Jicarilla Apache tribal permit to hunt Deer, $15.00; Mescalero Apache tribal permits (Bear, Deer), each, $20.00; Mescalero Apache tribal combination (Bear, Deer) permit, $25.00.

Nonresident license fees: Fishing, $8.00; fishing 5 consecutive days, $3.00; hunting upland game birds, $15.25; big game hunting (including nongame animals), $50.25; Bear hunting before or after big game season, $25.00; Antelope hunting, $40.00; Elk hunting, $50.00; Barbary Sheep hunting, $100.00; Bighorn Sheep hunting, $100.00; nongame animal hunting, $10.00; trapping, $50.00; special Deer season tag (in addition to big game license), $2.00; bow hunting Deer tag (in addition to big game license), $2.00; federal "Duck" stamp, $3.00; hunting game birds on private shooting preserves, $5.25. Indian Tribal permit fees are similar to those for residents.

HUNTING AND TRAPPING

Big game: Pronghorn Antelope, Bear, Deer, Elk, Barbary Sheep, Bighorn Sheep, Chickaree, and Tassel-eared Squirrels. OPEN SEASONS IN DESIGNATED AREAS:* Antelope—two or more days in mid-September in the Northeast; a few days in late September in the Southeast; a few days in mid-October in the Southwest and Northwest. Bear—Sept. 1–Nov. 30. Deer—archery, for about 2 weeks in late October and one week in mid-December; firearms, late October to mid-December including seasons set for from 2–35 days. Elk—early October to late December including general seasons for periods of about one week. Barbary and Bighorn Sheep—open seasons are rare, but usually set for about one week in November. Squirrels—about one week in late September. BAG LIMITS: Antelope, Bear, Deer, Elk, Sheep—1 each per year. Squirrels—5 per season singly or in the aggregate.

A legal Buck is a male Deer with 2 or more distinct points on at least one antler.

Furbearing animals: Badger, Beaver, Ring-tailed Cat, Coati-mundi, Fox, Marten, Muskrat, Nutria, Otter, Raccoon, Skunk, Weasel, Wolf. OPEN SEASONS:* Beaver (local exceptions)—Nov. 1–March 31 north of

_____
* Check current state regulations.

U.S. Highway 66; Dec. 1–March 31 south of the highway. Marten, Mink, Ring-tailed Cat—Dec. 1–31. FULLY PROTECTED: Otter—no open season. Barbary and Bighorn Sheep hunting may be permitted in odd years. NOT PROTECTED: Badger, Bobcat, Coyote, Prairie Dog, Fox, Gopher, Mountain Lion, Nutria, Porcupine, Rabbits, Raccoon, Skunk, Weasel, and Wolves may be taken at any time.

Beaver may be taken only by the use of traps, and other furbearing animals may be taken by traps, firearms, longbow and arrow.

Game birds: Coot, Lesser Sandhill (Little Brown) Crane, Doves (Mourning, White-winged), Ducks (except Canvasback and Redhead) Gallinule, Geese, Dusky Grouse, Merganser, Cock Pheasant, Prairie Chicken, Quail (Bobwhite, Gambel, Scaled) Rails, Sora, Wild Turkey. OPEN SEASONS: Coot, Ducks, Merganser—east of the Continental Divide, from late November to early January; west of the divide, from mid-October to early January. Crane—during November in Chaves, Curry, Eddy, De Baca, Lea, Quay, and Roosevelt counties. Dove— Sept. 1–Oct. 31; Jackson Lake Game Management Area, Sept. 1–30. Gallinule, Rails, Sora—Sept. 1 to mid-October. Geese—east of Continental Divide, from late November to mid-January; west of the divide, from mid-October to early January. Dusky Grouse—about one week in late September in designated areas. Cock Pheasant—a few days in late November. Prairie Chicken—a few days in mid-October in designated areas. Quail—late November to late December. Wild Turkey—late September to late November in designated areas. Game birds on private shooting preserves—Sept. 1–March 31. FULLY PROTECTED: Canvasback, Redhead and Wood Ducks—no open seasons. NOT PROTECTED: Crow, Golden Eagle, all Hawks, Magpies, and all Owls may be taken at any time.

FIREARMS

Antelope, Bear, and Deer may not be taken with semiautomatic rifles capable of holding more than 6 rounds in magazine and chamber combined; with an M-1 carbine; with a gun or rifle capable of discharging more than once with one pull of the trigger; with a shotgun smaller than 20 gauge and capable of holding more than 3 shells in the magazine and chamber combined, or using any ammunition except slugs. Hard-pointed or full metal case bullets, and cartridges with bullets less than 40 grains in weight, or with rated impact energy at muzzle of less than 1,000 foot-pounds are prohibited. All firearms used to hunt Elk must be fired from the shoulder. Cartridges with bullets less than 87 grains in weight, or with rated impact energy from muzzle of less than 1,000 foot-pounds are prohibited.

Longbow and arrows, pistols, centerfire, rimfire rifles, or shotguns not larger than 10 gauge and holding not more than 3 shells in magazine and chamber combined are legal for taking Turkey in the Northwest area, and Grouse and Squirrels in open areas. Turkey may be hunted in other areas with longbow and arrows, with big game rifles using a full metal case or patched bullets, and with shotguns not larger than 10 gauge, or capable of holding more than 3 shells in magazine and chamber combined.

Other game birds may be taken with longbow and arrows, and shotguns not larger than 10 gauge or capable of holding more than 3 shells in magazine and chamber combined. Legal longbows must be capable of propelling arrows at least 130 yards, and carrying of firearms by archers during a bow hunting season is unlawful. A table listing approximately 75 legal or illegal firearms, and ballistics of some cartridges is included in the big game regulations.

The use of dogs to hunt Wild Turkey and big game (except Bear and Squirrels) is prohibited, and during the archery big game season, Bear may not be hunted with dogs.

Shooting hours: One-half hour before sunrise to sunset. Exceptions: migratory game birds east of Continental Divide, sunrise to sunset. Shooting starts at 12:00 o'clock noon on the opening day of the Antelope and Duck seasons. If an open season for Geese is in progress on the opening day of a Duck season, then shooting Ducks starts either at sunrise or one-half hour before sunrise according to the area.

FISHING

Game fish: Black Bass (Largemouth), White Bass, Bluegill, Catfish (except Bullheads), Crappie, Northern Pike, Trout (Brook, Brown, Cutthroat, Rainbow), Walleyed or Yellow Pike-perch. OPEN SEASONS:* All game fish except Trout—April 1–March 31, except in the Bitter Lake National Wildlife Refuge, April 1–Oct. 15; Bosque del Apache, May 30–Oct. 15; Tucumcari Lake, June 1–March 31. Trout—April 1–March 31 on all Trout waters south of U.S. Highway 66, except Bonito Lake, June 1 to Labor Day; early May to November 30 on all Trout waters north of U.S. Highway 66 except in Lower Charlotte Lake, early May to October 31; Upper Charlotte Lake, Wahon Mound Salt Lake, early May to September 30; Chicos Lake, Clayton Lake (except waterfowl area), and Santa Cruz Lake, April 1–Oct. 31; Clayton Lake in waterfowl area, La Junta Creek, and tributaries, July 1–Sep. 30; McAllister Lake, April 1–Sept. 30; San Gregorio Lake, June 1–Nov. 30. Many lakes, ponds, reservoirs, and streams are open for 24-hour fishing of all species of game fish.

Game fish may be taken by angling with only one rod or one line per

---

* Check current state regulations.

person, except that trotlines and set lines may be used in designated areas of the Canadian, Gila, Mora, Pecos, Rio Grande, San Francisco, and San Juan rivers and watersheds. Warm water fish may be taken by gig, spears, bow and arrows discharged beneath the water, except in the Alamogordo, Avalon, Cabello, Conchas, Elephant Butte, and McMillan lakes.

Nongame fish may be taken by angling, set line, trotline, gigs, spears, or bow and arrows in some waters containing game fish.

Bullfrogs: Jumbo Bullfrogs may be taken by angling, gigging, grappling, spearing, or bow and arrow between sunrise and sunset. OPEN SEASONS: August 1–31 except at Tucumcari Lake.

The Pecos River and Rio Grande Valley are flyways for migratory birds, and La Joya, Jackson Lake, and the Madera Game Management Area are open for waterfowl hunting. Federal game refuges, national and state parks are closed to hunting, except for the San Andres–Organ Deer season in the Organ Mountain State Game Management Area and the San Andres National Wildlife Refuge.

STATE PARKS (fishing)

Bluewater Lake (3,500 acres) southeast of Thoreau—McKinley and Valencia counties; *Bottomless Lakes* (1,600 acres) containing Cottonwood, Devil's Inkwell, Figure 8, Lea, Mirror, and Pasture lakes, east of Roswell—Chaves County; and *Conchas Lake* (1,488 acres) on Canadian River, 30 miles northwest of Tucumcari—San Miguel County.

Licenses, regulations, and information about current seasons, bag and possession limits may be obtained from the New Mexico Department of Game and Fish, State Capitol, Santa Fe. Applications for special Deer season entry permits should be mailed to headquarters, or to offices at 1255 South Main St., Las Cruces, or 1727 S. E. Main St., Roswell. Special Deer season tags are available at the Santa Fe, Albuquerque, Las Cruces, Raton, and Roswell field offices, or from license vendors at Alamogordo, Capitan, Deming, Glenwood, Las Cruces, Lordsburg, Silver City, and Tularosa.

NEW YORK

Area: 49,204 square miles (land area—47,939 square miles); rank in nation–30
Bird: Bluebird (*Sialia sialis*)
Capital city: Albany on the Hudson River in Mohawk Valley, Albany County; population (1960)—129,726; rank in state–6

Counties: 62
Elevations: Highest, Mount Marcy (5,344 ft.) in Essex County; lowest, Atlantic Ocean
Flower: Rose
Geographic center: 6 miles east of south of Oneida in Madison County
Nicknames: Empire State, Excelsior State, Knickerbocker State
Population (1960): 16,782,304; rank in nation—1. *See* California.
Tidal shoreline: 1,850 miles (including islands, bays, and streams to a point where tidal waters narrow to 100 ft.)
Tree: Sugar Maple (*Acer saccharum*), adopted 1956

New York is bordered by Connecticut and Vermont on the east, Pennsylvania on the south, and separated from Canada on the north and west by the St. Lawrence River, Lake Ontario, and Lake Erie.

Tidal waters of the Hudson River flow from New York City on the Atlantic Ocean to Albany 150 miles upstream. The New York State Barge Canal System connects the Hudson River at Waterford to Lake Erie at Buffalo, to Lake Ontario via the Oswego Canal, and to the 110-mile-long Lake Champlain on the Vermont boundary by the Champlain Canal at Whitehall. Beautiful Lake Champlain is linked with the St. Lawrence River by the Richelieu River in Canada. There are more than 200 lakes or ponds and 800 miles of connecting rivers and canals in the system.

The Adirondack Forest Preserve (2,273,378 acres) in northern New York contains hundreds of lakes, Mount Marcy, and 45 other mountains over 4,000 feet high. Lake George in the foothills at Ticonderoga is 32 miles long and contains more than 150 private and public islands. Lake Placid at the base of Whiteface Mountain (4,867 ft.) is within sight of Mount Marcy and the Colden, MacIntyre, Saddleback, and Wallface mountains. The Raquette River region provides canoe routes from Old Forge through the Fulton Chain of Lakes, Raquette, Forked, and Long Lakes to Tupper Lake near the Saranac Lakes. The Marion River flows between Blue Mountain Lake and Raquette Lake. The Sacandaga Reservoir on the southern edge of the preserve is 6 miles northeast of Gloversville.

The famous Thousand Islands are between Cape Vincent and Ogdensburg on the St. Lawrence River and number many more than a thousand in all shapes and sizes. The Great Lakes–St. Lawrence Seaway consists of a series of locks, canals, and channels on a 2,342-mile system of waterways from the Atlantic Ocean through the Great Lakes. Lake St. Lawrence (38,000 acres) was formed by the Long Sault Dam and Moses-Saunders Dam at Barnhart Island. The magnificent American Falls (167 ft. high, about 1,075 ft. wide) and the Horseshoe or Canadian Falls

(160 ft. high, on a 2,000 foot curving escarpment) are above a series of rapids known as the Whirlpool on the Niagara River between Niagara on Lake Ontario and Buffalo on Lake Erie.

In the lakes region between Lake Erie and Lake Ontario on the north and Pennsylvania on the south are the Finger Lakes and the Genesee River from Pennsylvania flowing through the Genesee Gorge in a series of sparkling cascades before reaching Lake Ontario at Rochester. The name Genesee was derived from an Indian word meaning "beautiful valley." The finger-shaped lakes, varying from 11 to 40 miles long, include Cayuga Lake between Ithaca and Seneca Falls, Seneca Lake between Geneva and Watkins Glen, Lake Keuka south of Penn Yan, Canandaigua Lake at Canandaigua, Owasco Lake south of Auburn, and the Skaneateles Lake west of Syracuse. The Cohocton River and Canisteo River merge near Corning to flow on to the Susquehanna River. The Chautauqua Lake is in the southwestern corner of New York between Jamestown and Lake Erie.

The Mohawk River on a westward course from the Hudson River flows through Schenectady, Utica, and Syracuse, and south of the Mohawk Valley are Otsego Lake, a source of the Susquehanna River; Cannonsville Reservoir on the Delaware River; the Chenango, Otselic, and Unadilla rivers. The Catskill Forest Preserve (237,640 acres), in the Hudson River Valley west of Catskill and Kingston, contains scenic mountains and streams including Slide Mountain (4,180 ft.) and the Ashokan, Neversink, and Pepacton reservoirs.

New York City consists of islands on the east, Harlem and Hudson Rivers which merge to form a water route through Upper New York Bay to The Narrows between Long Island and Staten Island before spreading out into the Lower Bay, which is rimmed by New Jersey, Long Island, and the Atlantic Ocean. Long Island is accessible from all parts of the New York City metropolitan area over several arteries. The Palisades Region along the west side of the Hudson River from Orange and Rockland counties to Fort Lee in New Jersey consists of almost 60,000 acres developed into a chain of parks.

LICENSES

Resident licenses are issued to citizens who have lived in the state for at least 3 months immediately preceding an application for a license; and to members of the U.S. Armed Forces officially stationed in New York; and to citizens who are college or university students upon proof of enrollment in a full-time course and residence within the state for the school year. A license to hunt wild animals and birds may be issued to any person 14 or more years of age who has a certificate proving satisfactory completion of a firearms safety course, or possession of a previous hunting license. Juveniles 14–15 years of age are not eligible for big game or special archery licenses. They may obtain hunting licenses if a parent, guardian, or person 21 or more years of age (designated in writing by parent or guardian) possesses a hunting license and signs the minor's license. Such a minor must be accompanied during hunts by the person responsible for his license. Any person under the age of 18 who hunts Bear or Deer, and has not previously held a big game or special archery license, must be accompanied by his parent, guardian, or other person 21 or more years of age, who holds such a license and has had at least one year's experience in big game hunting.

Citizen resident owners or lessees, and members of their immediate families occupying and cultivating farm lands, are not required to possess licenses except to take Bear, Deer, Beaver, Fisher, and Otter on their lands.

Free fishing licenses are issued to citizen residents 70 or more years of age and to blind persons. Any legal resident stationed outside of New York as a member of the U.S. Armed Forces who returns on leave or furlough for not more than 30 days may fish, hunt, and trap without licenses except for the special archery and big game licenses required for Bear, Deer, and licenses to trap Beaver, Fisher and Otter. No licenses are needed to fish in the Marine District, and in the Hudson River south of the barrier dam at Troy. Patients at any U.S. Veterans Administration facility, and at any state or municipal hospital or sanitarium for treatment of tuberculosis, or any institution of the Department of Mental Hygiene, or any rest camp maintained by the state through the Division of Veterans Affairs, may fish without licenses. All persons 16 or more years of age must possess a federal "Duck" stamp to take migratory game birds. No license is required to hunt game birds on private shooting preserves.

Regardless of residence, all aliens must purchase nonresident licenses to fish, hunt, or trap. License period, Oct. 1–Sept. 30.

Citizen resident license fees: Fishing, $3.25; hunting (except Bear and Deer), $3.25; combination hunting and fishing (except Bear and Deer), $5.75; archery big game (Bear and Deer), $5.25; firearms big game (Bear and Deer), $3.25; trapping, $3.25; federal "Duck" stamp, $3.00.

Nonresident and alien license fees: Fishing, $5.50; fishing 6 consecutive days, $4.25; hunting (except Bear and Deer), $10.75; archery big game (Bear and Deer), $10.00; firearms big game (Bear and Deer), $10.00; trapping, $25.00; federal "Duck" stamp, $3.00.

HUNTING AND TRAPPING

Game animals: Bear, Deer, Varying Hare (Snowshoe Rabbit), Cottontail Rabbit, Raccoon, Squirrels (Black, Fox, Gray). OPEN SEASONS:*

* Check current state regulations.

Bear—late October to early December in Northern Zone except in Washington County; mid-November to mid-December with seasons varying from 2–4 weeks in designated counties. The archery season for Bear and Deer starts 14 days immediately preceding the regular seasons. Deer—late October through December including periods varying from 2–8 weeks in designated areas. Varying Hare—late October to early December in Northern Zone; early December to March 15 in Southern Zone including shorter seasons in designated counties. Cottontail Rabbit —early October through February with open season starting 2 weeks later in some counties, and from Nov. 1–Jan. 31 on Long Island. Raccoon —early October through February in Clinton, Essex, Franklin, Hamilton, Jefferson, Lewis, Warren (except town of Queensbury), and St. Lawrence counties; and extended for an additional 3 weeks in remainder of state except Long Island, November 1 through February. Squirrels—3 weeks in October throughout the state, except Long Island: Nov. 1–Dec. 31. BAG LIMITS: Bear—1 per year. Deer—1 per year, except holders of Deer hunting party permits may also take 1 extra Buck per party in designated areas. Deer of either sex may be taken only in Westchester County. Varying Hare—3 per day except in Cortland, Onondaga (east of Route 11), Chenango and Madison counties—1 per day. Cottontail Rabbit—4 per day in 19 counties, 5 on Long Island, 6 in other counties. Racoon—no limit. Squirrels—5 per day.

A legal Buck is a male Deer with antlers 3 or more inches in length.

Furbearing animals: Beaver, Bobcat, Coyote, Fisher, Fox, Marten, Mink, Muskrat, Opossum, Otter, Racoon, Skunk, Weasel. OPEN TRAPPING SEASONS: Beaver—late October to late March in designated areas with open seasons varying from 4–8 weeks. Fisher—late October to December 31 in Northern Zone. Mink, Raccoon, Skunk—late October to December 31 in Northern Zone, and from November 1 to late March in Southern Zone. Muskrat; Otter—from late October to April 30 in designated areas with shorter periods varying from 5–9 weeks. FULLY PROTECTED: Marten—no open season. NOT PROTECTED: Bobcat, Coyote, Fox, Opossum, and Weasel may be taken at any time.

Game birds: Brant, Coot, Ducks (except Canvasback and Redhead), Eider, Gallinule, Geese (except Snow Geese), Ruffed Grouse (Partridge), Merganser, Old Squaw, Hungarian Partridge (Grouse), Pheasant, Quail, Rails, Scaup, Scoter, Sora, Wilson's Snipe, Wild Turkey, Woodcock. OPEN SEASONS: Brant, Geese—mid-October to late December. Coot, Ducks, Gallinule, Merganser, Rails, Scaup, Sora—mid-October to early December. Eider, Old Squaw, Scoter—Oct. 1–Jan. 15 in coastal waters lying in Long Island and Block Island sounds, and Gardiner's Bay lying east of a line from Long Beach Lighthouse to the most easterly point of Ram Head on Shelter Island, but not including coastal waters south of

Long Island. Ruffed Grouse—early October through December except Long Island, Nov. 1–30. Hungarian Partridge—3 weeks in October in Clinton, Franklin, Jefferson, and St. Lawrence counties. Pheasant—3 weeks in October in 8 counties; late October to mid-November in remainder of state except Long Island, Nov. 1–Dec. 31. Quail—mid-October to mid-November in Orange, Putnam, and Westchester counties; Long Island, Nov. 1–Dec. 31. Wilson's Snipe and Woodcock—early October to late November. Wild Turkey—generally limited to 5 days in designated areas of Allegany, Cattaraugus, Chautauqaua, Delaware, and Steuben counties. Game birds on shooting preserves—Sept. 1–March 31. FULLY PROTECTED: Doves, Canvasback and Redhead Ducks and Snow Geese—no open seasons. NOT PROTECTED: Crow, Purple Grackle, Kingfisher, Wild Pigeon, English Sparrow, and Starlings may be killed at any time.

FIREARMS

Bear may be taken with pistols, rifles, shotguns and longbows in the Northern Zone, in the counties of Columbia, Delaware, Greene, Orange, Rensselaer, Sullivan, Ulster, and in parts of Broome, Chenango, Fulton, Otsego, Saratoga, and Washington counties in the Southern Zone. Only longbows may be used to take Deer in Westchester County, but longbows and shotguns are legal in other areas. The longbow must be capable of propelling a big game hunting arrow 150 yards, and the arrowhead used to take Bear and Deer should have at least 2 cutting edges.

Only shotguns holding not more than 3 shells in magazine and chamber combined may be used to take migratory game birds, and any shotgun capable of holding more than 3 shells must be plugged with a one-piece filler which cannot be removed without disassembling the gun. Shooting Pheasants with a pistol or rifle is prohibited, and Bear or Deer may not be hunted with rimfire cartridges, shotguns smaller than .20 gauge, or shotgun loads other than a single ball or slug. It is unlawful to possess in fields and forest automatic firearms, or an autoloading firearm with a capacity of more than a total of 6 shells, except one using .22 rimfire ammunition or except a pistol having a barrel length under 8 inches. It is unlawful to carry a rifle afield on Long Island or in Westchester County; or carry a rifle (larger than .22 rimfire) or shotgun (loaded with slug, ball, or buckshot) afield in the Adirondack Park if accompanied by a dog, unless engaged in hunting Coyote or Wolf under a special permit obtained from the local game protector.

Shooting hours: Hunting on Sunday is prohibited, except that small game may be hunted in the counties of Clinton, Delaware, Essex, Franklin, Greene, Orange, Putnam, Rockland, St. Lawrence, Sullivan, and

Ulster. Hunting hours, 7:00 A.M.–5:00 P.M. for native game, and from sunrise to sunset for migratory waterfowl. The Raccoon season opens at 7:00 A.M., but hunting may be during day or night during the open season.

Traps may not be staked out or set before 7:00 A.M. on the opening day for protected furbearing animals, and traps must be visited at least once every 24 hours in the Southern Zone and within every 48 hours in the Northern Zone.

Northern Zone: North of a line extending along the Salmon River from Lake Ontario to Pulaski, and along Route 11 to Trenton, Route 28 to Middleville, Route 29 to Route 4, Route 22, and Route 30-B to the state line. Southern Zone: South of the above region.

FISHING

Game fish: Black Bass, Striped Bass, Muskellunge, Pickerel, Pike-perch (Walleye Pike), Northern Pike, Landlocked Salmon, Shortnosed Sturgeon, Trout (Lake, Brook, Brown, Rainbow), Whitefish (Otsego Bass). OPEN SEASONS (local exceptions): Black Bass—July 1–Nov. 30. Otsego Bass—Jan. 1–Oct. 31. Muskellunge—July 1–Dec. 1. Perch, Pickerel, Northern Pike, Pike-perch—May 1–March 1. Shortnosed Sturgeon—July 1–April 30. Landlocked Salmon, Trout, Whitefish—April 1–Sept. 30. All other fish including Striped and White Bass, Bullheads, Crappie, White and Yellow Perch, Sauger, Lake and Sea Sturgeon—no closed seasons.

It is unlawful to use more than 2 lines with or without a rod (except tie-ups); leave a line unattended in the water; or use more than 15 single hooks, or 7 double hooks, or 5 triple hooks, or any combination exceeding 15 hook points. Game fish may be taken by use of hands, nets, snatch hooks, spears, firearms, bow and arrow. Rough fish such as Bullheads, Carp, Eels, Mullets, and Suckers may be taken with snatch hooks in designated waters. Blind snatching of Whitefish is permitted in Otsego Lake and Piseco Lake from Jan. 1–Oct. 31.

A hunting license is required to take rough fish by longbow and arrow, and a fishing license permits the use of spears and longbows, but spear guns may be used only in the Marine District. The use of longbow and spears is prohibited in all waters inhabited by Trout in the counties of Chemung, Genesee, Greene, Montgomery, Nassau, Orleans, Putnam, Schenectady, Schoharie, Suffolk, Sullivan, Westchester, and in all waters (except the Hudson River and tidal waters) of the Bronx, Columbia, Kings, New York, Queens, Rensselaer, Richmond, and Wyoming counties, and in designated areas of other counties.

Frogs: A fishing license is required to take Frogs by the use of hands, club, hook, or spear, and a hunting license permits the use of a gun or longbow. OPEN SEASON: June 16–Sept. 30 (7:00 A.M.–5:00 P.M.). No bag limits.

New York State offers an exceptional diversity of outdoor activities and a well developed park system. There is good fishing in the following state parks.

STATE PARKS

Allegany (58,420 acres) 10 miles southwest of Salamanca—Cattaraugus County; *Bear Mountain* (4,924 acres) contains the 1,314 ft. mountain near West Point—Orange County; *Beaver Island* (1,081 acres) at southern tip of Grand Island in Niagara River, north of Buffalo —Erie County; *Belmont Lake* (459 acres) north of Babylon—Suffolk County; *Braddock Bay* (2,050 acres) on Lake Ontario, 10 miles west of Rochester—Monroe County; *Buckhorn Island* (896 acres) 16 miles north of Buffalo—Erie County; *Burnham Point* (12 acres) 3 miles east of Cape Vincent—Jefferson County; *Buttermilk Falls* (675 acres) 2 miles south of Ithaca—Tompkins County; *Canoe-Picnic Point* (70 acres) on Grindstone Island in the St. Lawrence River near Clayton—Jefferson County; *Captree* (298 acres) on Atlantic Ocean Island south of Babylon —Long Island; *Caumsett* (1,426 acres) on Long Island Sound near Huntington—Suffolk County; *Cayuga Lake* (188 acres) east of Seneca Falls—Seneca County; *Cedar Island* (10 acres) at Chippewa Bay— Jefferson County; *Cedar Point* (48 acres) 6 miles west of Clayton— Jefferson County; *Chenango Valley* (983 acres) 13 miles north of Binghamton—Broome County; *Chittenango Falls* (123 acres) 4 miles north of Cazenovia—Madison County; *Clark Reservation* (228 acres) 3 miles southeast of Syracuse—Onondaga County; *Coles Creek* 2 miles northeast of Waddington—St. Lawrence County; *Crown Point Reservation* (103 acres) 9 miles north of Crown Point on Lake Champlain—Essex County; *Cuba Reservation* (650 acres) 2 miles north of Cuba—Allegany County; *Devil's Hole* (42 acres) at Niagara Falls—Niagara County; *DeWolf Point* (13 acres) 4 miles north of Thousand Islands Bridge, on Wellesley Island—Jefferson County; Evangola (759 acres) on Lake Erie, 27 miles southwest of Buffalo—Erie County; *Clarence Fahnestock Memorial* (4,415 acres) 9 miles east of Cold Spring—Putnam County; *Fair Haven Beach* (824 acres) on Lake Ontario, 2 miles north of Fair Haven—Cayuga County; *Fire Island* (1,000 acres) on the Atlantic Ocean, south of Long Island—Suffolk County; *Fort Niagara* (289 acres) at mouth of Niagara River, north of Youngstown—Niagara County; *Four Mile Creek Annex* (228 acres) at Fort Niagara; *Gilbert Lake* (1,569 acres) 12 miles northwest of Oneonta—Otsega County; *Grass Point* (27 acres) east of Fishers Landing—Jefferson County; *Hamlin Beach* (1,118 acres) on Lake Ontario, north of Hamlin—Monroe County; *Harriman* (40,829 acres) in highlands of the Hudson, west of Stony Point—Orange County; *Heckscher* (1,538 acres) near East Islip on Long Island—Suffolk County; *Hither Hills* (1,755 acres) west of Montauk on Long Island—Suffolk County; *Jacques Cartier* (461 acres) on St. Lawrence River, 2 miles south of Morristown—St. Lawrence County; *Jones Beach* (2,413 acres) on the Atlantic Ocean, south of Freeport—Nassau County; *Keewaydin* (177 acres) west of Alexandria Bay on St. Lawrence River—Jefferson County; *Kring Point* (38 acres) 10 miles northeast of Alexandria Bay—Jefferson County; *Lake Eria* (354 acres) on Lake Erie, 7 miles southwest of Dunkirk—Chatauqua County; *Lake George Islands* consists of 48 islands on Lake George—Warren County; *Lake Taghkanic* (1,002 acres) 11 miles south of Hudson—Columbia County; *Lakeside Beach* (693 acres) on Lake Ontario, 10 miles north of Albion—Orleans County; *Letchworth* (13,941 acres) on Genesee River near Castile (Wyoming County) and Mount Morris—Livingston County; *Long Point* (22 acres) 14 miles from Three Mile Bay on Lake Ontario—Jefferson County; *Mary Island* (13 acres) at foot of Wellesley Island on St. Lawrence River—Jefferson County; *Ogden and Ruth Livingston Mills Memorial* (315 acres) on Hudson River, 10 miles north of Poughkeepsie—Dutchess County; *Mohansic* (609 acres) on Taconic State Parkway, east of Peekskill—Westchester County; *Montauk Point* (724 acres) on southeastern tip of Long Island—Suffolk County; *Margaret Lewis Norris* (323 acres) 9 miles north of Poughkeepsie—Dutchess County; *Nyack Beach* (61 acres) on Hudson River near Tappan Zee Bridge—Rockland County; *Orient Beach* (357 acres) on Gardiners Bay, eastern Long Island—Suffolk County; *Rockland Lake* (962 acres) 3 miles north of Nyack—Rockland County; *Rudd Pond* (210 acres) 2 miles north of Millerton—Duchess County; *St. Lawrence* (3,607 acres) on St. Lawrence River near Massena—St. Lawrence County; *Selkirk Shores* (967 acres) on Lake Ontario, 13 miles west of Pulaski—Oswego County; *Seneca Lake* (141 acres) east of Geneva—Seneca County; *Silver Lake* (477 acres) east of Silver Springs—Wyoming County; *Sunken Meadow* (1,266 acres) near Kings Park on Long Island Sound—Suffolk County; *Taconic* (3,943 acres) at Copake Falls—Columbia County; *Taughannock Falls* (607 acres) 8 miles north of Ithaca—Tompkins County; *Robert H. Treman* (989 acres) 7 miles southwest of Ithaca—Tompkins County; *Verona Beach* (1,355 acres) at eastern shore of Oneida Lake—Oneida County; *Waterson Point* (6 acres) on north side of Wellesley Island in St. Lawrence River—Jefferson County; *Wellesley Island* (2,610 acres) on St. Lawrence River—Jefferson County; *Westcott Beach* south of Sacketts Harbor on Lake Ontario—

Jefferson County; *Wildwood* (699 acres) on Long Island Sound, west of Wading River—Suffolk County.

Licenses, regulations, information about current seasons, bag and possession limits may be obtained from the Commissioner for Fish and Game, New York State Conservation Department, Albany 1. All checks for licenses should be made payable to the New York State (NYS) Conservation Department. Sportsmen will find valuable information in the magazine *The Conservationist*, and the annual subscription fee of $2.00 should be sent to the NYS Conservationist, Albany 1. Free material is available from the Division of State Parks, State Campus Site, Albany; Thousand Islands State Park Commission, 832 Washington St., Watertown; Long Island State Park Commission, Belmont Lake State Park, Babylon; Forest Preserve Region, Division of Lands and Forests, State Campus Site, Albany; Finger Lakes State Parks Commission, Taughannock Falls State Park, R.D. #3, Trumansburg; and Palisades Interstate Park Commission, Bear Mountain State Park, Bear Mountain. The attractive 192-page booklet *New York State Vacationlands* is issued without cost by the New York State Department of Commerce, 112 State St., Albany 7.

NORTH CAROLINA

Area: 52,426 square miles (land area—49,067 square miles); rank in nation–29
Bird: Cardinal (*Richmondena cardinalis*), adopted 1943
Capital city: Raleigh near the Neuse River in Wake County; population (1960)—93,931; rank in state–4
Counties: 100
Elevations: Highest, Mount Mitchell (6,684 ft.) in Yancey County; lowest, Atlantic Ocean
Flower: Dogwood (*Cornus florida*), adopted 1941
Geographic center: 10 miles northwest of Sanford, Chatham County
Nicknames: Tarheel State, Old North State, Turpentine State
Population (1960): 4,556,155; rank in nation–12
Tidal shoreline: 3,375 miles (including islands, bays, and streams to a point where tidal waters narrow to 100 ft.)

North Carolina on the Atlantic Ocean is bordered by Virginia on the north, Tennessee on the west, South Carolina and Georgia on the south.

The Blue Ridge Parkway in western North Carolina links the Blue Ridge and Great Smoky mountains of the Southern Appalachians. Numerous swift streams and waterfalls are among more than 200 peaks over 5,000 feet high, including Mount Mitchell, the tallest peak east of the Mississippi River, Clingman's Dome (6,642 ft.) in the Great Smoky National Park, and Roan Mountain (6,285 ft.) on the Tennessee border. The foothills of the Blue Ridge Divide drop to the Piedmont Plateau, and in southeastern Cumberland, Moore, Richmond and Scotland counties are sandhills and longleaf pine forests. The broad, level coastal plain with fertile farms, forested swamplands, large estuaries, and sounds, is protected from the open sea by a chain of slender sandy islands or banks that vary in size from a few miles to only hundreds of feet wide. The 135-foot high Jocky Ridge on Bodie Island is a sand dune south of Nags Head on Roanoke Island Sound. Currituck Sound in the northeast opens into Albemarle Sound, and the Cape Hatteras National Seashore Recreational Area (28,500 acres) on the Outer Banks is east of Pamlico Sound, a sportsman's paradise. The great cold Atlantic current flowing down from the north collides with the warm Gulf Stream and creates shifting shoals and fogs on a treacherous coastline known as the "Grave yard of the Atlantic." The turbulent waters east of Cape Hatteras offer superlative deep sea fishing, and the state-operated ferries provide free transportation to the Outer Banks.

From Roanoke Rapids Lake (5,000 acres) near Gaston, the Roanoke River flows to Albemarle Sound near the mouth of the Chowan River. The Tar River from northern Granville County, and the Neuse River from Person County reach the Atlantic Ocean through Pamlico Sound. Other major eastern rivers include the Black and South rivers merging to join the Cape Fear River flowing to Wilmington and Cape Fear. The Yadkin River leaves the mountains to form High Rock Lake near Salisbury, Bladin Lake east of New London, Lake Tillery at the confluence of the Uwharrie River near Albemarle, and with other streams continues as the Pee Dee River to South Carolina. Other large rivers entering South Carolina include the French Broad River from Lake Lure in Rutherford County, the Lumber River, and Waccamaw River from Lake Waccamaw (8,938 acres) in the southeast; the Catawba River from Lake James (6,500 acres) west of Morgantown, to Lake Rhodhiss, Lake Hickory, and Lookout Shoals Lake near Hickory, Mount Island Lake northwest of Charlotte, and Catawba Lake on the boundary. Fontana Lake (10,670 acres) on the Little Tennessee River, the Aquone or Nantahala Lake (1,610 acres), Chatuga Lake (7,000 acres), Lake Hiwassee (6,240 acres) and Lake Santeetlah are in the mountainous southwestern corner of the state. Bugs Island Lake (130 square miles), formed by the John H. Kerr Reservoir in Virginia, is north of Henderson in Vance County. There are dense forests and canals in the Great Dismal Swamp covering about 600 square miles in Virginia and North Carolina, and the Dismal Swamp Canal is a waterway between Hampton Roads in Virginia and Elizabeth City on the Pasquotank River flowing into Albemarle Sound.

LICENSES

Resident licenses are issued to persons who have lived in the state for at least 6 months immediately preceding an application for a license; and to members of the U.S. Armed Forces assigned to military facilities in the state, and their wives and children under the age of 21 years; and to legal residents of North Carolina home on leave from military service. All nonresidents 12 or more years of age must obtain a license to fish by any method. Residents over 16 years of age, and nonresidents 12 or more years of age may not fish in any lake or streams designated as Public Mountain Trout Waters without a special Trout license in addition to a general fishing license. A county or statewide license must be obtained if a resident fishes in his county with artificial bait. No licenses are required to fish in the Atlantic Ocean and coastal sounds; in Cape Fear River below Highway 74 bridge at Wilmington; in Trent below Highway 70 bridge at New Bern; in Neuse River below Highway 17 bridge at New Bern; in the Pamlico and Tar rivers below the Norfolk & Southern Railroad bridge at Washington; in New River below Highway 17 bridge at Jacksonville; in White Oak River below Highway bridge at Stella; and in private waters.

Resident children under the age of 16 may hunt if accompanied by a parent or guardian holding a valid license. Special permits in addition to hunting licenses may be obtained to hunt on some wildlife management areas. Owners of private lands located within game lands managed by the Wildlife Resources Commission may hunt on their own lands in accordance with the open seasons and bag limits prescribed for surrounding game land, or under open season and bag limits prescribed in the statewide regulations. The latter apply to private holding unless the owner declares his choice in writing to the Wildlife Resources Commission before September 1. Local laws prevail where county laws govern hunting and fishing. All persons 16 or more years of age must obtain a federal "Duck" stamp to take migratory game birds. License periods are Jan. 1–Dec. 31 except for the resident statewide combination hunting and fishing license, which is valid Aug. 1–July 31.

Resident license fees: Statewide fishing (except Mountain Trout waters), $4.25; County fishing (except Mountain Trout waters), $1.65; fishing one day (except Mountain Trout waters), $1.25; fishing Mountain Trout waters, $1.00; taking nongame fish with bow and arrow, $1.00; statewide combination hunting and fishing, $6.25; statewide hunting, $4.25; county hunting, $1.65; special controlled shooting preserve hunting, $5.25; statewide trapping, $3.25; county trapping, $2.25; federal "Duck" stamp, $3.00; hunting guide, $5.25.

Nonresident license fees: Statewide fishing (except Mountain Trout waters), $8.25; fishing 5 consecutive days (except Mountain Trout waters), $3.75; fishing one day (except Mountain Trout waters), $1.65; fishing in Mountain Trout waters, $3.25; statewide hunting, $20.00; hunting 6 consecutive days, $15.75; special controlled shooting preserve hunting, $5.25; trapping, $25.25; federal "Duck" stamp, $3.00.

HUNTING AND TRAPPING

Game animals: Black Bear, White-tailed Deer, European Wild Boar, Fox (Gray, Red), Opossum, Rabbits, Raccoon, Squirrels. OPEN SEASONS: Bear—Oct. 15–Jan. 1. Deer—Oct. 15–Jan. 1 except no open season in the Atlantic Township and Roanoke Island, Dare County; or from several days to weeks in designated areas, and for the entire season in 31 counties; no open season for Deer in 25 counties. Wild Boar—Oct. 15–Jan. 1 in Cherokee, Clay, Graham, and Macon counties. Fox —may be taken with guns during open seasons for hunting game animals and birds according to county regulations. Opossum and Raccoon—Oct. 1–Feb. 15. Rabbit—late November to mid-February. Squirrels—Oct. 10–Jan. 15. SEASON BAG LIMITS: Bear–2, except in and east of Alexander, Catawba, Cleveland, Surrey, and Yadkin counties, no limits. Deer—2. Wild Boar—2. Rabbit—75. Raccoon—20. Squirrels— 75.

Only male Deer with visible antlers may be hunted, except in designated areas and periods set aside for taking antlerless Deer. Chasing or taking Deer with dogs is prohibited in and west of Anson, Guilford, Montgomery, Randolph, and Rockingham counties. A Bear weighing less than 50 pounds is considered to be a Cub Bear, and taking a Cub Bear, or a female Bear with one or more cubs at its side is prohibited.

Furbearing animals: Beaver, Fox, Mink, Muskrat, Opossum, Otter, Raccoon, Skunk, Weasel, Wildcat. OPEN SEASONS: Mink, Muskrat, Opossum, Otter, Raccoon—December 1 through February, except in Fruitville Township, Currituck County, Jan. 1–March 16. Otter may be taken only in Currituck County, Dec. 15 through February. Otter and Raccoon may not be trapped west of U.S. Highway no. 1. It is unlawful to set steel traps for Mink and Muskrat in and west of Alexander, Catawba, Cleveland, Surrey, and Wilkes counties except in and adjacent to waters of lakes, ponds, and streams. FULLY PROTECTED: Beaver—no open season. NOT PROTECTED: Groundhog, Skunk, Weasel, and Wildcat may be taken at any time. Bears inflicting, or attempting to inflict, injury to a person or to any person's property may be killed on the spot; or if authorized by a wildlife protector, a Bear may be pursued after such an offense.

Game birds: Brant, Coot, Mourning Dove, Ducks (except Canvasback and Redhead), Eider, Gallinule, Geese (except Snow Geese), Ruffed Grouse, Merganser, Old Squaw, Pheasant, Quail, Rails, Scaup, Scoter, Sora, Wilson's Snipe, Wild Turkey, Woodcock. OPEN SEASONS: Brant, Geese—early November to mid-January. Coot, Ducks, Eider, Merganser, Scaup, Scoter—mid-November to early January. Dove—early September to mid-October, and mid-December to mid-January. Gallinule, Rails, Sora—early September to mid-November. Ruffed Grouse—Oct. 1–Feb. 16 except in Alleghany County, late November to mid-February. Pheasant—late November to mid-February except that in 24 counties, Pheasant may be taken only on licensed shooting preserves. Quail—late November to mid-February. Wilson's Snipe—late November to early January. Wild Turkey—mid-November to mid-February, except no open season in Anson, Beaufort, Carteret, and Richmond counties, or in and west of Gaston, Iredell, Lincoln, Stokes, and Yadkin counties. Woodcock—mid-November to early January. Private shooting preserves—Oct. 1–March 31. Except on licensed shooting preserves, Quail and Wild Turkey may not be hunted or killed while the ground is covered with snow in and west of Bladen, Brunswick, Chatham, Columbus, Durham, Granville, Harnett, New Hanover, and Sampson counties. FULLY PROTECTED: Canvasback and Redhead Ducks, and Snow Geese—no open season. NOT PROTECTED: Buzzards, Crows, Cooper's Hawks, Sharp-shinned Hawks, and Great Horned Owls may be taken at any time.

FIREARMS

Migratory game birds may be taken with shotguns not larger than 10 gauge and capable of holding only 3 shells in the magazine and chamber combined. Longbows used in hunting must have a rated pull of not less than 45 pounds, and arrows should have a minimum broadhead width of seven-eighths of an inch for big game, and blunt heads for small game. Barbed arrows are prohibited.

Shooting hours: Daylight hours. Exceptions: Migratory game birds from sunrise to sunset; Raccoons may not be shot during the daytime west of U.S. Highway 1 except in Richmond County, or at any time in 14 counties.

FISHING

Game fish: Black Bass (Largemouth, Smallmouth), Kentucky or Spotted Bass, Striped Bass, White Bass, Muskellunge, Chain Pickerel (Jack), Pike-perch (Sauger, Walleye), Kokanee Salmon, Trout (Brook, Brown, Rainbow), Weakfish (Sea Trout), and Panfish including Rock Bass (Redeye), Bluegill, Bream, Crappie, White and Yellow Perch, Warmouth (Openmouth), and all species of Perch, Pickerel, and Sunfish.

OPEN SEASON:* Kokanee Salmon and Trout—early April to September, and in some waters a season is extended to September 30. There are no closed seasons for taking Kokanee Salmon and Trout from impounded waters of power reservoirs open to public fishing. Other fish—open season all year.

A portion of Neals Creek in the Mount Mitchell Wildlife Management Area (Yancey County) and of the Pigeon River in the Sherwood Wildlife Management Area are set aside for juveniles under the age of 12 and women to fish for Trout on scheduled dates.

All species of Herring, Mullet, and Shad are classified as freshwater fish when found in inland waters and may not be taken without a valid fishing license. Trotlines and set hooks may be set in the inland waters provided no live bait is used; except that no such lines and hooks may be set in designated Trout waters, or in New River (in Alleghany and Ashe counties) including North and South forks, where the water is clear.

There is top Trout fishing in and near Fontana Lake, Cheoah Reservoir, Nantahal Reservoir and River, and in other Trout waters. Surf casting for Channel Bass, and deep sea fishing for Blue and White Marlin, Amberjack, Barracuda, Dolphin, King Mackerel, and Tuna have landed record-sized fish in and around the Outer Banks and the Cape Hatteras National Seashore Recreational Area. Many areas have been set aside for access to public waters in addition to national- and state-landowner agreements on privately owned lands in the South Mountain Wildlife Management Area in Burke County.

PUBLIC FISHING WATERS (with access areas)

Badgen Reservoir west of El Dorado—Montgomery County; *Black River* 8 miles east of Kelly—Bladen County; *Blewitt Falls Reservoir* on Pee Dee River—Anson County; *Cape Fear River* in Bladen, Chatham, Cumberland, and Harnett counties; *Catawba Lake* 11 miles southwest of Charlotte—Mecklenburg County; *Chatuge Reservoir* 5 miles east of Hayesville—Clay County; *Cheoah Reservoir* on the Little Tennessee River—Graham County; *Chowan River* at Edenhouse Bridge—Chowan County; *Contentnea Creek* at Snow Hill—Greene County; *Dan River* at Milton—Caswell County; and at Leaksville—Rockingham County; Deep River south of Carbonton—Moore County; *East Lake* north of Manns Harbor—Dare County; *Fontana Reservoir* east of Fontana Village—Graham County; *Hickory Lake* 2 miles north of Hickory—Alexander County; *High Rock Lake* southeast of Salisbury—Rowan County; *Hiwassee Reservoir* northwest of Murphy—Cherokee County; *Inland Waterway* one mile east of Coinjock—Currituck County; *James Lake*

---

* Check current state regulations.

west of Morgantown—Burke County; *Kerr Reservoir* (Buggs Island Lake)
north of Bullock—Granville County; *Kitty Hawk Bay* on Albermarle
Sound—Dare County; *Lookout Shoals Lake* northeast of Conover—
Catawba County; *Meherrin River* at Murfreesboro—Hartford County;
Mountain Island Lake northwest of Charlotte—Gaston and Mecklenburg
counties; *Nantahala Reservoir* east of Andrews—Macon County; *Neuse
River* near Bridgeton—Craven County, and near Goldsboro—Wayne
County; *Northeast Cape Fear River* between Beulaville and Kenans-
ville—Duplin County; *Pasquotank River* east of Elizabeth City—Camden
County; *Pee Dee River* 8 miles north of Wadesboro—Anson County;
Rhodhiss Lake northeast of Morgantown—Burke and Caldwell counties;
Roanoke River at Weldon—Halifax County; *Santeetlah Lake* west of
Robbinsville—Graham County; *Scuppernong River* west of Columbia—
Tyrrell County; *Shelter Creek* 9 miles east of Burgaw—Pender County;
South River southwest of Garland—Bladen County; *South Yadkin River*
at Cooleemee—Davie County; *Tar River* north of Tarboro—Edgecombe
County; and northwest of Greenville—Pitt County; *Tillery Lake* north-
west of Mount Gilead—Montgomery County; *Waccamaw Lake* west of
Bolton—Columbus County; *White Oak River* southeast of Maysville—
Jones County.

STATE PARKS

Cliffs of the Neuse (355 acres) on the Neuse River south of Goldsboro—Wayne County; *Fort Macon* (390 acres) at Beaufort Inlet to
Bogue Sound near Morehead City—Carteret County; *Hanging Rock*
(3,865 acres) in the Sauratown Mountains, near Danbury—Stokes
County; *Jones Lake** (2,000 acres) near Elizabethtown—Bladen County;
Morrow Mountain (4,135 acres) in the Uwharrie Mountains on Pee
Dee River, east of Albermarle— Stanley County; *Pettigrew* (16,830
acres) around Lake Phelps (16,600 acres) south of Creswell—Tyrrell
and Washington counties; *Singletary Lake* (1,287 acres) near Elizabeth-
town—Bladen County; *William B. Umstead* (3,846 acres) between
Durham and Raleigh—Wake County.

STATE WILDLIFE MANAGEMENT AREAS

Angola Bay in Duplin and Pender counties; *Caswell* (exclusive of
the Turkey refuge) in Caiswell County; *Goose Creek* in Beaufort and
Pamlico counties; *Gull Rock* in Hyde County; *Holly Shelter* in Pender
County; *Northwest River Marsh* in Currituck County; *Sandhills* in
Moore, Richmond, and Scotland counties; *Thurmond* in Chatham and
Wilkes counties.

---

* Established for Negroes.

NATIONAL WILDLIFE MANAGEMENT AREAS

Croatan in Carteret, Craven, and Jones counties; *Daniel Boone* in Avery, Burke, and Caldwell counties; *Fires Creek* in Clay County; *Flat Top* in Mitchell and Yancey counties; *Harmon Den* in Haywood County; *Mattamuskeet* in Hyde County; *Mount Mitchell* in McDowell and Yancey counties; *Pisgah* in Buncombe, Henderson, and Transylvania counties; *Rich Laurel* in Madison County; *Santeetlah* in Graham County; *Standing Indian* in Macon County; *Uwharris* in Montgomery County; *Wayah Bald* in Macon County.

Licenses, regulations, information about current seasons, bag and possession limits may be obtained from the Director, North Carolina Wildlife Resources Commission, P.O. Box 2919, Raleigh. Official highway maps issued free by the North Carolina State Highway Commission show the national forests. Detailed information about state forests and parks, resorts, and other places of interest is available from the State Department of Conservation and Development, Raleigh. A map of Buggs Island Lake (Kerr Reservoir) may be obtained from the U.S. Army Corps of Engineers, Wilmington District, P.O. Box 1890, Wilmington.

NORTH DAKOTA

Area: 70,837 square miles (land area—69,457 square miles); rank in nation–17
Bird: Western Meadowlark (*Sturnella neglecta*), adopted 1947
Capital city: Bismarck on the Missouri River in Burleigh County; population (1960)—27,670; rank in state–4
Counties: 53
Elevations: Highest, Black Butte (3,468 ft.) in Slope County; lowest, Pembina (790 ft.) in Pembina County
Flower: Wild Prairie Rose (*Rosa blanda*), adopted 1907
Geographic center: 5 miles southwest of McClusky, Sheridan County
Nicknames: Flickertail State, Great Central State, Sioux State
Population (1960): 632,446; rank in nation–44
Tree: American Elm (*Ulmus americana*), adopted 1947

North Dakota is bordered by Montana on the west, South Dakota on the south, and shares the Bois de Sioux River and Red River of the North with Minnesota on the east; and the provinces of Manitoba and Saskatchewan are on the northern Canadian boundary.

The state is a great fertile prairie rising in a series of plains to the

Missouri Plateau region. The Missouri River has been impounded to create the Garrison Reservoir (640 square miles) with a 1,600-mile shore-line extending through the Fort Berthold Indian Reservation from the Snake Creek National Wildlife Refuge in the eastern end to the Williston area near the junction of the Yellowstone River close to the Montana border. The Little Missouri, Cedar, Cannonball, Green, and Heart rivers are in the southwest where buttes project above the terrain in the region known as the Badlands. The Little Knife, Little Muddy, and White Earth rivers flow into the Garrison Reservoir from the northwest. The DeLacs River and Mouse or Souris River flow into central North Dakota from Canada, and the Forest, Park, Pembina, and Tongue rivers wander through the northeastern part of the state. The James, Maple, Rush, Sheyenne, and Wild Rice rivers meander throughout the southeast. There are numerous large and small natural and man-made lakes, particularly in central North Dakota.

LICENSES

Resident licenses are issued to bona fide residents of the state including members of the U.S. Armed Forces, but servicemen stationed outside of North Dakota must obtain nonresident licenses. Farmers and members of their families permanently residing on land owned or leased by them may fish, hunt, and trap on their property without licenses, except to take Deer. Residents under the age of 16, or more than 65 years of age, and nonresidents under the age of 12, may fish without licenses. Regardless of age, all persons must obtain licenses to hunt and trap on land other than their own, except that no license is required to hunt varmints. Juveniles under the age of 15 must be accompanied by a parent or guardian when using firearms. There is no age limit for archers hunting Deer, but juveniles under fifteen may not hunt big game with guns. Mule Deer hunting stamps are issued as mailed applications are received by the Game and Fish Department between October 1 and November 1, and any remaining stamps may be purchased in person or by mail after November 1. A Mule Deer stamp attached to a hunting license permits a choice of taking a Mule or White-tailed Deer. A limited number of free permits in the form of stamps are issued to hunt Wild Turkey. Persons owning or leasing at least 160 acres of land located in a Turkey-hunting region, may request only one permit for a family, and any remaining permits are issued on a lottery basis. All persons 16 or more years of age must purchase a federal "Duck" stamp to take migratory game birds. A license is required to erect or maintain a fish house on ice.

Resident license fees: Fishing, $2.00; family fishing (husband and wife), $3.00; hunting small game, $2.00; hunting big game (firearms), $6.00; hunting big game (bow and arrow), $6.00; trapping, $1.00; Mule

Deer permit (attach to big game license), $1.00; federal "Duck" stamp, $3.00; ice fishing house permit, $1.00.

Nonresident license fees: Fishing, $5.00; fishing 7 consecutive days, $1.00; hunting small game, $25.00; hunting Antelope and Deer with bow and arrow $25.00; hunting big game with firearms (except Antelope), $50.00; Mule Deer permit (attach to big game license), $1.00; federal "Duck" stamp, $3.00; ice fishing house permit, $1.00.

HUNTING AND TRAPPING

Game animals: Pronghorn Antelope, Deer (Mule, White-tailed), Tree Squirrels. OPEN SEASONS:* Antelope—archery, early September for about 2 weeks and a similar period in October; firearms, generally in late September. Deer—archery, early September to early November and from mid-November to mid-December; firearms, about 8 or 10 days in November. Tree Squirrels—late September to December 31 except during the firearms Deer season. BAG LIMITS: Antelope—1 per year. Deer—1 per year. Tree Squirrels—5 per day.

A legal Buck is a male Deer with forked antlers on at least one side. Only archers may take Deer of either sex.

Furbearing animals: Badger, Beaver, Bobcat, Cougar, Coyote, Canada Lynx, Fox, Mink, Muskrat, Rabbit, Raccoon, Skunk, Weasel, Wolf. OPEN SEASONS:* Badger, Beaver—mid-November to mid-May. Mink, Weasel—mid-November to mid-December. *Bag limits*—none. FULLY PROTECTED: Muskrat—no open season. NOT PROTECTED: Bobcat, Cougar, Coyote, Fox, Gopher, Canada Lynx, Porcupine, Prairie Dog, Rabbit, Raccoon, Ground Squirrels, Skunk, Wolf, and Woodchuck may be taken at any time.

Only traps may be used to take Mink and Weasel.

Game birds: Coot, Mourning Dove, Ducks (except Canvasback and Redhead), Geese, Grouse (Ruffed, Sharptail), Merganser, Hungarian Partridge, Cock Pheasant, Wilson's Snipe, Wild Turkey. OPEN SEASONS:* Coot, Duck, Merganser—early October to early November. Dove—late September to mid-October. Geese: Oct. 1–Nov. 30 in designated areas. Ruffed Grouse—late September to early November in Bottineau, Cavalier, Pembina, and Rolette counties. Sharptail Grouse—late September to early November and mid-November to mid-December throughout the state except in a designated area. Hungarian Partridge—late September to early November, and mid-November to mid-December. Cock Pheasant —mid-October to early November statewide, and mid-November to December 31 in units I and III. Wilson's Snipe—3 weeks in October. Wild Turkey—about 5 or 6 days in late November in Burleigh, Emmons,

---

* Check current state regulations.

Grant, McLean, Mercer, Morton, and Oliver Counties. FULLY PRO-
TECTED: Canvasback and Redhead Ducks, Gallinule, Rails, Sora, and
Woodcock—no open seasons. NOT PROTECTED: Crow, Cooper's Hawk,
Sharp-shinned Hawk, Great Horned Owl, Snow Owl, and Magpies may
be taken at any time.

FIREARMS

Game birds may be taken only by the use of longbow, and shotgun
not larger than 10 gauge and capable of holding not more than 3 shells
in the magazine and chamber combined. Deer may be hunted with
muzzle-loading rifles of at least .36 caliber, and shotguns of .410 gauge
or larger with a minimum barrel length of 18 inches. Rifles firing centerfire cartridges of .22 caliber or larger, and rifled slugs are permitted, but
fully automatic guns, rimfire firearms, and full metal jacket or altered
projectiles are prohibited. Shotguns with rifled slugs only may be used
to take Deer in the Bismarck area and on the Riverdale Game Management Area. Archers hunting Deer must use longbows which are capable of propelling a hunting arrow at least 130 yards, and the arrows should
be at least 24 inches long and tipped with steel points not less than
three-quarters of an inch or more than 1½ inches in width. Rifles and
traps may be used to take Beaver; and Badger, Coyote, Fox, Raccoon,
and Skunk may be shot with any rifle or shotgun.

Shooting hours: Sunrise to sunset; and opening day of the big game
and migratory game birds seasons start at 12:00 o'clock noon. Exceptions: archery big game hunting season, one-half hour before sunrise
to sunset; except that opening day starts at 12:00 o'clock noon. The season for taking Beaver with rifles or traps starts and ends at noon. Mink
and Weasel traps may be set at 12:00 noon on opening day and remain
until sunset of the last day.

FISHING

Game fish: Black Bass, Muskellunge, Northern Pike, Walleyed Pike,
Sauger, Trout. OPEN SEASONS:* Black Bass: from early June to Decem-
ber 31. Muskellunge—no open season. Northern Pike, Walleyed Pike,
Sauger—January 1 to mid-March, and mid-May to December 31 in Cat
Coulee Lake, Garrison Reservoir and Tailrace, Jund Dam, Lake Meti-
goshe, Nieuwsma Pond, and North Lemmon Lake; mid-May to mid-
October in other designated waters. Other fish—all year.

Each fisherman may use not more than 2 poles equipped with one
line each to which is attached one hook or lure, and any artificial lure is
considered as one hook. Snagging or spearing fish is unlawful, but the

---

* Check current state regulations.

use of bow and arrow is permitted providing that an arrow with a harpoon style point (or barbed wire point) is attached by a line to the bow. Game fish may not be taken with bow equipment, and the open season for other fish is from mid-May to mid-October. Bow fishing is prohibited in the Missouri River including Dickinson Reservoir and tributaries and Lake Tschida; the James River and all tributaries including Dakota Lake and Jamestown Reservoir; Long Lake and tributaries in Burleigh County; and all streams tributary to the Red River except the portion of Sheyenne River lying upstream from Baldhill Dam, Lake Ashtabula, and Baldhead Creek.

All species of fish may be taken through ice from January 1 to mid-March, but taking Largemouth Black Bass, White Bass, Northern Pike, Walleyed Pike, and Sauger is prohibited from mid-March to mid-May.

The Garrison Reservoir is the largest and most popular pike-fishing water in the state, and there are also large Rainbow Trout, Channel Catfish, Crappies, Goldeyes, Ling, and Perch. There is also excellent pike fishing in Lake Ashtabula, Brush Lake, Heart Butte Reservoir, Lake Darling, Jamestown Reservoir, Lake Metigoshe, Lake Tewaukon, Spiritwood, and Strawberry lakes, and top Trout fishing in the Missouri and Yellowstone rivers, Spring Lake, and Hammon and Gordon lakes. The following state parks and public waters are well stocked with fish.

PUBLIC WATERS

Blacktail Dam Reservoir north of Williston—Williams County; *Braddock Dam Reservoir* southwest of Braddock—Emmons County; *Brush Lake* north of Mercer—McLean County; *Cat Coulee Lake* northeast of Carson—Grant County; *Crooked, Long,* and *Strawberry lakes* south of Ruso—McLean County; *Crystal Springs* near town of Crystal Springs—Kidder County; *Danzig Reservoir* (Storm Creek) northwest of New Salem—Morton County; *Des Lacs Reservoir* on Des Lacs River at Kenmare—Ward County; *Devils Lake* bordering Fort Totten Indian Reservation—Ramsey County; *Dickinson Reservoir* southwest of Dickinson—Stark County; *George* and *Round lakes* north of Drake—McHenry County; *Golden Lake* northeast of Finley—Steele County; *Hamman Lake* west of Amidon—Slope County; *Homme Reservoir* at Park River—Walsh County; *Jamestown Reservoir* on the James River, north of Jamestown—Stutsman County; *Jund Dam* east of Zeeland—McIntosh County; *Lake Ashtabula* on Sheyenne River, northwest of Valley City—Barnes County; *Lake Darling* in the Upper Souris Wildlife Refuge at Grano—Renville County; *Lake Elsie* southwest of Hankinson—Richland County; *Lake Hoskins* west of Ashley—McIntosh County; *Lake Ilo* west of Dunn Center—Dunn County; *Lake Isabel* south of Dawson—Kidder County; *Lake Metigosh* (2 lakes) 9 miles north of Bottineau—Bottineau County;

Lake Tewauken south of Cayuga—Sargent County; *Lake Tobiason* north-east of Sharon—Steele County; *Lake Tschida* formed by the Heart Butte Dam on Heart River, south of Glen Ullin—Morton County; *Lake Williams* west of Pettibone—Kidder County; *McLeod Lake* near Ray—Williams County; *McVille Dam* east of McVille—Nelson County; *Nieuwsma Pond* 15 miles southeast of Strasburg—Emmons County; *North Lemmon Lake* near boundary—Adams County; north of Lemmon in South Dakota; *Raleigh Reservoir* west of Raleigh—Grant County; *Red Willow Lake* northwest of Binford—Griggs County; *Rice Lake* southeast of Strasburg—Emmons County; *Silver Lake* southwest of Rutland—Sargent County; *Spiritwood Lake* north of Jamestown—Stutsman County; *Springs Lake* west of Rhame—Bowman County; *Sterling Reservoir* southeast of Hensler—Oliver County; *Williams Creek Dam* southeast of Sentinel Butte—Golden Valley County; *Wolf Butte Dam* northeast of Bucyrus—Adams County; *Yanktonai Reservoir* northwest of Wilton—Burleigh County.

STATE PARKS

Beaver Lake (9,340 acres) at Beaver Lake southeast of Napoleon—Logan County; *Fort Lincoln* (740 acres) at confluence of Heart and Missouri rivers near Mandan—Morton County; *Lake Metigoshe* (728 acres) at North and South Metigoshe lakes near the Canadian boundary, north of Bottineau—Bottineau County; *Turtle River* (486 acres) near Arvilla—Grand Forks County.

Licenses, permits, regulations, and information about current seasons, bag and possession limits may be obtained from the Commissioner, State Game and Fish Department, Bismarck. The very interesting monthly magazine *North Dakota Outdoors* is published for $1.00 per year by the State Game and Fish Department.

OHIO

Area: 41,040 square miles (land area—40,972 square miles); rank in nation–35
Bird: Cardinal (*Richmondena cardinalis*), adopted 1933
Capital city: Columbus at the confluence of the Olentangy and Scioto rivers in Franklin County; population (1960)—471,316; rank in state–3
Counties: 88
Elevations: Highest, Campbell Hill (1,550 ft.) in Logan County; lowest, Ohio River (425 ft.) in Hamilton County
Flower: Scarlet Carnation (*Dianthus*), adopted 1904
Geographic center: 25 miles east of north of Columbus, Delaware County

Nicknames: Buckeye State, Mother of Presidents, Yankee State
Population (1960): 9,706,397; rank in nation—5
Tree: Buckeye (*Aesculus glabra*), also called Horse Chestnut Tree

Ohio is a Great Lakes state with Michigan and Lake Erie on the north, Indiana on the west, Pennsylvania on the northwest, and the Ohio River flowing 436 miles as a boundary between West Virginia on the southwest and Kentucky on the south.

The range of hills above rolling prairie land extends from western Drake County to Trumble County in the eastern Allegheny Plateau region, and divides the drainage system of the state. Many northern streams flow rapidly through narrow valleys, and the Black, Huron, and Vermillion rivers follow direct courses to Lake Erie. The Cuyahoga River meanders for miles before reaching Cleveland's 30-mile waterfront on Lake Erie. The Catawba Peninsula and a lighthouse on rugged Marblehead Peninsula overlook the Sandusky River flowing into beautiful Sandusky Bay, and Port Clinton at the mouth of Portage River. Catawba Island, Put-in-Bay on South Bass Island, Gibraltar, Kelleys, Middle Bass, and North Bass Islands are accessible by aircraft, ferry, or other watercraft. On the northwestern shore of Lake Erie, Toledo stretches for about 15 miles along the Maumee River. The Ashtabula River, in Ashtabula County, and Grand River, in Lake County, flow into the northeastern shore of Lake Erie.

Grand-St. Mary's Lake (13,500 acres) at Celina in western Mercer County, is south of St. Mary's River, a tributary of the Great Miami River. The long eastern Muskingum River joined by the Licking River at Zanesville flows under a unique Y-shaped bridge on a southward course through the Allegheny Plateau to Marietta on the Ohio River. The Scioto River, increased by many tributaries, drains central Ohio at Columbus, and is joined by the Olentangy River before moving southward to Portsmouth on the Ohio River. The Great Miami River, which flows through Dayton on a long journey, the Little Miami River in southeastern Ohio, and the Hocking River flowing through Athens in the Allegheny Plateau are tributaries of the Ohio River. There are 10 beautiful, large lakes within the Muskingum Conservancy District at New Philadelphia in eastern Ohio.

LICENSES

Resident licenses are issued to United States citizens who have lived in the state for at least 6 months immediately preceding an application for a license. Fishing licenses are not required for juveniles under the age of 18 or for persons receiving old age pensions from the Ohio Division of Aid for the Aged, but the latter exemption does not apply to persons receiving other pensions, such as social security. Members of the U.S. Armed Forces carrying proper identification may fish, hunt, or trap without licenses while on leave or furlough. Landowners, tenants, or managers actually living on farms may fish, hunt and trap on their lands without licenses, but must obtain a Deer permit to transport Deer from their property. Otherwise, hunting and trapping licenses are required regardless of age, and nonresidents may not trap Beaver unless the state of their home residence permits Ohio citizens to take Beaver. No juvenile under the age of 16 may hunt unless he is accompanied by an adult at least 21 years old. Ohio licenses are required to fish in all public waters including Lake Erie. Fish, Frogs, and Turtles may not be taken from the Pennsylvania shore of Pymatuning Lake, except by the holder of a Pennsylvania license. Aliens must obtain nonresident licenses, and all persons 16 or more years of age must possess a federal "Duck" stamp to take migratory game birds. Any duplicate of a lost, destroyed or stolen license may be made only by the agent who issued the original license. No person may possess a live wild animal without a permit issued by a game protector. License period: fishing, March 1 through February; hunting and trapping, Sept. 1–Aug. 31.

Resident license fees: Annual fishing, $2.00; hunting and trapping, $2.00; permit to take Deer (in addition to hunting license), $5.00; federal "Duck" stamp, $3.00.

Nonresident license fees: Annual fishing, $5.00; fishing 15 consecutive days, $3.00; hunting and trapping, $20.00; permit to take Deer (in addition to hunting license), $5.00; federal "Duck" stamp, $3.00; hunting on private shooting preserves, $5.00.

HUNTING AND TRAPPING

Game animals: White-tailed Deer, Snowshoe Hare, Cottontail Rabbit, Squirrels. OPEN SEASONS:** Deer—archery, Oct. 15–Dec. 31; shotgun, a few days in mid-December. Cottontail Rabbit—Nov. 15–Jan. 31. Squirrel—private land, from early September to November in the North Zone, and extended 2 weeks longer in South Zone; state public hunting areas, from early September through December. BAG LIMITS: Deer—1 per year. Cottontail Rabbit—3 per day. Squirrel—4 per day.

Furbearing animals: Badger, Beaver, Fox, Mink, Muskrat, Opossum, Raccoon, Skunk, Weasel. OPEN SEASONS:** Beaver—about 2 weeks in late February by trapping only on private land, and in Ashtabula, Carroll, Columbiana, Jackson, Jefferson, Mahoning, Portage, Trumbull, and Williams counties. Mink, Muskrat, Opossum, Raccoon—November 15

---

* Plus 25-cent issue fee.
** Check current state regulations.

through February. BAG LIMITS: Beaver—2 per season. Raccoon—4 per day. Mink, Muskrat, Opossum—no limits. FULLY PROTECTED: Snowshoe Hare—no open season. NOT PROTECTED: Badger, Fox, Skunk, Weasel, and Woodchuck may be taken at any time.

Game birds: Brant, Coot, Mourning Dove, Ducks (except Canvasback and Redhead), Eider, Gallinule, Geese (except Snow Goose), Ruffed Grouse, Merganser, Old Squaw, Hungarian Partridge, Pheasant (Reeve's, Ringnecked), Quail, Rails, Scaup, Scoter, Sora, Wilson's Snipe, Wild Turkey, Woodcock. OPEN SEASONS:* Brant, Geese—late October to late December. Coot, Ducks, Eider, Merganser, Old Squaw, Scaup, Scoter—late October to mid-November and another week in late December. Mourning Dove, Gallinule, Rails, Sora—early September to late October. Ruffed Grouse—mid-October to mid-February. Hungarian Partridge, Cock Pheasant—mid-November to mid-December on private land; mid-November to January 31 on state public hunting areas. Cock or Hen Pheasant—in the Auburn Marsh, Hambden Orchard, Pleasant Valley, and Spring Valley wildlife areas, Nov. 15–Jan. 31. Quail—mid-November to mid-December on state-owned and controlled lands; and season extended to mid-January on the Delaware Reservoir and on Cooper Hollow, Indian Creek, Pleasant Valley, Ross, Rush Run, Spring Valley, Tranquility, and Wolf Creek wildlife areas. Wilson's Snipe, Woodcock—October 1 to mid-November. Hunting on private shooting preserves—Sept. 1–April 30. FULLY PROTECTED: Canvasback and Redhead Ducks, Snow Geese, Reeve's Pheasant, and Wild Turkey—no open seasons. NOT PROTECTED: Crows, Hawks, or Owls may be killed in the act of damaging or destroying poultry or property.

FIREARMS

Pistols, rifles, or shotguns larger than 10 gauge or capable of holding more than 3 shells in the magazine and chamber combined may not be used to take game birds. Shotguns loaded with a single ball or rifled slug may be used to hunt Deer, and there are no restrictions on longbows and arrows except that explosive or poisoned arrows are prohibited. It is unlawful to use pistols and rifles during the Rabbit season on public hunting areas, and at any time in state parks, on the Auburn Marsh Wildlife Area, and the Muskingum Conservancy district lands.

Shooting hours: Hunting on Sunday is prohibited. Deer, Rabbit, Partridge, Pheasant, Quail—9 A.M.–5 P.M.; except that Deer may be taken by bow and arrow from daylight to dark. Ruffed Grouse and Squirrel—daylight to dark. Migratory game birds—sunrise to sunset. Mink, Muskrat, Opossum, Raccoon—6:00 P.M.–6:00 A.M. A continuous

---

* Check current state regulations.

white light visible for at least one-quarter of a mile must be carried during night hunting.

FISHING

Game fish: Black Bass, Muskellunge, Yellow Pike-perch (Walleye). OPEN SEASONS: All year. There are no closed seasons, minimum or maximum lengths, bag or possession limits for fish, except in Magee Marsh and Pymatuning Lake. Magee Marsh: March 1–Oct. 1; anglers may take fish, frogs, and turtles; no bag or possession limits. Pymatuning Lake: Daily bag limits—Black Bass, 10; Muskellunge, 2; Yellow Pike-perch (Walleye), 10; other fish, no limit.

Not more than 2 handlines, or 2 units of rod and line, or a combination of one handline and one rod and line may be used at the same time by one sportsman. Handlines are limited to not more than 10 single hooks, and the use of treble hooks is prohibited. Float lines, trotlines, bank or set lines may be used in designated areas.

Rough fish such as Buffalo, Carp, Dogfish, Gar, Quillback, Gizzard Shad, Sheepshead (Lake Erie), and Suckers may be taken by bow and arrow or handline, but not by any person swimming under water with or without a self-contained breathing apparatus or other equipment designated for swimming under water. Gizzard Shad and Smelt may be taken with a hand landing net, minor dip net, or minnow seine.

Ice fishermen may not use more than 6 tip-ups or fish through holes cut larger than 12 inches in diameter.

Frogs may be taken by bow and arrow, hook and line, but not by firearms or the use of lights. Open seasons: June 16–April 30, except in Pymatuning Lake, July 2–Oct. 31; daily bag limit, 10; Pymatuning Lake, 15.

There are several wooded tracts on Lake Erie reserved for recreational purposes with excellent deepwater fishing nearby. The Interlake Yacht Regatta at Put-in-Bay is held in August, and Camp Perry (5 miles west of Port Clinton) is the site of the annual National Rifle Association Match. The following lists include only the largest fishing or hunting areas provided for public use throughout the state.

PUBLIC LAKES

Acton Lake (625 acres) northwest of Oxford—Preble County; *Belmont Lake* (822 acres) at Loomis—Belmont County; *East Branch Reservoir* (450 acres) at Clarendon—Geauga County; *Ferguson Lake* (305 acres) east of Lima— Allen County; *Findlay Reservoir* (187 acres) southeast of Findlay—Hancock County; *Fostoria Reservoir* southwest of Fostoria—Hancock County; *Griggs Reservoir* (364 acres) 4 miles north of Columbus—Franklin County; *Hinckley Lake* (100 acres) northeast of

Medina—Medina County; *Hoover Reservoir* (3,300 acres) 4 miles east of Westerville—Delaware and Franklin counties; *Lost Creek Reservoir* (112 acres) east of Lima—Allen County; *Mill Creek Park* (2,750 acres) at Youngtown—Mahoning County; *Milton Reservoir* (1,685 acres) 15 miles west of Youngstown—Mahoning County; *Metzer Reservoir* (167 acres) east of Lima—Allen County; *Mogadore Reservoir* (1,000 acres) south of Kent—Portage County; *O'Shaughnessy Reservoir* (832 acres) north of Dublin—Delaware County; *Springfield Lake* (600 acres) at Springfield Center—Summit County; *Winton Woods Lake* (181 acres) south of Greenhills—Hamilton County.

PUBLIC RESERVES

Alma Lake (244 acres, lake 73 acres) northeast of Wellston—Vinton County; *Atwood Reservoir* (4,135 acres, lake 1,540 acres) south of New Cumberland—Tuscarawas County; *Auburn Marsh* (431 acres) at Auburn Center—Geauga County; *Avondale* (3,589 acres) 10 miles southwest of Zanesville—Muskingum County; *Beach City Reservoir* (1,258 acres, lake 420 acres) south of Beach City—Tuscarawas County; *Berlin Reservoir* (6,745 acres, lake 3,650 acres) north of Alliance—Mahoning, Portage, and Stark counties; *Big Island* (1,043 acres) west of Marion— Marion County; *Boliver* (1,450 acres) at Boliver—Stark County; *Buckeye Lake* (4,000 acres, lake 3,300 acres) south of Hebron—Fairfield, Licking, and Perry counties; *Caldwell Lake* (9,354 acres) 9 miles south of Chillicothe—Ross County; *Catawba Island* (7 acres) in Lake Erie, 10 miles northwest of Port Clinton—Ottawa County; *Charles Mill Reservoir* (3,432 acres, lake 1,350 acres) near Mifflin—Richland County; *Clear Lake* (389 acres, lake 100 acres) near Harmony—Clark County; *Clear Fork Reservoir* (1,072 acres, lake 944 acres) northwest of Lexington—Richland County; *Clendening Reservoir* (6,219 acres, lake 1,800 acres) at Tippecanoe—Harrison County; *Cooper Hollow* (3,478 acres) 11 miles southeast of Jackson—Jackson County; *Cumberland* (800 acres) south of Cumberland—Noble County; *Deer Creek Reservoir* (314 acres) at Limaville—Stark County; *Delaware Reservoir* (7,378 acres, lake 1,300 acres) 8 miles north of Delaware—Delaware, Mason, and Morrow counties; *Dillon Reservoir* (11,761 acres, lake 1,325 acres) 4 miles northwest of Zanesville—Muskingum County; *Dover* (366 acres) 3 miles northeast of Dover—Tuscarawas County; *Dow Lake* (160 acres) 5 miles east of Athens—Athens County; *Fallsville* (1,071 acres) near New Vienna—Highland County; *Grand St. Marys Lake* (15,537 acres, lake 13,500 acres) 2 miles west of St. Marys—Auglaize County; *Grand River* (4,188 acres) 5 miles northeast at junction of state routes 88 and 534— Trumbull County; *Grant Lake* (376 acres, lake 207 acres) south of Mount Orab—Brown County; *Guilford Lake* (496 acres, lake 396 acres) northwest of Lisbon—Columbiana County; *Hambden Orchard* (695 acres) south of Hambden—Geauga County; *Hargus Creek* (427 acres, lake 146 acres) northwest of Circleville—Pickaway County; *Harrison Lake** (196 acres, lake 105 acres) southwest of Fayette—Fulton County; *Harrison County Reclamation* (1,321 acres) north of Cadiz; *Highlandtown* (1,560 acres) northwest of Highlandtown—Columbiana County; *Indian Creek* (1,580 acres) near Fayettville—Brown County; *Indian Lake** (544 acres, lake 5,800 acres) 12 miles northwest of Bellefontaine—Logan County; *Jackson Lake* (406 acres, lake 243 acres) west of Oak Hill—Jackson County; *Jefferson County Reclamation* (2,107 acres) near Bloomfield; *Kaul* (1,000 acres) 5 miles west of Toronto—Jefferson County; *Kelleys Island* (412 acres) in Lake Erie, north of Marblehead Peninsula; *Kipton Reservoir* (166 acres, lake 20 acres) at Kipton—Lorain County; *Kiser Lake* (653 acres, lake 385 acres) south of Quincy—Champaign County; *Knox Lake* (1,241 acres, lake 495 acres) east of Fredericktown—Knox County; *Lake Loramie* (1,950 acres, lake 1,650 acres) south of Minster—Shelby County; *Lake White** (360 acres, lake 337 acres) southwest of Waverly—Pike County; *Leesville Reservoir* (3,607 acres, lake 1,000 acres) south of Sharrodsville—Carroll County; *Liberty* (145 acres) northwest of Jackson near county line—Jackson County; *Little Portage River* (357 acres) 5 miles west of Port Clinton—Ottawa County; *Lordstown* (950 acres) at junction of state Route 45 and Turnpike—Tumbull County.

Madison Lake (187 acres, lake 107 acres) east of London—Madison County; *Magee Marsh** (2,198 acres) 17 miles west of Port Clinton—Lucas and Ottawa counties; *A. W. Marion* (427 acres, lake 146 acres) north of Circleville—Pickaway County; *Mead* (2,242 acres) northwest of Jackson—Jackson County; *Mount Gilead Lakes* (172 acres) east of Mount Gilead—Morrow County; *Metzger Marsh* (558 acres) east of Bono—Lucas County; *Milan* (296 acres) west of Milton—Erie County; *Mohawk* (4,572 acres) west of Warsaw—Coshocton County; *Mohican River* (370 acres) west of Walhonding—Coshocton and Knox counties; *Monroe Lake* (778 acres, lake 39 acres) south of Malaga—Monroe County; *Mosquito Creek Reservoir* (11,364 acres, lake 7,850 acres) at Mecca—Trumbull County; *New Lyme* (529 acres) east of New Lyme—Ashtabula County; *Nimisila* (1,225 acres) 7 miles south of Akron—Summit County; *Oldaker* (145 acres) 6 miles west of Hillsboro—Highlands County; *Orwell* (197 acres) north of Orwell—Ashtabula County; *Oxbow Lake* (415 acres, lake 36 acres) 8 miles north of Defiance—Defiance County; *Perry County Reclamation* (4,400 acres) northeast of Lexington; *Piedmont Reservoir* (6,332 acres, lake 2,270 acres) northeast of Smyrna—Belmont and Harrison counties; *Pleasant Hill Reservoir* (2,394 acres,

---

* Waterfowl hunting; special permit for Magee Marsh.

lake 850 acres) west of Perrysville—Ashland and Richland counties; *Pleasant Valley* (1,410 acres) 5 miles west of Chillicothe—Ross County; *Portage Lakes* (2,780 acres including 8 reservoirs—total 2,150 acres of water) south of Akron—Summit County; *Powelson* (2,687 acres) south of Dresden—Muskingum County; *Resthave* (2,507 acres, lake 300 acres) at Castalia—Erie County; *Roosevelt Lake* (250 acres, lake 11 acres) northwest of Friendship—Scioto County; *Ross Lake* (1,100 acres) 3 miles east of Chillicothe—Ross County; *Rush Run* (1,101 acres) 4 miles southeast of Camden—Preble County; *Salt Fork* (7,886 acres) 8 miles northeast of Cambridge—Guernsey County; *Seneca Reservoir* (7,165 acres, lake 3,550 acres) east of Senecaville—Guernsey and Noble counties; *Shreve Lake* (228 acres, lake 58 acres) west of Shreve—Wayne County; *South Bass Island* (32 acres) in Lake Erie, north of Marblehead Peninsula, access from Catawba Point or Port Clinton; *Spencer Lake* (575 acres, lake 70 acres) northeast of Spencer—Medina County; *Spring Valley* (913 acres, lake 104 acres) south of Spring Valley—Green County; *Stonelick Creek* (1,027 acres, lake 171 acres) at Edenton—Clermont County; *Tappan Reservoir* (6,641 acres, lake 2,350 acres) at Tappan—Harrison County; *Tranquility* (2,743 acres) northeast of Tranquility—Adams County; *Trimble* (2,089 acres) west of Glouster—Athens County; *Tycoon Lake* (776 acres, lake 100 acres) northeast of Rio Grande—Gallia County; *Van Buren Lake* (189 acres, lake 53 acres) southeast of Van Buren—Hancock County; *Veto Lake* (451 acres, lake 160 acres) 8 miles northwest of Belpre—Washington County; *Waterloo* (1,254 acres) at New Marshfield—Athens County; *Willard Marsh* (1,508 acres) near Celeryville—Huron County; *Wills Creek Reservoir* (4,364 acres, lake 900 acres) at Marquand Mills—Coshocton and Muskingum counties; *Woodbury* (1,758 acres) south of Warsaw—Coshocton County; *Wolf Creek* (2,882 acres) 8 miles southwest of McConnelsville—Morgan County; *Wolf Run* (932 acres) at Belle Valley—Noble County; *Wyandot* (383 acres) south of Carey—Wyandot County; *Zepernick Lake* (221 acres, lake 36 acres) east of New Alexander—Columbiana County.

STATE FORESTS

Athens (2,554 acres) east of Athens—Athens County; *Blue Rock* (4,892 acres) south of Taylorsville—Muskingum County; *Brush Creek* (11,311 acres) northeast of Rarden—Adams and Scioto counties; *Dean* (1,796 acres) south of Vernon—Lawrence County; *Hocking* (9,080 acres) 10 miles west of Logan—Hocking County; *Maumee* (2,975 acres) west of Whitehorse— Fulton and Henry counties; *Mohican Memorial* (4,366 acres) southwest of Loudenville—Ashland County; *Pike County* (9,420 acres) north of Morgantown—Pike County; *Raccoon* (5,650 acres) east of Dundas—Vinton County; *Richland Furnace* (2,186 acres) northwest of Wellston—Vinton County; *Scioto Trail* (9,354 acres) south of Chillicothe—Pike and Ross counties; *Shade River* (2,744 acres) south of Longbottom—Meigs County; *Shawnee-Roosevelt* (56,209 acres, 6 small lakes) east of Henley—Adams and Scioto counties; *Tar Hollow* (16,553 acres) south of Laurelville—Hocking, Ross, and Vinton counties; *Yellow Creek* (677 acres) near Salineville—Columbiana County; *Zaleski* (18,823 acres) around Brown Township—Vinton County.

STATE PARKS*

Beaver Creek (1,232 acres) about 10 miles north of East Liverpool —Columbiana County; *John Bryan* (751 acres) on Little Miami River, east of Yellow Springs—Greene County; *Burr Oak* (2,104 acres, lake 664 acres) northeast of Glouster—Morgan County; *Clear Fork* (545 acres) on the Clear Fork of Mohican River, near Perrysville—Ashland County; *Cowan* (1,700 acres, lake 700 acres) southwest of Wilmington—Clinton County; *Crane Creek Beach* (650 acres) on Lake Erie, and adjacent to Magee Marsh near Oak Harbor—Lucas and Ottawa counties; *East Harbor* (1,256 acres) on Lake Erie east of Port Clinton—Ottawa County; *Findlay* (915 acres, lake 92 acres) 5 miles south of Wellington—Lorain County; *Forked Run* (794 acres, lake 102 acres) in Shade River State Forest; *Hocking* (1,555 acres, water 636 acres) in Hocking State Forest; *Hueston Woods* (3,508 acres, Acton Lake 625 acres) near Oxford—Butler and Preble counties; *Independence Dam* (58 acres) on Maumee River and Miami-Erie Canal, east of Defiance—Defiance County; *Jefferson Lake* (892 acres, lake 270 acres) northwest of Richmond—Jefferson County; *Lake Hope* (1,062 acres, lake 120 acres) in Zaleski State Forest; *Pike* (326 acres, lake 13 acres) south of Bainbridge—Pike County; *Punderson* (505 acres, lake 90 acres) west of Burton—Geauga County; *Pymatuning* (4,877 acres, lake 2,580 acres) partly in Pennsylvania, near Andover—Ashtabula County; *Rocky Ford* (3,574 acres, lake 2,080 acres) east of Hillsboro—Highland County; *Stonelick Creek* (1,056 acres, lake 200 acres) near Edenton—Claremont County; *Strouds Run* (630 acres) east of Athens—Athens County; *Tar Hollow* (540 acres, lake 15 acres) in Tar Hollow State Forest.

Licenses, permits, regulations, and information about current seasons, bag and possession limits may be obtained from the Ohio Department of Natural Resources, 1500 Dublin Road, Columbus 12. Additional information is available at the following Wildlife Districts: no. 1—Ohio

---

* Only parks with fishing waters are listed.

Fisheries Building, Sandusky; no. 2—952 Lima Ave., Findlay; no. 3—
P.O. Box 2751, Firestone Park Station, Akron; no. 4—360 East State
St., Athens; no. 5—345 Allen Ave., Chillocothe. Maps of many public
fishing and hunting areas may be obtained by sending a large self-
addressed envelope to the Department of Natural Resources, Publication Room, 1500 Dublin Road, Columbus 12. The attractive *Ohio Conservation Bulletin* is published monthly for $1.00 per year by the Ohio
Department of Natural Resources.

OKLAHOMA

Area: 70,057 square miles (land area—68,887 square miles); rank in
nation—19
Bird: Scissor-tail Flycatcher (*Muscivora forticata*), adopted 1951
Capital city: Oklahoma City on the North Canadian River in Oklahoma
County; population (1960)—324,253; rank in state—1
Counties: 77
Elevations: Highest, Black Mesa (4,978 ft.) in Cimarron County; lowest,
Red River (300 ft.) in McCurtain County
Flower: Mistletoe (*Phoradendron flavescens*), adopted 1893
Geographic center: 8 miles north of Oklahoma City, Oklahoma County
Nicknames: Sooner State, Boomers Paradise
Population (1960): 2,328,284; rank in nation—27
Tree: Redbud (*Cercis canadensis* or *Cercis reniformis*), adopted 1937

Oklahoma is bordered by Arkansas on the east and Missouri on the
northeast; by Kansas on the north and Colorado at the northwestern
end of the panhandle; by Texas on the southwest; and the Red River
outlines the southern Texas border.

Rolling, treeless prairies cover a large portion of the state, and a
flat bed of salt deposits in the north near the towns of Cherokee and Jet,
known as the Salt Plains and partially covered by water, have been set
aside as the Great Salt Plains National Wildlife Refuge (31,129 acres).
The wooded Ozark Range in the northeast is a plateau region with
spring-fed streams; the swift-flowing Caney, Grand, Illinois, Spring, and
Verdigris rivers; the Grand Lake or Lake O' the Cherokees (46,300
acres) formed by Pensacola Dam on Grand River; Fort Gibson Reservoir
(19,100 acres) in the Cookson Hills where the Indians' Trail of Tears
ended; the Upper Sparvinaw (3,100 acres) and Lower Sparvinaw (1,638
acres) lakes in the Ozarks, not far from Greenleaf Lake (900 acres);
Lake Tenkiller (12,500 acres) on the Illinois River. Lake Wister (4,000
acres) is southwest of Poteau in the San Bois Mountains near the Jack

Fork Mountains, and north of Winding Stair Mountain (2,428 ft.) and the Kiamichi Mountains in the Ouachita (WASH-i-taw) National Forest which extends from Arkansas into southeastern Oklahoma.

Rapid streams flow through canyons in the Arbuckle Mountains of south central Oklahoma. Lake Texoma Recreational Area (195,326 acres), on the Texas border, contains the 93,000-acre lake impounded by Denison Dam on the Red River. Lake Murray (5,728 acres), at Ardmore south of the Arbuckle Mountains in the old Chickasaw Nation region, was built exclusively for recreation purposes. Lake Altus-Lugert (6,800 acres) in the Quartz Mountains, and Lake Lawtonka (1,868 acres) adjacent to the Wichita Mountains Wildlife Refuge (59,099 acres) and Fort Sill Military Reservation are in southwestern Oklahoma. About 400,000 persons attend the annual Easter Sunrise Service in a natural amphitheater in the Wichita Mountains near Lawton.

The Arkansas River enters from Kansas east of Chiloco and follows a southeasterly course to be joined by the Cimarron River from the northwest, and continues on to Fort Smith across the Arkansas border. The North Canadian River from Fort Supply Reservoir (1,550 acres) near Woodward moves on a southeasterly course through Oklahoma city to merge with the Arkansas River near Muskogee. The South Canadian River from Texas loops around Antelope Hills south of Arnett, and meanders through southern Oklahoma to reach the Arkansas River south of Weber Falls. Clear Mountain Fork River, Fourche Maline, Little River, and Kiamichi River are mountain streams in southeastern Oklahoma.

LICENSES

Resident licenses to fish, hunt, and trap are issued to all persons 16 or more years of age who are bona fide residents of Oklahoma, except noncitizens, who must purchase alien hunting licenses. No permits or licenses are required of residents 65 or more years of age, of honorably discharged war veterans with at least 60 per cent disability, or of citizens in the U.S. Armed Forces stationed outside the state and home on a 10-day leave or furlough; but all should carry proof of such exemption. A totally blind person and one companion may fish without licenses. No license is required of residents who hunt exclusively on land occupied as their permanent year-round residence; or fish in streams, natural lakes, and mine pits within or bordering their own county when using bait other than artificial or commercial bait, blood, cutfish, minnows, shrimp, or stink bait. Nonresident hunting license fees are reciprocal with nonresident fees charged in a hunter's home state, and the minimum nonresident license fee for all game except Deer is $15.

All persons 16 or more years of age must purchase a federal "Duck" stamp to take migratory game birds. Texans may purchase a special license to hunt migratory waterfowl in the bed of the Red River between Oklahoma and Texas for the duration of the Oklahoma open season. Residents and nonresidents may hunt on private game farms (hunting preserves) on an Oklahoma hunting license, or for a $1.00 fee for 10 days. Except for owners or tenants hunting and trapping exclusively on their own lands, all other persons must possess a hunting license before applying for a trapping license. An amateur trapping license permits the use of 20 traps to take furbearing animals, and the holder of a professional trapping license may use 50 traps.

In addition to the annual license fee, commercial game propagation and hunting preserve operators must file a $5,000 surety bond to propagate Pheasant and Quail on private game farms for hunting or other commercial purposes. A wildlife breeder's license is necessary if any lawfully acquired game animals, birds, or fish are bred and/or raised commercially. An applicant for a license to collect protected wildlife for scientific study must be 15 years of age or older, and must present two written testimonials of well-known scientists or scientific institutions certifying to his fitness and good character.

Resident license fees: Sport fishing, $2.00; hunting, $2.00; alien hunting, $25.00; hunting Deer (in addition to hunting license), $5.00; combination hunting and fishing (except aliens), $3.50; federal "Duck" stamp, $3.00; hunting on commercial shooting preserves (10 days), $1.00; amateur trapping (not more than 20 traps), $1.25; professional trapping (not more than 50 traps), $50.00; fur buyer, $15.00; scientific collecting of wildlife, $1.00; wildlife breeder, $35.00; commercial hunting preserve game breeder, $500.00. Permits for designated areas: Pheasant, $1.00; Prairie Chicken, $1.00; Wild Turkey, $3.00.

Nonresident license fees: Annual fishing, $5.00; fishing 10 consecutive days, $2.25; hunting (reciprocal—check home state nonresident fee), $15.00; alien hunting, $25.00; Red River hunting of waterfowl (Texas residents only), $2.50; trapping, $250.00; fur buyer, $50.00; federal "Duck" stamp, $3.00; hunting on commercial shooting preserves (10 days), $1.00. Pheasant, Prairie Chicken, and Wild Turkey permits, fees same as for residents.

HUNTING AND TRAPPING

Game animals: Antelope, Bear, Deer, Elk, Opossum, Raccoon, Squirrel. OPEN SEASONS: Buck Deer—archery, about 2 weeks in November; firearms, a few days in late November or early December; some counties are closed to Deer hunting. Opossum, Raccoon—Dec. 1–Jan. 31. Squirrels—May 15–Jan. 31. BAG LIMITS: Buck Deer–1 per year. Opossum, Raccoon—no limit. Squirrels—6 per day.

A legal Buck Deer must have antlers or pronghorns at least 6 inches long.

Furbearing animals: Badger, Beaver, Bobcat, Civet Cat, Coyote, Fox (Gray, Red), Mink, Muskrat, Opossum, Otter, Raccoon, Skunk, Wolf. OPEN TRAPPING SEASONS: Badger, Fox, Mink, Muskrat, Opossum, Raccoon, Skunk—Dec. 1–Jan. 31. *Bag limits*—none. FULLY PROTECTED: Antelope, Bear, Beaver, Elk, Otter—no open seasons. NOT PROTECTED: Bobcat, Coyote, Gopher, Porcupine, Prairie Dog, Wolf, and Woodchuck may be killed at any time. Fox may be taken if destroying animals or fowl at any time.

Game birds: Coot (Mud hen), Mourning Dove, Ducks (except Canvasback and Redhead), Gallinule, Geese, Jacksnipe, Merganser, Pheasant, Prairie Chicken, Quail (Bobwhite, Blue, Stubble), Rails, Sora, Wild Turkey, Woodcock. OPEN SEASONS: Coot, Ducks, Merganser—mid-November to mid-December. Mourning Dove—about 6 weeks after the first of September. Gallinule, Rails, Sora—mid-September to late October. Geese—mid-October to late December. Jacksnipe—about 6 weeks after November 1. Pheasant—a few days in November. Prairie Chicken —a few days in October. Quail—mid-November to mid-January on Tuesdays, Thursdays, Saturdays, and legal holidays. Wild Turkey—during October to early November in designated areas. Woodcock—mid-November to early January. There are no season limits for hunting upland game birds on private shooting preserves. FULLY PROTECTED: Crane, Curlew, Plover, Canvasback and Redhead Ducks—no open seasons. NOT PROTECTED: Crow, Cooper's Hawk, Goshawk, and Sharp-shinned Hawk (commonly called Blue Darter) may be taken at any time.

FIREARMS

Deer may be hunted with rifles in some areas, and only with shotguns loaded with slugs in other designated areas. Quail and migratory game birds may be taken only with shotguns not larger than 10 gauge or not capable of holding more than 3 shells in the magazine and chamber combined.

Shooting hours: Sunrise to sunset, and Raccoon may be taken at night.

FISHING

Game fish: Black Bass (Largemouth, Smallmouth), Rock Bass (Goggle-eye), Spotted Bass, Catfish (Blue, Channel, or Forktailed), Crappie (Black, White), Trout. OPEN SEASON: All year from midnight to midnight except during a special season set annually for Trout in the Cimarron County Lake. Private, club, and municipal lakes have their own regulations.

Game fish may be taken only by hook and line. Artificial devices used in taking fish may contain not more than 15 hooks, and trotlines with not more than 100 hooks (spaced not less than 24 inches apart) may be used statewide unless prohibited by an individual owner, municipal or club ordinance, or regulations. Commercial fishing is prohibited on Saturday, Sunday, or any legal holiday in public lakes open to commercial fishing including Canton, Carl Blackwell, Fort Gibson, Fort Supply, Grand, Greenleaf, Heyburn, Hulah, Lugert, Murray, Salt Plains, Tenkiller, Texoma (except Washita Arm), and Wister Lakes. The term "lakes" means the main bodies or stationary waters and does not include tributaries or parts of tributaries flowing into the lakes.

Rough fish may be taken in all public waters by means of nets and seines except during April and May, but not at any time in lakes open to commercial fishing. Nongame fish may be taken only in the above lakes, and in all lakes and streams of Delaware and Mayes counties (except an area south of Grand River Dam in Mayes County) by the use of gigs, grab hooks, ropes, bows and arrows, underwater spear guns, and other similar devices providing that arrows, gigs, and spears do not have more than 3 points with not more than 2 barbs on each point.

On many large lakes, there are enclosed fishing docks, heated in winter and cooled in warm weather. Other large lakes and reservoirs include Canton Lake (6,700 acres) on the North Canadian River near Canton; Hulah Lake (3,200 acres) at the Kansas line northwest of Bartlesville on the Caney River; Lake Carl Blackwell (3,000 acres) near Perry; Lake Hefner (2,530 acres) in the Nichols Hills and Lake Overholser (1,750 acres) west of Oklahoma City; Lake McAlester (2,100 acres) north of McAlester. State parks are also well stocked with fish. Float trips are popular on the Illinois River and Mountain Fork River, and the best Deer hunting is in eastern Oklahoma.

STATE PARKS AND RECREATION AREAS

Beavers Bend (1,300 acres) on Mountain Fork River in the Kiamichi Mountains, 10 miles northeast of Broken Bow—McCurtain County; *Black Mesa* (349 acres) surrounding Carl Etling Lake (240 acres) in the panhandle, about 30 miles northwest of Boise City—Cimarron County; *Boiling Springs* (880 acres) northeast of Woodward—Woodward County; *Cherokee* (48 acres) at south end of Grand Lake or Lake O' the Cherokees, northwest of Jay—Delaware County; *Clayton Lake* (410 acres, lake 25 acres) in the Kiamichi Mountains, south of Clayton—Pushmataha County; *Fort Cobb* (4,028 acres) northwest of Fort Cobb—Caddo County; *Great Salt Plains* (741 acres) at dam of Great Salt Plains Lake (10,700 acres) and Salt Fork of Arkansas River, 7 miles north of Jet—Alfalfa County; *Greenleaf Lake* (1,475 acres, lake 900 acres) near Braggs

—Muskogee County; *Heyburn Lake* (438 acres) at Heyburn Lake (1,070 acres) between Bristow and Sapulpa—Creek County; *Honey Creek* (28 acres) at Grand Lake near Grove—Delaware County; *Lake Murray* (21,-000 acres, lake 5,728 acres) between Ardmore and Marietta—Carter County; *Lake Raymond Gary* (60 acres) at lake (291 acres), 15 miles east of Hugo—Choctaw County; *Lake Tenkiller* (12,500 acres) including 3 areas and series of islands in the lake, northeast of Gore—Cherokee and Sequoia counties; *Lake Texoma* (2,600 acres) at Lake Texoma, east of Kingston—Marshall County; *Lake Wister* (4,000 acres) south of Wister —Le Flore County; *Osage Hills* (1,005 acres, lake 18 acres) on clear Sand Creek, southwest of Bartlesville—Osage County; *Quartz Mountains* (11,000 acres) at Lake Altus (7,000 acres) and Lugert—Greer and Kiowa counties; *Robbers Cave* (8,400 acres, Lake Carlton 52 acres) in the San Bois Mountains north of Wilburton—Latimer County; *Roman Nose* (560 acres) on a bluff overlooking Lake Boecher, north of Watonga— Blaine County; *Sequoyah* (2,880 acres) at Fort Gibson Reservoir, east of Wagoner—Cherokee County; *Sparvinaw Hills* (35 acres) at Sparvinaw Creek, southwest of Jay—Delaware County; *Twin Bridges* (63 acres) at north end of Grand Lake, southeast of Miami—Ottawa County.

Licenses, permits, regulations, information about current seasons, bag and possession limits may be obtained from the Director, Department of Wildlife Conservation, State Capitol, Oklahoma City. The following licenses are issued only from headquarters at Oklahoma City: Alien hunting, wildlife breeder, fur buyer, professional trapping, nonresident trapping, and scientific collector. Other licenses are sold in sporting goods, drug, hardware, and general merchandise stores throughout the state, and at many concession stands at public fishing lakes. There are 80 State Game Ranger offices with headquarters at 2222 North Walnut, Oklahoma City. The interesting sportsman's magazine *Oklahoma Wildlife*, published by the Oklahoma Wildlife Conservation Department, is only $1.50 per year.

OREGON

Area: 96,699 square miles (land area—96,248 square miles); rank in nation—10
Bird: Western Meadowlark (*Sturnella neglecta*), adopted 1927
Capital city: Salem on the Willamette River in Marion County; population (1960)—49,142; rank in state—3
Elevation: Highest, Mount Hood (11,245 ft.) in Clackamas and Hood counties; lowest, Pacific Ocean
Flower: Oregon Grape (*Berberis aquifolium*), adopted 1899

Geographic center: 25 miles east of south of Prineville, Crook County
Nicknames: Beaver State, Webfoot State
Population (1960): 1,768,687; rank in nation–32
Tidal shoreline: 1,410 miles (including islands, bays, and streams to a point where tidal waters narrow to 100 ft.)
Tree: Douglas Fir (*Pseudotsuga taxifolia*) also called a Douglas Spruce or Oregon Pine, adopted 1937

Oregon is a northwestern state on the Pacific Ocean bordered by California and Nevada on the south and partially separated from Washington on the north by the Columbia River; on the east, the Snake River flows through spectacular Hells Canyon and for nearly 200 miles forms a portion of the Idaho-Oregon boundary.

The magnificent Cascade Range extending from California into Washington is dominated by Mount Hood and other glistening white peaks rising above dense evergreen forests, blue alpine lakes, swift streams, and sparkling waterfalls. The Willamette River, joined by the McKenzie, North Santiem, and Clakamas rivers from the western slopes of the Cascades, flows through a broad fertile valley to Portland and the Columbia River. Sauvie Island is at the confluence of the Columbia and Willamette rivers. The Coast Range has several streams rushing among lateral spurs, to the rugged Pacific Coast, and mountains rise to the highest elevation at Marys Peak (4,097 ft.) southwest of Corvallis. From the southern town of Brookings at the mouth of the Chetco River, the 400 miles of beaches and rocky headlands are open to public recreation except for 23 miles, and Seaside at the end of the Old Oregon Trail in Tillamook County has an aquarium with hundreds of marine life exhibits.

From the southern Cascades, the Rogue River moves along a westward course through Grants Pass to Gold Beach. The Hundred Valleys of the Umpqua River system from the western slopes of the Cascades are formed by tributaries to the North and South Umpqua rivers which mingle waters 5 miles north of Roseburg and continue as the Umpqua River to Winchester Bay. Across the California-Oregon boundary, several ridges of the Cascade and Coast ranges merge, and are called Klamath and Siskiyou mountains. The Deschutes River, from the eastern slopes of the Cascades, is fed by the Crooked and Metolius rivers on a northwest course to the Columbia River. At Bonneville Dam on the mighty Columbia River, there are fish ladders for Salmon on their way upstream to spawn. The Columbia River Highway between Crown Point and Umatilla passes about a dozen sparkling cascades including Multnomah Falls plunging 680 feet from a basaltic cliff.

Two-thirds of the state is east of the Cascade Range, and grasslands, sagebrush, and timber cover the southeastern semiarid region containing the Steen Mountains rising to 9,354 feet, the Harney and Malheur lakes connected by the Narrows, the Silver River, Donner and Blitzen River south of Burns in Harney County; the Antelope Reservoir, Owyhee Reservoir on the Owyhee River, Malheur River, and the Snake River bordering Malheur County. The Blue Mountains and Wallowa Mountains in the northeast are known as the "Switzerland of America." The Matterhorn (10,004 ft.) is in the Wallowa Mountains overlooking the Snake River Canyon, Gronde Ronde, Powder, and Wallowa rivers. The John Day River from headwaters in the Blue Mountains flows into the Columbia River between Gilliam and Sherman counties. The High and Low deserts in central Oregon are north of the Warner Range containing Drakes Peak (8,402 ft.), Hart Mountain (8,020 ft.), Lake Abert, Drew, Goose, and Summer lakes in Lake County at the California line.

The Hart Mountain National Antelope Refuge near Lakeview, the Malheur National Wildlife Refuge south of Burns, and the Upper Klamath National Wildlife Refuge near Klamath Falls are in southern Oregon. The McKay Creek National Wildlife Refuge in northeastern Oregon is near Pendleton on the Umatilla River where the famous Pendleton Round-up is held annually in mid-September.

LICENSES

Resident licenses to fish, hunt, and trap are issued to persons 14 or more years of age who have lived in the state for at least 6 months immediately preceding an application for a license; and to members of the U.S. Armed Forces who are assigned to permanent duty within the state, or who are legal residents stationed outside of Oregon and return home on furlough or leave. Noncitizens must possess a $25 alien gun license before applying for a license to hunt or trap. Lawful owners or renters of established agricultural lands are not required to purchase a trapper's license to hunt or trap furbearing animals on their premises, but must register the location of such lands with the Oregon State Game Commission each year, and possess the receipt of the registration before hunting or trapping. If registered landowners or renters and licensed trappers purchase Beaver tags, each tag authorizes the holder to take and sell one Beaver. A trapper may obtain not more than 100 tags, and fees will be refunded for unused tags sent to the commission before April 15. No person may hunt big game on his own or other lands without a valid hunting license and appropriate big game tags. Established agricultural lands are defined as not less than 10 acres used for domestic crops, or an orchard covering at least one acre containing 25 or more live fruit trees.

All juveniles under the age of 17 must possess a hunting safety certificate to hunt with firearms on lands other than their own premises, and no juvenile under 12 years of age may hunt big game. A juvenile under the age of 14 may hunt small game without a license, but must be accompanied on lands other than his family's property by at least one licensed hunter over 21 years of age. Juvenile hunting licenses are not issued to nonresidents, and a resident juvenile must possess a general hunting license to secure big game tags. All persons 16 or more years of age must purchase a federal "Duck" stamp to take migratory game birds.

Disabled veterans and Pioneers of Oregon may purchase licenses and Elk tags at special prices, and free angler's licenses arc issued to blind persons. Permits are issued to hunt big game in 66 management units, but only residents may hunt Antelope. Sportsmen who received Antelope tags and/or antlerless Elk permits in 1963 are not eligible to apply for them again until 1969. Party applications are limited to two persons, and fees must accompany all controlled hunt application forms, which are available at licensed agencies. Permit applications to hunt Deer and/or Elk in designated areas are issued with Deer and Elk tags.

An angler license is required to catch game fish in the tidewaters of streams and all coastal waters of the Pacific Ocean within the 3-mile limit. All anglers (including juveniles fishing without licenses) must use a Salmon-Steelhead punch card to record the type of fish, date, and name of waters from which the fish was taken. Whoever hooks a Salmon or Steelhead is responsible for recording the catch and returning the card not later than July 1 to the commission or a license agency. No license is necessary to take nongame fish.

Resident license fees: Sport fishing (angler), $4.00; fishing one day, $1.00; disabled war veterans and Pioneers of Oregon fishing, 50 cents; juvenile angler (14–17 years inclusive), $2.00; hunting, $4.00; disabled war veterans and Pioneers of Oregon hunting, 50 cents; juvenile hunter (14–17 years inclusive), $2.00; combination angler and hunter, $7.00; federal "Duck" stamp, $3.00; hunting on private shooting preserves, $3.00; trapping furbearing animals, $6.00; fur dealer, $10.00; taxidermist, $5.00; game breeders permit, $5.00. Tags: Antelope, $5.00; Beaver, $5.00; Deer, $1.00; Elk, $7.50; Elk—for disabled war veterans and Pioneers of Oregon, $2.50; guide, $15.00. Game management areas shooting fees per day: Government Island, $2.00; Sauvie Island, $2.00; Summer Lake, $2.00; Warner Valley, $1.00; blinds on Sauvie Island, $3.00.

Nonresident license fees: Sport fishing (angler), $10.00; fishing 7 consecutive days, $5.00; fishing one day, $1.00; hunting, $35.00; federal "Duck" stamp, $3.00; hunting upland game birds on private shooting preserves, $3.00. Tags: Deer, $15.00; Elk, $35.00.

HUNTING AND TRAPPING

Game animals: Pronghorn Antelope, Bear, Deer (Black-tailed, Mule, White-tailed), Elk (Roosevelt, Rocky Mountain), Mountain Goat,

Mountain Sheep, Gray Squirrel. OPEN SEASONS:* Antelope—a few days in mid-August in designated units. Bear—Aug. 31–Dec. 15 in national forests between U.S. Highway 97 and U.S. 99, and all lands within one mile of the Rogue River from the confluence of Graves Creek to Agness; and at any time in the remainder of the state. Deer—about 3 weeks from late September to mid-October, or a choice of either sex in designated areas for a number of days; special seasons are limited to residents and may precede or follow the general season, which is usually held during the first 3 weeks in October. Elk—generally extends from late October to middle of November for Bull or antlerless Elk. Gray Squirrel—Sept. 1–Oct. 31 in southwest area, and at any time in remainder of the state. BAG LIMITS: Antelope—1 adult Buck with horns longer than his ears. Bear—1 in open area; no limit in remainder of the state. Deer—1 Buck with forked antlers or visible antlers on a general Deer tag; one of either sex on general Deer tag and management unit permit. Elk—1 Bull with antlers longer than ears, or one antlerless Elk on tag and/or unit permit. Gray Squirrel—4 daily in southwest area, and no limit in remainder of state.

Furbearing animals: Beaver, Bobcat, Ringtail Cat, Cougar, Coyote, Fisher, Fox, Marmot, Marten, Mink, Muskrat, Nutria, Opossum, Otter, Raccoon, Weasel. OPEN SEASONS: Beaver, Otter—Nov. 1–Feb. 15 in Grant, Harney, Lake, and Malheur counties; Nov. 15–Feb. 15 in 32 counties. Ringtail Cat, Marten, Mink, Muskrat—Nov. 15–Feb. 15. BAG LIMITS: None, except not more than 100 Beaver tags are issued to one trapper. FULLY PROTECTED: Fisher, Mountain Goat, Mountain Sheep—no open seasons. NOT PROTECTED: Bobcat, Cougar, Coyote, Fox, Gopher, Mole, Marmot, Nutria, Opossum, Jack Rabbit, Ground Squirrels, and Weasels may be killed at any time.

Game birds: Black Brant, Coot, Mourning Dove, Ducks (except Canvasback and Redhead), Geese, Grouse (Blue, Ruffed, Sage), Merganser, Partridge (Chukar, Hungarian), Cock Pheasant, Band-tailed Pigeon, Quail (Bobwhite, Mountain, Valley), Snipe. OPEN SEASONS: Brant—mid-November through January. Coot, Ducks, Geese, Merganser—early October to early November. Dove, Grouse, Pigeon—opens late August or early September. Partridge, Cock Pheasant, Quail—late October and early November. Wilson's Snipe—late October to early November. Upland game birds on private shooting preserves—Aug. 1–March 31. Open seasons for juveniles, Wilson Game Management Area in Benton County: Pheasant and Quail—a few days in October and November; Waterfowl—several days in late December and early January. FULLY PROTECTED: Canvasback and Redhead Ducks—no open season. NOT PROTECTED: Black-

---

* Check current state regulations.

bird, Crow, Double-crested Cormorant, Scrub Jay, Steller Jay, Kingfisher, Magpie, Raven, House Sparrow, and Starling may be killed at any time.

FIREARMS

Game birds may be taken with shotguns not larger than 10 gauge and capable of holding not more than 3 shells in the magazine and chamber combined. Antelope and Deer rifles should have a caliber designation of not less than .23 inches, and it is unlawful to hunt Elk with a rifle having a caliber designation of less than .25 inches and developing less than 1,220 foot-pounds of energy at 100 yards. The longbow for Deer should have at least 40 pounds pull and be capable of casting an arrow at least 150 yards at the normal draw length; not less than 50 pounds pull for Elk. The arrow should weigh not less than one ounce (437½ grains) for Deer and not less than 500 grains for Elk. The head of a big game hunting arrow should be not less than seven-eighths of an inch wide. Longbows and crossbows may be used during the firearms season instead of shotguns and rifles, but a crossbow may not be used in any specific archery season. It is unlawful to use pistols, revolver, shotguns loaded with buck or bird shot; any semiautomatic rifle with a magazine capacity of more than 5 cartridges; or any military, or full metal-jacketed bullet in the original or altered form to hunt or kill Antelope, Deer, or Elk. Rifle hunting is not permitted on public shooting grounds during a waterfowl season.

Shooting hours: Big game—one-half hour before sunrise to one-half hour after sunset. Small game and migratory game birds—one-half hour before sunrise to sunset. Exceptions: Shooting starts on the opening day at 1:00 P.M. for waterfowl and at 8:00 A.M. for Quail and Pheasant; traps may not be set until 8:00 A.M. for Beaver, Marten, Mink, Muskrat, Otter, Ring-tailed Cat on the opening day. Shooting is not permitted after 4:00 P.M. during the waterfowl season at the Sauvie Island Public Shooting Ground. No light of any kind may be used to hunt game animals and birds.

FISHING

Game fish: Black Bass, Striped Bass, Bullhead and Channel Catfish, Salmon (Chinook, Kokanee, Silver), Shad, Steelhead, Sturgeon, Trout (Cutthroat, Eastern Brook, German Brown, Lake, Rainbow). OPEN SEASONS: Salmon, Steelhead, Trout—mid-April to October 31 and Nov. 1– March 31. The state is divided into 10 zones, and regulations should be carefully read to note local exceptions.

A sport fisherman may use only one line closely attended, or a line and rod with not more than 3 hooks on a line except on floating Bass plugs.

A gaff or net may be used to land fish caught by hook and line, but it is unlawful to shoot, snag, spear, club, gaff, net, or trap game fish.

Frogs: Bullfrogs may be taken at any time of the day or night and by any means except firearms or explosives. BAG LIMIT: 12 in possession.

The Oregon Skyline Trail may be followed by hiking or on horseback through national forests along the crest of the Cascades. There are more than 15,000 miles of fishing streams, hundreds of lakes, and 400 miles of coastline for surf and deepwater fishing. The Columbia, John Day, Deschutes, McKenzie, Rogue, Siuslaw, Umpqua, and Willamette rivers are famous Salmon, Steelhead, and Trout streams. There is top Striped Bass fishing from July through October, and Chinook Salmon from March through June and August through October. Silver Salmon may be caught in the Columbia River from October through December; and Steelhead, in coastal streams from December through February. Salmon derbies are held at Astoria, Gold Beach, Newport, Taft, Warrenton, and at many other places.

STATE PARKS

Armitage (41 acres) northeast of Eugene—Lane County; *Ben and Kay Dorris* (79 acres) west of Vida—Lane County; *Ben Hur Lampman* (23 acres) at Gold Hill—Jackson County; *Benson* (84 acres) on Multnomah Lake near Multnomah Falls—Multnomah County; *Beverly Beach* (69 acres) north of Newport—Lincoln County; *Cape Arago* (134 acres) 14 miles southwest of Coos Bay—Coos County; *Cape Lookout* (1,451 acres) 12 miles southwest of Tillamook—Tillamook County; *Cascadia* (322 acres) on South Santiem River, west of Sweet Home—Linn County; Casey (80 acres) 30 miles northeast of Medford—Jackson County; *Catherine Creek* (160 acres) southeast of Union—Union County; *Collier Memorial* (349 acres) at Indian Reservation on Williamson River—Klamath County; *Cove-Palisades* (4,029 acres) Lake Chinook, west of Culver—Jefferson County; *Dabney* (79 acres) on Sandy River near Troutdale—Multnomah County; *Detroit Lake* (45 acres) on Santiem River, west of Detroit—Marion County; *Devil's Elbow* (97 acres) north of Florence—Lane County; *Devil's Lake* (110 acres) at Delake and Pacific Ocean—Lincoln County; *Devil's Punchbowl* (5 acres) north of Newport—Lincoln County; *Ecola* (1,107 acres) near Seaside on Pacific Ocean—Clatsop County; *Farewell Bend* (65 acres) at Brownlee Reservoir southeast of Huntington—Baker County; *Fern Ridge* (54 acres) at Fern Ridge Reservoir west of Eugene—Lane County; *Fogerty Creek* (104 acres) 15 miles north of Newport—Lincoln County; *Fort Stevens* (793 acres) at mouth of Columbia River, south of Warrington—Clatsop County; *Harris Beach* (141 acres) north of Brookings—Curry County; *Hat Rock* (369 acres) at McNary Reservoir east of Umatilla—Umatilla County; *Jessie M. Honeyman Memorial* (522 acres) at Cleawox and Woahink lakes, south of Florence—Lane County; *Humbug Mountain* (1,821 acres) south of Port Orford—Curry County; *Illinois River* (178 acres) south of Grants Pass—Josephine County; *Jackson F. Kimball* (19 acres) north of Fort Klamath—Klamath County; *Lake Owyhee* (730 acres) about 30 miles southwest of Nyssa—Malheur County; *Laurelhurst* (317 acres) on Rogue River about 35 miles northeast of Medford—Jackson County; *Lewis and Clark* (56 acres) on Sandy River near Troutdale—Multnomah County; *Loeb* (160 acres) east of Brookings—Curry County; *Lost Creek* (78 acres) south of Newport—Lincoln County; *Mayer* (308 acres) west of The Dalles—Wasco County; *McLeod Wayside* (80 acres) east of McLeod—Jackson County; *Neptune* (331 acres) on Pacific Ocean near Yachats—Lincoln County; *Ocho Lake* (10 acres) east of Prineville—Crook County; *Ona Beach* (138 acres) on Beaver Creek with access to the ocean, south of Newport—Lincoln County; *Oswald West* (2,502 acres) on Pacific Ocean north of Manzanita —Tillamook County; *Prineville Reservoir* (365 acres) 15 miles southeast of Prineville—Crook County; *Red Bridge* (37 acres) west of Hilgard Junction—Union County; *Rooster Rock* (825 acres) on the Columbia River east of Troutdale—Multnomah County; *Saddle Mountain* (3,054 acres) northeast of Necanicum—Clatsop County; *Sarah Helmick* (31 acres) on Luckiamute River, south of Monmouth—Polk County; *Silver Falls* (8,059 acres) 25 miles east of Salem—Marion County; *Sunset Bay* (88 acres) on Cape Arago, south of Charleston—Coos County; *Susan Creek* (176 acres) on North Umpqua River, east of Winchester—Douglas County; *Tou Velle* (35 acres) on the Rogue River, 10 miles north of Medford—Jackson County; *W. M. Tugman* (405 acres) 20 miles north of Coos Bay—Coos County; *Tumalo* (117 acres) on Deschutes River, north of Bend—Deschutes County; *Ukiah-Dale Forest* (3,000 acres) on Camas Creek and North Fork of John Daly River near Ukiah—Umatilla County; *Umpqua Lighthouse* (2,747 acres) south of Winchester Bay— Douglas County; *Unity Lake* (39 acres) north of Unity—Baker County; *Valley of the Rogue* (209 acres) three miles east of Rogue River—Jackson County; *Wallowa Lake* (166 acres) at south end of the lake near Joseph— Wallowa County.

Licenses, permits, regulations, and information about current seasons, bag and possession limits may be obtained from the Oregon State Game Commission, P.O. Box 4136, Portland 8; and from authorized agents throughout the state. The synopsis of current fishing regulations is usually available by March 1; and hunting regulations, after September 1. State highway maps and information about camping in state parks are issued by the Travel Information Division, Oregon State Highway Department, Salem.

PENNSYLVANIA

Area: 45,126 square miles (land area—45,007 square miles); rank in state–33
Bird: Ruffed Grouse (*Bonasa umbellus*), adopted 1931
Capital city: Harrisburg on the Susquehanna River in Dauphin County; population (1960)—79,697; rank in state–7
Counties: 67
Elevations: Highest, Negro Mountain (3,213 ft.) in Somerset County; lowest, Delaware River (sea level)
Flower: Mountain Laurel (*Kalmia latifolia*), adopted 1933
Geographic center: 2.5 miles southwest of Bellefonte, Center County
Nicknames: Keystone State, Coal State, Quaker State, Steel State
Population (1960): 11,319,366; rank in nation–3
Tidal shoreline: 89 miles (including islands, bays, and streams to a point where tidal waters narrow to 100 ft.)
Tree: Hemlock (*Tsuga canadensis*), adopted 1931

Pennsylvania is bordered on the north by New York, and the Delaware River flows from New York to form a boundary between New York on the northeast and New Jersey on the east. Maryland and West Virginia are on the southern border, with Delaware arching into the southeast corner. Ohio and West Virginia share the western border, and about 70 miles of Lake Erie's shoreline is on the northwest.

The Appalachians in a series of parallel mountains and narrow valleys extend for over 200 miles in a southwesterly direction from New York to Maryland. The Northern Tier is a wilderness of rugged hills and steep gorges, rapid streams, waterfalls, and the "Grand Canyon Country of the East" near Wellsboro in the north central region. There are shallow valleys among pine and hemlock forests, over 200 lakes, and cascading streams among the scenic Pocono Mountains in northeastern Pennsylvania. The western Allegheny Plateau covers more than half of the state, and the network of narrow valleys and ravines changes west of the Allegheny River to uplands with wider and shallower valleys. In the south central region are fertile farms and orchards among rolling hills in the Pennsylvania Dutch country. The Susquehanna River from New York rushes through the Northern Tier, and fed by many streams broadens on a wandering course to Maryland. The Delaware River is joined at Easton by the Lehigh River from the Poconos, and the Schuylkill River at Philadelphia, to continue on the long journey to Delaware Bay. The Allegheny meanders from New York through western Pennsylvania, and at Pittsburgh unites with the Monongahela to form the Ohio River. The Youghiogheny River, joined by the Casselman River at Confluence, moves on a northwesterly course from the Youghiogheny Reservoir on the Maryland border to merge with the Monongahela River at McKeesport. A few short streams flow across the sandy shores to Lake Erie. The Appalachian Trail leads through the beautiful Delaware Water Gap in a southwesterly direction along the Blue Mountains through Indiantown Gap in Dauphin County, across the Susquehanna River and South Mountains to Maryland.

LICENSES

Resident licenses are issued to citizens who have been bona fide residents of the commonwealth for at least 60 days immediately preceding an application for a license. Foreign-born citizens should present their naturalization papers to a county treasurer or to the Department of Revenue in order to obtain resident licenses; otherwise an alien must purchase nonresident licenses. Any citizen residing upon land continuously cultivated on a commercial basis is not required to possess licenses to fish, hunt, or trap on his premises or an adjacent privately owned lands, providing the owner (or lessee) gives his written consent. Free fishing licenses are issued to war veterans who are either totally blind, disabled by loss (or loss of use) of one or more limbs, hospitalized, or in a convalescent camp due to service during a war or armed conflict. A war veteran disabled by loss of one or more limbs may also secure a free hunting license from a county treasurer.

Juveniles 16 or more years of age must possess a license to fish in all public waters. Hunting licenses are issued to juveniles under the age of 16 only if written consent signed by a parent or legal guardian is presented to the county treasurer or the Department of Revenue. Hunting licenses are not issued to persons under the age of 12. A parent, legal guardian, or member of his family at least 21 years of age must accompany any juvenile 12 or 13 years old; and hunters 14 or 15 years old should be accompanied by an adult 21 or more years of age. Aliens and nonresidents 12 or more years of age are required to possess licenses to fish in public waters. A Trout stamp must be purchased by a nonresident to take Trout if his home state requires a Trout stamp. Residents under the age of 18 may trap furbearing animals and predators without a license, except Bear and Raccoon.

An antlerless Deer license is not required during the open archery season for Deer. The holder of a hunting license may obtain an antlerless Deer license only from the county treasurer of the county in which he plans to hunt, and a license to take antlerless Deer is not issued to a nonresident until 30 days prior to the opening date of the season. The nonresident trapping license does not permit hunting, but animals and birds may be trapped (except Beaver) during an open season.

The big game tag attached to a license should be used for Deer only, and a hunter may tag a Bear with a self-made card similar to a printed big game tag.

A fishing license is required to fish in Lake Erie, Presque Isle Bay, and peninsular waters, and to take Frogs, Tadpoles, and Turtles throughout the commonwealth. Licenses are not reciprocal, and a person with a Pennsylvania license may fish only within the Pennsylvania border of Conowingo Reservoir on the Lower Susquehanna River, and the Youghiogheny Reservoir on the Youghiogheny River unless he holds a Maryland license. Maryland sportsmen must possess Pennsylvania nonresident licenses to· fish anywhere in these reservoirs except within the Maryland boundary. A person from New Jersey, New York, or Pennsylvania with a license issued by his state may fish from a boat anywhere on the waters of the Delaware River; but a nonresident license must be obtained to fish on the shores of any state other than that of one's own legal residence.

All persons 16 or more years of age must possess a federal "Duck" stamp to take migratory game birds. Special licenses are issued to operate regulated fishing lakes and shooting grounds, commercial hatcheries, and for commercial fishing in Lake Erie. A nonresident 3-day license is issued by the operator of any regulated shooting grounds to hunt for game on such premises.

License period: Fishing, Jan. 1–Dec. 31; hunting, Sept. 1–Aug. 31.

Resident license fees: Fishing, $3.25; hunting (permits trapping except Beaver and Raccoon), $3.15; archery Deer hunting (in addition to regular hunting license), $2.00; antlerless Deer (in addition to regular hunting license), $1.15; federal "Duck" stamp, $3.00.

Nonresident license fees: Annual fishing, $7.50; tourist fishing 5 consecutive days, $3.25; hunting, $20.00; hunting on regulated shooting grounds (3 days), $3.15; federal "Duck" stamp, $3.00; trapping (except Beaver), $25.00; archery Deer hunting (in addition to regular hunting license), $2.15; antlerless Deer (in addition to regular hunting license), $1.15.

HUNTING AND TRAPPING

Game animals: Bear (over 1 year old), Deer, Elk, Hare (Snowshoe Rabbit), Cottontail Rabbit, Squirrel, Woodchuck (Groundhog). OPEN SEASONS:* Bear—generally last week in November. Deer—archery, about 3 weeks in October; firearms (including bow and arrow), about 2 weeks in December. Hare—generally last week in December, but no open

---

* Check current state regulations.

scason in Bedford, Blair, Cambria, Centre, Elk, Forest, Huntingdon, Jefferson, McKean, Somerset, and Warren counties. Cottontail Rabbit, Squirrels (Black, Fox, Gray)—usually during the month of November and a few days in late December. BAG LIMITS: Bear—1 per year. Deer—1 per year. Hares—2 daily and 6 per season. Cottontail Rabbits—4 daily and not more than 20 in combined seasons. Squirrels—6 daily and not more than 30 in the aggregate during combined seasons.

A legal Buck is a male Deer with 2 or more points to an antler, or a spike 3 or more inches long.

Furbearing animals: Beaver, Fox, Mink, Muskrat, Opossum, Otter, Skunk, Weasel, Wildcat. OPEN SEASONS:* Beaver—mid-February to mid-March. Mink, Muskrat—mid-November to mid-January. FULLY PROTECTED: Cub Bear (under 1 year old), Elk, Otter—no open seasons. NOT PROTECTED: Chipmunk, Fox, Opossum, Porcupine, Raccoon, Skunk, Red Squirrels, Weasel, and Wildcat may be taken at any time.

Game birds: Brant, Coot, Mourning Dove, Ducks (except Canvasback and Redhead), Eider, Gallinule, Geese (except Snow Goose), Grouse (Ruffed, Sharp-tailed), Merganser, Old Squaw, Hungarian Partridge, Ring-necked Pheasant, Bobwhite Quail, Rails, Scaup, Scota, Sora, Wilson's Snipe, Wild Turkey, Woodcock. OPEN SEASONS:* Brant, Geese—mid-October to early December in Crawford County and Pymatuning Goose Management Area, but may open a week earlier in the remainder of the state. Coot, Ducks, Eider, Merganser, Old Squaw, Scaup, Scota—mid-October to early December. Dove, Gallinule, Rails, Sora—from early September to early November. Ruffed Grouse—during November and about one week in late December. Cock Pheasant and Bobwhite Quail—during November. Wilson's Snipe—mid-September through October. Wild Turkey—about 4 weeks from late October in designated areas. Upland game birds on private shooting preserves—Oct. 1–March 30. FULLY PROTECTED: Canvasback and Redhead Ducks, Snow Geese, Sharp-tailed Grouse, Hungarian Partridge, Hen Pheasants—no open seasons. NOT PROTECTED: Crow, Cooper's Hawk, Goshawk, Grackles, Sharp-shinned Hawk, Blue Jay, Kingfisher, Great Horned Owl, Snow Owl, English Sparrow, and European Starling may be killed at any time, except that all Hawks are protected during September and October in a designated area.

FIREARMS

Hand-operated repeating shotguns or rifles loaded with single ball may be used to take big game, but it is unlawful to use air pistols,

---

* Check current state regulations.

air rifles, automatic or semiautomatic loading pistols and rifles; or .22 and .25 caliber rifles with rimfire cartridges. Game may be hunted with a hand-operated or single shot rifle and telescope sights, if the hunter shoots one all-lead, lead alloy, or soft-nosed or expanding ball or bullet at a single discharge. Shotguns not larger than 10 gauge and capable of holding only 3 shells in the magazine and chamber combined may be used to take small game. Bow and arrow may be used to hunt any wild animals or birds that may be killed with firearms. It is unlawful to use a crossbow or any bow held, drawn, or released by mechanical means. There are no restrictions on the draw weight of a longbow, on the weight or materials in shafts and heads, or types of broadheads; but only a single shaft arrow may be used in hunting.

Dogs may not be used to hunt Wild Turkey and big game. However, they may be trained from August 1 to March 31 including Sundays, but not with rifles or shotguns.

Shooting hours: Hunting game on Sunday is prohibited. Resident game: 7:00 A.M.—5:00 P.M.; except July 1–Sept. 30, 6:00 A.M.–7:30 P.M. Migratory game birds including Dove—sunrise to sunset, except that shooting does not start until 12:00 o'clock noon on the opening day of the Dove and Duck seasons. Traps for furbearing animals must not be placed, set, or staked before 7:00 A.M. on the opening day of the season. Special hours may be established in controlled shooting areas.

FISHING

Game fish: Black Bass (Largemouth, Smallmouth), Rock Bass, Striped Bass, Catfish (Black Bullhead, Brown Bullhead, Yellow Bullhead, Channel, White), Crappie (Black, White), Muskellunge, Yellow Perch, Pickerel (Chain, Grass, Redfin), Northern Pike, Sunfish (all species including Bluegill and Warmouth), Trout (Brook, Brown, Lake, Rainbow), Walleye. OPEN SEASONS:* In all waters: Black Bass, Muskellunge, Pickerel, Pike, Walleye—all year except from mid-March to mid-May; Trout (except Lake)—mid-April to September; in lakes or ponds 10 or more acres, mid-April to October 31. Lake Erie: Rainbow Trout—mid-April to October 31. Conowingo and Youhiogheny Reservoirs: Muskellunge—June 1–Nov. 15; Trout (all species)—mid-April to mid-March; Walleye—April 1–Nov. 15. Delaware River: Striped Bass—March 1–Dec. 31; Trout (all species)—April 15–Sept. 30. All other fish—no closed seasons.

Unless a special permit is issued, sport fishing must be under the immediate control of one person using not more than 2 rods and 2 lines, and one handline with not more than 3 hooks attached to a line. Five tip-ups or any combination of 5 devices that include tip-ups may be used

---

* Check current state regulations.

when fishing through ice. Portions of more than 25 streams have been set aside for fishing only with artificial flies and streams, and such lures as plugs, spinners, or spoons made of metal, plastic, rubber, or wood are prohibited.

Spearing in waters stocked with fish is prohibited, but in other waters Carp, Gar, and Suckers may be taken by spear (not mechanically propelled) or longbow and arrow at any hour, and aided by light at night. Catfish, Eels, Herring, and Shad may also be taken by such methods in the Delaware River.

Frogs: Any person holding a fishing license may take Frogs; and it is lawful to take them by shooting, except in the Pymatuning Reservoir. No lights may be used at night. OPEN SEASON: July through October. DAILY BAG LIMIT: 15.

There are more than 45,000 miles of flowing waters including over 4,300 miles of streams and 60 lakes annually stocked with about 2,500,000 legal-sized Trout. Boat launching ramps, fishing and boating access sites throughout the commonwealth have been developed for public use. The following state parks provide fishing waters, and many are in state forests where additional camping and picnic sites provide scenic attractions. Surf and deepwater fishing is excellent in Lake Erie, and popular inland waters are so numerous that only those over 100 acres have been mentioned.

STATE PARKS*

Black Moshannon (2,150 acres, lake 250 acres) 9 miles east of Philipsburg—Centre County; *Blue Knob* (5,597 acres) east of Beaverdale—Bedford County; *Chapman* (803 acres, lake 68 acres) south of Clarendon—Warren County; *Clear Creek* (923 acres) north of Sigel—Jefferson County; *Colonel Deming* (62 acres) north of Newville—Cumberland County; *Cook Forest* (7,820 acres)on Clarion River, northwest of Sigel—Jefferson County; *Cowans Gap* (1,346 acres, lake 42 acres) northeast of McConnellsburg—Fulton County; *Crooked Creek* (2,480 acres, reservoir 350 acres) 4 miles south of Ford City—Armstrong County; *French Creek* (5,794 acres) contains Hopewell Lake (68 acres) and Scotts Run Lake (21 acres), south of Birdsboro—Berks and Chester counties; *George W. Childs* (154 acres) on Dingman's Creek west of Dingman's Ferry—Pike County; *Gifford Pinchot* (2,300 acres, lake 340 acres) 14 miles northwest of York—York County; *Gouldsboro* (2,800 acres, water area 255 acres) at Gouldsboro—Wayne County; *Greenwood Furnace* (382 acres, water area 5 acres) west of Belleville—Huntingdon County; *Hickory Run* (15,500 acres) southeast of Whitehaven—Carbon

---

* Subject to continual change due to an extensive expansion program and the establishment of additional parks with fishing waters.

County; *Hills Creek* (513 acres, reservoir 137 acres) near Mansfield—Tioga County; *Hyner Run* (17 acres) at Hyner—Clinton County; *Kettle Creek* (40 acres) west of Renovo—Clinton County; *Keystone* (807 acres, lake 78 acres) between Latrobe and New Alexandria—Westmoreland County; *Kooser* (375 acres, lake 4 acres) west of Somerset—Somerset County; *Laurel Hill* (4,082 acres, lake 65 acres) north of Rockwood—Somerset County; *Leonard Harrison* (961 acres) at Pine Creek Gorge southwest of Wellsboro—Tioga County; *Linn Run* (1,500 acres) south of Ligonier—Westmoreland County; *Little Pine* (500 acres, lake 90 acres) north of Waterville—Lycoming County; *Lyman Run* (800 acres, reservoir 40 acres) southwest of Galeton—Potter County; *Ole Bull* (67 acres) on Kettle Creek 17 miles south of Galeton—Potter County; *Parker Dam* (960 acres, reservoir 22 acres) southeast of Penfield—Clearfield County; *Poe Valley* (760 acres, reservoir 25 acres) east of Potters Mills—Centre County; *Pennsylvania* (3,200 acres) on the Erie Peninsula at Lake Erie, and includes the Bay of Presque Isle and Erie Harbor—Erie County; *Prince Gallitizin* (6,600 acres, lake 1,740 acres) northeast of Patton—Cambria County; *Promised Land* (2,328 acres, Lower Lake 173 acres, Promised Land Lake 422 acres) in the Pocono Mountains about 12 miles southwest of Hawley—Pike County; *Pymatuning* (20,075 acres, reservoir 16,420 acres) north of Jamestown—Crawford County; *Raccoon Creek* (7,600 acres, lake 101 acres) west of Clinton—Beaver County; *Ravensburg* (423 acres, lake 3 acres) 9 miles south of Jersey Shore—Clinton County; *Reeds Gap* (250 acres) on New Lancaster Creek 15 miles north of Lewistown—Mifflin County; *Ricketts Glen* (13,133 acres, Lake Jean 254 acres) contains 28 cascades north of Nanticoke—Columbia, Luzerne, and Sullivan counties; *Shawnee* (3,832 acres, lake 451 acres) 9 miles north of Bedford—Bedford County; *Sinnemahoning* (670 acres, reservoir 142 acres) north of Sinnemahoning—Cameron County; *Synder-Middlesworth* (500 acres) in Bald Eagle State Forest, west of Beaver Springs—Snyder County; Tobyhanna (4,187 acres, lake 170 acres) north of Tobyhanna—Monroe and Wayne counties; *Trough Creek* (500 acres) 20 miles south of Huntingdon—Huntingdon County; *Whipple Dam* (254 acres, lake 22 acres) 8 miles south of State College —Huntingdon County; *Raymond B. Winter* (580 acres, lake 7 acres) 20 miles west of Lewisburg—Union County; *Worlds End* (1,891 acres) on Loyalsock Creek 9 miles northwest of Laporte—Sullivan County.

Denton Hill State Park (500 acres) 5 miles west of Walton is a winter sports area in the Black Forest.

FAVORITE FISHING WATERS (over 100 acres)

Austin County—Chambersburg Reservoir (175 acres) near Calendonia. *Bedford County*—Evitts Creek (3,669 acres, lake 391 acres) south of Bedford Valley; Gordon Lake (275 acres) and Koon Lake (268 acres) near Centreville. *Berks County*—Ontelaunee Reservoir (1,080 acres) near Leesport. *Chester County*—Canadohta Lake (169 acres) near Union City; Conneaut Lake (928 acres) west of Meadville; Sugar Lake (150 acres) northeast of Cochranton. *Cumberland County*—Opossum Creek Lakes (214 acres) northwest of Carlisle. *Delaware County*—Springton Reservoir (435 acres) near Newton Square. *Erie County*—H. S. Eaton Reservoir (246 acres) southeast of North East; Edinboro Lake (120 acres). *Forest County*—Tionesta Reservoir (480 acres) at Tionesta. *Lackawanna County*—Crystal Lake (190 acres) and Newton Lake (112 acres) near Scranton. *Lancaster County*—Conowings Reservoir (6,000 acres) near Drumore; Hottwood Reservoir (2,400 acres) near Peguea; Safe Harbor Reservoir (5,000 acres) near Columbia. *Luzerne County*—Harveys Lake (658 acres). *Mercer County*—Sandy Lake (150 acres) at Sandy Lake. *Monroe County*—Brady's Lake (190 acres) northeast of Blakeslee. *Montgomery County*—Green Lane Reservoir (814 acres) at Green Lane. *Pike County*—Fairview Lake (246 acres) south of Tafton; Lake Wallenpaupack (5,670 acres) near Hawley. *Schuylkill County*—Sweet Arrow Lake (175 acres) near Pine Grove. *Snyder County*—Middle Creek Lake (100 acres) south of Selingsgrove. *Somerset County*—Lake Somerset (468 acres, lake 253 acres) north of Somerset; and Youghiogheny Reservoir (2,172 acres, lake 1,000 acres) south of Confluence. *Sullivan County*—Hunters Lake (2,473 acres, lake 127 acres), north of Muney Valley. *Wayne County*—Duck Harbor Pond (6,234 acres, lake 300 acres) south of Lookout; Lake Quinsigamond (100 acres) near South Canaan; White Oak Pond (350 acres) at Aldenville. *Wyoming County*—Lake Carey (250 acres) near Tunkhannock; Lake Winola (200 acres).

Regulations, information about current seasons, bag and possession limits may be obtained from the Executive Director, Pennsylvania Game and Fish Commission, State Capitol, Harrisburg. Licenses may be purchased from the Miscellaneous License Division, Pennsylvania Department of Revenue, Harrisburg; and from any county treasurer or local agent such as a sporting goods store. For interesting monthly reports on wildlife, subscribe to *Game News*, published by the Pennsylvania Game and Fish Commission for $1.00 a year. Information about state parks may be obtained from the Chief, Division of State Parks, Department of Forests and Waters, Harrisburg. The official Pennsylvania Road Map published by the Pennsylvania Department of Highways is also issued without cost. The Vacation and Travel Development Bureau, Bureau of the Department of Commerce, issues an excellent guide to *Fishing and Boating in Pennsylvania*.

RHODE ISLAND

Area: 1,248 square miles (land area—1,058 square miles); rank in nation—50

Bird: Rhode Island Red Hen, adopted 1954

Capital city: Providence at the confluence of the Moshassuck, Woonasquatucket, Providence, and Seekonk rivers, which flow through Narragansett Bay and Rhode Island Sound to the Atlantic Ocean in Providence County; population (1960)—207,498; rank in state—1

Counties: 5

Elevations: Highest, Durfee Hill (805 ft.) in Providence County; lowest, Atlantic Ocean

Flower: Purple Violet (*Viola*)

Geographic center: 1 mile west of Compton, Kent County

Nicknames: Little Rhody, Plantation State

Population (1960): 859,488; rank in nation—39

Tidal shoreline: 384 miles (including islands, bays, and streams to a point where tidal waters narrow to 100 ft.)

Tree: Red Maple (*Acer rubrum*)

Rhode Island is a New England state on the Atlantic Ocean bordered by Connecticut on the west and by Massachusetts on the north and east.

Beautiful Narragansett Bay, extending 28 miles inland to Providence, contains many islands, estuaries, and protected saltwater harbors. The largest islands are Rhode or Aquidneck Island (15 miles long) accessible by ferry and connected with mainland towns at the northern end by a toll bridge over Mount Hope Bay to Bristol and the Sakonnet River Bridge to Tiverton. Conanicut Island, also at the mouth of Narragansett Bay, is reached by ferry service and a toll bridge between Jamestown and Kingston on the western shore of the bay. Farther up the bay, a ferry runs between Prudence Island and Bristol. Block Island (7 miles long) is 9 miles southeast of Point Judith at the western entrance to Narragansett Bay, and accessible by aircraft, ferries from New London (Conn.), Newport, Point Judith, and Providence. Sandy beaches and marshlands fringe coastal lagoons, called ponds, along Block Island Sound and Rhode Island Sound.

LICENSES

Resident licenses are issued to citizens 15–65 years of age who have lived in the state for at least 6 months immediately preceding an application for a license and to members of the U.S. Armed Forces and Merchant Marine. Noncitizens residing in Rhode Island for one year prior to the date of application may purchase resident alien fishing licenses, but otherwise must obtain nonresident licenses. Owners or tenants and their immediate families may fish, hunt, and trap on their property without licenses if actually living on such lands. Any totally disabled veteran may fish without a license but must observe all other regulations pertaining to fishing. A hunting license issued to a legal resident inducted into the U.S. Armed Forces remains valid for 6 months after termination of his military service. If a person has not held a prior hunting license, or served as a member of the Armed Forces, he must complete a course in safe hunting practices and present a certificate of competency in order to obtain a license.

Permits are required to hunt on state-owned areas, and no person may fish, hunt, or trap on another person's private property without obtaining permission whether or not the land is posted. A license should be plainly visible at all times, and failure to present it for inspection makes a person liable to the penalty imposed for hunting without a license. Trappers without a valid hunting license may not carry guns. All persons 16 or more years of age must purchase a federal "Duck" stamp to take migratory game birds. Special permits are required to take live Raccoons for breeding purposes.

All males under the age of 16 and females of any age may fish without licenses. Fishing licenses are reciprocal with Connecticut for the Beach, Hazard, Killingly, and Peck Ponds; and with Massachusetts for Wallum Lake. Permanent licenses are issued to persons 65 or more years of age.

Annual license periods: Fishing and hunting, March 1 to the last day of February; trapping, April 1–March 31; fur buyer, July 1–June 30.

Resident license fees: Annual fishing (male citizens 16–65 years of age), $3.25; annual fishing (aliens 16–65 years of age), $5.25; permanent fishing (65 or more years of age), $3.25; hunting (citizens 15–65 years of age), $3.25; hunting (over 65 years of age), 25 cents; archery Deer hunting, $5.00; combination hunting and fishing, $5.25; hunting on shooting preserve, $3.00; federal "Duck" stamp, $3.00; trapping (over 15 years of age), $2.00; raw fur buyer, $5.00; commercial raising of game animals and birds, $5.00; shooting preserve, $10.00.

Nonresident license fees: Annual fishing (citizen), $7.25; annual fishing (alien), $9.25; tourist fishing 3 consecutive days, $3.25; hunting, $10.25; archery Deer hunting, $20.00; federal "Duck" stamp, $3.00; hunting on shooting preserve, $3.00; raw fur buyer, $25.00. Trapping fee is reciprocal with home state, but not less than $15.00.

HUNTING AND TRAPPING

Game animals: Deer, Snowshoe Hare, Cottontail Rabbit, Raccoon, Gray Squirrel. OPEN SEASONS:* Deer—archery, during October and from late December to late January; firearms, no open season. Hare and Rabbit —Nov. 1–Jan. 31; except in Portsmouth, from late December to late January; and remainder of Newport County, Nov. 1–Feb. 15. Raccoon— mid-October through January. Gray Squirrel—Nov. 1–Dec. 31. BAG LIMITS: Deer—1 per year. Hares—2 per day. Rabbits—5 per day. Raccoons—2 per day and 20 per season.

Furbearing animals: Bobcat, Fox, Mink, Muskrat, Otter, Raccoon, Skunk, Weasel. OPEN SEASONS:* Mink, Muskrat, Otter—mid-November through January, except that Muskrat may be trapped in Jamestown (Island of Conanicut) Jan. 15–Feb. 15 only. Raccoon—November 15 through January. Skunk—mid-November to mid-March. NOT PROTECTED: Bobcat, Fox, Weasel, and Woodchuck may be taken at any time.

Game birds: Brant, Coot, Mourning Dove, Ducks (except Canvasback and Redhead), Eider, Gallinule, Geese (except Snow Goose), Ruffed Grouse (Partridge), Merganser, Old Squaw, Pheasant, Quail, Rails, Scaup, Scoter, Sora, Wilson's Snipe, Woodcock. OPEN SEASONS:* Brant, Geese—early November to mid-January. Coot, Ducks, Eider, Merganser, Old Squaw, Scaup, Scoter—mid-November to early January. Dove— mid-September to mid-October, November 1 to mid-December. Gallinule, Rails, Sora—mid-September to mid-November. Ruffed Grouse, Pheasant, Quail—Nov. 1–Dec. 31. Wilson's Snipe, Woodcock—November 1 to mid-December. Shooting Preserves: Sept. 1–April 15. FULLY PROTECTED: Hawks and Owls—no open seasons. NOT PROTECTED: Crows, English Sparrows, and Starlings may be killed at any time.

FIREARMS

Deer may be hunted only with longbow and arrow. The use of any rifle larger than a .22 caliber long rifle is prohibited Oct. 1–March 31; and shotguns having shot larger than no. 2 may not be used at any time. Shotguns not larger than 10 gauge but capable of holding more than 3 shells must be altered so as to reduce the capacity to not more than 3 shells in the magazine and chamber combined when hunting game birds.

Shooting hours: Sunday hunting is prohibited by ordinances in the towns of Jamestown, Little Compton, Middletown, Portsmouth, and Tiverton. Doves—12 o'clock noon to sunset daily during open season. Duck season starts at 12:00 o'clock noon on opening day to sunset, but

---

* Check current state regulations.

otherwise hours arc from sunrise to sunset. Traps may not be set, staked, or placed before 12:00 o'clock noon on the opening day. Raccoons may be pursued and taken with a gun and dog only from 5:00 P.M. on the opening day until midnight of the closing day of a season and may be trapped from midnight to midnight.

FISHING

Game fish: Black Bass (Largemouth, Smallmouth), Striped Bass, Brown Bullhead (Horned Pout), White Perch, Yellow Perch, Chain Pickerel, Sunfish including Bluegill, Trout (Brook, Brown, Rainbow). OPEN SEASONS:* Black Bass, Chain Pickerel—third Saturday in April to mid-February. Trout (all species)—third Saturday in April to October 31; and through ice only, from December 1 to last day of February. Other fish—all-year; except fishing in designated Trout ponds and streams is prohibited from mid-February to the third Friday in April.

A single line on a rod or pole (or operated by hand) with not more than 2 hooks on a line may be used by any angler catch fish, but a licensed fisherman may use 2 rods or handlines when fishing from a boat. All ice fishermen must be licensed and may use 5 lines with a single hook on each line. Licensed fishermen may also use snares, spears, bow and arrows to take Carp and Sucker at any time.

Record catches of saltwater fish have been made in Narragansett Bay, Block Island Sound, and Rhode Island Sound. The Open Salt Water Fishing Derby extends from mid-August to early November. Surfcasters have taken Striped Bass weighing 63 pounds at Sachusett Point (Middletown) and a 59-pound Striper at Point Judith.

Fishing and hunting are permitted in state management areas, but only fishing is lawful in the following state parks, state beaches, and public fishing areas.

STATE MANAGEMENT AREAS

Arcadia (7,335 acres) east of Millville—Washington County; *Buck Hill* (1,357 acres) in northwestern corner of state near Wallum Lake at Burrillville—Providence County; *Burlingame* (825 acres) west of Charlestown—Washington County; *Carolina* (1,422 acres) north of Wood River Junction—Washington County; *Durfee Hill* (688 acres) in town of Glocester—Providence County; *Dutch Island* west of Conanicut Island in Narragansett Bay—Newport County; *George Washington* (3,341 acres) west of Pascoag—Providence County; *Great Swamp* (2,748 acres) west of Kingston—Washington County; *Harrisville* (1,000

---

* Regulations may vary in state-controlled fishing areas.

acres) west of Glendale—Providence County; *Indian Cedar Swamps* (921 acres) south of Wood River Junction—Washington County; *Rockville* (132 acres) south of Centerville—Washington County; *Round Top* (135 acres) northwest of Harrisville at Massachusetts line—Providence County; *Sapowet Marsh* (162 acres) on Sakonnet River near Tiverton Four Corners—Newport County; *Wickaboxet* (288 acres) near Greenwich Center—Kent County; *Woody Hill* (723 acres) south of Bradford —Washington County.

STATE BEACHES

Block Island (19 acres) on easterly side of New Shoreham, Black Island; *East Matanuck* (102 acres) on Block Island Sound near Jerusalem —Washington County; *Misquamicut* (57 acres) on Block Island Sound between Weckapaug and Watch Hill—Washington County; *Sand Hill Cove* (27 acres) west of Point Judith—Washington County; *Scarsborough* (23 acres) between Point Judith and Narragansett Pier— Washington County.

STATE PARKS

Arcadia (48 acres including Arcadia Pond) near Millville—Washing County; *Beach Pond* (3,200 acres) at the Connecticut line, west of Millville—Washington County; *Burlingame* (2,100 acres including Watchaug Pond 934 acres) west of Charlestown—Washington County; *Diamond Hill* (373 acres) on Silver Brook, west of Grant Mills—Providence County; *Goddard Memorial* (472 acres) on Greenwich Bay at city of Warwick—Kent County; *Haines Memorial* (101 acres) at Bullock's Cove on town lines of Barrington and East Providence; *Lincoln Woods* (627 acres including Olney Pond 126 acres) near Saylesville— Providence County; *Meshanticut* (33 acres, lake 9 acres) at Cranston— Providence County; *Casimir Pulaski Memorial* (100 acres, Pecks Pond 20 acres) at the Connecticut line adjacent to the George Washington Game Management Area near West Glocester; *Ten Mile River* (104 acres) near state line at Pawtucket.

PUBLIC FISHING AREAS

Barber Pond (28 acres) near West Kingston; *Locustville Pond* (83 acres) near Hope Valley; *Ocean Drive* and *Prices Neck* at Newport on Rhode Island Sound; *Pongansett River* (70 acres) in town of Foster; *Stafford Pond* (476 acres) east of Tiverton; *Tucker Pond* (101 acres) east of Tuckertown; *Worden Pond* (1,043 acres) adjacent to the Great Swamp State Management Area, west of Tuckertown.

There are many other access areas where fishing is open to the public, and more than 50 ponds and streams are stocked with Trout.

Licenses, permits, regulations, and information about current seasons, bag and possession limits may be obtained from the Department of Agriculture, Division of Fish and Game, Veterans Building, Providence. Hunting permits are also issued by conservation officers, and at checking stations at Arcadia, Carolina, and Great Swamp managament areas during November. A list of approved hunter safety instructors is available at any license agency or from a conservation officer.

SOUTH CAROLINA

Area: 30,989 square miles (land area—30,272 square miles); rank in nation—40
Bird: Carolina Wren (*Thryothorus ludovicianus*), adopted 1948
Capital city: Charleston at the confluence of the Ashley and Cooper rivers flowing into Charleston Bay on the Atlantic Ocean; population (1960)—97,433; rank in state—1
Counties: 46
Elevations: Highest, Sassafras Mountain (3,548 ft.) in Pickens County; lowest, Atlantic Ocean
Flower: Yellow Jasmine (*Gelsemium sempervirens*), adopted 1924
Geographic center: 13 miles southeast of Columbia, Richland County
Nicknames: Palmetto State, Pirate State, Rice State
Populations (1960): 2,382,594; rank in nation—26
Tidal shoreline: 2,876 miles (including islands, bays, and streams to a point where tidal waters narrow to 100 ft.)
Tree: Palmetto (*Sabal palmetto*), adopted 1939

South Carolina is a southeastern state on the Atlantic Ocean bordered on the north and northeast by North Carolina, by Georgia separated by the Savannah River on the west, and by the Chattanooga and Tugaloo rivers in the northwest.

An eastward-facing escarpment of the forested Blue Ridge Mountains rises 2,000 feet across the northwestern corner of the state. The Piedmont Plateau region gradually changes to a low coastal plain about 125 miles wide and crisscrossed with streams among woodlands and sandy beaches, islands and marshes between estuaries. From Caesars Head (3,227 ft.) north of Marietta in the Blue Ridge Mountains, the Saluda River flows southward to unite with the Broad River at Columbia, and continues on as the Congaree River until joined by the Wateree River at Lake Marion, and finally emerges as the Santee River on the journey to the Atlantic Ocean. Major rivers flow in a southeasterly direction. The Pee Dee River from North Carolina is fed by The Little Pee Dee River; the Lynch River, on a parallel course, merges on the coastal plain within a few miles of the Waccamaw River from the east and Black River from Williamsburg County joining the Pee Dee River near Georgetown on Winyah Bay. The Edisto River, rising west of Columbia, the Ashepoo River, and the Combahee River, formed by the union of the east and west branches of the Salkehatchie River in Colleton County, empty their waters in St. Helena Sound. The Coosawatchie and Pocotaligo rivers merge as the Broad River on a course passing the U.S. Marine base on Parris Island at Port Royal Sound. The New River flows through Beaufort County in the southeastern corner of the state to reach the sea.

Historic Fort Moultrie on Sullivan Island, the Isle of Palms, and Folly Island are among several islands near the mouth of scenic Charleston Harbor, a deepwater port for ocean steamships. The famous fishing waters of Santee-Cooper Reservoir include Lake Marion (157 square miles) on the Santee River, joined by a navigation canal to Lake Moultrie which is linked via the Cooper River with Charleston. Lake Murray (78 square miles), impounded by the Dreher Shoals Dam west of Columbia, and Greenwood Lake (16,000 acres), formed by Buzzard Roost Dam east of Greenwood, are on the Saluda River. The Clark Hill Reservoir (122 square miles) on the Savannah River north of Clark Hill, extends into Georgia; and Hartwell Reservoir (97 square miles) near Anderson is in the northwestern part of the state.

LICENSES

Licenses to fish and hunt are required of all persons 12–65 years of age, except residents of South Carolina on active duty with the U.S. Armed Forces during a furlough or leave, providing they present official papers. Military personnel stationed in the state may obtain resident licenses, but all other persons not living in the state must purchase nonresident licenses regardless of whether or not they own property and pay taxes. Legal residents of Georgia and South Carolina may fish in the waters of the Savannah River, Tugaloo River, and Yonah Lake, including backwaters of Clark Hill from the North Carolina line to the Atlantic Ocean with their state licenses. Nonresidents of Georgia and/or South Carolina are required to hold South Carolina nonresident licenses to fish in the South Carolina portions of such waters. Any resident using artificial bait, a casting rod, fly rod, or any manufactured equipment other than an ordinary hook and line must obtain a resident angler's license. Any person using more than 3 baskets or trotlines must procure a commercial fishing license. A nonresident may not fish in any manner anywhere in the state without a fishing license and permits required for special lakes except the Hartwell and Clark Hill lakes. Permits are required to fish in the Santee-Cooper Reservoir (Lake Marion-Lake Moultrie), the Catawba-Wateree, Clark Hill, and Hartwell lakes, Lake Greenwood and Lake Murray. A resident may procure a special annual fishing license entitling him to fish in all waters of the state without the regular fishing license or permits. This special fishing license does not include lakes where a daily fee is charged, such as lakes of the Sandhills National Wildlife Refuge. Nongame fish tags and trapping and county hunting licenses may be purchased from local or county game wardens. All persons 16 or more years of age must purchase a federal "Duck" stamp to take migratory game birds.

Resident license fees: Annual anglers, $1.10; annual fishing lake permit (each lake), $1.10; fishing in all lakes and other waters, $3.00; nongame fish tags for each basket or trotline, $1.00; commercial fishing (not more than 25 baskets), $25.00; county hunting (county of residence only), $1.35; state hunting (all counties), $4.25; trapping, $10.00; federal "Duck" stamp, $3.00.

Nonresident license fees: Annual fishing, $10.25; fishing 10 consecutive days, $3.10; lake fishing permit (each lake), $1.10; annual hunting, $22.25; hunting 3 consecutive days, $11.25; hunting upland game birds on private preserves, $5.00; federal "Duck" stamp, $3.00.

HUNTING AND TRAPPING

Game animals: Alligator, Bear, Buck Deer, Fox, Opossum, Rabbit, Raccoon, Squirrel. OPEN SEASONS: Bear—Nov. 15–Dec. 1 in Zone 1 only. Buck Deer—Sept. 15–Jan. 1 in designated areas with open seasons varying from 7 days to the entire period. Opossum, Raccoons—Sept. 1–March 31 with shorter periods in some zones. Rabbits—Sept. 1–March 1 with shorter periods in some zones; and generally firearms may not be used until Thanksgiving Day. Squirrels—Sept. 15–March 1, and shorter seasons in designated zones. BAG LIMITS: Bear—1 per season. Buck Deer—varies from 1 per season in Zone 1 (Greenville, Oconee, Pickens counties) to 5 per season in most other counties. Rabbits—generally 5 per day. Squirrels—generally 10 per day. There are no bag limits for Rabbits and Squirrels in several counties.

Furbearing animals: Bobcat, Fox, Mink, Muskrat, Opossum, Otter, Rabbit, Raccoon, Skunk. TRAPPING SEASONS: Jan. 1–March 1, except in Laurens County, Dec. 1–Jan. 31, and in 3 game zones, Thanksgiving Day to January 31. Trapping is prohibited in Greenville County. Rabbits may not be trapped in Zone 2, or Raccoons in zones 1 and 2 except by owners or tenants on their lands. PROTECTED: Alligators may not be shot or killed except in Baumberg, Colleton, and Dorchester counties. NOT PROTECTED: Bobcat, Skunk, Weasel, and Woodchuck may be taken at any time, except that Fox may not be taken with firearms Jan. 2–Aug. 15 in 4 zones.

Game birds: Brant, Coot, Mourning Dove, Ducks (except Canvasback and Redhead), Geese, (except Snow Geese), Marsh Hens (Gallinule, Rails, Sora), Merganser, Partridge (Quail), Pheasant, Scaup, Wilson's Snipe (Jacksnipe), Gobbler Turkey, Woodcock. OPEN SEASONS: Brant, Geese—early November to mid-January. Coot, Merganser, Scaup—mid-November to early January. Dove—mid-September to early October, 2 or 3 weeks in late November, and mid-December to mid-January. Marsh Hens—October 1 to early December. Partridge (Quail)—Thanksgiving Day to February 15 in 2 zones, and extended to March 1 in 6 zones. Wilson's Snipe—early December to mid-January. Wild Turkey—Thanksgiving Day to April 15 with various open seasons in designated counties ranging from a few days in some areas to 10 or 12 weeks in other zones. Woodcock—late November to mid-January. Shooting preserves—Oct. 1–March 31. FULLY PROTECTED: Canvasback and Redhead Ducks, Snow Geese, and Swans—no open seasons. NOT PROTECTED: Buzzards, Crows, Cooper's Hawk, Sharp-shinned Hawk, and Great Horned Owls may be taken at any time.

FIREARMS

Shotguns not larger than 10 gauge and capable of holding only 3 shells in the magazine and chamber combined may be used to take migratory game birds. If originally capable of holding more than 3 shells, it must be plugged with a one-piece filler incapable of removal without disassembling the gun. Deer may be taken in most zones by the use of bow and arrows, guns, dogs, and three blinds. Raccoons may not be hunted with firearms in Zone 4 between September 1 and Thanksgiving Day. No person may possess or fire a rifle within 100 yards of the Clark Hill Reservoir and Hartwell Reservoir shorelines. It is unlawful to discharge any firearms other than shotguns within one-quarter of a mile from the Waterlee Reservoir at any time; or within the same distance of the backwaters of the Catawba River and tributaries up to and including all waters impounded by India Hook Dam in York County, between February 16 and Thanksgiving Day.

Shooting hours: Sunrise to sunset. Exceptions: Doves—12 o'clock noon to sunset daily. Coot, Ducks—12 o'clock noon on the opening day of season to sunset; otherwise sunrise to sunset. Fox, Mink, Opossum, Raccoon, and Skunk may be hunted at night, and the only artificial light permitted is a headlight attached to a hunter's head or body.

FISHING

Game fish: Black Bass (Pond Trout), Rock Bass, Striped Bass (Rockfish), White Bass, Copper-faced or Ball-faced Bream, Red Belly Bream, Crappie, Flyer, Goggle-eye, Jackfish (Pickerel), Sun Perch, Yellowbelly Perch, White Perch, Pike, Trout (Brown, Rainbow), Warmouth. Jackfish and Pike are classified as nongame fish in Zone 7. OPEN SEASONS: Trout—Oct. 1–March 1 in Zone 1, except in boundary streams between Georgia and South Carolina, no closed season. All species of fish, including Trout in other zones, may be taken at any time; and there are no size limits for any fish throughout the state.

Game fish may be caught only with handlines, hook and line, pole and line, casting rod, or fly rod, and not more than 2 such devices may be used at one time by any angler. The use of baskets, gill nets, seines, traps, or trotlines to catch game fish are prohibited in any clearwater streams. Nongame fish may be caught with such devices in muddy streams and inland waters, but not from sundown Saturday to sunrise Wednesday except in 3 zones where they may be used throughout the week. Basket and trotlines may be used to catch only nongame fish in the Santee-Cooper Reservoir; Catawba-Wateree Reservoir, Clark Hill Reservoir, Hartwell Reservoir, Lake Greenwood, Lake Murray, and the north and south branches of the Cooper River down to their confluence.

Record size game fish have been taken from the Santee-Cooper Reservoir and other well-stocked waters throughout the state. Fishing and waterfowl hunting draw sportsmen to the Georgetown area on Winyah Bay, and U.S. Highways 17 and 21, interwoven with state roads, provide easy access to exceptional saltwater fishing along the coast.

GAME MANAGEMENT AREAS

Bear Island (3,080 acres) between the Edisto and Ashepo Rivers near Bennetts Point in Colleton County; *Clark Hill* (5,000 acres). District 1—Chauga, The Forks, Key Bridge, Parsons Mountain; District 2—Belmont (5,700 acres), Broad River (15,200 acres), Dutchman's Creek (40,000 acres), Carlisle (19,500 acres), Enoree (51,100 acres), Wateree (18,000 acres); District 3—Buist, Francis Marion, Santee-Cooper, Walker Farm; District 4—Gapway Bay, Santee Delta, Big Pee Dee (2,670 acres) on narrows of Pee Dee River.

The Santee National Wildlife Refuge is open to fishing in all areas except Pinopolis Point, Jacks, Potato, and Taw Caw creeks, which are closed Oct. 15–March 15. Large areas are open to waterfowl hunting in season, and also at the Barnwell Lake and Wildlife Refuge on Turkey Creek in Barnwell County. The following state parks have good fishing waters, but hunting is prohibited.

STATE PARKS

Aiken (1,067 acres) on South Edisto River, north of Windsor—Aiken County; *Barnwell* (307 acres, lake 39 acres) south of Blackwell—Barnwell County; *Campbells Pond** in Sand Hills State Forest, 10 miles south of Cheraw—Chesterfield County; *Cheraw* (7,361 acres) 4 miles southwest of Cheraw—Chesterfield County; *Chester* (523 acres, lake 160 acres) southwest of Chester—Chester County; *Croft* (7,135 acres) 5 miles southeast of Spartanburg—Spartanburg County; *Givhans Ferry* (1,235 acres) on Edisto River, northwest of Givhans—Dorchester County; *Greenwood* (914 acres) at Lake Greenwood near Ninety-Six—Greenwood County; *Hunting Island* (5,000 acres) on St. Helena Sound, 16 miles southeast of Beaufort—Beaufort County; *Kings Mountain* (6,141 acres) 12 miles north of York—York County; *Lee* (2,839 acres) on Lynches River, near Bishopville—Lee County; *Little Pee Dee* (835 acres) near Little Pee Dee River, north of The Fork—Dillon County; *Mill Creek** in Manchester State Forest near Pinewood—Sumter County; *Myrtle Beach* (312 acres) on the Atlantic Ocean, 3 miles south of Myrtle Beach—Horry County; *Paris Mountain* (1,275 acres) 7 miles north of Greenville—Greenville County; *Poinsett* (1,000 acres) north of Pinewood—Sumter County; *Rivers Bridge* (390 acres) on *Salkehatchie River* near Ehrhardt—Bamberg County; *Santee* (2,364 acres) on Lake Marion, east of Elloree—Orangeburg County; *Sesquicentennial* (1,500 acres) near Dents—Richland County; *Table Rock* (2,860 acres) at Table Mountain (3,000 ft.) near Pumpkintown—Pickens County.

Licenses, permits, regulations, and information about current seasons, bag and possession limits may be obtained from local game wardens, or the Director, Wildlife Resources Department, Division of Game, Columbia.

SOUTH DAKOTA

Area: 77,615 square miles (land area—76,378 square miles); rank in nation—16
Animal: Coyote (*Canis latrans*), adopted 1949
Bird: Ring-necked Pheasant (*Phasianus colchicus*)
Capital city: Pierre on the eastern bank of the Missouri River in Hughes County; population (1960)—10,088; rank in state—8
Counties: 67 (3 unorganized)
Elevations: Highest, Harney Peak (7,242 ft.) in Pennington County;

---

* Established for Negroes.

lowest, Big Stone Lake (962 ft.) in Roberts County
Flower: Pasque Flower (*Pulsatilla hirutissima*), adopted 1903
Geographic center: 8 miles northeast of Pierre, Hughes County
Nicknames: Coyote State, Land of the Sioux, Sunshine State
Population (1960): 680,514; rank in nation—40
Tree: Black Hills Spruce (*Picea glauca densata*), adopted 1947

South Dakota is a north central state bordered by Nebraska on the south, Iowa and Minnesota on the east, Montana and Wyoming on the west, and North Dakota.

The historic Missouri River from North Dakota flows into Campbell County, and cutting through high bluffs continues southward along the eastern edge of the Cheyenne River Indian Reservation to be impounded north of Pierre to form the Oahe Reservoir (588 square miles), and then move through the Crow Creek and Lower Brule Indian Reservations to be harnessed at Pickstown to create the Fort Randall Reservoir (185 square miles); and in southern Charles Mix County, the Missouri River etches an irregular Nebraska boundary line swollen by the Lewis and Clark Lake formed by Gavin's Dam at Yankton.

The eastern half of the state, known as East-river, is a fertile rolling prairie sprinkled with lakes and streams. Big Stone Lake and Lake Traverse on the Minnesota River form the northeastern boundary of the lakes and sloughs region known as the Coteau des Prairies (Hills of the Rivers) since early fur trading days. The Waubay Lakes at Grenville are well named, for Waubay was derived from the Indian *wamay* meaning "where wildfowl build their nests." The Big Sioux River flowing between Iowa and South Dakota unites with the Missouri River south of Union County at Sioux City, Iowa.

The West-river region changes from farmlands and ranches to the desolate Pierre Clay or gumbo area. It is of mud when wet and crinkled ground when dry, but it sprouts sparse gumbo grass relished by cattle and sheep. The White River flows from the Pine Ridge Indian Reservation in the southwest through the weird erosions of the "Big Badlands" to merge with the Missouri River south of Chamberlain. The Black Hills at the Wyoming line are west of Rapid City and south of Belle Fourche, and contain the highest mountains east of the Rockies, the Black Hills National Forest, Custer State Park with scenic Sylvan Lake, the Norbeck Wildlife Preserve, Harney Peak (7,242 ft.), Crazy Horse Monument on Thunder Mountain, Mount Rushmore National Monument ("Shrine of Democracy"), Hot Springs, and the Wind Cave National Park. The Belle Fourche Reservoir is connected by an inlet canal with the Belle Fourche River flowing eastward to join the Cheyenne River which empties into the Missouri. The southwestern Bad River moves through Jackson, Jones, and Stanley counties to reach Pierre. The North Fork and South Fork of the Grand River unite at Shadehill Reservoir in National Grasslands, and continue as the Grand River to the Missouri near Mobridge. The Moreau River, also rising in the northwest, joins the Missouri River in the Dewey County area of the Cheyenne River Indian Reservation. The Terry Peak (7,071 ft.) Winter Sports Area is 4 miles west of Lead (Leed), site of the Homestake Mine, largest producing gold mine in North America.

LICENSES

Resident licenses are issued only to persons actually living as residents for at least 90 days preceding an application for a license. All persons must hold a valid basic or general hunting license before applying for other permits or licenses to hunt in the state. Resident juveniles under the age of 16 who pass a hunter safety course may obtain a general hunting license free of charge from the Department of Game, Fish, and Parks in Pierre. Nonresident juveniles under the age of 16 are not required to pass a firearms safety course, and must purchase the general hunting license. No juvenile under the age of 16 may hunt unless accompanied by a parent or guardian. Residents may obtain special licenses to hunt Antelope and Deer during limited permit seasons only once in every 3 years, except that landowners living on or operating land within hunting zones open to limited seasons may apply annually for the landowners' preference clause for such a license. Applications may be obtained from county treasurers, but the licenses are sold only at the Pierre office of the Department of Game, Fish, and Parks.

Nonresidents may hunt Grouse, Partridge, Pheasants, Quail, Cottontail Rabbits, Prairie Dogs, Crows, and Magpies under the small game hunting license. They may not hunt Antelope and Deer east of the Missouri River, or Elk, migratory waterfowl, Wild Turkey, Jack Rabbits, and predatory animals west of the Missouri River. Deer may be hunted by nonresidents, who may also take Antelope by bow and arrow in designated areas. Trapping licenses are issued only to residents of South Dakota. All persons 16 or more years of age must purchase a federal "Duck" stamp to take migratory game birds.

Most hunting takes place on privately owned lands, although about 250 shooting areas are owned or leased by the Department of Game, Fish, and Parks for public hunting. Landowners may post notices at entrance gates to their properties, and it is unlawful to hunt on land posted against hunting, on land enclosed by woven wire fences, or within 40 yards of an inhabited building, or on land containing livestock or unharvested crops unless permission is obtained from the owner or occupant of the land. Certain areas of Indian reservations may be opened to non-Indians, but permits must be purchased from tribal councils. National Councils, National Grasslands, public domain lands administered by the Bureau of Land Management, and military reservations are not posted against trespassers; but hunters should request permission to hunt on any privately owned lands within such federal tracts. Most public domain land is located in Butte, Haakon, and Meade counties in the western part of the state; and the Ellsworth Air Force Base Aerial Gunnery Range (Badlands Bombing Range) covers about 500,000 acres in northern Shannon County. Special permits to hunt Antelope with firearms in Custer State Park are issued only to residents. There are 6 controlled Geese shooting areas on the Missouri River and one at Hecla north of Aberdeen open only to residents.

Juveniles under the age of 16 are not required to possess fishing licenses. A nonresident under the age of 16 may fish without a license only if accompanied by a parent or guardian holding a valid fishing license, and any fish caught by the juvenile is counted as part of the adult's daily bag limit. Hunting and fishing on boundary waters are permitted under a South Dakota license providing that the person does not trespass beyond boundary lines.

Resident license fees: Fishing, $2.00; hoop net license and tag, $5.00; setline license and tag, $1.00; general hunting, 50 cents; hunting small game (in addition to general hunting), $2.00; hunting big game including Deer (in addition to general hunting), $7.50; federal "Duck" stamp (in addition to general hunting), $3.00; hunting Antelope (in addition to general hunting), $7.50; hunting Wild Turkey (in addition to general hunting), $2.00.

Nonresident license fees: Annual fishing, $5.00; fishing 3 consecutive days, $1.00; hoop net license and tag, $5.00; setline license and tag, $1.00; general hunting, 50 cents; hunting small game (in addition to general hunting), $25.00; hunting big game (in addition to general hunting), $35.00; federal "Duck" stamp (in addition to general hunting), $3.00.

HUNTING

Game animals: Antelope, Bison, Deer (Mule, White-tailed), Elk, Cottontail Rabbit. OPEN SEASONS:* Antelope—archery, from mid-August to late September plus about 3 weeks in October; firearms, a few days in late September in any of the 11 units open to archery hunting. Deer—archery, during October west of the Missouri River, and opens a month later east of the Missouri River; firearms (including bow and arrow), during month of November in the Black Hills Unit, and shorter

---

* Check current state regulations.

periods in designated areas. Elk—about 12 days divided into 2-day periods in September. Rabbit—no closed season. BAG LIMITS: Antelope, Deer, Elk—1 each.

The Antelope license is valid only in a designated unit. In some counties, Deer of either sex may be taken; in others, either Buck Deer with 2 or more points on one antler, or not less than 4 points on one antler are legal.

Furbearing animals: Beaver, Bobcat, Black Fox (Cross, Silver), Mink, Muskrat, Opossum, Otter, Raccoon, Wolf. OPEN SEASONS: Set annually in August. FULLY PROTECTED: Bison—no open season. NOT PROTECTED: Bobcat, Coyote, Fox, Mountain Lion, Prairie Dog, Cottontail and Jack Rabbits, Squirrels, and Wolf may be taken at any time.

Game birds: Coot, Ducks (except Canvasback and Redhead), Geese, Grouse (Sage, Sharp-tailed), Merganser, Hungarian Partridge, Chinese Ring-necked Pheasant, Prairie Chicken, Quail, Wilson's Snipe, Wild Turkey. OPEN SEASONS:* Coot, Ducks, Merganser—mid-October to mid-November. Geese—early October to mid-December. Sage Grouse —several days in late August. Sharp-tailed Grouse and Hungarian Partridge west of the Missouri River—season opens on same date, usually in mid-September. Hungarian Partridge east of the Missouri River and Pheasant—generally opens on the same date in mid-October. Wild Turkey—from mid-October to mid-November in the counties of Custer, Fall River, Lawrence, and portions of Mead and Pennington counties west of State Highway 79.

FIREARMS

It is unlawful to hunt big game animals with any rifle or firearm which discharges a projectile less than 22/100ths of an inch in diameter. or to use any muzzle-loading rifle which discharges a projectile less than 42/100ths of an inch in diameter; or to use autoloading or self-loading firearms that hold more than 6 cartridges. Big game animals may be hunted with firearms fired from the shoulder, and cartridges must not be less than 2 inches in length (including cartridge case and bullet) and contain a soft point or expanding bullet. Fully automatic firearms and buckshot are prohibited to take big game, and a single ball or rifled slug must weigh not less than one-half ounce. Pistols, revolvers, or other firearms; crossbows; explosive, poisonous, or barbed points may not be used or carried by an archer while hunting big game. All longbows for hunting big game and Wild Turkey must have at least 40 pounds pull.

Migratory game birds may be taken only with shotguns not larger than 10 gauge, and capable of holding not more than 3 shells in the

---

* Check current state regulations.

magazine and chamber combined. If originally capable of holding more than 3 shells, magazines should be plugged with one-piece or metal fillers incapable of being removed through the loading end.

Game animals and birds may be taken with birds trained in falconry.

Shooting hours: One-half hour before sunrise to one-half hour after sunset; except migratory game birds—sunrise to sunset; on opening day of the Duck season, shooting does not start until 12:00 o'clock noon.

FISHING

Game fish: Black Bass, Rock Bass, White Bass, Bluegill, Bullhead, Catfish, Crappie, Paddlefish, Perch, Northern Pike, Sauger, Sturgeon, Sunfish, Walleye. OPEN SEASONS (local exceptions):* Area 1, all year; Area 2 (Brown, Codington, Day, Grant, Marshall, Roberts counties), Jan. 1– Feb. 28, and first week in May to December 31; Area 3 (waters forming eastern boundary of state), same as Area 2 for Black Bass, Northern Pike, Sauger and Walleye, and no closed season for other fish. Paddlefish may be taken downstream from Fort Randall Dam to the Nebraska state line Nov. 15–Jan. 31 only. Area 1 includes all counties except those in Area 2.

Anglers may use 2 lines with not more than 3 hooks on each line to take game fish. Artificial lures are counted as one hook regardless of the number of attached gang hooks. A landing net, gaff, or similar device may be used to land fish taken by legal methods.

Hoop lines and setlines may be used by South Dakota residents to take rough fish from portions of the Missouri River and impoundments. There is no closed season on such devices downstream from the u.s. Highway 81 bridge at Yankton, but upstream from this point, the open season is May 1–Oct. 15, and a fisherman may use one hoop net and not more than 2 setlines. Game and rough fish may be taken by use of spears in the Fort Randall and Oahe reservoirs sunrise to sunset from the first week in May to November 30. Bows and arrows, spears and spear guns may be used to take rough fish throughout the year in Area 1, but such devices may be used only from the first week in May to early November in areas 2 and 3. All fish houses used by ice fishermen must be removed before the second week in March.

Frogs: OPEN SEASON: May 1–Oct. 15. BAG LIMITS: none; but only residents may take frogs for commercial purposes.

There are 33 varieties of fish caught in the "Great Lakes" of the Missouri River, and the Big Bend Dam at Fort Thompson, to be completed in 1966, will add another lake (80 miles long) with exceptional fishing. About 250 public shooting areas are open to big and small game

---

* Check current state regulations.

hunters, although the majority of hunting takes place on private lands. There are Pheasants in every county of the "Pheasant Capital of the World," and although hunting is prohibited there is good fishing in state parks and recreation areas. The following public shooting areas are open to big and small game hunting, and other areas provide good upland game and waterfowl hunting.

PUBLIC SHOOTING AREAS

Brown County: North Putney Slough (2 areas, 160 acres each) north and northwest of Claremont; North Putney Slough (920 acres) west of Claremont; Renziehauzen Slough (1,080 acres) 7 miles north of Claremont. *Clark County:* Dry Lake no. 2 (1,975 acres) 4 miles west of Vienna; Swan Lake (320 acres); and another 40 acres northeast of Bradley. *Day County:* Bitter Lake (2,373 acres) 5 miles south of Waubay; Breske Pass (126 acres) 8 miles northeast of Webster; Lohner Area (160 acres) 12 miles south of Waubay; Lily Area (400 acres) 5 miles west of Lily; Mydland Pass (440 acres); and another 346 acres about 10 miles west of Roslyn. *Fall River County:* Battle Mountain (3,080 acres) 5 miles east of Hot Springs; Buffalo Gap (156 acres) south of Buffalo; Oral Area (640 acres) east of Oral. *Hamlin County:* Sioux-Poinsett Area (1,539 acres) 10 miles northwest of Estelline. *Lake County:* Wentworth Slough (280 acres) east of Wentworth. *Lawrence County:* Badger-Trucano areas, Beilage-Hepler Area (2,043 acres), and McNenny-Coxes Area (1,079 acres) near Spearfish. *Meade County:* Bear Butte (79 acres) and Marcotte Area (763 acres) near Sturgis; Opal Lake (200 acres) northeast of Opal. *Pennington County:* Spring Creek (48 acres) 6 miles west of Custer. *Perkins County:* Bison Lake (226 acres) southeast of Buffalo; Strool Lake (320 acres)southeast of Sorum; Vobejde Area (83 acres) northeast of Lodgepole.

STATE PARKS AND RECREATION AREAS

Angostura (2,323 acres) in the Black Hills at Angostura Reservoir on Cheyenne River, south of Hot Springs—Fall River County; *Clear Lake* (3 acres) at Clear Lake and near Red Iron Lake, southeast of Lake City —Marshall County; *Cold Brook* (220 acres) north of Hot Springs—Fall River County; *Custer* (72,000 acres) in the Black Hills between Custer and Hermosa—Custer County; *De Smet Forest* (160 acres) near Henry and Thompson lakes, south of De Smet—Kingsburg County; *Farm Island* (1,800 acres) in the Missouri River, south of Pierre—Hughes County; *Fisher Grove* (120 acres) east of Redfield—Spink County; *Gavins Point* (1,234 acres) at Lewis and Clark Lake, west of Yankton—Yankton County; *Hartford Beach* (60 acres) north of Milbank—Grant County; *Lake Faulkton* (320 acres) near Faulkton—Faulk County; *Lake Byron*

(15 acres) north of Huron—Beadle County; *Lake Hendricks* (6 acres) at Lake Hendricks, east of White—Brookings County; *Lake Herman* (128 acres) west of Madison—Lake County; *Lake Hiddenwood* (160 acres) north of Selby—Walworth County; *Lake Louise* (320 acres) northwest of Miller—Hyde County; *Lake Osceola* (40 acres) near Bancroft—Kingsbury County; *Little Moreau* (160 acres) 5 miles south of Timber Lake—Dewey County; *Llewellyn Johns Memorial* (80 acres) at Flat Creek Lake near Shadehill, south of Lemmon—Perkins County; *Newton Hills* (640 acres) south of Canton—Lincoln County; *Oakwood Lakes* (800 acres) about 10 miles north of Volga—Brookings County; *Palisades* (44 acres) at Split Rock Creek, south of Garretson—Minnehaha County; *Parmley Lake* (856 acres) west of Aberdeen—Brown County; *Pickerel Lake* (60 acres) northeast of Grenville—Day County; *Richmond Lake* (480 acres) north of Aberdeen—Brown County; *Roy Lake* (632 acres) southwest of Lake City—Marshall County; *Sandy Shore* (10 acres) west of Watertown—Codington County; *Shadehill* (6,053 acres) at junction of North and South Fork Grand River, south of Lemmon—Perkins County.

The State Department of Game, Fish, and Parks also cooperates with the State Highway Department in the administration of more than 40 roadside parks along main highways, and with about 40 counties and municipalities in the development of recreation areas in the state. Open fires are prohibited in state parks, but campers may use cooking stoves or the fireplaces furnished in the public camping areas.

Licenses, permits, regulations, and information about current seasons, bag and possession limits may be obtained from the Director, South Dakota Department of Game, Fish and Parks, New Office Building, Pierre. Resident licenses are available from the office of any county treasurer. Permits to hunt on Indian reservations are issued by the tribal council having jurisdiction over the reservation. The Soil Conservation Service has information about hunting on military reservations and public domain lands. The South Dakota Department of Highways, Publicity Division (Pierre) issues maps, booklets about camps and campgrounds, etc. The Black Hills and Badlands Association at Sturgis lists accommodations in that area. The *Guide to Public Shooting Areas*, and *Important Game Birds and Animals of South Dakota* are published by the Department of Game, Fish, and Parks.

TENNESSEE

Area: 42,022 square miles (land area—41,762 square miles); rank in nation—34

Bird: Mocking bird (*Mimus polyglottus*), adopted 1933
Capital city: Nashville on the Cumberland River in Davidson County; population (1960)—170,874; rank in state–2
Counties: 95
Elevations: Highest, Clingman's Dome (6,642 ft.) in Sevier County; lowest, Mississippi River (182 ft.) in Shelby County
Flower: Iris (*Iris versicolor*), adopted 1933; known as Blue Flag
Geographic center: 5 miles northeast of Murfreesboro, Rutherford County
Nicknames: Big Bend State, Volunteer State
Population (1960): 3,567,089; rank in nation–17
Tree: Tulip (*Liriodendron tulipifera*), adopted in 1947

Tennessee is bordered by Alabama, Georgia, and Mississippi on the south, North Carolina on the east, Kentucky and Virginia on the north; and on the west, the Mississippi River flows along the boundary between Arkansas and Missouri.

The irregular, forested ridges of the Unaka Mountains in the eastern Appalachian Range contains several mountains above 6,000 feet including Clingman's Dome, the Cherokee National Forest, and the Great Smoky Mountains shared with North Carolina. Parallel ridges and valleys in the Great Valley of East Tennessee rise abruptly to the Cumberland Plateau west of the Tennessee River. Streams cut deeply into this rolling region, and the terrain drops 1,000 feet to the Highland Rim of Middle Tennessee. The broad fertile central basin below the Highland Rim slopes gradually to the bluffs and low bottom lands of the Mississippi River.

In eastern Tennessee, the Clinch, Holston, French Broad, and Little Tennessee rivers form the mighty Tennessee River which runs south into Alabama and returns to follow a northward course between middle and west Tennessee to Kentucky. Impounded waters of the Tennessee River include Watts Bar Lake (38,600 acres) near Kingston and Chickamauga Lake (34,500 acres) north of Chattanooga in the Great Valley; Pickwick Lake (42,800 acres) on the Alabama-Mississippi boundaries, south of Savannah; Kentucky Lake (407 square miles) with a 2,380-mile shoreline extending into Kentucky west of Dover. The Cumberland River rising in Kentucky flows through Gainesboro, Carthage, Nashville, Clarksville, and Dover in the northern region of middle Tennessee before swerving northward into Kentucky east of the Tennessee River. Holston Lake on the South Fork Holston River extending 24 miles across the Virginia line at Bristol; Fort Patrick Henry Lake (37-mile shoreline) and Daniel Boone Lake (4,520 acres) near Kingsport; Watauga Lake (6,430 acres) and Wilbur Lake near Elizabethton; and the Kettlefort Area are in the northeastern corner of the state. Norris Lake (34,200 acres) at the confluence of the Clinch and Powell rivers north of Clinton; the Cherokee Lake (30,200 acres) on the Holston River near Morristown; Davy Crockett Lake on the Nolichucky River near Greeneville and the Unicoi Area; Douglas Lake (30,600 acres) on the French Broad River west of Newport; Fort Loudon Lake (14,600 acres) and Melton Hill Lake near Knoxville are among the mountain streams of eastern Tennessee. Ocoee Lake and Parksville Lake are on the Ocoee River which joins the Hiwassee River to flow into Chickamauga Lake.

Dale Hollow Lake (30,000 acres) extending into Kentucky is connected with the Cumberland River by the Obey River northeast of Carthage. Center Hill Lake (23,000 acres) is on the Caney Fork Cumberland River southeast of Carthage; and Old Hickory Lake south of Gallatin, Cheatham Lake west of Nashville, and Lake Barkeley (150 square miles) extending into Kentucky are on the Cumberland River. Reelfoot Lake (14,500 acres) at Tiptonville in the northwestern corner of the state is connected by Reelfoot Running Bayou; and the Obion and Deer rivers, with the Mississippi River. The Hatchie, Loosahatchie, and Wolf rivers drain through western Tennessee into the Mississippi River. In middle Tennessee, the Buffalo and Duck rivers flow into Kentucky Lake, and the Elk River wanders into Alabama. The Sequatchie River from the Cumberland Plateau leaves Tennessee west of Chattanooga.

LICENSES

Resident licenses are issued to persons who have established a bona fide residence in the state for at least 90 days immediately preceding an application for a license, but members of the U.S. Armed Forces stationed in Tennessee on active duty and their families may purchase resident licenses at any time. Free fishing licenses are issued to blind residents, and sport fishing, commercial fishing, hunting, and trapping licenses may be obtained without cost by residents 70 or more years of age. Any resident veteran certified by the Veterans Administration as being 80 per cent disabled by reason of war service may procure a free hunting and sport fishing license. Military personnel home on leave or furlough may fish and hunt without licenses if carrying copies of their official orders. Owners of land in Tennessee who do not live within the state must purchase nonresident licenses. Owners or tenants and their dependent children living on their farm may fish, hunt, and trap on their lands without licenses. A resident may use natural or cut bait with a hook and line, or a trotline of not more than 50 hooks in the county of his residence without a license, except that Trout may not be taken, or minnows used for bait. Other persons 16 or more years of age must purchase fishing licenses.

Juveniles under the age of 16 may fish in state lakes without a license if accompanied by an adult relative. Free daily permits to take rough fish with bow and arrow, gig, or spear guns during a special winter season may be obtained by holders of fishing licenses from county court clerks or game and fish officers in Hardin, Hickman, Lawrence, Lewis, Perry, and Wayne counties. Fish taken under a sport fishing license may not be sold, and anyone using fishing equipment other than methods listed as legal sport fishing is considered to be a commercial fisherman and must obtain such a license.

Regardless of age, all residents and nonresidents are required to possess licenses to hunt or trap any wildlife. Hunting licenses will not be issued to nonresidents if their home state does not grant similar privileges to residents of Tennessee. North Carolina and Tennessee county or state fishing licenses are valid in the Great Smoky Mountains National Park. Juveniles under the age of 16 are not permitted to participate in big game hunts. Application forms for quota hunts in wildlife management areas are available about July 1, and permits are sold at the Nashville Fish and Game office on a first-come basis to persons holding hunting licenses. A drawing is held in September if there are more applications than openings, and fees are refunded to unsuccessful applicants. Permits for hunting in wildlife management areas without quotas may be purchased on the day of a hunt at checking stations set at fixed points. A season small game permit may be obtained to hunt on all wildlife management areas except those within the Cherokee National Forest. No hunting or collecting of any sort of wildlife is permitted in the Great Smoky Mountains National Park, federal and state game refuges, or other public areas set aside for special purposes, except during special seasons. A regular hunting license must be obtained by a nonresident to hunt on private shooting preserves. All persons 16 or more years of age must purchase a federal "Duck" stamp to take migratory game birds.

Resident license fees: Combination annual hunting and sport fishing, $3.00; sport fishing one day, 50 cents; Trout stamp (affix to license), $1.00; state lake fishing (per day), 75 cents; wildlife management area fishing per day (except Catoosa Area), $1.00; slat basket tag in Humphreys County, $3.00; commercial fishing, $15.00; trapping, $2.00; taxidermy, $5.00; retail fur buyer, $2.00; wholesale fur buyer, $100.00; breeding furbearers, $10.00; breeding game birds, $10.00; keeping a wild pet, $1.00; federal "Duck" stamp, $3.00. Permits: Hunting Bear, Wild Boar, Wild Turkey for each 2-day hunt in the Catoosa, Central Peninsula, Fall Creek Falls, Oconee, and Tellico areas, $2.00; each 2-day hunt in the Shelby Area, $3.00; small game hunting season permit in all areas (except in the Cherokee National Forest), $5.00.

Nonresident license fees: Annual sport fishing, $3.00; sport fishing 10 consecutive days, $2.00; sport fishing 3 consecutive days, $1.50; Trout stamp (affix to license), $1.00; commercial fishing, $50.00; hunting,

$15.00; big game stamp (Bear, Boar, Deer, Turkey), $5.00; small game hunting for 3 consecutive days, $6.00; breeding game birds, $20.00; wholesale fur buyer, $250,000; federal "Duck" stamp, $3.00. State lake fishing and wildlife management area fees are same as for residents.

HUNTING AND TRAPPING

Game animals: Bear, Wild Boar, Deer, Fox (Gray, Red), Opossum, Raccoon, Squirrel. OPEN SEASONS (statewide, exclusive of wildlife management areas): Bear—about 3 weeks in October and one week in November in Blount, Cooke, Greene, Monroe, and Sevier counties. Boar—concurrent with Bear except only in Blount and Monroe counties. Buck Deer*—one week in November and one week in December. Gray Fox—any time except in counties regulated by private acts. Red Fox—no open season except by county regulations. Opossum, Raccoon—mid-October to late January. Rabbit—mid-November to late January. Squirrels—Sept. 1–Jan. 1. Controlled or commercial shooting of Bear, Boar, Deer, Turkey—Sept. 1–May 31. BAG LIMITS: Statewide: Bear—1 per year. Wild Boar—1 per year. Buck Deer—1 per year. Gray Fox, Opossum—no limit. Rabbits—5 per day. Raccoon—1 per night in counties east of Kentucky Lake and no limit in Hardin County and counties west of Kentucky Lake. Squirrels— 6 per day. Wildlife Management Areas: Bear, Boar, Deer—1 per permit. Fox, Opossum, Raccoon, Squirrel—limits conform with statewide regulations.

Furbearing animals: Beaver, Bobcat, Fox, Groundhog, Mink, Muskrat, Opossum, Raccoon, Skunk, Weasel. OPEN TRAPPING SEASON: Beaver —mid-November to mid-December in counties of Bradley, Hardin, Houstin, Humphreys, Montgomery, Perry, Stewart, Wayen, and all counties west of Kentucky Lake. Gray Fox, Mink, Muskrat, Opossum— mid-November to mid-January. NOT PROTECTED: Bobcat, Skunk, Weasel, Woodchuck may be taken at any time.

Game birds: Coot, Mourning Dove, Ducks (except Canvasback and Redhead), Gallinule, Geese, Ruffed Grouse, Merganser, Bobwhite Quail, Rails, Sora, Wilson's Snipe, Wild Turkey, Woodcock. OPEN SEASONS: Coot, Ducks, Gallinule, Merganser, Rails, Sora—early October to early November. Dove—generally month of November and about 10 days in early January. Geese—early November to mid-January. Ruffed Grouse —Nov. 1–Feb. 15. Bobwhite Quail—mid-November to late January. Wilson's Snipe, Woodcock—mid-November to early January. Wild Turkey—about 1 week in early April and 2 weeks in early May except in Benton, Henry, and Lauderdale counties. Controlled and commercial shooting of upland game birds—Oct. 1–April 1. FULLY PROTECTED:

---

* A legal buck Deer should have antlers visible above the hairline.

Canvasback and Redhead Ducks—no open seasons. NOT PROTECTED: Bluejay, Buzzard, Crow, Cooper's Hawk, Sharp-shinned Hawk, Great Horned Owl, English Sparrow, and Starling may be taken at any time.

FIREARMS

Shotguns capable of holding not more than 3 shells in the magazine and chamber combined may be used with shot smaller than no. 2 for small game and Wild Turkey, and with a single ball or rifled slug for Bear, Boar, and Deer. A shotgun should be 20 gauge or larger to take big game including Turkey. Shot larger than no. 2 is prohibited for all species except big game and waterfowl. Migratory game birds may not be hunted with rifles, and during Bear, Boar, and Deer open seasons no centerfire ammunition may be used to hunt any wildlife except big game. The use of rifles with rimfire cartridges or rifles of less than .24 caliber to hunt Bear, Boar, and Deer is prohibited. Hand guns are not permitted in wildlife management areas, or for big game; and on the A.E.D.C. Wildlife Management Area, rifles and sidearms are prohibited.

Longbows used for shooting big game must be capable of propelling a hunting arrow 150 yards. Legal big game hunting arrows should be at least 24 inches in length and equipped with steel broadhead blades of barbless design, and not less than seven-eighths of an inch or more than 1½ inches at the widest point for single two-inch blades, or less than 3 inches in circumference for 3 or more blades. All broadheads must weigh at least 100 grains.

Red or yellow caps or jackets must be worn during managed big game hunts.

Shooting hours: Sunrise to sunset, except that shooting starts at 12:00 o'clock noon on the opening day of the Duck season. Opossum and Raccoon—sunset to sunrise.

FISHING

Game fish: Black Bass (Largemouth, Smallmouth), Coosa (Redeye) Bass, Kentucky Bass, Rock Bass, White Bass, Yellow Bass, Bluegill, Catfish (Blue, Channel, Yellow), Crappie (Black, White), Muskellunge, Pickerel, Rockfish (Striped Bass), Sauger, Sunfish (all species), Trout (Brook, Brown, Cutthroat, Kamloops, Kokanee, Rainbow), Walleye, Warmouth. OPEN SEASONS: All year, except in the following wildlife management areas: Catoosa Area—March to October 31 except on dates of managed hunts; Andrew Johnson, Kettlefoot, Laurel Fork, Unicoi areas —mid-April to early October on Wednesday, Saturday, Sunday, and legal holidays; Ocoee Area—mid-April to late July on Saturdays, Sundays, and legal holidays; Tellico Area—mid-April to March 1 on Thursdays, Fridays, Saturdays, Sundays, and national holidays except on dates of big game hunts. Trout streams in the Great Smoky Mountain National Park—mid-May to August 31.

Sport fishermen may use 3 closely attended cane or natural poles, or manufactured rods at one time, and one trotline with not more than 100 hooks. The use of slat baskets is prohibited except in Hickman, Humphreys, Jackson, and Smith counties. Dip nets and seines may be used to capture bait minnows, and rough fish may be taken in July and August with seines in De Kalb County except in Center Hill Lake, Pine Creek, and Caney Fork River.

Grab hook and grabbling are permitted in designated areas of the Cumberland, Duck, Elk, French Broad, Harpeth, Holston, Nolichucky, Red, Sequatchie, and Smith Fork rivers, Lick Creek (Greene County), Shoals Creek (Lawrence County), and all streams west of Kentucky Lake and the tributary streams of Dale Hollow Lake, and in Wolf River only from the Highway 28 bridge downstream to the Dale Hollow backwaters.

Buffalo, Carp, Drum, Gar, Shad, Spoonbill, Suckers, and other rough fish may be taken by bow and arrow, gig, or speargun in all impounded waters during daylight hours, and at any hour in other waters including streams west of Kentucky Lake; tributaries to Center Hill, Dale Hollow, and Great Falls reservoirs; and from designated areas of the Clinch, French Broad, Holston, Lick, and Powell rivers. Snatch hooks may be used to take rough fish in all public waters except within 100 yards below dams.

Bullfrogs: May be taken by use of gigs in all public waters except in the Anderson-Tully, Andrew Johnson, Catoosa, Central Peninsula, Fall Creek Falls, Kettlefoot, Laurel Fork, Natchez Trace, Ocoee, Prentice Cooper, Shelby Forest, Tellico, and Unicoi wildlife management areas. Center Hill and Dale Hollow Lakes are closed to bullfrogging Feb. 1–May 31. DAILY BAG LIMIT: 10.

Turtles may be taken at any time from waters open to commercial fishing.

Tailwater Trout fishing is superb in such storage reservoirs as Appalachia, Daniel Boone, Calderwood, Center Hill, Dale Hollow, Fort Patrick Henry, Norris, South Holston, Watauga, and Wilbur lakes. Fishing and hunting is permitted in wildlife management areas, but hunting is prohibited in state parks.

STATE LAKES

Bedford Lake (47 acres) near Normandy—Bedford County; *Brown's Creek Lake* (167 acres) in Natchez Trace Forest, northeast of Lexington —Henderson County; *Burgess Falls Lake* (400 acres) 7 miles south of Cookeville on the boundary of Putnam and White counties; *Carroll Lake* (100 acres) south of McKenzie-Carroll County; *Fisherville Lake*

(177 acres) near Collierville—Fayette County; *Garrett Lake* (183 acres) near Como—Weakly County; *Humboldt Lake* (87 acres) west of Humboldt—Crockett County; *Laurel Hill Lake* (327 acres) 14 miles west of Lawrenceburg—Lawrence County; *Laurel Lake* (34 acres) northeast of Maryville—Blount County; *Maples Creek Lake* (90 acres) in Natchez Trace Forest, 5 miles east of Yuma—Carroll County; *Marrowbone Lake* (60 acres) near Joelton—Davidson County; *Whiteville Lake* (158 acres) east of Whiteville—Hardman County.

STATE PARKS

Big Ridge (3,600 acres) on Norris Lake near Maynardville—Union County; *Booker T. Washington* (350 acres) on Chickamauga Lake near Chattanooga—Hamilton County; *Chickasaw* (11,215 acres) west of Henderson—Chester County; Cove Lake (850 acres) north of Caryville—Campbell County; *Cumberland Mountain* (1,425 acres) south of Crossville—Cumberland Mountain (1,425 acres) south of Crossville—Cumberland County; *Fall Creek Falls* (15,777 acres) includes Cane Creek Falls (85 ft.), Fall Creek Falls (256 ft.), and Rock House Falls (125 ft.) west of Pikeville—Bledsoe County; *T. O. Fuller* (1,000 acres) on the Mississippi River, south of Memphis—Shelby County; *Harrison Bay* (1,500 acres) on a forested peninsula at Chickamauga Lake, 10 miles east of Chattanooga—Hamilton County; *Montgomery Bell* (5,000 acres) including Lake Acorn and Lake Woodhave near Burns—Dickson County; *Natchez Trace Forest* (42,000 acres) north of Lexington—Carroll and Henderson counties; *Norris Dam* (4,000 acres) at Norris Lake—Anderson County; *Paris Landing* (1,200 acres) at Kentucky Lake, near Buchanan—Henry County; *Pickett* (11,952 acres) east of Byrdstown—Pickett County; *Reelfoot Lake* (85 acres) near the Islom Lake Bird Refuge, east of Tiptonville—Lake County; *Shelby Forest* (12,512 acres) overlooking the Mississippi River north of Memphis—Shelby County; *Standing Stone* (8,764 acres) 5 miles from Dale Hollow Lake, northeast of Livingston—Overton County; *Warrior's Path* (1,000 acres) at Lake Patrick Henry, southeast of Kingsport—Sullivan County.

WILDLIFE MANAGEMENT AREAS

Anderson-Tully (30,000 acres) on the Mississippi River, west of Ripley; *Andrew Johnson* (9,000 acres) in the Cherokee National Forest, southeast of Newport; Arnold Engineering Development Center (A.E.-D.C.) (42,000 acres) south of Manchester; *Catoosa* (85,000 acres) east of Crossville; *Central Peninsula* (27,000 acres) at Norris Lake, north of Knoxville; *Cheatham* (19,852 acres) on the Cumberland River, at Ashland City; *Cove Creek* (2,120 acres) north of Clinton; *Kettlefoot* (35,230 acres) in the Cherokee National Forest, west of Mountain City; *Laurel*

Fork (7,900 acres) on Laurel Fork Creek in the Cherokee National Forest, southeast of Elizabethton; *Ocoee* (44,000 acres) in the Cherokee National Forest, east of Cleveland; *Old Hickory* at Old Hickory Lake (97 miles long) on the Cumberland River, 15 miles northeast of Nashville; *Prentice Cooper* (26,800 acres) northwest of Chattanooga; *Reelfoot* (9,210 acres) at Reelfoot Lake near Tiptonville; *Tellico* (79,370 acres) east of Madison, and *Unicoi* (40,000 acres) east of Greenville, both in the Cherokee National Forest.

There are wildlife management areas in the following state parks: Chickasaw, Fall Creek Falls, Laurel Hill Lake, Natchez Trace Forest, Pickett, Shelby Forest, and Standing Stone.

Regulations, information about current seasons, bag and possession limits, disabled veterans and old-age licenses may be obtained from license agents, or the Director, Tennessee Game and Fish Commission, Cordell Hull Building, Nashville. Game and Fish personnel do not sell licenses. They are issued by county court clerks, sporting goods and hardware stores, dock operators, and other merchants. Permits for management area fishing and hunting (except quota hunting) are available at nearby checking stations, and permits to fish in the Great Smoky Mountains National Park should be obtained at the park headquarters, Gatlinburg, Tennessee. In addition to the *Tennessee Conservationist* published monthly and issued free to interested sportsmen, the Information and Education Division, Tennessee Game and Fish Commission, also publishes a *Pocket Guide to Tennessee Hunting, A Guide to Tennessee Fishing, Wildlife in Tennessee,* and other booklets. Information and maps of TVA lakes are available from the Information Office, Tennessee Valley Authority, Knoxville.

TEXAS

Area: 265,896 square miles (land area—262,840 square miles); rank in nation—2
Bird: Mocking Bird (*Mimus polyglottus*), adopted 1927
Capital city: Austin on the Colorado River in Travis County; population (1960)—186,545; rank in state—6
Counties: 254
Elevations: Highest, Guadalupe Peak (8,751 ft.) in Culberson County; lowest, Gulf of Mexico (sea level)
Flower: Bluebonnet (*Lupinus subcarnosus*), adopted 1901
Geographic center: 15 miles northesat of Brady, McCulloch County
Nicknames: Lone Star State, Beef State, Jumbo State

Population (1960): 9,579,677; rank in nation–6
Tidal shoreline: 3,359 miles (including islands, bays, and streams to a point where tidal waters narrow to 100 ft.)
Tree: Pecan (*Cary illinoesis,* or *Hickoria pecan*), adopted 1919

Texas on the Gulf of Mexico is bordered on the east by Louisiana and Arkansas on the northeast, Oklahoma on the north, New Mexico on the west, and separated from the Republic of Mexico on the south by the Rio Grande wandering from El Paso to the Gulf of Mexico east of Brownsville.

The terrain of Texas varies from the semitropical low coastal plain fringed with marshes, sandy lagoons, and bays to the highest point, Guadalupe Peak, near the New Mexico border north of Pine Springs; the fertile Black Prairie belt from San Antonio to the Red River on the Oklahoma border; the irregular north central plain rising sharply to grassy Staked Plains, or Llano Estacado, a plateau region between the Panhandle and the Rio Grande. The rugged Panhandle bordered by New Mexico and Oklahoma includes the counties of Bailey, Cottle, Floyd, Hale, Lamb, and counties north of them transvered by the Canadian River. The Palo Duro Canyon State Park (15,103 acres), at a spectacular gorge on the Prairie Dog Town Fork of the Red River, contains 20 miles of bridle paths and 30 miles of hiking trails.

The Trans-Pecos country between the Pecos River and the Rio Grande is an arid wilderness region of isolated ridges and broad plains with the Apache, Delaware, and Guadalupe mountains in Culberson County; Mount Livermore (8,382 ft.) and McDonald Observatory near Fort Davis in Jeff Davis County; the Quitman Mountains, Sierra Vieja, and Chanati Mountains along the Rio Grande north of the Chisos (Ghost) Mountains in the Big Bend National Park. San Antonio is on the southeastern edge of the Balcones Escarpment extending between the Colorado River and the Rio Grande. South of the Nueces River flowing into Corpus Christi Bay on the Gulf of Mexico is the vast King Ranch covering 726,924 acres. There are approximately 2 million acres of bayous, ponds, and dense forests in the Big Thicket northwest of Beaumont.

The Highland Lakes, a 150-mile chain in the Colorado River, vary in size from Little Lake Inks (3 miles long) to Lake Travis 65 miles long) and also include the Austin, Buchanan, Granite Shoals, and Marble Falls lakes, and farther north, the Pecan Bayou is a connecting waterway with Lake Brownwood. In the Lake Kemp region west of Wichita Falls, the Brazos River starts on a long journey to be impounded near Mineral Springs and create the Possum Kingdom Reservoir, and downstream, the Whitney Reservoir (78 sq. miles) before flowing through Waco to the Gulf of Mexico at Freeport. Rising in Archer County, the West Fork

Trinity River forms Lake Bridgeport, Eagle Mountains Lake, and Lake Worth at Fort Worth, and from Cooke County, the Elm Fork of the Trinity River forms the Garza–Little Elm Reservoir (61 sq. miles) north of Dallas, and continues on a southward course to mingle waters in Galveston Bay with the San Jacinto River from Lake Houston northeast of Houston. The Sabine River marks the Louisiana-Texas border from Hunt County to Sabine Lake at Port Arthur and flows through a ship channel to the Gulf. Lake Texoma (225 sq. miles) on the Red River at Denison is shared with Oklahoma. Among many other large lakes is the McGee Bend Reservoir (187 sq. miles) on Sulphur River near Texarkana in northeastern Texas. The Laguna Atascosa National Wildlife Refuge is near Port Isabel at the southern end of Laguna Madre which is connected by a causeway with Padre Island (80 miles long). The Padre Island National Seashore is a strip of sand dunes similar to other islands along the Gulf Coast. Port Aransas is on the northern end of Mustang Island at Corpus Christi Bay south of the Aransas National Wildlife Refuge on Aransas Bay protected by the St. Joseph and Matagorda islands. Galveston on the north end of Galveston Island is linked by causeways with Texas City and the mainland, and by ferry with Port Bolivar on High Island at the entrance of Galveston Bay.

LICENSES

Resident licenses to fish and hunt are issued to U.S. citizens 17–65 years of age who have been bona fide residents of Texas for at least 6 months immediately preceding an application for any license. No license is required to fish within the county of a person's residence if the fisherman uses only a throwline, trotline, or an ordinary pole and line without any reel or winding device attached to it. Owners and tenants are not required to purchase licenses to fish, hunt, or trap on their private lands, and any citizen may hunt in the county of his residence without a license. No person may hunt Deer or Turkey anywhere in the state without either a hunting license or a special exemption license issued upon request to landowners and tenants hunting on their lands and to citizens less than 17 years of age or more than 65 years of age. Special licenses must be obtained by the manager or owner of a shooting resort (600–2,000 acres) where game birds are released for hunting, and by the manager for a club or shooting preserve used for hunting purposes. Any person raising game birds in captivity for sale should purchase a commercial game breeder's license. No fees are charged for private blinds used to hunt waterfowl, but the operation of commercial blinds in Harrison and Marion counties requires a license.

Every person who is paid to operate a power- or sailboat for hunters must hold a hunting boat license. Deer hides may be sold, and taxidermists are permitted to sell unclaimed specimens; but otherwise it is unlawful for any person except game breeders, fur buyers, and trappers to buy or sell dead or living game animals and birds. General laws protecting wildlife are supplemented by special regulations issued by the Texas Parks and Wildlife Department for counties grouped into regulatory districts. General, special, county, and lake laws should be carefully checked in the current *Digest* and *Digest Supplement* of Game and Fish Regulations. All persons 16 or more years of age must purchase a federal "Duck" stamp to take migratory game birds.

Resident license fees: Sport fishing (fresh- and saltwater), $2.15; commercial fishing, $3.00; fish boat (freshwater, motor, or sail), $3.00; commercial fishing boat (saltwater), $6.00; skiff propelled by oars or poles, $1.00; hunting, $3.15; federal "Duck" stamp, $3.00; manager of shooting preserve, $5.00; owner or manager of a shooting resort, $10.00; game breeder (propagation of game animals or birds), $2.00; commercial game breeder, $25.00; trapping, 1.00; Beaver-Otter permit (outside county of residence), $50.00; propagation of furbearing animals, $5.00; retail fur buyer, $5.00; wholesale fur buyer, $25.00.

Nonresident license fees: Sport fishing (fresh- and saltwater), $2.15; hunting (regardless of age), $25.00; migratory bird hunting 5 consecutive days, $5.00; hunting upland birds on private shooting preserves, $3.15; migratory waterfowl license (reciprocal basis only), $10.00; trapping, $200.00.

HUNTING AND TRAPPING

Game animals: Pronghorn Antelope, Black Bear, Buffalo, Deer (Mule, White-tailed), Elk, Javelina, Sheep (Aoudad, Bighorn), Squirrels (Cat, Gray, Red). OPEN SEASONS:* Antelope—several days in late September or early October in Borden, Mitchell, Nolan, and Taylor counties, in Possum Kingdom, and in Trans-Pecos Regulatory District; 2 or 3 days in the Panhandle Regulatory District. Bear—mid-November through December. Deer—archery, during October including shorter seasons in designated areas; firearms, Nov. 1–Dec. 31. Elk—several days early December in the Trans-Pecos Regulatory District. Javelina—Nov. 1–Dec. 31, and no closed season in Bowie, Brooks, Harrison, Jim Hogg, Maverick, Red, and Zapata counties, or in the Edwards Plateau and South Central Regulatory Districts. Squirrels—May 1–Dec. 31 including shorter seasons in designated areas, and no closed seasons in the Edwards Plateau and South Central Regulatory District, or in 16 counties. BAG LIMITS: Antelope—1 per permit. Bear—1 annually. Deer—under general law, 2 Bucks per season; special laws, 2 or 3 in designated areas, except only 1 per sea-

---

* Check current state regulations.

son in the Panhandle Regulatory District and in Falls, McLennan, Milam, Smith, Upshur, and Wood counties. Elk—1 per permit. Javelina—2, except in counties open all year, no limit. Squirrels—5 to 10 per day in designated areas except in counties open all year, no limit.

A Buffalo may be taken only by special permit, and hunting Aoudad Sheep has been allowed for 3 days during December in the Panhandle Regulatory District. Alligator may not be taken in Harrison, Jefferson, Liberty, and Marion counties.

Furbearing animals: Badger, Beaver, Civet Cat, Ring-tailed Cat, Coypu, Fox, Mink, Muskrat, Opossum, Raccoon, Polecat. OPEN PELT-TAKING SEASONS:* General: Dec. 1–Jan. 31 and extended to February 15 in Cherokee County. Exceptions: Beaver—Jan. 1–15 in Maverick County and Trans-Pecos Regulatory District; from December 1 through February in the Panhandle Regulatory District; no open season in the South Central Regulatory District. Fox—Dec. 1–31 in Cass County; no trapping in Navarro; shooting, trapping, and sale of pelts prohibited in Camp Rusk, Shelby and Upshur counties; pelts may be taken at any time in Robertson County. Mink—general season, Nov. 15–Jan. 15; Regulatory Districts, Dec. 1–Jan. 31 except Southeast Texas Regulatory District, Nov. 15–March 15. Muskrat—general season, Nov. 15–March 15; Panhandle Regulatory District Dec. 1–Feb. 28; Oak-Prairie, Possum Kingdom, and Trinity Brazos regulatory districts, Dec. 1–Jan. 31. BAG LIMITS: none. FULLY PROTECTED: Buffalo and Bighorn Sheep—no open season. NOT PROTECTED: Armadillo, Russian Boar, Bobcat, Wild Cats, Coyote, Cougar, Mountain Lion, Ocelot, Rabbits, Rats, Weasel, and Wolf are classified as predatory animals and may be killed at any time.

A legal Buck is a male Deer with a pronged antler, and any Deer without hardened antlers protruding through the skin is an "antlerless" Deer, except in Eastland County, where the term refers only to a female Deer.

Game birds: Brant, Chachalaca, Coot, Lesser Sandhill Crane, Dove (Mourning, White-winged), Ducks (except Canvasback, Redhead, Black-bellied Tree Ducks), Gallinule, Geese, Merganser, Partridge, Pheasant, Pigeon, Plover, Prairie Chicken (Pinnated Grouse), Quail, Rails, Wilson's Snipe, Sora, Wild Turkey, Woodcock. OPEN SEASONS:* Brant, Geese—November to mid-January. Chachalaca—December to mid-January, and no closed season in LaSalle County. Coot, Ducks, Merganser, Plover—December. Crane—November in designated areas. Mourning Dove—September and October in designated counties, and extended to mid-November in several counties. Gallinule, Rails, Sora—September to mid-October. Pheasant—one week in December in several Panhandle counties; about

---

* Check current state regulations.

6 weeks in December and January in Ellis County; and all year in Kaufman, LaSalle, Lee, and Smith counties. Quail—Nov. 1–Jan. 31 with shorter seasons in designated areas. Wilson's Snipe, Woodcock—early December to mid-January. Wild Turkey—Dec. 1–Jan. 31 including shorter seasons in designated areas. Hunting on shooting preserves—Oct. 1–March 31. FULLY PROTECTED: White-winged Dove, Canvasback, Redhead, and Black-bellied Tree Ducks, Brown Pelican, Prairie Chicken—no open seasons. NOT PROTECTED: Blackbirds, Blue Darters, Butcherbirds, Buzzards (Vultures), Crows, Golden Eagles, Goshawks, Cooper's Hawk, Duck Hawk, Sharp-shinned Hawk, Jays, Great Horned Owl, White Pelican, Ravens, Ricebirds, Roadrunner, Sapsucker, English Sparrow, Starling, and Woodpeckers may be taken at any time.

FIREARMS

Game animals and birds may be hunted with rifles and shotguns capable of being fired from the shoulder, except that it is unlawful to use rifles to hunt migratory game birds, Chachalacas, Pheasants, Quails, and Turkeys. Shotguns used to hunt game birds must be plugged to hold not more than 3 shells in the magazine and chamber combined. Except in Kendall County, the use of a .22 caliber rifle loaded with rimfire ammunition to shoot Antelope, Deer, and Elk is prohibited. Deer, Javelina, and Turkey may be hunted with a longbow capable of propelling a broadheaded hunting arrow 150 yards. The broadhead point should be at least seven-eighth inches and not more than 1½ inches in width. During the October archery season, only Buck Deer, Javelina of either sex, and Turkey Gobblers may be hunted, but any game may be taken with bow and arrow during the regular hunting season.

Shooting hours: Game animals—one-half hour before sunrise to one-half hour after sunset, except Deer in Marion County, sunrise to sunset. Mourning Dove—12:00 o'clock noon to sunset daily. Migratory game birds—sunrise to sunset, except opening day of the Duck season, 12 o'clock noon to sunset. Hunting fur-bearing animals at night with an artificial light is prohibited where Deer are known to range. The use of artificial lights to hunt game animals and birds is prohibited.

FISHING

Game fish: Black Bass (Largemouth, Smallmouth), Spotted Bass, White Bass, Bream, Catfish (Blue, Channel), Flathead Catfish, Crappie (White Perch). OPEN SEASONS: All year.

An ordinary pole and line, fly rod, rod and reel, set line, trotline, artificial lures, seines and nets (not less than 3-inch square mesh) may be used for taking freshwater fish. A bow and arrow, spear, or spear gun may be used to take Buffalo, Carp, Gar, Gaspergou, and Rio Grande Perch. County and Lake laws should be checked for special regulations.

There are hundreds of lakes and 3,700 freshwater streams, and the forested hill country in central Texas is easily accessible and provides excellent hunting and fishing. The Gulf Coast offers superlative saltwater fishing and waterfowl hunting. The annual Texas-International Fishing Tournament in August is centered at Port Isabel, and new records are constantly being made by sport fishermen. Hunting is prohibited in state parks, and permission to fish should be obtained from the person in charge of the park.

STATE PARKS

Atlanta (1,475 acres) on Lake Texarkana, north of Atlanta—Cass County; *Bentsen–Rio Grande Valley* (587 acres) southwest of Mission—Hidalgo County; *Blanco* (110 acres) on Blanco River, near Blanco—Blanco County; *Bonham* (555 acres, lake 60 acres) south of Bonham—Fannin County; *Caddo Lake* (485 acres) at Caddo Lake, east of Jefferson—Harrison and Marion counties; *Cleburne* (498 acres) 10 miles southwest of Cleburne—Johnson County; *Daingerfield* (580 acres) southeast of Daingerfield—Morris County; *Eisenhower* (416 acres) on Lake Texoma, northwest of Denison—Grayson County; *Fort Parker* (1,496 acres) on Navasota River, north of Grosbeck—Limestone County; *Frio* (51 acres) on the Rio Frio, south of Pearsall—Frio County; *Garner* (640 acres) on the Rio Frio in the Balcones Escarpment, 26 miles north of Uvalde—Uvalde County; *Goose Island* (307 acres) about 10 miles northeast of Rockport—Aransas County; *Huntsville* (2,100 acres) 5 miles south of Huntsville—Walker County; *Inks Lake* (1,202 acres) west of Burnet—Burnet County; *Kerrville* (500 acres) on Guadalupe River, southeast of Kerrville—Kerr County; *Lake Brownwood* (538 acres) on Pecan Bayou, 24 miles northwest of Brownwood—Brown County; *Lake Corpus Christi* (14,111 acres) on the Nueces River, west of Mathis—San Patricio County; *Lake Whitney* (1,315 acres) on the Brazos River, west of Whitney—Hill County; *Meridian* (468 acres) southwest of Meridian—Bosque County; *Palmetto* (198 acres) 7 miles southeast of Luling—Caldwell County; *Possum Kingdom* (2,621 acres) at Possum Kingdom Lake near Mineral Wells—Palo Pinto County; *Stephen F. Austin* (664 acres) on the Brazos River, east of Sealy—Austin County; *Tyler* (992 acres, lake 65 acres) 10 miles north of Tyler—Smith County.

POPULAR PUBLIC LAKES AND RESERVOIRS

Belton Reservoir on the Santee River; *Ellison Creek Reservoir* in Morris County; *Fort Phantom Hill Lake* in Jones County; *Lake Baird* in

Callahan County; *Highland Lakes*; *Lake Bosque* in Bosque County; *Lake Casa Blanca* east of Laredo; *Lake Colorado City* in Mitchell County; *Lake Dallas* (Garza–Little Elm Reservoir) north of Dallas; *Lake Houston* in Harrison County; *Lake Kemp* north of Seymour; *Lake Kickapoo* in Archer County; *Lake Texoma* at Denison; *Lavon Lake* in Collin County; *Lake Murvaul* in Panola County; *Lake-o-the-Pines* or Ferrels Bridge Reservoir west of Jefferson; *Lake Thomas* near Synder; *Lake Waco* on the Brazos River; *Lake Wichita* near Wichita Falls; *Lake Winters* in Runnels County; *McGee Bend Reservoir*; *North Concho Reservoir* northwest of San Angelo; *Rockland Reservoir* on the Neches River; *Sweetwater Oak Creek Lake* in Coke County; *Texarkana Lake* in northeastern Bowie, Cass, and Morris counties; *Wood County*—Hawkins, Holbrook, Quitman, and Winsboro lakes.

Licenses, permits, regulations, information about current seasons, bag and possession limits may be obtained from the Director, Parks and Wildlife Department, State Office Building, Austin. Regional offices: 105 San Jacinto St., La Porte; P.O. Box 117, Rockport; Drawer 1590, San Angelo; 530 South Beckham, Tyler; 3725 Franklin, Waco.

UTAH

Area: 84,990 square miles (land area—82,339 square miles); rank in nation–11
Bird: Sea Gull (*Larus californicus*), adopted 1955
Capital city: Salt Lake City on the Jordan River at the base of Wasatch Mountains; population (1960)—189,454; rank in state–1
Counties: 29
Elevations: Highest, King's Peak (13,498 ft.) in Duchesne County; lowest, Beaverdam Creek (2,000 ft.) in Washington County
Flower: Sego Lily (*Calochortus nuttallii*), adopted 1911
Geographic center: 3 miles north of Manti, Sanpete County
Nicknames: Beehive State, Land of the Saints, Mormon State, Salt Lake State
Population (1960): 890,627; rank in nation–38
Tree: Blue Spruce (*Picea pungens kosteriana*), adopted 1933

Utah is a western state with Idaho on the northern boundary, which is shared by Wyoming cutting into the northeast corner to meet Colorado on the eastern border. Nevada extends along the western boundary, and Arizona on the south is joined at the common Four Corners by Colorado and New Mexico.

Extreme contrasts are found among the snow-crowned mountains, lake-studded plateaus, exquisitely colored and sculptured cliffs and canyons, fertile green valleys, barren alkalai deserts, and huge inland salty sea. Lofty peaks and deep canyons characterize the Wasatch Range which stretches from Bear Lake on the Idaho line in the northeast, and the Cache National Forest southward for about 150 miles to Mount Nebo (11,887 ft.) in central Utah. Pioneers passed through Emigration Canyon to found Salt Lake City, and in this region are Big Cottonwood, City Creek, Little Cottonwood, Mill Creek, and Parleys canyons. In the western valleys of the Wasatch Mountains are Ogden, at the junction of the Ogden and Weber rivers near Pineview Lake 10 miles up Ogden Canyon, and Logan, on the North Branch of the Logan River.

Mount Timpanogos (11,750 ft.) looms above the Utah Valley, and Provo Peak (11,068 ft.) overlooks Provo and freshwater Lake Utah which spreads over about 150 square miles before draining through the Jordan River into the Great Salt Lake. This huge body of water is approximately 75 miles long, 30 miles wide, and 20–50 feet deep with a salt content of 15–28 per cent according to the water stage, and contains several islands inhabited by Pelicans and Sea Gulls. Many mountains are scattered through this dry region including the Cedar, Grouse Creek, Hogup, Lakeside, Mineral, Oquirrh, Promontory, and Tintec mountains rising abruptly from desert plains; and travelers' landmarks are Desert Peak (6,984 ft.) west of Lakeside; Granite Peak (9,780 ft.) north of the old Pony Express and Stage route; Montezuma Peak (7,360 ft.), Ochre Mountain (7,735 ft.), South Peak (8,185 ft.), and Haystack Peak (12,101 ft.) near the Nevada line. The world's largest open-cut copper mine is at Bingham Canyon in the Oquirrh Mountains south of the Great Salt Lake. The Sevier Dry Lake is among mountains and valleys in an arid region south of the Great Salt Lake Desert.

A series of plateaus in central and western Utah are interspersed with glacial lakes and streams, bare, wooded and snow-covered mountains, deep canyons, and countless creeks. North of U.S. Highway 40 and south of the Wyoming border, the High Uintas Primitive Area lies like a frosted green saddle of wilderness accessible only by pack trips. There are mountains, lakes, and streams including Brown Duck, Big Elk, Mirro, Moon, and Grandaddy lakes, and Paradise Park Reservoir. Above all is Kings Peak not far from Gilbert Peak (13,422 ft.), Mount Emmons (13,428 ft.), Mount Lovinia (13,227 ft.), and Red Castle (13,134 ft.). The Flaming Gorge Reservoir (66 sq. miles) extending into Wyoming was created by impounding Green River which runs through the Dinosaur National Monument near Vernal, and fed by many streams, continues southward between West Tavaputs Plateau and the Hill Creek Extension of the Uintah and Ouray Indian Reservation to merge with the Colorado River at Still Water Canyon.

The Colorado River enters Utah northeast of Cisco and moves past the Arches National Monument near Moab to be joined by such tributaries as the Dolores, Green, Fremont, and Escalante rivers. The twisting San Juan River bordering the Navajo Indian Reservation in southeastern Utah flows into the Colorado River at Lake Powell which is part of the Glen Canyon Recreation Area containing 1,336,844 acres in Utah and 92,163 acres in Arizona.

There are lakes, reservoirs, and streams in southcentral Utah on the massive Wasatch Plateau in the Manti-LaSal and Fishlake national forests, and the Tushar Mountain region of Mount Belknap (12,139 ft.) and Delano Peak (12,173 ft.) near Marysvale. The Sevier River meanders between and around the Aquarius and Sevier plateaus of the Dixie National Forest in the southwestern corner of the state. In this region, the spectacular Cedar Breaks National Monument and the intricate erosion of the Bryce Canyon National Park are separated by the Markagunt and Paunsaugunt plateaus. The fantastic formations of Zion National Park are east of the Pine Valley Mountains and south of Cedar City. The Virgin River wanders through this area before crossing the Arizona line southwest of St. George in Washington County.

LICENSES

Resident licenses are issued to bona fide residents who have lived in Utah for at least 6 months immediately preceding any application for a license, and to members of the U.S. Armed Forces on active duty within the state and their immediate families. Residents of Utah attending school, employed in federal service, or on active military duty outside the state are entitled to resident licenses provided that they have not established legal residence in another state. All persons 12 or more years of age must possess a license to fish in any public waters. A blind person may receive a fishing license upon payment of a 5-cent issue fee. Nonresidents under the age of 12 must be accompanied by a licensed angler, and any game fish caught by the juvenile is counted in the possession limit of the license holder. Disabled veterans of the U.S. Armed Forces in veterans hospitals may receive a license to fish in the Red Butte Reservoir on the Fort Douglas Military Reservation upon payment of 10 cents. Portions of the Uintah-Ouray Indian Reservations are set aside for the use of full-blooded Indians, and nonresidents must procure a tribal permit to fish on Indian reservations in addition to any state license.

Hunting licenses are required for all persons 14 or more years of age to take game birds, and juveniles under the age of 16 are not permitted to hunt big game. No hunting license is issued to any resident under the age of 21 unless he presents (a) satisfactory proof of having held a resident license issued by the Department of Fish and Game; or (b) a certificate of competency in the safe handling of firearms; or (c) satisfactory proof that he has passed a National Rifle Association or Rescue Officers Training Corps gun training course, or that he is a serviceman or veteran who has completed training equivalent to a certificate of competency. Nonresidents are exempt from the above requirements. Mule Deer is the only species of big game that nonresidents may hunt, and special permits for designated areas are issued only to holders of hunting licenses. Each possessor of a valid hunting license may procure one special Deer permit, which is not issued at the Salt Lake City office except to archers. Gun hunters must first obtain a big game license number, and may then apply for special permits to the regional offices indicated on the annual Deer proclamation, which is generally available around July 15. Deer permits for archery hunting go on sale in early August, and for the gun season in mid-September. A Ute tribal license and a regular big game hunting license are required to hunt on the Uintah-Ouray Indian reservations, and regulations vary in different sections in Duchesne, Uintah, and Grand counties. Hunters may not apply for a permit to hunt Antelope for either of the two Antelope seasons next following a successful hunt, or for an Elk during the next 4 years. All persons 16 or more years of age must purchase a federal "Duck" stamp to take migratory game birds. Every person hunting big game must wear red, yellow, blaze orange, or fluorescent orange headgear, shirt, sweater, or jacket, except archers, who may wear only bright headgear.

No hunting or trapping licenses are necessary to kill nongame "varmints" or unprotected animals and birds. Shooting preserves of not more than 640 acres or less than 160 acres must be owned or leased for a term of not less than 5 years from the date of application for a hunting preserve license. On a licensed shooting preserve, a bird hunting license issued by the state of Utah is required in addition to a hunting permit issued by the owner or operator.

Resident license fees: Fishing (juveniles 12–15 years of age), $1.00; fishing (16–64 years of age), $3.50; fishing (65 years of age or older), $1.00; hunting game birds (juveniles 14–15 years of age), $2.00; hunting upland game birds (16 years of age or older), $3.50; combination fishing and hunting (16 years of age or older), $6.00; Deer hunting throughout state (16 years of age or older), $3.50. Special permits: Antelope, $10.00; Buffalo, $25.00; archery Deer season, $3.00; antlerless Deer from a designated area, $3.00; one Deer of either sex from a designated area, $3.00; two Deers (1 antlerless, both taken from a designated area), $5.00; Elk, $15.00; Moose, $25.00; federal "Duck" stamp, $3.00; trapping (any age), $6.00; guide, $6.00; fur dealer, $5.00; private fish pond permit, $1.00; permit to seine, $10.00.

Nonresident license fees: Fishing (juveniles 12–15 years of age),

$5.00; fishing 5 consecutive days (juveniles 12–15 years of age), $2.00; fishing (16 years of age or older), $10.00; fishing 5 consecutive days* (16 years or older), $4.00; Deer hunting throughout state (1 Deer), $40.00. Special permits: archery Deer season, $3.00; one Deer of either sex from a designated area, $5.00; two Deer (1 antlerless, both taken from a designated area), $8.00; federal "Duck" stamp, $3.00.

HUNTING AND TRAPPING

Game animals: Antelope, Buffalo, Deer, Elk, Moose, Mountain Goat, Mountain Sheep. OPEN SEASONS:** Antelope—a few days in August. Buffalo—set for Henry Mountain unit only. Deer—archery, late August and early September for about 2 weeks; general state season, opens on Saturday nearest October, usually lasts into November, and varies in length from a few days to 3–4 weeks; plus a special late November–December short season on the Dolores River unit east of Dewey on the Colorado River. Elk—special days between mid-September and November in designated areas. Moose—special days between mid-September and mid-October. BAG LIMIT: Antelope—1 every 3 years. Buffalo—1. Deer—2 or 3 according to license and permits. Elk—1 every 4 years. Moose—1.

Furbearing animals: Beaver, Marten (Sable), Mink, Otter. OPEN SEASON set annually by the Fish and Game Commission.** FULLY PROTECTED: Mountain Goat, Mountain Sheep—no open seasons. NOT PROTECTED: Bobcat, Coyote, Fox, Mountain Lion, Prairie Dog, Muskrat, Porcupine, Rabbits, Raccoon, Skunk, Weasel, and Woodchuck may be taken at any time. Bears are not protected, but killing is discouraged because they are not plentiful.

Game birds: Mourning Dove, Ducks (except Canvasback and Redhead), Geese, Grouse, Chukar and Hungarian Partridge, Pheasant, Quail, Whistling Swan. OPEN SEASONS:** Dove—September. Ducks, Geese—early October to January. Grouse—September. Partridge—September to November. Pheasant—November. Quail—November–December. Whistling Swan—taken on permit basis by lottery system and public drawing; applications must be made in person at offices of the State Department of Fish and Game during September. FULLY PROTECTED: Canvasback and Redhead Ducks—no open season. NOT PROTECTED: Crow, Prairie Falcon, Goshawk, Cooper's Hawk, Sharp-shinned Hawk, Magpie, Raven, and Starling may be killed at any time.

FIREARMS

Deer hunters must use rifles of .23 caliber or larger, and shells at least 2 inches long. The use of pistols, revolvers, shotguns, rimfire car-

---

* Each successive day, $1.00 up to period in excess of 10 days.
** Check current state regulations.

tridges, or nonexpanding type bullets to hunt Deer is prohibited. Deer may not be hunted with crossbows, and longbows must have a minimum pull of 40 pounds. The archer should be capable of shooting an arrow at least 130 yards, and the arrowhead must have 2 or more sharp cutting edges making a broadhead not less than seven-eighths of an inch in width. It is unlawful for an archer to have any firearms in his possession during an archery hunt. Unless accompanied by a parent or guardian, any person under the age of 14 years who carries, or has in his possession, any pistol, gun, target gun, or other firearms is considered to be a delinquent juvenile.

Shooting hours: Deer—during daylight hours. Other game—sunrise to sunset; except that on the opening day of Duck season shooting starts at 12:00 o'clock noon.

FISHING

Game fish: Black Bass, White Bass, Catfish, Bonneville Cisco, Grayling, Walleyed Pike, Salmon, Trout, Whitefish. OPEN SEASONS:* General fishing opens on the Saturday nearest June 1 and closes November 30, and some waters are open all year.

A sport fisherman may use a single line attached to a pole or rod, with not more than 2 baited hooks or 2 artificial flies. Not more than 3 gangs of hooks are permitted on mechanical lures, and multiple prongs attached to a single shaft are defined as one hook. Anglers must remain within 10 feet of their equipment at all times. Trolling is permitted, but chumming and snagging are prohibited. Setlines with not more than 50 hooks in the aggregate may be used day or night by one fisherman in the Bear River downstream from the Idaho border, in the Little Bear River below Highway 69, and in Colorado, Green, Malad, and San Juan rivers and Utah Lake. Setlines do not have to be closely attended, but should be securely anchored at one end to a nonmoving object.

Bonneville Cisco may be taken with dip nets in Bear Lake Jan. 1–Feb. 15. Taking nongame fish for personal noncommercial use with a fyke, gill, hoop, trammel net, trawl net, or with chemicals, electrical devices, explosives, and firearms is prohibited.

Angling from boats, rafts, or other floating devices is permitted on the following waters: Indian Creek Reservoir, Middle Kents Lake, Minersville Reservoir, Otter Lake, Puffers Lake, Three Creek Reservoir—Beaver County; Cutler Reservoir, Hyrum Reservoir, Newton Reservoir, Pelican Ponds, Bear River downstream from Idaho State line, and Little Bear River downstream from Highway 69—Cache County; Scofield Reservoir —Carbon County; Green River and Spirit Lake—Daggett County; Borham Lake, Mirror Lake, Moon Lake, Red Creek Reservoir, and Scout

---

* Check current state regulations.

Lake—Duchesne County; Cleveland Reservoir, Miller's Flat Reservoir, and Green River—Emery County; Colorado River, Lower Bowns Reservoir, North Creek Reservoir, Panguitch Lake, Pine Lake, Posey Lake, Tropic Reservoir, Wide Hollow Reservoir—Garfield County; Colorado and Green Rivers—Grand County; New Castle Reservoir, Paragonah (Red Creek) Reservoir, Yankee Meadow Reservoir—Iron County; Yuba Reservoir—Juab County; Colorado River, Navajo Lake—Kane County; East Canyon Reservoir, Gunnison Bend Reservoir, and Diversion Dam north of Delta on Sevier River—Millard County; Otter Creek Reservoir, Piute Reservoir—Piute County; Bear Lake—Rich County; Jordan River —Salt Lake County; Colorado and San Juan rivers—San Juan County; Ferron Reservoir, Gooseberry Reservoir, Gunnison Reservoir, Huntington Reservoir, Miller's Flat Reservoir, None-Miles Reservoir, Palisades Lake, Forsythe Reservoir, Johnson Reservoir, Koosharem Reservoir, Rex Reservoir—Sevier County; Echo Reservoir, Hoops Lake, Rockport Lake, Trial Lake—Summit County; East Park Reservoir, Montez Creek Reservoir, Oakes Park Reservoir, Paradise Park Reservoir, Stanaker Reservoir, and Green River—Uintah County; Jordan River and Utah Lake—Utah County; Deer Creek Reservoir—Wasatch County; Bakers Reservoir, Kolob Reservoir, Lower and Upper Enterprise reservoirs, Lower and Upper Sand Cove reservoirs—Washington County; Blind Lake, Mill Meadow Reservoir, Colorado and Green rivers—Wayne County; Pineview Reservoir—Weber County.

STATE PARKS

Bear Lake (799 acres) north of Garden City—Rich County; *Green River* (53 acres) at Green River City—Emery County; *Hyrum Lake* (3.22 acres) at Hyrum Reservoir (480 acres)—Cache County; *Rockport Lake* (lake 1,100 acres) on Weber River, south of Hoytsville—Summit County.

Migratory game bird hunting is excellent on the Great Salt Lake marshes, and there are special shooting sites.

WATERFOWL MANAGEMENT AREAS

Farmington Bay near Salt Lake City; *Howard Slough* and *Ogden Bay* west of Ogden; *Public Shooting Grounds* west of Corinne; *Salt Creek* near Penrose; *Locomotive Springs* south of Snowville; *Temple Springs* near Temple.

Licenses, permits, regulations, and information about current seasons, bag and possession limits may be obtained from the Director, Utah Department of Fish and Game, 1596 West North Temple, Salt Lake City

16. Regional offices: Northern Regional Office, 3930 Washington Boule vard, Ogden; Southern Regional Office, 622 North Main St., Cedar City; Eastern Regional Office, 513 East Main St., Price; Central Regional Office, 176 East Center St., Provo. No special permits (except archery) are mailed from Salt Lake City, but they may be obtained from regional offices by mail, and from license vendors throughout the state upon personal application. The interesting *Utah Fish and Game* magazine published 6 times annually ($1 per year) may be obtained at the Salt Lake City office.

VERMONT

Area: 9,564 square miles (land area—9,276 square miles); rank in nation —43
Bird: Hermit Thrush (*Hylocichla gutta pallasi*)
Capital city: Montpelier on the Winooski River in Washington County; population (1960)—8,782; rank in state–5
Counties: 14
Elevations: Highest, Mount Mansfield (4,393 ft.) in Lamoille County; lowest, Lake Champlain (95 ft.) in Franklin County
Flower: Red Clover (*Trifolium pratense*), adopted 1894
Geographic center: 3 miles east of Roxbury, Washington County
Nicknames: Green Mountain State, Maple Syrup State
Population (1960): 389,881; rank in nation–47
Tree: Sugar Maple (*Acer saccharum*), adopted 1949

Vermont is a New England state with the Connecticut River, from Massachusetts on the south, marking the entire New Hampshire boundary on the east to Beecher Falls; and New York on the west is partially separated by the Poultney River and Lake Champlain (360 square miles) extending into the Canadian province of Quebec on the north.

The Green Mountains dominate the state from Canada to Massachusetts, and Mount Mansfield rising above all others is also noted for projections named the Adams Apple, the Chin, the Lips, the Nose, and the Forehead, suggesting the profile of a face. Other high summits include the Camel's Hump (4,083 ft.) near North Duxbury, Cuffs Peak (4,085 ft.) and Mount Ellen (4,135 ft.) northwest of Warren, Killington Mountain (4,241 ft.) near West Bridgewater, Mount Abraham (4,052 ft.) and Lincoln Peak (4,013 ft.) near Lincoln. In southwestern Vermont, Mount Equinox (3,816 ft.), west of Manchester, is the highest summit in the Taconic Range extending from Massachusetts and New York.

Vermont's claim to the Connecticut River is only to the low water mark on the western bank. Streams flowing into the Connecticut River include the West River at Brattleboro, Saxtons River at Bellows Falls, Williams River south of Springfield, White River at White River Junction, Wells River at Wells River, Ompompanoosuc River at Pompanoosuc, Passumpsic River at Barnet, and Nulhegan River at Bloomfield. The Batten Kill River flows from the Taconic Mountains into New York southwest of Manchester. The largest streams draining into Lake Champlain are the Missisquoi River to Swanton and north to Missisquoi Bay on the Canadian boundary; the Lamoille River running westward to Milton and the Sand Bar Bridge area; and the Winooski River flowing through Montpelier, Waterbury, and Winooski. At Newport in northern Vermont, the swift Barton, Black, and Clyde rivers flow into Lake Memphremagog (30 miles long) on the Canadian boundary. On the northern end of lovely Lake Champlain, framed by the Green Mountains of Vermont and the New York Adirondacks, are Grand Island, North Hero Island, Isle La Motte, Butler Island, Savage Island, and the Albury Peninsula on the Canadian border within the county of Grand Isle.

There are numerous natural and man-made lakes, and among the largest are Lake Bomoseen (3.69 sq. miles) south of Hubbardton; the Somerset Reservoir on East Branch Deerfield River near Stratton; Whitingham Reservoir on North Branch Deerfield River north of Chittenden; Townshend Lake on West River; Great and Little Averill lakes, and Norton Pond on the Coaticook River near Averill and Norton in northeastern Vermont; Willoughby Lake near Westmore; Lake Salem and Seymour Lake near East and West Charleston; and Moore Reservoir between Gilman and Lower Waterford.

The Long Trail maintained by the Green Mountain Club follows crests of the Green Mountains for 255 miles. Hikers cross the Massachusetts line at Bennington County to reach Killington Mountain, and at Pico Peak (3,967 ft.), the Appalachian Trail turns eastward to New Hampshire, but the Vermont Long Trail continues northward through the Presidential Mountains—Mount Wilson (3,756 ft.), Mount Roosevelt (3,440 ft.), Mount Grant (3,661 ft.), Mount Cleveland (3,500 ft.), and Jay Peak (3,861 ft.) to enter Canada near North Troy.

LICENSES

Resident licenses are issued to any person who has lived in Vermont for at least 6 months immediately preceding the date of an application for a license, providing that he has not claimed legal residence in another state during that period. A nonresident who pays taxes on Vermont real estate appraised at not less than $3,000 may procure resident licenses, but the spouse and minor children are entitled only to resident fishing licenses. Any member of the U.S. Armed Forces officially stationed on active duty within the state is entitled to purchase resident fishing and hunting licenses, if he obtains from a commanding officer (or designated agent) of his military, air, or naval base a certificate proving his eligibility, and presents it with his application for a license to the local town clerk. A nonresident college student currently enrolled in an educational institution at which he has completed two or more successive semesters within the state may also obtain resident fishing and hunting licenses upon presentation of his admission card to the local city or town clerk.

Any owner or tenant of agricultural lands, and his spouse and minor children residing on and engaged in farming such lands may fish, hunt, and trap on their lands without licenses. All other persons 15 or more years of age must possess licenses to fish, and a hunting license may be obtained by a juvenile under the age of 16 only if the consent of his parent or guardian is written in the presence of the clerk issuing the license. A regular license to hunt is required in addition to a bow and arrow license for taking Deer during the special archery season.

Fish may not be taken beyond the ordinary low water mark on the Vermont side of the Connecticut River by holders of Vermont nonresident fishing licenses. Persons possessing Vermont or New Hampshire resident licenses may take fish anywhere in the Connecticut River. A fishing or combination fishing and hunting license is required to take rough fish by spearing or with bow and arrow. All persons 16 or more years of age must purchase a federal "Duck" stamp to take migratory game birds.

Resident license fees: Fishing, $1.75; hunting, $2.25; combination fishing and hunting, $3.50; bow and arrow hunting (in addition to hunting license), $1.00; trapping, $1.75; fur buyer, $2.00; federal "Duck" stamp, $3.00; Beaver tag (per pelt), $1.00.

Nonresident license fees: Annual fishing, $6.25; fishing 14 consecutive days, $4.25; fishing 3 consecutive days, $2.25; hunting, $22.00; combination hunting and fishing, $26.00; bow and arrow hunting (in addition to hunting license), $3.50; trapping, $50.00; fur buyer, $10.00; federal "Duck" stamp, $3.00; Beaver tag (per pelt), $1.00.

HUNTING AND TRAPPING

Game animals: Black Bear, Caribou, White-tailed Deer, Elk, Moose, Cottontail Rabbit, Snowshoe Rabbit, Gray Squirrel. OPEN SEASON:* Black Bear—Sept. 1–Nov. 30. Deer—archery, from second Saturday in October for 16 days; regular (guns, bows and arrows), from second Saturday in November for 16 days. Rabbits—Oct. 1–Feb. 28. Gray Squirrel—October. BAG LIMITS: Black Bear—no limit. Deer—1 per year. Rabbits—3 per day. Squirrels—4 per day.

---

* Check current state regulations.

Only Buck Deer may be taken during the regular season, and the antlers of a legal Buck Deer must be 3 or more inches in length.

Furbearing animals: Beaver, Bobcat, Fisher, Fox, Marten, Mink, Muskrat, Otter, Raccoon, Skunk, Weasel. OPEN TRAPPING SEASONS: Beaver —regulated annually by the fish and game department. Fox, Mink, Otter, Skunk—late October to mid-February, Muskrat—late October to mid-April. Raccoon—late October to December 31. OPEN SHOOTING SEASONS:* Fox—dog and gun, Oct. 1–Feb. 15; without dogs, all year. Muskrat— 10 days in April. Raccoon—Aug. 1–Dec. 31. BAG LIMITS: Raccoon— 25 by shooting and 25 by trapping each season. Other furbearers —no limits. FULLY PROTECTED: Caribou, Elk, Fisher, Marten, Moose— no open seasons. NOT PROTECTED: Bobcat, Porcupine, Red Squirrels, Weasel, and Woodchuck may be killed at any time.

Game birds: Brant, Coot, Ducks (except Canvasback and Red-head), Gallinule, Geese (except Snow Geese), Merganser, Partridge, Pheasant, Rails, Sora, Wilson's Snipe, Wild Turkey, Woodcock. OPEN SEASONS: Brant, Coot, Ducks, Geese, Merganser—mid-October for about 2 weeks, and mid-November to mid-December. Gallinule, Rails, Sora —September 1 to early November. Partridge—October. Pheasant, Wild Turkey—first 2 weeks in October. Wilson's Snipe, Woodcock—October 1 to mid-November. FULLY PROTECTED: Dove, Canvasback and Redhead Ducks, Snow Geese—no open seasons. NOT PROTECTED: Crow, Purple Grackle, Kingfisher, English Sparrow, and Starling may be taken at any time.

FIREARMS

It is unlawful to carry or have in possession any kind of autoloading rifle with a magazine capacity of more than 6 cartridges, except a .22 caliber rifle using rimfire ammunition when hunting wild animals. Deer may be taken with a gun fired at arm's length or by use of bow and arrow, and the arrowhead should be at least seven-eighths of an inch at the widest point, and have not less than 2 sharp cutting edges without barbs. Migratory game birds may not be hunted with a shotgun larger than 10 gauge or capable of holding more than 3 shells in the magazine and chamber combined. The possession of crossbows or firearms during the special bow and arrow Deer hunting season is prohibited.

Shooting hours: Sunrise to sunset, except Deer, 6:00 A.M.–5:00 P.M.; shooting starts on the opening day of the Duck season at 12:00 o'clock noon. Bear, furbearers, and Raccoon may be hunted day and night during open seasons.

---

* Check current state regulations.

FISHING

Game fish: Black Bass, Muskellunge, Pickerel, Walleyed Pike (Pike-perch), Northern Pike, Salmon, Smelt, Trout (Brook, Brown, Lake, Rain-bow). OPEN SEASONS* (local exceptions): Black Bass—second Saturday in June to November 30. Muskellunge, Pickerel, Pike-perch, Northern Pike, Walleyed Pike—last Saturday in April to March 15. Salmon and all species of Trout—last Saturday in April to September 30. Smelt—last Saturday in May to March 15.

A sport fisherman may catch fish with a baited hook on a line held in his hands or attached to a hand rod, and by 2 such hooks and lines from a boat, and by casting or trolling not more than 3 artificial flies, or one plug, lure, or spoon, with or without bait. It is unlawful to use a spear gun, or any fyke, gill, set or trap nets, seines, snares, set lines, electrical, or other devices unless regulations specifically provide otherwise.

Muskellunge, Pickerel, Northern and Walleyed Pike, Perch, Smelt, and nongame fish may be taken through ice with not more than 2 lines with a single hook on each line, or with bobs and tip-ups. On Lake Champlain, 15 lines, tip-ups, or bobs may be used, and all ice fishermen should check their lines at least once every hour.

Shooting Pickerel in Lake Champlain March 15–May 15 is permitted by the holder of a hunting license. Bowfin, Carp, Garfish, Mullet, and Suckers may be speared in Lake Champlain (not including tributaries) April 1–June 15.

Many anglers consider the Batten Kill River the best Brown Trout stream in New England, and there are several outstanding Trout streams including the Nulhegan, West, and White rivers. Fishing and waterfowl hunting are particularly popular on Lake Champlain, and there are over 400 lakes and ponds throughout the state. The Green Mountain Horse Association at South Woodstock annually sponsors the 100-mile Trail Ride held in August. The average snowfall reaches 120 inches annually, and there are numerous winter sports areas including 30 major well-equipped ski resorts. Several state forests and parks are enjoyed summer and winter.

STATE FORESTS

Calvin Coolidge (10,035 acres, several segments) near the Calvin Coolidge birthplace at Plymouth, and near other areas, contains Killington Mountain (4,241 ft.) and Smith Peak (3,230 ft.) near West Bridge-water—Rutland and Windsor counties; *Camel's Hump* (7,778 acres) southwest of Waterbury—Chittenden and Washington counties; *Grafton*

---

* Check current state regulations.

(240 acres) near Grafton on Saxons River—Windham County; *Groton* (15,300 acres) contains Lake Groton and several ponds on the Wells River, northwest of Groton—Caledonia and Washington counties; *Jay Peak* west of Jay—Orleans County; *Maidstone* (450 acres) at Maidstone Lake, south of Bloomfield—Essex County; *Mount Mansfield* (20,944 acres, 2 segments) contains Big Spring, Bingham Falls, Mount Mansfield, Horse Mountain (3,468 ft.), Spruce Peak (3,300 ft.), White Face Mountain (3,715 ft.), and Smugglers Notch northwest of Stowe, and Bolton Mountain (3,725 ft.), Ricker Mountain (3,401 ft.), and Waterbury Dam on Little River north of Waterbury and west of Moscow— Chittenden, Lamoille, and Washington counties; *Proctor-Piper* (1,487 acres) near Proctorsville—Windsor County; *Okemo* (4,461 ft.) contains Okemo Mountain (3,372 ft.) west of Ludlow—Rutland and Windsor counties; *Thetford Hill* (260 acres) north of Union Village—Orange County; *Townshend* (700 acres) contains Bald Mountain (1,690 ft.) west of Townshend—Windham County; *Victory* contains Burke Mountain (3,267 ft.) east of Lyndonville—Caledonia and Essex counties.

STATE PARKS

Allis (470 acres) at Brookfield—Orange County; *Ascutney* (1,530 acres) contains Ascutney Mountain (3,144 ft.) north of Ascutney— Windsor County; *Bomoseen* (300 acres) at Lake Bomoseen, north of Castleton Corners—Rutland County; *Branbury* (98 acres) at Lake Dunmore, east of Salisbury—Addison County; *Brighton* at Island Pond on the Clyde River, at Island Pond village—Essex County; *Crystal Lake* (15 acres) at Barton—Orleans County; *D.A.R.* (120 acres) on Lake Champlain, north of Chimney Point Bridge—Addison County; *Darling* (1,725 acres) east of Lydonville—Essex County; *Elmore* (427 acres) southeast of Morrisville—Lamoille County; *Emerald Lake* (462 acres) at North Dorset near Netop Mountain (3,020 ft.)—Bennington County; *Grand Isle* (222 acres) near South Hero, on Lake Champlain—Grand Isle County; *Granville* (1,060 acres) north of Granville—Addison County; *Lake Carni* (499 acres) near West Berkshire—Franklin County; *Molly Stark* (148 acres) southeast of Wilmington—Windham County; *Monroe* (200 acres), a bird sanctuary at Camel's Hump State Forest; *Mount Philo* (160 acres) near Lake Champlain, southeast of Charlotte—Chittenden County; *St. Albans Bay* (45 acres) on Lake Champlain, west of St. Alabans—Franklin County; *St. Catherine* (16 acres) at Lake St. Catherine between Poultney and Wells—Rutland County; *Sandbar* (10 acres) on Lake Champlain at Sandbar Bridge to Grand Isle—Chittenden County; *Wilgus* (125 acres) on the Connecticut River—Windsor County.

Licenses may be purchased at the office of any city clerk or town clerk; and regulations, information about current seasons, bag and possession limits are issued by the Commissioner, Vermont Fish and Game Department, State Office Building, Montpelier. Town clerks and local chambers of commerce can also supply information about guides and accommodations, and the Vermont Department of Forests and Parks at Montpelier issues lists of state camp sites. A detailed guide to the Long Trail is available for $1.00 from the Green Mountain Club at Woodstock. Vermont information centers are at 1268 Avenue of the Americas, New York 20, N.Y.; the Laurentian Hotel, Montreal, Province of Quebec, Canada; and the New England Vacation Center, 2051 East 14th St., Cleveland, Ohio. The attractive *Vermont Life* magazine, issued quarterly, and published at Montpelier, is $1.85 a year.

VIRGINIA

Area: 42,627 square miles (land area—39,838 square miles); rank in nation—37
Bird: Cardinal (*Richmondena cardinalis*)
Capital city: Richmond, along the James River and adjacent to but not part of any county; population (1960)—219,958; rank in State—2
Counties: 98
Elevations: Highest, Mount Rogers (5,719 ft.) in Grayson and Smyth counties; lowest, Atlantic Ocean
Flower and Tree: Dogwood (*Cornus florida*), adopted 1918
Geographic center: 11 miles southeast of Amherst, Appomattox County
Nicknames: The Old Dominion, Cavalier State
Population: (1960): 3,966,949; rank in nation—14
Tidal shoreline: 3,315 miles (including islands, bays, and streams to a point where tidal waters narrow to 100 ft.)

Virginia on Chesapeake Bay and Atlantic Ocean is separated from the District of Columbia and Maryland on the northeast by the Potomac River. North Carolina and Tennessee are on the southern boundary, Kentucky on the southwest, and West Virginia on the west and northern borders.

The level coastal plain known as Tidewater Virginia is unevenly edged with large and small bays, inlets, marshes and islands. On the Eastern Shore, Accomack and Northampton counties on the lower Delmarva Peninsula are separated by Chesapeake Bay from the remainder of the state except by a bridge and tunnel connecting Cape Charles with the Hampton Roads area. The waters of landlocked Back Bay (25,000 acres), in Princess Anne County, flow into Currituck Sound at the head of the North Carolina outer banks. Canals from Norfolk and Portsmouth on

Hampton Roads provide waterways through the Great Dismal Swamp (750 square miles) to Albemarle Sound in North Carolina.

The rolling Piedmont Plateau west of the fall line varies in elevation from 150 to 300 feet on the east and 700 to 1,200 feet in the west. The Blue Ridge Mountains rising above 5,000 feet in the southwest—Mount Rogers (5,719 ft.) and White Top Mountain (5,520 ft.), the Great Valley of Virginia—and the Allegheny Mountains dominate the parallel ridges, ravines, and valleys of the Appalachian System in western Virginia. The Cumberland Gap National Historical Park (20,193 acres) in the southwest tip of Lee County is shared by Kentucky, Tennessee, and Virginia. The Shenandoah River flows northward between highlands to the Potomac River; and the Clinch and Holston rivers run through south-western Virginia into Tennessee. The James River, formed by such swift mountain streams as the Jackson, Calfpasture, and Cowpasture rivers among western mountains, follows an erratic course to Richmond; and joined, by the Appomattox River at Hopewell and the Chickahominy River at Glasshouse Point, the James passes Newport News, Portsmouth, and Norfolk to empty into Chesapeake Bay and the Atlantic Ocean.

The Rappahannock River from the Blue Ridge flows between Fauquier and Rappahannock counties, and joined by the Rapidan west of Falmouth, it reaches Chesapeake Bay between Lancaster and Middlesex counties. The Mattaponi River from Spottsylvania County and the Pamunkey River on the southern border of King William County unite near West Point to continue as the York River to Chesapeake Bay. The Meherrin, Nottoway, and Blackwater rivers of southeastern Virginia are tributaries of the Chowan River in North Carolina. The Dam River, Staunton River, and Roanoke River are tributaries of Buggs Island Lake (48,900 acres) impounded by the John H. Kerr Dam in Mecklenburg County at the North Carolina border. South Holston Lake (7,500 acres), extending into Tennessee, is south of Abingdon in Washington County. The New River was impounded south of Radford to form Claytor Lake (4,485 acres), and Philpott Reservoir near Bassett covers 3,370 acres.

The scenic Skyline Drive from Front Royal in northern Virginia traverses the Blue Ridge through the Shenandoah National Park (212,303 acres), and continues as the Blue Ridge Parkway through the George Washington National Forest to North Carolina south of Galax.

LICENSES

Resident licenses are issued to citizens who have physically lived in the state for at least 6 consecutive months immediately preceding the date of application for a license; and to alien owners of real property in Virginia who have lived in a county for 5 years immediately preceding an application for a license; and to members of the U.S. Armed Forces stationed on active duty; to legal voters; and to students enrolled in a bona fide educational institution in Virginia. Any member of the U.S. Armed Forces on active duty may purchase resident licenses to fish, hunt, or trap on his military reservation, but only when authorized by the commanding officer of the reservation. All persons are required to purchase national forest stamps to fish, hunt, or trap in national forests. All persons 16 or more years of age must purchase a federal "Duck" stamp to take migratory game birds.

Juveniles under the age of 16 and adults 70 or more years of age may fish without licenses. A landowner, spouse, and children, or tenants residing on the property and with the written permission of the owner, may fish, hunt, or trap on the landowner's property without licenses. Guests may fish without licenses in private ponds owned by individuals, but licenses are required to hunt or trap on lands owned by clubs or corporations. No license is required for residents under the age of 16 to trap, and Rabbits may be taken with box traps only on private property without a license, if permission to do so is granted by the landowner.

Land or water blinds used to shoot at waterfowl on or over public waters must be licensed, except on or along the shores of the James River above tidewater; and in Princess Anne County outside of Back Bay, its tributaries, and North Landing River; and in the counties of Accomack, Northampton, and York. Owners of riparian rights, their lessees and permittees have the exclusive privilege of licensing and erecting blinds on their shorelines and the prior right of erecting and licensing blinds in public waters in front of their shorelines. Riparian owners, their lessees or permittees may obtain licenses July 1–Aug. 31. Licenses for floating blinds are limited to one mat blind and one other floating blind per season to a single applicant, and such licenses may be purchased July 1–Oct. 31. Holders of blind licenses may renew their privileges annually, and the exclusive privileges given owners and their lessees and permittees are recurrent each year even if such privileges were forfeited in the preceding year.

Floating blinds are prohibited in Essex and Richmond counties in the public marshes and other waters flowing into the Rappahannock River, or in Green Bay and Port Tobaggo Bay in the Rappahannock River. No floating or stationary blinds are permitted in Red Wing Lake and Tucumseh Lake waters in Princess Anne County, or in waters adjacent to the Free School and Michael Marshes near the town of Saxis in Accomack County which make up the posted boundaries of the Saxis Wildlife Management Area. Any boat or other floating devices used to hunt waterfowl in the tidal portion of the Potomac River and its tidal tributaries under the jurisdiction of Virginia must be licensed and used according to regulations for such blinds.

Special stamps purchased from the county clerks are required to hunt Bear and Deer in Bath, Bland, Botetourt, Craig, Grayson, Giles, Highland, Patrick, Rockbridge, Smyth, Tazewell, Warren, Washington, Wise, and Wythe counties. Other counties are authorized to require Bear and Deer hunting stamps, and hunters should inquire about them.

State fishing licenses and permits legally obtained from representatives of the Virginia Commission of Game and Inland Fisheries or the North Carolina Wildlife Resources Commission permit anglers to fish in waters lying east of the mouth of Hyco River on the Dan River arm of Kerr Reservoir and the mouth of Difficult Creek on the Staunton River arm of Kerr Reservoir to the Gaston Dam on the Roanoke River, including all tributary waters lying in either Virginia or North Carolina which are accessible by boat from the main bodies of the reservoirs, or from sub-impoundments lying within this area. The nonresident Kerr Reservoir 3-day license is good only in the waters of Kerr Reservoir.

Resident license fees: Fishing and hunting in city or county of residence, $3.50; statewide fishing, $3.50; statewide fishing 3 consecutive days in waters not stocked with Trout, $1.50; fishing for Trout in designated waters (in addition to regular fishing license), $1.00; fishing 3 consecutive days for Trout in Shenandoah National Park (not required if holding state or county license), $3.00; county dip net to take Herring, Mullet, Shad, $1.00; seine for taking nongame fish for personal use, $2.50; stamp to fish, hunt or trap in national forests, $1.00; gill or fyke net to take nongame fish in Princess Anne and Southampton counties, $1.00; to erect a stationary shore blind, $5.00; to erect a stationary water blind, $5.00; to use a floating blind, $10.00; Duck blind stamp in Accomack or North-ampton counties, $5.00; floating blind in Princess Anne County, $15.00; stationary water blind, $15.00; stationary shore blind, $25.00; federal "Duck" stamp, $3.00; statewide hunting Bear, Deer, and Wild Turkey (in addition to regular hunting license), $1.00; special county stamp to hunt Bear and Deer, $1.00; statewide trapping, $7.50; trapping in county of residence, $3.00; state forest permit to hunt and/or trap (in addition to regular hunting license), $1.00.

Nonresident license fees: Statewide fishing, $10.00; fishing 3 consecutive days in Kerr Reservoir, $1.00; statewide fishing in waters not stocked with Trout, $1.50; fishing for Trout in designated waters (in addition to regular fishing license), $5.00; fishing 3 consecutive days for Trout in Shenandoah National Park (not required if holding statewide license), $3.00; county dip net to take Herring, Mullet, Shad, $1.00; stamp to fish, hunt, or trap in national forests, $1.00; federal "Duck" stamp, $3.00; statewide hunting, $15.75; statewide hunting Bear, Deer, and Wild Turkey (in addition to regular hunting license), $5.00; statewide trapping, $50.00; state Forest permit to hunt and/or trap (in addition to regular hunting license), $1.00; hunting on shooting preserves only (obtain in each county), $3.00; special stamp to hunt Bear and Deer in Bath, Bland, Botetourt, Craig, Giles, Highland, Patrick, Rockbridge, Tazewell, Warren, Washington, or Wise counties, $1.00; special stamp to hunt Bear and Deer in Grayson, Smyth, or Wythe counties, $5.00.

HUNTING AND TRAPPING

Game animals: Bear, White-tailed Deer, Elk, Fox, Rabbit, Squirrel. OPEN SEASONS:* Bear—firearms, Oct. 1–Nov. 30 in Dismal Swamp; mid-November to January statewide, except in designated areas, season open one or two weeks earlier. Bear, Deer, and Squirrel—archery, Oct. 15–Nov. 15, Deer—firearms, Oct. 1–Nov. 30 in Dismal Swamp; mid-November to mid-January in designated areas. Fox—firearms, Oct. 1–March 31 in Rockingham County, shorter seasons in other counties, and no closed season (except during Deer season) in Richmond and Rockbridge counties; no open season in 12 counties; Fox may be taken by dogs only all year in Amelia County; April 1–Sept. 1 and Oct. 12–Jan. 31 in Newport News City; Sept. 1–March 1 (except during Deer season) in counties of Clarke, Fairfax, Fauquier, Loudoun, and Rappahannock. Rabbit—mid-November to mid-January in Accomack and Northampton counties; mid-November to January 31 in Lunenburg County and west of the Blue Ridge; mid-November to mid-February in all other counties east of the Blue Ridge. Rabbits may also be taken with box traps Oct. 15–Jan. 31. Squirrel—Sept. 1–Feb. 15 including shorter seasons in designated areas. BAG LIMITS: Bear—1 (over 75 pounds live weight) per year. Deer—1 or 2 (in designated areas) per year. Fox, Squirrel—no limits. Rabbits —6 per day; 75 per year.

Furbearing animals: Beaver, Fox, Mink, Muskrat, Opossum, Otter, Raccoon. OPEN TRAPPING SEASONS:* Beaver, Mink, Muskrat, Opossum, Otter—December 1 to mid March. Fox—Nov. 15–Jan. 31, except Albemarle County, Nov. 1–30; Nelson County, November 1 to mid-January; no closed season in Augusta, Buchanan, and Richmond counties. Trapping Fox is prohibited in Fauquier, Loudoun, and Rappahannock counties. Raccoon—December 1 to mid-March, except Essex County, Jan. 1–March 15; Accomack, Charles City, Gloucester, James City, Mathews, New Kent, Northampton, and York counties, Hampton, Newport News, and Virginia Beach cities, Oct. 1–Jan. 31. Trapping Raccoon is prohibited in 28 counties. Rabbit—Oct. 15–Jan. 31 by box trap only. FULLY PROTECTED: Elk—no open season. NOT PROTECTED: Bobcat, Skunk, Weasel, and Woodchuck may be killed at any time. Fox may be killed at any time (except Sunday) by owners or tenants on their lands.

---

* Check current state regulations.

Game birds: Brant, Coot, Dove, Ducks (except Canvasback and Redhead), Gallinule, Geese (except Snow Geese), Grouse, Jacksnipe, Merganser, Pheasant, Quail, Clapper Rail, Scaup, Sora, Wild Turkey, Woodcock. OPEN SEASONS:* Brant, Coot, Ducks, Geese, Merganser, Scaup —mid-November to early January. Dove—mid-September to November and mid-December to January. Gallinule, Rails, Sora—mid-September to late November. Grouse, Quail—mid-November to January 31 west of the Blue Ridge, and Accomack, Lunenburg, and Northampton counties; mid-November to mid-February in counties east of the Blue Ridge. Jacksnipe —mid-November to January. Wild Turkey—mid-November to January 31 in Pittsylvania County; shorter seasons in 41 counties; and no open seasons in remaining counties. A spring Turkey season may also be set annually. Woodcock—mid-November to early January. Shooting preserves—Oct. 1–March 31. FULLY PROTECTED: Pheasant hunting is prohibited except on licensed shooting preserves. Canvasback and Redhead Ducks and Snow Geese—no open seasons. NOT PROTECTED: Bluejays, Buzzards (Vultures), Crows, House or English Sparrows, and Starling may be taken at any time. A landowner or his agent may kill Hawks and Owls if necessary to protect his game birds or poultry.

FIREARMS

Shotguns not larger than 10 gauge and capable of holding only 3 shells in the magazine and chamber combined may be used to hunt all wild animals and birds. Any shotgun capable of holding more than 3 shells must be plugged with a one-piece metal or wooden filler which cannot be removed through the loading end. There are no restrictions on shot sizes, except that slugs may not be used in Goochland, King Williams, Louisa, Northumberland, Prince George, Prince William, and Richmond counties.

Rifles may not be used to take migratory game birds, and they must be .23 caliber or larger to hunt Bear and Deer. Rifles larger than .22 caliber are prohibited in the counties of Appomattox, Buckingham, Caroline (.22 long rifle maximum), Charles City, Cumberland, Goochland, Halifax, King and Queen, King George, Lancaster, Louisa, Northumberland (only rimfire .22 permissible), and Prince William. Hunting Deer with any rifle is prohibited in all the above counties, and also in Chesterfield, Essex, Hanover, Isle of Wight, King William, New Kent, Prince George, Richmond, Southampton, Surry, and Sussex counties. The use of a rifle to hunt Bear and Deer is not permitted in Chesapeake City and Nansemond County, except in that part of Dismal Swamp located at least 100 yards from any railroad or public highway. Any size rifle may

---

* Check current state regulations.

be used to kill Woodchucks in King George County during the general closed season for hunting game. Wild animals and birds may not be killed with pistols.

Archers hunting Bear and Deer must use a longbow capable of propelling an arrow 125 yards; and big game hunting arrows should have broadheads with blades at least seven-eighths of an inch wide.

Dogs may not be used to hunt Deer west of the Blue Ridge, or in designated areas east of the Blue Ridge.

The possession of any firearms is prohibited on the Blue Ridge Parkway, in the Colonial National Historical Park, Prince William Forest State Park, and the Shenandoah National Park. No hunting is permitted in Arlington County, or in a portion of Fairfax County, except that waterfowl may be hunted from shore blinds on the Potomac River. Waterfowl hunting is prohibited in Princess Anne County in the waters and from the shores of Crystal Lake, Linkhorn Bay, Broad Bay, Long Creek, and their tributaries. Hunting and trapping are not permitted on Hog Island in Surry County, and in all waters of the James River within a radius of 1,000 yards around that island, except that Bear, Deer, and Squirrel may be hunted during an archery season.

Shooting hours: Hunting on Sunday is prohibited. Game animals and upland game birds—one-half hour before sunrise to one-half hour after sunset. Migratory game birds—sunrise to sunset, except that on opening day of the Duck season, shooting does not start until 12:00 o'clock noon; Dove—12 noon to sunset daily. Fox, Mink, Opossum, and Raccoon may be hunted day or night.

FISHING

Game fish: Black Bass (Largemouth, Smallmouth), Rock Bass, Spotted Bass, Striped Bass, White Bass, Bluegill and other Sunfish, Crappie, Pickerel, Trout (Brook, Brown, Rainbow), Walleye. OPEN SEASONS:* Trout—first Saturday in April to October 15 in Shenandoah National Park; and extended to December 31 statewide, with local exceptions; the opening day does not start until noon. Continuous open season for all other fish; except that Sunday fishing in public waters is prohibited in the counties of Alleghany, Bath, Botetourt (except James River and Carvins Cove), Craig, Highland, Rockbridge, Surry (in Blackwater River and Cypress Swamp), and in Silver Lake in Rockingham County.

Game fish may be taken from inland waters by angling with one hook and line, or rod and reel held in the hand. A hand net may be used to land fish legally hooked in any waters. Set poles, or trotlines using any

---

* Check current state regulations.

bait except live bait, may be used statewide to take nongame fish and turtles except in designated Trout waters. Nongame fish may be taken at any time by gigging, grabbling, snagging, snaring, or striking iron in all waters, except public impoundments and those waters stocked by the Game and Inland Fisheries Commission in the counties of Amelia, Appomattox, Brunswick, Campbell, Charlotte, Cumberland, Dinwiddie, Greensville, Halifax, Louisa, Lunenburg, Mecklenburg, Nottaway, Pittsylvania, and Prince Edward.

Nongame fish may be taken with gig and grabhook during the daytime April 1–May 15 and Oct. 1– Nov. 30 in the counties of Buchanan (except Dismal River), Grayson (in New River), Lee (in Powells River), Russell (in Clinch River), Scott (in Clinch and Holston rivers and tributaries), and Washington (in 3 forks of the Holston River). Licensed fishermen may use a long bow and arrow to take Carp and Gar in all public waters (except designated Trout waters) March 1–Oct. 31 during daylight hours. Carp, Redhorse, and Suckers may be shot with a rifle during daylight hours April 15–May 31 in the shoals of the Clinch River waters within Scott County (except within 200 yeards of Speers Ferry Dam) and in the South Fork Holston River in Washington County. Mullet and other Suckers may be taken with dip nets Feb. 1–April 30, except in Rockbridge County, Jan. 1–Feb. 28. Shad season—October 16 to late May statewide, except that in the Nottoway River, the season is extended to June 30.

Lake Drummond (5,000 acres) and surrounding Dismal Swamp have proven to be a paradise for fishermen, hunters, and naturalists. The waters of Chesapeake Bay and the ocean side of the Eastern Shore provide superlative fishing and waterfowl hunting, and throughout the state are countless lakes and streams stocked with Bass, Trout, and other game fish. The Virginia Salt Water Fishing Tournament is held annually at Virginia Beach from May 1 to November 1. The Commission of Game and Inland Fisheries has developed wildlife management areas for hunting and fishing in Piedmont and tidewater Virginia.

STATE FORESTS

Appomattox-Buckingham (19,282 acres) contains Holiday Lake (145 acres) and Horsepen Lake (20 acres) south of Mount Rush—Appomattox and Buckingham counties; *Cumberland* (16,016 acres) contains Bear Creek Lake (55 acres), Winston Lake (10 acres), and borders Willis River, north of Cumberland Court House—Cumberland County; *Prince Edward* (7,000 acres) contains Prince Edward Lake (37 acres) and Goodwin Lake (10 acres) north of Green Bay—Prince Edward County.

STATE PARKS

Claytor Lake (438 acres) at Claytor Lake (4,485 acres) near Dublin —Pulaski County; *Douthat* (4,493 acres, lake 60 acres) 9 miles east of Clifton Forge—Bath County; *Fairy Stone* (4,561 acres, lake 168 acres) north of Bassett—Patrick County; *Hungry Mother* (2,139 acres, lake 108 acres) 3 miles north of Marion; *Pocahontas* (7,605 acres) near Chesterfield Court House—Chesterfield County; *Staunton River* (712 acres) at Buggs Island Lake (Kerr Reservoir) 18 miles east of South Boston— Halifax County; *Westmoreland* (1,355 acres) on the Potomac River, north of Montrose—Westmoreland County.

WILDLIFE MANAGEMENT AREAS

Appomattox-Buckingham Forest (18,534 acres) southwest of Buckingham Court House, south of Route 24 near intersection Route 636; *Berry-Aylor* (500 acres) adjacent to Shenandoah National Park, near Criglersville; *Buggs Island Lake* (38,000 acres) near Clarksville—Charlotte, Halifax, and Mecklenburg counties; *Camp A. P. Hill* (77,000 acres) near Bowling Green—Caroline County; *Camp Picket* (47,000 acres) east of Blackstone—Brunswick, Dinwiddie, and Nottaway counties; *Chesapeake #1* (3,000 acres) near Bacon's Castle—Surry County; *Chesapeake #2* (2,645 acres) on Staunton River, south of Leesville—Bedford and Campbell counties; *Clinch Mountain* (18,500 acres) on Flat Top Mountain, 6 miles north of Saltville—Smyth County; *Cumberland Forest* (15,105 acres) north of Route 60 near Cumberland; *Fairystone Farms* (6,000 acres) near Philpott Reservoir—Patrick County; *Game Farm Marsh* (568 acres) near Virginia tree nursery—New Kent County; *Gathright* (18,500 acres) about 15 miles north of Covington on the Jackson River—Alleghany and Bath counties; *George Washington Forest* (957,- 000 acres) north of Lynchburg and the James River; *Goshen* (15,594 acres) south of Goshen—Rockbridge County; *Havens* (6,200 acres) on Fort Lewis Mountain, northwest of Salem; *Hidden Valley* (6,400 acres) on Brumley Mountain, 12 miles northwest of Abingdon; *Highland County* (17,700 acres) 5 miles southeast of Monterey, on Shenandoah, Bullpasture, and Jack mountains; *Hog Island* (2,100 acres) 6 miles northeast of Bacon's Castle—Surry County; *Jefferson Forest* (543,000 acres) near Marion, south of James River; *Kerr Reservoir* (see Buggs Island Lake); *Lee Forest* (2,500 acres) south of Buckingham Court House; *Lehigh-Portland* (6,100 acres) near Craigsville and extending into Rockbridge County; *Lester* (3,800 acres) adjacent to Martinsville Reservoir in Henry County; *Little North Mountain* (4,726 acres) north of Craigsville on Route 42; *Mockhorn Island* (9,110 acres) on ocean side of Eastern Shore in Northampton County and accessible by boat from Oyster; *Philpott*

(4,750 acres) at Philpott Lake near Basset—Franklin, Henry, and Patrick counties; *Prince Edward Forest* (6,365 acres) north of Green Bay—Prince Edward County; *Saxis* (4,630 acres) at town of Saxis and includes Freeschool Marsh (2,500 acres) and Michael's Marsh (1,130 acres)—Accomack County; *Seward Forest* (3,600 acres) in southern Brunswick County; *Smith Mountain* (2,684 acres) 9 miles southwest of Leesville on the Roanoke River; *Union-Bag Camp* (15,000 acres) in several small tracts near Edgarton in southeastern Brunswick County; *Ward-Rue* (8,400 acres) adjacent to Shenandoah National Park near Criglersville; *Wunder* (1,335 acres) 7 miles northwest of Broadway on the Sours Run, and adjoins the George Washington National Forest.

Licenses, permits, information about current seasons may be obtained from city corporation court clerks, county circuit court clerks, and other authorized agents of the Commission of Game and Inland Fisheries, P.O. Box 1642, Richmond. The *Virginia Wild Life* magazine published monthly at $1.50 per year offers valuable information to all sportsmen. Send subscription to the Commission of Game and Inland Fisheries, but make the check payable to the Treasurer of Virginia. Information and maps—Buggs Island Lake (Kerr Reservoir) U.S. Army Corps of Engineers, Wilmington District, P.O. Box 1890, Wilmington, N. C.; Philpott Reservoir: U.S. Army Corps of Engineers, Norfolk District, P.O. Box 119, Norfolk, Va.; South Holston Reservoir: Information Officer, Tennessee Valley Authority, Knoxville, Tenn. Virginia state parks and forest lakes are under the jurisdiction of the Department of Conservation and Economic Development. Official state highway map is issued by the Virginia Department of Highways, 1221 East Broad St., Richmond 19.

WASHINGTON

Area: 69,127 square miles (land area—66,709 square miles); rank in nation—20
Bird: Willow Goldfinch (*Astragalinus tristis salicamans*), adopted 1951
Capital city: Olympia on the Deschutes River in Thurston County; population (1960)—18,273; rank in state—13
Counties: 39
Elevations: Highest, Mount Rainier (14,408 ft.) in Pierce County; lowest, Pacific Ocean
Flower: Western Rhododendron (*Rhododendron macrophyllum*), adopted 1949
Geographic center: 10 miles south of west of Wenatchee, Chelan County

Nicknames: Chinook State, Evergreen State
Population (1960): 2,853,214; rank in nation–23
Tidal shoreline: 3,026 miles (including islands, bays, and streams to a point where tidal waters narrow to 100 ft.)
Tree: Western Hemlock (*Tsuga heterophylla*), adopted 1947

Washington on the Pacific Ocean is bordered by California on the south, Idaho on the east, and the province of British Columbia in Canada on the north with the Juan de Fuca archipelago on the northwest.

Juan de Fuca Strait and Haro Strait separate Canadian Vancouver Island from Washington's Puget Sound, which is filled with more than 170 evergreen habitable islands and sheltered harbors of all sizes and shapes. Hood Canal is a narrow fish-hook-shaped fiord projecting about 60 miles from Admiralty Inlet into the eastern shore of Olympic Peninsula. Seattle, on Elliott Bay, several hills and waterways, overlooks Puget Sound. Ocean vessels move from Shilshone Bay and are raised by the Chittendon Locks, and continue through Salmon Bay, Lake Washington Ship Canal, Lake Union and Portage Bay into Lake Washington in eastern Seattle. Fisherman's Terminal on Salmon Bay is the hub of a huge fishing industry and a dense sea of masts when the fleet is in port. Majestic Mount Rainier (14,408 ft.), glistening with active glaciers and the Paradise Glacier Ice Caves, rises above the summits of the snow-frosted Cascade Range which divides the busy seacoast from the broad treeless plains of the Inland Empire.

The Columbia.River, joined by the Pend Oreille from Idaho in the northeastern corner of the state, continues on a tortuous southwesterly course to be impounded several times before marking the Oregon boundary from Lake Wallula to the ocean at Pacific County. The Grand Coulee Dam created the F. D. Roosevelt Lake (132 square miles) reaching northward for about 150 miles, and the Equalizing Reservoir spreads southward to Coulee City near the spectacular Dry Falls. The spillway of Coulee Dam is floodlighted with a fantastic display of colors from May 30 to Labor Day annually. Lake Rufus Woods impounded by the Chief Joseph Dam near Bridgeport; Bonneville Dam noted for the ladders and weirs provided for Salmon on their way upstream to spawn; Lake Wallula south of Kennewick; Pasco formed by McNary Dam; and The Dalles are among the important dams harnessing the mighty Columbia River. Lovely Lake Chelan (55 miles long, 1,500 feet deep) is north of a series of valleys known as the Wenatchee Valley and "Apple Capital of the World." Yakima Valley between the Cascades and the Columbia River is called the "Fruitbowl of the Nation." The Spokane River flows into the Columbia at Miles, west of Spokane; and the Snake

River, veering from Idaho at Clarkston, joins the Columbia between Franklin and Walla Walla counties. Eastern Washington is also cattle country, and the fertile Palouse Hills are covered with wheat.

LICENSES

Resident licenses are issued to any citizen of the United States who has maintained a permanent place of abode within the state for at least 90 days immediately preceding an application for a license; and at any time to members of the U.S. Armed Forces stationed at military reservations in Washington. An alien who has not in good faith declared his intention to become a citizen of the United States must purchase nonresident licenses. Free fishing permits are issued to any blind person who is a bona fide resident in the state, and to any person 70 or more years of age who has lived in Washington for at least 10 years. Free hunting and fishing licenses may be obtained by residents who are veterans of the Spanish-American War, and by persons aged 65 years or more with service-connected disabilities who are honorably discharged veterans of the U.S. Armed Forces and have been residents of Washington for 5 or more years. Affidavit forms are available at all license dealers and at offices of the State Department of Game. Any person of Indian ancestry may hunt and fish without licenses on land originally ceded to his tribe under the Stevens Treaty, and is not required to possess tags to take Deer, Elk, and Mountain Goat, or permit cards. Treaty Indians may submit applications for controlled hunts within the boundaries of lands originally ceded by their tribes, and a letter sent to the State Game Department in Olympia, containing the applicant's name, address, tribal name, game management unit number, and county is considered an application for a controlled hunt. Nonresident and nontreaty Indians are not eligible for such privileges and must procure licenses to hunt and fish except on their own reservations. All other persons regardless of age must obtain licenses to hunt and trap. A trapping license is required to take Canada Lynx, Marten, Mink, Muskrat, and Otter.

A juvenile under the age of 18 must present an accredited firearm safety certificate in order to purchase a hunting license. All persons 16 or more years of age must possess a federal "Duck" stamp to take migratory game birds.

Application forms for controlled Deer and Elk hunts are attached to Deer and Elk cards. A partnership application form may be used by two persons desiring to hunt together. Any person entering his name on more than one Deer hunt application and one Elk hunt application will be eliminated from drawings. A Deer tag is issued free with the nonresident hunting license.

A juvenile under the age of 16 may fish without a license, but all persons fishing for Steelhead in any waters designated as "Steelhead Management Waters" must have in his possession a free Steelhead fishing permit. Immediately after catching a Steelhead, the fisherman should remove one punch from the card and enter the name of the water in which the Steelhead was taken and the date. A fishing license and a Steelhead punch card are also required to fish for sea-run Cutthroat, Dolly Varden, and Steelhead Trout throughout the year below the mouths of rivers emptying into Puget Sound, Hood Canal, Strait of Juan de Fuca, and all connecting bays, harbors, and sounds. No license is required to catch saltwater fish or dig clams for personal use along the Pacific Coast.

Resident license fees: Statewide fishing, $4.50; county fishing only, $3.00; statewide hunting, $4.50; statewide hunting and fishing, $8.00; county fishing and hunting, $4.25; trapping, $5.00; Deer tag (in addition to hunting license), $2.00; Elk tag (in addition to hunting license), $7.50; Mountain Goat tag (in addition to hunting license), $7.50; fishing guide, $10.00.

Nonresident license fees: Statewide fishing, $15.00; fishing 7 consecutive days, $4.00; hunting, $35.00; Elk tag (in addition to hunting license), $25.00; Mountain Goat tag (in addition to hunting license), $25.00; fishing guide, $100.00.

HUNTING AND TRAPPING

Game animals: Bear, Deer, Elk, Mountain Goat, Rabbits (Cottontail, Snowshoe). OPEN SEASONS:* Bear—archery, from September 1 for about 8 weeks in the Nason Creek Game Reserve (Chelan County) and about 3 weeks from mid-October into November on Long Island in Pacific County; firearms, in eastern Washington, early September to early November, except season opens August 1 outside national forests in King, Skagit, and Snohomish counties; and all year in Clallam, Clark, Cowlitz, Grays Harbor, Island, Jefferson, Kitsop, Klickitat (west of White Salmon River), Lewis (except in national forest and north of White Pass Highway), Mason, Pacific, San Juan, Skamania, Thurston, and Wahkiakum counties; western Washington, September 1 to mid-November including shorter seasons in several counties, plus a spring season March 1–April 30 in Asotin, Columbia, Ferry, Garfield, Pend Oreille, Spokane, Stevens, and Walla Walla counties. Deer—archery, early September to December 31 including shorter seasons in designated areas; firearms, about 2 weeks during September in special areas on the Cascade Range, and from mid-October to November 30 including various seasons of a few days up to 5 or 6 weeks in designated counties and game management areas. A special orchard season is generally established to pre-

---

* Check current state regulations.

vent damage by Deer to cultivated orchards, and all hunters who have not killed a Deer during other seasons may hunt Dec. 1–31 in designated areas. Elk—firearms (including bow and arrow), from mid-November to January 31 with open seasons varying from several days to the entire period in designated areas. Mountain Goat—about 2 weeks in mid-September by permit in 21 separate areas. Rabbits—early September to March 31 in western Washington, from mid-October through February in eastern Washington, and all year in Clark and Island counties; except that Rabbits may not be hunted with dogs April 1–July 31 or during the Deer season on Whitbey Island. ANNUAL BAG LIMITS: Bear—1 in eastern Washington and no limit in western Washington. Deer—1. Elk—1. Mountain Goat—1. Rabbits—5 per day (mixed or straight bag), and no limit in Clark, Island, Skagit, Snohomish, and Whatcom counties.

A legal Buck Deer and Bull Elk should have visible antlers described as "a bony growth with velvet shed that is visible above the hair." It is unlawful to kill cubs under 6 month of age, or female Bears with such cubs during the spring Bear season.

Furbearing animals: Badger, Beaver, Bobcat, Cougar, Fox, Fisher, Canada Lynx, Marten, Mink, Muskrat, Opossum, Otter, Raccoon, Skunk, Weasel, Wolverine. OPEN SEASONS:* Canada Lynx, Marten, Otter— Dec. 1–Jan. 31. Mink—mid-November to mid-January. Muskrat—mid-November to mid-March. FULLY PROTECTED: Beaver, Fisher—no open seasons. NOT PROTECTED: Badger, Bobcat, Cougar, Coyote, Fox, Gopher, Opossum, Porcupine, Raccoon, Skunk, Weasel, Wolverine.

Game birds: Brant, Coot, Dove (Mourning, White-winged), Ducks (except Canvasback and Redheads), Gallinule, Geese, Grouse (Blue, Franklin, Ruffed, Sage, Sharp-tailed), Merganser, Partridge (Chukar, Hungarian), Chinese Pheasant, Quail, Wilson's Snipe. OPEN SEASONS:* Brant—mid-November through January. Coot, Ducks, Gallinule, Geese, Merganser—mid-October to early January. Dove—Sept. 1–30. Blue, Franklin, and Ruffed Grouse—mid-September to mid-November, except shorter seasons in Asotin, Columbia, Garfield, and Walla Walla counties. Sage Grouse (Sage Hen)—about 1 week during October in Benton, Douglas, Grant, Kittitas, Lincoln, and Yakima counties. Sharp-tailed Grouse: about 1 week during October in Douglas, Lincoln, and Olanogan counties. Partridge, Pheasant, Quail—generally opens in mid-October, and closing dates are established annually. An early Partridge season may extend Sept. 15–30 in Asotin and Garfield counties and in portions of Columbia and Whitman counties. Wilson's Snipe—opens on first day of Duck season and continues for about 45 consecutive days. Grouse and

---

* Check current state regulations.

Rabbits may be taken by bow and arrow during an open season in the Nason Creek Game Reserve in Chelan County. FULLY PROTECTED: Canvasback and Redhead Ducks—no open seasons. NOT PROTECTED: Cormorants, Crows, Magpies, and Great Horned Owls may be killed at any time.

FIREARMS

An archer hunting Bear, Deer, and Mountain Goat must be equipped with a longbow which will cast a legal hunting arrow at least 120 yards; and the arrow should weigh not less than one ounce (437 grains) with single-bladed broadheads at least one inch in width, or multiple-bladed broadheads (3 blades or more) at least seven-eighths of an inch in width at the widest point of the blade. Elk hunters should use a longbow capable of casting a hunting arrow a minimum distance of 150 yards, and the Elk hunting arrow should weigh at least 500 grains, and have single or multiple broadheads of not less than one inch at the widest point of the blade.

It is unlawful to hunt Bear, Deer, Elk, and Mountain Goat with any weapon which fires the following loads: any and all rimfire cartridges; 218B, .25-20, .38-40, .32-20, .44-40, .22 Hornet, .30 U.S. Army carbine, .45 A.C.P. Deer may not be hunted with a shotgun containing any load other than buckshot or slugs. The use of a shotgun to hunt Elk, or any pistol, revolver, or fully automatic firearm to hunt Bear, Deer, Elk, and Mountain Goat is prohibited.

Game birds may be hunted with shotguns not larger than 10 gauge, and capable of holding only 3 cartridges in the magazine and chamber combined, but the use of pistols and rifles is prohibited except to take Blue, Franklin, and Ruffed Grouse.

It is unlawful for a juvenile under the age of 14 years to possess, handle, or have in his control any firearms for hunting, target practice, or other purposes, except while accompanied by, or under the immediate charge of, his parent or guardian.

Shooting hours: One-half hour before sunrise to sunset; except that on the opening day of the Duck season, shooting starts at 12:00 o'clock noon.

FISHING

Game fish: Bass, Bluegill, Catfish, Crappie, Perch, Salmon, Steelhead, Trout, Whitefish. OPEN SEASONS: The Columbia River and many major streams and lakes are open all year, but the general summer seasons open in mid-April or mid-May, and the Steelhead and Whitefish winter seasons start on December 1 or January 1. The detailed *Game Fish Seasons and Catch Limits* covering each county should be carefully checked before planning to fish.

An angler may take game fish only with one line or rod held in the hand and under his absolute control, and not more than 2 hooks or flies, or one plug with any number of hooks attached to the line. The use of live bait or artificial lights to take game fish is prohibited.

Bullfrogs: May be taken by angling, hand dip netting, spearing, or bow and arrow only in the waters and during the open season for taking game fish. DAILY BAG LIMIT: 10.

STATE PARKS

Alta Lake (176 acres) 2 miles northwest of Pateros—Okanogan County; *Bay View* (19 acres) west of Burlington—Skagit County; *Beacon Rock* (3,026 acres) between North Bonneville and Skamania—Clark County; *Birch Bay* (194 acres) on Strait of Georgia, 10 miles south of Blaine—Whatcom County; *Bogachiel* (123 acres) on Bogachiel River, south of Forks—Olallam County; *Blake Island* on Puget Sound, west of Seattle—Kitsap County; *Bridgeport* on Rufus Woods Lake at Bridgeport—Douglas County; *Brooks Memorial* (156 acres) at Satus Pass, 14 miles north of Goldendale—Klickitat County; *Bush Pacific Pioneer* (42 acres on Wallapa Bay) at South Bend—Pacific County; *Camano Island* (174 acres) northwest of Everett—Island County; *Conconully* (46 acres) at Conconully—Okanogan County; *Curlew Lake* (122 acres) in the Kettle River Range, northeast of Republic—Ferry County; *Deception Pass* (1,746 acres) on Whidbey Island, west of Mount Vernon—Island County; *Dosewallips* (500 acres) at the confluence of Dosewallips River and Hood Canal, near Brinnon on the Olympic Peninsula; *Fay Bainbridge* (16 acres) on the north end of Bainbridge Island west of Seattle on Puget Sound—Kitsap County; *Fields Spring* (253 acres) in the Blue Mountains south of Anatone—Asotin County; *Fort Casey* (110 acres) on Whidbey Island, 3 miles south of Coupville—Island County; *Fort Flagler* (700 acres) on Admiralty Inlet to Puget Sound, southeast of Port Townsend—Jefferson County; Illahee (70 acres) 3 miles north of Bremerton on Puget Sound—Kitsap County; *Kamiak Butte* (280 acres) southwest of Palouse—Whitman County; *Kitsap Memorial* (40 acres) on Hood Canal, southwest of Port Gamble—Kitsap County; *Kiopachuck* (84 acres) on Cook Inlet, west of Tacoma; *Lake Chelan* (140 acres) in the Wenatchee Range, west of Chelan—Chelan County; *Lake Cushman* (480 acres) northwest of Hoodsport on the Olympic Peninsula; *Lake Easton* (276 acres) northwest of Cle Elum on Yakima River in the Cascade Range—Kittitas County; *Lake Sammish* (253 acres) 2 miles north of Issaquah—King County; *Lake Sam-*

mish (253 acres) 2 miles north of Issaquah—King County; *Lake Sylvia* (234 acres) north of Montesano—Grays Harbor County; *Lake Wenatchee* (358 acres) on Wenatchee River, north of Cole—Chelan County; *Larrabee* (1,980 acres) at Samish Bay, north of Edison—Skagit County; *Leadbetter Point* between Willapa Bay and Pacific Ocean, north of Ocean Park—Pacific County; *Millerslyvania* (833 acres) 11 miles south of Olympia—Thurston County; *Moran* (4,804 acres) on Orcas Island southwest of Bellingham, (but access by ferry is from Anacortes on Whidbey Island)—San Juan County; *Moses Lake* (15 acres) 4 miles south of the town of Moses Lake—Grant County; *Mount Pilchuck* (2,000 acres) 20 miles southeast of Granite Falls—Snohomish County; *Mount Spokane* (24,240 acres) 34 miles northeast of Spokane—Spokane County; *Mukilteo* (14 acres) on Possession Sound at Mukilteo—Snohomish County; *Ocean City* (82 acres) on the Olympic Peninsula at Ocean City—Grays Harbor County; *Old Fort Townsend* on Admiralty Inlet, southeast of Port Townsend—Jefferson County; *Osoyoos Lake* (38 acres) north of Oroville—Okanogan County; *Pend Oreille* (393 acres) 15 miles southwest of Newport—Pend Oreille County; *Palouse Falls* (95 acres) on Palouse River, southeast of Washtuca—Adams County; *Pearygin Lake* (500 acres) near Winthrop—Okanogan County; *Penrose Point* (125 acres) at Carr Inlet on Puget Sound, 3 miles north of Longbranch—Mason County; *Potlatch* (142 acres) on Hood Canal, south of Hoodsport—Mason County; *Rainbow Falls* (116 acres) on Chehalis River, 18 miles west of Chehalis—Lewis County; *Riverside* (5,500 acres) 3 miles northwest of Spokane—Spokane County; *Rockport* (447 acres) on Skagit River—Skagit County; *Sacajawea* (30 acres) at Lake Sacajawea (9,200 acres) formed by the Ice Harbor Dam east of Pasco—Franklin County; *Saltwater* (90 acres) on East Passage of Puget Sound, west of Kent—King County; *Schafer* (106 acres) on East Fork Satsop River, northwest of Elma—Grays Harbor County; *Seaquest* (154 acres) at Silver Lake, east of Castle Rock—Cowlitz County; *Sequin Bay* (73 acres) on Strait of Juan de Fuca, near Sequin—Clallam County; *Squillchuck* (290 acres) in the Wenatchee Mountains, southwest of Wenatchee—Chelan County; *Sun Lakes* (2,400 acres) contains 3 lakes and spectacular Dry Falls, near Coulee City—Grant County; *Twanoh* (210 acres) on the Hood Canal, east of Union—Mason County; *Twin Harbors* (87 acres) on the Pacific Ocean between Grayland and Westport—Grays Harbor County; *Wenberg* (55 acres) 18 miles northwest of Everett—Snohomish County; *Yakima* (232 acres) in Yakima Valley, east of Yakima—Yakima County.

Licenses, regulations, and information about current seasons, bag and possession limits may be obtained from the Director, Washington

State Department of Game, 600 North Capitol Way, Olympia; also at 3117 Pacific Ave., Hoquiam; 150 "A" St., N.W. Ephrata; 509 Fairview Ave., North Seattle; 8702 Division St., Spokane; 2802 Naches Highway, Yakima; and on the Chelan Highway, Wenatchee. The Washington State Parks and Recreation Commission, General Administration Building, Box 335, Olympia, issues information about boats and state parks.

WEST VIRGINIA

Area: 24,170 square miles (land area—24,079 square miles); rank in nation–41
Animal: Black Bear (*Euarctos americanus*)
Bird: Cardinal (*Richmondena cardinalis*), adopted 1949
Capital city: Charleston at the confluence of the Elk and Kanawha rivers in Kanawha County; population (1960)—85,796; rank in state–1
Counties: 55
Elevations: Highest, Spruce Knob (4,860 ft.) in Pendleton County; lowest, Potomac River (240 ft.) in Jefferson County
Flower: Rhododendron (*Rhododendron maximum*), adopted 1903
Geographic center: 4 miles east of Sutton, Braxton County
Nicknames: Mountain State, Panhandle State, Scenic Wonderland
Population (1960): 1,869,421; rank in nation–30
Tree: Sugar Maple (*Acer saccharum*), adopted 1949

West Virginia is bordered by Virginia on the east and southeast, Maryland and Pennsylvania on the north, Ohio on the west separated by the Ohio River, and Kentucky on the southwest across the Big Sandy and Tug Fork rivers.

An irregular line following crests of the Allegheny Mountains marks the boundary between Virginia and West Virginia. The North Branch Potomac River outlines the northern border of the Eastern Panhandle, a region of fruit orchards and streams between Maryland and Virginia. The Northern Panhandle between Pennsylvania and the Ohio River narrows to less than 5 miles wide in Hancock County north of Weirton. Mountain ridges separated by parallel valleys are in the northeastern portion of the state where streams drain into the Potomac River. The southern mountains are a maze of canyons and branching streams among broader rounded summits. On the Allegheny Plateau west of the mountains are less rugged hills sloping to rolling land drained by the Ohio River system. Large tributaries of the Ohio River include the Kanawha River flowing through Charleston to Point Pleasant in Mason County; the Little Kanawha mingling waters at Parkersburg; and the Guyandot

River in the southwestern portion of the state merging with the Ohio at Huntington. South Fork and North Fork unite near Moorefield in Hardy County to form the swift South Branch Potomac River; and the Cacapon River flows through the Eastern Panhandle to join the Potomac River at Great Capacon. The Monongahela River runs through Clarksburg, Fairmont, and Morgantown on a northward course to Pennsylvania.

Tygart Lake (3,860 acres), and a series of cascades in a gorge known as Valley Falls, are on the Tygart River near Grafton in Taylor County. Dairy and beef cattle are raised in the southeastern bluegrass region, and the Greenbrier River moves through fertile farmland in mountain valleys. Sutton Reservoir (1,520 acres) on the Elk River is north of the Gauley River in the central part of the state. Harper's Ferry National Monument (1,500 acres) is at the confluence of the Potomac and Shenandoah rivers in the Blue Ridge Mountains, the meeting point of Maryland, Virginia, and West Virginia.

LICENSES

Resident licenses to fish, hunt, and trap are issued to bona fide residents 15–65 years of age, and no licenses are required before a resident has reached his fifteenth birthday or after his sixty-fifth birthday. Bona fide resident landowners and their children, (or tenants residing on their lands) may fish and hunt on such lands without licenses. Any bona fide resident who is totally blind may fish without obtaining a license. Nonresidents, regardless of age, must secure licenses to fish, hunt, trap or catch any fish, amphibians, or aquatic life of any kind. All persons 16 or more years of age must purchase federal "Duck" stamps to take migratory game birds. National forest fishing and hunting stamps are required to fish or hunt on the George Washington and Monongahela national forests in addition to valid statewide fishing or hunting licenses. The nonresident statewide bow and arrow hunting and fishing license is not required if an archer has obtained a nonresident statewide hunting license. The nonresident state park and forest family fishing license (valid for one week) is available at the state forests and parks. Special nonresident licenses to fish and hunt on the Ohio River are sold only to residents of Ohio.

*Resident license fees:** Statewide fishing, $3.00; statewide hunting, $3.00; combined statewide hunting and fishing, $5.00; statewide Beaver trapping, $2.00; federal "Duck" stamp, $3.00; national forest fishing stamp, $1.00; national forest hunting stamp, $1.00.

*Nonresident license fees:** Statewide fishing, $10.00; statewide

---

* Issue fee 25 cents when bought from license agents.

tourist fishing 6 consecutive days, $3.00; statewide hunting, $20.00; state-wide bow and arrow hunting and fishing, $5.00; Ohio River fishing, $2.00; Ohio River hunting, $2.00; federal "Duck" stamp, $3.00; national forest fishing stamp, $1.00; national forest hunting stamp, $1.00. State parks and forests family fishing: Head of the family (one week only), $3.00; each additional member of the family, 50 cents.

HUNTING AND TRAPPING

Game animals: Bear, Deer (must have antlers at least 3 inches long), Opossum, Rabbit (Cottontail, Snowshoe), Raccoon, Squirrel. OPEN SEA-SONS:* Bear—archery, mid-October through February; firearms, 2 or 3 weeks in November. Deer—archery, opens in designated areas on same day as the Bear season; firearms, in designated areas, several days after the Monday nearest December 1. Opossum, Raccoon—mid-October to early January in 21 counties and extended through February for remainder of the state. Rabbits, Squirrels—mid-November to early January.

Furbearing animals: Beaver, Bobcat, Fox (Gray, Red), Mink, Muskrat, Opossum, Raccoon, Skunk, Weasel. OPEN TRAPPING SEASONS:* Beaver—season set for residents only. Mink, Muskrat, Opossum, Raccoon, Skunk—generally from mid-November. NOT PROTECTED: Bobcat, Fox, Weasel, and Woodchuck may be taken at any time.

Game birds: Brant, Coot, Mourning Dove, Ducks (except Canvas-back and Redhead), Gallinule, Geese (except Snow Geese), Ruffed Grouse, Merganser, Ring-necked Pheasant, Quail, Rails, Wilson's Snipe, Wild Turkey, Woodcock. OPEN SEASONS:* Brant, Dove, Gallinule, Geese, Rails—mid-October to mid-December. Coot, Ducks, Grouse, Merganser —mid-October to early January. Pheasant, Quail—mid-November to early January. Wild Turkey—one week in mid-October in Mercer, Monongalia, Preston, and Summer counties; mid-October to early January in 16 other counties; no open seasons in remainder of the state. Wilson's Snipe, Woodcock: mid-October to late November. FULLY PROTECTED: Snow Geese, Canvasback and Redhead Ducks—no open seasons. NOT PRO-TECTED: Crow, Cooper's Hawk, Sharp-shinned Hawk, Goshawk, and Starling may be killed at any time.

FIREARMS

Migratory game birds may be hunted with a shotgun not larger than 10 gauge, and capable of holding not more than 3 shells in the magazine

---

* Check current state regulations.

and chamber combined. If originally capable of holding more than 3 shells, the magazine must be plugged with a one-piece metal or wooden filler incapable of removal through the loading end.

Shooting hours: Migratory birds may be taken from sunrise to sunset, except that on the opening day of the Duck season, shooting does not start until 12:00 o'clock noon. The opening day of hunting Opossum, Raccoon, and Skunk starts at 6:00 o'clock P.M., and traps may not be set out or staked for furbearing animals until 8:00 A.M. on the opening day of a trapping season.

FISHING

Game fish: Black Bass (Largemouth, Smallmouth), Kentucky or Spotted Bass, Rock Bass, White Bass, Bluegill and other Sunfish, Crappie, Muskellunge, Pickerel, Walleyed Pike, Trout (Brook, Brown, Rainbow). OPEN SEASONS: Trout—from 6:00 A.M. on the last Saturday in April to midnight December 31, except on the Elk River below Sutton Dam, open all year. Other fish—no closed seasons.

Nongame fish (except Catfish) may be taken by underwater spear fishing during daylight hours in the following waters: West of U.S. Route 19, any open waters; Cheat Lake; Monongalia, Greenbrier River; Summers and Greenbrier counties; New River and Bluestone Reservoir, except from Bluestone Dam downstream to the lower bridge at Hinton; Shenandoah River; Sutton Reservoir; Tygart Reservoir and Tygart River below Reservoir. The Elk River is closed to underwater spearing from the Sutton Dam to the bridge of Route 19. Spear guns may be discharged only beneath the surface of the water; and it is unlawful for skin divers to fish in marked swimming areas, heavily traveled boat lanes, areas set aside for water skiing, or in any manner to interfere with hook and line fishermen.

Nongame fish may be taken by dip nets in open waters Feb. 1–April 15; by gigging, west of U.S. Route 19 Jan. 1–April 30 and July 1–Dec. 31, and east of U.S. Route 19, from Jan. 1–April 30, Nov. 1–Dec. 31; Carp and other nongame species, by longbow and arrow, during all the months except May and June. Carp, Creek Chub, Fallfish, and Suckers may be caught by snaring through ice.

Frogs: Bullfrog and Green Frog may be taken from 8:00 P.M. on June 15 to midnight July 31, except on the Big Sandy and Tug Fork rivers, May 15 to mid-October. Nightly limit (noon–noon), 10.

Hunting is prohibited in state parks, but state forests and public hunting areas provide good hunting and fishing throughout the state.

STATE FORESTS

Cabwaylingo (8,126 acres) on Twelvepole Creek, east of Missouri Branch—Wayne County; *Calvin Price* (10,658 acres) on Greenbrier River, south of Huntersville—Pocahontas County; *Camp Creek* (5,578 acres) north of Camp Creek—Mercer County; *Coopers Rock* (13,479 acres) on Cheat River, east of Morgantown—Monongalia and Preston counties; *Kanawha* (6,705 acres) on Davis Creek, 7 miles south of Charleston—Kanawha County; *Kumbrabow* (9,585 acres) on Mill Creek, west of Elkwater—Randolph County; *Panther* (7,724 acres) near Tug Fork Sandy River, west of Iaeger—McDowell County; *Senecca* (11,492 acres) near Greenbrier River, west of Frost—Pocahontas County.

STATE PARKS

Audra (306 acres) on Middle Fork Buckhannon River, 10 miles west of Belington—Barbour County; *Babcock* (3,227 acres) near Clifftop —Fayette County; *Blackwater Falls* (1,679 acres) on Blackwater River, southwest of Davis—Tucker County; *Bluestone* (211 acres) at Blackstone Reservoir (1800 acres) near Hinton—Summers County; *Cacapon* (5,814 acres, lake 6 acres) in Eastern Panhandle, 10 miles from Berkeley Springs—Morgan County; *Cedar Creek* (2,000 acres) about 7 miles south of Glenville—Gilmer County; *Holly River* (7,592 acres) contains Laurel Fork of Holly River, near Hacker Valley—Webster County; *Lost River* (3,610 acres) contains Lee White Sulphur Springs, near Mathias and Moorefield—Hardy County; *Mont Chateau* (42 acres) at Cheat Lake, and adjacent to Coopers Rock State Forest, 8 miles east of Morgantown—Monongalia County; *North Bend* (1,420 acres) on the Hughes River, east of Cairo—Ritchie County; *Tomlinson Run* (1,387 acres, lake 27 acres) near Pughtown—Hancock County; *Tygart Lake* (1,803 acres) south of Grafton—Barbour and Taylor counties; *Watoga* (10,057 acres, lake 11 acres) adjacent to the Calvin Price State Forest, southwest of Huntersville—Pocahontas County.

PUBLIC HUNTING AREAS

Bluestone south of Hinton—Sumner County; *Chief Cornstalk* west of Southside—Mason County; *Elk River* east of Sutton—Braxton County; *Lew Wetzel* south of Jacksonburg—Wetzel County; *Nathaniel Mountain* south of Romney and *Short Mountain* south of Hanging Rock —Hampshire County; *Sleepy Creek* west of Martinsburg—Berkeley County.

Resident Managers are at the following wildlife management areas in the Monongahela National Forest: *Beaver Dam* at Glady; *Canaan* at

Davis; *Cheat Mountain* at Huttonsville; *Cranberry* at Marlington; *Flat Rock Plains* at Dry Fork; *Gatewood* at Circleville; *Little River* at Bartow; *Neola* at Neola; *Otter Creek* at Alpena; *Richwood* at Richwood; *Rimel* at Minnehaha Springs. The *Wardensville* Wildlife Management Area is in the George Washington National Forest, and the resident manager is at Wardensville.

Licenses, regulations, and information about current seasons, bag and possession limits may be obtained from the Director, West Virginia Department of Natural Resources, Charleston 5; or from county clerks and authorized hunting and fishing license agents. The attractive *Conservation Magazine* is published monthly at $2.00 for a 3-year subscription. Address Education Division, West Virginia Conservation Commission, Charleston 5. The *Sportsman's Map of National Forests in West Virginia* is available from national forest supervisors.

WISCONSIN

Area: 56,066 square miles (land area—54,705 square miles); rank in nation—25
Animals: Badger (*Taxidea taxus*) and White-tailed Deer (*Odocoileus virginianus*)
Bird: Robin (*Merula migratoria*)
Capital city: Madison on Mendota, Monona, and Wingra lakes in Dane County; population (1960)—126,706; rank in state—2
Counties: 72
Elevations: Highest, Rib Hill (1,940 ft.) in Marathon County; lowest, Lake Michigan (581 ft.)
Fish: Muskellunge (*Esox masquinongy*)
Flower: Wood Violet (*Viola*)
Geographic center: 9 miles southeast of Marshfield, Wood County
Nicknames: Badger State, Copper State, Green Bay State
Population (1960): 3,951,777; rank in nation—15
Tree: Sugar Maple (*Acer saccharum*)

Wisconsin is bordered by Lake Superior and the Michigan Upper Peninsula on the north, Lake Michigan and its long arm, Green Bay, on the east, Illinois on the south, Iowa separated on the southwest by the Mississippi River, and Minnesota on the west by the Mississippi and St. Croix rivers.

There are more than 8,700 inland lakes among large and small streams on rolling plains broken by buttes, mesas, and ridges such as the northern highlands with Rib Hill near Wausau in central Wisconsin, the Trempealeau County bluffs including Bald Knob, Perrot Ridge, and Thunder Mountain, and Grandad Bluff rising 570 feet above La Crosse. The St. Croix River, from the northwestern portion of the state, starts to etch the Wisconsin-Minnesota border west of Riverside, and joins the Mississippi River at Prescott. The Wisconsin River rising among numerous lakes in the north flows over sparkling falls and rapids on a southern course through Rhinelander, Tomahawk, Merrill, Wausau, Stevens Point, Wisconsin Rapids, Wisconsin Dells; and at Portage swings on a southwesterly course through Merrimac to reach the Mississippi River south of Prairie du Chien. A 10-mile channel carved into fantastic formations between the Coldwater Canyon and Witches Gulch of the Upper Dells, and the caverns and rocky islands of the Lower Dells at Lake Dalton, are north of Portage on the Wisconsin River. The Chippewa River fed by many streams forms a 100-mile shoreline at Lake Wissota near Chippewa Falls, and south of Durand enters Lake Pepin on the Mississippi River. In eastern Wisconsin, the Wolf River flows from northern lakes on a meandering course through Shawam, Poygan, and Butte des Morte lakes to Oshgosh on the western shore of lovely Lake Winnebago (215 square miles) with a 92-mile shoreline. The Fox River links Lake Winnebago and Appleton with Green Bay. The famous Trout stream Brule River leaves the Upper St. Croix on a northern course to Lake Superior. The 22 Apostle Islands are clustered around a peninsula thrust into Lake Superior at Bayfield. The long protective peninsula between Green Bay and Lake Michigan is separated by a strait at Sturgeon Bay, and provides an exceptional recreation area.

LICENSES

Resident licenses are issued to any person who has maintained a place of permanent abode in the state for at least one year immediately preceding an application for a license; to members of the U.S. Armed Forces stationed in Wisconsin; and to registered full-time undergraduate students in residence at a recognized college or university. Settler's Deer and settler's small game hunting licenses may be issued by the Conservation Commission to persons living in the state not less than 60 days prior to the date of application. Hunting licenses are not issued to juveniles under the age of 12 years, and any person 12–16 years of age may hunt only when accompanied by a parent or guardian or by an adult over 21 years of age designated by his parent or guardian.

Big game licenses must be purchased before November 16 to be valid during a Deer season. All persons 16 or more years of age must purchase a federal "Duck" stamp to take migratory game birds. Regardless of age, a trapping license is required to trap any wild animal. The voluntary sportsman's license to hunt, fish, and trap is issued to any person who voluntarily pays a fee over $10.

Licenses for fishing inland waters are required of all persons 16 or more years of age, and residents may fish without licenses after reaching the age of 65 years. No licenses are necessary to catch rough fish and minnows by dip net, landing net, or minnow seines. License periods: Annual fishing, Jan. 1–Dec. 31; Deer hunting, small game hunting, and voluntary sportsman's licenses, Sept. 1–Aug. 31.

Resident license fees: Annual fishing, $3.00; spearing Sturgeons, $2.50; hunting small game, $4.00; hunting Bear and Deer, $5.00; voluntary sportsman's (fishing, hunting, trapping), not less than $10.00; federal "Duck" stamp, $3.00.

Nonresident license fees: Annual fishing, $5.00; combination fishing 15 consecutive days (husband and wife), $6.00; bow and arrow Deer hunting, $10.00; hunting exclusive of Deer, $25.00; hunting including Deer, $50.00; hunting on licensed shooting preserves, $5.00; federal "Duck" stamp, $3.00.

HUNTING AND TRAPPING

Game animals: Black Bear, White-tailed Deer, Cottontail Rabbit, White-tailed Jack Rabbit, Snowshoe Hare, Raccoon, Squirrels (Gray, Western Fox). OPEN SEASONS:* Bear, Deer—archery, usually from late September to mid-November and the month of December; firearms (including bow and arrow), for several days after mid-November in designated areas. Hare and Rabbit—Oct. 1–Jan. 31, and no closed season on Cottontails in Milwaukee County, or on Snowshoe Hare in a majority of the counties. Raccoon—Oct. 1–Dec. 31 north of Fox River, State Highway 21, and U.S. Highway 16; Oct. 15–Dec. 31 south of that line; and no closed season in Kenosha, Racine, and Walworth counties. Squirrels—Oct. 1–31 west of designated highways, and open about 3 weeks later east of that boundary. BAG LIMITS: Bear—1 per year. Deer— 1 per year. Cottontail Rabbit—3 per day. Jack Rabbit and Snowshoe Hare—4 each per day, and no limits on Snowshoe Hare in areas open all year.

Furbearing animals: Badger, Beaver, Bobcat, Coyote, Fisher, Fox (Gray, Red), Canada Lynx, Marten, Mink, Muskrat, Opossum, Otter, Raccoon, Skunk, Wolf, Wolverine. OPEN TRAPPING SEASONS:* Beaver— Feb. 1–March 31 including shorter seasons in several counties; April 1– 30 in designated areas of Bayfield, Forest, Iron, Langlade, Lincoln, Marathon, Oneida, and Shawne counties; and no open season in Buffalo, Crosses, Trempeauleau, and portions of Jackson, Monroe, Pierce, Pepin,

---

* Check current state regulations.

and Vernon counties. Mink, Muskrat—November to mid-December in northern counties, and generally opens a week later in central counties; and Nov. 15–Jan. 15 in southern counties. Raccoon—may be trapped during the open season for hunting. FULLY PROTECTED: Badger, White Deer, Elk, Fisher, Canada Lynx, Marten, Moose, Flying Squirrel, Timber Wolf, Wolverine, and Woodchuck—no open seasons. NOT PROTECTED: Bobcat, Coyote, Fox, Gopher, Opossum, Porcupine, Skunk, Weasel, and other animals not specifically mentioned as game or protected may be taken at any time.

The owner or occupant of any land, and members of his family without licenses, may kill Rabbits and Squirrels damaging property, except during 5 days prior to the season open for hunting Deer with guns. Rabbits may also be taken with box traps if the use of guns is prohibited in the area. Landowners should apply in writing to the Conservation Department in Madison for a permit to destroy other animals causing damage.

The antlers of a legal Buck Deer must be not less than 3 inches in length. Sportsmen hunting any game except waterfowl during the Deer season are required to wear red, orange, or bright yellow colors on at least 50 per cent of the visible portion of caps and jackets (except sleeves) and also to attach the tag to the center of the back of the jacket, sweater, shirt, or similar outer garment.

Game birds: Coot, Ducks (except Canvasback and Redhead), Gallinule, Geese, Ruffed Grouse (Partridge), Sharp-tailed Grouse, Merganser, Chukar and Hungarian Partridge, Pheasant, Prairie Chicken, Bobwhite Quail, Rails, Sora, Wilson's Snipe, Woodcock. OPEN SEASONS:* Coot, Ducks, Gallinule, Merganser, Rails, Sora, Wilson's Snipe—early October to early November. Geese—early October to mid-December. Ruffed Grouse—Oct. 1–Dec. 15 including shorter periods in designated areas; and no open season in southeastern counties. Sharp-tailed Grouse— first 2 weeks in October in northern counties, and no open season in remainder of state. Hungarian Partridge—mid-October to mid-November east of designated highway boundaries, and no open season in remainder of state. Pheasant—mid-October to mid-November statewide; and Milwaukee County open to bow and arrow hunting during Hungarian Partridge seasons. Woodcock—for about 6 weeks after the opening date in late September or early October. FULLY PROTECTED: Bitterns, Crane, Mourning Dove, Canvasback and Redhead Ducks, Canada Spruce Grouse (Spruce Hen), Eagles, Hawks, Owls (except Great Horned Owl), Plover, Prairie Chicken, Sandpipers, Swan, and Wild Turkey—no open season. NOT PROTECTED: Red-winged Blackbird, Cowbird, Crow, Great

---

* Check current state regulations.

Horned Owl, Chukar Partridge, Coturnix Quail, English Sparrow, and Starling may be taken at any time.

FIREARMS

Bear and Deer may not be hunted with any .22 rimfire rifle or any .410 bore shotgun, or any shotgun or musket charge other than single ball or slug. Smoothbore muskets of .45 caliber or larger, and rifled muskets of .40 caliber or larger may be used for hunting Deer in counties having a shotgun-only season, but the possession of a rifle larger than .22 rimfire is prohibited. It is unlawful in 39 counties to possess any rifle other than a .22 rimfire chambered for cartridges less than one inch in length, or any shotgun shells loaded with shot larger than no. BB, or any divided or cut shells, or any shells loaded with single slug or ball from June 1 to December 31 in areas frequented by Deer. Lawful firearms and ammunition may be carried into such areas for 5 days prior to the Bear and Deer season and until the third day after the season ends. Hunting with any means other than the use of a gun discharged from the shoulder or a bow and arrow is not permitted except that .22 rimfire handguns and pellet guns of .177 caliber (or larger) may be used in the same manner for the same purposes and subject to the same restrictions as .22 rimfire rifles. The use of any hand gun by a minor is prohibited. Longbows with a pull of not less than 30 pounds may be used to hunt big game, and the arrows should have sharp metal broadhead blades at least seven-eighths of an inch and not more than 1½ inches in width.

Shooting hours: One-half hour before sunrise, except that on the opening day of the season for Ducks, upland game birds, Rabbits, and Squirrels shooting is not permitted until 12:00 o'clock noon. There are no hunting hour restrictions on Raccoon or unprotected animals and birds. It is unlawful to set a trap or attend a trapline from sunset to one hour before sunrise.

FISHING

Game fish: Black Bass (Largemouth, Smallmouth), Catfish, Muskellunge, Pickerel (Mud), Northern Pike, Walleye (Pike-perch), Sauger, Sturgeon, Trout (Brook, Brown, Lake, Rainbow). OPEN SEASONS:* Black Bass—from first Saturday in May to February 15 in inland waters south of Highway 64; from first Saturday in June to February 15 in waters north of Highway 64 and all outlying waters; Wisconsin-Michigan boundary waters, June 1–Dec. 31; Wisconsin-Iowa boundary waters, continuous open season; St. Louis River and St. Croix River downstream to

---

* Check current state regulations.

Highway 64 bridge at Houlton, first Saturday in June to March 1; all other Wisconsin-Minnesota boundary waters, first Saturday in May to March 1. Northern Pike, Sauger, Walleye—concurrent with Black Bass except that inland waters north of Highway 64 open on the third Saturday in May. Muskellunge—first Saturday in May to November 15 in waters south of Highway 64, and open on the third Saturday in May north of Highway 64 and in the Wisconsin–Michigan boundary waters. Lake Trout—first Saturday in January to September 30 in waters inland; first Saturday in November to September 30 in Lake Superior; second Saturday in December to September 30 in Lake Michigan—Green Bay outlying waters. Rock or Lake Sturgeon—first Saturday in May to October 31 in Wisconsin-Minnesota boundary waters; first Saturday in September to October 15 in Wisconsin-Michigan boundary waters and all inland waters except Lakes Little Buttes des Mortes, Poygan, Winneconne, Winnebago, and connecting waters downstream to the uppermost dam in the City of Appleton (Outagamie County), the Wolf River from the dam at Shewano downstream to Lake Poygan, and Fox River downstream from milepost 63 (Johnson Creek–Green Lake County) to Lake Buttes des Mortes. Shovenose Sturgeon—continuous season, except no open season in inland waters north of Highway 64 or in the St. Louis River and St. Croix River downstream to St. Croix Falls Dam. Trout (except Lake)—first Saturday in May to first Saturday in September in waters inland south of Highway 64 and the Wisconsin-Michigan boundary waters; and opens 2 weeks later north of Highway 64; Lake Superior, continuous except for about one week in May. The Trout season is extended to February 15 in numerous inland lakes. Catfish—from first Saturday in May to March 1 in the St. Croix River downstream to St. Croix Falls Dam, and other Wisconsin-Minnesota boundary waters; continuous in all other waters. Paddlefish (Spoonbill Cat)—no open season. All other fish may be taken at any time.

No person may catch any game fish with more than 2 lines or 2 poles with 1 line attached to each pole (or rod) and 1 hook or bait to each line, but if using only one line, the fisherman may attach 2 lures, or 2 hooks, or 2 baits to his line. Northern Pike may be speared through ice in Lake Superior. The hole cut in ice must not be larger than 12 inches in diameter except for dip-netting, taking minnows by traps, or for skin diving. Fishing through ice with hook and line is prohibited from 8:00 P.M. to 6:00 A.M. in any waters of the state. Any person fishing through ice with hook and line in Lake Winnebago may use 3 lines with not more than one hook attached to each line. Portable structures must be removed from the ice on or before March 1 on the Wisconsin-Minnesota boundary waters, and not later than March 5 south of Highway 64, and March 15 north of Highway 64.

Panfish (Rock, Warmouth, White and Yellow Bass, Bluegill, Black, Brown, and Yellow Bullheads, Crappie, Perch, Pumpkinseed) and rough fish may be taken by skin divers using spears or spear guns in the following waters: Crooked and Jordan Lakes, Adams County; Lake Arbutus, Clark and Jackson counties; Long Lake, Chippewa County; Lake Mendota, Dane County; Helen and Wolf lakes, Portage County; Cyclone and Stone lakes, Washburne County; Spencer and Stratton lakes, Waupaca County. Skin divers may also spear Carp in Lake Michigan and take rough fish in the Barron, Eau Claire, Iron, and Jefferson counties. Rough fish—Buffalo, Burbot, Carp, Drum, Garfish, Dogfish, Sheepshead and Suckers—may be taken by dip nets, gill nets, hoop nets, seines, spears bow and arrows in designated waters.

Hunting and fishing is excellent throughout the state, with ice fishing and skiing favorite winter sports. Top Trout streams include the Brule River, the Mecan in Waushara County, and Tomorrow in Portage County. Wisconsin owns 196,536 acres and has leased 304,483 acres for public lands open to hunting and fishing. These areas are in all counties and easily accessible, but only those containing more than 1,000 acres are included in the following list.

PUBLIC LANDS

Adams County—Big Spring (2,005 acres) northeast of Wisconsin Dells; Colbum (4,889 acres) northeast of Friendship. *Ashland County*— Hoffman Lake (5,562 acres) east of Butternut. *Brown County*—Bellevue (1,571 acres) 2 miles north of Bellevue; Holland (1,008 acres) southeast of Greenleaf. *Buffalo County*—Big Swamp (2,313 acres) west of Mondovi; Tiffany (8,371 acres) northwest of Nelson. *Burnett County*—Amsterdam Sloughs (3,407 acres) southwest of Webster; Clam River (1,000 acres) 8 miles northeast of Clam Falls; Crex Meadows (22,775 acres) northeast of Grantsburg, Danbury (1,233 acres) 2 miles southwest of Danbury; Fish Lake (6,413 acres) southwest of Grantsburg; Kiezer Lake (1,352 acres) northeast of Webster; Kohler-Peet (3,329 acres) 13 miles northeast of Grantsburg; Namekagon Barrens (5,687 acres) northeast of Webb Lake. *Calumet County*—Brillion (7,834 acres) west of Brillion; New Holstein (1,345 acres) north of New Holstein. *Chippewa County*— Jim Falls (1,443 acres) south of Jim Falls. *Columbia County*—French's Creek (3,195 acres) 7 miles north of Portage; Pine Island (3,739 acres) 3 miles west of Portage. *Dane County*—Deansville (2,671 acres) east of Sun Prairie; Mazomanie (9,750 acres) north of Mazomanie. *Dodge County*—Horicon Marsh (10,483 acres) north of Horicon; Mud Lake (2,156 acres) south of Reesville; Westford (1,063 acres) 6 miles west of Beaver Dam; Wildcat Swamp (1,915 acres) north of Hustisford. *Door*

County—Lost Lake (1,154 acres) northwest of Jacksonport. *Douglas County*—(2,760 acres) south of Solon Springs. *Dunn County*—Dunnville (3,670 acres) east of Dunnville, Elk Mound (4,159 acres) west of Elk Mound; *Eau Claire County*—Augusta (1,940 acres) north of Augusta; Pleasant Valley (2,185 acres) 9 miles south of Eau Claire. *Florence County*—Spread Eagle (4,338 acres) 7 miles east of Florence. *Fond du Lac County*—Eden (2,170 acres) southeast of Eden; Eldorado (2,836 acres) 8 miles northwest of Fond du Lac; St. Cloud (3,352 acres) west of St. Cloud. *Forest County*—Little Rice (1,566 acres) 7 miles west of Crandon. *Grant County*—Blue River (2,224 acres) at Within and Wolf Blue River. *Green County*—Albany (2,276 acres) north of Albany; Brodhead (3,063 acres) southwest of Brodhead; Brooklyn (4,498 acres) 7 miles west of Brooklyn; Browntown (4,004 acres) east of Brownstown; New Glarus (3,756 acres) south of New Glarus. *Green Lake County*—Silver Creek (2,405 acres) east of Green Lake. *Iowa County*—Avoca (4,391 acres) 2 miles east of Avoca. *Iron County*—Hay Creek (3,535 acres) 12 miles east of Park Falls; Underwood (1,602 acres) 9 miles north of Mercer. *Jefferson County*—Jefferson Marsh (2,552 acres) southeast of Jefferson; Princess Point (5,948 acres) northwest of Palmyra; Rome Pond (1,220 acres) east of Rome; Waterloo (7,645 acres) 10 miles west of Watertown. *Juneau County*—Meadow Valley (57,000 acres) west of Necedah. *Kenosha County*—New Munster (1,845 acres) at New Munster; Paris (3,264 acres) 10 miles west of Kenosha; Salem (1,010 acres) 6 miles southeast of New Munster. *La Crosse County*—Val Loon (3,942 acres) north of Holmen. *Lafayette County*—Argyle (2,922 acres) north of Argyle; Benton (2,120 acres) northeast of Benton; Spafford Creek (4,074 acres) southwest of South Wayne; Yellowstone (1,954 acres) 7 miles northwest of Argyle. *Langlade County*—Ackley (2,237 acres) 11 miles west of Antigo. *Lincoln County*—New Wood (1,600 acres) 17 miles northwest of Merrill. *Manitowoc County*—Collins (9,519 acres) southwest of Valders. *Marathon County*—McMillan Marsh (2,239 acres) east of Spencer; George W. Mead (20,125 acres) 7 miles southwest of Mosinee; Nine Mile Swamp (4,117 acres) 6 miles southwest of Wausau; Plover River (993 acres) east of Hogarty. *Marinette County*—Amberg (1,150 acres) southwest of Amberg; Athelstane (1,797 acres) west of Athelstane; Coleman (1,234 acres) southeast of Coleman; Dunbar (4,404 acres) west of Dunbar; Lake Noquebay (1,300 acres) 10 miles northeast of Crivitz; Peshtigo Harbor (2,845 acres) 7 miles south of Peshtigo. *Marquette County*—Germania (2,373 acres) 8 miles north of Montello. *Monroe County*—Bangor (5,850 acres) west of Sparta. *Oconto County*—Peshtigo Brook (2,160 acres) 10 miles north of Suring. *Oneida County*—Thunder Lake (1,814 acres) northwest of Three Lakes. *Outagamie County*—Deer Creek (1,010 acres) west of Leeman; Mack

(1,358 acres) near Shicton. *Ozaukee County*—Cedarburg (1,331 acres) northwest of Grafton. *Polk County*—McKenzie Creek (2,731 acres) south of Clam Falls; Rice Beds Creek (1,715 acres) 16 miles southeast of Luck. *Price County*—Price Creek (1,466 acres) 16 miles west of Phillips. *Racine County*—Beulah Station (2,320 acres) northwest of Waterford; Tichigan (1,100 acres) north of Waterford. *Richland County*—Richland (2,978 acres) at Gotham. *Rock County*—Evansville (2,920 acres) 5 miles south of Evansville; Footville (7,734 acres) at Footville; Lima (1,900 acres) at Lima Center. *Rusk County*—Silvernail (1,038 acres). *Sauk County*—Dell Creek (1,112 acres) 6 miles northeast of Reedsburg; Reedsburg (1,782 acres) at Reedsburg. *Sawyer County*—Chief River (1,183 acres) 22 miles north of Radisson; Totagatic River (2,714 acres) 9 miles north of Hayward; Weirgor Springs (1,900 acres) 1 mile north of Weirgor. *Shawano County*—Navarino Marsh (4,505 acres) 10 miles south of Shawano. *Sheboygan County*—Adell (1,678 acres) at Adell; Nicholas Creek (1,186 acres) west of Waldo; Sheboygan Falls (2,154 acres) 3 miles north of Sheboygan Falls. *Taylor County*—Pershing (3,640 acres) 3 miles northwest of Hannibal. *Vilas County*—Dorothy Dunn (2,240 acres) 6 miles north of Star Lake; Powell Marsh (10,398 acres) 10 miles north of Lac du Flambeau. *Walworth County*—Clover Valley (2,007 acres) south of Whitewater; Richmond (2,349 acres) north of Delavan; Troy (7,588 acres) west of East Troy. *Washington County*—Allenton (2,059 acres) at Allenton; Hartford (1,494 acres) northeast of Hartford; Theresa (4,652 acres) 8 miles west of Kewaskum. *Waukesha County*—Scuppernong (2,709 acres) north of Eagle; Vernon Marsh (3,014 acres) north of Mukwonago. *Waupaca County*—Marion (2,466 acres) west of Marion; Clintonville (1,467 acres) 7 miles southeast of Clintonville; Mukwa (1,555 acres) west of New London. *Waushara County*—Greenwood Farms (1,603 acres) south of Hancock; Pine River (1,053 acres) at Wild Rose; Willow Creek (1,181 acres) north of Redgranite. *Winnebago County*—Bay Boom (2,286 acres) 4 miles west of Winchester. *Wood County*—Wood County (19,671 acres) west of Babcock.

On the White River, there are 960 acres of hunting grounds 3 miles south of Ashland and 307 acres only 1 mile from Wautoma, providing Brook, Brown, and Rainbow Trout fishing.

STATE FORESTS

American Legion (38,385 acres) north of Rhinelander—Oneida County; *Black River* (59,200 acres) east of Black River Falls—Jackson County; *Brule River* (22,461 acres) south of Brule—Douglas County; *Council Grounds* (278 acres) on Wisconsin River, west of Merrill—Lincoln County; *Flambeau River* (73,825 acres) north of Hawkins—

Rusk, Price, and Sawyer counties; *Kettle Moraine* (19,000 acres) north unit (11,952 acres) west of Plymouth—Sheboygan, Fond du Lac, and, Washington counties, and south unit (7,048 acres) west of Waukesha—Jefferson, Walworth, and Waukesha counties; *Northern Highland* (124,121 acres) near Boulder Junction—Iron and Vilas counties; *Point Beach* (2,258 acres) on Lake Michigan, 4 miles north of Two Rivers—Manitowoc County.

STATE PARKS

Big Foot Beach (261 acres) south of Lake Geneva—Walworth County; *Brunet Island* (179 acres) at confluence of Chippewa and Fisher rivers, north of Cornell—Chippewa County; *Copper Falls* (1,480 acres) north of Mellen—Ashland County; *Devil's Lake* (2,538 acres) south of Baraboo—Sauk County; *Governor Dodge* (2,675 acres) contains Cox Hollow Lake, 3 miles north of Dodgeville—Iowa County; *High Cliff* (288 acres) overlooking Lake Winnebago—Calumet County; *Interstate* (675 acres) on The Dalles of St. Croix River, south of St. Croix Falls—Polk County; Wisconsin and Taylors Falls in Minnesota; *Lucius Woods* (37 acres) at Lake St. Croix, south of Solon Springs—Douglas County; *Merrick* (133 acres) at Fountain City Bay on the Mississippi River—Trempealeau County; *Ojibwa* (353 acres) on the Chippewa River—Sawyer County; *Pattison* (1,160 acres) contains Gitchee Monido (Manitou) Falls on the Black River, 10 miles south of Superior—Douglas County; *Peninsula* (1,028 acres) on Mississippi River, contains Trempealeau Mountain (530 ft.)—Trempealeau County; *Potawatomi* (1,046 acres) on eastern shore of Green Bay 2 miles northeast of Sturgeon Bay—Door County; *Terry Andrae* (167 acres) on Lake Michigan, 4 miles south of Sheboygan—Sheboygan County; *Tower Hill* (108 acres) on southern side of Wisconsin River, near Spring Green—Iowa County; *Wildcat Mountain* (1,600 acres) south of Ontario—Vernon County; *Wyalusing* (1,671 acres) at the confluence of the Mississippi and Wisconsin rivers, 4 miles south of Prairie du Chief—Crawford County.

Licenses, regulations, and information about current seasons, bag and possession limits may be obtained from the Director, Wisconsin Conservation Department, Box 450, Madison 1. Interesting illustrated publications about the animals, birds, and fish in Wisconsin will be sent without cost if requested from the Conservation Department.

WYOMING

Area: 97,914 square miles (land area—97,411 square miles); rank in nation—9

Bird: Meadow Lark (*Sturnella neglecta*), adopted 1927
Capital city: Cheyenne on a rolling plain in Laramie County; population (1960)—43,505; rank in state–1
Counties: 23
Elevations: Highest, Gannett Peak (13,785 ft.) in Fremont County; lowest, Belle Fourche River (3,100 ft.) in Crook County
Flower: Indian Paint Brush (*Castillija linariaefolia*), adopted 1917
Geographic center: 58 miles north of east of Lander, Fremont County
Nicknames: Equality State, Cowboy State, Wonderful Wyoming
Population (1960): 330,066; rank in nation–48
Tree: Cottonwood (*Populus balsamifera*), adopted 1947

Wyoming is bordered by Montana on the north, Nebraska and South Dakota on the east, Colorado on the south, Idaho on the west, and Utah around the southwest corner of the state.

The Continental Divide of the Rocky Mountain system crosses the state from the southeastern Medicine Bow country to the magnificent Wind River Range and Yellowstone National Park in the northwest. It is a land of contrasts, with vast treeless plains about 6,000–7,000 feet above sea level; ranches on rolling hills covered with sage and buffalo grass in the east, the Devil's Tower looming 1,280 feet above Belle Fourche River in the northeastern Black Hills; the scenic sand dunes of Red Desert (10,000 square miles) in the southwest; the high-mountain 50-mile valley Jackson Hole surrounded by majestic Tetons and Teton National Forest at the entrance to Yellowstone National Park. The incredible Yellowstone National Park (2,221,772 acres extending into Idaho and Montana) contains nearly 3,000 hot springs and geysers, Atkins Peak (11,063 ft.), several peaks above 10,000 feet, and Lower Falls plunging 306 feet to colorful Yellowstone River Canyon.

Thermapolis Hot Springs State Park (956 acres) at Thermapolis in the northern Big Horn Basin contains hundreds of springs including Big Horn Spring, which sends 18,600,000 gallons of mineral water to the Big Horn River daily.

The Snake River rushes from Jackson Lake (39 square miles) in the Jackson Hole country on a long journey to the Columbia River in Washington. The Big Horn River rising on the eastern slopes of the Wind River Range flows north through central Wyoming, the Powder River from the Hell's Half Acre region, and Tongue River in the northeast all move into Montana. The Sweetwater River runs between the Green Mountains and Rattlesnake Range to join the North Platte River at the Alcova Reservoir linked with Pathfinder Reservoir southwest of Casper. The Medicine Bow River merges with the North Platte at the Seminoe Reservoir (31 square miles) northwest of Medicine Bow; and the Laramie River connects

Wheatland Reservoir, Lake Ione, and Lake Hattie near Laramie in southeastern Wyoming. The turbulent Green River flows through the southwest to be impounded and form the Flaming Gorge Reservoir (66 square miles) extending into Utah. Wyoming Peak (11,388 ft.) overlooks Grey's River on its course to join the Snake River at Alpine on the Idaho border.

LICENSES

Resident licenses are issued to citizens of the United States who have lived in the state at least one year immediately preceding the date of application for a license, and to members of the U.S. Armed Forces stationed in Wyoming. Aliens who have not taken out naturalization papers must purchase nonresident licenses. Juveniles under the age of 14 years are not permitted to hunt game animals, but they may fish without a license if accompanied by an adult in possession of a valid fishing license. Any person 14 or more years of age is required to obtain a hunting license to take game animals and birds, but a license is not necessary to kill unprotected wildlife. All persons 16 or more years of age must purchase a federal "Duck" stamp to take migratory game birds.

Any hunter holding a regular $20 Deer license and the special $25 2-Deer license may take 1 antlerless Deer and 2 Deer of either sex in any multiple Deer area. There are no quotas on Deer licenses, and nonresidents may secure any Deer license from the Cheyenne Office of the Game and Fish Commission, or from authorized agents throughout the state after arriving in Wyoming. Multiple-area Deer licenses are valid only on designated areas and cannot be transferred. Applications for Antelope permits may be made at any time after January 1, and although the commission does not set seasons until late April, permits are issued immediately afterward on a first-come basis from the Cheyene office. The nonresident combined hunting and fishing license includes the right to take 1 Bear, 1 Deer, and 1 antlered Elk in addition to small animals, birds, and fish. Elk may only be hunted by nonresidents who possess combination licenses, which are usually sold out by early spring. About 25 per cent of the permits to hunt Moose and Mountain (Bighorn) Sheep are issued to nonresidents. Applications (separate registrations for each species) must be accompanied by fees, and registrations are accepted until June 30. Fees are returned if an applicant was not successful in the drawing. Only 1 Moose permit or 1 Mountain Sheep permit may be issued to a successful hunter in any 3-year period. Applications for other hunting licenses or permits should not be sent in a Moose or a Mountain Sheep application envelope because unsuccessful applicant's envelopes are returned unopened after drawings.

Nonresident hunters of Bear, Deer, Elk, Moose, and Mountain Sheep must be accompanied by licensed guides on any land within a national forest, national park, or national game refuge. Only 1 guide for each 2 persons is required for a hunting group; and no licensed guide is necessary for not more than 2 nonresidents hunting together if they are accompanied by a resident hunter who holds a valid big game hunting license, a resident guide permit, and does not charge for his services. Out-of-state hunters should obtain a free list of guides and outfitters from the Wyoming Game and Fish Commission and make arrangements with a qualified guide before arriving in Wyoming.

Resident license fees: Fishing, $3.00; hunting birds, $2.00; federal "Duck" stamp, $3.00; hunting birds, Bear, Deer, $5.00; hunting birds, Bear, Elk, $5.00; hunting Antelope, $5.00; special Bear permit, $5.00; hunting Moose, $15.00; hunting Mountain Sheep, $15.00.

Nonresident license fees: Annual fishing, $12.00; tourist fishing 5 consecutive days, $4.00; hunting birds, $10.00; federal "Duck" stamp, $3.00; hunting Antelope, $25.00; hunting Bear (2-Bear permit), $25.00; regular Deer hunting, $20.00; hunting Deer in special areas only (2-Deer permit), $25.00; hunting Moose, $75.00; hunting Mountain (Bighorn) Sheep, $75.00; combined fishing and hunting birds, 1 Bear, 1 Deer, 1 antlered Elk, $100.00.

HUNTING

Big game animals: Antelope, Bear, Deer (Mule, White-tailed), Elk, Moose, Mountain (Bighorn) Sheep. OPEN SEASONS:* Antelope—usually from late August to mid-October; some areas close early September; others open according to area, until December 31. Bear—during Deer and Elk seasons. Deer—designated areas open September 1 and continue to open according to area until early November and close according to area ending December 31. Elk—opens and closes by area between mid-September and November 30. Moose—opening and closing dates in designated areas between September 1 and December 31. Mountain Sheep—opening and closing dates in designated areas between September 1 and November 15. BAG LIMITS: Antelope—1. Bear—2. Deer—3 with proper permits and licenses. Elk—1. Moose—1. Mountain Sheep—1.

Furbearing animals: Badger, Bobcat, Coyote, Fisher, Fox, Lynx, Mink, Opossum, Otter, Raccoon, Weasel. Trapping licenses are required to take Fisher, Fox, Marten and Mink. NOT PROTECTED: Badger, Bobcat, Coyote, Gopher, Opossum, Porcupine, Prairie Dog, Rabbits (Cottontail, Jack, Snowshoe), Skunk, Weasel, and Woodchuck.

Game birds: Ducks (except Canvasback and Redhead), Geese, Grouse (Blue, Ruffed, Sage, Sharp-tailed), Partridge (Chukar, Hungarian) Pheasant, Wild Turkey. OPEN SEASONS:* Ducks—early November to early December east of the Continental Divide; early October to December

---

* Check current state regulations.

31 west of the Continental Divide. Geese—about 2 weeks in late October and from mid-November to mid-January east of the Divide; and concurrent with the Duck season west of the Divide. Grouse, Partridge, Pheasant—check current regulations. Sage Grouse is found throughout southern and central Wyoming and in the Big Horn Basin. NOT PROTECTED: Crow, Cooper's Hawk, Goshawk, Sharp-shinned Hawk, and Great Horned Owls may be killed at any time.

FIREARMS

A big game hunter may use any rifle having not less than 23/100-inch bore, and cartridges not less than 2 inches over-all measurement, and containing a soft-point bullet. Hollow-point and other expanding bullets are legal. An archery hunter must be equipped with a nonmechanical bow having at least a 40-pound pull, and capable of projecting the hunting arrows 150 yards. The arrow should be not less than 24 inches long with a steel cutting head.

Ducks and Geese may be hunted with bow and arrow, or a shotgun not less than 10 gauge and capable of holding not more than 3 shells in the magazine and chamber combined.

The Oneshot Hunt is held annually on the first day of the Antelope season at Lander. All hunters are required to wear red on hat or clothing while hunting game animals.

Shooting hours: Ducks, Geese—sunrise to sunset east of the Continental Divide, and from one-half hour before sunrise to sunset west of the Divide.

FISHING

Game fish: Largemouth Bass, Channel Catfish, Grayling, Kokanee Salmon, Sunfish, Trout (Brook, Brown, Cutthroat, Golden, Rainbow), Walleye, Whitefish. OPEN SEASONS: Drainage Area 1, June 1–Dec. 31; Drainage Area 2, 4, 5, May 1–Oct. 31; Drainage Area 3, all year. Regulations should be carefuly checked to note local exceptions.

There are over 5,000 lakes and 20,000 miles of streams in Wyoming, and top fishing is available in state parks, national forests and parks. The Grand Teton National Park (310,350 acres) in the northwestern Teton Range contains the Snake River rushing through Jackson Hole; Jackson Lake (11,257 acres), Bradley, Jenny, Leigh, Phelps, and Taggart lakes among pine forests; Cascade and Death canyons; 11 superb peaks including the Grand Teton (13,776 ft.), Mount Owen (12,922 ft.), Middle Teton (12,798 ft.), Mount Moran (12,594 ft.), South Teton (12,505 ft.), Mount Teewing (12,317 ft.), Thor Peak (12,018 ft.) Buck Mountain (11,923 ft.), Nez Perce Peak (11,900 ft.), Mount Wister (11,840 ft.) and Mount St. John (11,412 ft.). There are float trips on rafts downstream, and excellent fishing in the Snake River and lakes in the park. Solo mountain climbing is forbidden, and climbers must register at the Jenny Lake Ranger Station where the Exum Mountain Climbing School prepares novices and experts for scaling the Tetons. In addition to natural wonders in nearby Yellowstone National Park, the Yellowstone Lake (29 miles long, 14 miles wide) on Yellowstone River and most lakes and streams contain Trout. The open fishing season dates vary from May 30 to July 15, and the season closes on October 31. No hunting is permitted in national and state parks.

The following lakes also offer exceptional fishing: *Fremont Lake* (6,000 acres), *Meadow Lake* (160 acres) and *Willow Lake* (1,992 acres) near Pinedale—Sublette County; *Ocean Lake* (4,062 acres) near Riverton —Fremont County; *Pathfinder Reservoir* (19,000 acres) on North Platte River, southwest of Casper—Carbon and Natrona counties.

STATE PARKS

Alcova at Alcova Reservoir on North Platte River, southwest of Casper—Natrona County; *Big Sandy* at Big Sandy Reservoir north of Farson—Sublette and Sweetwater counties; *Boysen* at Boysen Reservoir (18,000 acres) on Wind River northwest of Shoshoni—Fremont County; *Buffalo Bill* at Buffalo Bill Reservoir on the Shoshoni River, west of Cody —Park County; *Glendo* at Glendo Reservoir (12,000 acres) on North Platte River, near Glendo—Platte County; *Guernsey* at Guernsey Reservoir on North Platte River, north of Guernsey—Platte County; *Keyhole* at Keyhole Reservoir (1,500 acres) on Belle Fourche River north of Moorcroft—Crook County; *Saratoga Hot Springs* northeast of Saratoga —Carbon County; *Seminoe* at Seminoe Reservoir on North Platte River, northeast of Rawlins—Carbon County.

Licenses, regulations, information about current seasons, bag and possession limits may be obtained from the Commissioner, Wyoming Game and Fish Department, State Office Building (Box 378), Cheyenne. The attractive and informative Wyoming Wildlife magazine is published monthly by the Wyoming Game and Fish Department for $1.00 a year. National park addresses: Superintendent, Grand Teton National Park, Moose, Wyoming; Superintendent, Yellowstone National Park, Yellowstone Park, Wyoming.

PART II

PART II

National Forests

Magnificent mountains, virgin stands of timber, clear water lakes and streams in national forests may be easily accessible or reached only by water courses, hiking, or riding trails if portions are in Primitive, Wild and Wilderness areas. Rangers of the Forest Service, U.S. Department of Agriculture, are responsible for the multiple use of resources for outdoor recreation, water supply, harvesting timber, grasslands for domestic livestock, and vegetation to sustain wildlife. Congress defined multiple use* as "the management of all the various renewable surface resources of the national forests so that they are utilized in the combination that will best meet the needs of the American people."

The storage capacity of watersheds draining into lakes and streams is improved by proper maintenance of timber and vegetation. Foresters select trees to be harvested under plans to insure perpetual sustained yield for current and future needs, and also provide openings for livestock and wildlife. Timber is sold under competitive bidding and removed by private industry. Seedlings replace harvested timber, and young forests are thinned for maximum-quality crops. Prospecting, locating, and developing mineral resources are subject to the mining laws of the United States. Land ownership may include private, federal, and state holdings within or adjacent to forests. Agreements are negotiated with private landowners to provide for sharing the construction and maintenance cost of roads.

One forest fire can destroy watersheds, timber, forage for livestock, vegetation for wildlife, and recreation sites. Aircraft are used to spray insect repellents and to prevent or control forest fires. Fire-retardant chemicals are loaded in tanks and dropped to hold small fires until the arrival of ground crews, and to cool hot areas so that crews may establish firelines in advance of fires. Smokejumpers are expertly trained aerial fire fighters who parachute to forest fires. Helicopters are used not only for forest needs, but in rescue operations for sick or injured fishermen, hunters, hikers, mountain climbers, and persons in distress.

Summer homes may be erected according to the Forest Service's architectural and construction standards on lots leased by the year. Home lots are not procurable near population centers, where all lands in national forests are needed for public use.

---

* Multiple Use-Sustained Yield Act (1960)

Roads for motor vehicles lead through superb surroundings to camp and picnic sites which generally have such facilities as fireplaces, tables, benches, toilets, community shelters, boat launching ramps, and space for tents and trailers. Forest rangers issue fire permits, and provide information about guides, outfitters, trails, mountain climbing, pack and saddle trips, photographing wildlife, historic background, and other matters pertinent to their districts. Approximately one-third of the Appalachian Trail from Mount Katahdin in Maine to Mount Oglethorpe in Georgia goes through 8 national forests. The Pacific Crest Trail System traverses the summits of California, Oregon, and Washington mountains in 19 national forests between Canada and Mexico.

Forest rangers manage the habitat of wildlife, and each state fish and game department controls the population of wildlife through annual regulations restricting open seasons, bag limits, and licenses to fish, hunt, and trap. Except for special managed hunts, no fees are charged to enter and enjoy national forests. National parks are often surrounded by national forests, and hunters should not follow trails going through national parks where the use or possession of firearms is prohibited except by official personnel. Game may be hunted on ranges open to livestock.

There are 10 Forest Service regions under regional foresters. A forest supervisor is responsible for the multiple use of the national forest under his jurisdiction, and district rangers are in charge of operations within their districts of a forest. The multiple use of national forests adds up to an income of more than $120,000,000 annually. The Treasury of the United States returns about 25 per cent of that amount to the states, and each county having national forest lands then receives a share of that revenue to use for public schools and roads.

Individual forest maps are available from the forest supervisor's office, or ranger stations. Each Forest Service Region issues campground directories listing location, accessibility, facilities, and recreation opportunities. *Alaska Region*—Fifth Street Office Building, Juneau; *California Region*— 630 Sansome St., San Francisco 11; *Eastern Region* (Ky., N.H., Pa., Vt., Va., W. Va.)—6816 Market St., Upper Darby, Pa.; *Intermountain Region* (Idaho, Nev. Utah, Wyo.)—Forest Service Building, Ogden, Utah; *North Central Region* (Ill., Ind., Mich., Minn., Mo., Ohio, Wis.) —710 North Sixth St., Milwaukee 3, Wis.; *Northern Region* (Idaho, Mont., Colville National Forest, Wash.)—Federal Building, Missoula, Mont.; *Pacific Northwest Region* (Ore., Wash.)—729 N.E. Oregon St., Portland 8, Ore.; *Rocky Mountain Region* (Col., Neb., S. D., Wyo.: Bighorn, Medicine Bow, Shoshone national forests)—Denver Federal Center, Building 85, Denver 25, Col.; *Southwestern Region* (Ariz., N.M.)— 517 Gold St., N.W., Albuquerque, N.M.

ALABAMA NATIONAL FORESTS

William B. Bankhead (178,895 acres) in northern Alabama: Bass fishing in Brushy Lake (33 acres); hunting Deer, Turkey, and Squirrel. Special features: Bee Branch Scenic Area of approximately 1,000 acres in a deep box canyon; Lewis Smith Reservoir; Sipsey River Recreation Area; Black Warrior Wildlife Management Unit (96,500 acres). Camp and picnic sites, 1; picnic only, 3. Nearby towns: Cullman, Decatur, Haleyville, Hamilton, Jasper, Moulton, Russelville. Highways: u.s. 31, 43, 78; State 5, 24, 31, 36. Forest supervisor at Montgomery.

Conecuh (83,790 acres) on the Florida border: Bass and Bream fishing; Deer, Turkey, and small game hunting. Special features: Open Pond (50 acres); Conecuh River; Blue Springs Wildlife Management Unit (27,268 acres) Camp and picnic site, 1; picnic only, 1. Nearby towns: Andalusia, Brewton, Geneva. Highways: u.s. 29, 31, 84; State 12, 15, 88. Forest supervisor at Montgomery.

Talladega (357 acres in 2 divisions): Bass, Bream, and Perch fishing; Deer, Turkey, Squirrel, waterfowl hunting. Special features: Oakmulgee District—Payne Lake (100 acres), Cahaba River, Perry Mountain, Oakmulgee Wildlife Management Area (45,000 acres); Talladega District—Lake Chinnabee (20 acres), Cheaha State Park containing Mount Cheaha (2,407 ft.), Choccolocco Wildlife Management Unit (39,000 acres). Camp and picnic sites, 4; picnic only, 7. Nearby towns: Alexander City, Anniston, Ashland, Calera, Greensboro, Heflin, Marion, Selma, Sylacauga, Talladega, Tuscaloosa. Highways: u.s. 11, 31, 43, 78, 241; State 5, 6, 9, 11, 22, 37. Forest supervisor at Montgomery.

Tuskegee (10,777 acres): Bream fishing in streams. Special feature: pine plantation; picnic sites—2. Nearby towns: Auburn, Tuskegee. Highways: u.s. 29, 80; State 81. Forest Supervisor, Federal Building, Montgomery, Ala.

ALASKA NATIONAL FORESTS

Chugach (4,726,145 acres) along shores of Prince William Sound and eastern part of Kenai Peninsula: Trout and saltwater fishing; Bear, Moose, Mountain Goat, Bighorn Sheep, Grouse, Ptarmigan, waterfowl hunting. Special features: Hanging, Piedmont, and Tidewater glaciers; Kenai Mountains; Afognak Island; fiords of Port Wells; Aleut villages and *bidarkis* (boats); salmon and shellfish canneries; Alyeska Ski Area. Camp and picnic sites, 5; picnic only, 16. Nearby towns: Anchorage, Cordova, Kodiak, Seward, Valdez, Whittier. Highways: State 3, 4. Transportation generally by air and watercraft. Forest supervisor at Anchorage.

Tongass (16,016,140 acres) on the southeastern coast: Trout and salt-water fishing; Bear, Deer, Moose, Mountain Goat, and small game hunting. Special features: western hemlock, Sitka spruce and cedar forests, lakes, fiords, snow-capped mountains, and maze of islands including Admiralty Island; "Trail of 98" to the Yukon; Behn and Portland canals; Indian villages; salmon canneries; Douglas Ski Bowl and Petersburg Ski Area. Camp and picnic sites, none in North Division, 2 in Southern Division; picnic only, 2 (North), 1 (South). Nearby towns: Juneau, Petersburg, Sitka, Skagway (North); Ketchikan, Wrangell (South). Highways: spur road from Alaska Highway in Canada to Haines. Ferry service to Juneau June 1–March 1; transportation generally by air and watercraft. Forest supervisors at Juneau and Ketchikan.

ARIZONA NATIONAL FORESTS

Apache (1,732,891 acres extending into New Mexico): Trout fishing; Antelope, Bear, Deer, Elk, and small game hunting. Special features: clear streams, deep ravines, and mountain meadows among aspen, pine, and spruce forests; White Mountains; Greens Peak (10,115 ft.); Big Crescent, Greer, and Luna lakes; headwaters of the Black, Blue, and Little Colorado rivers; Blue Range and Mount Baldy primitive areas; historic Coronado Trail; hiking trails, pack and saddle trips. Camp and picnic sites, 26; picnic only, 1; motels and resorts. Nearby towns: Alpine, Greer, Springerville; Luna and Reserve in New Mexico. Highways: u.s. 60, 260, 666. Forest supervisor at Springerville.

Coconino (1,801,091 acres) adjacent to the Kaibab (southern division), Prescott, Sitgreaves and Tonto National Forests: Bass, Bluegill, Crappie and Trout fishing in lakes and streams; Pronghorn Antelope, Deer (Rocky Mountain Mule, White-tailed), Javelina, Wild Turkey, upland game, predator hunting. Special features: San Francisco Mountains; Humphreys Peak (12,670 ft.); O'Leary Peak (8,925 ft); Mormon Mountain (8,440 ft.); Sunset Crater National Monument (3,040 acres); Mogollon Plateau and Rim; Verde River; Bear, Clear and Oak Creeks; Lake Mary; Ashurst, Kinnikinick, Knoll, Rogers, Soldier, Stehr, and Stoneman lakes; Blue Ridge Reservoir; Sycamore Canyon Primitive Area; Oak Creek Canyon; Arizona Snow Bowl. Camp and picnic sites, 18; picnic only, 5; dude ranches and resort hotels. Nearby towns: Cameron, Camp Verde, Clarkdale, Cottonwood, Flagstaff, Sedona, Winslow. Highways: u.s. 66, 89, 89A. Forest supervisor at Flagstaff.

Coronado (1,796,534 acres) scattered in southeastern Arizona with a small segment in New Mexico: Bass and Trout fishing in lakes; Black Bear, Deer (Mule, White-tailed), Javelina, Wild Turkey, Pigeon, Quail, Rabbit, Coati-mundi, Jaguar, and other predator hunting. Special features:

desert cactus and evergreen forests; Chiricahua Mountains; Chiricahua and Galiuro Wild Areas; Mount Graham (10,714 ft.) in the Pinaleno Mountain Recreation Area. Riggs Flat Lake; Rose Canyon Lake, Sabino Canyon, and Mount Lemmon Snow Bowl in Santa Catalina Mountains; Peña Blanca Lake (52 acres) near Arizona-Mexico boundary; Pole Bridge Canyon Natural Area; Cochise Head (8,109 ft.); Portal Peak (8,544 acres); pack trips and hiking trails. Camp and picnic sites, 32; picnic only 17; dude ranches and winter resorts. Nearby towns: Benson, Bisbee, Douglas, Fort Huachuca, Nogales, Patagonia, Safford, San Simon, Tombstone, Tucson, Wilcox. Highways: u.s. 80, 84, 89, 666; State 82, 86. Forest supervisor at Tucson.

Gila (75,666 acres adjacent to Apache National Forest) . . . Special features: Hannagan Meadows (9,092 ft. elevation); Blue River. Nearby towns: Clifton, Morenci. Highways: u.s. 70; Arizona 75,666. See NEW MEXICO NATIONAL FORESTS.

Kaibab (1,715,190 acres in 4 divisions): Trout fishing in lakes; Black Bear, Rocky Mountain Mule Deer, Buffalo, Elk, upland game, predator hunting. Special features: Aspen, ponderosa pine, fir, and spruce forests; north and south of Grand Canyon National Park (673,203 acres); Tusayan and Williams divisions south of the Grand Canyon; North Kaibab or Kaibab North, called Kaibabitz (Mountain-lying-down) by Piute Indians, a plateau 60 miles long and 40 miles wide at 6,000–9,000 elevation; Sycamore Canyon Primitive Area; Mount Logan (7,700 ft.); Mount Trumbull (8,028 ft.); Sitgreaves Mountain (8,984 ft.); Kendrick Mountain (10,418 ft.); Bill Williams Mountain (9,264 ft.); McClellan Reservoir; Cataract, Jacob, Kaibab, and Whitehorse lakes; Grand Canyon National Game Preserve (Buffalo and Deer hunts); pack and saddle trips. Camp and picnic sites, 6; hunting camps in season; guest ranches, motels, and resorts. Nearby towns: Ashfork, Cottonwood, Flagstaff, Fredonia, Grand Canyon, Williams. Highways: u.s. 66, 67, 89; State 64, 67, 79. Forest supervisor at Williams.

Prescott (1,248,210 acres in 2 segments): Trout fishing; Antelope, Deer, Dove, Quail, and other small game hunting. Special features: Granite Basin Lake; Hassayampa Lake; Verde River; Horse Mountain (7,059 ft.); Mount Union (7,971 ft.); Pine Mountain and Sycamore Canyon Primitive Areas; hiking and saddle trails. Camp and picnic sites, 8; picnic only, 8; dude ranches, motels, and resorts. Nearby towns: Clarkdale, Cottonwood, Jerome, Mayer, Prescott. Highway: u.s. 89. Forest supervisor at Prescott.

Sitgreaves (744,820 acres) adjacent to Apache and Coconino national forests: Perch and Trout fishing; Antelope, Bear, Deer, and small game hunting. Special features: Show Low Lake; Woods Canyon Lake; Mogollon Plateau; pack and saddle trips. Camp and picnic sites, 4; guest ranches, hotels, and resorts. Nearby towns: Holbrook, Lakeside, Pinetop, Show Low, Snowflake, Winslow. Highways: u.s. 66; State 77, 173. Forest supervisor at Holbrook.

Tonto (2,902,820 acres) adjacent to, and south of, Coconino, Prescott and Sitgreaves national forests: Bass, Bluegill, Catfish, Crappie, Perch, and Trout fishing; Black Bear, Deer (Rocky Mountain Mule, White-tailed), Elk, Javelina, Wild Turkey, small game, predator hunting. Special features: elevation 1,500–7,905 feet from saguaro cactus desert to evergreen forests on Mogollon Rim; Mazatzal Wilderness Area; Pine Mountain Primitive Area; Sierra Peak (7,905 ft.); Tonto Basin; Roosevelt Reservoir on the Salt River and Tonto Creek; Apache, Canyon, and Saguaro lakes also formed by dams on the Salt River; Bartlett and Horseshoe lakes on the Verde River; Apache Trail through Tonto National Monument (1,120 acres) to Roosevelt, and southwest to Horse Mesa and Superstition Mountains; pack and saddle trips. Camp and picnic sites, 22; picnic only, 4; dude ranches and resorts. Nearby towns: Globe, Mesa, Miami, Payson, Phoenix, Pine, Superior, Young. Highways: u.s. 60, 70, 80, 89. Forest supervisor at Phoenix.

ARKANSAS NATIONAL FORESTS

*Ouachita** (1,543,361 acres) extends into Oklahoma: Bass and Trout fishing in lakes and streams; White-tailed Deer, Wild Turkey, Bobwhite Quail, small animal hunting. Special features; pine forests and stands of hardwood trees on series of long narrow ridges; Fourche La Fave, Little Missouri, and Ouachita rivers; Lake Ouachita (75 square miles); Three Sisters Springs in Lake Ouachita State Park; Blakely Dam Spillway near Mountain Pine; Crystal Mountain near Lake Winona; Nimrod Lake south of Plainview; Lake Sylvia (40 acres) near Chinquapin Mountain; Shady Lake (35 acres) near Caney Creek Scenic Area; Belle Starr Caves in 1,000-foot cliffs at Rock Creek; Cedar Lake (84 acres) and Winding Stair Mountain in Oklahoma area; hiking trails. Camp and picnic sites, 20; picnic only, 7; cabin camps, hotels, and resorts. Nearby towns: Boonville, Briggsville, Cove, Crystal Springs, Danville, Glenwood, Hot Springs, Jessieville, Joplin, Langley, Mount Ida, Mena, Mountain Pine, Perryville, Plainview, Waldron in Arkansas; Big Cedar, Haworth, Heavener, Hodgens, Idabel, Muse, Talihina and Whitesboro, Oklahoma. Highways: u.s. 70, 71, 270; Arkansas 7, 8, 10, 23, 27, 28, 60, 70, 80, 84, 88; Oklahoma 63, 269. Forest supervisor at Hot Springs.

Ozark (1,046,309 acres) several segments in the northwestern Boston and Ozark mountains: Bass and Trout fishing in lakes and streams; White-tailed Deer, Wild Turkey, and small game hunting. Special fea-

* Pronounced wash-i-taw

tures: oaks forests and picturesque bluffs; Cove Lake (166 acres) north of Magazine Mountain (2,830 ft.); Lake Wedington (102 acres) west of Fayetteville; Horsehead Lake (98 acres) near Clarkesville; Shores Lake (80 acres) southwest of Cass; Spring Lake (82 acres) north of Belleview; Blanchard Springs north of Mountain View in the wilderness "Land of the Bow and Arrow" (crossbow and longbow archery field); White Rock Mountain; Buffalo and Mulberry rivers; hiking trails. Camp and picnic sites, 10; cabins and resorts. Nearby towns: Belleville, Calico Rocks, Cass, Clarksville, Fayetteville, Fort Smith, Harrison, Ozark, Paris, Russellville. Highways: u.s. 64, 71; State 7, 9, 14, 16, 22, 23, 27, 44, 164. Forest supervisor at Russellville.

St. Francis (20,000 acres) on the Mississippi River: Fishing in lakes and streams; White-tailed Deer, Turkey, and waterfowl hunting. Special features: Storm Creek Lake (510 acres); Bear Creek Lake Recreation Area. Camp and picnic sites, 1 (9 units); rental boats and cabins. Nearby towns: Helena, Marianna. Highways: u.s. 79; State 1, 20.

CALIFORNIA NATIONAL FORESTS

Angeles (648,754 acres) west of the Mojave Desert in southern California: Trout fishing; Deer and small game hunting. Special features: mountains, canyons, springs, and streams; Mount San Antonio or Old Baldy Peak (10,059 ft.) north of San Antonio Canyon; Mount Baden Powell (9,399 ft.); Throop Peak (9,134 ft.); Waterman Mountain (8,038 ft.) above Kratka Ridge; Telegraph Peak (9,008 ft.) overlooking adjacent San Bernardino National Forest; Mount Lewis (8,395 ft.); Mount Williamson (8,214 ft.) above Pleasant View Ridge; Mount Wilson Observatory (5,736 ft.) between Mount Lowe (5,650 ft.) and Big Santa Anita Recreation Area; Smithsonian Observatory at Big Pines Recreation Area; Twin Peaks (7,760 ft.) in Devils Canyon–Bear Canyon Wild Area; Big Dalton Canyon, Big Tujunga Creek, Little Rock Creek, Pacoima, and San Dimas Canyon Reservoirs; Morris, San Gabriel, and Cogswell Reservoirs on the San Gabriel River; Boquet Reservoir in Sierra Pelona; Crystal Lake Recreation Area; Blue Ridge, Holiday Hill, Kratka Ridge, Mount Baldy, Mount Waterman, Movie Slope, and Table Mountain ski areas; hiking and riding trails. Camp and picnic sites, 82; picnic only, 11 (open camp fires prohibited); cabins and resorts. Nearby towns: Arcadia, Azusa, Castaie, Glendora, Gorman, Monrovia, Newhall, Palmdale, Pasadena, San Fernando, Saugus, Sunland, Tujunga. Highways: u.s. 6, 66, 99; State 2, 14, 39, 118, 134. Forest supervisor at Pasadena.

Cleveland (391,682 acres, in several segments) in southwestern California: Bass, Bluegill, Catfish, and Crappie fishing; Deer, Pigeon, Quail, waterfowl hunting. Special features: Los Pinos Peak (4,507 ft.),

Sierra Peak (3,045 ft.), Sugar Loaf Peak (4,007 ft.), and Santiago Lookout (5,687 ft.) in the Santa Ana Mountains; San Juan Canyon in the Elsinore Mountains; San Mateo Canyon in the Santa Margarita Mountains; El Cajon Mountain (3,684 ft.) and Rock Mountain (3,300 ft.) near El Capitan Reservoir and adjacent Capitan Grande Indian Reservation; San Diego River; Loveland Reservoir on Sweetwater River; Barber Mountain (3,248 ft.) east of Barrett Lake; Los Pinos Mountain Lookout above Morena Lake and Valley; Chiquito Peak (4,110ft.), Poser Mountain (3,919 ft.), and Viejas Mountain (4,178 ft.) overlooking adjacent Viejas Indian Reservation; San Luis Rey River in Barker Valley; Agua Tibia Wilderness Area adjacent to the Pechanga Indian Reservation; Birch Hill (5,157 ft.) near La Jolla Indian Reservation; Lake Henshaw; Black Mountain Lookout (4,051 ft.) north of Lake Sutherland; hiking and riding trails. Camp and picnic sites, 22; picnic only, 4 (open fires prohibited); dude ranches, motels, and resorts. Nearby towns: Aguanga, Alpine, Corona, Cuyamaca, Desano, Escondido, Julian, Pomona, Ramona, San Diego. Highways: u.s. 80, 101, 395; State 67, 71, 74, 78, 79, 94. Forest supervisor at San Diego.

Eldorado (640,619 acres) in the Sierra Nevada east of Sacramento: Trout fishing; Bear, Deer, and small game hunting. Special features: mountain streams and hundreds of lakes, including Cascade Lake, Emerald Bay, and southwestern shore of Lake Tahoe; Brown Mountain (7,144 ft.), Devils Peak (7,541 ft.), Guide Peak (7,741 ft.), Jerrett Peak (7,504 ft.) and Red Mountain (6,872 ft.) overlooking Loon Lake Reservoir; Big Hill (6,155 ft.) and Deer Knob (5,621 ft.) near Union Valley Reservoir; Ice House Reservoir on Silver Creek; Echo Peak (8,895 ft.), Flagpole Peak (8,363 ft.), and Talking Mountain (8,824 ft.) above Upper and Lower Echo lakes; Ralston Peak (9,235 ft.) near Lake of the Woods, Cagwin, Ralston, and Tamarack lakes; American Bar Reservoir on the Middle Fork American River near Ralston Ridge; Angora Peak (8,588 ft.) south of Fallen Leaf Lake; Lookout Mountain (5,159 ft.) near Lake Edison; Round Top Lookout (10,380 ft.) above Lake Winnemucca; Blue Mountain (8,772 ft.) east of Wrights Lake; Salt Springs Reservoir on North Fork Mokelumne River; Twin Lakes west of Carson Pass; Silver Lakes near Thimble Peak (9,827 ft.); Mokelumne Peak (9,332 ft.); Bear River and Lower Bear River Reservoirs near Peddler Hill; Dicks Peak (9,974 ft.) in the Desolation Valley Primitive Area; Hornblende Mountains; South Fork American River; Rubicon River; Echo Summit, Heavenly Valley, Peddler Hill, Sierra Ski Ranch, and Strawberry Lodge Winter Sports areas; pack and saddle trips. Camp and picnic sites, 28; picnic only, 3; dude ranches, motels, and resorts. Nearby towns: Auburn, Coloma, Georgetown, Jackson, Placerville, Truckee in California; Carson City and Reno, Nevada. Highways: u.s. 50; State 4, 49, 88, 89. Forest supervisor at Placerville.

Inyo (1,774,176 acres in 2 divisions) in the Sierra Nevada near Bishop: Trout fishing; Deer and small game hunting. Special features: mountain meadows, numerous natural lakes, and streams in the High Sierra accessible by paved roads up to 9,700-foot elevation; adjacent to Kings Canyon National Park (454,650 acres) and Yosemite National Park (760,951 acres), and encircles the Devils Postpile National Monument (798 acres); Mount Whitney (14,496 ft.); John Muir Wilderness Area containing 34 peaks above 13,000 feet; Kern River; Mount Stanford (13,938 ft.); Mount Kaweah (13,816 ft.); Strawberry Meadows; White Mountains east of Owens Valley and the Paiute Indian Reservation; White Mountain Peak (14,242 ft.); Mount DuBois (13,545 ft.); Montgomery Peak (13,465 ft.); Boundary Peak (13,145 ft.) on the Nevada border; Black Mountain (9,724 ft.) and Mustang Mountain (10,252 ft.) in Nevada; the Ancient Bristlecone Pine Forest (28,000 acres) containing gnarled and twisted 4,000-year-old trees; Minarets Wilderness Area: Crystal Crag (10,364 ft.) and Mammoth Mountain (11,053 ft.) overlooking Mammoth Lakes; Mono Lake; Reversed Peak (9,473 ft.) Recreation Area at Grant, Gulf, Junc, and Silver lakes; Mono Craters; June Mountain, Mammoth Mountain, and Onion Valley Winter sports areas. Camp and picnic sites, 61; picnic only, 4; motels and resorts. Nearby towns: Big Pine, Bishop, Independence, Lone Pine. Highways: u.s. 6,395; State 120, 168. Forest supervisor at Bishop.

Klamath (1,697 acres) extending north of Yreka into Oregon: Salmon and Steelhead fishing in lakes and streams; Deer and small game hunting. Special features: thick forests and deep narrow canyons; Klamath, Salmon, and Scott rivers; Kings Castle (7,396 ft.) in Marble Mountain Wilderness Area; Black Rock (7,468 ft.) in the Salmon Trinity Alps Wilderness Area; Big Red Mountain (6,054 ft.), Doe Peak (5,218 ft.), and Siskiyou Peak (7,147 ft.) in Oregon; McKinley Mountain (6,229 ft.) north of Gunsight Peak (6,140 ft.); Grizzly Peak (7,956 ft.) near Russian Peak (8,183 ft.); Bear Mountain (6,437 ft.) near Devils Punchbowl; Bear Peak (5,740 ft.) source of Bear Valley creeks; Herd Peak (7,060 ft.) near Grass Lake; Caribou Mountain (8,563 ft.); Scott Bar Mountains; Preston Peak (7,310 ft.) above Rattlesnake Meadow; Lower, Middle, and Upper Devils peaks; hiking trails, pack and saddle trips. Camp and picnic sites, 28; picnic only, 2; dude ranches, motels, and resorts. Nearby towns: Callahan, Fort Jones, Happy Camp, Somes Bar, Sawyers Bar, Yreka in California; Medford, Oregon. Highways: u.s. 97, 99; California 96.

Lassen (1,047,372 acres in several segments) in northern California: Steelhead and other Trout fishing in lakes and streams; Bear, Deer, and small game hunting. Special features: northern tip of Sierra Nevada and southern end of Cascade Range; Lake Almanor on North Fork Feather River near Chester; Lassen Volcanic National Park (106,933 acres) con-

taining Mount Lassen (10,457 ft.); Silver Lakes east of the Caribou Peak
Wild Area; Thousand Lakes Wild Area; Crater Lake Mountain (7,429 ft.)
above Crater Lake; Burney Mountain (7,863 ft.) north of Burney Springs;
Eagle Rock (7,063 ft.) and Humboldt Peak (7,087 ft.) near Robbers
Roost; Butler Mountain (7,866 ft.); Philbrook Lakes west of Spring Valley Mountain (6,862 ft.); Lava Peak (6,613 ft.) and Slate Mountain
(7,136 ft.) above Gooch Valley; Cave Mountain (6,578 ft.) north of Ice
Cave Ridge; Alcohol Jack and Bainbridge Reservoirs; Subway Cave in
Devils Half Acre; West Prospect Peak (8,338 ft.); Red Rock Mountain
(7,555 ft.); McCoy Flat Reservoir; Eagle Lake east of Whale back Mountain (6,924 ft.); Coppervale and Stover Winter Sports areas; hiking and
riding trails. Camp and picnic sites, 59; picnic only, 5; cabins, hotels, and
resorts. Nearby towns: Burney, Chester, Chico, Fall River Mills, Greenville, Oroville, Red Bluff, Susanville. Highways: u.s. 40A, 99; State 32,
36, 44, 89. Forest supervisor at Susanville.

Los Padres (1,749,245 acres in 2 divisions) north and south of San
Luis Obispo in the Coast Range: Fishing in freshwater lakes and streams
and the Pacific Ocean; Deer, Wild Pig, and small game hunting. Special
features: Northern division—Santa Lucia Range; Ventana Primitive Area,
Pico Blanco (3,710 ft.), Junipero Serra Peak (5,862 ft.), Cone Peak
(5,155 ft.) north of Hunter Liggett Military Reservation, Tassajara Hot
Springs; Southern division—La Panza, San Rafael, Sierra Madre, and
Santa Inez ranges, San Rafael Primitive Area, Zaca Peak (4,333 ft.) above
Zaca Lake, Matilija Reservoir, Santa Barbara Reservoir south of Lake
Cachuma, Mount Pinos (8,826 ft.) west of Frazier Park, Frazier Moun-
tain (8,013 ft.), Tejon Pass (4,183 ft.), Reyes Peak (7,488 ft.), Cuyama
Peak (5,880 ft.) north of Apache Canyon Recreation Area, Santa Inez
River, Topatopa Peak (6,120 ft.) in Sespe Wildlife Area, Mount Abel
Ski Area. Camp and picnic sites, 49; picnic only, 7 (open campfires pro-
hibited); cabins, dude ranches, hot springs resorts, hotels. Nearby towns:
Atascadero, Carmel, Frazier Park, Gorman, King City, Maricopa, Ojai,
Paso Robles, San Luis Obispo, Santa Barbara, Santa Maria, Ventura.
Highways: u.s. 99, 101, 399; State 1, 33, 41, 58, 150. Forest supervisor at
Santa Barbara.

Mendocino (867,425 acres) north of Lakeport and Clear Lake in
northern California: Trout fishing in lakes and streams; Columbian Black-
tailed Deer and small game hunting. Special features: brush (chaparral),
grass ranges, numerous forested ridges, lakes, springs, and streams; Lake
Pillsbury on the Eel River; South Yolla Bolly (8,092 ft.); Hammerhorn
Mountain (7,593 ft.); Snow Mountain (7,056 ft.); Black Butte (7,448
ft.); East Snow Mountain (7,040 ft.); Anthony Peak (6,954 ft.); Bald
Mountain (6,739 ft.); Hull Mountain (6,873 ft.); St. John Mountain
(6,743 ft.); Sheetiron Mountain (6,503 ft.); Uhl Mountain (6,635 ft.);

Mendocino Pass near Oak Knoll (5,262 ft.); Yolla Bolly–Middle Eel Wilderness Area; pack and saddle trips. Camp and picnic sites, 49; dude ranches and motels. Nearby towns: Corning, Covelo, Lakeport, Laytonville, Paskenta, Ukiah, Williams, Willits, Willows. Highways: u.s. 99 West, 101; State 20, 29. Forest supervisor at Willows.

Modoc (1,688,789 acres in 2 divisions) in northern California: Trout fishing in lakes and streams; Mule Deer, waterfowl, and other small game hunting. Special features: numerous reservoirs, natural lakes, and streams; Clear Lake National Wildlife Refuge north of Double Head Mountain (5,582 ft.); Big Sage Reservoir at Whittemore Ridge west of Raker, Thomas, and Wood Flat Reservoirs; Egg and Little Egg lakes east of Barnum Flat and Whittemore Flat reservoirs; South Warner Wild Area in South Warner Mountains division between Upper Goose Lake and Upper Alkali Lake; Tule Lake National Wildlife Refuge north of the Lava Beds National Monument (46,238 acres); Medicine Lakes; Glass Mountain (7,622 ft.); Indian Butte (6,818 ft.); Buck Mountain (8,636 ft.); Cedar Pass Ski Course west of Cedarville; hiking and riding trails. Camp and picnic sites, 25; picnic only, 2; hunters' camps during Deer seasons, cabins, and hotels. Nearby towns: Adin, Alturas, Canby, Cedarville, Fort Bidwell, Lake City, Tulelake. Highways: u.s. 299, 395; State 139. Forest supervisor at Alturas.

Plumas (1,147,611 acres) between Lassen and Tahoe national forests in northeastern California: Trout fishing in lakes and streams; Bear, Mule Deer, waterfowl, and other small game hunting. Special features: Feather River country with evergreen forests, Feather River Falls (640 ft.), Middle Fork Feather River, and Lake Almanor; Bald Eagle Mountain (7,176 ft.); Spanish Peak (7,017 ft.) and Bucks Lakes west of Quincy; Grizzly Peak or Lone Tree Lookout (7,704 ft.) above Devils Punchbowl; Taylor Rock (7,338 ft.); Lower Taylor (7,024 ft.); Mount Hough 7,232 ft.) at Crystal Lake; Frenchman Reservoir near Bald Rock (7,171 ft.); Reconnaissance Peak (7,631 ft.); Dixie Mountain (8,923 ft.); Adams Peak (8,197 ft.) and Crystal Peak in the Diamond Mountains; Squaw Valley Peak (6,846 ft.); Elephant Playground between Babcock Peak (7,007 ft.) and Wheeler Peak (7,374 ft.), Eisenhower Peak (7,500 ft.) Rattlesnake Peak (7,431 ft.) north of Kettle Rock (7,820 ft.); Thompson Peak Lookout (7,795 ft.) and Clarks Peak (7,177 ft.) near Honey Lake just east of the national forest; Bagley Pass (6,300 ft.) into Red Clover Valley; Plumas-Eureka Ski Bowl; Pacific Crest Trail. Camp and picnic sites, 27; picnic only, 2; cabins, hotels, and resorts. Nearby towns: Blairsden, Hallelujah Junction, Oroville, Quincy, Taylorsville, Sierraville. Highways: u.s. 40A, 395; State 24, 49, 89. Forest supervisor at Quincy.

San Bernardino (613,912 acres) west of Joshua Tree National Monument (505,226 acres) in southern California: Trout fishing; Deer and small game hunting. Special features: mountain meadows, canyons, creeks and springs; Big Bear Lake Recreation Area near San Gorgonio Wild Area; Galena Peak (9,330 ft.); Sugarloaf Mountain (9,952 ft.); Lake Arrowhead Recreation Area; Keller Peak (7,882 ft.); Slide Peak (7,779 ft.); Cleghorn Ridge; Cleghorn Mountain (5,333 ft.); Circle Mountain (6,875 ft.); Upper Lytle Creek Ridge; Cucamonga Wild Area; San Jacinto Wild Area; Hemet Reservoir on South Fork San Jacinto River below Horse Creek Ridge; Black Mountain Scenic Area (7,772 ft.); Indian Mountain Lookout (5,790 ft.); Coahuila Mountain Lookout (5,624 ft.); Green Valley Snow Bowl; Lynn Ski Lifts, Moon Ridge, Snow Summit, and Snow Valley Winter Sports Areas; hiking and riding trails. Camp and picnic sites, 41; picnic only, 10 (open camp fires prohibited); cabins, hotels, resorts. Nearby towns: Banning, Beaumont, Cabezon, Palm Desert, Palm Springs, San Bernardino, West Palm Springs. Highways: u.s. 60, 66, 70, 91, 99; State 2, 18, 30, 74, 111, 138. Forest supervisor at San Bernardino.

Sequoia (1,118,551 acres) adjacent to Sequoia National Park (385,-418 acres) and north of the Mojave Desert: Trout (including Golden Trout) fishing in mountain lakes and streams; Bear, Mule Deer, and small game hunting. Special features: numerous meadows, mountain streams and springs; Dome Land Wild Area; John Muir Wilderness Area; Kern River and Kings River canyons; Quaking Aspen Meadow; Mineral Peak (11,535 ft.) in the Mineral King Game Refuge; Sunday Peak (8,320 ft.) and Tobias Peak (8,305 ft.) in the Greenhorn Mountains; Piute Peak (8,432 ft.); Cannell Peak (9,453 ft.); Crag Peak (9,555 ft.) and Finger Rock (9,181 ft.) near Deer Mountain (9,530 ft.); Granite Knob (9,140 ft.); Lookout Mountain (9,826 ft.); Jackass Peak (9,305 ft.); Sherman Peak (9,974 ft.); Siretta Peak (9,956 ft.); Hume Lake, California Hot Springs; Isabella Reservoir just outside national forest; Shirley Meadows and Sugar Loaf Ski Areas; hiking and riding trails. Camp and picnic sites, 45; picnic only, 8. Nearby towns. Bakersfield, Ducor, Freeman Junction, Isabella, Kernville, Lone Pine, Porterville, Three Rivers. Highways: u.s. 6, 395; State 65, 178, 190, 198. Forest supervisor at Porterville.

Shasta-Trinity (2,036,836 acres in 2 divisions) in northern California: Salmon and Trout fishing; Bear, Deer, waterfowl, and other small game hunting. Special features: heavy stands of timber, jagged peaks, deep valleys, lava and limestone caves; Salmon-Trinity Alps Primitive Area; Yolla Bolly–Middle Eel Wilderness Area; Mount Shasta (14,162 ft.) covered with perpetual snow and 5 living glaciers; access to Shasta Lake (46 square miles); Hay Fork, McCloud, Pit and Trinity Rivers; Coffee Creek Lakes; Lewiston Lake; Jackass Springs below Jackass Peak (4,487 ft.) at Trinity Lake (shoreline 145 miles); Soda Creek Ridge; Shoein Horse Mountain (5,261 ft.) and Little Shoein Horse (5,252 ft.) near Van Sicklin Butte (5,059 ft.); Blake Mountain (5,848 ft.) in South Fork

Mountain; Picket Peak (5,781 ft.) in North Fork Mountains; Grizzly Peak (6,253 ft.); Trout Creek Butte (5,494 ft.); Mount Shasta Ski Bowl; hiking trails, pack and saddle trips. Camp and picnic sites, 75; picnic only, 5; dude ranches, motels, and hotels. Nearby towns: Callahan, Douglas City, Dunsmuir, Lewiston, McCloud, Shasta, Redding, Trinity Center, Weaverville, Weed. Highways: u.s. 99, 299; State 36, 44, 89, 96. Forest supervisor at Redding.

Sierra (1,295,832 acres) adjacent to Kings Canyon and Yosemite national parks on western slopes of the Sierra Nevada: Trout fishing in lakes and streams; Bear, Deer, and small game hunting. Special features: meadows, ridges, clear mountain lakes and streams; Bear Butte (8,598 ft.), Black Point (8,111 ft.), Chinese Peak (8,709 ft.), Jumpoff Point (8,549 ft.), and Kaiser Peak (10,320 ft.) within sight of Huntington Lake; Ely Mountain (6,886 ft.), Flume Peak (5,979 ft.), Musick Mountain (6,807 ft.), and Mount Stevenson (6,404 ft.) overlooking Shaver Lake; Kerckoff Lake and Redinger Lake near Horseshoe Bend, and Mammoth Reservoir about 20 miles upstream on the San Joaquin River; Wishon Reservoir on the North Fork Kings River near Loper Peak (10,059 ft.) in Woodchuck Country; Pine Flat Reservoir on Kings River; Spanish Mountain (10,051 ft.) and Lakes; Bass Lake near South Fork Bluffs; Little Shuteye Peak (8,362 ft.) above Chiquito Ridge; John Muir Wilderness Area; Minarets Wilderness Area; Florence Lake near Mount Givens (10,648 ft.); Lake Thomas A. Edison below Bear Ridge; Chowchilla Mountains; Courtright Reservoir guarded by Eagle Peak (10,318 ft.), Long Top Mountain (9,375 ft.) and Maxson Dome (9,547 ft.); several lakes between Bear Mountain (9,512 ft.), Black Peak (9,771 ft.), Brown Peak (10,349 ft.) Dinkey Dome (7,697 ft.), Marble Point (8,858 ft.), and Nelson Mountain (10,218 ft.); Nelder Grove of redwood trees (*Sequoia gigantea*) near Grouse Meadow and Speckerman Mountain (7,137 ft.); China Peak Ski Area; hiking trails, pack and saddle trips. Camp and picnic sites, 79; picnic only, 19; dude ranches, hotels, and resorts. Nearby towns: Badger, Dunlap, Fresno, Hume, Kingsburg, Mariposa. Highways: u.s. 99; State 41, 168, 180. Forest supervisor at Fresno.

Six Rivers (935,268 acres) in the northwestern Coast Range extending into Oregon: Salmon and Trout fishing; Bear, Deer, and small game hunting. Special features: Redwood (*Sequoia sempervirens*) and fir forests; Black Mountain (3,209 ft.) near the Klamath River; Mount Lassic (4,663 ft.), Red Lassic (5,903 ft.), Green Mountain (5,302 ft.), and Goat Hill (5,463 ft.) in the Mule Ridge region of the Van Duzen River; Mad River flowing parallel to South Fork Mountains; Trinity River between Brannan Mountain (4,002 ft.) and Waterman Ridge; Lower and Upper Coon mountains between the Middle Fork and South Fork Smith rivers; High Plateau near the North Fork Smith River; Grizzly Mountain

(5,456 ft.) above Big Meadow Creek; Hayden Roughs (4,663 ft.) near Jones Ridges; Pigeon Roost (3,267 ft.) and Springs; Baldy Peak (5,775 ft.) at Bear Wallows; Bear Basin Butte (5,303 ft.) and Hurdygurdy Butte (5,281 ft.) on Blue Ridge; Broken Rib Mountain (5,824 ft.) near Wounded Knee Mountain (4,778 ft.)–Redwood Empire region; adjacent Hoopa Valley Indian Reservation; Horse Mountain Ski Area; hiking and riding trails. Camp and picnic sites, 33; picnic only, 1. Nearby towns: Arcata, Crescent City, Eureka, Fortuna, Klamath, Orick, Orleans, Weitchpec. Highways: u.s. 101, 199, 299; State 36, 96. Forest supervisor at Eureka.

Stanislaus (896,165 acres) in the Sierra Nevada between Eldorado National Forest and Yosemite National Park: Trout fishing in mountain lakes and streams; Bear, Deer, and small game hunting. Special features: Emigrant Basin Primitive Area; Merced River below Eagle Peak (4,578 ft.) and Trumbull Peak (5,004 ft.); Sonora Peak (11,462 ft.); Sonora Pass (9,628 ft.); Stanislaus Peak (11,220 ft.); Tuolumne River and Clavey Creek divided by Jawbone Ridge; Pilot Peak (6,004 ft.) on Pilot Ridge; Cherry Lake separated by Kibbee Ridge from Eleanor Lake in Yosemite National Park; Lyons Reservoir downstream from Pinecrest Lake on the South Fork Stanislaus River; Beardsley Lake and Donnell Lake on the Middle Fork Stanislaus River; Calaveras Big Tree (*Sequoia gigantea*) National Forest near Big Trees State Park on the North Fork Stanislaus River; Spicer Meadow Reservoir on Highland Creek; Union Reservoir and Utica Reservoir between Elephant Rock (7,425 ft.) and Sapps Hill (7,303 ft.); Dardanelles Cone (9,524 ft.) near The Dardanelles (8,875 ft.); Airole Peak (9,938 ft.) and Iceberg Peak (9,720 ft.) near Lightning Mountains (rising to 9,326 ft.); Hiram Peak (9,760 ft.) above Highland Lakes; Bull Run Peak (9,352 ft.) near Lookout Peak (9,584 ft.) and Peep Sight Peak (9,727 ft.); Ebbets Pass (8,731 ft.); Salt Spring Reservoir on the North Fork Mokelumne River; Middle Fork and South Fork Mokelumne rivers between Bailey Ridge and Summit Level Ridge; Dodge Ridge Ski Area at Pinecrest Winter Sports Area on Highway 108; hiking trails, boat, pack, and saddle trips. Camp and picnic sites, 55; cabins and resorts: Nearby towns: Angels Camp, Coulterville, Columbia, Groveland, Jamestown, San Andrews, Sonora, Tuolumne, Twain Harte. Highways: u.s. 99, 395; State 4, 49, 108, 120, 132, 140. Forest supervisor at Sonora.

Tahoe (694,112 acres) in northeastern California between Eldorado and Plumas national forests: Trout fishing in numerous lakes and streams; Bear, Deer, and small game hunting. Special features: Western slopes of the Sierra Nevada; Lake Tahoe; Donner Lake on the Truckee River; Donner Pass (7,088 ft.); Donner Peak (8,019 ft.), Mount Judah (8,243 ft.), Mount Lincoln (8,383 ft.), Mount Disney (7,953 ft.), Crows Nest (7,896 ft.), Lake Van Norden, Angela, Ice, Kidd, Kilborn, Long, Mary, and Palisade lakes in a popular recreation region west of Truckee; Squaw Peak

(8,885 ft.) at Squaw Valley State Park; Ward Peak (8,637 ft.) near Scott Peak (8,289 ft.); Granite Chief (9,006 ft.); Needle Peak (8,971 ft.) and Lake; Forest Hill Divide, Deadwood Ridge, Secret Canyon, and Red Star Ridge between the Middle Fork and North Fork American rivers; Deadman Peak (7,494 ft.) and Sierra Buttes (8,587 ft.) near North Yuba River; Jackson Meadow Reservoir on the Middle Yuba River; French Lake between English Mountain (8,383 ft.) and Old Man Mountain (7,789 ft.); Webber Peak (8,092 ft.) above Webber Lake on the Little Truckee River; Boca and Prosser Reservoirs; Mount Lola (9,143 ft.) west of Independence Lake; Brady Mountain (5,956 ft.) and Zion Hill (6,204 ft.) in sight of Spaulding Lake; Meadow Lake Hill (7,813 ft.); Buzzard Roost near Fordyce Lake; winter sports areas include Alpine Meadows, Deer Park, Granlibakken, Mount Lincoln, Squaw Valley, and Yuba Ski Land; hiking and riding trails. Camp and picnic sites, 54; picnic only, 2; cabins, hotels and resorts. Nearby towns: Comptonville, Downieville, Grass Valley, Nevada City, Sierra City, Sierraville, Taho City, Truckee. Highways: U.S. 40, 80; State 20, 28, 49, 89. Forest supervisor at Nevada City.

Toiyabe (3,118,966 acres, largest portion in Nevada): Trout fishing in lakes and streams; Bear, Deer, and small game hunting. Special features in California: Eastern slopes of the Sierra Nevada; Mount Rose (10,778 ft.); Ebbets Pass (8,731 ft.) near Kinney Lakes; Reynolds Peak (9,690 ft.) and Meadows; Highland Peak (10,934 ft.); Whitecliff Peak (10,833 ft.) between Boulder Peak (9,381 ft.) and Fish Valley Peak (10,571 ft.); Lost Cannon Mountain (11,099 ft.), Wells Peak, (10,833 ft. and White Mountain (11,398 ft.) within a few miles of Sonora Peak (11,462 ft.) and Stanislaus Peak (11,220 ft.); Peavine Peak (8,266 ft.) north of the Truckee River. Nearby town: Truckee, California. See NEVADA NATIONAL FORESTS.

COLORADO NATIONAL FORESTS

Arapaho (1,074,185 acres, federal 990,371 acres) in central Colorado south and west of Rocky Mountain National Park: Trout fishing in alpine lakes and streams; Black Bear, Mule Deer, Elk, Bighorn Sheep hunting. Special features: Straddles Continental Divide with only about one-fifth of the area on the eastern slopes; ponderosa pine and Douglas fir at lower elevations, alpine fir, lodgepole pine, Engelmann spruce, quaking aspen, and grasslands up to about 11,500 feet; Gore Range–Eagle Nest Primitive Area; scenic highway to Mount Evans (14,260 ft.); Fletcher Peak (13,917 ft.), Pacific Peak (13,964 ft.), and Quandary Peak (14,256 ft.) between Blue River and Ten Mile Creek; Argentine Peak (13,738 ft.), Mount McClellan (13,644 ft.), Kelso Mountain (13,070 ft.), Grays Peak (14,274 ft.), Torreys Peak (14,264 ft.), Murray and Silver Dollar lakes north of

Santa Fe Peak (13,180 ft.) and east of Grizzly Peak (13,420 ft.) above the Arapaho Basin Ski Area; nearby Loveland Pass (11,992 ft.); Breckenridge Peak (12,845 ft.); Bard Peak (13,634 ft.), Engelmann Peak (13,037 ft.), Mount Parnassus (13,576 ft.), and Robeson Peak (13,122 ft.) south of Berthoud Pass (11,314 ft.); Arapaho Peak (13,506 ft.), Navajo Peak (13,406 ft.), Ogalallah Peak (13,147 ft.), and Pauite Peak (13,082 ft.) within sight of Granby Reservoir, Monarch and Strawberry lakes; James Peak (13,261 ft.) east of Fraser River; Williams Fork River and Mountains; Mount Goliath Natural Area; Fraser Experimental Forest (22,000 acres); Moffat Tunnel (6.2 miles) under the Continental Divide; Moffat Road first known as the Hell Hill route; winter sports at Berthoud Pass, Breckinridge, Loveland Basin, and Loveland ski areas; pack and saddle trips, camp and picnic sites, 33; picnic only, 20; dude ranches, cabin camps, hotels, and resorts. Nearby towns: Boulder, Denver, Dillon, Fraser, Frisco, Georgetown, Golden, Granby Hot Sulphur Springs, Idaho Springs, Kremmling. Highways: u.s. 6, 40; State 9, 74, 84, 91, 103, 119, 125. Forest supervisor at Golden.

Grand Mesa–Uncompahgre (1,317,865 acres, 2 forests) in western Colorado: Trout fishing in lakes and streams; Bear, Mule Deer, Elk, Mountain Sheep, Grouse, Ptarmigan, Wild Turkey, waterfowl hunting. Special features: Grand Mesa Plateau 5,000 feet above surrounding region (average elevation 10,300 ft.) north of the Gunnison River; fir, spruce, aspen, and ponderosa pine forests, grass ranges, and nearly 300 lakes and reservoirs on the top and side benches including popular Beaver, Butts, Eggleston, Granby, Island, Jumbo, Leon, and Mesa lakes; Bonham, Colby Horse Park, Cole, Paonia, and Vega reservoirs; Lands End Observatory; Mesa Creek Winter Sports Area on Route 65. Ouray-Norwood division: Level alpine grasslands among deep canyons, jagged peaks, streams and waterfalls; Uncompahgre Primitive Area known as the Switzerland of America; Alta Lakes in the Wilson Mountains Primitive Area; Hayden Peak (12,990 ft.); North Pole Peak (12,197 ft.), Sheep Mountain (13,180 ft.), and Coxcomb Peak (13,660 ft.) feed tributaries of the Cimarron, San Miguel, and Uncompahgre rivers. Uncompahgre Plateau division south of the Gunnison River: Aspen, pine, and spruce forests, steep rough canyons among piñon-Juniper hills and countless creeks flowing toward the Dolores and Uncompahgre rivers; Columbine Pass (8,500 ft.); hiking and riding trails. Camp and picnic sites, 31; picnic only, 6. Nearby towns: Collbran, Cedaredge, Delta, Grand Junction, Mesa, Montrose, Naturita, Ouray, Placerville, Ridgeway, Telluride. Highways: u.s. 6, 50, 550; State 4, 6, 19, 23, 62, 65. Forest supervisor at Delta.

Gunnison (1,773,589 acres, federal 1,660,147 acres) on the western slope of the Rocky Mountains: Trout fishing in lakes and streams; Bear, Mule Deer, Elk, Bighorn Sheep, Mountain Lion, and small game hunting.

Special features: Engelmann spruce forests, sage brush, grazing lands, 3,000 miles of streams, 55 natural and man-made lakes; Elk, Gunnison and Ruby ranges; East and Taylor rivers mingling waters at Almont to form the Gunnison River; Avery Peak (12,659 ft.) near the Gothic Natural Area (900 acres); West Elk Wild Area south of Mount Owen (13,102 ft.), Ruby Peak (12,749 ft.) and Lake Irwin; La Garita Wild Area southeast of San Luis Peak (14,149 ft.); Matchless Mountain (12,383 ft.) overlooking Taylor Reservoir; White Rock Mountain (13,532 ft.) at Queen Basin; Grizzly Peak (13,300 ft.) in the Gunnison Mountains above Taylor Park; Gunnison Peak (12,688 ft.) in the Minnesota Creek region; mining operations; Crested Butte Ski Area; pack and saddle trips. Camp and picnic sites, 34; cabin camps and resorts. Nearby towns: Almont, Baldwin, Crested Butte, Crawford, Delta, Gunnison, Montrose, Ohio City, Paonia, Pitkin, Sargent, Somerset, Tincup. Highways: u.s. 50; State 92,114, 135, 149. Forest supervisor at Gunnison.

Pike (1,258,825 acres, federal 1,084,947 acres) in the Rampart Range of the Rocky Mountains: Trout fishing in lakes and streams; Antelope, Bear, Deer, Elk, Bighorn Sheep, and small game hunting. Special features: Nearly 1,000 lakes and 400 miles of streams among meadows, quaking aspen groves, ponderosa pine, Douglas fir, and Engelmann spruce forests; Eleven Mile Canyon Reservoir north of Saddle Mountain (10,815 ft.) Natural Area; Pikes Peak (14,110 ft.) reached by the Auto Highway, Cog Railway, or by hiking up 13-mile Barr Trail; Tarryall Bighorn Research and Management Station at the Tarryall Reservoir and Creek; Mount Lincoln (14,234 ft.), Mount Brass (14,169 ft.), Mount Cameron (14,238 ft.), Mount Buckskin (13,858 ft.), and Horseshoe Mountain (13,903 ft.) in the Mosquito Range; Mount Bierstadt (14,046 ft.) and Mount Evans (14,260 ft.) near Deer, Duck, and Geneva creeks; Mount Boreas (13,058 ft.), Hoosier Pass (11,541 ft.), and Mount Silverheels (13,825 ft.) north of Fairplay; Manitou Recreation Area above Woodland Park; Abyss Lake Scenic Area; Blodgett Peak (9,435 ft.) overlooking the U.S. Air Force Academy adjacent to the national forest; winter sports at Indianhead and Pikes Peak ski areas; hiking and riding trails. Camp and picnic sites, 37; picnic only, 40; motels, hotels, and resorts. Nearby towns: Breckenridge, Colorado Springs, Cripple Creek, Fairplay, Florissant, Hartsel, Jefferson, Lake George, Sedalia, Woodland Park. Highways: u.s. 24, 85, 87, 285; State 4, 89, 67, 77. Forest supervisor at Colorado Springs.

Rio Grande (1,800,322 acres) framing San Luis Valley in Southern Colorado: Trout fishing in lakes and streams; Antelope, Black Bear, Mule Deer, Elk, Bighorn Sheep, Wild Turkey, and waterfowl hunting. Special features: Kit Carson Mountain (14,100 ft.), Crestone Needle (14,197 ft.) and Crestone Peak (14,291 ft.) on the western slopes of the Sangre de Cristo Range towering above the Great Sand Dunes National Monument (36,740 acres); La Garita Wild Area; San Juan Mountains on the Continental Divide; Upper Rio Grande Primitive Area; Weminuche Pass (10,622 ft.); Mount Nebo (13,192 ft.) above Hunchback Pass; Cochetopa Pass (10,032 ft.); Poncha Pass (9,010 ft.); Pole Mountain (13,740 ft.); Grouse Mountain (10,122 ft.); Continental Reservoir (26,700 acres); Beaver Creek, Rio Grande, and Santa Maria reservoirs; Wolf Creek Pass (10,850 ft.) Winter Sports Area; pack and saddle trips. Camp and picnic sites, 31; picnic only, 5. Nearby towns: Alamosa, Capulin, Creede, Del Norte, Gunnison, Moffat, Monte Vista, Pagosa Springs, Saguache. Highways: U.S. 50, 160, 285; State 10, 15, 17, 114, 149. Forest supervisor at Monte Vista.

Roosevelt (1,085,000 acres) north, east, and south of the Rocky Mountain National Park (260,018 acres) in north central Colorado: Trout fishing in lakes and streams; Bear, Deer, Elk, Bighorn Sheep, Mountain Lion, and small game hunting. Special features: Front, Mummy, and Medicine Bow ranges; Arapaho Glacier, Arapaho Peak (13,506 ft.), Navajo Peak (13,406 ft.), Isabelle Glacier, Paiute Peak (13,082 ft.), Mount Audubon (13,223 ft.), Sawtooth Mountain (12,304 ft.), St. Vrain Glacier, and Ogalallah Peak (13,147 ft.) on the Continental Divide; Indian Peaks Recreation Area with many lakes including Blue, Brainerd, Isabelle, Long, Mitchell, and Red Rock lakes; Beaver Reservoir; Rainbow Lakes; St. Vrain, Big and Little Thompson rivers; Chambers Lake (300 acres) at the confluence of the Cache La Poudre and Laramie rivers near the Rawah Wild Area; Cameron Pass (10,285 ft.); Comanche and Hourglass Reservoir below Comanche Peak (12,716 ft.); Dowdy Lakes Recreation Area near Parvin and Red Feather lakes; Creedmore Lakes; Fort Collins Mountain Recreation Area along the Cache La Poudre River; Seaman Reservoir (1,320 acres) on North Fork Cache La Poudre River; Lake Eldora Ski Area near Nederland; hiking trails, pack and saddle trips. Camp and picnic sites, 21; picnic only, 18; dude ranches and motels. Nearby towns: Allenspark, Bellevue, Boulder, Central City, Drake, Estes Park, Fort Collins, Livermore, Loveland, Lyons, Nederland, Pinecliff. Highways: U.S. 34, 87, 287; State 7, 14, 16, 28, 66, 72, 119, 160. Forest supervisor at Fort Collins.

Routt (1,264,850 acres, federal 1,145,111 acres) in 4 segments on western slope of the Continental Divide in the Park Range and Medicine Bow Range in northern Colorado: Trout fishing in lakes and streams; Bear, Deer, Elk, Grouse, waterfowl, and other small game hunting. Special features: Mount Zirkel–Dome Peak Wild Area in the Park Range; Big Creek Lakes Recreation Area; Fish Creek Reservoir and Fish Creek Falls (200 ft.) near Steamboat Springs; Dumont Lake west of Rabbit Ears Pass (9,680 ft.); Gore Pass (9,524 ft.) to the Arapaho National Forest; Elkhead Mountains; Elk River; Flattop Mountain (12,493 ft.) above Stillwater Reservoir on Bear River; Gardner Park Reservoir; several lakes and reservoirs in the Pyramid Peak (11,611 ft.) region; Willow Creek Pass (9,683 ft.); Seven Utes (11,438 ft.) south of the Colorado State Forest in the Medicine Bow Range; pack and saddle trips, camp and picnic sites, 48; picnic only, 5; cabins and motels. Nearby towns: Clark, Cowdry, Kremmling, Steamboat Springs, Toponas, Weldon, Yampa. Highways: U.S. 40; State 14, 84, 125. Forest supervisor at Steamboat Springs.

San Isabel (1,104,042 acres in 4 segments) in south central Colorado: Trout fishing in lakes and streams; Antelope, Bear, Deer, Elk, Grouse, Turkey, waterfowl, and other small game hunting. Special features: Independence Pass on the Continental Divide; Mount Elbert (14,431 ft.) and Mount Massive (14,418 ft.) north of Twin Lakes; Grizzly Peak (14,020 ft.), Huron Peak (14,005 ft.), La Plata Peak (14,340 ft.), Quail Mountain (13,461 ft.), and Missouri Mountain (14,067 ft.) near the Collegiate Peaks: Mount Columbia (14,073 ft.), Mount Harvard (14,399 ft.), Mount Oxford (14,153 ft.), Mount Princeton (14,197 ft.), and Mount Yale (14,172 ft.); Antero Peak (14,245 ft.), Shavano Peak (14,179 ft.), Tabequache Mountain (14,155 ft.) and Mount Aetna (14,163 ft.) north of the Arkansas River; Monarch Pass (11,302 ft.), Marshall Pass (10,846 ft.), Pahlone Peak (12,035 ft.), and Mount Ouray (13,955 ft.) north of Sheep Mountain (13,855 ft.); Bushnell Lakes, Balman Reservoir, and Rainbow Lake near Hayden Pass Trail; Lake of the Clouds, Venable Falls and Lakes, Humboldt Peak (14,044 ft.), Kit Carson Peak (14,100 ft.), and Little Bear Peak (14,040 ft.) above several lakes in the Sangre de Cristo Range; Lake Isabel Recreation Area southwest of Pueblo; winter sports at Cooper Hill near Tennessee Pass (10,424 ft.) north of Leadville, and Monarch Pass northeast of Doyleville; pack and saddle trips. Camp and picnic sites, 26; dude ranches and motels. Nearby towns: Buela, Buena Vista, Canon City, La Veta, Leadville, Nathrop, Pueblo, Salida, Trinidad, Twin Lakes, Walsenburg, Westcliffe, Wetmore. Highways: U.S. 24, 50, 85, 87, 285; State 69, 76, 82, 96, 111, 165, 306. Forest supervisor at Pueblo.

San Juan (2,0846,462 acres, federal 1,850,053 acres) adjacent to the Southern Ute Indian Reservation in southwestern Colorado: Trout fishing in lakes and streams; Bear, Deer, Elk, Bighorn Sheep, Wild Turkey, and other small game hunting. Special features: San Juan Mountains; Wilson Mountains Primitive Area; Needle Mountains on the Continental Divide between the Animas River and Vallecito Creek include Mount Aeolus (14,086 ft.), Sunlight Peak (14,060 ft.), and Windom Peak (14,091 ft.); Weminuche Pass (10,622 ft.) between the San Juan Primitive Area and Upper Rio Grande Primitive Area; Highland Mary Lakes; Williams Creek Reservoir; Vallecito Reservoir (1,720 acres) north of Bayfield; Dolores, La Plata, Mancas, Piedra, and Los Pinos or Pine rivers; Narraguinnep Natural Area south of Glade Lake; Montezuma Peak (13,181 ft.) and Summit Peak (13,272 ft.) south of Wolf Creek Pass (10,850 ft.) and Stoner Ski Area on u.s. 160; Narrow-gauge railroad daily trips during summer months between Durango and Silverton; pack and saddle trips. Camp and picnic sites, 34; picnic only, 7; dude ranches and motels. Nearby towns: Arboles, Bayfield, Chromo, Cortez, Dolores, Durango, Pagosa Springs, Silverton. Highways: u.s. 84, 160, 550; State 17, 145, 331, 789. Forest supervisor at Durango.

White River (2,076,000 acres, federal 1,961,798 acres) north and south of the Colorado River in western Colorado: Trout fishing in lakes and streams; Bear, Mule Deer, Elk, Bighorn Sheep, Bobcat, and small game hunting. Special features: Aspen, Engelmann spruce, and lodgepole pine forests, piñon and juniper, mountain meadows, mineral springs, and caves; Crystal, Frying Pan, Roaring Fork, and White rivers; Gore Range–Eagle Nest Primitive Area; Maroon Bells–Snowmass Wild Area; several lakes north of Baxter Peak (11,188) including Duck, Monument, Deep, and Heart Lakes; Trappers Lake (noted for Cutthroat Trout) on the North Fork White River; many lakes north of the Flat Top Primitive Area; Glenwood Canyon; Spouting Creek Lake plunges over Bridal Veil Falls into Hanging Lake on a precipitous cliff 1,200 feet above Dead Horse Gulch, northeast of Glenwood Springs; Tennessee Pass (10,424 ft.) to San Isabel National Forest; Aspen Highlands and Buttermilk ski areas near Aspen; Husky dog team trips (Dec.–April) at Toklat Lodge 12 miles south of Aspen; hiking trails, pack and saddle trips. Camp and picnic sites, 58; dude ranches and motels. Nearby towns: Aspen, Basalt, Buford, Carbondale, Craig, Eagle, Glenwood Springs, Gypsum, Leadville, Meeker, Minuturn, Rifle. Highways: u.s. 6, 16, 24; State 13, 65, 82, 131, 133, 330. Forest supervisor at Glenwood Springs.

FLORIDA NATIONAL FORESTS

Apalachicola (556,480 acres) in northwestern Florida: Bass, Bream, and Perch fishing in lakes and streams; Bear, Deer, Quail, Squirrel hunting. Special features: Coastal Plain pine-hardwood forests, natural sinks, and swamps along large rivers; Apalachicola and Ochlockonee rivers flowing into Gulf of Mexico region of the Big Bend; Camel Lake (37 acres); Silver Lake (23 acres); Hitchcock Lake north of Carrabelle; Wright Lake south of Sumatra; Leon-Wakulla Wildlife Management Area (67,000 acres); Liberty Wildlife Management Area (133,120 acres). Camp and picnic sites, 4; picnic only, 10. Nearby towns: Apalachicola, Blountstown, Bristol, Carrabelle, Panama City, Tallahassee, Wakulla Springs. Highways: u.s. 98, 319; State 20, 65, 67, 260, 369. Forest supervisor at Tallahassee.

Ocala (361,029 acres) in eastern Florida, bordered by the St. John River, Lake George, Little Lake George, and Lake Dexter on the east, and the Oklawaha River on the north and west: Black Bass, and warm water fish in famous Lake George, St. Johns River, and hundreds of clear sandy-bottomed lakes and streams; Bear, Deer, Turkey, Squirrel, waterfowl hunting. Special features: Subtropical vegetation, palms, hardwood trees draped with Spanish moss; "Big Scrub" stands of sand pines; Alexander Springs pouring 76 million gallons of water per day into a creek; Juniper Springs Recreation Area and Farless Lake in the Ocala Wildlife Refuge; Ocala Wildlife Management Area (203,680 acres); Clearwater, Door, and Nicotoon lakes near Altoona. Camp and picnic sites, 30; picnic only, 1; hunting camps. Nearby towns: Altoona, Astor, Barberville, Deland, Eustis, Fort McCoy, Fruitland, Leesburg, Mount Dora, Ocala, Oklawaha, Palatka, Silver Springs, Weirsdale. Highways: u.s. 17, 301, 441; State 19, 21, 40, 42, 44, 314, 315, 316, 318, 452. Forest supervisor at Tallahassee.

Osceola (157,233 acres) in northeastern Florida: Bass, Bream, and Perch fishing in numerous ponds; Bear, Deer, Dove, Quail, Turkey hunting. Special features: Level land with numerous ponds, sinks, and cypress swamps; Osceola Wildlife Management Area (92,000 acres); Steinhatchee Wildlife Management Area (225,000 acres); Ocean Pond (2,000 acres) with boat dock and launching ramp. Camp and picnic sites, 1 (24 units); picnic only, 3. Nearby towns: Jacksonville, Lake City, Olustee (in forest). Highways: u.s. 41, 90, 441; State 100. Forest supervisor at Tallahassee.

GEORGIA NATIONAL FORESTS

Chattahoochee (680,333 acres) in the Blue Ridge Mountains of northern Georgia: Bass, Bream, Muskellunge, and Trout fishing; Deer and small game hunting. Special features: Brasstown Bald (4,784 ft.); Rabun Bald (4,663 ft.); Tallulah River and Gorge; Soque and Toccoa rivers; Morgantown Point Recreation Area at Lake Blue Ridge (3,290 acres); Lake Rabun; Lake Russell (100 acres) east of Cornelia; Lake Winfield Scott (18 acres) near Suches; Lake Conasauga (25 acres) near Chatsworth; Rock Creek Lake; Blood Mountain Archaeological Area; Annie Ruby Falls, Cooper Creek, De Soto Falls, and Sosebee Cove Scenic Areas; southern end of the Appalachian Trail. Camp and picnic sites, 10; picnic only, 23. Nearby towns: Blairsdale, Blue Ridge, Chatsworth, Clarkesville, Clayton, Cleveland, Cornelia, Dahlondega, Dalton, Lakemont, Morganton, Suches in Georgia; Chattanooga, Tenn. Highways: u.s. 19, 23, 27, 41, 76, 123, 129, 411; State 2, 17, 60, 66, 71, 75, 180, 197. Forest supervisor at Gainesville.

Oconee (96,066 acres) northeast of Macon in central Georgia: Bass and Bream fishing in lakes and streams; Deer and small game hunting.

Special features: Thickly forested Piedmont Hills; Oconee River, Sinclair Lake (15,330 acres); Rock Eagle Lake (110 acres); Piedmont Wildlife Refuge; Indian Mound Archaeological Area; Mammoth 4-H Center. Camp and picnic sites, none; picnic only, 2. Nearby towns: Eatonton, Greensboro, Madison, Sugar Valley. Highways: U.S. 129, 278; State 15, 44, 77, 156, 212. Forest supervisor at Gainesville.

IDAHO NATIONAL FORESTS

Boise (2,950,000 acres, Federal 2,629,465 acres) in southwestern Idaho: Salmon and Trout fishing in lakes and streams; Black Bear, Deer (Mule, White-tailed), Elk, Mountain Goat, Moose, Bighorn Sheep, and small game hunting. Special features: Ponderosa pine forests, mountain meadows, towering cliffs, canyons, and cascading streams in the Sawtooth Range; Idaho Primitive Area; Sawtooth Primitive Area; Middle Fork and South Fork Salmon rivers; Scott Mountain (8,260 ft.); Whitehawk Mountain (8,374 ft.); Deadwood Reservoir on the Deadwood River; South Fork Payette River; Grape Mountain (5,910 ft.) above Arrow Rock Reservoir on the Boise River Middle Fork; Little Camas Reservoir near Anderson Ranch Reservoir on South Fork Boise River; Big Roaring River Lake near Rainbow and Trout lakes; Danskin Peak (6,745 ft.) northwest of Dixie; Cascade Reservoir (35,000 acres); Sage Hen Reservoir west of Smith's Ferry; North Fork Payette River; Bernard Mountain (8,203 ft.) above Deer and Elk creeks; Bogus Basin Ski Area north of Boise; boating, pack, and saddle trips. Camp and picnic sites, 121, picnic only, 22; dude ranches, motels, and resorts. Nearby towns: Boise, Cascade, Dixie, Garden City, Horseshoe Bend, Idaho City, McCall, Mountain Home, Stanley. Highways: U.S. 20, 26, 30, 93; State 15, 17, 52, 68. Forest supervisor at Boise.

Cache (651,909 acres) extending from the Soda Point Reservoir in Idaho to the Weber River in Utah: Idaho portion: Bear River Range with ice caves, Minnetonka Cave, and Bloomington Lake. Nearby towns: Bloomington, Garden City, Montpelier, Ovid, Paris, Preston, St. Charles, Soda Springs. Highways: U.S. 30, 89, 91; Idaho 34. Forest supervisor at Logan, Utah. See UTAH NATIONAL FORESTS.

Caribou (976,041 acres in 5 segments) in southwestern Idaho: Cutthroat and Rainbow Trout fishing; Black Bear, Deer, Elk, Moose, Bobcat, and small game hunting. Special features: Aspen, fir, and lodgepole pine forests, wide valleys, ridges, waterfalls; Poker Peak (8,435 ft.) above Palisades Reservoir on the Snake River; Mount Baldy (7,380 ft.), Red Peak (8,750 ft.), Big Elk Mountain (9,478 ft.), Little Elk Mountain (8,745 ft.), Caribou Mountain (9,805 ft.), Old Baldy Peak (8,330 ft.), Tincup Mountain (8,216 ft.), and Stump Peak (8,600 ft.) in the Caribou

Range; Henry Peak (8,320 ft.) in Grays Range; Dry Ridge (8,975 ft.) near Schmid Mountain (8,994 ft.); Sulphur Peak (8,316 ft.) in the Aspen Range; Green Mountain (8,777 ft.) and Harrington Peak (8,554 ft.) north of Meade Peak (9,953 ft.); Bonneville Peak (9,260 ft.) and Haystack Mountain (9,025 ft.) in the Portneuf Range between Inkom and Pebble; Justice Park Scout Mountain (8,710 ft.) in the Bannock Range; Elkhorn Peak (9,001 ft.), Oxford Peak (9,281 ft.), and Old Baldy Peak (8,360 ft.) near Malad City; Skyline Ski Area east of Inkom; pack and saddle trips. Camp and picnic sites, 19; Picnic only, 6; motels and resorts. Nearby towns: Dayton, Freedom, Georgetown, Herman, Idaho Falls, Inkom, Malad City, Montpelier, Pebble, Pocatello, Soda Springs, Weston in Idaho; Afton, Wyoming. Highways: u.s. 30 N, 91, 191; Idaho 34. Forest supervisor at Pocatello.

Challis (2,468,067 acres, federal 2,447,696 acres) in central Idaho: Salmon and Trout fishing in lakes and streams; Antelope, Bear, Deer, Elk, Mountain Goat, Moose, Bighorn Sheep, Mountain Lion, and small game hunting. Special features: Douglas fir and lodgepole pine forests; numerous springs, headwaters of the Salmon River, Big and Little Lost rivers; Idaho Primitive Area on the Middle Fork Salmon River; Sawtooth Primitive Area on South Fork Payette River; Big Lost River Game Preserve containing Big Black Dome (11,357 ft.), Hyndman Peak (12,078 ft.), Ryan Peak (11,900 ft.); Standhope Peak (11,700 ft.) and Copper Basin Knob (10,779 ft.) in the White Knob Mountains; Mount Borah (12,655 ft.), Leatherman Peak (12,230 ft.), Mount McCaleb (11,593 ft.), Invisible Mountain (11,343 ft.) in the Lost River Range; Dickey Peak (11,140 ft.) in the Pahsimero Mountains above Thousand Springs Valley; Flatiron Mountain (11,025 ft.) in the Lemhi Range; Little Soldier Mountain (8,820 ft.), Big Soldier Mountain (8,993 ft.), Greyhound Ridge, and Sheep Mountain (9,195 ft.) in the Rapid River region; Salmon River Mountains with 18 peaks over 9,000 ft. including the highest: Twin Peaks (10,328 ft.), Bald Mountain (10,314 ft.), General Mountain (10,325 ft.); Castle Peak (11,820 ft.) overlooking several alpine lakes and meadows among the Whitecloud Peaks; hiking trails, pack and saddle trips. Camp and picnic sites, 19; dude ranches, cabins, hotels, and resorts. Nearby towns: Arco, Challis, Howe, Ketchum, Mackay, Salmon, Stanley. Highways: u.s. 20, 93, 93A; Idaho 22, 27. Forest supervisor at Challis.

Clearwater (1,677,000 acres, federal 1,248,455 acres) on western slopes of the Bitterroot Range on the Montana boundary: Trout and Whitefish in about 75 lakes and 11,000 miles of streams; Bear, Deer (Mule, White-tailed), Elk, Mountain Goat, Mountain Lion, and small game hunting. Special features: Steep river canyons, evergreen forests, and large stands of virgin white pine; Bernard De Voto Memorial Grove of cedars on the Lochsa River; Middle Fork and North Fork Clearwater River; Selway-Bitterroot Wilderness Area; Ranger Peak (8,810 ft.), Eagle

Mountain (7,414 ft.), Rhodes Peak (7,940 ft.), Rocky Point (6,805 ft.), The Nub (6,928 ft.); Lookout Point (6,903 ft.); Lunde Peak (6,217 ft.); Jerry Johnson Hot Springs near Colgate Warm Springs; Lolo Pass (5,233 ft.) on the Lolo Indian Trail followed by the Lewis and Clark Expedition in 1805; fast river boating in canoes and rafts; hiking trails, pack and saddle trips, camp and picnic sites, 8; cabins and motels. Nearby towns: Greer, Kamiah, Kooskia, Lewiston, Orofino, Pierce in Idaho; Hot Springs and Missoula in Montana. Highways: u.s. 12, 95A; Idaho 7, 9, 11. Forest supervisor at Orofino.

Coeur d'Alene (802,177 acres, federal 723,235 acres) in northwestern Idaho: Trout fishing in lakes and streams; Bear, Deer, Elk, waterfowl, and other small game hunting. Special features: Forested mountains and valleys; Coeur d'Alene Lake (30 miles long, shoreline 104 miles); Hayden Lake; Coeur d'Alene River; Downy Peak (6,024 ft.); Granite Peak (6,810 ft.), Kellogg Peak (6,296 ft.), Stevens Peak (6,826 ft.), and Striped Peak (6,329 ft.) highest among several mountains over 5,000 feet; Mount Coeur d'Alene (4,440 ft.); Lookout Pass (4,727 ft.) on the Idaho-Montana border; Deception Creek Experimental Forest; extensive mining operations; Lookout Pass Winter Sports Area; hiking and riding trails. Camp and picnic sites, 7; picnic only, 2; cabins and resort hotels. Nearby towns: Avery, Coeur d'Alene, Harrison, Kellogg, Pritchard, Spirit Lake, St. Maries, and Wallace in Idaho; Spokane in Washington. Highways: u.s. 10, 95; Idaho 5, 53. Forest supervisor at Coeur d'Alene.

Kaniksu (1,625,383 acres, partly in Montana and Washington) along the Canadian boundary: Trout fishing in lakes and streams; Bear (Black, Grizzly), White-tailed Deer, Elk, Mountain Goat, Moose, Bighorn Sheep, and small game hunting. Special features: Glacial lakes and swift streams among Douglas fir, ponderosa and white pine forests; rugged Cabinet and Selkirk Mountains; Chimney Rock (7,136 ft.); Mount Casey (6,735 ft.); Pend Oreille River flowing into Lake Pend Oreille (147 square miles, 1150 ft. deep) noted for huge Kamloop Trout and a dozen varieties of game fish; Upper and Lower Priest lakes on the Priest River; Noxon Rapids Dam on the Clark Fork River; Cabinet Mountains Primitive Area; Roosevelt Grove of Ancient Cedars near Upper Priest Lake; Kootenai and Moyie rivers flowing through the Purcell Mountains to Canada; Myrtle Creek Game Preserve west of Bonners Ferry; Chewelah Mountain Ski Area. Camp and picnic sites, 19; cabins, resort lodges, and hotels. Nearby towns: Bonners Ferry, Clark Fork, Nordman, Priest River, and Sandpoint in Idaho; Libby and Thompson Falls in Montana; Cusick, Metaline Falls and Newport in Washington. Highways: u.s. 2, 10A, 95, 195; State 1, 57. Forest supervisor at Sandpoint.

Nezperce (2,196,029 acres, federal 2,195,962 acres) extending south-westerly across Idaho from the Bitterroot Mountains on the Montana border to the Snake River on the Oregon boundary: Trout fishing in lakes and streams; Black Bear, Deer, Elk, Mountain Goat, Moose, Bighorn Sheep, and small game hunting. Special features: Deep canyons and jagged peaks; Douglas, alpine and grand fir, lodgepole and ponderosa pine forests; Salmon River Breaks Primitive Area; Selway-Bitterroot Wilderness Area; Selway River; South Fork and Middle Fork Clearwater River; Red River Hot Springs; Seven Devils Range above the Snake River Hells Canyon (100 miles long, 4–9 miles wide, 5,500–7,900 feet deep); He Devil Mountain (9,387 ft.); Big Rock Mountain (7,000 ft.); Cove Peak (7,608 ft.); Lone Knob (5,295 ft.); annual Chinook Salmon and Steelhead runs in the Salmon and Snake rivers; Boating, pack and saddle trips. Camp and picnic sites, 6; picnic only, 1; cabins, hotels, and resorts. Nearby towns: Clearwater, Dixie, Elk City, Grangeville, Kooskia, Riggens, Stites, Whitebird. Highways: U.S. 95; State 9, 13, 14. Forest supervisor at Grangeville.

Payette (2,417,977 acres, federal 2,307,150 acres) in west central Idaho: Chinook Salmon and Trout fishing; Bear, Deer (Mule, White-tailed), Elk, Mountain Goat, Bighorn Sheep, and small game hunting. Special features: Numerous mining operations; elevations from 1,440 to over 9,000 feet in a generally rugged terrain with about 150 fishing lakes and 1,300 miles of streams; Hells Canyon on the Snake River; Salmon, Middle Fork Salmon, Weiser, and Wild Horse rivers; Idaho Primitive Area; Payette Lake on North Fork Payette River; Goose, Granite, and Upper Payette lakes near the Hazard Lakes south of Elk Meadows; access to adjoining Cascade Reservoir (35,000 acres) at Rainbow Point west of Donnelly; Lost Valley Reservoir west of Tamarack; Parks Peak (8,822 ft.), No Business Mountain (7,330 ft.), and Smith Mountain (8,005 ft.) in the Snake River region; Brundage Mountain and Payette Lakes winter sports areas near McCall; hiking and saddle trails. Camp and picnic sites, 31; dude ranches and mining camps. Nearby towns: Cambridge, Council, Donnelly, Fruitvale, McCall, New Meadows, Pollock, Riggens. Highways: U.S. 95; State 1, 9, 11, 12, 15, 26, 28. Forest supervisor at McCall.

Salmon (1,792,351 acres in 4 segments) in the Bitterroot Range on the Idaho-Montana border: Chinook Salmon and Trout fishing; Antelope, Bear, Deer (Mule, White-tailed), Elk, Mountain Goat, Bighorn Sheep, Cougar, and small game hunting. Special features: Western slopes of the Continental Divide with elevations from 2,840 feet at Horse Creek on the Salmon River to 11,324 feet on Gunsight Peak, west of Leadore; Douglas fir, ponderosa pine, and Engelmann spruce forests; Bighorn Crags in the Idaho Primitive Area; several mountains over 8,000 feet including Allen Mountain (9,137 ft.), Black Mountain (9,521 ft.), Blackbird Mountain (9,113 ft.), Blue Nose Lookout (9,660 ft.), Lake Mountain (9,267 ft.), and Taylor Mountain (9,968 ft.); magnificent Salmon River Gorge;

Middle Fork Salmon River Canyon; headwaters of the Lemhi and North Fork Salmon rivers, Horse and Panther Creeks; historic Lewis and Clark Trail and monument marking first camp on the Pacific slope; mining operations; Lost Trail Pass (6,995 ft.) Ski Course north of Gibbonsville; boat trips on the "River of No Return"; 2,400 miles of hiking and horse trails. Camp and picnic sites, 4; picnic only, 2; dude ranches. Nearby towns: Baker, Carmen, Gibbonsville, Leadore, Lemhi, Salmon, Tendoy. Highways: u.s. 93; State 28, 29. Forest supervisor at Salmon.

St. Joe (866,269 acres) on western slopes of the Bitterroot Range in northeastern Idaho: Bass and Trout fishing in lakes and streams; Bear, Deer, Elk, Mountain Goat, and small game hunting. Special features: Cedar, fir, hemlock, and virgin stands of white pine; St. Joe River drainage; St. Maries River Valley; Little North Fork Clearwater River; Palouse River; Little Joe Mountain (7,052 ft.); Illinois Peak (7,684 ft.); Fishhook Peak (6,516 ft.); Quarles Peak (6,565 ft.); Simmons Peak (6,650 ft.); Siwash Peak (5,829 ft.); Snow Peak (6,762 ft.); North-South Winter Sports Area between Moscow and St. Maries; hiking and riding trails. Camp and picnic sites, 8; cabins on St. Joe River, dude ranch. Nearby towns: Avery, Clarkia, Emida, Moscow, Palouse, Potlach, St. Maries, Wallace. Highways: u.s. 10, 95A; State 7, 8, 43. Forest supervisor at St. Maries.

Sawtooth (1,802,680 acres) in south central Idaho and 5 segments at the Idaho-Utah boundary: Kokanee Salmon and Trout fishing in lakes and streams; Beer, Deer, Elk, Mountain Goat, Bighorn Sheep, Cougar, and small game hunting. Special features: Douglas fir, ponderosa and lodgepole pine forests, several hot springs, and mining operations among the mountains of the Sawtooth Range Division; Big Wood River; headwaters of South Fork Boise, East Fork and West Fork Salmon rivers; Glassford Peak (11,500 ft.) and Ryan Peak (11,900 ft.) in the Boulder Mountains; Alturas, Petit, Redfish, and Yellowbelly lakes near the Sawtooth Primitive Area; The Devils Bedstead (11,000 ft.) and Hyndman Peak (12,078 ft.) in the Pioneer Mountains; Norton Peak (10,179 ft.) in the Smoky Mountains; Soldier Mountains Game Preserve north of Fairfield. Minidoka Division: Cleveland Lake and Cache Peak (10,340 ft.) above Independence Lakes in the Albion Mountain District east of Lower Goose Creek Reservoir; Black Pine and Eagle Peak in the Black Pine District, and Hartley Peak in the Sublette District east of Raft River; several mountains, canyons, and creeks in the Cassia District south of Lake Murtaugh; Raft River District in Utah. Magic Mountain Ski Area at Rock Creek Canyon in the Cassia District; Mount Harrison Ski Area 11 miles southwest of Albion; Pomerelle, Soldier Mountain, and Sun Valley winter sports areas in the Big Wood River region; hiking trails, pack and saddle trips. Camp and picnic sites, 57, picnic only, 15; dude ranches, camps, and motels. Nearby towns: Gooding, Hailey, Ketchum, Shoshoe, Stanley, Sun Valley in Sawtooth Division; Albion, Burley, Elba, Hansen, Malta, Oakley, Rockland, Rogerson, Strevell, Twin Falls in Minidoka Division. Highways: u.s. 30 North, 30 South, 93; State 22, 27. Forest supervisor at Twin Falls.

Targhee (1,666,370 acres) on the Idaho-Montana border, and adjacent to Yellowstone National Park in Wyoming: Silver Salmon and Trout fishing in lakes and streams; Antelope, Bear, Deer, Elk, Moose, and small game hunting. Special features: Numerous canyons, creeks, mountain meadows, forests of Douglas fir, lodgepole pine, and Engelmann spruce; Bannock Pass (7,672 ft.), Monida Pass (6,823 ft.), Red Rock Pass (7,000 ft.), Reynolds Pass (7,400 ft.), and Targhee Pass lead across the Continental Divide to Montana; Saddle Mountain (10,325 ft.) in the Lemhi Range; Signal Peak (5,883 ft.) and Frazier Reservoir northeast of Spence; Buffalo and Warm Rivers; Upper Mesa Falls (106 ft.) and Lower Mesa Falls (45 ft.) on Henrys Fork Snake River; Island Park Reservoir on Yale Creek; Palisades Reservoir on Snake River at Big Elk and Little Elk creeks; western slopes of the Teton Range; Teton Pass (8,431 ft.) southwest of Victor; Lake of the Woods and Grassy Lake near the southern edge of Yellowstone National Park in Wyoming; Bear Gulch Ski Area north of Ashton; Pine Basin Ski Area southwest of Victor; hiking trails. Camp and picnic sites, 16; picnic only, 7; dude ranches, fishing camps, pack outfits for hunters, motels, and resorts. Nearby towns: Ashton, Driggs, Dubois, Gilmore, Idaho Falls, St. Anthony, Swan Valley, and Victor in Idaho; Jackson in Wyoming. Highways: u.s. 9, 20, 26, 89, 91, 191; Idaho 22, 28, 29, 31, 32. Forest supervisor at St. Anthony.

ILLINOIS NATIONAL FOREST

Shawnee (211,013 acres in 2 divisions) in southern Illinois: Black Bass, Bluegill, Catfish, and Crappie fishing; Quail, waterfowl, Fox, and Raccoon hunting. Mississippi River division: Crab Orchard, Devils Kitchen, and Little Grassy lakes, and Marion Reservoir in the Crab Orchard National Wildlife Refuge near Marion; Fountain Bluffs on the Mississippi River; Pine Hills Scenic Area; Union State Forest and Nursery; Union County Game Refuge adjacent to the forest near Pottsville; Horseshoe Lake Game Refuge northwest of Cairo. Ohio River division: Cave and Wildcat Hills; Garden of the Gods; Pounds Hollow Recreation Area; Kaskaskia Experiment Forest; Bell Smith Springs and Lake Glendale recreation areas. Camp and picnic sites, 1; picnic only, 24; cabins and motels. Nearby towns: Anna, Cairo, Carbondale, Elizabethtown, Harrisburg, Jonesboro, Marion, Metropolis, Murphysboro, Sellers Landing in Illinois; Paducah in Kentucky; Cape Girardeau in Missouri. Highways:

u.s. 45; Illinois 1, 3, 13, 34, 37, 127, 144, 146, 151. Forest supervisor at Harrisburg.

INDIANA NATIONAL FOREST

Hoosier (129,000 acres in 2 divisions) in southern Indiana: Bass, Catfish, and Bluegill fishing; Quail, Rabbit, Raccoon, Squirrel hunting. Special features: Ponds, creeks, meadows, and woodland areas. Northern division is adjacent to Brown County State Game Preserve near Nashville; southern division extends to Ohio River: Pioneer Mothers' Memorial Forest, East Fork White River, Sulphur Springs, German Ridge Recreation Area, historic trail of migratory Bison between French Lick and the West. Camp and picnic sites, 2; picnic only, 2; motels. Nearby towns: Bedford, Bloomington, Brownstown, Columbus, Evansville, Paoli, Tell City. Highways: u.s. 3, 50, 150, 231, 460; State 37, 46, 56, 58, 60, 62, 64, 66, 70, 145, 164, 450. Forest supervisor at Bedford.

KENTUCKY NATIONAL FOREST

Cumberland (460,680 acres) in eastern Kentucky: Bass, Rainbow Trout, and Walleye fishing; Deer, Wild Turkey, and upland game hunting. Special features: About 500 miles of fishable streams, mineral springs, limestone caves, and massive sandstone cliffs; Lake Cumberland (99 sq. miles) formed by Wolf Creek Dam; Natural Arch Scenic Area (945 acres) at Parker's Lake; Laurel Recreation Area; Red River Gorge; Stone Sky Bridge (75 ft. long, 18 ft. high), Yahoo Falls (116 ft.); Primitive Weapons Hunting Area (7,000 acres) in Bath and Menifee counties, south of Morehead, reserved for hunters using crossbows, longbows, muzzle-loading shotguns, and rifles during open seasons; Cumberland Falls and Natural Bridge state parks; boat launching ramps at Lake Cumberland. Camp and picnic sites, 7; picnic only, 5; cottages and motels. Nearby towns: Corbin, London, Morehead, Pine Ridge, Richmond, Somerset, Williamsburg, Winchester. Highways: u.s. 25, 27, 60, 421, 460; State 15, 52, 80, 90. Forest supervisor at Winchester.

LOUISIANA NATIONAL FOREST

Kisatchie (560,543 acres in 6 segments): Ranger Districts: Catahoula, Evangeline, Leesville, Winn. Bream, Catfish, and other warm water fish in lakes and bayous; Deer, Wild Turkey, waterfowl, and small game hunting. Special features: Plantations of longleaf, loblolly, and splash pines. Catahoula District: Catahoula Game Management Area (36,117 acres); Stuart Forest Service Nursery (77 acres) with annual production capacity of 40 million seedlings; Lake Iatt. Evangeline District: Evangeline Wildlife Management Area (15,000 acres); Valentine Lake (80 acres) west of Alexandria. Leesville District: Fullerton Lake (28 acres) north of Cravens; Red Dirt Game Management Area (40,082 acres). Winn District: Caney Lakes (165 and 226 acres) north of Minden; Corney Lake (2,100 acres) northeast of Homer; Saline Bayou and Lake. Longleaf Trail Vista between Alexander and Natchitoches. Camp and picnic sites, 2; picnic only, 6. Nearby towns: Alexandria, Ball, Bellwood, Cravens, Derry, Homer, Leesville, Minden, Natchitoches, Oakdale, Winnfield. Highways: U.S. 71, 84, 165, 167; State 9, 10, 19, 21, 28, 117, 119, 156, 159, 399. Forest supervisor at Alexandria.

MICHIGAN NATIONAL FORESTS

Hiawatha-Marquette (832,631 acres, 2 forests) in eastern region of the Upper Peninsula: Black Bass, Trout, Northern and Walleyed Pike fishing in lakes and streams; Black Bear, White-tailed Deer, waterfowl, and other small game hunting. Special features: Numerous chains of large and small lakes and streams among evergreen and hardwood forests. Hiawatha Division: Au Train Bay on Lake Superior connected via White-fish River East Branch, Trout Lake, Cleveland Cliffs Basin, Au Train River and Lake, and other streams with little Bay de Noc and Green Bay on Lake Michigan; Rapid River flowing into Little Bay de Noc; Fishdam, Ogontz, and Sturgeon rivers flow from lakes into Big Bay de Noc; Indian River and other streams fill Indian Lake near Manistique on Lake Michigan; Miners Falls on Miners River east of Grand Island on Lake Superior; Thunder Bowl Winter Sports Area in the Indian River Country of countless lakes northeast of Manistique; Upper Peninsula Experimental Forest west of Laughing Whitefish Falls State Park. Marquette Division between Whitefish Bay on Lake Superior and Straits of Mackinac, Lake Huron and Lake Michigan: Carp, Frenchman, and Wegwas lakes source of Carp River flowing into Lake Huron near Pine River; Brevoort Lake and River on Lake Michigan, Monocle and Spectacle lakes near Point Iroquois Lighthouse on Lake Superior; McNarney, Pendills, and Platt lakes west of Dollar Settlement; Mission Hill or Iroquois Winter Sports Area east of Dollar Settlement on Lake Superior. Hiking trails, canoe routes. Camp and picnic sites, 22; picnic only, 5; cabins, hotels, and resorts. Nearby towns: Au Train, Chatham, Escanaba, Gladstone, Manistique, Munising, Rapid River in Shingleton-Hiawatha Division; Brevoort, Brimley, Charles, Dollar Settlement, Rudyard, St. Ignace, Sault Ste. Marie, Trout Lake in Marquette Division. Highways: U.S. 2, 41; Interstate 75; State 28, 48, 94, 123, 149. Forest supervisor at Escanaba.

Huron (414,819 acres) on Lower Peninsula in northeastern region: Trout fishing in lakes and streams; Deer, game birds, and other small game hunting. Special features: Lake Huron; Middle Branch and South Branch Au Sable rivers; Black and Pine rivers; impounded waters of Au Sable River: Mio Dam Pond near Mio, Alcona Dam Pond east of Curtis and Loud Dam, Five Channels Dam, Cooke Dam, and Foote Dam ponds in Iosco County west of Oscoda; Lake Jewel near Barton City; Kiwanis Monument (10,000 acres of red pine trees), Lumbermans Monument, Indian, Island, and Sand lakes north of Tawas City; Mack and Wagner lakes north of Rose City; Canoe Harbor on South Branch Au Sable River north of Roscommon; Silver Valley Winter Sports Area north of Tawas City; canoeing and float trips. Camp and picnic sites, 9; picnic only, 8; cabins, hotels, and resorts. Nearby towns in and near forest: Alcona, East Tawas, Grayling, Harrisville, Mio, Oscoda, Roscommon, Rose City, Tawas. Highways: u.s. 23, 27; State 18, 33, 55, 65, 72, 76, 144, 171. Forest supervisor at Cadillac.

Manistee (445,775 acres) in northwestern portion of Lower Peninsula: Trout and deepwater fishing; Deer, game birds, and other small game hunting. Special features: Lake Michigan; numerous lakes among pine, spruce, and hardwood forests; Hamlin Lake on Big Sable River, north of Ludington; Big Bass Lakes; Big Star Lake; Lake Mitchell west of Cadillac; Hodenpyle Dam and Tippy Dam ponds on the Manistee River southwest of Mesick, Muskegon, and Pere Marquette rivers; adjacent Pere Marquette State Forest; Caberfae Winter Sports Area west of Cadillac; Big M or Manistee Winter Sports Area east of Manistee; canoe and float trips. Camp and picnic sites, 12; picnic only, 17; cabins, hotels, and resorts. Nearby towns: Benson, Big Rapids, Cadillac, Fremont, Ludington, Manistee, Mesick, Reed City. Highways: u.s. 10, 31, 33; State 20, 37, 46, 55, 63, 82, 115. Forest supervisor at Cadillac.

Ottawa (861,479 acres) on Lake Superior at western end of the Upper Peninsula: Bass, Muskellunge, Pike, and Trout fishing in numerous lakes and streams; Bear, Deer, and small game hunting. Special features: About 400 lakes and 1,200 miles of streams with over 30 beautiful waterfalls including the Agate, Bond, Mex-i-min-ee, and Sparrow Rapids falls on the Ontonagon River, the Sturgeon River Falls southwest of Baraga, the Conglomerate, Gorge, Potowatomi, Rainbow, and Sandstone falls on the Black River; Lake Gogebic at Bergland; Lake Ottawa (551 acres), Bass Lake (96 acres) and Hagerman Lake (584 acres) near Brule Lake (251 acres) head of the Brule River canoe route west of Iron River; Prickett Dam Reservoir on the Sturgeon River near Baraga; Cranberry, Iron, and Presque Isle Rivers flowing into Lake Superior; Multiple Use Demonstration Area at Imp Lake; Old Indian Pony Trail, Indian Head Ski Area and Mount Joy Winter Sports Area near Wakefield; Mount Kimberly

Winter Sports Area northeast of Marenisco at Lake Gogebic; cabins and motels. Camp and picnic sites, 16; picnic only, 10. Nearby towns: Baraga, Bergland, Bessemer, Covington, Iron River, Ironwood, Ontonagon, Presque Isle, Silver City, Trout Creek, Wakefield, Watersmeet. Highways: u.s. 2, 45; State 28, 35, 64, 73. Forest supervisor at Ironwood.

MINNESOTA NATIONAL FORESTS

Chippewa (639,452 acres) in north central Minnesota: Bass, Trout, Northern and Walleyed Pike fishing in lakes and streams; Black Bear, White-tailed Deer, waterfowl, and other small game hunting. Special features: Mississippi River connecting Leech Lake (251 sq. miles) and Big Winnie or Winnibigosh Lake (179 sq. miles); Big Fork, Boy, Leech Lake rivers and several other streams linking numerous chains of lakes; large stands of jack and red pines; wild rice areas; Chippewa Indian villages of Ball Club, Inger, and Oniqum; Cut Foot Sioux and Pike Bay experimental forests; Lake Windigo on Star Island near Knutson Dam; Shingobee Winter Sports Area south of Walker; Old Red Lake Trail. Camp and picnic sites, 60; cabins, hotels, and resorts. Nearby towns: Alwood, Big Fork, Black Duck, Cass Lake, Deer River, Grand Rapids, Northome, Park Rapids, Walker. Highways: u.s. 2, 71, 371; State 6, 34, 38, 46, 84, 92. Forest supervisor at Cass Lake.

Superior (1,957,981 acres in 2 segments) on Lake Superior in northeastern Minnesota: Smallmouth Bass, Trout, Northern and Walleyed Pike fishing in lakes and streams; Black Bear, White-tailed Deer, game birds, and other small game hunting. Special features: Boundary Waters Canoe Area bordering Quetico Provincial Park in Canada; nearly 2,000 inland lakes including large Basswood, Crooked, Gunflint, Knife, Moose, Mountain, Namakan, and Saganaga lakes and Lac La Croix on the Canadian boundary; Whiteface River Reservoir in southern portion; Bear Island Lake; Birch Lake on South Kawishiw River; Burntside Lake connected by waterways with Trout and Vermillion lakes on Vermillion River; Eagle Mountain (2,301 ft.) near Brule Lake and River in the northeast; Echo Trail extending from Crane Lake in the northwest to the Farm Lake and West Iron Lakes region; Gunflint Trail from Grand Marais; the Caribou Trail near Lutsen, and Sawbill Trail from Toft start on u.s. 61 bordering Lake Superior and lead to the northern Boundary Waters Canoe Area; magnetic rock near Gunflint Lake; boat launching sites at Whiteface Reservoir, Bearskin, Caribou, Crane, Crescent, Devils Track, Fall, Greenwood (Route 2), McFarland, Pike, Sand, and Windy lakes, all outside of the Boundary Waters Canoe Area. Camp and picnic sites, 29; picnic only, 12; cabins, hotels, and resorts. Nearby towns: Buyck, Duluth, Ely, Grand Marais, International Falls, Orr, Vermillion, and

Virginia in Minnesota; Port Arthur and Winnepeg in Canada. Highways: U.S. 53, 61, Minnesota 1, 2, 23, 24, 35, 73, 135, 169. Forest supervisor at Duluth.

MISSISSIPPI NATIONAL FORESTS

Bienville (175,657 acres) in central Mississippi: Bass and Bream fishing; Deer and Quail hunting. Special features: Coastal Plain hardwood and pine forest; Marathon Lake (48 acres) north of Raleigh; 80 acres of loblolly pine at Bienville Ranger Station; forest management demonstration areas. Camp and picnic sites, 2, picnic only, 3. Nearby towns: Forest, Jackson, Meridian, Raworth. Highways: U.S. 80; State 18, 35. Forest supervisor at Jackson.

De Soto (500,335 acres) in southeastern Mississippi: Bass, Bluegill, and Perch fishing; Quail and other small game hunting. Special features: Big Biloxi River; bottomland hardwoods and pines; Ashe Lake (14 acres) near Ashe Forest Service Nursery; Black, Red, Thompson, and Tuxachanie creeks; South Mississippi Gun and Dog Club field trials area; boating and swimming. Camp and picnic sites, 3; picinic only, 8. Nearby towns: Biloxi, Columbia, Gulfport, Hattiesburg, Laurel, Wiggins. Highways: U.S. 11, 49, 90, 98; State 13, 15, 26, 29, 55, 63, 67. Forest supervisor at Jackson.

Holly (143,352 acres) in northern Mississippi: Bass and Bream fishing; Quail and other small game hunting. Special features: Rolling hills heavily wooded; Sardis Reservoir, Paskus Lake (80 acres), Tillatoba Lake (40 acres); annual bird dog field trials at Holly Springs. Camp and picnic sites, 4. Nearby towns: Holly Springs, New Albany, Oxford. Highways: U.S. 2, 51, 78; State 5, 7, 15, 30. Forest supervisor at Jackson.

Homochitto (189,069 acres) in southwestern Mississippi: Bass and Bream fishing; Quail and other small game hunting. Special features: Bald cypress and hardwood trees; Homochitto River watershed; Mount Nebo Lake, Pipe's Lake (26 acres), Clear Springs Lake (13 acres); Woodman Springs; several forest management demonstration areas. Camp and picnic sites, 1; picnic only, 3. Nearby towns: Brookhaven, Gloster, Meadville, Natchez. Highways: U.S. 61, 84, 98; State 33. Forest supervisor at Jackson.

Tombigbee (65,232 acres) in northeastern Mississippi: Bass, Bream, and Crappie fishing; Deer, Quail, and other small game hunting. Special features: Upper Coastal Plain pine and hardwood forest; Davis Lake (200 acres) Choctaw Lake (100 acres) recreation areas; Indian Mounds; Natchez Trace Parkway. Camp and picnic sites, 1; picnic only, 2; cabins and resort lodge at Choctaw Lake. Nearby towns: Ackerman, Houston,

Kosciusko, Tupelo; Highways: u.s. 82; State 8, 15. Forest supervisor at Jackson.

MISSOURI NATIONAL FORESTS

Clark (902,662 acres in 4 segments) on the Ozark Plateau in central and southeastern Missouri: Black Bass, Catfish, Jack Salmon (Walleye) and Rainbow Trout fishing; small game hunting. Special features: Oak and pine forests interlaced with springs and streams in a mountainous region; Lake Killarney east of Ironton; Silver Mine Dam on St. Francis River west of Fredericktown; Castor River in the Marquand region; Big River near Belgrade; Huzzah Creek near Steelville; Indian Trail State Park northeast of Salem; Loggers Lake south of Bunker; Black River and Cook Springs near Centerville, Sunnen Lake west of Potosi; Keith Springs Recreational Area near Goodland; McCormack Lake, Greer Springs, and Eleven Mile River near Alton; Buffalo Creek and Current River near Doniphan; Lake Wappapelo (shoreline 150 miles), Black and St. Francis rivers near Poplar Bluff; "John-boat" float trips. Camp and picnic sites, 2; picnic only, 6. Nearby towns: Alton, Belgrade, Bunker, Centerville, Doniphan, Fredericktown, Ironton, Marquand, Poplar Bluff, Potosi, Salem, Steelville. Highways: u.s. 60, 61, 67, 160; State 19, 21, 32, 49, 72, 117. Forest supervisor at Rolla, Missouri (northern portion), and at Harrisburg, Illinois (southern portion).

Mark Twain (451,085 acres in 4 segments) in Ozark Mountains near Arkansas border: Black Bass, Catfish, Jack Salmon (Walleye), and Rainbow Trout fishing; waterfowl and other small game hunting. Special features: Numerous clear streams, springs, caves, stands of pine and hardwood trees; White River east of Gainesville; Gasgonde River near Fort Leonard Wood; Table Rock Lake (shoreline 850 miles) east of Cassville; Beaver Creek near Bradleyville; Brush Creek Recreation Area north of Rueter; Big Springs Recreation Area near West Plains; Washington Bald Lookout, Lake Taneycomo, and the Mincy Wildlife Area outside are close by and between portions of forest near Branson. Camp and picnic sites, 8; picnic only, 14; hotels and resorts. Nearby towns: Ava, Bradleyville, Branson, Cassville, Fort Leonard, Wood, Lebanon, Rotta, Springfield, Summit, Taneyville, West Plains, Willow Springs. Highways: u.s. 60, 63,66, 160; State 14, 17, 32, 39, 76, 86, 95, 125. Forest supervisor at Springfield.

MONTANA NATIONAL FORESTS

Beaverhead (2,131,136 acres in several segments) in southwestern Montana: Grayling and Trout fishing in lakes and streams; Antelope, Bear,

Deer, Elk, Moose, Mountain Goat, Bighorn Sheep, and small game hunting. Special features: Bitterroot Range on the Continental Divide and Idaho boundary; Anaconda-Pintlar Wilderness Area; numerous mountain meadows, lakes, and streams; Bloody Dick Creek Reservoir in the Big Hole Divide north of Lemhi Pass (8,000 ft.); Ajax Peak (10,900 ft.) above several lakes including Miners and Twin lakes; Mussigbrid Lake near the North Fork Big Hole River; Alder Peak (9,210 ft.), Odel Mountain (9,446 ft.) and headwaters of the Wise River in the Pioneer Mountains; Potosi Hot Springs; Branham, Meadow, and Twin lakes in the Tobacco Root Mountains; Cherry Lakes and Vigilante Experimental Range east of Ruby River; Sphinx Mountain (10,860 ft.) in the Medicine Range; Wade, Cliff, Conklin, Hidden, and Elk lakes near the Red Rock Migratory Bird Refuge at Lakeview, east of Monida Pass (6,823 ft.) to the Targhee National Forest; Rainy Mountain Winter Sports Area west of Dillon near Polaris and Elkhorn Hot Springs; pack and saddle trips. Camp and picnic sites, 28; dude ranches, cabins, and resorts. Nearby towns: Alder, Armstead, Dillon, Ennis, Jackson, Lima, Sheridan, Virginia City, Wisdom. Highways: u.s. 91, 93; State 1, 34, 36, 41, 43, 46. Forest supervisor at Dillon.

Bitterroot (1,547,563 acres) straddles the Continental Divide on the Idaho-Montana boundary: Trout fishing in lakes and streams; Bear, Deer, Elk, Mountain Goat, Moose, Bighorn Sheep, and small game hunting. Special features: Ponderosa and lodgepole pine, Douglas fir, Engelmann spruce, and western larch forests, alpine lakes and streams; Anaconda-Pintlar Wilderness Area; Selway-Bitterroot Wilderness Area; Salmon River Breaks Primitive Area; Skalkaho Pass (7,258 ft.) in the Skalkaho Game Preserve in the Sapphire Range south of Missoula; East Fork and West Fork Bitterroot rivers; Lake Como northwest of Darby; St. Joseph Peak (9,570 ft.), Bass Peak (8,840 ft.), and Bass Lake near Florence in the Bitterroot Range; Shook Mountain (7,550 ft.) above Medicine Springs; Gallogly Hot Springs north of Saddle Mountain (8,842 ft.) and Thunder Mountain (7,720 ft.); Lost Trail (6,951 ft.) on the Bitterroot–Salmon River Divide; Lost Trail Pass Winter Sports Area on u.s. 93 south of Sula; pack and saddle trips. Camp and picnic sites, 11; dude ranches, cabins, hotels, and resorts. Nearby towns: Darby, Corvallis, Florence, Hamilton, Missoula, Stevensville, Sula. Highways: u.s. 93; State 38, 43. Forest supervisor at Hamilton.

Custer (1,171,476 acres in several segments) east of the Stillwater River region in southern Montana and South Dakota: Trout fishing in mountain lakes and streams; Antelope, Bear, Deer, Elk, Moose, Mountain Goat, Bighorn Sheep, and small game hunting. Special features: Beartooth Primitive Area; Stillwater River, Emerald and Mystic lakes on West Rosebud Creek; and Silver Run Peak (12,610 ft.) near Red Lodge in the

Beartooth Division. Big Ice and Crater Ice Caves west of Big Horn River; Powder River Game Preserve, Horse Creek, Wild Horse Creek, and Wild Horse Buttes at East Fork Hanging Woman Creek, and several wells east of the Tongue River Northern Cheyenne Indian Reservation in the Ashland Division. Chalk Buttes, Ekalaka Park, Capital Rock, Lantis Spring, Carter, Snow Creek, and Wood Gulch wells in the Long Pines Division near Ekalaka. Cave Hills north of Buffalo, Moreau Peak in the Short Pine Hills, and Slim Buttes east of South Dakota State Park in the South Fork Grand River region of South Dakota; Grizzly Peak Ski Area near Red Lodge; hiking trails, pack and saddle trips. Camp and picnic sites, 13; picnic only, 2. Nearby towns: Absaroke, Ashland, Billings, Broadus, Ekalaka, Red Lodge, and Warren in Montana; Buffalo, Ludlow, Redig, and Reva in South Dakota. Highways: u.s. 12, 85, 212, 310; State 7, 8. Forest supervisor at Billings.

Deerlodge (1,134,639 acres in several segments) on the Continental Divide in southwestern Montana: Grayling and Trout fishing in about 100 lakes and 290 miles of streams; Antelope, Black Bear, Deer (Mule, White-tailed), Elk, Moose, Grouse, and other small game hunting. Special features: Evergreen forests, mountain meadows, and valleys with elevations from about 4,600 ft. to 10,635 ft. on summit of Mount Evans in the Pintlar Range; Moose Lake and East Fork Reservoir of the Anaconda-Pintlar Primitive Area; Mount Emerine (8,640 ft.), West Fork Buttes (7,100 ft.), Bare Hill (8,749 ft.), and Medicine Lake in the Sapphire Mountains; Echo, Fred Burr, Georgetown, and Silver lakes, Goat Mountain (9,321 ft.), Mount Princeton (7,916 ft.), and Pikes Peak (9,359 ft.) above Rock Creek Lake in the Flint Creek Range; John Long Mountains; Mount Fleecer (9,445 ft.), Nigger Mountain (8,392 ft.), Table Mountain (10,217 ft.), and Basin Creek Reservoir in the Highland Mountains; Pipestone Pass; Delmoe Lake on Big Pipestone Creek; Whitetail Peak (8,476 ft.) above Whitetail Reservoir; Haystack Mountain near Little Boulder River; Sheepshead Mountain (7,779 ft.) north of Butte; Mount Jackson (10,380 ft.), Mount Jefferson (10,604 ft.), and South Boulder River in the Tobacco Root Mountains; Cable Mountain Winter Sports Area west of Anaconda; hiking trails, pack and saddle trips. Camp and picnic sites, 27; picnic only, 4; dude ranches, cabins, hotels, and resorts. Nearby towns: Anaconda, Boulder, Butte, Deer Lodge, Phillipsburg, Whitehall. Highways: u.s. 10, 10A, 91; Interstate 15, 90; State 38, 41, 48, 274, 348. Forest supervisor at Butte.

Flathead (2,335,565 acres in several segments) west of the Continental Divide in northwestern Montana: Bass, Silver Salmon, and Trout fishing in lakes and streams; Bear, Deer, Elk, Mountain Goat, Moose, Bighorn Sheep, and small game hunting. Special features: Alpine and Douglas fir, spruce, western larch, lodgepole, ponderosa, and white pine forests, alpine lakes, glaciers, and rugged mountains; Bob Marshall Wilderness Area; Mission Mountains Primitive Area; Flathead Lake (30 miles long, 10 miles wide, average depth 220 ft.) on Flathead River; Hungry Horse Reservoir (35 sq. miles) on the South Fork Flathead River; Mount Orvis Evans (7,440 ft.) and Three Eagles Mountain (7,445 ft.) near Swan Lake; Elk Calf Mountain (7,610 ft.), Trinity Mountain (7,535 ft.), and Big Lodge Mountain (7,665 ft.) on the Continental Divide; Middle Fork Flathead River on the Glacier National Park (1,013,129 acres) boundary; Big Hawk Mountain (7,540 ft.), Circus Peak (7,810 ft.), Grant Glacier, Great Bear Mountain (7,600 ft.), Great Northern Mountain (8,700 ft.), Mount Aeneas (7,530 ft.), Mount Cameohwait (7,895 ft.), Mount Grant (8,620 ft.), Mount Murray (7,140 ft.), Mount Penrose (7,810 ft.), Nyack Mountain (7,760 ft.), Red Sky Mountain (8,155 ft.), and Triangle Peak (7,645 ft.) in the Flathead Range; Bald Mountain (7,000 ft.), Coal Ridge (7,123 ft.), Diamond Peak (7,285 ft.), Moose Peak (7,521 ft.), Werner Peak (7,000 ft.), and Whitefish Lake in the Whitefish Range; Tally Lake near the Stillwater River; Big Mountain Winter Sports Area north of Whitefish; hiking trails, boating, canoeing, pack and saddle trips. Camp and picnic sites, 15; picnic only, 1. Dude ranches, cabins, hotels, and resorts. Nearby towns: Big Fork, Columbia Falls, Coram, Eureka, Kalispell, Missoula, Polson, Swan Lake, Whitefish. Highways: u.s. 2, 93; State 35, 40. Forest supervisor at Kalispell.

Gallatin (1,700,139 acres) adjacent to the Yellowstone National Park (2,221,772 acres) and 2 districts north of Livingston in southern Montana: Trout fishing in mountain lakes and streams; Pronghorn Antelope, Bear (Brown, Grizzly), Deer (Mule, White-tailed), Elk, Mountain Goat, Bighorn Sheep, Grouse, waterfowl, and other small game hunting. Special features: Grazing lands among lodgepole pine and Douglas fir forests; Absaroka Primitive Area; Earthquake and Hebgen lakes in the Madison River Canyon Earthquake Area (37,000 acres) near Ennis and West Yellowstone; Targhee Pass (7,078 ft.) on the Continental Divide; Kotch Peak (11,293 ft.) south of Spanish Peaks Primitive Area; Gallatin Game Preserve and Gallatin River in the Madison Range; Mount Blackmore (10,196 ft.), Mount Delano (10,200 ft.), Mount Cowen (11,190 ft.), Emigrant Peak (10,960 ft.), and Montanapolis Springs in the Absaroka Range; Colter Pass (8,066 ft.) south of Beartooth Primitive Area; Bridge Range northwest of Livingston; several lakes including Campfire, Cave, and Rock lakes between Crazy Peak (11,214 ft.) and Porcupine Butte (6,970 ft.) in the Crazy Mountains; Indian paintings in caves at Natural Bridge on the Boulder River south of Big Timber; Yellowstone River; Bridger Ski Bowl 20 miles north of Bozeman; hiking trails, pack and saddle trips. Camp and picnic sites, 33; dude ranches, cabins, hotels, and resorts. Nearby towns: Big Timber, Bozeman, Cook, Emigrant, Gardiner, Livingston, Red Lodge, West Yellowstone. Highways: u.s. 10, 12, 89, 191; State 19, 287. Forest supervisor at Bozeman.

Helena (966,613 acres in 4 districts) in west central Montana: Trout fishing in lakes and streams; Deer, Elk, and small game hunting. Special features: Douglas fir, lodgepole, and ponderosa pine forests, and grazing lands; Continental Divide; MacDonald Pass (6,325 ft.), Little Blackfoot River, Chessman and Scott reservoirs southwest of Helena; Mulland Pass (5,800 ft.), Greenhorn Mountain (7,400 ft.). Stemple Pass (6,373 ft.) and Flesher Pass (6,350 ft.) between the Blackfoot River, Nevada and Prickly Pear creeks; Indian Meadows, Big Horn, Heart, Silver King, Twin, and Webb lakes north of Lincoln; Rogers Pass (5,609 ft.) near South Fork Deerhorn River; Gates of the Mountain Wild Area; Big Belt Mountains east of the Missouri River impounded by Hauser Dam to form Lake Helena and Hauser Lake, and Canyon Ferry Dam creating a 25-mile long lake; Dry Range between Lingshire and the Smith River; Grass Mountain Winter Sports Area 25 miles east of Townsend; hiking trails, pack and saddle trips. Camp and picnic sites, 10; dude ranches, cabins, hotels, and resorts. Nearby towns: Avon, Boulder, East Helena, Helena, Lincoln, Townsend, White Sulphur Springs, Wolf Creek. Highways: u.s. 10, 89, 91; State 6, 20. Forest supervisor at Helena.

Kaniksu (1,625,383 acres) in northwestern Montana with largest portion in Idaho: Cabinet Mountains Primitive Area; Bull River; Eagle Peak (7,554 ft.), Squaw Peak (6,166 ft.); Noxon Rapids Dam on Clark Fork. Nearby towns: Thompson Falls in Montana; Clark Fork in Idaho. Highway: u.s. 10A. See IDAHO NATIONAL FORESTS.

Kootenai (1,817,975 acres) bordering Idaho and Canada in northwestern Montana: Trout fishing in lakes and streams; Black Bear, Deer (Mule, White-tailed), Elk, Moose, Mountain Goat, Bighorn Sheep, and small game hunting. Special features: Northwest Peak (7,700 ft.), Boulder Mountain (7,072 ft.), Grizzly Peak (6,500 ft.), Lost Horse Mountains (6,560 ft.), Newton Mountain (6,534 ft.), Parsnip Mountain (6,150 ft.), Turner Mountain (5,952 ft.), Yak River, Kilbrennan and Loon lakes in the Purcell Range; Blue Mountain (6,042 ft.) north of Libby; Cabinet Mountains Primitive Area; Fisher River; Spar Peak (6,565 ft.) and Lake; Bull Lake east of Ross Creek Scenic Area; Kootenai River; Pinkham Mountain Lookout, Twin Meadows, and Wolf Peak (6,115 ft.) in the Flathead Mountains; Mount Locke (7,190 ft.), Green Mountain (7,830 ft.), and Poorman Mountain (7,800 ft.) north of Dickey and Murphy lakes; several lakes in the Tobacco River region; Turner Mountain Ski Area north of Libby; 1,600 miles of foot and horse trails. Camp and picnic sites, 23; dude ranches, cabins, and hotels. Nearby towns: Eureka, Kalispell, Libby, Ruxford, Trout Creek, Troy. Highways: u.s. 2, 93; State 37. Forest supervisor at Libby.

Lewis and Clark (1,862,011 acres) in the Rocky Mountain Division south of the Glacier National Park and east of the Flathead National Forest in northwestern Montana, and several segments south and east of Great Falls in the Jefferson Division: Trout fishing in mountain lakes and streams; Antelope, Bear (Black, Grizzly), Deer, Elk, Mountain Goat, and small game hunting. Special features: Rocky Mountain Division: eastern slope of the Continental Divide; Arsenic Mountain (8,500 ft.); Bear Top Mountain (8,090 ft.); Mount Field (8,595 ft.); Teton Peak (8,400 ft.); Bob Marshall Wilderness Area; Sun River Game Preserve west of North Fork Sun River; Teton River. Jefferson Division: Gibson Highwood Mountains west of Great Falls; Big Baldy (9,191 ft.), Kings Hill (8,000 ft.), Porphyry Peak (8,026 ft.), Hoover Springs, Lost Fork and Musselshell rivers in the Little Belt Mountains; White Sulphur Springs; Old Baldy (8,600 ft.), Snow Mountains Game Preserve, Crystal Lake, Ice Cave, Big Snowy and Little Snowy mountains south of Lewistown; Little Rocky Mountains Game Preserve at Landusky; Kings Hill Winter Sports Area north of White Sulphur Springs. Camp and picnic sites, 12; dude ranches, cabins, and resorts. Nearby towns: Augusta, Choteau, Dupuyer, East Glacier Park in Rocky Mountains Division; Armington, Garneil, Great Falls, Hobson, Landusky, Lewiston, Martinsdale, Musselshell, White Sulphur Springs in Jefferson Division. Highways: u.s. 2, 87, 89; State 6, 19, 21, 33. Forest supervisor at Great Falls.

Lolo (2,502,698 acres in several segments) in western Montana: Trout fishing in mountain lakes and streams; Bear, Deer, Elk, and small game hunting. Special features: Clark Fork, Siamese Lakes, Crater Mountain (7,600 ft.), Oregon Peak (7,290 ft.) above Missoula and Oregon lakes, Ninemile Divide, Keystone Game Preserve near Superior, Driveway Peak (6,030 ft.) west of Thompson Falls, Lolo Pass (5,178 ft.) south of Lolo Hot Springs, and Lookout Pass (4,738 ft.) near Shoshone Peak in the Bitterroot Range on the Idaho-Montana boundary; Mount Headley (7,424 ft.) and Thompson River in the Cabinet Mountains north of Thompson Falls; Cleveland Mountain (7,182 ft.) and Quigg Peak (8,450 ft.) in the Sapphire Range; Selway-Bitterroot Wilderness Area (10,010 acres); Seeley Lake Game Refuge, Clearwater Lake north of Alva, Inez, and Rainy lakes, Placid Lake near Salmon Lake on the Clearwater River, and Blackfoot River northwest of Missoula; Baldy Mountain (7,934 ft.) Ski Area north of Plains; Missoula Snow Bowl on Grant Creek Road northwest of Missoula; hiking trails, pack and saddle trips. Camp and picnic, 18; picnic only, 1; dude ranches and resorts. Nearby towns: Alberton, Drummond, Missoula, Ovando, Plains,

St. Regis, Superior, Thompson Falls. Highways: U.S. 10, 10A, 93; State 93. Forest supervisor at Missoula.

NEBRASKA NATIONAL FOREST

Nebraska (206,082 acres): fishing; no hunting—entire area is a Mule Deer game refuge, and a nesting ground for Great Blue Heron, Grouse, and Prairie Chicken. Special features: Forest plantations on sandhills, and Bessey Nursery near Halsey ships more than 5 million seedlings annually to federal, state, and private planting projects in 5 states; Middle Loup River; Nebraska 4-H Club Camp, Niobrara District is south of Nenzel, and Pine Ridge District is south of Chadron. Camp and picnic sites, 3; picnic only, 2. Nearby towns: Alliance, Broken Bow, Crawford, Halsey, Thedford, Nenzel, Valentine. Highways: U.S. 20, 83; State, 2. Forest supervisor at Lincoln.

NEVADA NATIONAL FORESTS

Humboldt (2,507,869 acres in 9 divisions); Humboldt division at the Idaho border, Santa Rosa division at the Oregon boundary, and other divisions in eastern Nevada: Bass and Trout fishing; Antelope, Mule Deer, Elk, Bighorn Sheep, and small game hunting. Special features: Grazing lands among Engelmann spruce, Douglas fir, and white fir forests; mining operations; Humboldt River watershed; Jarbidge Wild Area; Mount Moriah (12,067 ft.) above Snake Valley at the Utah border; Wheeler Scenic Area southeast of Ely, containing Wheeler Peak (13,063 ft.) glistening with a perpetual ice field; Baker, Johnson, and Stella lakes; Baker and Snake creeks; ancient bristlecone pine, and enormous mountain mahogany trees; Hole-in-the-Mountain Peak (11,276 ft.) in the East Humboldt Range; Harrison Pass (7,247 ft.), Pearl Peak (10,198 ft.) above Ruby Lake, and Ruby Dome (11,349 ft.) south of Elko and Wells; Copper Mountain (9,911 ft.), Jacks Peak (10,198 ft.), Matterhorn (10,839 ft.), and Wild Horse Reservoir north of Elko; Calico Mountain (8,365 ft.), Hinkey Summit (7,867 ft.), Santa Rose Peak (9,728 ft.), Spring Peak (9,728 ft.), and North Fork Little Humboldt River north of Paradise Valley and Winnemucca; Current Mountain (11,513 ft.), Duckwater Mountain (11,268 ft.), Mount Hamilton (10,745 ft.), Hamilton Lake, White River, and Timber Mountain (10,280 ft.) near Troy Peak (111,268 ft.) north and south of Currant; Ward Mountain (10,936 ft.) Winter Sports Area south of Ely and Ruth; hiking trails, pack and saddle trips, camp and picnic cites, 24; picnic only, 5; dude ranches and resorts at Wild Horse Reservoir. Nearby towns: Currant, Elko, Ely, Paradise Valley, Pioche, Ruth, Wells, Winnemucca. Highways: u.s. 6, 40, 50, 93, 95; State 8B, 11, 20, 43, 46. Forest supervisor at Elko.

Toiyabe (3,118,966 acres in several segments with one portion extending into California): Bass, Perch and Trout fishing in lakes and streams; Antelope, Deer, Elk, Bighorn Sheep, and small game hunting. Special features: High Sierra region: Mount Rose Summit (8,933 ft.) north of Lake Tahoe; Desert Creek Peak (8,969 ft.), Lucky Boy Pass (8,001 ft.), Sweetwater Summit (7,120 ft.), and Boundary Peak (13,145 ft.) near Hawthorne practically on the California line; Sherman Peak (8,672 ft.) in the Quartz Mountains; Arc Dome (11,775 ft.), Bunker Hill (11,474 ft.), North Shoshone Peak (10,313 ft.), South Shoshone Peak (10,063 ft.), Scott Summit (7,267 ft.), and Ichthyosaur Fossil Area State Park near Austin's Bald Mountain (9,275 ft.), Mount Jefferson (11,807 ft.), and Wild Cat Peak (10,534 ft.) in the Toquima Range; and Antelope Peak (10,220 ft.), Monitor Peak (10,856 ft.), Piñon Peak (9,327 ft.), and Summit Mountain north of Tonopah; Charleston Peak (11,910 ft.) at the head of Kyle Canyon and Mummy Mountain (11,534 ft.) west of Las Vegas; Hoover Wild Area north of Mono Lake in California; Kyle Canyon and Lee Canyon Winter Sports Area in the Charleston segment; and Reno Ski Bowl northeast of Lake Tahoe; pack and saddle trails. Camp and picnic sites, 33; dude ranches, motels, and resorts. Nearby towns: Austin, Carson City, Eureka, Hawthorne, Las Vegas, Luning, Minden, Reno, Tonopah. Highways: u.s. 6, 95, 395; State 3, 8, 21, 22, 23, 27, 28, 31, 52, 88, 91. Forest supervisor at Reno.

NEW HAMPSHIRE NATIONAL FOREST

White Mountains (724,311 acres in 2 segments) in north central New Hampshire and a small portion in western Maine: Bass, Perch, Pickerel, and Trout fishing; Bear, Deer, Wildcat, and small game hunting. Special features: Stands of spruce, fir, and hardwoods; Mount Adams (5,798 ft.); Mount Clay (5,532 ft.), Mount Franklin (5,004 ft.); Mount Lafayette (5,249 ft.); Mount Lincoln (5,408 ft.); Mount Madison (5,362 ft.); Mount Monroe (5,385 ft.); Mount Washington (6,288 ft.); Ammonoosuc, Baker, Mad, Peabody, Pemigewasset, Saco, and Wild rivers in Maine; Crawford Notch State Park; Franconia Notch State Reservation containing Cannon Mountain (4,060 ft.) and a rocky formation known as the Old Man of the Mountain; Echo Lake and Moose Brook state parks; Dolly Capp Recreational Area; Rocky Gorge Scenic Area; Great Gulf Wild Area; Appalachian Mountain Club trails with 47 shelters and high country cabins for hikers. Camp and picnic sites, 14; picnic only, 12; cabins, motels, and resorts. Nearby towns: Ashland, Bartlett, Berlin, Bretton Woods, Campton, Conway, Franconia, Gorham, Glencliff, Jackson, Lincoln, Littleton, North Woodstock, Pinkham Notch in New Hampshire; Bethel, Fryeberg, Gilead in Maine. Highways: u.s. 2, 3, 202; State 16, 18, 25, 112, 113, 175; Maine 5, 35. Forest supervisor at Laconia.

NEW MEXICO NATIONAL FORESTS

Carson (1,225,408 acres in 3 segments) in north central part of state: Trout fishing in mountain streams; Bear, Deer, and small game. hunting. Special features: Adjacent to Jicarilla Apache Indian Reservation; Sangre de Cristo Range; Wheeler Peak (13,180 ft.), Canjilon Mountain (10,700 ft.); Latir Lakes and Peak (12,708 ft.); Ortiz Peak (12,583 ft.); Santa Barbara Canyon near Penasco; Kit Carson Memorial State Park; Red River; Pecos Wilderness Area; Wheeler Peak Wild Area; Tres Piedras–Lagunitas Lake country; Agua Piedra Winter Sports Area; Taos Ski Valley at Hondo Canyon. Camp and picnic sites, 34; picnic only, 1. Nearby towns: Abiquiu, Brazos, Arroyo Hondo, Canjilon, Cebolla, Chama, Chimayo, Cimarron, Costilla, Eagle Nest, Las Vegas, Ojo Caliente, Questa, Red River, Taos. Highways: u.s. 64, 84, 285; State 3, 38, 76, 96, 111. Forest supervisor at Taos.

Cibola (1,696,703 acres in several segments): Fishing in McGaffey Lake; Antelope, Bear, Deer (Rocky Mountain Mule, White-tailed), and small game hunting. Special features: Mount Powell, Zuni Mountains, and Oso Ridge on the Continental Divide; McGaffey Lake and Lookout Mountain Rim in McKinley and Valencia counties; Horace, La Jara, and San Mateo mesas, Mount Taylor (11,389 ft.) in the San Mateo Mountains near Grant; Bear, Datil, Gallinas, and Magdalena mountains, San Mateo Peak (10,141 ft.), and Mount Washington (10,116 ft.) in San Mateo Mountains of Socorro County; Capillo Peak (9,368 ft.), Manzano Mountain, cave dwellings, springs, Sandia Crest Vista Point (10,678 ft.), and La Madera Ski Area in the Sandia Mountains east of the Rio Grande in Bernalillo, Sandoval, and Torrence counties. Camp and picnic sites, 15; picnic only, 14; dude ranches, motels, and hotels. Nearby towns: Albuquerque, Belen, Bernalillo, Bluewater, Chilili, Corona, Datil, Gallup, Grants, Magdalena, Mountainair, Socorro, Wingate. Highways: u.s. 60, 66, 85; State 6, 10, 42, 44, 52, 53, 55, 78. Forest supervisor at Albuquerque.

Gila (2,715,520 acres in 2 divisions): Bass, Bluegill, Catfish, and Trout fishing; Antelope, Black Bear, Deer (Rocky Mountain Mule, White-tailed), Elk, Wild Turkey, predators, and small game hunting. Special features: Black Range, Pinos Altos, and Tularosa ranges, Elk and

Long Canyon mountains on the Continental Divide; Gila Cliff Dwellings National Monument; Black Range Gila Primitive and Wilderness Areas; Diablo Range; Black Mountain (9,303 ft.); Boiler Peak (7,878 ft.); John Kerr Peak (8,862 ft.); Eagle Peak (9,802 ft.); Elk Mountain (9,780 ft.), Bear Wallow (9,920 ft.), Mogollon Baldy (10,778 ft.), and Whitewater Baldy (10,892 ft.) in the Mogollon Range; Gila River; San Francisco River; Bear Canyon Reservoir; numerous creeks and canyons, grassy meadows, ponderosa pine forests; hiking and riding trails. Camp and picnic sites, 13; picnic only, 5; dude ranches, motels, and resorts. Nearby towns: Buckhorn, Deming, Gila, Las Cruces, Lordsburg, Silver City, Truth or Consequences, White Signal. Highways: u.s. 60, 70, 85, 180, 260; State 12, 32, 52, 61, 78, 90. Forest supervisor at Silver City.

Lincoln (1,087,855 acres in 3 divisions): Trout fishing in lakes and streams; Black Bear, Deer (Rocky Mountain Mule, White-tailed), Wild Turkey, upland game, predator hunting. Special features: Canyons, creeks, springs, juniper-covered foothills, ponderosa pine and fir forests; Capitan Mountains (birthplace of Smoky the Bear); Capitan Peak (10,083 ft.); Jicarilla Mountains; Carrizo Mountain (9,656 ft.); Tucson Mountain (8,308 ft.); Nogal Lake; Bonita Lake and Creek; White Mountain Wild Area; Monjeau Skyline; Sierra Blanca Recreation Area; Women's Clubs Memorial Forest; Rio Ruidoso; which are separated by Mescalero Apache Indian Reservation from division containing Sacramento Mountains, Rio Penasco, Sacramento River, Alamo Peak (9,700 ft.), Mule Peak (8,097 ft.); Guadalupe Mountain division, adjacent to Carlsbad Caverns National Park (49,448 acres), includes Deer Hill (7,059 ft.); Sitting Bull Falls; pack and saddle trails in all divisions. Camp and picnic sites, 10; picnic only, 2; Cloudcroft (9,100 ft.) and Ruidoso (7,000 ft.) resorts, dude ranches, organization camps, and hotels. Nearby towns: Almogordo, Artesia, Capitan, Carlsbad, Carrizozo, Roswell, Tularosa. Highways: u.s. 54, 70, 380; State 24, 37, 48, 83, 214, 386. Forest supervisor at Alamogordo.

Santa Fe (1,233,550 acres in 2 divisions): Trout fishing in mountain lakes and streams; Black Bear, Rocky Mountain Mule Deer, Elk, Wild Turkey, predator, and small game hunting. Special features: Mountain grasslands, ponderosa pine and spruce forests, numerous springs and streams; headwaters of Gallinas, Jemez, and Pecos rivers, Rio Frijoles, and Rio En Medio; Nichols and Two Mile reservoirs on Santa Fe River; Lake Katherine; Pecos Baldy and Truchas Lakes; Sangre de Cristo Range; Pecos Wilderness Area; Truchas Peak (13,102 ft.); Thompson Peak (10,554 ft.); Jemez and San Pedro ranges west of the Rio Grande and Santa Fe; Chicomo Peak (11,950 ft.); Nacimiento Peak (10,624 ft.); San Miguel Mountain (9,457 ft.); Rio Chama; Jemez State Monument; San Pedro Parks Wild Area; Santa Fe Ski Basin; pack and saddle trips. Camp and picnic sites, 29; picnic only, 9; guest ranches, hotels, and resorts on Jemez and Pecos rivers. Nearby towns: Albuquerque, Cuba, Espanola, Las Vegas, Pecos, Santa Fe. Highways: u.s. 64, 84, 85, 285; State 4, 50, 63, 96, 105, 121, 126. Forest supervisor at Santa Fe.

NORTH CAROLINA NATIONAL FORESTS

Croatan (152,351 acres): Fishing in lakes, streams, and at Bogue Sound on the Atlantic Ocean; Bear, Deer, Quail, Turkey, and waterfowl hunting. Special features: Pine and swamp hardwoods on coastal area between Neuse River estuary, White Oak River, and Bogue Sound; Ellis, Great, Havelock, Little, and Long lakes. Camp and picnic sites, none; picnic only, 2; motels and resorts. Nearby towns: Bogue, Croatan, Maysville, Morehead City, New Bern. Highways: u.s. 17, 70; State 24, 58, 101. Forest supervisor at Asheville.

Nantahala (448,278 acres) in southwestern corner of state: Bass and Trout fishing in lakes and streams; Bear, Wild Boar, Deer, and small game hunting. Special features: Adjacent to Great Smoky Mountains National Park (511,714 acres); Wayah Bald (5,335 ft.); Wayah Gap (4,180 ft.); Hangover Mountain (5,160 ft.); Hogback Mountain (4,935 ft.); Satulah Mountain (4,520 ft.); Scaly Mountain (4,200 ft.); Whiteside Mountain (4,930 ft.); scenic waterfalls in Blue Valley; Aquone, Chatuge, Cheoha, Fontana, Glenville, Hiwassee, and Santeetlah lakes; Little Tennessee River; Cullasaja Gorge and waterfall; Nantahala Gorge (8 miles long); Bridal Veil, Toxaway, and Whitewater falls; Joyce Kilmer Memorial Forest; Appalachian Trail (60 miles); Indian "Trail of Tears" crossing Snowbird Mountains from Andrews to Robbinsville; boating and hiking. Camp and picnic sites, 10; picnic only, 15; cabins and tourist accommodations. Nearby towns: Andrews, Bryson City, Dillsboro, Fontana, Franklin, Highlands, Murphy, Robbinsville. Highways: u.s. 19, 23, 64, 129; State 28, 107. Forest supervisor at Asheville.

Pisgah (479,697 acres in 2 segments): Bass, Perch, and Trout fishing; Bear, Deer, and small game hunting. Special features; Mount Mitchell (6,684 ft.) north of Blue Ridge Parkway; Cold Mountain (6,030 ft.); Mount Pisgah (5,721 ft.); Beach Gap (5,345 ft.); Grandfather Mountain (5,964 ft.); Roan Mountain (6,285 ft.); Linville Gorge; Craggy Gardens; Daniel Boone and Mount Mitchell wildlife management areas; Pisgah National Game Preserve; Davidson River, North Mills, Sliding Rock, and White Pine recreation areas; Appalachian Trail and riding trails. Camp and picnic sites, 28; picnic only, 23. Nearby towns: Brevard, Burnsville, Canton, Hot Springs, Lenoir, Marion, Waynesville. Highways: u.s. 19, 23, 25, 64, 70, 221, 276, 321; Blue Ridge Parkway; State 80, 90, 128, 191. Forest supervisor at Asheville.

North Carolina National Forests, 42, North French Broad Avenue, Asheville.

OHIO NATIONAL FOREST

Wayne (112,000 acres in segments): Bass, Catfish, and panfish of all types; Deer and small game hunting. Special features: Ohio River; Lake Vesuvius (143 acres) created by a dam on Stern Creek about 9 miles from Ironton; coniferous and hardwood trees; small caves; Hanging Rock iron district; strip mining (coal); hiking and horseback trails; boat facilities (no motorboats) at the Vesuvius Recreation Area. Family units for camping, 92; picnic only, 83. Nearby towns: Albany, Ashland, Athens, Chillicothe, Coolville, Crown City, Huntington, Ironton, Jackson, Logan, Marietta, New Lexington, Woodsfield. Highways: u.s. 21, 23, 33, 35, 50, 52; State 7, 8, 37, 75, 77, 141. Forest supervisor at Bedford, Indiana.

OKLAHOMA NATIONAL FOREST

Ouachita (1,543,361 acres). See ARKANSAS NATIONAL FORESTS

OREGON NATIONAL FORESTS

Deschutes (1,659,368 acres): Trout in lakes and streams; Antelope, Black Bear, Mule Deer, Elk, and small game hunting. Special features: Cascade Range; forests of ponderosa, white, and sugar pines, grazing meadows, more than 200 lakes, canyons, caves, and cascades; Deschutes and Metolius rivers; Mount Jefferson Primitive Area; Diamond Peak and Mount Washington wild areas; Three Sisters Wilderness Area; Three Fingered Jack (7,481 ft.); Mount Washington (7,802 ft.); North Sister (10,095 ft.), Middle Sister (10,053 ft.), and South Sister (10,354 ft.); Crane Prairie and Wickiup reservoirs; Crescent, Cultus, Davis, Miller, Odell, Pauline, Summit, and Suttle lakes; Tumalo Falls (96 ft.); Lava Cast Forest Geological Area; Bachelor Butte and Willamette Pass winter sports areas; Santiam Pass Ski Area; pack and saddle trails. Camp and picnic sites, 76; picnic only, 11; dude ranches, motels, and resorts. Nearby towns: Bend, Chemult, Lapine, Madras, Millican, Oakridge, Redmond, Sweet Home. Highways: u.s. 20, 97, 126; State 31, 58, 230. Forest supervisor at Bend.

Fremont (1,254,595 acres in 2 segments) between Deschutes National Forest and the California-Oregon line: Bass, Perch, and Trout fishing in lakes and streams; Mule Deer and waterfowl hunting. Special features: Ponderosa pine forests, grazing land, and numerous shallow lakes; Chewaucan River; Sprague River and headwaters of Sycan River;

Crook Peak (7,834 ft.); Abert Rim, a geologic fault about 2,500 feet above Lake Abert; Mule Deer Game Refuge west of Drews Reservoir; Gearhart Mountain Wild Area; Campbell and Deadhorse lakes northeast of Gearhart Mountain (8,364 ft.); Dog Lake at head of Dog Creek; Mitchell Recreation Area northeast of Bly; Thompson Reservoir south of Silver Creek Marsh; Sugarpine Mountain (6,388 ft.); Warner Canyon Ski Area near Lakeview. Camp and picnic sites, 21. Nearby towns: Bly, Chemult, Klamath Falls, Lakeview, Paisley, Valley Falls. Highways: u.s. 51, 395; State 31, 66. Forest supervisor at Lakeview.

Malheur (1,410,548 acres in 2 segments): Steelhead and Trout fishing in lakes and streams; Mule Deer, Rocky Mountain Elk, and small game hunting. Special features: Southwestern Blue Mountains; ponderosa pine forests, mountain meadows, and grasslands; headwaters of John Day, Malheur, and Silvies rivers; Magone and Strawberry lakes; Strawberry Mountain Wild Area; Canyon Creek Archery Area; Aldrich Mountain (6,215 ft.); Cinnabar Mountain (6,166 ft.); Cougar Rock (6,162 ft.); Lake Butte (6,227 ft.); McClellan Mountain (7,042 ft.); Moon Mountain (7,044 ft.); Nipple Butte (6,156 ft.); Second Peak (6,647 ft); Hi-desert and Starr Ridge ski areas; pack and saddle trails. Camp and picnic sites, 39; cabins and motels. Nearby towns: Burns, Canyon City, John Day, Mount Vernon, Prairie City. Highways: u.s. 20, 26, 395. Forest supervisor at John Day.

Mount Hood (1,108,000 acres): Steelhead and Trout fishing in mountain lakes and streams; Black Bear, Deer (Mule, Columbian Black-tailed, White-tailed), Elk (Rocky Mountain, Roosevelt), and small game hunting. Special features: Douglas fir and hemlock forests, glaciers, alpine meadows, about 100 lakes and 400 miles of fishable streams in the Cascade Range; Bull Run, Clackamas, Columbia, Hood, Roaring, Salmon, Sandy, White, and Zigzag rivers; Mount Hood and Mount Jefferson wild areas; Mount Hood (11,245 ft.); Multnomah Falls (620 ft); Columbia River Gorge; Bagby Hot Springs; Badger Butte (5,992 ft.); East Mountain (5,321 ft.); Granite Peak (5,160 ft.); Pinhead Buttes (5,604 ft.); Silver King Mountain (5,242 ft.); Squaw Mountain (4,771 ft.); Mount Hood Recreation Area; Olallie and Timothy lakes on the Oregon Skyline Trail; pack and saddle trails. Camp and picnic areas, 110; picnic only, 8; Multnomah Falls Lodge, Timberline Lodge, and other resorts. Nearby towns: Bonneville, Clackamas, Estacada, Gresham, Hood River, Maupin, Oregon City, the Dalles, Troutdale, Warm Springs. Highways: u.s. 26, 30; State 22, 35, 52, 211, 213, 281. Forest supervisor at Portland.

Ochoco (845,876 acres): Trout fishing in lakes and streams; Antelope, Mule Deer, Elk, and small game hunting. Special features: Ponderosa pine forests at western end of Blue Range; Maury Mountains;

agate, opal, and thunder egg deposits; Mount Pisgah (6,675 ft); Wolf Mountain (6,372 ft.); Bald Butte (6,000 ft.); Wildcat Mountain (5,985 ft.); Paulina Butte (5,572 ft.); Spanish Peak (6,885 ft.); Ochoco Summit (4,720 ft.); Crooked River; Ochoco Reservoir; Delintment and Walton lakes. Camp and picnic sites, 28; cabins and motels. Nearby towns: Bend, Burns, Hines, Mitchell, Prineville. Highways: u.s. 20, 26, 126; State 27, 380. Forest supervisor at Prineville.

Rogue River (839,290 acres): Steelhead and Trout fishing in lakes and streams; Bear, Mule, Deer, Elk, migratory game bird hunting. Special features: Cascade Range; adjoins Crater Lake National Park (160,290 acres); forests of Douglas fir, sugar, white, and ponderosa pines, incense-cedar; Applegate and Rogue rivers; Fish Lake; Willow Creek Reservoir; Dead Indian and McAllister soda springs; Wrangle Butte (6,600 ft.); Parker Meadows; pack and saddle trails. Camp and picnic sites, 47; picnic only, 3; cabins, motels, and resorts. Nearby towns: Ashland, Grants Pass, Klamath Falls, Medford. Highways: u.s. 97, 99, 199; State 42, 62, 66, 232. Forest supervisor at Medford.

Siskiyou (1,046,607 acres) in western Oregon on the California line: Salmon, Steelhead, and Trout fishing; Black Bear, Black-tailed Deer, Cougar, and game bird hunting. Special features: Coast Range; Douglas fir, ponderosa and sugar pines, maple. Pacific madroña and golden chinquapin trees; Port Orford Cedar Experimental Forest; special areas of weeping spruce (*Picea breweriana*), saddler oak (*Quercus sadleriana*) and rock rhododendron (*Kalmiopsis leachiana*); gold, copper, silver, chrome, and cinnabar mines; Grayback Mountain (7,043 ft.); Little Grayback (6,145 ft.); Lake Mountain (6,668 ft.) near Oregon Caves National Monument (480 acres); Kerby Peak (5,555 ft.); Canyon Peak (4,895 ft.); Kalmiopsis Wild Area; Rogue River; headwaters of the Chetco, Coquille, Elk, Illinois, Pistol, Sixes, South Fork, and Winchuck rivers; boat trips on Rogue River; pack and saddle trips. Camp and picnic sites, 18; picnic only, 2; cabins and resorts. Nearby towns: Brooking, Cave Junction, Coquille, Gold Beach, Grants Pass, Sixes in Oregon; Crescent City, and Smith River in California. Highways: u.s. 99, 101, 199; State 43, 46. Forest supervisor at Grants Pass.

Suislaw (621,044 acres in several segments): Bass, Bluegill, Crappie, Salmon, Steelhead, and Trout in freshwater lakes and streams, plus surf and deep sea fishing in the Pacific Ocean; Black-tailed Deer, Roosevelt Elk, Grouse, Band-tailed Pigeon, and waterfowl hunting. Special features: Dense forests of Douglas fir, Sitka spruce, western hemlock, and red cedar, broad sandy beaches and towering rock cliffs from Cape Lookout to Coos Bay; Cape Perpetua Overlook 800 feet above the sea; Marys Peak (4,097 ft.); Sea Lion Caves; Alsea, Nestucca, Siuslaw, Smith, and Yachats rivers. Camp and picnic sites, 29; motels and resorts. Nearby towns: Corvallis, Dallas, Drain Hill, Eugene, Hemlock, McMinnville, North Bend, Pacific City, Tillamook, Toledo, Waldorf, Yachats. Highways: u.s. 20, 99, 101; State 18, 22, 34, 36, 38, 229. Forest supervisor at Corvallis.

Umatilla (1,514,053 acres) extending into Washington: Trout fishing in lakes and streams; Mule Deer, Elk, and game bird hunting. Special features: Blue Mountains of northwestern Oregon; ponderosa pine forests, range lands, meadows, hot sulphur springs; Grande Ronde, Tucannon, Umatilla, and North Fork John Day rivers; Langdon and Olive lakes; Tower Mountain (6,600 ft.); Big Butte (5,009 ft.); Diamond Peak (6,379 ft.); Oregon Butte (6,401·ft.); Saddle Butte (5,873 ft.) and Table Rock (6,250 ft.) in the Washington portion; Spout Springs; Tollgate Ski Area; pack and saddle trails. Camp and picnic sites, 44; dude ranches and resorts. Nearby towns: Hepner, La Grande, Pendleton, Tollgate, Ukiah in Oregon; Dayton, Pomeroy, Walla Walla in Washington. Highways: u.s. 30, 395, 410; Oregon 82, 204, 207, 341. Forest supervisor at Pendleton.

Umpqua (978,704 acres) in the Cascade Range: Trout fishing in lakes and streams; Black Bear, Columbia Black-tailed Deer, Cougar, and small game hunting. Special features: Douglas fir, sugar pine, incense-cedar forests; Clearwater Falls; Little, Watson, North and South Umpqua rivers; Diamond Lake (3,000 acres) stocked with Kamloop Trout; Mount Thielsen (9,173 ft.); Mount Bailey (8,363 ft.); Black Rock (6,170 ft.); Hersheberger Mountain (6,200 ft.); Hills Peak (6,147 ft.); Twin Lakes Mountain (5,190 ft.); Kelsay Mountain (5,980 ft.); Elephant Mountain (5,950 ft.); Oregon Skyline Trail; pack and saddle trips. Camp and picnic sites; dude ranches, motels, and resorts. Nearby towns: Eugene, Medford, Roseburg. Highways: u.s. 97, 99; State 42, 58, 62, 230. Forest supervisor at Roseburg.

Wallowa-Whitman (2,285,206 acres in 2 major divisions) in northeastern Oregon: Trout fishing in lakes and streams; Black Bear, Mule Deer, Elk, and small game hunting. Special features: Snow-capped peaks, range lands, ponderosa pine, larch, Engelmann spruce, Douglas and white fir forests; Blue Mountains division: Burnt, Grande Ronde, Imnaha, Lostine, and Powder rivers; Anthony and Horseshoe Lakes; Bald Mountain (6,675 ft.); Chicken Hill (7,018 ft.); Ireland Mountain (8,330 ft.); Anthony Lakes Ski Area. Wallowa Mountains division: Bear Point (6,905 ft.); Black Mountain (6,881 ft.); Hat Point (7,000 ft.) and Lookout Mountain (6,795 ft.) overlooking the Snake River on the Idaho boundary and the Grand Canyon of the Snake; Imnaha, Minam, and Wallowa rivers; Eagles Cap (9,675 ft.) Petes Point (9,600 ft.), Sacajawea Peak, (10,033 ft.) and Sentinel Peak (9,500 ft.) in the Eagle Cap Wilderness Area. Pack and saddle trips. Camp and picnic sites, 40;

picnic only, 2; dude ranches, motels, and resorts. Nearby towns: Baker, Bridgeport, Copperfield, Enterprise, La Grande, Medical Springs, Starkey, Unity, Wallowa. Highways: u.s. 26, 30; State 7, 82, 86, 203, 341. Forest supervisor at Baker.

Willamette (1,666,036 acres): Trout fishing in mountain lakes and streams; Black Bear, Mule Deer, and small game hunting. Special features: Douglas fir forests, snow-capped mountains, hot springs, lava beds, waterfalls in the Cascade Range; Mount Jefferson (10,495 ft.); Mount Washington (7,802 ft.); Three Fingered Jack (7,841 ft.); Hills Peak (6,147 ft.); Potter Mountain (6,137 ft.); Three Pyramids (5,685 ft.); Diamond Peak and Mount Washington Wild Areas; Mount Jefferson Primitive Area; Three Sisters Wilderness Area; headwaters of the Middle Fork and North Fork of the Willamette River, Mackenzie, North and South Santiam rivers; Detroit Reservoir; Clear, Elk, Scott, and Waldo lakes; Oregon Skyline Trail; Mackenzie River Recreational Area; Hoodoo Ski Bowl, Santiam Lodge, and Willamette Pass winter sports areas; canoe, pack and saddle trips. Camp and picnic sites, 69; picnic only, 2; dude ranches, cabins, and motels. Nearby towns: u.s. 20, 99, 126; State 22, 58. Forest supervisor at Eugene.

Winema (908,985 acres in several segments; about half of the area was formerly the Klamath Indian Reservation): Trout fishing in lakes and streams; Deer, waterfowl, and other small game hunting. Special features: Adjacent to Crater Lake National Park on the eastern face of the Cascade Range; numerous escarpments, creeks, lakes, and springs; ponderosa pine forests; Mount McLoughlin (9,493 ft.); Lake of the Woods (1,113 acres); Four Miles Lake (900 acres); Miller Lake (554 acres); Mountain Lakes Wild Area; Sky Lakes region on a 20,000-acre plateau near Cold Springs; Upper Klamath Lake; Klamath Marsh; Sprague, Sycan, and Williamson rivers; site of Fort Klamath Military Reservation; Tomahawk Ski Bowl; Oregon Skyline Trail; Cascade Pack Station (guides and horses); logging camps, ranches, cabins, motels, and resorts. Camp and picnic sites, 6; picnic only, 3. Nearby towns: Beatty, Chemult, Chiloquin, Crescent, Fort Klamath, Klamath Falls, Modoc-Point, Sprague River. Highways: u.s. 97; State 31, 39, 58, 62, 66, 230, 232. Forest supervisor at Klamath Falls.

PENNSYLVANIA NATIONAL FOREST

Allegheny (470,197 acres) in northwestern part of state: Bass fishing in the Allegheny and Clarion rivers (85 miles) and 260 miles of Trout streams; Bear, Deer, and small game hunting. Special features: Allegheny Plateau region; Hearts Content Natural Area; Tionesta Scenic Area;

Beaver Meadows Pond; Twin Lakes Recreation Area; Bear and Minister creeks. Camp and picnic sites, 7; picnic only, 4; roadside tables, 27; cabins in Allegheny and Cook Forest state parks. Nearby towns: Bradford, Kinzua, Marienville, Ridgway, Sheffield, Tionesta, Warren, Wilcox. Highways: u.s. 6, 62, 219; State 59, 68. Forest supervisor at Warren.

SOUTH CAROLINA NATIONAL FORESTS

Francis Marion (245,650 acres) between Charleston and Georgetown on the Atlantic Ocean: Bass fishing in lakes and streams, coastal saltwater fishing; Alligator, Deer, Quail, Turkey, and waterfowl hunting. Special features: Longleaf and loblolly pines, live oak stands of timber; numerous "Carolina bays"; Santee River; Winyah Bay. Camp and picnic sites, 3; picnic only, 10. Nearby towns: Charleston, Georgetown, Huger, Jamestown, McClellanville, Moncks Corner. Highways: u.s. 17, 52, 701; State 41, 45. Forest supervisor at Columbia.

Sumter (341,624 acres): Bass and Trout fishing in lakes and streams; Deer, Turkey, and small game hunting. Special features: Piedmont and Blue Ridge foothills; Lick Fork Lake (12 acres); Parsons Mountain Lake (32 acres); Fork Wildlife Area; hiking and riding trails. Camp and picnic sites, 2; picnic only, 20. Nearby towns: Abbeville, Clarks Hill, Clinton, Edgefield, Greenwood, Newberry, Union, Walhalla. Highways: u.s. 25, 76, 123, 176, 221, 378; State 28, 72, 107. Forest supervisor at Columbia.

SOUTH DAKOTA NATIONAL FOREST

Black Hills (1,045,441 acres extending into Wyoming): Trout fishing in lakes and streams; Largemouth Black Bass, Catfish, and Pike in Angostura Reservoir; Mule and White-tailed Deer, and small game hunting. Special features: Canyons, crystal caves, and cataracts; Harney Peak (7,242 ft.); Terry Peak (7,071 ft.); Flag Mountain (6,900 ft.); Custer Peak (6,794 ft.); Sylvan Lake; Chief Crazy Horse Memorial; Mount Rushmore National Memorial; Wind Cave National Monument; Mead Federal Game Refuge; Norbeck Wildlife Preserve; Pactola Reservoir; Spearfish Federal Fish Hatchery; Hot Springs called the "Vale of the Minnekahta" by Indians; petrified forest known as the "Timber of Ages"; granite spire "The Needles" near Custer; Homestake Mine and other large mining operations; Stratosphere Bowl; Terry Peak Winter Sports Area; boat, pack and saddle trips. Camp and picnic sites, 21; picnic only, 45; dude ranches and motels. Nearby towns: Belle Fourche, Custer, Deadwood, Fort Mead, Hot Springs, Lead, Rapid City, Spearfish and Sturgis,

S. D.; Newcastle and Sundace, Wyo. Highways: u.s. 14, 16, 85, 385; State, 34, 40, 71, 79, 87, 89. Forest supervisor at Custer.

TENNESSEE NATIONAL FOREST

Cherokee (595,097 acres divided by Great Smoky Mountains National Park) in eastern Tennessee: Brook and Rainbow Trout fishing; Deer, Wild Boar, and small game hunting. Special features: Rugged mountains, river gorges, and several tributaries of the Tennessee River; Watauga Lake (6,400 acres); Parksville Lake (1,900 acres), Tellico River; Laurel Lake; Andrew Johnson, Kettlefoot, Laurel Fork, and Ocoee wildlife management areas; Unaka Mountain (5,000 ft.), Ducktown Copper Basin; boating, hiking, and riding. Camp and picnic sites, 17; picnic only, 27. Nearby towns: Cleveland, Damascus, Etowah, Hampton, Johnson City, Madisonville, Mountain City, Newport, Parksville, Tellico Plains, Unicoi. Highways: u.s. 11, 19, 23, 25, 64, 411, 421; State 7, 67, 68, 70, 91, 107, 133. Forest supervisor at Cleveland.

TEXAS NATIONAL FORESTS

Angelina (154,392 acres) in eastern Texas: Bass and Catfish in lakes and streams; Dove and Quail hunting. Special features: Angelina and Neches rivers; Boykin Lake (10 acres); Bouton Lake (7 acres); flat and rolling sandy areas, springs, pine and hardwood stands along river bottom. Camp and picnic sites, 2; picnic only, 3. Nearby towns: Jasper, Lufkin, San Augustine, Zavalla. Highways: u.s. 59, 69; State 147. Forest supervisor at Lufkin.

Davy Crockett (161,556 acres): Bass and Catfish in lakes and streams; Deer and small game hunting. Special features; Flat country with stands of shortleaf and loblolly pines and hardwood stands along streams; Ratcliff Lake (60 acres); Neches River. Camp and picnic sites, 2; picnic only, 3. Nearby towns: Highways: u. s. 287; State 7, 94, 103, Forest supervisor at Lufkin.

Sabine (183,842 acres): Bass and Catfish; Deer and small game hunting. Special features: Pine and hardwood stands along the Sabine River; Patroon Creek; Red Hills Lake (17 acres); Fox Hunter's annual national meet at Boles Field. Camp and picnic sites, 2; picnic only, 3. Nearby towns: Center, Hemphill, Jasper, Milam, San Augustine, Shelbyville. Highways: u.s. 96; State, 21, 87. Forest supervisor at Lufkin.

Sam Houston (158,205 acres): Bass and Catfish in lakes and streams. Special features: Numerous lakes in a flat country with pine and hardwood stands along small streams; part of the "Big Thicket" area; Stubble Field Lake (25 acres); Double Lake Recreation Area. Camp and picnic sites, 2; picnic only, 3. Nearby towns: Cleveland, Cold Springs, Conroe, Huntsville. Highways: u.s. 59, 75, 190; State 105, 150. Forest supervisor at Lufkin.

UTAH NATIONAL FORESTS

Ashley (1,282,829 acres) north and south of the Uinta and Ouray Indian Reservation in northeastern Utah: Grayling and Trout fishing in lakes and streams; Antelope, Black Bear, Mule Deer, Elk, and small game hunting. Special features: Numerous streams and hundreds of lakes, virgin forests of lodgepole and ponderosa pines; Douglas fir and Engelmann spruce in the Uinta Range; Kings Peak (13,498 ft.) in the High Uinta Primitive Area; Uinta River; Flaming Gorge Reservoir (66 square miles) on the Green River near Dutch John and north of Vernal; Icy Cave Peak (10,118 ft.) overlooking Whiterocks River; Paradise Park Reservoir; Marsh Peak (12,219 ft.) surrounded by lakes; Trout Peak (10,509 ft.) near East Park, Oak Park, and Long reservoirs; Leidy Peak (12,020 ft.) in sight of several lakes; Sheep Creek Canyon Geological Area; Mount Emmons (13,428 ft.) near a chain of lakes; Moon Lake Resort; East Grandaddy Mountain (11,265 ft.) above Rock Creek Resort; Duchesne River; Tabby Mountain (10,015 ft.) between Fruitland and Hanna; Grizzly Ridge Winter Sports Area north of Vernal; hiking trails; pack and saddle trips. Camp and picnic sites, 34; picnic only, 3; dude ranches and resorts. Nearby towns: Duchesne, Manila, Roosevelt, Vernal in Utah; Green River, Rock Springs in Wyoming. Highways: u.s. 40; Utah 33, 35, 36, 43, 44, 86, 87, 121, 245, 246. Forest supervisor at Vernal.

Cache (651,909 acres) in several segments from the Weber River to Soda Point Reservoir in Idaho: Trout fishing in lakes and streams; Black Bear, Mule Deer, Elk, Cougar, Grouse, and other small game hunting. Special features: Caves, canyons, rangeland, aspen and evergreen forests in the Bear River Range and northern end of the Wasatch Mountains; Logan Peak (9,723 ft.), and Naomi Peak (9,980 ft.) at White Pine Lake in the Logan River region; Blacksmith Fork Little Bear River near Hardware Ranch; Pineview Reservoir on Ogden River; Beaver Mountain Ski Area northeast of Logan; Snow Basin Ski Area between Huntsville and Logan; hiking and riding trails. Camp and picnic sites, 46; picnic only, 17. Nearby towns: Brigham City, Huntsville, Hyrum, Logan, Mendon, Ogden, Richmond, Smithfield, Wellsville in Utah; Franklin, Preston, St. Charles in Idaho. Highways: u.s. 30, 89, 91; Utah 2, 23, 32, 39, 101, 163. Forest supervisor at Logan.

Dixie (1,839,547 acres in 4 segments) in southwestern corner of Utah: Trout fishing in lakes and streams; Bear, Mule Deer, Grouse,

Partridge, and predator hunting. Special features: Broad plateaus, forested slopes, colorful cliffs, and deep gorges in this "Land of Rainbow Canyons"—Bryce Canyon National Park (36,010 acres) and Cedar Breaks National Monument (6,154 acres); Jacobs Reservoir, Big and Cyclone lakes on the Aquarius Plateau; Long Lake and Oak Creek Reservoir between Boulder and Deer mountains; Pine Lake south of Widtsoe; Adams Head (10,360 ft.) south of Mount Dutton (10,800 ft.); Tropic Reservoir on East Fork Sevier River; Brain Head (11,307 ft.) near Cedar Breaks National Monument; Panguitch Lake south of Red Creek Reservoir; Navajo Lake near Cascade Falls on the North Fork Virgin River; Bear Valley Peak (10,557 ft.); Enterprise Reservoir, Mountain Meadow Monument, and Pine Valley in the Santa Clara River District; Cedar Canyon Ski Area southeast of Cedar City. Camp and picnic sites, 13; picnic only, 8; dude ranches, motels, and resorts. Nearby towns: Cedar City, Circleville, Escalante, Hurricane, Koosharem, Marysvale, Newcastle, Panguitch, Parowan, St. George, Salina. Highways: u.s. 89, 91; State 12, 14, 15, 16, 18, 22, 24, 54, 56, 117, 120, 143. Forest supervisor at Cedar City.

Fishlake (1,415,673 acres in 4 divisions) in south central Utah: Trout fishing in lakes and streams; Bear, Mule Deer, Elk, Mountain Lion, Grouse, and other small game hunting. Special features: Fishland and Pahvant plateaus, and portions of the Aquarius, Sevier, Tushar, and Wasatch plateaus with elevations between 5,500–11,000 feet; mining operations and grazing ranges; Crater Lakes, and Johnson Valley Reservoir near 2,600-acre Fish Lake (maximum depth 120 ft.) stocked with Mackinaw and Rainbow Trout; Mill Meadow Reservoir on Fremont River; Hilgard Mountain (11,527 ft.) above Willes Flat Reservoir; Thousand Lake Mountain (11,259 ft.) north of Wayne Wonderful and the adjacent Capitol Reef National Monument (39,172 acres); Mount Marvin (11,599 ft.); Signal Peak (11,223 ft.) above Annabella and Scrub Flat reservoirs east of Monroe; Tushar Mountains streams flowing into Beaver River; Canyon Mountains near Scipio; Sevier River winding between segments of the national forest; Gooseberry Ski Area southeast of Salina; hiking and riding trails. Camp and picnic sites, 24; picnic only, 5; motels, hotels, and resorts. Nearby towns: Beaver, Delta, Elsinore, Fillmore, Marysvale, Monroe, Richfield, Salina, Scipio. Highways: u.s. 6, 50, 89, 91; State 10, 13, 24, 62, 63, 72, 118, 125, 132, 153. Forest supervisor at Richfield.

Manti–La Sal (1,237,128 acres) including Manti Division west of Price in central Utah and the Moab and Monticello districts in La Sal Division near the Colorado border: Trout fishing in lakes and streams; Black Bear, Mule Deer, Elk, Mountain Lion, and small game hunting. Special features: Aspen, Engelmann spruce, Douglas fir, and ponderosa pine forests, grazing lands, mining operations, Indian pictographs and petroglyphs in caves and on cliffs. Manti Division on rugged Wasatch Plateau. Grove of the Aspen Giants Scenic Area west of Ferron Reservoir and Willow Lake; numerous mountains, ridges, canyons, and creeks among Seeley Mountain (10,362 ft.) near Cleveland, Huntington, and Rolfson Reservoirs; South Tent (11,282 ft.); Lower Gooseberry Reservoir north of Fairview Lake and Bougler; Skyline Drive. Moab District: Mesas and mountains; Mount Peale (13,089 ft.) between Blue and Medicine lakes; Fisher and Oowah lakes; Buckeye Reservoir. Monticello District: Canyons, creeks, and mountains including Abajo Peak (11,357 ft.) and Mount Linnaeus (11,019 ft.) above Dry Wash Reservoir; Great. Basin Research Center; Blue Mountain Ski Area west of Monticello. Hiking and riding trails. Camp and picnic sites, 15; picnic only, 5. Nearby towns: Manti Division: Castle Dale, Ephraim, Fairview, Huntington, Manti, Mount Pleasant, Price, Spring City; La Sal Division: Blanding, Grand Junction, Monticello, Moab. Highways: u.s. 6, 50, 89, 91, 160; State 10, 29, 31, 46, 47, 95, 96, 128. Forest supervisor at Price.

Uinta (774,721 acres) near Utah Lake in central Utah: Trout fishing in lakes and streams; Deer, Elk, and small game hunting. Special features: Extensive stands of Engelmann spruce, lodgepole pine, alpine and Douglas fir, and range lands in the Wasatch Range; Mount Timpanogas (11,957 ft.); Mount Nebo (11,928 ft.) above Devils Kitchen; Dry Mountain (9,847 ft.) overlooking Utah Valley; Provo Peak (11,068 ft.); Spanish Fork Peak (10,185 ft.); Current Creek Peak (10,584 ft); Bald Knob (10,073 ft.); Timpanogos Cave; Strawberry Reservoir; American Fork; Hobble Creek; Provo and Santaquin Creek canyons; Payson Lake; Payson Winter Sports Area near Provo; Alpine Scenic Loop; hiking trails. Camp and picnic sites, 42; picnic only, 6; motels and hotels. Nearby towns: American Fork, Heber, Nephi, Payson, Pleasant Grove, Provo, Santaquin, Spanish Fork. Highways: u.s. 6, 40, 50, 89, 91, 189; State 11, 80. Forest supervisor at Provo.

Wasatch (827,441 acres in several scattered districts); Kamas, Salt Lake, and Toole districts in Utah; Evanston and Mountainview districts in Wyoming: Trout fishing in mountain lakes and streams; Deer, Elk, and small game hunting. Special features: High Uintas Primitive Area near Mount Elizabeth (10,353 ft.), Mount Notch (11,155 ft.), Mount Watson (11,527 ft.), North Burro Peak (12,680 ft.), Thompson Peak (11,813 ft.) and China Meadows; Bridger, Hoop, Island, Mirror, Red Castle and Trial Lakes. Toole District south of the Great Salt Lake: Canyons, creeks, Dutch Peak and Red Pine Mountain adjacent to Skull Valley Indian Reservation. Salt Lake District in Wasatch Mountains: several canyons; Grandeur Peak (7,866 ft.), Mount Aire (8,620 ft.); Mount Olympus (9,753 ft.); Porter Peak (10,239 ft.); Alta and

Brighton ski areas in Cottonwood Canyon region 28 miles southeast of Salt Lake City; Little Mountain Winter Sports Area at Emigration Canyon, 11 miles east of Salt Lake City. Hiking trails, pack and saddle trips. Camp and picnic sites, 51; picnic only, 20; dude ranches, motels, and resorts. Nearby towns: Alta, Brighton, Grantsville, Heber, Lofgreen, Kamas, Murray, Oakley, Ogden, Provo, Salt Lake City in Utah; Evanston, Lonetree, Mountain View in Wyoming. Highways: u.s. 30 South, 40, 80, 89, 91, 189; Utah 35, 36, 65, 150. Forest supervisor at Salt Lake City.

VERMONT NATIONAL FOREST

Green Mountain (230,954 acres): Trout fishing in lakes and 400 miles of streams; Black Bear, Deer, Grouse, and Rabbit hunting. Special features: Heavily wooded mountains and picturesque valleys; headwater tributaries of the Connecticut and Hudson rivers; Mount Abraham (4,052 ft.); Bread Loaf Mountain (3,823 ft.); Mount Cleveland (3,500 ft.); Mount Grant (3,661 ft.); Mount Ellen (4,135 ft.); Glastonbury Mountain (3,763 ft.); Lincoln Peak (4,013 ft.); Nancy Hanks Mountain (3,860 ft.); Stark Mountain (3,585 ft.); Mount Wilson (3,756 ft); Chittenden, Somerset, and Whittingham reservoirs; the hikers Long Trail known as "A Footpath in the Wilderness"; winter sports facilities at Big Bromley and Snow Valley northeast of Manchester, Dutch Hill near Readsboro, Snow Bowl near Middlebury, Sugar Bush Valley near Warren, Mad River Glen northwest of Irasville. Camp and picnic sites, 8, including 5 Adirondack shelters on the Long Trail; picnic only, 2; cabins, motels, and resorts. Nearby towns: Arlington, Bennington, Brattleboro, Brandon, Hancock, Ludlow, Manchester, Middlebury, Rochester, Rutland, Warren, Wallingford, West Dover, Weston. Highways: u.s. 4, 7; State 8, 9, 11, 30, 73, 100, 103, 107, 125. Forest supervisor at Rutland.

VIRGINIA NATIONAL FORESTS

Jefferson (546,285 acres) in the southwest "Valley of Virginia": Bass, Bream, and Trout fishing; Bear, White-tailed Deer, Wild Turkey, Grouse, Squirrel hunting. Special features: Cave Mountain Recreation Area near Buchanan; Arcadia Game Management Unit on portions of Bedford, Botetourt, and Rockbridge counties; Barbours Creek, Broad Run, and Cuba game management units in Craig County near Newcastle; Dismal and Stoney Creek Game management units in Giles County north and south of Pearisburg; Comers Rock and Gullion Fork game management units near Wytheville; Feather Camp and Hurricane game management units in the Iron Mountains; Mount Rogers (5,719 ft.); White Top Mountain (5,520 ft.); Poor Valley Game Management Unit near Tazewell; Breaks Game Management Unit near Clintwood in

Dickinson County along the Kentucky line; High Knob (4,162 ft.); High Knob Game Management Unit near Norton in Wise County; Scott-Wise Lake (65 acres); Blue Ridge Parkway; Appalachian Trail. Camp and picnic sites, 6; picnic only, 60; cabins, hotels, and resorts. Nearby towns: Abingdon, Bristol, Clintwood, Damascus, Fincastle, Marion, Newcastle, Norton, Pearisburg, Pulaski, Radford, Roanoke, Tazewell, Wytheville. Highways: u.s. 11, 19, 21, 23, 52, 58, 221; Interstate 81; State 16, 42, 43, 65, 72, 91, 94, 100, 311. Forest supervisor at Roanoke.

George Washington (1,005,372 acres in 3 segments) in northwestern Virginia extending into West Virginia: Bass and Trout in more than 400 miles of fishing streams; Bear, White-tailed Deer, upland game, and waterfowl hunting. Special features: Narrow, wooded valleys and numerous streams; Fort Valley Game Management Unit around Passage Creek gorge in Page, Shenandoah, and Warren counties east of Edinburg; Lost River Game Management Unit on North Mountain west of Woodstock in Shenandoah County along the West Virginia line; Shenandoah River; New Market Gap (1,850 ft.) Recreation Area; Massanutten Game Management Unit on Middle and Massanutten mountains in Page and Rockingham counties east of New Market; Blue Hole Game Management Unit west of Broadway in Rockingham County; Shenandoah Lake (39 acres) Recreation Area on Congers Creek east of Harrisburg; Dry River and North River game management units near Bridgewater; Reddish Knob (4,398 ft.); Cowpasture, Deerfield, and East Slope game management units; Elliott Knob (4,458 ft.) and Ramseys Draft west of Staunton; Big Levels Wildlife Management Area in Augusta County near Greenville; St. Marys River, and the Pedlar River Game Management Unit near Buena Vista on the Blue Ridge; Dolly Ann and Potts Creek game management units north and south of Covington in Allegheny County; James River; Back Creek Game Management Unit and Jackson River in the Allegheny Mountains west of Warm Springs; Brattons Run Game Management Unit on Pads Creek south of Millboro Springs and northeast of Clifton Forge; Blue Ridge Parkway; Appalachian Trail. Camp and picnic sites, 6; picnic only, 7; cabins, hotels, and resorts. Nearby towns: Clifton Forge, Covington, Edinburg, Front Royal, Greenville, Harrisonburg, Lexington, Luray, New Market, Staunton, Strasburg, Warm Springs, Waynesboro, Winchester, Woodstock. Highways: u.s. 11, 33, 50, 60, 211, 220, 340, 501; State 39, 42, 55, 251, 257, 259, 260. Forest supervisor at Harrisonburg.

WASHINGTON NATIONAL FORESTS

Colville (928,332 acres in several segments) west of the Columbia River in northeastern Washington: Cutthroat, Eastern Brook, and Rainbow Trout fishing in lakes and streams; Black Bear, Deer (Mule, White-tailed), Elk, Grouse, waterfowl hunting. Special features: Kettle and Pend Oreille rivers; F. D. Roosevelt Lake (125 sq. miles) on the Columbia River; Pierre Lake; Lake Thomas; Metaline Mining District; Gardner Caves in Crawford State Park north of Metine; Snow Peak (7,103 ft.), Copper Butte (7,135 ft.), Graves Mountain (5,947 ft.), and Marble Mountain (5,978 ft.) west of Kettle Falls; Abercrombie Mountain (7,306 ft.); Sherlock Peak (6,362 ft.); Sullivan Lake near Hall Mountain (6,305 ft.) and Sullivan Mountain (6,483 ft.); Round Top Mountain (6,242 ft.); Molybdenite Mountain (6,790 ft.); Leo, Niles, Scotsman, and Thomas lakes in the Selkirk Mountains; Little Pend Oreille Wildlife Refuge east of Colville; Chewelah Peak Winter Sports Area. Camp and picnic sites, 16; cabins and resorts. Nearby towns: Chewelah, Colville, Curlew, Gifford, Kettle Falls, Metaline, Newport, Pollard, Torada. Highways: u.s. 395; State 3, 4, 6, 22. Forest supervisor at Colville.

Gifford Pinchot (1,263,380 acres): Trout fishing in lakes and streams; Bear, Black-tailed Deer, and small game hunting. Special features: Dense Douglas fir forests, mountain meadows, huckleberry fields, white water streams from central Washington to the Columbia River; Goat Rocks and Mount Adams Wild Areas; Dog Mountain (2,989 ft.); South Twin Buttes (4,200 ft.), Steamboat Mountain (5,425 ft.), and Tumac Mountain (6,300 ft.) on the Cascade Crest Trail; Cowlitz River and East Fork Lewis River spawning beds for Salmon and Steelhead; Cispus, Ohanapecosh, and Toutle rivers; Blue, Chambers, Council, Goose, Horseshoe, St. Helens, and Takhlakh lakes; Mount Adams (12,307 ft.) flanked by the Adams, Lava, and Mazama glaciers; Cold Springs (base for mountain climbers); Mount Saint Helens (9,671 ft.) overshadowing Spirit Lake; Tatoosh Ridge Lookout (6,307 ft.); Sunset Falls; Twin Falls; Trout Lake Creek; Packwood Lake fed by Upper Lake Creek; Bird Creek Meadows; Wind River Experimental Forest producing about 20 million trees to regenerate cut areas in 19 national forests; White Pass Ski Area; pack and saddle trails. Camp and picnic sites, 54; picnic only, 2; cabins, motels, and resorts. Nearby towns: Carson, Castle Rock, Glenwood, Morton, Randle, Tacoma, Vancouver, White Salmon, Woodland. Highways: u.s. 99, 830; State 1R, 1S, 5, 8C, 8D. Forest supervisor at Vancouver.

Mount Baker (1,818,283 acres): Steelhead and Trout fishing in lakes and streams; Black Bear, Deer, and small game hunting. Special features: Douglas fir forests, 30 mountains over 8,000 feet elevation, turbulent streams, alpine lakes and glaciers; Glacier Peak (10,528 ft); Mount Baker (10,778 ft.); Mount Shuksan (9,127 ft.); Heather Meadows; Picture Lake, Park Butte, and Panorama Dome in Mount Baker Recreation Area; Anderson Butte (5,420 ft.); Mount Challenger

(8,326 ft.); Pugh Mountain (7,224 ft.); Baker Lake on Baker River; Diablo and Ross lakes on Skagit River in the North Cascade Primitive Area; Lake Twenty-two and Long Creek natural areas on Stillaguamish River; Suiattle River in Glacier Peak Wilderness Area; Kennedy Hot Springs (base for Glacier Peak); Monte Cristo Lakes of Sauk River; Mount Baker and Mount Pilchuk winter sports areas; pack and saddle trips. Camp and picnic sites, 40; picnic only, 45; hotels and resorts. Nearby towns: Arlington, Bellingham, Darrington, Ellingham, Everett, Granite Falls, Snohomish. Highways: u.s. 2, 10, 99, 410; State 1, 15, 16, 17A. Forest supervisor at Bellingham.

Okanogan (1,520,340 acres in several segments) extends from the Canadian boundary to the Methow-Chelan Divide and from the Cascade Range east to the Okanogan County line: Fishing in lakes and streams; Black Bear, Deer (Mule, White-tailed), Mountain Goat, and small game hunting. Special features: Large stands of ponderosa pine, Douglas fir, western larch, and Engelmann spruce, division west of Okanogan River: Glacier Peak Wilderness Area; North Cascade Primitive Area; Chewack, Lost, and Twisp rivers, tributaries to Methow River; Pasayten River; Lake Chelan (55 miles long, 1,500 ft. deep) on the Stehekin River; Abernathy Peak (8,300 ft.); Flora Mountain (8,320 ft.); Martin Peak (8,200 ft.); Remmel Mountain (8,688 ft.); Reynolds Peak (8,400 ft.); Seven Fingered Jack (9,077 ft.); and several other mountains 6,000–8,000 feet; Cascade Crest Trail; Loup Loup Ski Bowl between Okanogan and Twisp. East of Okanogan River: Haley Mountain (5,112 ft.) and Mount Hull (4,617 ft.) above Summit Lake near Oroville; Buckhorn Mountain (5,602 ft.) east of Chesaw; Mount Bonaparte (7,258 ft.) near Bonaparte Lake and Strawberry Mountain (4,742 ft.) south of Chesaw; Fir Mountain (5,690 ft.) and Mount Annie (6,054 ft.) in sight of Beaver, Beth, and Lost lakes near Wauconda; Bailey Mountain (5,786 ft.), Crawfish Lake and Tunk Mountain (6,054 ft.) southwest of Tonasket. Boating, pack and saddle trips. Camp and picnic sites, 51; dude ranches and motels. Nearby towns: Brewster, Carlton, Chelan, Coconully, Loomis, Methow, Okanogan, Omak, Oroville, Tonasket, Toroda, Twisp, Winthrop. Highways: u.s. 97; State 4, 10, 10A, 10B, 10C, 16. Forest supervisor at Okanogan.

Olympic (621, 746 acres in 2 divisions) on north, east, and southern sides of Olympic National Park (896,559 acres) on the Olympic Peninsula dominated by Mount Olympus (7,195 ft.): Salmon, Steelhead, and Trout fishing in lakes and streams; Black Bear, Black-tailed Deer, Roosevelt Elk, Grouse, Pigeon, Rabbits, and predator hunting. Special features: Douglas fir, hemlock, red cedar, Sitka spruce, and white pine on mountains with winding ridges and deep canyons; Lake Quinault and Willaby Gorge in rain forest on a trail in the Quinault Recreation Area; Big Tree

Grove west of Willaby Creek; about 300 miles of Steelhead and Trout streams including turbulent Humptulips and Wynoochee rivers near Capitol Peak (5,056 ft.), Chapel Peak (4,250 ft.), and Lightning Peak (4,664 ft.) in the southern portion; Mount Henderson (6,445 ft.); Mildred Lakes, source of Hamma Hamma River; Copper Mountain (5,400 ft.); Mount Ellinor (5,840 ft.); Mount Washington (6,250 ft.); St. Peters Dome (4,515 ft.) near Duckabush River; Mount Constance (7,735 ft.) between Dosewallips and Big Quilcene rivers; Quilcene Range; Calawah and Soleduck rivers; Mount Muller (3,760 ft.) and Baldy Ridge (4,875 ft.) overlooking the Strait of Juan de Fuca; pack and saddle trips. Camp and picnic sites, 14; picnic only, 2; dude ranches, motels, and resorts. Nearby towns: Aberdeen, Hoodsport, Montesano, Port Angeles, Queete, Quilcene, Shelton. Highways: u.s. 99, 101, 410; State 9, 9A. Forest supervisor at Olympia.

Snoqualmie (1,207,877 acres): Salmon, Steelhead, and Trout fishing in lakes and streams; Bear, Deer (Mule, Blacktailed), Elk, and small game hunting. Special features: Douglas and other firs, hemlock, red cedar, and ponderosa pine trees; more than 300 lakes and 670 miles of fishing streams along the Cascade Range from Mount Baker National Forest to the Goat Rocks Wild Area; Chinook Pass (5,443 ft.) and White Pass (4,467 ft.) to Mount Rainer National Park (241,782 acres); Bumping Lake on American River between American Ridge (6,494 ft.) and Mount Aix (7,772 ft.); Tieton Peak (7,775 ft.), Bear Creek, Tieton Meadow, Pinegrass Ridge, Clear and Rimrock lakes in the Tieton River region; Snoqualmie Mountain (6,270 ft.) and Mount Thompson (6,500 ft.) north of Snoqualmie Pass, (3,004 ft.); Columbia Peak (7,134 ft.) near Silver Lake; Cedar, Green Skykomish, and Snoqualmie rivers; Cascade Crest Trail; pack and saddle trips. Camp and picnic sites, 210; motels and outfitters. Nearby towns; Cle Elum, Elbe, Ellensburg, Everett, Monroe, Seattle, Tacoma, Tieton, Yakima. Highways: u.s. 10, 99, 410; State 2, 5. Forest supervisor at Seattle.

Wenatchee (1,728,086 acres): Trout fishing in mountain streams; Bear, Deer, and small game hunting. Special features: Alpine lakes and meadows amid snow-covered peaks; Mount Stuart (9,470 ft.); Belwett Pass (4,071 ft.); Lake Chelan (55 miles long, 1,500 ft. deep); Cle Elum, Kachess, Keecheluss, and Wenatchee lakes; Glacier Peak Wilderness Area; Cascade Crest Trail from Blowout Mountains to Rainy Pass; Tumwater Botanical Area; Hyak, Leavenworth, and Stevens Pass winter sports areas; boating, pack and saddle trips. Camp and picnic sites, 93; picnic only, 4; dude ranches and motels. Nearby towns: Cashmere, Chelan, Cle Elum, Ellensburg, Leavenworth, Wenatchee. Highways: u.s. 2, 10, 97. Forest supervisor at Wenatchee.

WEST VIRGINIA NATIONAL FORESTS

George Washington (1,005,372 acres): Only a small portion is in Hampshire and Hardy counties. See VIRGINIA NATIONAL FORESTS.

Monongahela (806,361 acres) in east central West Virginia: Bass and Trout fishing in lakes and 1,900 miles of streams; Bear, White-tailed Deer, Wild Turkey hunting. Special features: Forested slopes of the Allegheny and Appalachian mountains; Spruce Knob (4,860 ft.); Blackwater Falls (60 ft.) and Canyon; Smoke Hole Recreation Area on South Branch of the Potomac River; Cheat, Cherry, and Cranberry rivers; Spruce Knob Lake (25 acres); Summit Lake (42 acres); Black Mountain Management Area; Seneca Rocks on the Seneca Indian Trail; the Devil's Garden; Eagle Rock. Camp and picnic sites, 21; picnic only, 15; motels and tourist homes. Nearby towns: Covington, Elkins, Franklin, Lewisburg, Monterey, Petersburg, Richwood, White Sulphur Springs. Highways: U.S. 33, 60, 219, 220, 250; State 4, 28, 33, 39. Forest supervisor at Elkins.

WISCONSIN NATIONAL FORESTS

Chequamegon (827,027 acres in 3 segments) in northern Wisconsin: Black Bass, Muskellunge, Trout, Northern and Walleyed Pike fishing; Black Bear, White-tailed Deer, waterfowl, and other small game hunting. Special features: Evergreen forests, clear streams, and hundreds of lakes; Chippewa, Jump, and Mauer rivers; Mondeaux River and Flowage below dam near North and South Twin lakes; rapids on the South Fork Flambeau River; Katheryn, Anderson, and Richter lakes near Perkinstown; Pike and Round lakes near Memorial Grove; Perkinstown Winter Sports Area; canoe trips on the Chippewa and Flambeau rivers. Camp and picnic sites, 9; picnic only, 14; cabins and resorts. Nearby towns: Ashland, Eau Claire, Fiefield, Hayward, Lublin, Ogema, Medford, Park Falls, Superior, Washburn. Highways: U.S. 2, 8, 63; State 13, 60, 70, 73, 182. Forest supervisor at Park Falls.

Nicolet (640,075 acres) in northern Wisconsin: Bass, Muskellunge, Pike, and Trout fishing in lakes and streams; Bear, White-tailed Deer, waterfowl, and other small game hunting. Special features: 367 lakes and 840 miles of streams among evergreen and hardwood forests; large rivers rising in lakes include the Pine River from Franklin Lake, Wisconsin River from Lac Vieux Desert, and Wolf River from Pine Lake; the Popple River runs eastward, and the Eagle River flows into a chain of lakes; Fisher Wildlife Management Area; Paul Bunyan Winter Sports Area north of Paul Bunyan Mountain; Sheltered Valley Winter Sports

Area east of Three Lakes; tours and trails at Alvin Creek near Alvin, Boulder Lake on the Oconto River southeast of Langlad, Butternut Lake northeast of Three Lakes; boating and canoe trips. Camp and picnic sites, 20; picnic only, 18; private cabins and resorts. Towns in or near forest: Alvin, Amberg, Argonne, Carney, Crandon, Crystal Falls, Eagle River, Gillette, Lily, Iron Mountain, Iron River, Langlade, Marinette, Monico, Norway, Rhinelander, Three Lakes, Watersmeet. Highways U.S. 2, 8, 45; State 32, 52, 55, 64, 70, 139. Forest supervisor at Rhinelander.

WYOMING NATIONAL FORESTS

Bighorn (1,113, 597 acres) between Black Hills and Rocky Mountains east of Continental Divide: Trout fishing in lakes and streams; Bear, Mule Deer, Elk and small game hunting. Special features: Evergreen forest of lodgepole, ponderosa, and limber pine, Engelmann spruce, Douglas and alpine fir on the Bighorn Range; Cloud Peak Primitive Area; Cloud Peak (13,165 ft.); Penrose Peak (12,443 ft.); Baldy Mountain (10,029 ft.) and Little Baldy Mountain (9,828 ft.); Hazelton Peak (10,545 ft.) near Hesse Mountain (10,399 ft.); Antelope Butte (9,955 ft.) in sight of Granite Creek; Little Goose Peak (9,334 ft.); Black Butte (9,249 ft.); Snowshoe Mountain (9,200 ft.); Bighorn, Powder, and Tongue rivers; numerous creeks and lakes including Tensleep Canyon south of Meadow Lark Lake; Last Chance, Martin, Park, and Western reservoirs; Sibley Reservoir; Lake Solitude; Dome, Sawmill, and Twin lakes; prehistoric Indian Medicine Wheel on mountain; Fun Valley and Meadow Lark ski areas; pack and saddle trips. Camp and picnic sites, 60; picnic only, 14; dude ranches and motels. Nearby towns: Buffalo, Dayton, Greybill, Lovell, Sheridan, Story, Ten Sleep, Worland. Highways: U.S. 14, 16, 87; State 789. Forest supervisor at Sheridan.

Bridger (1,699, 087 acres in 2 divisions): Trout (all species including Golden) fishing in alpine lakes and streams; Bear, Mule Deer, Elk, Moose, Bighorn Sheep hunting. Special features: 1,700 miles of trails to magnificent peaks, mountain meadows, hundreds of lakes and streams. Wind River Range on the Continental Divide; Gannett Peak (13,785 ft.); Bridger Wilderness Area; Green River Lakes; New Fork River and Lake; Island and Titcomb lakes below Fremont Peak (13,730 ft.); Mount Helen (13,600 ft.); Sweetwater Needles (10,480 ft.); Wild Cat Butte (9,624 ft.); Boulder, Half Moon, and Willow lakes; Fremont Lake near Pinedale noted for record Mackinaw Trout; Salt River Range; Snake River; Greysalt (10,750 ft.); Haystack Mountain (10,105 ft.); Mount Wagner (10,745 ft.); Stewart Peak (10,080 ft.); Cottonwood Lake. Wyoming Range: Headwaters of Grey's River; Wyoming Peak (11,363 ft.); Piney Lakes; Lander Peak (10,456 ft.); Bare Mountain (10,725 ft.); Bald Knoll (10,343 ft.); Fontenette Mountain (10,015 ft.); Mount Thompson (9,748 ft.); Greyfall Lookout (10,365 ft.) at Moore Flat; Elk Peak Lookout (8,505 ft.) near Forks of Grey's River; Divide and Surveyor Park winter sports area northeast of Pinedale, pack and saddle trips. Camp and picnic sites, 24; picnic only, 2; dude ranches, cabins, and resorts. Nearby towns: Afton, Alpine, Big Piney, Kemmerer, La Barge, Pinedale. Highways: u.s. 26, 30 North, 187, 189. Forest supervisor at Kemmerer.

Medicine Bow (1,063,537 acres): Fishing in lakes and streams; Deer and small game hunting. Special features: Alpine lakes, sheer granite cliffs, and evergreen forests; northern portion below Douglas is in rugged Laramie Range; small Pole Mountain segment is between Cheyenne and Laramie; Sierra Madre Area on Continental Divide is west of Encampment; largest area is in Medicine Bow or Snowy Range extending to the Colorado border; Bow River; North Platte River; Brooklyn, Lewis, Mirror, and Silver lakes at elevations above 10,400 feet west of Centennial; Medicine Bow Peak (12,005 ft.); Happy Jack, Medicine Bow, and Ryan Park ski areas. Pack and saddle trips. Camp and picnic sites, 23; picnic only, 25; dude ranches and motels. Nearby towns: Casper, Centennial, Cheyenne, Douglas, Encampment, Laramie, Rawlins. Highways: u.s. 26, 30, 87; State 130, 230. Forest supervisor at Laramie.

Shoshone (2,429,510 acres) in northwestern Wyoming: Trout fishing in mountain lakes and streams; Antelope, Bear (Black, Grizzly), Mule Deer, Elk, Moose, Bighorn Sheep hunting. Special features: Large glaciers, swift streams, and hundreds of lakes in the Absaroka Mountains, Beartooth Plateau, and portions of the Wind River Range; Wapiti Valley between the North and South Absaroka wilderness areas; Glacier, Popo Agie, and Stratified primitive areas; North Fork and South Fork Shoshone River; Gannett Peak (13,785 ft.); Fremont Peak (13,730 ft.); Citadel Mountain (12,100 ft.); Francis Peak (13,140 ft.); Trout Peak 12,259 ft.); Needle Mountain (12,130 ft.); Sunlight Peak (11,977 ft.); Indian Peak (10,983 ft.); Sleeping Giant Winter Sports Area in Wapiti Valley west of Cody; scenic Cody-Yellowstone Road; Sunlight Basin Road; hiking trails, pack and saddle trips. Camp and picnic sites, 34; picnic only, 2; dude ranches, lodges, and resorts. Nearby towns: Cody, Dubois, Lander, South Pass City in Wyoming; Cook City, Red Lodge in Montana. Highways: u.s. 12, 14, 20, 287. Forest supervisor at Cody.

Teton (1,700,766 acres) in the Jackson Lake country adjacent to Yellowstone National Park (2,221,772 acres): Trout fishing in lakes and streams; Bear, Deer, Elk, Moose, Bighorn Sheep hunting. Special features: Portions of Gros Ventre, Teton, and Wind River ranges on the Continental Divide; forests of lodgepole pine, Douglas fir, and Engelmann spruce; Two Ocean Pass where waters of Two Ocean Creek divide to send one stream toward the eastern Atlantic Ocean, and the other westward to the Pacific via the Snake River; Teton Pass (8,429 ft.); Togwotee Pass (9,658 ft.); Buffalo, Gros Ventre, Hogback, and Snake rivers with many tributaries; Lower Slide Lake 6 miles east of Kelly, and Upper Slide Lake about 15 miles upstream formed by mountains sliding into and across the Gros Ventre River at different times; picturesque Red Hills of the Gros Ventre region; National Elk Refuge; Crystal Peak (10,054 ft.) at Six Lakes; Darwin Peak (11,645 ft.); Goodwin Peak (10,707 ft.); Hogback Peak (10,864 ft.); Hodges Peak (11,130 ft.); Pass Peak (9,970 ft.); Pyramid Peak (11,087 ft.); Triangle Peak (11,525 ft.); Snow King Mountain near Jackson, Teton Pass, and Togwotee Pass ski areas. Camp and picnic sites, 4; picnic only, 7; outfitting camps for pack and saddle trips; dude ranches, cabins, hotels, and resorts. Nearby towns: Daniel, Dubois, Jackson in Wyoming; Alpine, Victor in Idaho. Highways: u.s. 26, 89, 187, 287; State 22. Forest supervisor at Jackson.

Wilderness Areas

These remote areas within National Forests contain awe-inspiring natural wonders and an abundance of wildlife that offer the priceless privilege of intimacy with a timeless world. There are no roads or other provisions for motorized transportation, and access is by watercraft, hiking over trails and trackless areas, or packing in on horseback. Commercial timber cutting (except in the Boundary Waters Canoe Area) and special use permits for resorts, summer homes, hotels, stores, organized camps, hunting and fishing lodges are prohibited in order to maintain the primeval character of a region. Roads necessary for the exercise of statutory right of ingress and egress may be allowed, and grazing domestic livestock, water storage projects not requiring road construction, and improvements for protection of forests are permitted in some areas. The prospecting, locating, and developing of mineral resources are regulated by mining laws of the United States. Although selected timber is harvested in the Boundary Waters Canoe Area of the Superior National Forest in Minnesota, commercial harvesting is not allowed in the northern zone, and no cutting is permitted within 400 feet of a shoreline in the southern zone so as to protect the natural appearance of the area.

Primitive areas were classified separately prior to 1939 if they had fire roads or other developments. Wild areas are single tracts of not less than 5,000 acres or more than 99,999 acres, and Wilderness areas contain at least 100,000 acres. There is a concentration of wildlife in all these areas. Local forest rangers recommend the best campsites, routes to follow, mountains to scale, and provide maps and information about guides, outfitters, and packers. Write to forest supervisors for detailed maps and specific information. Private, state, or other public ownership represents the difference between gross and net federal acreage. See NATIONAL FORESTS and state regulations for descriptions of available game.

ARIZONA

Blue Range Primitive Area (181,566 acres, net 180,139 acres) in the Apache National Forest. Special features: Canyons, creeks, and

Mogollon Rim; fir and spruce forests in high country and ponderosa pine in lower broken areas.

Chiricahua Wild Area (18,000 acres) in the Coronado National Forest. Special features: Rare plants, pine-clad peaks, springs, precipitous canyons on crest of the Chiricahua Mountains; Sentinel Peak (8,999 ft.); former hunting grounds of Chiricahua Apache Indians.

Galiuro Wild Area (55,000 acres) in the Coronado National Forest. Special features: Jagged mountains and hazardous slopes limit hiking to established trails.

Mazatzal Wilderness Area (205,346 acres, net 205,000 acres) in the Tonto National Forest. Special features: Piñon and juniper; East Verde River; Mazatzal Peak (7,905 ft.); Mazatzal High Trail.

Mount Baldy Primitive Area (7,400 acres) in the Apache National Forest. Special features: Mount Baldy (11,496 ft.) at head of the West Fork Little Colorado River.

Pine Mountain Primitive Area (17,500 acres, net 17,445 acres) in the Prescott and Tonto national forests. Special features: Heavy cover, step canyons, and rough terrain; west side of Verde River.

Sierra Ancha Wild Area (20,850 acres) in the Tonto National Forest. Special features: Prehistoric cliff dwellings; scarped mountains; Piñon and juniper near Aztec Peak.

Superstition Wilderness Area (124,140 acres) in the Tonto National Forest. Special features: Oak and Piñon growth south of the Roosevelt Reservoir; extremely rough; Fish Creek Mountain; Weavers Needle, and other prominent peaks.

Sycamore Canyon Primitive Area (48,230 acres, net 45,952 acres) in the Coconino, Kaibab, and Prescott national forests. Special features: A tremendous gorge of the Mogollon Rim with unusual geologic formations, with flora and fauna common to canyon types of landscape.

CALIFORNIA

Agua Tibia Primitive Area (26,760 acres, net 25,995 acres) in the Cleveland National Forest. Special features: Virgin brush; Palomar Divide; Wild Horse Peak (3,277 ft.); Crosley Saddle near Agua Tibia Mountain (4,779 ft.); Dripping Springs; Mission Indian Reserve.

Caribou Peak Wild Area (19,080 acres) in the Lassen National Forest. Special features: Rolling, forested plateau; adjacent to Lassen Volcanic National Park (106,934 acres); numerous lakes including Black, Beauty, Long, Posey, Triangle, Turnaround, and Twin lakes connected by trails; Black Butte (7,884 ft.); Black Cinder Rock (7,761 ft.); Red Cinder (8,374 ft.); North Caribou Mountain (7,784 ft.).

Cucamonga Wild Area (9,022 acres) in the San Bernardino National

Forest. Special features: gentle to rugged topography; Big Horn (8,441 ft.); Cucamonga Peak (8,859 ft.); Telegraph Peak (8,985 ft.); Timber Mountain (8,303 ft.).

Desolation Valley Primitive Area (41,383 acres) in the Eldorado Forest. Special features: Numerous mountain lakes and streams above 6,500-foot elevation in rugged region; Rubicon Reservoir on Rubicon River in Rockbound Valley; Rockbound Lake; Lake Aloha; Dicks Peak (9,974 ft.); Jacks Peak (9,856 ft.); Maggies Peaks (8,699 ft.); McConnell Peak (9,099 ft.); Middle Mountain (8,333 ft.); Mount Price (9,975 ft.); Phipps Peak (9,234 ft.); Pyramid Peak (9,983 ft.); Rubicon Peak (9,183 ft.); Mount Tallac (9,735 ft.).

Devils Canyon–Bear Canyon Primitive Area (35,267 acres) in the Angeles National Forest. Special features: Chaparral and deep canyons; Bear Creek, Chileno, and Devils canyons; Twin Peaks (7,760 ft.); Cogswell Dam on San Gabriel River.

Dome Land Wild Area (62,561 acres, net 62,121 acres) in the Sequoia National Forest. Special features: Bare rock domes and spires rising from 3,000 to 9,529 feet at the South Fork of Kern River Canyon.

Emigrant Basin Primitive Area (98,043 acres, net 97,020 acres) in the Stanislaus National Forest. Special features: Numerous meadows, lakes, and streams; Emigrant Pass to Emigrant Meadows and Lakes; Relief Reservoir in Lower Relief Valley; headwaters of South Fork Stanislaus River; Horse Meadow Reservoir; Huckleberry Lake; Bigelow Peak (10,539 ft.) and Lake; Granite Dome (10,322 ft.); Black Hawk Mountain (10,348 ft.); Cooper Peak (9,603 ft.); Gillett Mountain (8,361 ft.); Kennedy Peak (10,718 ft.); Leavitt Peak (11,570 ft.); Hell's Mountain (6,998 ft.) at Cherry Ridge; Relief Peak (10,808 ft.); Wheeler Peak (9,001 ft.).

Hoover Wild Area (42,800 acres) in the Inyo and Toiyabe national forests. Special features: Mountain lakes and meadows, cascades, clear streams, remnants of 5 perennial snow fields; East, Gilman, Green, Hoover, Summit, Virginia, and West lakes; Black Mountain (11,794 ft.); Dunderberg Peak (12,374 ft.); Excelsior Mountain (12,440 ft.); Lee Vining Peak (11,600 ft.); North Peak (12,256 ft.); Mount Warren (12,327 ft.); Tioga Peak (11,532 ft.).

John Muir Wilderness Area (502,978 acres) in the Inyo, Sequoia, and Sierra national forests. Special features: Several glaciers, alpine meadows, hundreds of lakes and streams in the High Sierra; large stands of Jeffrey pine; John Muir and other trails; Glacier and Le Conte divides; Whitney Mountain (14,495 ft.); Mount Williamson (14,334 ft.); North Palisade (14,254 ft.); Mount Muir (14,025 ft.); Langley Mountain (14,042 ft.); Bear Creek Spire (13,713 ft.); Birch Mountain (13,885 ft.); Diamond Peak (13,105 ft.); Junction Peak (13,903 ft.); Kearsage

Peak (13,650 ft.); Mount Abbott (13,715 ft.); Mount Agassiz (13,891 ft.); Mount Barnard (13,747 ft.); Mount Bradley (13,280 ft.); Mount Bolton Brown (13,527 ft.); Mount Gabb (13,711 ft.); Mount Goode (13,068 ft.); Mount Haeckel (13,435 ft.); Mount Hilgard (13,361 ft.); Mount Humphrey (13,972 ft.); Mount Irvine (13,335 ft.); Mount Keith (13,990 ft.); Mount Le Conte (13,960 ft.); Mount Merriam (13,067 ft.); Mount Mills (13,468 ft.); Mount Pinchot (13,471 ft.); Mount Prater (13,601 ft.); Mount Royce (13,238 ft.); Mount Tom (13,649 ft.); Red Slate Mountain (13,152 ft.); Seven Gables (13,075 ft.); Temple Crag Peak (13,016 ft.); Tunnabora Peak (13,593 ft.); University Peak (13,588 ft.); and several other mountains rising above 12,000 feet.

Marble Mountain Wilderness Area (214,543 acres, net 213,283 acres) in the Klamath National Forest. Special features: Numerous lakes and streams including Burney, Campbell, Cliff, Granite, Hancock, Sky High, Ukonom, and Wright lakes; Solomon River; Buckhorn Mountain (6,917 ft.); Chimney Rock (6,871 ft.); English Peak Lookout (7,316 ft.); Kings Castle or Marble Mountain (7,396 ft.); Red Mountain or Boulder Peak (8,317 ft.); Red Rock Valley.

Minarets Wilderness Area (109,559 acres, net 109,484 acres) in the Inyo and Sierra national forests. Special features: Numerous alpine lakes and streams among spire-like rock formations adjacent to the Yosemite National Park and along the central crest of the Sierra Nevada; Alger, Garnet, Gem, Thousand Island, Walker, and Waugh lakes; Spooky Meadow; Banner Peak (12,957 ft.); Blacktop Peak (12,710 ft.); Donohue Peak (12,023 ft.); Foerster Peak (12,062 ft.); Mono Pass (elevation 10,644 ft.); Mount Dana (13,052 ft.); Mount Davis (12,311 ft.); Mount Gibbs (12,764 ft.); Mount Lewis (12,296 ft.); Mount Ritter (13,157 ft.); Mount Wood (12,637 ft.); Parker Peak (12,861 ft.).

Salmon Trinity Alps Primitive Area (285,756 acres, net 223,300 acres) in the Klamath and Shasta-Trinity national forests. Special features: Numerous lakes and swift clear streams; Battle Mountain (7,920 ft.); Black Mountain (8,012 ft.); Black Rock (7,468 ft.); Caribou Mountain (8,563 ft.) and Lakes; Gibson Peak (8,400 ft.); Sawtooth Ridge; Siligo Peak (8,162 ft.); Tri Forest Peak (7,681 ft.); Yeatapom Peak (7,602 ft.).

San Gorgonio Wild Area (34,718 acres, net 33,898 acres) in the San Bernardino National Forest. Special features: Meadows and streams; desert to alpine vegetation; High Meadow, Lodgepole, Limber Pine, Manzanita, and Trail Fork springs; Ten Thousand Foot Ridge; Anderson Peak (10,864 ft.); Charlton Peak (10,815 ft.); Dobbs Peak (10,454 ft.); San Bernardino Peak (10,624 ft.); San Gorgonio Peak (11,502).

San Jacinto Wild Area (21,955 acres, net 20,565 acres) in the San Bernardino Forest. Special features: Many meadows, streams, valleys and precipitous cliffs; game refuge; Snow Lookout (3,027 ft.); Tahquitz Peak

(8,823 ft.); Apache, Little Rock, Red Tahquitz, and South peaks.

San Rafael Primitive Area (74,990 acres, net 74,160 acres) in Los Padres National Forest. Special features: San Rafael Mountain (6,596 ft.); Jack Rabbit Flat; Mission Pine Basin; Condor Sanctuary on the Sisquoc River.

South Warner Primitive Area (70,682 acres, net 68,870 acres) in the Modoc National Forest. Special features: Numerous streams flowing east and west from a central ridge mostly over 9,000 feet elevation; summit trails from Squaw Peak, Patterson Lake near Warren Peak, Duxenberry Peak, Cole Peak, Emerson Peak, and Bear Camp Mountain.

Thousand Lakes Wild Area (16,335 acres, net 15,695 acres) in the Lassen National Forest. Special features: Thousand Lake Valley (200 acres); Lake Eiler; Barrett, Box, Durbin, Everett, Huford, Magee, Upper and Lower Twin lakes; Crater Peak (8,677 ft.); Freaner Peak (7,485 ft.); Fredonyer Peak (8,054 ft.); Hall Butte (7,187 ft.); Magee Peak (8,550 ft.); Red Cliff (8,224 ft.).

Ventana Primitive Area (54,857 acres, net 52,129 acres) in Los Padres National Forest. Special features: Rugged Santa Lucia Range; Bear Basin; Boulder Peak or Mount Carmel (4,430 ft.); Island Mountain (3,169 ft.); Ventana Cone (4,734 ft.); Ventana Double Cone (4,833 ft.); Carmel River; Little Sur River.

Yolla Bolly–Middle Eel Wilderness Area (111,091 acres, net 109,315 acres) in the Mendocino and Shasta-Trinity national forests. Special features: Ridges and streams; Four Corners Rock (5,406 ft.); Hammerhorn Peak (7,567 ft.); Harvey Peak (7,361 ft.); Hopkins Peak (6,749 ft.); Horsehead Mountain (5,864 ft.); The Knob (6,486 ft.); Lazyman Butte (6,541 ft.); Linn Peak (8,083 ft.) in the South Yolla Bolly Mountains; Shell Mountain (6,700 ft.); Sugarloaf Mountain (7,567 ft.); Solomon Peak (7,581 ft.); Vinegar Peak (6,549 ft.); Windy Mountain (7,078 ft.).

COLORADO

Flat Tops Primitive Area (117,800 acres) in the White River National Forest. Special features: White River Plateau; alpine lakes and streams; Flat Top Mountain (12,493 ft.); Sheep Mountain (12,246 ft.) east of Island Lake; Shingle Peak (12,001 ft.); Big Marvine Peak (11,875 ft.) above Marvine Lake; Little Marvine Peaks near Mary Loch Lake; Turret Peak (11,500 ft.); Trappers Peak (11,990 ft.); Horseshoe, Indian, Rim, Shepherd, Twin, and Walt lakes; headwaters of the South Fork White River; Chinese Wall; Devils Causeway.

Gore–Eagle Nest Primitive Area (61,275 acres, net 61,204 acres) in the Arapahoe and White Rivers national forests. Special features:

Mountain lakes and streams, craggy ridges of the Gore Range; Eagle Nest Mountain (13,397 ft.); Mount Powell (13,534 ft.); Red Peak (13,183 ft.); Slate Ridge; Black, Cliff, Mirror, Slate, Upper and Lower Cataract lakes.

La Garita Wild Area (49,000 acres) in the Rio Grande National Forest, adjacent to the Gunnison National Forest. Special features: La Garita Mountain (13,725 ft.); Mesa and Sheep mountains; Half Moon Pass near Wheeler National Monument; summer range of Elk and Bighorn Sheep in La Garita Mountains.

Maroon Bells–Snowmass Wild Area (66,280 acres, net 66,100 acres) in the White River National Forest. Special features: Many mountain lakes and streams; Elk Mountains; Maroon Bells (14,158 ft., 14,000 ft.); Snowmass Peak (14,077 ft.) overlooking Snowmass Lake and Trail Rider Pass; Cathedral Peak (14,000 ft.) between Electric Pass and Castle Peak (14,259 ft.); Pyramid Peak (14,000 ft.); Avalanche, Capitol, and Pierre lakes near Capitol Peak; Conundrum Hot Springs.

Mount Zirkel–Dome Peak Wild Area (53,400 acres) in the Routt National Forest. Special features: Park Range on the Continental Divide; 40 alpine lakes among lodgepole pine and Engelmann spruce forests; Mount Zirkel (12,200 ft.); Bighorn, Gilpin, Katherine, Roxy Ann, and Seven lakes; headwaters of the Encampment and North Fork Elk rivers.

Rawah Wild Area (26,797 acres, net 25,597 acres) in the Roosevelt National Forest. Special features: Numerous glacial lakes in the Medicine Bow Range; Cameron Peak (12,124 ft.); Clark Peak (12,965 ft.); Rawah Lakes.

San Juan Primitive Area (240,000 acres, net 238,080 acres) in the San Juan National Forest. Special features: Needle Mountains; Mount Eolus (14,159 ft.); Sunlight Peak (14,060 ft.); Windom Peak (14,091 ft.); Rio Grande Pyramid (13,830 ft.); Mount Nebo (13,192 ft.); White Dome (13,607 ft.); Eagle Mountain (12,007 ft.); Pagosa Peak (12,634 ft.); Quien Sabe Mountain (10,224 ft.); Fourmile Lakes; Emerald, Granite, Hossick, Turkey Creek, and Vallecito lakes among numerous alpine lakes and virgin forests; Durango Reservoir adjacent to the area; Weminuche Pass (10,622 ft.) to the Upper Rio Grande Primitive Area.

Uncompahgre Primitive Area (69,253 acres, net 53,252 acres) in the Uncompahgre National Forest. Special features: Alpine lakes, streams, and waterfalls in rugged mountains; Uncompahgre Mountain (14,306 ft.); Mount Sneffels (14,143 ft.); Wetterhorn Peak (14,020 ft.); Dallas Peak (13,700 ft.); Matterhorn (13,589 ft.); Mears Peak (13,490 ft); Potosi Peak (13,790 ft.); Whitehouse Mountain (13,490 ft.); Wild Horse Peak (13,271 ft.); Red Mountain no 2 (13,339 ft.); Mount

Abrams (12,800 ft.); Blue Lake Trail; mining operations in the Pierson, Silver, and Yankee Boy basins.

Upper Rio Grande Primitive Area (56,600 acres) in the Rio Grande National Forest. Special features: Headwaters of the Rio Grande in the San Juan Mountains on the Continental Divide; numerous mountain lakes, and streams including Black, Red, Twin, and Ute lakes; Rio Grande Pyramid (13,830 ft.); Mount Nebo (13,192 ft.) above Hunchback Pass; Weminuche Pass (10,622 ft.) to adjacent San Juan Primitive Area; Rio Grande Reservoir just outside of the northern border.

West Elk Wild Area (62,000 acres) in the Gunnison National Forest. Special features: Fantastic formations with walls hundreds of feet high and known as The Castles; mountain meadows, lakes, and streams; Mount Baldy (12,809 ft.); West Elk Peak (12,920 ft.); Costo, Rainbow, and Sheep lakes; Beckwith Pass Trail to Storm Ridge, North, Middle, and South Baldy mountains.

Wilson Mountains Primitive Area (26,347 acres) in the San Juan and Uncompahgre national forests. Special features: Mount Wilson (14,250 ft.) above Alta Lakes; Wilson Peak (14,026 ft.); Dolores, Dunn, Gladstone, Middle, San Bernardino, Sheep, and Sunshine mountains; Lizard Head; headwaters of the Dolores River; Navajo Lake stocked with Golden Trout.

IDAHO

Idaho Primitive Area (1,232,744 acres, net 1,224,576 acres) in the Boise, Challis, Payette, and Salmon national forests. Special features: Network of trails to spectacular waterfalls, grassy meadows, numerous mountain lakes, and hundreds of streams; Middle and South Forks of the Salmon River; Pistol Creek Ridge, Walkers Peak (8,904 ft.), Chinook Mountain (9,120 ft.), Pistol Lakes, and Pistol Hot Springs near the Snowshoe Summit Entrance; Chilcoot Mountains (9,020 ft.) at Chilcoot Pass; Big Baldy Lookout (9,722 ft.), Baldy Ridge, Papoose Lake, and Pistol Rock near Trapper Creek Entrance; Murphy Peak (9,288 ft.), Red Ridge, Red Peak (9,475 ft.), Quis Quis Hot Springs, Rainbow Peak (9,329 ft.), Thunder Mountain (8,538 ft.), Cougar Peak (9,128 ft.), and Lookout Mountain (8,660 ft.) near Stibnite Entrance; Big Creek Ridge, Center Mountain (9,324 ft.), Snowslide Mountain (9,094 ft.), Acorn Butte Lookout (7,750 ft.), McFadden Point (8,544 ft.), Ramey Mountain (8,390 ft.), Mosquito Peak (8,769 ft.), and Rock Rabbit Lookout in the Big Creek Entrance region; Horse Creek Bridge Entrance to Bend Peak (9,302 ft.), Cottonwood Butte (9,321 ft.), Farrow Mountain (8,987 ft.), and Black Butte (8,694 ft.); Stoddard Bridge Entrance to the Middle Fork Salmon River rapids and Box Canyon; Big Horn Crags near the Cathedral Rock (9,411 ft.) Entrance include Aggipah Peak (9,929 ft.), Bee Hive (9,599 ft.), Mount McGuire (10,070 ft.), Pudding Mountain (9,684 ft.), and Wilson Mountain (9,556 ft.); Yellow Jacket Mountains Entrance to Middle Fork Lookout (9,130 ft.) and Sugar Loaf (9,141 ft.); Sleeping Deer–Cache Creek Entrance to Sleeping Deer Mountain (9,885 ft.) and the Middle Fork Salmon River.

Salmon River Breaks Primitive Area (217,185 acres, net 216,870 acres) in the Bitterroot and Nez Perce national forests. Special features: Adjacent to the Idaho Primitive Area; rugged terrain extending more than 40 miles on north side of the Salmon River about midway between North Fork and Riggins; river canyon and white waters; game preserve; Indian writings; access by boat from road end below Shoup in Idaho, and from west end, or by trail from each end.

Sawtooth Primitive Area (200,942 acres) in the Boise, Challis, and Sawtooth national forests. Special features: Headwaters of the South Fork Payette River, Middle Fork and North Fork Boise rivers; Alice, Alpine, Hell Roaring, Imogene, and Toxaway lakes among more than 150 mountain lakes and numerous streams; Barron Peak (10,307 ft.); Heyburn Mountain (10,229 ft.); Redfish Lake Mountain (10,629 ft.); Browns Peak (9,724 ft.); Elk Peak (10,605 ft.); Snowside Mountain (10,659 ft.).

Selway-Bitterroot Wilderness Area (1,239,840 acres) in the Bitterroot, Clearwater, and Nez Perce national forests. Special features: Bitterroot Range including parts of the Lochsa and Selway River drainages in Idaho and the Bitterroot River drainage in Montana; Big Creek Canyon; Moose Ridge; Lake Como; Emerald and Indian lakes; Bass Peak (8,840 ft.); Big Rock Mountain (7,100 ft.); Blodgett Mountain 8,400 ft.); Cove Peak (7,608 ft.); Diablo Peak (7,465 ft.); Eagle Mountain (7,414 ft.); Grave Peak (7,878 ft.); Hunter Peak (8,422 ft.); McConnell Mountain (7,415 ft.) in the Selway Game Preserve; Trapper Peak (10,131 ft.); Stuart Hot Springs.

MINNESOTA

Boundary Waters Canoe Area (1,034,852 acres, net 886,673 acres) in the Superior National Forest. Special features: Dense evergreen forests interlaced with large and small lakes, and streams on the Canada–United States boundary. See SUPERIOR NATIONAL FOREST; CANOE TRIPS.

MONTANA

Absaroka Primitive Area (64,000 acres) in the Gallatin National Forest. Special features: Evergreen forests and rugged peaks in the

Absaroka Range; Hell Roaring Creek; trails from the Yellowstone National Park, Mill Creek, Boulder and Stillwater Rivers.

Anaconda-Pintlar Wilderness Area (159,086 acres, net 157,803 acres) in the Beaverhead, Bitterroot, and Deerlodge national forests. Special features: Wooded mountains with high barren and precipitous peaks on the Continental Divide; glacial cirques, mountain meadows, alpine lakes and streams; Mount Howe (10,475 ft.); Mount Tiny (9,857 ft.); Maloney Basin; trails from Rock Creek and Bitterroot River in the Columbia River Basin and Big Hole River in the Missouri River Basin; Hiline Trail.

Beartooth Primitive Area (230,000 acres) in the Custer and Gallatin national forests. Special features: Majestic peaks, waterfalls, alpine meadows, lakes and streams; glaciers including the one-mile-long Grasshopper Glacier (elevation 11,000 ft.); Granite Peak (12,850 ft.); Black, Broadwater, Crazy, and Rainbow lakes; trails from the East and West Rosebud rivers, Stillwater River, Red Lodge Creek, Rock Creek, and Cook City.

Bob Marshall Wilderness Area (950,000 acres) in the Flathead and Lewis and Clark national forests. Special features: Towering crags, alpine lakes, meadows and streams; 1,000-foot cliffs of the Chinese Wall on the Continental Divide extending for about 15 miles from Larch Hill southward to Haystack Mountain; South Fork Flathead River; Sun River; Big Salmon Lake; Big Horn Mountain (8,199 ft.); Beartop Mountain (8,090 ft.); Cliff Mountain (8,585 ft.); Greek Cliffs near Silvertip Mountain (8,890 ft.); Lookout Mountain (8,184 ft.); Pentagon Mountain (8,877 ft.); Redhead Peak (8,802 ft.); Sphinx Mountain (9,510 ft.); Signal Mountain (8,255 ft.); and Winter Elk Range.

Cabinet Mountains Primitive Area (89,900 acres) southwest of Libby in the Kaniksu and Kootenai national forests. Special features: White pine and red cedar forests below snowy peaks, lakes, streams and waterfalls; Snowshoe Peak (7,621 ft.) above Granite and Leigh lakes; Wanless Lake south of Rock Peak.

Gates of the Mountain Wild Area (28,562 acres) in the Helena National Forest. Special features: Mountain meadows, streams, and narrow canyons in the Big Belt Range; Candle, Moors, Sacajawea, Sawtooth, and Sheep Mountains; access by boat from Lewis and Clark Landing to spectacular 2,000-foot limestone walls of the Missouri River.

Mission Mountains Primitive Area (75,500 acres, net 73,340 acres) in the Flathead National Forest. Special features: Mission Range; glaciers, alpine country, stands of spruce, fir, and western larch; Crystal, Glacier, and Turquoise lakes.

Selway-Bitterroot Wilderness Area. See IDAHO.

Spanish Peaks Primitive Area (50,000 acres, net 49,800 acres) in the

Gallatin National Forest. Special features: Mountain meadows, lakes, streams, and waterfalls in the Madison Range including Hellroaring Creek and Gallatin Peak (11,015 ft.).

NEVADA

Jarbridge Wild Area (64,827 acres, net 64,667 acres) in a portion of the Humboldt National Forest near the Idaho border and north of Elko. Special features: Rugged terrain with elevations from 6,000 feet to the Matterhorn (10,839 ft.); Emerald Lake; headwaters of St. Marys River; East Fork Jarbridge River.

NEW HAMPSHIRE

Great Gulf Wild Area (5,400 acres) in the White Mountains National Forest. Special features: Rough forested basin on eastern slopes of Mount Washington (6,288 ft.) with elevations ranging from 1,700 to 5,800 feet; Spaulding and Star lakes; West Branch Peabody River and numerous tributary streams.

NEW MEXICO

Black Range Primitive Area (169,984 acres, net 169,196 acres) in the Gila National Forest. Special features: Numerous creeks and canyons, evergreen forests; Reeds Peak (10,011 ft.) and Diamond Peak on the Continental Divide.

Blue Range Primitive Area (36,598 acres) in the Apache National Forest. Special features: Adjacent to the Gila National Forest; ponderosa pine, fir, and spruce woodlands, canyons and creeks; Blue River; Bear Mountain; Mogollon Rim.

Gila Primitive Area (132,788 acres, net 129,639 acres) adjoins the *Gila Wilderness Area* (438,626 acres, net 438,360 acres) in the Gila National Forest. Special features: Narrow rock-walled canyons, springs, mountain meadows, aspen glades, ponderosa pine and spruce-fir forests; Middle Fork and West Fork of Gila River; Gila Canyon; numerous creeks including Mogollon, Turkey, and Whitewater creeks; Mogollon Baldy (10,778 ft.) and Whitewater Baldy (10,892 ft.) in the Mogollon Range; Granite Peak (8,699 ft.) in the Diablo Range; Grouse Mountain (10,132 ft.); Brushy Mountain (8,008 ft.); Jerky Mountains; Iron Creek Mesa Lake; Roberts Lake on Sapillo Creek.

Pecos Wilderness Area (165,000 acres) in the Carson and Santa Fe national forests. Special features: Sangre de Cristo Range; Truchas Peak (13,102 ft.); East Pecos Baldy (12,529 ft.); Pecos Baldy (12,500 ft.); Santa Fe Baldy (12,622 ft.); Aspen Peak (11,109 ft.); Lake Peak (12,409 ft.); headwaters of the Pecos River; Lake Katherine; Pecos Baldy, Spirit, Stewart, and Truchas lakes; Rio Santa Barbara; Trailriders Wall.

San Pedro Parks Wild Area (41,132 acres) in the Santa Fe National Forest. Special features: High mountain plateau about 10,000 feet elevation; small Trout streams, dense stands of spruce, and open meadows.

Wheeler Peak Wild Area (6,051 acres) in the Carson National Forest. Special feature: Scenic Wheeler Peak (13,151 ft.) in the Sangre Cristo Range north of Taos.

White Mountain Wild Area (28,230 acres, net 28,118 acres) in the Lincoln National Forest. Special features: Located north of the Muscalero Apache Indian Reservation; juniper and piñon on mountains rising to 11,000 feet; Church Mountain; Nogal Peak.

NORTH CAROLINA

Linville Gorge Wild Area (7,655 acres) in the Pisgah National Forest. Special features: Cascades in a deep gorge, flowering shrubs, and virgin timber; approximately 2,500 feet elevation.

OREGON

Diamond Peak Wild Area (35,440 acres) in the Deschutes and Willamette national forests. Special features: 33 mountain lakes, small meadows, and swift streams on the Cascade Range; Diamond Peak (8,750 ft.) near Crescent, Odell, and Summit lakes.

Eagle Cap Wilderness Area (220,280 acres, net 216,250 acres) in the Wallowa-Whitman National Forest. Special features: Numerous deep canyons and more than 50 lakes in the Wallowa Mountains; headwaters of the Imnaha, Lostine, Minam, and Wallowa rivers; Eagle Cap (9,675 ft.); Pete's Point (9,600 ft.); Sentinel Peak (9,500 ft.); Sacajawea Peak (10,033 ft.)

Gearhart Mountain Wild Area (18,709 acres) in the Fremont National Forest. Special features: Rough, mountainous area with elevations from 6,000 to 8,364 feet at the summit of Gearhart Mountain; Blue Lake; Gearhart Marsh; tributaries of the Sprague River.

Kalmiopsis Wild Area (78,850 acres) in the Siskiyou National Forest. Special features: Mountain meadows, rushing streams, and deep rough canyons; Chetco River; Canyon Peak (4,895 ft.); Johnson Butte; Pearsoll Peak Lookout and Vulcan Peak Lookout; an abundance of rare flora including the rock rhododendron (*Kalmiopsis leachiana*) and 17 species of conifer; red peaks of peridotite.

Mount Hood Wild Area (14,160 acres) in the Mount Hood National Forest. Special features: Superb high country with alpine meadows north and west of snow-capped Mount Hood (11,245 ft.) in the Cascade Range; Cathedral Ridge; Timberline Trail.

Mount Jefferson Primitive Area (86,700 acres) in the Deschutes, Mount Hood, and Willamette national forests. Special features: Perpetual glaciers; Mount Jefferson (10,495 ft.); Three Fingered Jack (7,848 ft.); Cinder Peak (6,700 ft.); Maxwell Butte (6,225 ft.); Marion and Pamelia lakes; Oregon Skyline Trail.

Mount Washington Wild Area (46,655 acres) in the Deschutes and Willamette national forests. Special features: Alpine meadows and extensive lava beds; Mount Washington (7,802 ft.); Mount Scott (6,125 ft.); Belknap Crater (6,877 ft.); McKenzie Pass; Coldwater Spring; Oregon Skyline Trail.

Mountain Lakes Wild Area (23,071 acres) in the Winema National Forest. Special features: Rugged region with major portion above 6,000-foot elevation; 5 hanging valleys (glacial cirques); Trout-stocked lakes varying from 2 to 70 acres: Avalanche, Como, Coyote, Echo, Harriette, Hemlock, Paragon, South Pass, and Storm lakes.

Strawberry Mountain Wild Area (33,653 acres, net 33,004 acres) in the Malheur National Forest. Special features: Mountain lakes, meadows, and streams; unique rock formations; Baldy Mountain; Strawberry Range; Strawberry Mountain Lookout above Strawberry Lake; High and Slide lakes. The adjacent Canyon Creek Archery Area is southeast of Canyon City.

Three Sisters Wilderness Area (196,708 acres) in the Deschutes and and Willamette national forests. Special features: Mountain streams and more than 100 lakes; several glaciers including the largest in Oregon, the Collier Glacier on North Sister (10,094 ft.); Middle Sister (10,053 ft.); South Sister (10,354 ft.); Substitute Point (6,340 ft.); Packsaddle Mountain (6,138 ft.); Irish Mountain (6,891 ft.); Oregon Skyline Trail.

UTAH

High Uintas Primitive Area (240,717 acres) in the Ashley and Wasatch national forests. Special features: Elevations are above 8,000 feet; extensive stands of lodgepole pine and Engelmann spruce; numerous streams and more than 250 fishing lakes including the larger Bluebell, Brown Duck, Grandaddy, Kidney, Moon, North Star, Pine Island, and Superior lakes; along crest of the Uinta Range: Kings Peak (13,498 ft.); Mount Lovenia (13,229 ft.); Brown Duck Mountain (11,910 ft.); Cleveland Peak (12,615 ft.); East Grandaddy Mountain (11,265 ft.); Brown Duck, Lake Fork, Swasey Hole, and Yellowstone canyon trails connecting with the Highline of the High Uintas.

WASHINGTON

Glacier Peak Wilderness Area (458,505 acres, net 458,105 acres) in the Mount Baker and Wenatchee national forests. Special features: Several glaciers, numerous lakes, mountains, and valleys; Glacier Peak (10,528 ft.); Seven Fingered Jack (9,077 ft.); Fortress Mountain (8,874 ft.); Flora Mountain (8,320 ft.); Miners Ridge; Lake Chelan; Suiattle River.

Goat Rocks Wild Area (82,680 acres) in the Gifford Pinchot and Snoqualmie national forests. Special features: Glaciers, several large lakes, meadows, and precipitous cliffs; Goat Ridge (6,240 ft.); Cispus Pass; Cowlitz River; Upper Lake Creek; Walupt Lake.

Mount Adams Wild Area (42,411 acres) in the Gifford Pinchot National Forest. Special features: Mountainous region above timberline; Mount Adams (12,307 ft.); Adams Lava and Mazama glaciers; Hellroaring Creek; Around the Mountain Trail; Cascade Crest Trail.

North Cascade Primitive Area (801,000 acres) in the Mount Baker and Okanogan national forests. Special features: Glaciers, Alpine lakes and streams; Remmel Mountain (8,688 ft.); Mount Challenger (8,236 ft.); Diablo and Ross Lakes on the Skagit River; Pasayter River; Cathedral, Hidden, Image, Lyman, and Remmel lakes.

WYOMING

Bridger Wilderness Area (383,300 acres) in the Bridger National Forest. Special features: Perpetual ice fields on mountain crags; cascades, alpine lakes and streams; Wind River Range; Gannett Peak (13,785 ft.); Downs Peak (13,344 ft.); Fremont Peak (13,730 ft.); Mount Helen (13,-600 ft.); West Atlantic Peak (12,445 ft.) on the Continental Divide; Bonneville Peak (12,530 ft.); Mount Lester (12,325 ft.); Mount Nystrom (12,101 ft.); Pyramid Peak (12,020 ft.); Stroud Peak (12,222 ft.); Temple Peak (12,976 ft.); Big Sheep Mountain (11,605 ft.); Dome Peak (11,210 ft.); Mount Baldy (11,855 ft.); Mount Washakie (11,490 ft.) near Hailey Pass; Salt Lick Mountain (11,521 ft.); Squaretop Mountain (11,679 ft.); Green River Lakes.

Cloud Peak Primitive Area (137,000 acres) in the Bighorn National Forest. Special features: Lowest elevation 8,500 feet at the Main Fork of Paint Rock Creek; mountainous region with several sheer walls 1,000–5,000 feet high; large stands of pine and spruce, swift streams, and more than 250 fishing lakes; Cloud Peak (13,165 ft.); Lake Geneva on East Fork of Big Goose Creek; trails to Lakes Angeline, Cliff, Elk, Emerald, Helen, Lame Deer, Lost Twins, Mirror, Old Crow, Seven Brothers, Solitude, and Lakes of the Rough.

Glacier Primitive Area (177,000 acres) in the Shoshone National Forest. Special features: Numerous lakes and several large living glaciers; Gannett Peak (13,785 ft.); Fremont Peak (13,370 ft.); Sacajewa Peak (13,607 ft.); Chimney Rock (13,340 ft.); Downs Peak (13,344 ft.) and Glacier above Downs Lake; alpine lakes and streams including Klondike, Milky, Ross, Simpson, and Trail lakes; Indian Pass (12,130 acres); Fish Lake Trail crossing the Sheridan Trail.

North Abasaroka Wilderness Area (359,700 acres) in the Shoshone National Forest. Special features: Abasaroka Range on eastern border of Yellowstone National Park; Hoodoo Peak (10,552 ft.); Trout Peak (12,259 ft.); Indian Creek and Meadow; Hurricane Mesa.

Popo Agie Primitive Area (70,000 acres) in the Shoshone National Forest. Special features: on the Continental Divide in the Wind River Range; Wind River Peak (13,200 ft.); 75 mountain lakes including Cathedral, Ice, South Fork, and Washakie lakes; Hailey Pass and Washakie Pass to the Bridger Wilderness Area.

South Abasaroka Wilderness Area (506,300 acres) in the Shoshone National Forest. Special features: Adjacent to Teton National Forest and Yellowstone National Park; Needle Mountain (12,130 ft.); Shoshone Trail along Greybull River; mountain lakes and streams including South Fork Shoshone River; Shoshone Pass; Eagle Pass; Crescent Mountain (11,875 ft.); Mount Crosby (12,435 ft.).

Stratified Primitive Area (202,000 acres) in the Shoshone National Forest. Special features: Narrow valley between broad flat-topped mountains; Ragged Top Mountain (11,848 ft.); Wiggins Peak (12,160 ft.); Wood River; Washakie Needles (12,496 ft.); Petrified Forest near Cougar Pass (11,364 ft.); Cottonwood Peak (10,900 ft.); Bear Creek Pass (11,202 ft.).

Teton Wilderness Area (563,500 acres) in the Teton National Forest. Special features on the Continental Divide: Numerous streams, large valleys, and mountain meadows adjacent to the south and southwestern borders of Yellowstone National Park; Two Ocean Pass (elevation 8,200 ft.); Snake River; Bridger Lake on Yellowstone River; Blue Lakes; Granite Falls and Hot Springs; summer range for the Jackson Hole Elk herd.

Ski Areas in National Forests

Some of the best ski areas in the country are in national forests. Snow rangers insure safety on winter playgrounds used for skiing, skating, ice-boating, and fishing through ice. Areas for winter sports are established and managed to meet national forest safety requirements, and all concessionaires operate under forest use permits. An affiliate of the National Ski Association, the National Ski Patrol System, works closely with the Forest Service to provide safety on slopes. During 1963, there were 2,028,-500 visits to winter sports sites in California national forests, and the number of visits over 100,000 in other states were: Colorado, 702,500; Idaho, 225,500; Michigan, 347,300; Montana, 254,100; New Hampshire, 224,200; New Mexico, 220,600; Oregon, 503,900; Utah, 662,000; Vermont, 445,000; Washington, 676,300; and Wyoming, 104,600. Detailed information about exact location, elevation, facilities, and overnight accommodations may be obtained from forest supervisors, and local or state chambers of commerce.

State	National forest	Ski areas
Alaska	Chugach	Alyeska
	North Tongass	Douglas Ski Bowl, Petersburg
Arizona	Coconino	Arizona Snow Bowl
	Coronado	Mount Lemmon
California	Angeles	Blue Ridge, Holiday Hill, Kratka Ridge, Mount Baldy, Mount Waterman, Movie Slope, Table Mountain
	Eldorado	Echo Summit, Heavenly Valley, Peddler Hill, Sierra Ski Ranch, Strawberry Lodge
	Inyo	June Mountain, Mammoth Mountain, Onion Valley
	Lassen	Coppervale, Stover
	Los Padres	Mount Abel
	Modoc	Cedar Pass
	Plumas	Plumas-Eureka Ski Bowl
	San Bernardino	Green Valley Snow Bowl, Lynn Ski Lifts, Moonridge, Snow Summit, Snow Valley
	Sequoia	Shirley Meadows, Sugar Loaf
	Shasta-Trinity	Mount Shasta Ski Bowl
	Sierra	China Peak
	Six Rivers	Horse Mountain
	Stanislaus	Dodge Ridge
	Tahoe	Alpine Meadows, Deer Park, Granlibakken, Mount Lincoln, Squaw Valley,* Yuba Ski Land

* Site of 1960 Winter Olympics.

State	National Forest	Ski Areas
Colorado	Arapaho	Arapaho Basin, Berthoud Pass, Breckenridge, Loveland Basin, Loveland Valley, Winter Park
	Grand Mesa– Uncompahgre	Mesa Creek
	Gunnison	Crested Butte
	Pike	Indianhead, Pikes Peak
	Rio Grande	Wolf Creek
	Roosevelt	Lake Eldora
	San Isabel	Cooper Hill, Monarch Pass
	San Juan	Stoner Ski Area
	White River	Aspen, Aspen Highlands, Buttermilk Ski Corporation, Vail
Idaho	Boise	Bogus Basin
	Caribou	Skyline
	Coeur d'Alene	Lookout Pass
	Payette	Brundage Mountain, Payette Lakes
	St. Joe	North-South
	Sawtooth	Magic Mountain, Pomerelle, Soldier Mountain, Sun Valley
	Targhee	Bear Gulch, Pine Basin
Michigan	Hiawatha	Mission Hill (Iroquois), Thunder Bowl
	Huron	Silver Valley
	Manistee	Caberfae, The Big M
	Ottawa	Indian Head
Minnesota	Chippewa	Shingobee
	Superior	Giants Ridge, Lookout Mountain
Montana	Beaverhead	Rainy Mountain
	Bitterroot	Lost Trail
	Custer	Grizzly Peak
	Deerlodge	Cable Mountain
	Flathead	Big Mountain
	Gallatin	Bridger Bowl
	Helena	Grass Mountain
	Kaniksu	Woodchuck Mountain
	Kootenai	Turner Mountain
	Lewis and Clark	Kings Hill
	Lolo	Baldy Mountain, Missoula Snow Bowl
Nevada	Humboldt	Ward Mountain
	Toiyabe	Reno Ski Bowl
New Hamp- shire	White Mountain	Cannon Mountain Mittersill, Tuckerman Ravine, Waterville Valley, Wildcat Mountain
New Mexico	Carson	Red River, Sipapu, Taos Ski Valley
	Cibola	La Madera
	Lincoln	Sierra Blanca
	Santa Fe	Santa Fe Ski Basin
Oregon	Deschutes	Bachelor Butte
	Fremont	Warner Canyon
	Mount Hood	Cooper Spur, Multorpor, Mount Hood Ski Bowl, Summit, Timberline

State	National Forest	Ski Areas
Oregon	Rogue River	Union Creek
	Umatilla	Arbuckle Mountain, Spout Springs
	Umpqua	Taft Mountain
	Wallowa–Whitman	Anthony Lake, Little Alps
	Willamette	Hoodoo Ski Bowl, Willamette Pass
	Winema	Tomahawk
South Dakota	Black Hills	Stewart Slope
Utah	Ashley	Grizzly Ridge
	Cache	Beaver Mountain, Snow Basin
	Dixie	Cedar Canyon
	Fishlake	Gooseberry
	Manti-LaSal	Blue Mountain
	Wasatch	Alta, Brighton, Little Mountain, Solitude
Vermont	Green Mountain	Bromley, Mount Snow, Sugarbush
Washington	Colville	Chewelah Peak
	Mount Baker	Mount Baker, Pilchuk
	Okanogan	Loup Loup
	Snoqualmie	Crystal Mountain, Snowqualmie Pass, White Pass
	Umatilla	Rose Spring
	Wenatchee	Hyak, Leavenworth, Stevens Pass
Wisconsin	Chequamegon	Perkinstown
	Nicolet	Sheltered Valley
Wyoming	Bighorn	Fun Valley, Meadowlark Ski Area
	Medicine Bow	Happy Jack, Medicine Bow, Ryan Park, Snowy Range
	Shoshone	Sinks Canyon, Sleeping Giant

Canoe Trips

The silent, light canoe of the American Indian has been modernized but remains essentially the ideal craft for traveling through wilderness waterways. Many persons own or rent canoes to paddle around campsites, leisurely enjoy fishing, drift with the current, or skillfully rush through rapids for thrills. States with lakes linked by streams and short portages encourage canoeing and have convenient campsites and water trails. Maine and Minnesota have charted routes for short and long trips through still and white waters.

BOUNDARY WATERS CANOE AREA

The Boundary Waters Canoe Area (1,034,852 acres) in the Northern portion of the Superior National Forest in Minnesota is a fabulous canoe country. There are no public roads, and after World War II, seaplanes were used by sportsmen to reach isolated, privately owned cabins, fishing camps, and resorts otherwise accessible only by canoes and portages. Today, all aircraft are prohibited from flying below a 4,000-foot elevation except for an emergency or on official Forest Service duty.

The international boundary between Canada and the United States, starting at Lake Superior follows an irregular watercourse through dense forests on the northern border of Minnesota along such large bodies of water as the Pigeon River, Moose, Mountain, South, North, Gunflint, Saganaga, Basswood, and Crooked lakes, Lac La Croix, Namakan and Rainy lakes, Rainy River, and Lake of the Woods. The first special wilderness area was set aside in the Superior National Forest by Secretary of Agriculture W. M. Jardine in 1926. The Caribou, Little Indian Sioux, and Superior wilderness areas were collectively renamed the Boundary Waters Canoe Area in 1958. Associated state lands and the adjacent Quetico Provincial Park in Canada form a unique vacation region containing an abundance of wildlife and excellent fishing. Ely and Grand Marais in Minnesota are major entry points, and the Visitor Center at Ely provides valuable information.

Local chambers of commerce sponsor the Canada-USA International Canoe Derby from Fall Lake near Ely to Atiokkan in Ontario, Canada, and it is held annually during the third week in July. Black flies and mosquitoes are a nuisance in June, and the best canoeing period is from July 15, to October 15. The campground season in the Superior National

Forest extends from May 30 through Labor Day. Campers bring their own tents, food, cooking and sleeping equipment. For addresses of outfitters who rent or sell equipment and supplies, write to the chambers of commerce at Ely and Grand Marais; the Commercial Club at Crane Lake in the Superior National Forest; the Minnesota Arrowhead Association at Duluth; or to the Atikokan Chamber of Commerce in Ontario, Canada.

Maps are available from the Forest Supervisor, Superior National Forest, and local outfitters; or write for an index of maps prepared by the U.S. Geological Survey, Map Information Offices, 18th and F St., N.W., Washington 25, D.C. These colored maps show portages, rapids, and similar features on waterproof paper in individual sheets, or in a bound atlas of the entire area. The Department of Lands and Forests, Toronto, Ontario, issues maps of the Canadian territory. Regular Minnesota licences are required for the American region, and an Ontario fishing license is necessary in Canada. The latter may be obtained from the Ontario Department of Lands and Forests, at Canadian ranger stations, or at Crane Lake. Firearms are prohibited in Canadian areas.

PRINCIPAL CANOE ROUTES

1. International Boundary Route, or Voyageurs Highway (235 miles paddling, 9 miles portaging) from McFarland Lake to Mountain Lake and continuing westward through boundary waters to Namakan and Rainy Lakes beyond the Boundary Waters Canoe Area in the Superior National Forest. The route from McFarland Lake eastward is through South Fowl Lake and the Pigeon River to the Grand Portage Trail which is between Grand Portage Bay on Lake Superior and Fort Charlotte on the Pigeon River in the northeastern corner of Minnesota. An attractive branch route from western boundary waters is to Kabetogama Lake from Namakan Lake. The Kabetogama and Woodenfrog campgrounds are outside the Superior National Forest.

2. Clearwater-Bearskin Loop (38 miles paddling, 5 miles portaging) from the Gunflint area at the East Bearskin or Flour Lake campgrounds to Hungry Jack, Bearskin, Clearwater, Duncan, West Pike, McFarland, Pine, Canoe, and Alder lakes to East Bearskin Campground.

3. Poplar-Brule Loop (47 miles paddling, 5 miles portaging) from the Gunflint area at Poplar Lake to Winchell, Brule, Temperance, Cherokee, Long Island, Omega, and Poplar lakes.

4. Little Saganaga Route (25 miles paddling, 4 miles portaging) from Gunflint area at Ham Lake to Snipe, Copper, Tuscarora, Gabimichigami, Ogishkemuncie, Alpine, and Sea Gull lakes.

5. Sea Gull–Red Rock Loop (23 miles paddling, one-half mile portaging) from Gunflint area at Sea Gull Lake to Alpine Red Rock, Saganaga, and Sea Gull lakes.

6. Sawbill Loop (62 miles paddling, 2 miles portaging) from Sawbill Lake Campground to Cherokee, Long Island, Snipe, Copper, Tuscarora, Gabimichigami, Little Saganaga, Polly, and Alton lakes to Sawbill Lake Campground.

7. Kawishiwi Loop (83 miles paddling, 9 miles portaging) from Ely area at Lake One to Lake Three, Hudson Lake, Lake Insula, Alice, Koma, Polly, Kawishiwi lakes, Perent River, Isabella Lake, Isabella River, Bald Eagle, and Gabbro lakes, South Kawishiwi River, Kawishiwi River to Lake One.

8. Kekekabic Loop (49 miles paddling, 4½ miles portaging) from Ely area at Lake One to Lakes Two, Three, Four, Insula, Kiana, Thomas, Fraser, Kekekabic, Eddy, Knife, Birch, and to Moose Lake Campground.

9. North and South Kawishiwi Rivers Loop (30 miles paddling, 2 miles portaging) from Ely area at White Iron Lake to Farm and Clear lakes, South Kawishiwi River Campground, Birch and White Iron lakes.

10. Winton-Basswood Lake Route (13 miles paddling, one-half mile portaging) from Ely area at Fall Lake to Newton Lake, Pipestone Bay, and Basswood Lake.

11. Stuart and Moose Rivers Loop (57 miles paddling, 11 miles portaging) from Ely area at Burntside Lake to Crab, Cummings, and Big Moose lakes, Moose River, Nina Moose Lake, Nina Moose River, Lac La Croix, Dahlgren River, Stuart Lake, Stuart River, Big Lake, and Big Moose Lake.

12. Vermillion and Little Indian Sioux Rivers (116 miles paddling, 7½ miles portaging) from McKinley Park Campground on Vermillion Lake to Vermillion River and Crane Lake; from Vermillion Lake to Trout Lake, Little Trout Lake, Little Indian Sioux River, Sioux River Campground, Indian Sioux River, Pauness Lakes, and other lakes to Lac La Croix.

MAINE

There are 351 public campsites and lunch grounds maintained by the Maine Forestry District, including 263 in wilderness areas and 83 in organized townships. Campsites are usually near springs or running water on trails, highways, and waterways. They are large enough to accommodate two or more parties, and yellow signs labeled AUTHOR-IZED are posted nearby. Fires may be kindled at campsites and lunch grounds maintained by the State Forestry Department, but it is unlawful to camp and to kindle out-of-door fires in the unorganized territory of the state (except at campsites) without securing a permit from the landowner or nearest state forest fire warden. Permits must be procured from landowners in all organized towns outside of the Maine Forestry District. Out-of-door fires include those using charcoal, gasoline, sterno, or other fuel fires in or out of tents or collapsible structures.

A list of authorized campsites and lunch grounds, maps, and detailed information about canoe cruises may be obtained from the State Department of Economic Development, State House, Augusta. Competent guides are recommended by town clerks, sporting camps, sporting goods stores, and hotels. Maine licenses are required for fishing and hunting.

POPULAR CANOE CRUISES

1. St. John River Trip (201 miles) from Northwest Carry at the upper end of Moosehead Lake to Seboomook Lake, West Branch of the Penobscot River, Baker Lake, Seven Islands, Big Black River, and Fort Kent through nearby virgin country. Guide recommended.

2. Allagash River Trip (145 miles) from Northeast Carry on Moosehead Lake to West Branch of the Penobscot River, Moosehorn, Deadwater, Fox Hole, Rocky Rips, and Pine streams, Chesuncook Lake, Umbazooksus Lake, Mud Pond Brook, Chamberlain Lake, Eagle Lake, Churchill Lake, Long Lake to St. Francis or Fort Kent. Guide recommended.

3. Fish River Chain of Lakes Trip (52–93 miles) from St. Agatha near northern end of Long Lake, through Mud (Salmon) Lake, Cross Lake, Square Lake, Eagle Lake to Portage Lake (60 miles), or to St. Agatha (65 miles), or Fish Lake (81 miles). Guide recommended.

4. East Branch of the Penobscot River (118 miles) from Northeast Carry at Moosehead Lake to Chesuncook Lake, Mud Pond, Chamberlain Lake, Telosmis and Telos Lakes, Webster Lake, Second Lake, Grand or Mattagamon Lake, Stair Falls, Grand Falls (Pond, Grand, and Hulling Machine Pitches, Bowlin Falls), to Grindstone. Guide recommended.

5. Fish Stream Trip (18 miles) from Patten through woods to Island Falls. Trout waters; no portage.

6. Molunkus Stream Trip (28 miles) from Sherman Mills to Macwahoc Village on Route 2. Trout waters; 3 portages.

7. Baskahegan Stream and Mattawamkeag River Trip (40–46 miles) from Baskahegan Lake or Danforth to Mattawamkeag on Route 2; Bass and Pickerel water; spring Trout fishing.

8. East Grand Lake and St. Croix River Trip (95 miles) from Orient at head of East Grand Lake through a chain of lakes to Forest City; Spednic Lake to Vanceboro, down St. Croix River to Calais Falls; 6 portages. Guide recommended.

9. Penobscot River Trip (82 miles to Bangor) from Wytopitlock or Mattawamkeag Village to Penobscot tidewater at Bangor; continue downstream to Penobscot Bay. Dangerous white water between Wytopit-

lock and Mattawamkeag; dams at Enfield, Old Town, Orono, Great Works, and Bangor.

10. Union River and Great Pond Trip (36 miles) from Amherst to Great Pond, Brandy Pond, and return. Trout waters.

11. Union River Trip (35 miles) from Amherst to Graham Lake, Union River Bay, to Bluehill Bay. Many harbors on Mt. Desert Island for more tidewater canoeing.

12. Attean Lake Trip (30 miles) from Holeb Pond to Moose, Attean, and Wood ponds. 1 portage of one-fourth mile at Holeb Falls.

13. Moose River Trip (29 miles) from Jackman near Moose River Post Office to Long Pond, Moose River, Brassua Lake, to Moosehead Lake; and may be continued down Moosehead Lake 20 miles to Greenville. Only expert canoeists should attempt this trip; Maine guide essential.

14. Moosehead Lake Trip (200 miles) from Greenville to Northwest Carry and return.

15. Kennebec River Trip (125 miles) from The Forks at the confluence of the Dead and Kennebec rivers to Merrymeeting Bay at mouth of Androscoggin River, to tidewater at Bath.

16. Chain of Ponds Trip (7 miles) northwest of Flagstaff Lake near the New Hampshire boundary; no portage.

17. Flagstaff Lake Flowage and Dead River Trip (22 miles) and continues 14 miles to The Forks of the Kennebec River. Fast water between Dead River Dam and The Forks.

18. Rangeley Lakes Trip (45 miles) from the village of Rangeley on the Rangeley Lake to Mooselookmeguntic Lake, Upper Richardson, Lake (Mollychunkamunk), Lower Richardson Lake (Welokennebacook), and Lake Umbagog. Trip can be continued to the Androscoggin River, Magalloway River, Sawyer Lake, to Parmachenee. Guide recommended. Upper Dam Pool between Mooselookmeguntic and Mollychunkamunk Lakes is a famous Salmon and Trout water.

19. Androscoggin River Trip (114 miles) from Gilead to Merrymeeting Bay and junction of Androscoggin and Kennebec rivers; continue to tidewaters at Bath. A long portage at cities of Auburn and Lewiston.

20. Belgrade Lakes "Big Circle" Trip (32 miles) from East Pond at Clement's Camps, North Pond, Great Pond, Long Pond, Messalonskee Lake (Snow Pond) to Oakland, 3 miles from starting point.

21. Cobbosseecontee Stream and Maranacook Lake Trip (34 miles) from Gardiner up Cobbosseecontee Stream, through Horseshoe and Oxbow ponds to Lake Cobbosseecontee, Juggernot Stream, Lake Annabessacook, Lake Maranacook, to Readfield.

22. Damariscotta River and Lake Trip (50 miles) from Damariscotta Pond into Damariscotta Lake, Muscongus Bay, Pemaquid Pond, Biscay Pond, Pemaquid River, Boyd's Pond to tidewater. Paddle across

John's Bay to Bristol "Gut" and Damariscotta River northeast to starting point. Bass and Pickerel fishing; Duck and Partridge in fall.

23. Kezar Lake and Saco River Trip (84 miles) from North Lovell to Kezar Lake, Saco River to Biddeford.

24. Ossipee River Trip (49 miles) from Effingham Falls, New Hampshire, down Ossipee River to Saco River to Biddeford.

25. Presumpscott River and Sebago Lake Trip (105 miles) from Back Cove in Portland to Sebago Lake, Songo River, village of Harrison on Long Lake, and return. Native waters of Sebago Salmon.

26. West Branch of the Penobscot River Trip (32–78 miles) from Big Eddy below Ripogenus Dam, or Northeast Carry at Moosehead Lake to Chesuncook Lake, Sourdnahunk Stream, Pockwockamus Deadwater, Debsconeag Deadwater, Ambajejus Lake, Pemadumcook Lake, North Twin Lake, to Norcross. Guide recommended.

27. Grand Lake–Machias River Trip (75 miles) from Princeton on Big Lake to Grand Lake Stream, Grand Lake, Pocumcus Lake, Sysladobsis Lake, Fourth Machias Lake, Third Lake, Second Lake, First Lake, Machias River to Whitneyville. Guide recommended.

NOTE: Portages are not listed because there are many alternatives for short and long carries of canoes around dams and shallow waters, and if the "pitch of water" is right a run can be made without a carry.

Wilderness Trips

Novice or expert, young or old, may paddle canoes through Trout waters, explore fantastic chasms, climb majestic peaks, hike through mountain meadows and evergreen forests, leisurely ride horses through primitive areas, or experience white water thrills on neoprene rafts down the "River of No Return," and sleep under a trillion stars according to his choice of relaxation.

There are free open-faced shelters for hikers along the Appalachian Trail through 8 national forests between Maine and Georgia, and closed shelters owned by local Appalachian Trail clubs may be rented for moderate fees. Maps and detailed information are issued by the Appalachian Trail Conference, 1916 Sunderland Place, N.W., Washington 6, D.C.

The Sierra Club provides outings at minimum cost and with maximum pleasures for single persons and families in groups of 6–120 persons under experienced leaders in Alaska, California, Hawaii, Idaho, Maine, New Jersey, New York, Oregon, Utah, Wyoming, and British Columbia. Choice of travel on wilderness outings has a wide range: "cache-and-carry" type traveling with only a knapsack to carry from one food cache previously laid by packstock to the next selected campsite; trips with burros packing in equipment and supplies; "wilderness threshold trips" with camps only 5 or 6 miles from a roadhead and a central commissary for 10 families; the "high trip" with several pack animals and camping for 2 weeks near scenic timberline country; the "highlight trip" combining the techniques of the knapsack and high trips; the sociable base camp not far from a roadhead; and river trips on quiet or rough waters along canyons and primeval forests.

Sierra Club lodges and recreation centers in California: Benson Memorial Hut on the north slope of Mount Anderson (8,687 ft.) 5 miles from Norden and 3 miles from the Cold Creek roadhead; Bradley Hut on the Benson-Ludlow route near the Sierra crest; Clair Tappaan Lodge more than a mile west of Donner Summit near Norden; Guymon Cabins in the Cleveland National Forest, San Diego County; Harwood Memorial Lodge in San Antonio Canyon above Pomona; Hutchinson Lodge at Norden (formerly known as the Sierra Ski Club); Keller Peak Ski Hut in Snow Valley on Big Bear Highway northeast of San Bernardino; Le Conte Memorial Lodge at the terminus of the John Muir Trail in

Yosemite National Park; Ludlow Ski Hut 6 miles west of Chambers Lodge at Lake Tahoe; Muir Shelter on the divide between watersheds of the Kings and San Joaquin rivers in Kings Canyon National Park; Parsons Memorial Lodge west of Lambert Dome in Tuolumne Meadows, Yosemite National Park; Peter Grubb Hut in a bowl at 7,600 feet below Castle Peak (9,114 ft.) north of Donner Pass; San Antonio Ski Hut on southern slope of Mount San Antonio (10,080 ft.) north of Claremont; Shasta Alpine Lodge at about 8,000 feet elevation on Mount Shasta (14,161 ft.). For further information address Sierra Club, 1050 Mills Tower, San Francisco 4, California.

The Wilderness Society sponsors wonderful pack and saddle trips during summer months to the Bob Marshall Wilderness Area in August; the Selway-Bitterroot Wilderness Area in July from Missoula, Montana; the Flat Tops Primitive Area from Glenwood Springs, Colorado; the Rio Grande and San Juan wilderness areas from Durango, Colorado, in August; the Pecos Wilderness Area from Santa Fe, New Mexico, in June and September; the Teton and Yellowstone wilderness regions from Jackson Lake Lodge at Moran, Wyoming, during July. Membership is not required to take these trips. Write to The Wilderness Society, 2144 P Street, N.W., Washington, D.C., for *A Way to The Wilderness*.

Information on hiking trips is also available from the American Forestry Association, a national organization for the advancement of intelligent management and use of forests and related resources of soil, water, wildlife, and outdoor recreation. The association publishes a monthly magazine, *American Forests*; subscription price is $6.00 a year. Write The American Forestry Association, 919 Seventeenth Street, N.W., Washington 6, D.C.

PART III

PART III

Land Mammals

To simplify recognition of protected and unprotected game, the following lists are restricted to species and subspecies named by federal and state regulations and names commonly used by sportsmen. Jackrabbits are separated from other Hares (genus *Lepus*) because many states permit all-year open seasons.*

AMERICAN SABLE. See **MARTEN.**

ANTELOPE, PRONGHORN (*Antilocapra americana*). Food: grasses, plants, shrubs. Habitat: deserts, prairies, sagebrush plains.

ARMADILLO (*Dasypus novemcinctus*). Food: fruit, insects, poultry, worms. Habitat: burrows in brush and open forests.

BADGER (*Taxidea taxus*). Food: birds, eggs, reptiles, squirrels, small mammals. Habitat: open country.

BEAR. Food: carnivorous, fish, fruit, grubs, insects, vegetation. Habitat: forest areas. Alaska Blue, or Glacier (*Euarctos americanus emmonsii*); Alaska Brown, or Yukatat (*Ursus dalli*); Alaska Grizzly (*Ursus alascensis*); Black or Cinnamon (*Euarctos americanus*); Brown or Alaska Peninsula Giant (*Ursus gyas*); California Grizzly (*Ursus californicus*); Grizzly or Silvertip (*Ursus horribilis*); Kodiak Brown (*Ursus middendorffi*); Polar (*Thalarctos maritimus*); Yellowstone Grizzly (*Ursus mirus*).

BEAVER (*Castor canadensis*). Food: roots of water plants, bark, and twigs of trees. Habitat: ponds, lakes, and streams.

BISON (*Bison bison*). Food: grasses. Habitat: plains, wooded areas.

BLARINA. See **SHREW.**

BOAR, WILD (*Sus scrofa*). Food: roots, tuberous plants. Habitat: forests, mountainous areas. See also **PECCARY.**

BOBCAT (*Lynx rufus*). Food: birds, rabbits, small mammals. Habitat: forests.

BRUSH WOLF. See **COYOTE.**

BUFFALO. See **BISON.**

BUSHYTAIL. See **SQUIRREL,** Gray.

CACOMISTLE. See **CAT, RING-TAILED.**

CARAJOU. See **WOLVERINE.**

CARIBOU (*Rangifer caribou*). Food: lichen, grasses, leaves, twigs. Habi-

---

* Information and scoring charts for North American big game trophies are available from the Boone and Crockett Club, 5 Tudor City Pl., New York 17, N.Y.

tat: tundra and forested areas. Dwarf (*Rangifer tarandus dawsoni*); Grant (*Rangifer tarandus granti*); Mountain, or Rocky Mountain (*Rangifer tarandus montanus*); Stone (*Rangifer tarandus stonei*); Woodland (*Rangifer tarandus caribou*).

CAT, RING-TAILED (*Bassariscus astutus*). Food: birds, fruit, poultry, small mammals. Habitat: forests, rocky areas.

CATAMOUNT. See COUGAR.

CHICKAREE. See SQUIRREL, Red.

CHIPMUNK. Food: berries, insects, mice, nuts, seeds. Habitat: brush and rocky areas, open forests. Eastern (*Tamias striatus*); Gray (*Tamias striatus griseus*); Least (*Eutamias minimus*).

CIVET CAT. See CAT, RING-TAILED.

COATI or COATI-MUNDI (*Nasua narica*). Food: birds, fruits, insects, worms, small mammals. Habitat: forests.

CONEY. See PIKA.

COON. See RACCOON.

COUGAR (*Felis concolor*). Food: deer, small mammals. Habitat: forests, mountains, dense swampy areas.

COYOTE (*Canis latrans*). Food: carrion, berries, birds, mammals, rodents. Habitat: brush or wooded areas, ranchlands.

COYPU. See NUTRIA.

DEER. Food: evergreens, grasses, moss, weeds, buds, twigs. Habitat: brush and woodlands. Axis, Hawaiian, or Spotted (*Axis axis*); Black-tailed or Mule (*Odocoileus hemionus*); California Mule (*Odocoileus hemionus californicus*); Columbia Black-tailed (*Odocoileus hemionus columbianus*); Coues, Fantail, or Dwarf White-tailed (*Odocoileus virginianus couesi*); Fallow (*Dama dama*); Kansas or Western White-tailed (*Odocoileus virginianus macrourus*); Sika (*Cervus nippon*); Sitka Black-tailed (*Odocoileus hemionus sitkensis*); Virginia, or White-tailed (*Odocoileus virginianus*).

ELK. Food: buds, twigs, vegetation, roots of waterplants. Habitat: prairies and forests near lakes and streams. American (*Cervus canadensis*); Arizona or Merriman's (*Cervus merriami*); Nelson (*Cervus canadensis nelsoni*); Roosevelt (*Cervus canadensis roosevelti*); Tule (*Cervus nannodes*).

ERMINE. See WEASEL.

EUROPEAN WILD BOAR or WILD PIG. See BOAR, WILD.

FERRET. Food: poultry, prairie dogs, rabbits, small mammals. Habitat: plains and prairies. American (*Mustela putorius*); Black-footed (*Mustela nigripes*).

FISHER (*Martes pennanti*). Food: birds, eggs, mice, rabbits, squirrels. Habitat: forests.

FITCHET. See FERRET.

Fox. Food: berries, birds, eggs, carrion, rabbits, rodents, snakes. Habitat: brush, deserts, fields and wooded areas. Arctic or Blue (*Alopex lagopus*); Black, Cross, Red, or Silver (*Vulpes fulva*); Gray, or Tree (*Urocyon cinereoargenteus*); Kit (*Vulpes macrotis*); Swift (*Vulpes velox*).

Glutton. See **Wolverine**.

Goat. Food: grasses, lichens, plants. Habitat: mountainous areas. Mountain or White (*Oreamnos americanus*); Wild Goat of Hawaii (*Capra hircus*).

Gopher. Food: bulbs, crops, roots, vegetation. Habitat: underground in fields, gardens, pastures, foothills. Botta's Pocket (*Thomomys bottae*); Gray—see **Squirrel**, Franklin's; Georgia (*Geomys pinetis*); Northern Pocket (*Thomomys talpoides*); Plains, or Prairie (*Geomys bursarius*); Yellow-faced (*Cratogeomys castanops*).

Ground hog. See **Woodchuck**.

Hare. Food: berries, evergreens, plants, bark, buds, leaves and twigs of trees. Habitat: fields and forests. Arctic (*Lepus arcticus*); European (*Lepus europaeus*); Little Chief—see **Pika**; Varying (*Lepus americanus*).

Hedgehog. See **Porcupine**.

Jackrabbit. Food: berries, farm crops, vegetation. Habitat: open country, fields and farmlands. Black-tailed (*Lepus californicus*); Prairie (*Lepus townsendii mearnsii*); White-sided (*Lepus alleni*); White-tailed (*Lepus townsendii*).

Jackass deer. See **Elk**.

Jackass hare. See **Jackrabbit**.

Jaguar. Food: aquatic animals, fish, mammals. Habitat: brush, forests, open country. American (*Felis onca*); Mexican (*Felis onca hernandesii*).

Javelina. See **Peccary**, Collared.

Leopard. See **Jaguar**.

Little chief hare. See **Pika**.

Loup-cervier. See **Lynx**.

Lynx. Food: birds, rabbits, small mammals. Habitat: forests. Bay, see **Bobcat**; Canada or Common (*Lynx canadensis*).

Marmot. Food: grasses, farm crops, plants. Habitat: rocky areas. Hoary or Whistler (*Marmota caligata*); Maryland—see **Woodchuck**; Yellow-bellied (*Marmota flaviventris*).

Marten or **martin** (*Martes americana*). Food: eggs, birds, mice, rabbits, raccoons, squirrels. Habitat: forests.

Mink (*Mustela vison*). Food: birds, fish, shellfish, frogs, small mammals, poultry. Habitat: marshlands and forests.

Mole. Food: earthworms, insects, plants, small mammals. Habitat: underground near gardens, crops, and fields. Brewer's or Hairy-tailed (*Parascalops breweri*); Common or Eastern (*Scalopus aquaticus*); Prairie (*Scalopus aquaticus machrinus*); Shrew (*Neürotrichus gibbsii*); Star-nosed (*Condylura cristata*); Western (*Scapanus townsendii*).

MOOSE. Food: water plants, vegetation. Habitat: near shallow water in forests. Alaska (*Alces americana gigas*); American (*Alces americana*); Shiras or Wyoming (*Alces americana shirasi*).

MOUNTAIN GOAT. See GOAT.

MOUNTAIN LION. See COUGAR.

MOUNTAIN SHEEP. See SHEEP.

MUSK HOG. See PECCARY, Collared.

MUSK OX (*Ovibos moschatus*). Food: grasses, lichens, leaves, twigs. Habitat: Arctic coast and tundra regions.

MUSKRAT. Food: small aquatic mammals, vegetation. Habitat: fresh- or saltwater marshes, ponds and streams. Common (*Ondatra zibethicus*); Dismal Swamp (*Ondatra zibethicus macrodon*); Southern (*Ondatra zibethicus rivalicus*).

MUSQUASH. See MUSKRAT.

NUTRIA (*Myocaster coypus*). Food: vegetation. Habitat: marshland.

OCELOT (*Felis pardalis*). Food: birds, small mammals. Habitat: dense forests.

OPOSSUM. Food: birds, poultry, small mammals, fruit, vegetables, eggs. Habitat: swamps, forests near farming areas. Common (*Didelphis marsupialus*); Texas (*Didelphis marsupialus texensis*).

OTTER. Food: crayfish, fish, frogs. Habitat: waterways. Canada, Land, or River (*Lutra canadensis*); Sea (*Enhydra lutris*).

PAINTER or PANTHER. See COUGAR.

PECCARY. Food: grains, nuts, roots, fruit, vegetables. Habitat: marshy woodlands. Collared or Sonora Collared (*Tayassu tajacu*); Texas Collared (*Tayassu tajacu angulatus*).

PEKAN. See FISHER; MARTEN.

PIG, WILD. See BOAR, WILD; PECCARY.

PIKA. Food: grasses, vegetation. Habitat: crevices of rocks. Colorado (*Ochotona princeps saxatilis*); Little Chief (*Ochotona princeps*); Sierra Nevada (*Ochotona princeps schisticeps*).

POLAR OX. See MUSK OX.

POLECAT. See SKUNK.

PORCUPINE. Food: plants, farm crops, nuts, bark, leaves and twigs. Habitat: forested areas. Eastern (*Erethizon dorsatum*); Yellow-haired (*Erethizon dorsatum epizanthus*).

PORKY. See PORCUPINE.

POSSUM. See OPOSSUM.

Prairie dog (*Cynomys ludovicianus*). Food: grasses, insects, plants. Habitat: underground burrows in prairies.

Prairie hare. See Jackrabbit.

Prairie wolf. See Coyote.

Pronghorn. See Antelope.

Puma. See Cougar.

Rabbit. Food: farm crops, vegetation. Habitat: open country, brush and forested areas, marsh or swamp lands. Audubon, Desert, or Sacramento (*Sylvilagus audubonii*); Brush (*Sylvilagus bachmani*); Marsh (*Sylvilagus palustris*); Mearns' Cottontail (*Sylvilagus floridanus mearnsii*); New England or Northeastern (*Sylvilagus transitionalis*); Nuttall's Cottontail (*Sylvilagus nuttallii*); Pygmy (*Sylvilagus idahoensis*); Snowshoe—see Hare, Varying; Swamp (*Sylvilagus aquaticus*).

Raccoon. Food: birds, eggs, crops, fruit, insects, poultry. Habitat: farmlands, forested areas and swamps. Desert (*Procyon lotor pallidus*); North American (*Procyon lotor*).

Rat. Food: birds, farm crops, insects, seeds, crustaceans. Habitat: deserts, fields, forests, fresh- and saltwater marshes. Black (*Rattus rattus*); Bushy-tailed Wood (*Neotama cinerea*); Cotton (*Sigmodon hispidus*); Coypu—see Nutria; Eastern, Packrat, or Wood (*Neotoma floridana*); Kangaroo (*Dipodomys deserti*); Rice (*Oryzomys palustris*); Southern Plains Wood (*Neotoma micropus*); White-throated Wood (*Neotoma albigula*).

Ring-tailed cat. See Cat, ring-tailed.

Ringtails. See Raccoon.

Russian boar. See Boar, wild.

Sable. See Marten.

Sheep. Food: vegetation. Habitat: open mountainous region. American Bighorn, Bighorn, Mountain, or Rocky Mountain Bighorn (*Ovis canadensis*); Aoudad or Barbary (*Ammotragus lervia*); Audubon or Badlands Bighorn (*Ovis canadensis auduboni*); Dall's (*Ovis dalli*); Hawaiian (*Ovis aries*); Rimrock Bighorn (*Ovis canadensis californiana*); Kenai (*Ovis dalli kenaiensis*).

Shrew. Food: earthworms, grubs, insects, plants, carrion. Habitat: marshes, meadows, brush, mountainous and tundra areas. Blarina, Mole, or Short-tailed (*Blarina brevicauda*); Least, Lesser, Short-tailed, or Little (*Cryptotis parva*); Masked (*Sorex cinereus*); Smoky (*Sorex fumeus*).

Skunk. Food: birds, eggs, fruit, insects, rodents. Habitat: fields, brush, farm, and woodlands. Civet (*Spilogale putorius interrupta*); Common (*Mephitis mephitis*); Eastern spotted or striped (*Spilogale* *putorius*); Hognose (*Conepatus mesoleucus*); Little Striped (*Spilogale putorius ambarvalis*).

SKUNK-BEAR. See **WOLVERINE.**

SQUIRREL. Food: birds, eggs, crops, insects, plants, pine cones, seeds, nuts, young mammals. Habitat: brush, meadows, forests. Flying (*Glaucomys volans*); Northern Flying (*Glaucomys sabrinus*). *Ground:* Arctic or Arctic Ground (*Citellus parryii*); Franklin's or Franklin's Ground (*Citellus franklinii*); Golden-mantled (*Citellus lateralis*); Richardson's or Richardson's Ground (*Citellus richardsonii*); Rock or Rock Ground (*Citellus variegatus*); Spotted or Spotted Ground (*Citellus spilosoma*); Striped, or Thirteen-Lined (*Citellus tridecimlineatus*). *Tree:* Abert, Tassel-eared, or Tuft-eared (*Sciurus aberti*); Cat or Fox (*Sciurus niger*); Eastern Red (*Tamiasciurus hudsonicus*); Gray (*Sciurus carolinensis*); Mountain Red (*Tamiasciurus hudsonicus fremontii*); Western Fox (*Sciurus niger rufiventer*); Western Red or Douglas (*Tamiasciurus douglasii*).

SWAMP COTTONTAIL. See **RABBIT,** Swamp.

TEXAS PECCARY. See **PECCARY.**

TIMBER WOLF. See **WOLF,** Gray.

TREE SQUIRREL. See **SQUIRREL.**

VARYING HARE. See **HARE,** Varying.

WAPITI. See **ELK.**

WEASEL. Food: birds, small mammals, snakes. Habitat: brush, farm lands, prairies, rocky areas, swamps, and woodlands. Bonaparte, Ermine, or Short-tailed (*Mustela erminea*); Eastern or New York (*Mustela frenata noveboracensis*); Least (*Mustela rixosa*); Long-tailed (*Mustela frenata longicauda*).

WHISTLING PIG. See **WOODCHUCK.**

WILD BOAR. See **BOAR,** WILD; **PECCARY.**

WILD CAT. See **BOBCAT; CAT,** RING-TAILED

WOLF. Food: birds, fish, fruit, mammals, snakes, carnivorous. Habitat: caves, plains, forests, and remote regions. Alaska Black (*Canis lupus pambasileus*); Alaska Tundra (*Canis lupus tundrarum*); Brush— see **COYOTE;** Florida Red (*Canis niger*); Gray, Loafer, or Timber (*Canis lupus*); Great Plains or Buffalo (*Canis lupus nubilus*); Kenai Peninsula (*Canis lupus alces*); Mississippi Valley Red (*Canis niger gregoryi*); Rocky Mountain (*Canis lupus irremotus*); Texas Gray (*Canis lupus monstrabilis*); Texas Red (*Canis niger rufus*).

WOLVERINE. (*Gulo luscus*). Food: carnivorous, carrion. Habitat: brush, forests, and mountainous regions.

WOODCHUCK. (*Marmota monax*). Food: farm crops, fruit, birds, mice, grasses. Habitat: underground in field, brush, and rocky areas. Western Rockchuck (*Marmota caligata*).

Marine Mammals

DOLPHIN. Food: fish, squid. Habitat: coastal and offshore waters. Black (*Globicephala melaena*); Black Short-finned (*Globicephala macrorhyncha*); Bottle-nosed (*Tursiops truncatus*); Common (*Delphinus delphis*).

ELEPHANT SEAL. See **SEA ELEPHANT**.

PORPOISE (*Phocoena phocoena*). Food: fish, squid. Habitat: coastal and offshore waters.

SEA BEAR. See **SEAL**, Northern.

SEA ELEPHANT. (*Mirounga augustirostris*). Food: fish. Habitat: offshore islands and waters.

SEA HORSE. See **WALRUS**.

SEA LION. Food: crustaceans, fish, mollusks. Habitat: coastal islands and offshore waters. Black or California (*Zalophus californianus*); Northern or Stellar (*Eumetopias jubata*).

SEAL. Food: crustaceans, fish, mollusks. Habitat: coastal and offshore islands and waters. Alaska Fur (*Callorhinus ursinus*), also called Northern Seal; Bearded (*Erignathus barbatus*); Gillespie's Hair— see **SEA LION**; Black; Harbor or Leopard (*Phoca vitulina*); Ribbon (*Phoca fasciata*); Ringed (*Phoca hispida*), called Netchek by Eskimos.

WALRUS (*Odobenus rosmarus*). Food: mollusks dug with tusks. Habitat: Arctic and Bering Sea ice floes, islands and waters.

WHALE, Beluga or White (*Delphinapterus leucas*). Food: fish. Habitat: coastal and offshore waters.

Auklet. Food: fish. Habitat: Aleutian Islands and North Pacific. Crested (*Aethia cristatella*); Least (*Aethia pusilla*); Rhinoceros (*Cerorhinca monocerata*).

American kestrel. See Falcon, Rusty-crowned.

Avocet (*Recurvirostra americana*). Food: crustaceans, insects, seeds. Habitat: shallow lakes and ponds.

Bald-crown, baldface, baldhead, baldpate duck. See Widgeon, American.

Bartram's tattler. See Plover, Upland.

Bastard broadbill. See Duck.

Bay blackhead, bay broadbill, bay shuffler, beachcomber, beetle-head. See Scaup, American.

Bittern. Food: amphibians, fish, insects. Habitat: fresh and saltwater marshes. American (*Botaurus lentiginosus*); Least (*Ixobrychus exilis*).

Black jack. See Duck, Black; Scaup, Marsh Bluebill.

Black warrior. See Hawk, Harlan's.

Blackbird. Food: fruit, grain, insects, weed seeds. Habitat: farmlands, fields, and swamps. Brewer's (*Euphagus cyanocephalus*); Cow—see Cowbird; Red-winged or Swamp (*Agelaius phoeniceus*); Rusty (*Euphagus carolinus*); Yellow-headed (*Xanthocephalus xanthocephalus*).

Black-headed broadbill, black-headed duck, black-headed raft duck. See Scaup, American.

Blatherskite. See Duck, Ruddy.

Blue darter. See Goshawk; Hawk, Cooper's, Sharp-shinned.

Blue peter. See Coot, American.

Bluebill. See Scaup.

Bobwhite. See Quail.

Bogsucker. See Woodcock.

Bottle-nosed diver. See Scoter, Surf.

Bracket or Breakhorn. See Merganser, American.

Brant. Food: eel grass, insects. Habitat: saltwater bays. American or Common (*Branta bernicla*); Bald, Bald-headed, Blue—see Goose, Blue; Black or Sea (*Branta nigricans*); Canada—see Goose, Canada; Gray, Prairie, Speckled, see Goose, White-fronted; White—see Goose, Snow.

BROADBILL. See SCAUP; SHOVELER.

BROAD-FACED MALLARD. See SHOVELER.

BUCKEYE, BULL-NECK, BUNTY. See SCAUP, Ring-necked.

BUFFLE-HEAD, BUTTERBALL. See DUCK.

BULL WHITEWING. See SCOTER, White-winged.

BUTCHER-BIRD. See SHRIKE.

BUTTER DUCK. See DUCK, Ruddy.

BUZZARD. See VULTURE.

BUZZ-BOMB. See DOVE.

CACCAWEE. See DUCK, Long-tailed.

CALICO-BACK. See TURNSTONE.

CAMP ROBBER. See JAY.

CANVASBACK. See DUCK, Canvasback.

CARRION CROW. See VULTURE, Black.

CHACHALACA (*Ortalis vetula*). Food: berries, fruit, insects. Habitat: thick chaparral bordering forests and streams.

CHAPARRAL COCK. See ROADRUNNER.

CHICACOCK. See GADWALL.

CHOCKS. See GRACKLES.

CLAPPER. See RAIL, Clapper.

COCK-OF-THE-PLAINS. See GROUSE, Sage.

COCK-PIE. See DUCK, Barrow's Golden-eye.

COCK ROBIN. See MERGANSER, Hooded.

CONDOR, CALIFORNIA (*Gymnogyps californianus*). Food: carrion. Habitat: canyons and rocky mountains.

COOT. Food: grains, grasses, aquatic vegetation, insects. Habitat: streams, fresh- and saltwater marshes. American, Ivory-billed, or White-billed (*Fulica americana*); Bay, Black, Broad-billed, Horsehead, River, Rock, Sea, Smutty, Whistling, Yellow-billed, Yellow-nosed—see SCOTER.

COPPERHEAD or CUBHEAD. See DUCK, American Golden.

CORMORANT. Food: aquatic life including fish. Habitat: lakes, rivers, and rocky seacoasts. Baird or Pelagic (*Phalacrocorax pelagicus resplendens*); Brandt (*Phalacrocorax penicillatus*); Double-crested (*Phalacrocorax auritus*); Great (*Phalacrocorax carbo*).

CORN THIEF. See CROW, American.

COTTONHEAD. See MERGANSER, Hooded.

COTTONTOP. See QUAIL, Blue.

COWBIRD (*Molothrus ater*). Food: berries, grains, insects, seeds. Habitat: fields, open woods.

COWEEN. See DUCK, Long-tailed.

CRAKE. See RAIL, Black, Yellow; SORA.

CRANE. Food: amphibians, aquatic vegetation, grain, insects, rodents, seeds. Habitat: marshlands. Little Brown or Sandhill (*Grus cana-densis*); Whooping (*Grus americana*).

CROCKER. See BRANT, American.

CROW. Food: bird eggs, carrion, crustaceans, grain, insects, seeds. Habitat: farmlands, fields, and forests. American (*Corvus brachyrhynchos*); Fish (*Corvus ossifragus*)—habitat: inland waters, seashores; Pond or Sea—see COOT, American.

CROW BLACKBIRD. See GRACKLE.

CROW DUCK. See COOT, American.

CUCKOO. Food: insects. Habitat: brush and farmlands. American or Yellow-billed (*Coccyzus americanus*); Blackbilled (*Coccyzus erythropthalmus*); Ground—see ROADRUNNER.

CURLEW. Food: berries, insects, larvae, shellfish, snails, worms. Habitat: prairie, tundra, and tidal shores. Buzzard, Long-billed, or Sickle-billed (*Numenius americanus*); Eskimo, Little, or Short-billed (*Numenius borealis*); Jack or Whimbrel (*Numenius phaeopus*); Spike-billed—see GODWIT, Marbled.

DABBLER. See DUCK, Mallard, Pintail.

DABCHICK, DIPCHICK, DIPPER. See GREBE, Pied-billed.

DARTER. See BLUE DARTER; SNAKEBIRD.

DIDAPPER. See MERGANSER, Hooded.

DIPPER. See DUCK, Bufflehead.

DIPTAIL DIVER, DOPPER. See DUCK, Ruddy.

DIVER. See DIVING DUCKS; GREBE; LOON.

DIVING DUCKS. Black-bellied Tree, Bufflehead, Canvasback, Fulvous Tree, Golden-eye, Harlequin, Old Squaw, Redhead, and Ruddy DUCKS; EIDER; MERGANSER; SCAUP; SCOTER.

DOODLER. See WOODCOCK.

DOVE. Food: grains, weed seeds. Habitat: farmlands, open forests. Barred (*Geopelia striata*); Ground (*Columbigallina passerina*); Key West Quaildove (*Geotrygon chrysia*); Lace-necked or Spotted (*Streptopelia chinensis*); Mourning, Rain, or Turtledove (*Zenaidura macroura*); Rock—see PIGEON, WILD; White-winged (*Zenaida asiatica*); Zenaida (*Zenaida aurita*).

DOWITCHER. Food: insects, mollusks, worms. Habitat: mudflats, fresh- and saltwater marshes. Long-billed (*Limnodromus scolopaceus*); Short-billed (*Limnodromus griseus*).

DUCK. Food: aquatic vegetation, grains, grasses, insects, small fish, mollusks, seeds. Habitat: beaches, lakes, streams, rice fields, fresh- and saltwater marshes. American Golden, American Golden-eye, Brass-eye, Brighteye, Conjuring, Fiddler, Whistler (*Bucephala clangula*); Barrow's Golden-eye, Rocky Mountain (*Bucephala islandica*); Big

Fish, Fisher, Fisherman, Redbreasted Fish Duck—see MERGANSER, American, Redbreasted; Big Sea, Isle of Shoals, Shoal, Squam Duck —see EIDER, American; Black, Black Mallard, Brown Mallard, Dusky, Marsh, Nigger, Pond, Redlegged (*Anas rubripes*); Black-bellied Tree (*Dendrocygna autumnalis*); Blaten, or Creek—see GAD-WALL; Booby, Deaf, Indian, Squaw, Siwash—see SCOTER, American; Buffle, Bufflehead, Buffalo-headed, Butterball, Dipper, Robin, Scotch, Spirit (*Bucephala albeola*); Can, Canvasback, Horse, Red-headed Bullneck, Whiteback (*Aythya valisineria*); Common Gold-eye (*Bucephala clangula*); Crow, Fan-crested, Frog, Oyster, Pheasant, Tufflehead—see MERGANSER, Hooded; Diamond, Wheat, Whistling —see WIDGEON, American; Fish—see MERGANSER, Hooded; Florida (*Anas fulvigula*); Fulvous Tree (*Dendrocygna bicolor helva*); Gray— see GADWALL; Harlequin, Blue Streak, Circus, Painted, Rock, Totem Pole (*Histrionicus histrionicus*); Long-tailed, Mammy, Old Squaw, Organ, Singing, Scolder, Son-Son-Sally, Swallowtail (*Clangula hyemalis*); Mallard, Green, Ice, Prairie, Redlegged, Snow, or Yellow-legged Mallard (*Anas platyrhynchos*); Broadfaced or Laughing Mallard—see SHOVELER; Mottled (*Anas fulvigula maculosa*); Mule— see SHOVELER; New Mexico (*Anas diazi*); Pintail, Picket-tail, Sharp-tail, Spiketail, Spindletail, Split-tail, Spring, Spring-tail, Trilby (*Anas acuta*); Ringbill, Ring-necked—see SCAUP, Marsh Bluebilled; Red-head (*Aythya americana*); Ruddy, Deaf, Dummy, Fool, Heavy-tailed, Rudder, Shanty, Sleepy, or Soldier (*Oxyura jamaicensis*); Tufted— see SCAUP, Marsh Bluebilled; Wood, Acorn, Crestwood, Swamp, (*Aix sponsa*); see also EIDER, GADWALL, MERGANSER, SCAUP, SCOTER, SHOVELER, TEAL, WIDGEON.

DUN-DIVER. See MERGANSER.

DUNLIN (*Erolia alpina*). Food: insects, worms. Habitat: beaches, flats.

DUSKY HEN. See GROUSE, Dusky.

DUSKY MALLARD. See DUCK, Black.

EAGLE. Food: birds, small mammals. Habitat: mountainous terrain. American, Bald, White-headed (*Haliaeetus leucocephalus*); Golden or War (*Aquila chrysaetos*).

EGRET. Food: amphibians, fish, insects. Habitat: streams, fresh- and saltwater marshes. American, Common, or White (*Casmerodius albus*); Snowy (*Leucophoyx thula*).

EIDER. Food: crustaceans, mollusks. Habitat: rocky seacoasts, islands, and large lakes. American or Common (*Somateria mollissima*); King (*Somateria spectabilis*); Spectacled (*Actonetta fischeri*); Steller's (*Polysticta stelleri*).

FALCON. Food: birds, insects, small mammals. Habitat: fields, forests, cliffs, and seacoasts. Gyrfalcon (*Falco rusticolus*); Peregrine (*Falco peregrinus*); Prairie (*Falco mexicanus*); Rusty Crowned (*Falco sparverius*).

FISH DUCK. See MERGANSER.

FISH HAWK. See OSPREY.

FOOL HEN. See GROUSE, Franklin's.

FOOL QUAIL. See QUAIL, Mearn's.

FROST BIRD. See PLOVER, American Golden.

FULMAR (*Fulmarus glacialis*). Food: crustaceans, fish, squid. Habitat: Atlantic Ocean islands.

FUZZYHEAD. See MERGANSER, Hooded.

GADWALL (*Anas strepera*). Food: aquatic vegetation, acorns, grains, insects, small fish. Habitat: lakes, streams, fresh- and saltwater marshes.

GALLINULE. Food: aquatic plants, berries, crustaceans, frogs, insects. Habitat: fresh- and saltwater marshes. Common (*Gallinula chloropus*); Purple (*Porphyrula martinica*).

GALOOT. See GOOSE, Ross's.

GANNET (*Morus bassanus*). Food: fish. Habitat: seacoasts.

GODWIT. Food: crustaceans, insects, shellfish, marine worms. Habitat: mudflats, fresh- and saltwater marshes. Hudsonian (*Limosa haemastica*); Marbled (*Limosa fedoa*).

GOGGLENOSE. See SCOTER, Surf.

GOLDEN-EYE. See DUCK.

GONY or GOOSANDER. See MERGANSER, American, Redbreasted.

GOOSE. Food: aquatic vegetation, grains, grasses, insects. Habitat: fields, lakes, streams, fresh- and saltwater marshes. Alaska, Arctic, Lesser Snow, White (*Chen hyperborea*); Barnacle (*Branta leucopsis*); Blue, Blue Snow, Blue-winged, Eagle, Eagle-headed (*Chen caerulescens*); Brant, Burnt, Clatter, Light-bellied—see BRANT, American; Bullneck, Cackling, Crow (*Branta canadensis minima*); Canada, Bay, Black-headed, Black-necked, Gray, Long-necked, Northern (*Branta canadensis*); Emperor, Japanese, Painted, White-headed (*Philacte canagica*); Gray, Mud, Lesser Canada, Short-necked, Southern (*Branta canadensis leucopareia*); Great Basin Canada (*Branta canadensis moffitti*); Greater Snow (*Chen hyperborea atlantica*); Hawaiian or Nene (*Branta sandwicensis*); Hutchin's Little Canada, Little Gray, Little Wild, Richardson's (*Branta canadensis hutchinsi*); Ross's (*Chen rossi*); Sea—see PHALAROPE, Wilson's; Western Canada (*Branta canadensis fulva*); White-fronted, Laughing, Mottled, Texas, Yellow-legged (*Anser albifrons*).

GOSHAWK (*Accipiter gentilis*). Food: birds, small mammals. Habitat: forests.

GRACKLE. Food: berries, crustaceans, grains, insects. Habitat: fields,

BLACK BEAR
(black and cinnamon phase)
Euarctos americanus

ALASKA PENINSULA GIANT
Ursus gyas

GRIZZLY BEAR
Ursus horribilis

POLAR BEAR
Thalarctos maritimus

WHITE-TAILED DEER
Odocoileus virginianus

BLACK-TAILED DEER
Odocoileus hemionus columbianus

MULE DEER
Odocoileus hemionus

MOOSE
Alces americana

ELK
Cervus canadensis

FALLOW DEER
Dama dama

SIKA DEER
Cervus nippon

AXIS DEER
Axis axis

WOODLAND CARIBOU
Rangifer caribou

PRONGHORN ANTELOPE
Antilocapra americana

WILD GOAT
Capra hircus

ROCKY MOUNTAIN GOAT
Oreamnos americanus

BARBARY SHEEP
Ammotragus lervia

BIGHORN SHEEP
Ovis canadensis

BOBCAT
Lynx rufus

CANADA LYNX
Lynx canadensis

COUGAR
Felis concolor

WILD BOAR
Sus scrofa

COLLARED PECCARY
Tayassu tajacu

GRAY FOX
Urocyon cinereoargenteus

RED FOX
Vulpes fulva

GRAY WOLF
Canis lupus

COYOTE
Canis latrans

RING-TAILED CAT
Bassariscus astutus

RACCOON
Procyon lotor

BADGER
Taxidea taxus

MARTEN
Martes americana

WOLVERINE
Gulo luscus

SHORT-TAILED WEASEL (winter and summer)
Mustela erminea

MINK
Mustela vison

RIVER OTTER
Lutra canadensis

SEA OTTER
Enhydra lutris

WOODCHUCK
Marmota monax

BLACK-TAILED PRAIRIE DOG
Cynomys ludovicianus

NUTRIA
Myocaster coypus

OPOSSUM
Didelphis marsupialus

STRIPED (THIRTEEN-LINED) SQUIRREL
Citellus tridecimlineatus

EASTERN RED SQUIRREL
Tamiasciurus hudsonicus

FRANKLIN'S GROUND SQUIRREL
Citellus franklinii

VARYING HARE (winter and summer
Lepus americanus

GRAY SQUIRREL (black and gray phase)
Sciurus carolinensis

MEARNS' COTTONTAIL
Sylvilagus floridanus

BLACK-TAILED JACKRABBIT
Lepus californicus

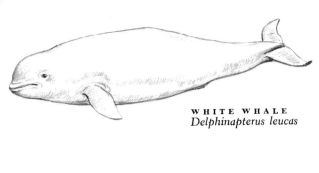

WHITE WHALE
Delphinapterus leucas

HARBOR PORPOISE
Phocoena-phocoena

CALIFORNIA SEA LION
Zalophus californianus

LEOPARD SEAL
Phoca vitulina

NORTHERN SEAL
Callorhinus ursinus

WALRUS
Odobenus rosmarus

WHISTLING SWAN
Olor columbianus

AMERICAN WIDGEON
Mareca americana

SHOVELER
Spatula clypeata

PINTAIL
Anas acuta

BLUE GOOSE
Chen caerulescens

CANADA GOOSE
Branta canadensis

(AMERICAN) WHITE-FRONTED GOOSE
Anser albifrons

ROSS'S GOOSE
Chen rossi

(AMERICAN) BRANT
Branta bernicla

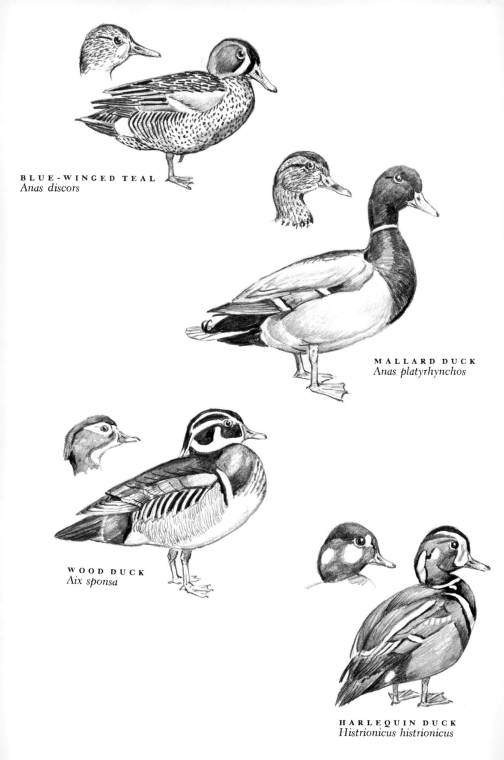

BLUE-WINGED TEAL
Anas discors

MALLARD DUCK
Anas platyrhynchos

WOOD DUCK
Aix sponsa

HARLEQUIN DUCK
Histrionicus histrionicus

RING-NECK SCAUP
Aythya collaris

GREATER SCAUP
Aythya marila

AMERICAN GOLDEN-EYE DUCK
Bucephala clangula

REDHEAD DUCK
Aythya americana

CANVASBACK DUCK
Aythya valisineria

RUDDY DUCK
Oxyurd jamaicensis

OLD SQUAW DUCK
Clangula hyemalis

BUFFLEHEAD DUCK
Bucephala albeola

BLACK DUCK
Anas rubripes

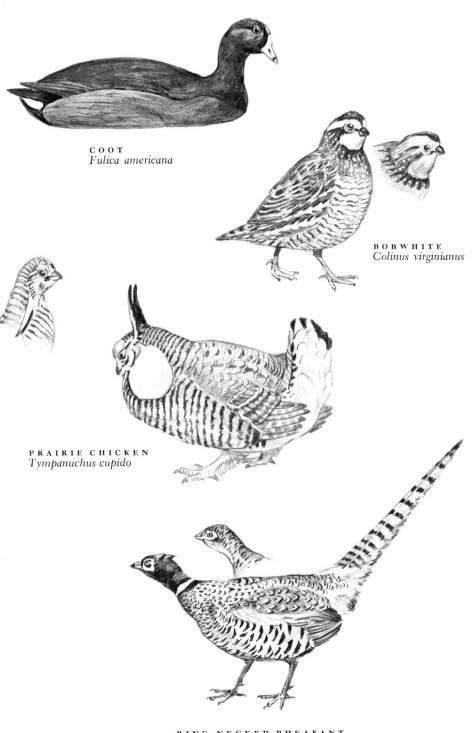

COOT
Fulica americana

BOBWHITE
Colinus virginianus

PRAIRIE CHICKEN
Tympanuchus cupido

RING-NECKED PHEASANT
Phasianus colchicus

HARLEQUIN QUAIL
Cyrtonyx montezumae

CALIFORNIA QUAIL
Lophortyx californica

SCALED QUAIL
Callipepla squamata

GAMBEL'S QUAIL
Lophortyx gambelii

MOUNTAIN QUAIL
Oreortyx pictus

CHUKAR PARTRIDGE
Alectoris graecia

GRAY (HUNGARIAN) PARTRIDGE
Perdix perdix

COMMON SNIPE
Capella gallinago delicata

AMERICAN WOODCOCK
Philohela minor

KING RAIL
Rallus elegans

VIRGINIA RAIL
Rallus limicola

SHARP-TAILED GROUSE
Pedioecetes phasianellus

RICHARDSON'S GROUSE
Dendragapus obscurus

SPRUCE GROUSE
Canachites canadensis

SAGE GROUSE
Centrocercus urophasianus

RUFFED GROUSE
Bonasa umbellus

COOPER'S HAWK
Accipiter cooperii

ACCIPITER

SHARP-SHINNED HAWK
Accipiter striatus

FALCON

HARRIS HAWK
Parabuteo unicinctus harrisi

SPARROW HAWK
(Rusty-Crowned Falcon)
Falco sparverius

BUTEO

RED-SHOULDERED HAWK *Buteo lineatus*

TURKEY VULTURE
Cathartes aura

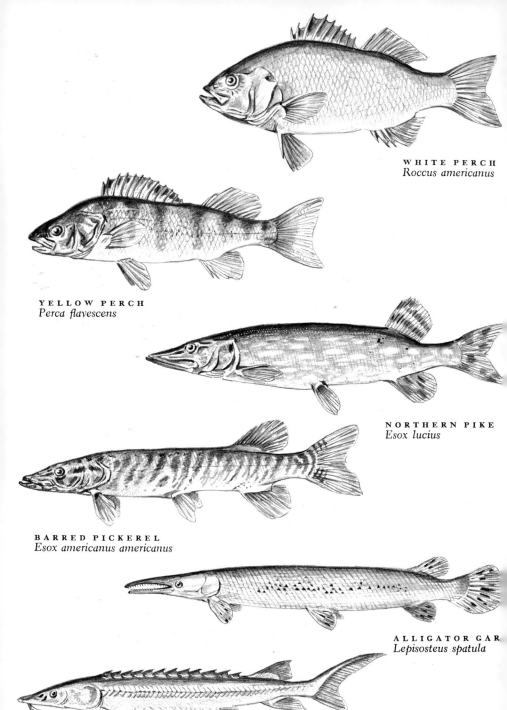

WHITE PERCH
Roccus americanus

YELLOW PERCH
Perca flavescens

NORTHERN PIKE
Esox lucius

BARRED PICKEREL
Esox americanus americanus

ALLIGATOR GAR
Lepisosteus spatula

WHITE (COLUMBIA RIVER) STURGEON
Acipenser transmontanus

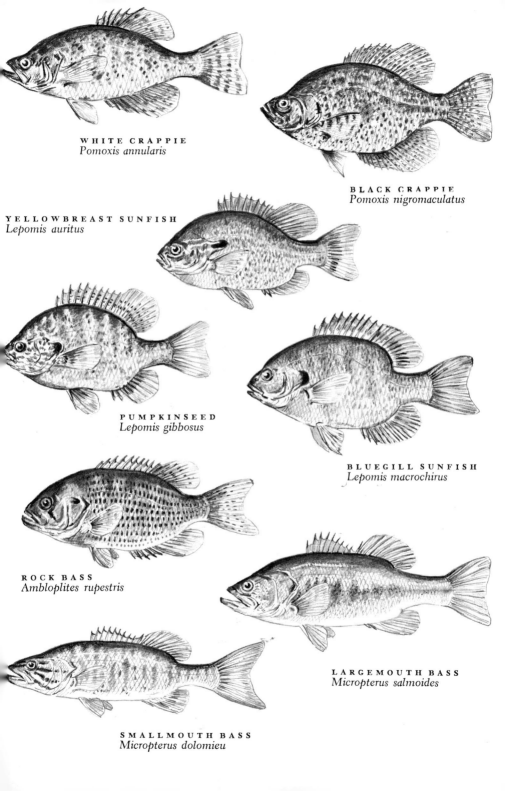

WHITE CRAPPIE
Pomoxis annularis

BLACK CRAPPIE
Pomoxis nigromaculatus

YELLOWBREAST SUNFISH
Lepomis auritus

PUMPKINSEED
Lepomis gibbosus

BLUEGILL SUNFISH
Lepomis macrochirus

ROCK BASS
Ambloplites rupestris

LARGEMOUTH BASS
Micropterus salmoides

SMALLMOUTH BASS
Micropterus dolomieu

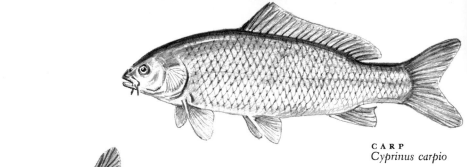

CARP
Cyprinus carpio

BROWN BULLHEAD
Ictalurus nebulosus

FLATHEAD CATFISH
Pylodictis olivaris

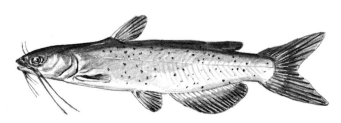

CHANNEL CATFISH
Ictalurus punctatus

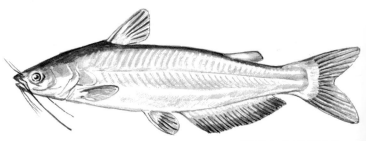

BLUE CATFISH
Ictalurus furcatus

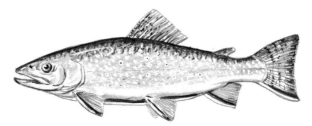

BROOK TROUT
Salvelinus fontinalis

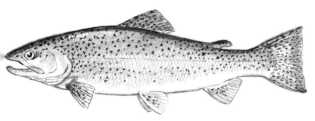

RAINBOW TROUT
Salmo gairdneri

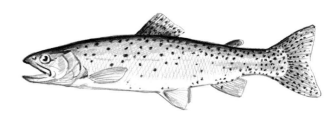

CUTTHROAT TROUT
Salmo clarki

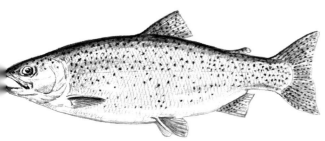

KAMLOOPS TROUT
Salmo kamloops

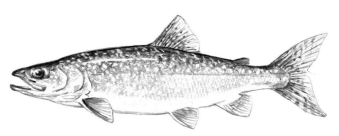

LAKE (MACKINAW) TROUT
Salvelinus namaycush

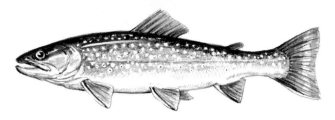

DOLLY VARDEN TROUT
Salvelinus malma

BROWN TROUT
Salmo trutta

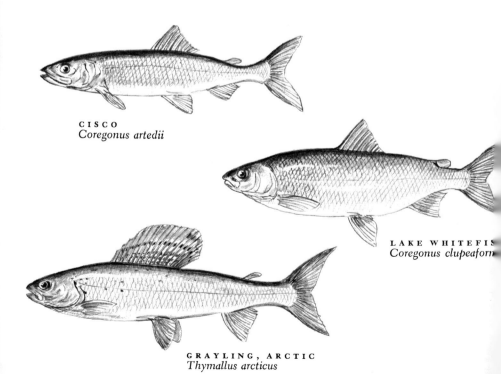

CISCO
Coregonus artedii

LAKE WHITEFIS
Coregonus clupeaforn

GRAYLING, ARCTIC
Thymallus arcticus

KOKANEE SALMON (young adult)
Oncorhynchus nerka kennerlyi

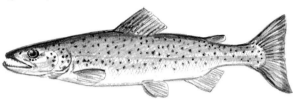

LANDLOCKED SALMON
Salmo salar sebago

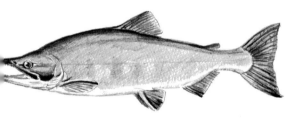

SOCKEYE SALMON (male at spawning time)
Oncorhynchus nerka

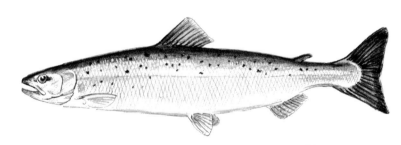

ATLANTIC SALMON
Salmo salar

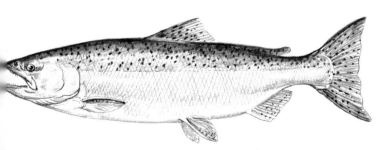

CHINOOK (KING) SALMON
Oncorhynchus tschawytscha

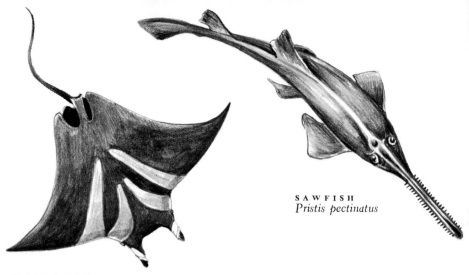

SAWFISH
Pristis pectinatus

MANTA RAY
Manta birostris

MUSKELLUNGE
Esox masquinongy

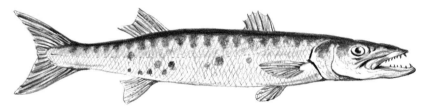

GREAT BARRACUDA
Sphyraena barracuda

MACKEREL (PORBEAGLE) SHARK
Lamna nasus

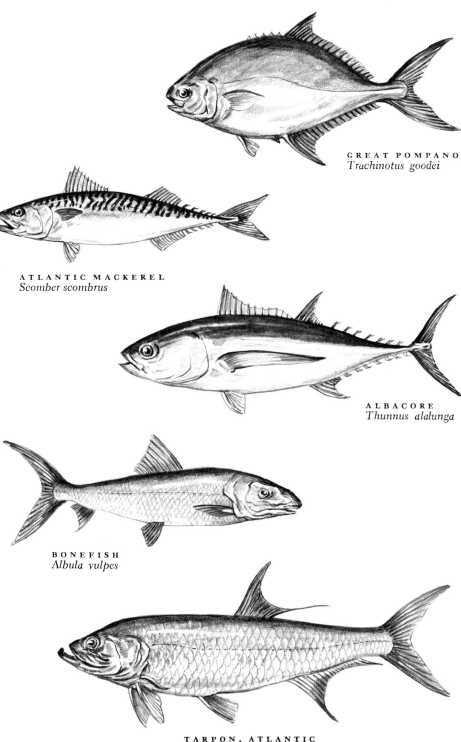

GREAT POMPANO
Trachinotus goodei

ATLANTIC MACKEREL
Scomber scombrus

ALBACORE
Thunnus alalunga

BONEFISH
Albula vulpes

TARPON, ATLANTIC
Tarpon atlanticus

ATLANTIC COD
Gadus callarias

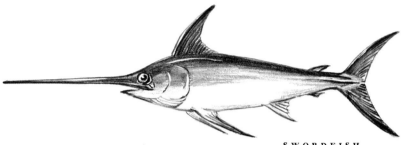

SWORDFISH
Xiphias gladius

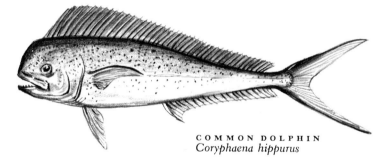

COMMON DOLPHIN
Coryphaena hippurus

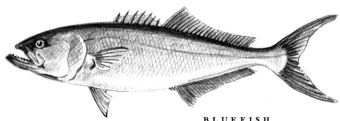

BLUEFISH
Pomatomus saltatrix

YELLOWFIN TUNA
Thunnus albacares

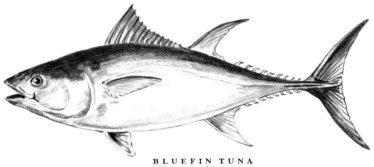

BLUEFIN TUNA
Thunnus thynnus

ATLANTIC BLUE MARLIN
Makaira ampla

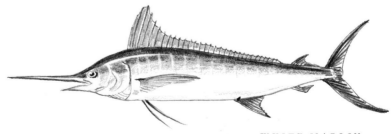

WHITE MARLIN
Makaira albida

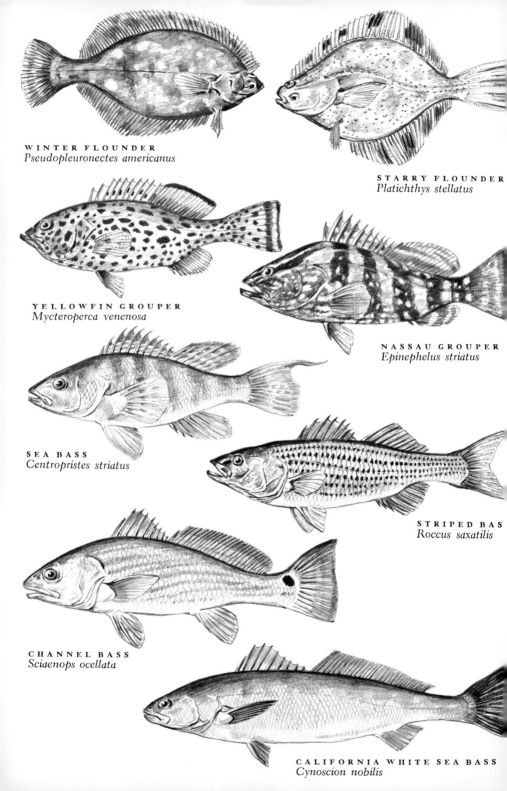

WINTER FLOUNDER
Pseudopleuronectes americanus

STARRY FLOUNDER
Platichthys stellatus

YELLOWFIN GROUPER
Mycteroperca venenosa

NASSAU GROUPER
Epinephelus striatus

SEA BASS
Centropristes striatus

STRIPED BAS
Roccus saxatilis

CHANNEL BASS
Sciaenops ocellata

CALIFORNIA WHITE SEA BASS
Cynoscion nobilis

forests, and marshlands. Boat-tailed (*Cassidix mexicanus*); Bronze (*Quiscalus quiscula versicolor*); Common (*Quiscalus quiscula*); Purple (*Quiscalus quiscula stonei*).

GREASER. See GOOSE, Bullneck.

GREATHEAD. See DUCK, American Golden.

GREBE. Food: fish, small aquatic animals, insects. Habitat: ponds, lakes, and saltwater areas. Eared (*Podiceps caspicus*); Horned (*Podiceps auritus*); Pied-billed (*Podilymbus podiceps*); Red-necked (*Podiceps grisegena*); Swan or Western (*Aechmophorus occidentalis*).

GREENHEAD. See DUCK, Mallard.

GROUSE. Food: buds, grain, insects, nuts, seeds. Habitat: fields, forests, and sheltered valleys. Blue, Dusky, Mountain, Pine, Richardson's, Sooty (*Dendragapus obscurus*); Canada, Spotted, Spruce, Wood (*Canachites canadensis*); Franklin's (*Canachites canadensis*); Pinnated—see PRAIRIE CHICKEN; Ruffed (*Bonasa umbellus*); Sage (*Centrocercus urophasianus*); Sharp-tailed or Willow (*Pedioecetes phasianellus*).

GUAN. See CHACHALACA.

GUILLEMOT. Food: fish. Habitat: rocky coasts. Black (*Cepphus grylle*); Foolish—see MURRE, Thick-billed; Pigeon (*Cepphus columba*).

GYRFALCON. See FALCON.

HAIRY CROWN or HAIRY HEAD. See MERGANSER, Hooded.

HAWK. Food: amphibians, birds, insects, reptiles, small mammals. Habitat: plains, fields, marshes, and wooded areas. Blue, Marsh, Mouse (*Circus cyaneus*); Broad-winged (*Buteo platypterus*); Cooper's, Chicken (*Accipiter cooperii*); Desert Sparrow, Killy, Sparrow—see FALCON, Rusty Crowned; Duck—see FALCON, Peregrine; Ferruginous (*Buteo regalis*); Fish—see OSPREY; Harlan's (*Buteo harlani*); Harris (*Parabuteo unicinctus harrisi*); Hen or Red-shouldered (*Buteo lineatus*); Night (*Chordeiles minor*); Pigeon (*Falco columbarius*); Red-legged (*Buteo lagopus*); Red-tailed (*Buteo jamaicensis*); Rough-legged (*Buteo lagopus*); Sharp-shinned (*Accipiter striatus*); Snake—see KITE, Swallow-tailed; Swainson's (*Buteo swainsoni*).

HEATHCOCK. See GROUSE, Canada.

HELL DIVER. See DUCK, Bufflehead; GREBE.

HERON. Food: amphibians, fish, insects. Habitat: lakes, streams, fresh- and saltwater marshes. Black Crowned Night (*Nycticorax nycticorax*); Great Blue (*Ardea herodias*); Great White (*Ardea occidentalis*); Green (*Butorides virescens*); Little Blue (*Florida caerulea*); Louisiana (*Hydranassa tricolor*); Yellow Crowned Night (*Nyctanassa violacea*).

HICKORY HEAD. See DUCK, Ruddy.

HICKORY QUACKER. See DUCK, Canvasback.

HONKER. See GOOSE, Canada.

HOOTAMAGANZY. See MERGANSER, Hooded.

HUN. See PARTRIDGE, Hungarian.

IBIS. Food: crayfish, insects, amphibians. Habitat: ponds, mudflats, fresh- and saltwater marshes. Glossy (*Plegadis falcinellus*); White (*Eudocimus albus*); White-faced (*Plegadis chihi*); Wood (*Mycteria americana*).

INDIAN HEN. See BITTERN, American.

JACKSNIPE. See SNIPE, Wilson's.

JAY. Food: berries, nuts, insects, mice, seeds. Habitat: farms, fields, and forests. Arizona (*Aphelocoma ultramarina*); Blue (*Cyanocitta cristata*); California, Scrub, Woodhouse (*Aphelocoma coerulescens*); Crested or Steller's (*Cyanocitta stelleri*); Gray (*Perisoreus canadensis*); Pinyon (*Gymnorhinus cyanocephala*); White-headed, Canada (*Perisoreus canadensis*).

JOHNNY BULL. See DUCK, Ruddy.

KESTREL. See FALCON, Rusty Crowned.

KILLDEER (*Charadrius vociferus*). Food: insects, larvae, worms. Habitat: marshy fields.

KINGBIRD. Food: insects. Habitat: brushlands, fields, and streams. Cassin's (*Tyrannus vociferans*); Eastern (*Tyrannus tyrannus*); Western (*Tyrannus verticalis*); see also EIDER, King.

KING DIVER. See DUCK, American Golden.

KINGFISHER (*Megaceryle alcyon*). Food: fish. Habitat: lakes, streams.

KITE. Food: insects. Habitat: fields and forests. Mississippi (*Ictinia misisippiensis*); Swallow-tailed (*Elanoides forficatus*); White-tailed (*Elanus leucurus*).

KNOCKMOLLY. See DUCK, Long-tailed.

KNOT (*Calidris canutus*). Food: crustaceans, worms. Habitat: tidal waters.

LAKE BLUEBILL. See SCAUP, American.

LAWYER. See STILT, Blacknecked.

LEATHERBACK, LEATHER BREECHES. See DUCK, Ruddy.

LITTLE HONKER. See GOOSE, Gray.

LITTLE SOLDIER. See DUCK, Ruddy.

LOON. Food: fish and aquatic life. Habitat: lakes, streams, and coastal waters. Arctic (*Gavia arctica*); Common (*Gavia immer*); Red-throated (*Gavia stellata*); Yellow-billed (*Gavia adamsii*).

MAGPIE. Food: berries, grains, insects, seeds. Habitat: farmlands, fields, and foothills. American or Black-billed (*Pica pica*); Yellow-billed (*Pica nuttalli*).

MALLARD. See DUCK, Mallard.

MARSH HEN. See BITTERN, American; COOT, American; GALLINULE; RAIL; SORA.

MARTIN, PURPLE (*Progne subis*). Food: grain, seeds, insects. Habitat: fields and open forests.

MERGANSER. Food: amphibians, crayfish, fish, water insects. Habitat: lakes, streams, fresh- and saltwater marshes. American or Common (*Mergus merganser*); Hooded, Mosshead, Peak-bill (*Lophodytes cucullatus*); Redbreasted (*Mergus serrator*).

MISSISSIPPI DUCK. See MERGANSER, Redbreasted.

MONGREL DRAKE. See EIDER, King.

MOORHEAD. See COOT, American.

MOOSE BIRD. See JAY, White-headed.

MOROCCO HEAD. See MERGANSER, American.

MUD HEN. See COOT, American; RAIL, Clapper.

MURRE. Food: fish, marine invertebrates. Habitat: rocky seacoasts. Atlantic or Common (*Uria aalge*); California (*Uria aalge californicus*); Thick-billed (*Uria lomvia*).

MURRELET. Food: fish. Habitat: Aleutian Islands. Ancient (*Synthliboramphus antiqum*); Marbled (*Brachyramphus marmoratum*).

NENE. See GOOSE, Hawaiian.

NIGGER GOOSE. See CORMORANT.

OLD GRANNY, OLD MOLLY, OLD SQUAW, OLD WIFE. See DUCK, Long-tailed.

OLD IRON POT. See SCOTER.

OSPREY (*Pandion haliaeetus carolinensis*). Food: small fish. Habitat: near lakes, streams, and other waters.

OWL. Food: birds, insects, rodents, small mammals. Habitat: fields, forests, marshes, and meadows. Acadian or Saw-whet (*Aegolius acadicus*); Barn, Cat, or Monkey-faced (*Tyto alba*); Barred, Hoot, or Wood (*Strix varia*); Boreal or Richardson's (*Aegolius funereus*); Burrowing or Prairie (*Speotyto cunicularia*); Cat or Long-eared (*Asio otus*); Elf (*Micrathene whitneyi*); Flammulated (*Otus flameolus*); Great Gray (*Strix nebulosa*); Great Horned (*Bubo virginianus*); Hawk (*Surnia ulula*); Little Horned, Red or Screech (*Otus asio*); Pigmy or Gnome (*Glaucidium gnoma*); Short-eared (*Asio flammeus*); Snowy or White (*Nyctea scandiaca*); Spotted (*Strix occidentalis*).

OYSTERCATCHER. Food: crustaceans, shellfish, seaworms. Habitat: rocky and sandy coastal areas. American (*Haematopus palliatus*); Black (*Haematopus bachmani*).

PADDYWACK. See DUCK, Ruddy.

PAPABOTTE. See SANDPIPER, Bartramian.

PARTRIDGE. Food: grain, insects, seeds. Habitat: brush areas, fields. Birch—see GROUSE, Ruffed; Black, Spring, or Swamp—see GOOSE,

Canada; Chukar, Redlegged (*Alectoris graecia*); Gambel's—see QUAIL, Gambel's; Gray or Hungarian (*Perdix perdix*); Night—see WOODCOCK; Plumed—see QUAIL, Mountain; Valley—see QUAIL, California Valley; Virginia—see QUAIL, Bobwhite; Water—see DUCK, RUDDY.

PEEP. See SANDPIPER, Baird's, Least Semipalmated, Western, White-rumped.

PEET-WEET. See SANDPIPER, Spotted.

PELICAN. Food: fish. Habitat: lakes, streams, saltwater shores. Brown (*Pelecanus occidentalis*); White (*Pelecanus erthrorhynchos*).

PHALAROPE. Food: crustaceans, insects, mosquito larvae. Habitat: marshes, fresh- and saltwater areas. Northern (*Lobipes lobatus*); Red (*Phalaropus fulicarius*); Wilson's (*Steganopus tricolor*).

PHEASANT. Food: grains, insects, vegetables, weed seeds. Habitat: brush and grasslands. Common or Ring-necked (*Phasianus colchicus*); Golden (*Chrysolophus pictas*); Japanese Blue (*Phasianus versicolor*); Reeves (*Phasianus reevesi*); Silver (*Euplocomus nycthemerus*); Water —see MERGANSER, Hooded.

PICKAXE. See MERGANSER, Hooded.

PIED FISHERMAN. See MERGANSER, American.

PIED WHISTLER. See DUCK, American Golden.

PIGEON, WILD. Food: grains, nuts, seeds. Habitat: farms and fields. Band-tailed, Blue, Wood, White-collared (*Columba fasciata*); Rock (*Columba livia*); White-crowned (*Columba leucocephala*).

PINTAIL. See DUCK, Pintail.

PLOVER. Food: crustaceans, insects, mollusks, worms. Habitat: mudflats, salt marshes, sand dunes. (Upland Plover—food: berries, insects, and weed seeds; habitat: deserts, fields, open country.) American Golden (*Pluvialis dominica*); Black-bellied, Black-breasted, or Whistling (*Squatarola squatarola*); Chicken—see TURNSTONE; Field or Upland (*Bartramia longicauda*); Killdeer—see KILLDEER; Mountain (*Eupoda montana*); Piping (*Charadrius melodus*); Ring-necked or Semipalmated (*Charadrius semipalmatus*); Ruddy—see TURNSTONE; Snowy (*Charadrius alexandrinus*); Upland (*Charadrius wilsonia*).

POACHER. See WIDGEON, American.

POND DUCKS. Black, Mallard, Pintail, and Wood DUCKS; SHOVELER; TEAL; WIDGEON.

POULE D'EAUX. See COOT.

PRAIRIE CHICKEN. Food: grain, insects, weed seeds. Habitat: tall grass. Greater or Square-tailed (*Tympanuchus cupido*); Lesser (*Tympanuchus pallidicinctus*); Sharp-tailed—see GROUSE.

PRAIRIE MALLARD. See GADWALL.

PRAIRIE PIGEON or **PRAIRIE SNIPE.** See PLOVER, Upland.

PTARMIGAN. Food: berries, insects, tree buds and twigs, vegetation. Habitat: plains, deserts, and valleys. Rock (*Lagopus mutus*); White-tailed (*Lagopus leucurus*); Willow (*Lagopus lagopus*).

PUFFIN. Food: fish, seafood. Habitat: seacoasts. Common (*Fratercula arctica*); Horned (*Fratercula corniculata*); Tufted (*Lunda cirrhata*).

PUDDLE DUCKS. Black, Florida, Mallard, Mottled, New Mexico, and Wood DUCKS; GADWALL; SHOVELER; TEAL; WIDGEON.

QUAIL. Food: berries, insects, seeds, vegetation. Habitat: brush, second growth areas, tall grasses, grain fields. Arizona, Desert, or Gambel's (*Lophortyx gambelii*); Blue, Mexican Blue, or Scaled (*Callipepla squamata*); Bobwhite (*Colinus virginianus*); California Valley, Crested, Helmet, Topknot, or Valley (*Lophortyx californica*); Clown, Harlequin, or Mearn's (*Cyrtonyx montezumae*); Coturnix or Japanese (*Coturnix japonica*); Mountain, Painted, or Plumed (*Oreortyx pictus*).

QUAWK. See HERON, Black-crowned Night.

QUINK. See BRANT, American.

RAIL. Food: aquatic plants, berries, insects, mollusks. Habitat: fresh- and saltwater marshes. Black (*Laterallus jamaicensis*); Blue—see GALLINULE; Clapper (*Rallus longirostris*); King (*Rallus elegans*); Virginia (*Rallus limicola*); Yellow (*Coturnicops noveboracensis*).

RAVEN. Food: carrion, grains, insects, seeds. Habitat: fields, forests, mountains, and coastal regions. American, Common, or Northern (*Corvus corax*); White-necked (*Corvus cryptoleucus*).

REDBREAST, RED-BREASTED FISH DUCK, RED-BREASTED GOOSANDER. See MERGANSER, Redbreasted.

RICE BIRDS. See BLACKBIRD, Red-winged; SORA.

ROADRUNNER (*Geococcyx californianus*). Food: insects, lizards, reptiles, rodents. Habitat: deserts, sage brush areas.

SABRE-BILL or **SICKLE-BILL.** See CURLEW, long-billed.

SAGE COCK or **SAGE HEN.** See GROUSE, Sage.

SANDERLING (*Crocethia alba*). Food: algae, insects, small marine life. Habitat: mudflats and sandy beaches.

SANDPIPER. Food: crustaceans, insects, seeds, small marine life. Habitat: fresh- and saltwater marshes, mudflats, rocky shores, and sandy beaches. Aleutian, or Rock (*Erolia ptiloenemis couesi*); Baird's (*Erolia bairdii*); Bartramian or Upland (*Bartramia longicauda*); Brant or Red-backed—see DUNLIN; Buff-breasted (*Tryngites subruficollis*); Least (*Erolia minutilla*); Pectoral (*Erolia melanotos*); Purple (*Erolia maritima*); Semipalmated or Peep (*Ereunetes pusillus*); Solitary (*Tringa solitaria*); Stilt or Long-legged (*Micropalama himantopus*); Spotted (*Actitis macularia*); Western (*Ereunetes mauri*); White-rumped (*Erolia fuscicollis*).

SAPSUCKER, COMMON or YELLOW-BELLIED (*Spyrapicus varius*). Food: sap of trees, insects. Habitat: orchards, wooded areas.

SAWBILL or SAWBUCK. See MERGANSER.

SCAUP. Food: insects, aquatic vegetation, mollusks, small fish. Habitat: fresh- and saltwater areas. American, Greater, Blackhead, Blue-billed (*Aythya marila*); Lesser (*Aythya affinis*); Marsh Bluebill, Pond Bluebill, Ringbill, Ring-billed Blackhead, Ring-neck, Ring-necked Blackhead (*Aythya collaris*).

SCOOPER. See AVOCET, American; SHOVELER.

SCOTCHMAN. See DUCK, Bufflehead.

SCOTER. Food: crustaceans. Habitat: large lakes, coastal areas. American or Common (*Oidemia nigra*); Surf (*Melanitta perspicillata*); White-winged (*Melanitta deglandi*).

SEA HORSE. See SCOTER, White-winged; Puffin.

SEA MOUSE. See DUCK, Harlequin.

SEA PIGEON. See GUILLEMOT.

SHAG. See CORMORANT.

SHEARWATER. Food: fish. Habitat: coastal and ocean waters. Audubon (*Puffinus lherminieri*); Cory's (*Puffinus diomedea*); Greater (*Puffinus gravis*); Manx (*Puffinus puffinus*); Sooty (*Puffinus griseus*).

SHELLDRAKE. See DUCK, Canvasback; MERGANSER.

SHOREBIRDS. CURLEW, DOWITCHER, DUNLIN, GODWIT, KILLDEER, KNOT, OYSTERCATCHER, PHALAROPE, PLOVER, SANDPIPER, SNIPE, STILT, TURNSTONE, WILLET, YELLOWLEGS.

SHOREYER. See EIDER, American.

SHOVELER (*Spatula clypeata*). Food: aquatic vegetation, mollusks, seeds, insects. Habitat: fresh- and saltwater marshes, coastal areas. Also called Shovelbill, Shovelmouth, and Shovelnose.

SHRIKE. Food: birds, insects, small mammals. Habitat: open forests, orchards, and swamps. Loggerhead or White-rumped (*Lanius ludovicianus*); Northern (*Lanius excubitor*).

SHUFFLER. See COOT; SCAUP.

SHUTTLECOCK. See GADWALL.

SKIMMER (*Rhynchops nigra*). Food: fish, plankton. Habitat: sandy coasts.

SKUNKHEAD or SKUNKTOP. See SCOTA, Surf.

SLEEPY BROADBILL, SLEEPYHEAD. See DUCK, Ruddy.

SLEEPY DIVER. See DUCK, American Golden.

SMOKER. See DUCK, Pintail.

SNAKEBIRD (*Anhinga anhinga*). Food: fish. Habitat: inland waters.

SNAKE-KILLER. See ROADRUNNER.

SNIPE. Food: earthworms, grubs, insects, seeds. Habitat: fresh- and salt-water marshes, wet brush, or forest lands. Brant or Horsefoot—see TURNSTONE. Common (*Capella gallinago*); Owl or Whistling—see

WOODCOCK; Jacksnipe, Sea, or Wilson's (*Capella gallinago delicata*); Quail—see DOWITCHER; White—see AVOCET.

SORA (*Porzana carolina*). Food: aquatic plants, mollusks, insects, seeds, wild rice. Habitat: fresh- and saltwater marshlands.

SPARLING FOWL. See MERGANSER.

SPARROW. Food: berries, fruit, grains, seeds, garbage. Habitat: farmlands, fields, residential areas. English or House (*Passer domesticus*); European or European Tree (*Passer montanus*); Le Contes (*Passerherbulus caudacutus*).

SPECKLEBELLY. See GADWALL; GOOSE, White-fronted.

SPIKEBILL. See MERGANSER.

SPIRIT DIPPER, SPIRIT DUCK. See DUCK, Bufflehead.

SPOONBILL. See SHOVELER.

SPRUCE HEN. See GROUSE, Canada.

SQUEALER. See DUCK, Harlequin and Wood.

STARLING (*Sturnus vulgaris*). Food: berries, fruit, grub, insects. Habitat: farmlands, fields, residential areas.

STILT, BLACK-NECKED (*Himantopus mexicanus*). Food: insects. Habitat: shallow fresh water.

STRAWBILL. See MERGANSER, Hooded.

STUB-TAIL, STUB-TWISTER. See DUCK, Ruddy.

SURF SCOOTER. See SCOTER, Surf.

SWAN. Food: aquatic vegetation, insects. Habitat: lakes, ponds, and coastal areas. American or Whistling (*Olor columbianus*); Mute (*Olor olor*); Trumpeter (*Olor buccinator*).

TATTLER. See WILLET; YELLOWLEGS.

TEAL. Food: crustaceans, aquatic vegetation, seeds. Habitat: fresh- and saltwater marshes, ponds, and streams. Bastard or Hairy Crown—see MERGANSER, Hooded; Blue-winged, Necktie, Southern, or White-faced (*Anas discors*); Cinnamon, Red-breasted, or Silver (*Anas cyanoptera*); Common (*Anas crecca*); Green-winged, Mud, or Red-headed (*Anas carolinensis*).

TEETER-TAIL. See SANDPIPER, Spotted.

TERN. Food: crustaceans, fish, frogs, insects, squid. Habitat: lakes, rivers, and seacoasts. Arctic (*Sterna paradisaea*); Black (*Childonias niger*); Caspian (*Hydroprogne caspia*); Common (*Sterna hirundo*); Forster's (*Sterna forsteri*); Gull-billed (*Gelochelidon nilotica*); Least (*Sterna albifrons*); Roseate (*Sterna dougallii*); Royal (*Thalasseus maximus*); Sandwich (*Thalasseus sandvicensis*); Sooty (*Sterna fuscata*).

TEXAS GUAN. See CHACHALACA.

TIMBERDOODLE. See WOODCOCK.

TREE DUCK. See DUCK, Black-bellied Tree, Fulvous Tree.

TROOP FOWL. See SCAUP, Greater.

TURKEY. Food: berries, insects, seeds, vegetation. Habitat: fields and open forests. Eastern (*Meleagris gallopavo silvestris*); Florida (*Meleagris gallopavo osceola*); Merriams (*Meleagris gallopavo merriami*); Water—see IBIS, Wood; SNAKEBIRD.

TURKEY BUZZARD. See VULTURE.

TURNSTONE (*Arenaria interpres*). Food: berries, crustaceans, mollusks. Habitat: beaches, mudflats, Great Lakes and coastal areas. Black (*Arenaria melanocephala*); Ruddy (*Arenaria interpres*).

TWEEZER. See MERGANSER.

VULTURE. Food: carrion. Habitat: beaches, fields, and mountains. Black (*Coragyps atratus*); Turkey (*Cathartes aura*).

WAMP. See EIDER, American.

WAMP'S COUSIN. See EIDER, King.

WATER TURKEY. See IBIS, Wood; SNAKEBIRD.

WAVEY. Blue—see GOOSE, Blue; Gray or White—see GOOSE, White-fronted, Greater, or Lesser Snow; Horned, Little, Wart-nosed Wavy —see GOOSE, Ross's.

WHIFFLER, WHISTLER, WHISTLER-WING. See DUCK, American Golden.

WHIMBREL. See CURLEW, Whimbrel.

WHISKEY JACK. See JAY, Gray.

WHISTLER, WIRECROWN. See MERGANSER, Hooded.

WHISTLING DICK. See WIDGEON.

WHITE-EYE, WHITE-WINGER, WHITE-WING DIVER. See SCOTER, White-winged.

WIDGEON. Food: eel grass, aquatic vegetation. Habitat: ponds and streams, fresh- and saltwater marshes. American, Baldfaced, Baldpate, Blue-billed, California, Green-headed, Southern (*Mareca americana*); Goose, Stiff-tailed—see DUCK, Ruddy; Gray—see GADWALL; Kite-tailed, Pintail, Sea, Spring-tailed—see DUCK, Pintail; Popping—see MERGANSER, Red-breasted; Wood—see DUCK, Wood.

WILLET (*Catoptrophorus semipalmatus*). Food: crustaceans, insects, mollusks. Habitat: saltwater marshes.

WOODCOCK (*Philohela minor*). Food: earthworms, grubs, insects. Habitat: swamps, wet brush and forest lands.

WOOLHEAD. See DUCK, Bufflehead.

WOOZER. See MERGANSER, American.

YELLOWLEGS. Food: crustaceans, fish, insects, mollusks. Habitat: mud-flats, marshes, and streams. Greater (*Totanus melanoleucus*); Lesser (*Totanus flavipes*).

YELPER. See GOOSE, Bullneck.

ZIN-ZIN. See MERGANSER, Hooded; WIDGEON, American.

Freshwater Fish

This list includes familiar freshwater fish living in lakes* and streams throughout the United States, and saltwater fish found in tidal waters, including some species that regularly leave the sea to spawn in fresh waters.

ACHIGAN. See BASS, Smallmouth Black.
ALEWIFE. (*Alosa pseudoharengus*). Food: insects, plankton. Habitat: streams and ocean waters.
ARCTIC CHAR. See TROUT.
BARFISH. See BASS, White, Yellow.
BASS. Food: crustaceans, fish, insects. Habitat: lakes and streams. Black, Largemouth Black, Bayou, Grass, Green, Marsh, or Oswego (*Micropterus salmoides*); Black, Smallmouth Black, Bronze-back, Brown, Gold, or Tiger (*Micropterus dolomieu*); Blue—see SUNFISH, Bluegill, Green; Coosa or Redeye (*Micropterus coosae*); Kentucky or Spotted (*Micropterus punctulatus*); Otsego—see WHITEFISH, Lake; Red-breasted—see SUNFISH, Bluegill; Roanoke (*Ambloplites cavifrons*); Rock (*Ambloplites rupestris*); Silver or White (*Roccus chrysops*); Strawberry—see CRAPPIE, Black; Striped (*Roccus saxatilis*); Sun—see SUNFISH, Pumpkinseed; Suwannee (*Micropterus notius*); Warmouth—see WARMOUTH; Yellow (*Roccus misisippiensis*).
BLACKEAR PONDFISH—see SUNFISH, Redbreast.
BLACKFISH, SACRAMENTO (*Orthodon microlepidotus*). Food: bottom feeders. Habitat: streams.
BLACK PERCH. See BASS; Smallmouth Black.
BLUEGILL. See SUNFISH, Bluegill.
BONNEVILLE CISCO. See CISCO.
BOWFIN (*Amia calva*). Food: crustaceans, fish, insects. Habitat: lakes and streams.
BREAM. Food: insects. Habitat: quiet streams and lakes. American—see SHINER, Golden; Ball-faced, Blue, Copper-faced, Copperhead, or Coppernosed—see SUNFISH, Bluegill; Red-bellied or Red Belly—see SUNFISH, Long-eared.
BUBBLER. See DRUM.

* Includes ponds and reservoirs.

BUFFALO. Food: crustaceans, insects, mollusks, vegetation. Habitat: shallow lakes and sluggish streams. Bigmouth, Gourdhead, or Redmouth (*Ictiobus cyprinella*); Black, Mongrel, or Round (*Ictiobus niger*); Highback, Razorback, or Smallmouth (*Ictiobus bubalus*).

BULLHEAD. See **CATFISH.**

BURBOT (*Lota lota*). Food: fish. Habitat: lakes and streams.

CALICO BASS. See **CRAPPIE,** Black.

CANDLEFISH or **EULACHON** (*Thaleichthys pacificus*). Food: insects, plankton. Habitat: northern Pacific coastal streams.

CARP (*Cyprinus carpio*). Food: crustaceans, insects, vegetation. Habitat: streams.

CARPSUCKERS. Food: insects, worms. Habitat: ponds and streams. Bluntnose or Highfin (*Carpiodes velifer*); Quillback (*Carpiodes cyprinus*); River (*Carpiodes carpio*).

CATFISH. Food: bottom feeder, crustaceans, fish, insects, mollusks. Habitat: lakes and streams. Apalcua, Flathead, Mud, Shovelhead, or Yellow (*Pylodictis olivaris*); Brown Bullhead, Speckled Bullhead, or Squaretail (*Ictalurus nebulosus*); Black Bullhead or Northern (*Ictalurus melas*); Blue, Forktail, or Mississippi (*Ictalurus furcatus*); Channel, Silver, or Speckled (*Ictalurus punctatus*); White (*Ictalurus catus*); Yellow or Yellow Bullhead (*Ictalurus natalis*).

CHAIN PIKE. See **PICKEREL,** Chain.

CHAR. See **TROUT.**

CICHLID. See **OSCAR.**

CHINQUAPIN PERCH. See **CRAPPIE,** White; **STUMPKNOCKER.**

CHISELMOUTH (*Acrocheilus alutaceus*). Food: bottom feeder. Habitat: streams.

CHUB. Food: algae, fish, insects. Habitat: clear lakes and streams. Butter, Cutlips, or Negro (*Exoglossum maxillingua*); Creek (*Semotilus atromaculatus*); Deepwater—see CISCO; Hornyhead (*Hybopsis biguttata*); Longjaw, Shortjaw, or Shortnose—see CISCO; Silver (Hybopsis storeriana); Tui (*siphateles bicolor*); White—see **FALLFISH.**

CHOUPIQUE. See **BOWFIN.**

CHUBSUCKER. Food: insects, mollusks. Habitat: ponds and streams. Creek (*Erimyzon oblongus*); Lake (*Erimyzon sucetta*).

CHUCKLEHEAD CAT. See **CATFISH.**

CISCO. Food: insects, fish. Habitat: deep lakes and streams. Arctic (*Coregonus autumnalis*); Blackfin (*Coregonus nigripinnis*); Deepwater (*Coregonus johannae*) Longjaw (*Coregonus alpenae*); Shortjaw (*Coregonus zenithicus*); Shortnose (*Coregonus reighardi*); Lake (*Coregonus artedii*), also called Whitefish.

CORPORAL. See **FALLFISH.**

COTTONFISH. See **BOWFIN.**

CRAPPIE. Food: crustaceans, fish, insects. Habitat: lakes and streams. Black (*Pomoxis nigromaculatus*); White (*Pomoxis annularis*).

CROAKER. See DRUM.

CUSK. See BURBOT.

DACE. Food: algae, insects. Habitat: clear small streams. Blacknose (*Rhinichthys atratulus*); Horned (*Semotilus atromaculatus*); Long-nose (*Rhinichthys cataractae*); Redside (*Clinostomus elongatus*); Southern Redbelly (*Chrosomus erythrogaster*).

DOGFISH. Scc BOWFIN.

DORY. See PIKE, Walleye.

DRUM (*Aplodinotus grunniens*). Food: crustaceans, mollusks. Habitat: lakes and streams.

DUCK-BILLED PIKE. See PICKEREL, Chain.

EEL (*Anguilla rostrata*). Food: crustaceans, fish. Habitat: lakes, streams, and coastal waters.

EELPOUT. See BURBOT.

FALLFISH (*Semotilus corporalis*). Food: algae, fish, insects. Habitat: lakes and streams.

FIDDLER. See CATFISH, Channel.

FLIER or FLYER (*Centrarchus macropterus*). Food: insects. Habitat: ponds and small streams.

FORKTAIL CAT. See CATFISH, Forktail.

GAR. Food: fish. Habitat: shallow lakes and streams. Alligator (*Lepisosteus spatula*); Longnose (*Lepisosteus osseus*); Shortnose (*Lepisosteus platostomus*); Spotted (*Lepisosteus oculatus*).

GASPERGOU. See DRUM.

GOGGLE-EYE. See BASS, Rock; WARMOUTH.

GOLDEN SHINER. See SHINER, Golden.

GOLDEYE. See MOONEYE.

GOLDFISH (*Carassius auratus*). Food: crustaceans, insects, vegetation. Habitat: streams.

GOUJON. See CATFISH, Flathead.

GRAYLING, Arctic (*Thymallus arcticus*). Food: insects. Habitat: clear streams.

GREEN PIKE. See PICKEREL, Chain.

GREEN TROUT. See BASS, Largemouth Black.

GRINDLE or GRINNEL. See BOWFIN.

GUDGEON. See BURBOT.

HACKLEBACK. See STURGEON, Shovelnose.

HALFBEAK (*Hyporhamphus unifasciatus*). Food: algae, small crustaceans. Habitat: coastal waters.

HARDHEAD (*Mylopharodon conocephalus*). Food: bottom feeder. Habitat: streams.

HERRING. Food: fish, insects, plankton. Habitat: streams and coastal waters. Blueback (*Alosa aestivalis*); Lake—see CISCO, Lake; Skipjack (*Alosa chrysochloris*); Toothed—see MOONEYE, Goldeye; Walleyed, Bigeye, and Gray Herring are popular names for Alewife.

HITCH (*Lavinia exilicauda*). Food: bottom feeder. Habitat: streams.

HOGMOLLY. See SUCKER, Hog.

HOOLIGAN. See SMELT.

HORNYHEAD. See CHUB, Hornyhead; STONEROLLER.

HORNED POUT. See CATFISH, Brown Bullhead.

HORSEFISH. See SAUGER.

INCONNU (*Stenodus leucichthys*). Food: fish. Habitat: streams.

INDIAN FISH. See WARMOUTH.

JACK FISH. See PICKEREL, Chain; SAUGER; SUNFISH, Pumpkinseed, Yellowbreast.

JACK SALMON. Refers to a Salmon under 20 inches in length.

KAMLOOP. See TROUT.

KIVER. See SUNFISH, Pumpkinseed, Yellowbreast.

KOI. See CARP.

KOKANEE. See SALMON.

LAMPREY. Food: fish. Habitat: large lakes, streams, coastal waters. Pacific (*Entosphenus tridentatus*); Sea (*Petromyzon marinus*); Silver (*Ichthyomyzon unicuspis*).

LAWYER. See BOWFIN; BURBOT.

LING. See BURBOT.

LING, Scaled. See BOWFIN.

LUKANANI. See TUCUNARE.

LUNGER. See TROUT, Lake.

LUNKER. See BASS, Largemouth Black.

MULLET. Food: vegetation. Habitat: coastal and tidal waters. Black or Striped (*Mugil cephalus*); Mountain (*Agonostomus monticola*).

MUSKELLUNGE, MUSCALLONGE, MUSKALONGE. Food: fish, frogs. Habitat: lakes and streams. Barred, Chautauqua, or Ohio River (*Esox masquinongy ohioensis*); Great or Tiger (*Esox masquinongy masquinongy*).

MUSKY. See MUSKELLUNGE.

NEEDLEFISH (*Strongylura marina*). Food: fish, shrimp. Habitat: coastal and tidal waters.

NERKA. See SALMON, Sockeye.

NORTHERN BULLHEAD. See CATFISH, Black Bullhead.

OPENMOUTH. See WARMOUTH.

OREGON CHAR. See TROUT, Dolly Varden.

OSWEGO. See BASS, Largemouth Black.

OSCAR (*Astronotus ocellatus*). Food: fish. Habitat: Hawaiian reservoirs and streams on islands of Kauai and Oahu, Hawaii.

OUANANICHE. See SALMON, Lake.

PADDLEFISH (*Polyodon spathula*). Food: bottom feeder. Habitat: lakes and the Mississippi River drainage.

PAPERMOUTH. See CRAPPIE, Black.

PAVON. See TUCUNARE.

PEACOCK. See TUCUNARE.

PEACOCK-EYE CICHLID. See OSCAR.

PEAMOUTH (*Mylocheilus caurinus*). Food: bottom feeder. Habitat: streams.

PERCH. Food: crustaceans, fish, insects. Habitat: lakes, streams. American, Yellow, or Yellowbelly (*Perca flavescens*); Black—see BASS, Smallmouth Black; Blue—see SUNFISH, Bluegill; Pirate (*Aphredoderus sayanus*); Pond—see SUNFISH, Pumpkinseed; Raccoon, Red, Ringed, or Striped—see American; Rio Grande (*Cichlasoma cyanoguttatum*); Sacramento (*Archoplites interruptus*); Silver or White (*Roccus americanus*); Speckled—see CRAPPIE, Black; Sun—see SUNFISH; Trout—see TROUTPERCH; Tule (*Hysterocarpus traskii*); Warmouth—see WARMOUTH.

PICKEREL. Food: fish. Habitat: lakes and streams. Barred, Bulldog, or Redfin (*Esox americanus americanus*); Chain, Eastern, Jack, Lake, Pond (*Esox niger*); Grass (*Esox americanus vermiculatus*); Great Northern—see PIKE, Northern; Walleye—see PIKE, Walleyed.

PIKE. Food: fish, insects. Habitat: large lakes and streams. Allegheny River, or Jack—see MUSKELLUNGE; American, Common, Grass, Great Lakes, or Northern (*Esox lucius*); Walleyed, Blue, Green or Yellow (*Stizostedion vitreum*); Duck-billed—see PICKEREL, Chain; Sacramento—see SQUAWFISH, Sacramento; Gray, Ground, or Sand Pike are popular names for SAUGER.

PIKE-PERCH. See PIKE, Walleyed; SAUGER.

PILOT (*Prosopium quadrilaterale*). Food: fish, insects, mollusks. Habitat: deep lakes and streams.

POISSON BLEU. See CATFISH, Blue.

POND PERCH. See SUNFISH, Pumpkinseed.

PONGEE. See SNAKEHEAD.

PUMPKINSEED. See SUNFISH, Pumpkinseed.

QUILLBACK. See CARPSUCKER.

REDBELLY BREAM. See SUNFISH, Longeared.

REDBREAST. See SUNFISH, Yellowbelly.

RED-EAR. See SUNFISH, Redear.

REDEYE. See BASS, Rock.

REDFIN. See PICKEREL, Redfin; REDHORSE, Northern.

REDHORSE. Food: insects, fish, mollusks. Habitat: clear lakes and streams. Black (*Moxostoma duquesnei*); Golden (*Moxostoma erythrurum*); Northern (*Moxostoma aureolum*); River (*Moxostoma carinatum*); Shorthead (*Moxostoma breviceps*); Silver (*Moxostoma anisurum*).

REDSIDE, LAHONTAN (*Richardsonius egregius*). Food: insects. Habitat: streams.

RIVERCARP. See CARPSUCKERS.

ROBIN. See SUNFISH, Yellowbreast.

ROCKFISH. See BASS, Rock, Striped.

SAC-A-LAIT. See CRAPPIE, White; WARMOUTH.

SACRAMENTO SQUAWFISH. See SQUAWFISH, Sacramento.

SACRAMENTO SALMON. See SALMON, King.

SALMON. Food: crustaceans, fish. Habitat: lakes, streams, and coastal waters. Atlantic, Kennebec, or Sea Run (*Salmo salar*); Blackmouth, Chinook, Columbia River, King, or Sacramento (*Oncorhynchus tschawytscha*); Blueback, Red, or Sockeye (*Oncorhynchus nerka*); Coho, Pacific, Silver, or White (*Oncorhynchus kisutch*); Calico, Chum, or Dog (*Oncorhynchus keta*); Colorado—see SQUAWFISH, Colorado; Gorbuscha, Haddo, Humpback, or Pink (*Oncorhynchus gorbuscha*); Kennerly's Kikanniny, or Kokanee (*Oncorhynchus nerka kennerlyi*); Lake, Landlocked, or Sebago (*Salmo salar sebago*).

SARGO (*Anisotremus davidsonii*). Food: bottom feeders, clams, crabs, shrimp, snails. Habitat: Salton Sea and coastal waters.

SAUGER (*Stizostedion canadense*). Food: fish. Habitat: lakes and streams.

SAWEYE. See SALMON, Sockeye.

SHAD. Food: crustaceans, fish, insects. Habitat: lakes and streams. American or Common (*Alosa sapidissima*)—often named for a region, i.e., Connecticut River, Delaware River, etc.; Golden—see HERRING, Blue; Gizzard or Stink (*Dorosoma cepedianum*); Hickory (*Alosa mediocris*); Ohio (*Alosa ohiensis*); White—see MOONEYE.

SHEEPHEAD. See DRUM.

SHELLCRACKER. See SUNFISH.

SHINER. Food: algae, insects, worms, small fish. Habitat: lakes, streams. Common (*Notropis cornutus*); Golden (*Notemigonus crysoleucas*).

SILVER CAT. See CATFISH, Channel.

SKIPJACK. See HERRING, Skipjack.

SMELT (*Osmerus mordax*). Food: crustaceans, insects, fish, plankton. Habitat: streams and coastal waters.

SNAKEHEAD (*Channa striata*). Food: fish. Habitat: reservoirs on islands of Kauai and Oahu, Hawaii.

Sockeye. See **Salmon**, Sockeye.

Speckled perch. See **Crappie**, Black.

Splittail (*Pogorichthys macrolepidotus*). Food: bottom feeder. Habitat: streams.

Spoonbill cat. See **Paddlefish**.

Squaretail. See **Trout**, Brook.

Squawfish. Food: insects, fish, frogs. Habitat: lakes and streams. Colorado (*Ptychocheilus lucius*); Northern (*Ptychocheilus oregonensis*); Sacramento (*Ptychocheilus grandis*).

Steelback. See **Stoneroller**.

Steelhead. See **Trout**, Rainbow. In many states, a Steelhead is identified as a Rainbow Trout over 20 inches in length.

Stonecat (*Noturus flavus*). Food: insects. Habitat: lakes and streams.

Stoneroller (*Campostoma anomalum*). Food: algae, insects. Habitat: small creeks and streams.

Straw bass. See **Bass**, Largemouth Black; **Crappie**, Black.

Strawberry bass. See **Crappie**, Black.

Streaker. See **Bass**, Yellow.

Striper. See **Bass**, Striped.

Stumpknocker (*Lepomis punctatus*). Food: insects, fish. Habitat: large streams.

Sturgeon. Food: crustaceans, fish, mollusks, vegetation. Habitat: rivers, lakes, coastal waters. Atlantic or Sea (*Acipenser oxyrhynchus*); Columbia River, Oregon, Sacramento, Washington, or White (*Acipenser transmontanus*); Green (*Acipenser medirostris*); Lake, Red, or Rock (*Acipenser fulvescens*); Pallid (*Scaphirhynchus albus*); Sand or Shovelnose (*Scaphirhynchus platorynchus*); Shortnose (*Acipenser brevirostris*).

Sucker. Food: bottom feeder, insects, vegetation, worms. Habitat: lakes and streams. Blue (*Cycleptus elongatus*); Hog (*Hypentelium nigricans*); Humpback (*xyrauchen texanus*); Large-scaled—see **Redhorse**, Northern; Pavement-toothed—see **Redhorse**, River; Plains or Mountain (*Pantosteus jordani*); Sacramento (*Catostomus occidentalis*); Spotted (*Minytrema melanops*); Tahoe (*Catostomus tahoensis*); Torrent (*Thoburnia rhothoeca*); White (*Catostomus commersonnii*).

Suckley perch. See **Crappie**, White.

Sun trout. See **Warmouth**.

Sunfish. Food: crayfish, fish, insects, mollusks. Habitat: lakes and streams. Banded (*Enneacanthus obesus*); Blackbanded (*Mesogonistius chaetodon*); Blackeye or Green (*Lepomis cyanellus*); Bluegill (*Lepomis macrochirus*); Bluespotted (*Enneacanthus gloriosus*);

Green (*Lepomis cyanellus*); Longeared (*Lepomis megalotis*); Orange-spotted (*Lepomis humilis*); Pumpkinseed (*Lepomis gibbosus*); Red-breast, Yellowbelly, Yellowbreast (*Lepomis auritus*); Redear (*Lepomis microlophus*); Rock—see BASS, Rock; Round—see FLIER; Spotted—see STUMPKNOCKER.

THUNDER PUMPER. See DRUM.

TILAPIA (*Tilapia machrochir, T. melanopleura, T. mossambica, T. zilli*). Food: aquatic vegetation, worms. Habitat: Hawaiian reservoirs and streams.

TOBACCOBOX. See SUNFISH, Longeared.

TOGUE. See TROUT, Lake.

TROUT. Food: crustaceans, fish, insects, worms. Habitat: lakes, streams, and tidal waters. Arctic Char (*Salvelinus alpinus*); Cutthroat, Black-spotted, Colorado River, or Native (*Salmo clarki*); Brook, Eastern Brook, Mountain, Speckled, or Squaretail (*Salvelinus fontinalis*); Brown, English, European or German Brown, Loch Leven (*Salmo trutta*); Dolly Varden, Bull, or Red-spotted (*Salvelinus malma*); Lake, Forktail, Great Lake, Mackinaw, Salmon, or Silver (*Salvelinus namaycush*); Golden (*Salmo aguabonita*); Kokanee—see SALMON; Lake Tahoe (*Salmo clarkii henshawi*); Rainbow, Salmon, or Steelhead (*Salmo gairdneri*); Kamloops (*Salmo kamloops*).

TROUTPERCH (*Percopsis omiscomaycus*). Food: insects, plankton. Habitat: large lakes.

TUCANARE (*Cichla ocellaris*). Food: crustaceans, fish, insects. Habitat: reservoirs and streams on islands of Hawaii.

TULLIBEE. See WHITEFISH, Tullibee.

TYEE. See SALMON. A Tyee is a Chinook or King Salmon weighing 30 or more pounds.

VELVET CICHLID. See OSCAR.

WALLEYE. See PIKE, Walleyed.

WALLEYED HERRING. See ALEWIFE.

WARMOUTH (*Chaenobryttus gulosus*). Food: fish, insects. Habitat: streams.

WAP. See MOONEYE, Goldeye.

WESTERN CHAR. See TROUT, Dolly Varden.

WHITE CAT. See CATFISH, Channel, White.

WHITEFISH. Food: fish, insects, mollusks. Habitat: lakes and streams. Lake (*Coregonus clupeaformis*); Menominee—see PILOT; Mountain (*Prosopium williamsoni*); Mule—see CISCO; Round (*Prosopium cylindraceum*) Tullibee (*Leucichthys nipigon*).

WINDFISH. See SHINER, Golden.

YELLOW JACK. See BASS, Yellow.

YELLOWBELLY. See SUNFISH, Yellowbelly.

RECORDS OF FRESHWATER FISH*

TAKEN BY ROD AND REEL

Bass, Black Largemouth–22 lbs. 4 oz., Montgomery Lake, Georgia
Bass, Black Smallmouth–11 lbs. 15 oz., Dale Hollow Reservoir, Kentucky
Bass, Silver (White)–5 lbs. 2 oz., Grenada Reservoir, Mississippi
Carp–55 lbs. 5 oz., Clearwater Lake, Minnesota
Catfish, Black Bullhead–8 lbs., Lake Waccabue, New York
Catfish, Blue–97 lbs., Missouri River, South Dakota
Catfish, Channel–57 lbs., Santee-Cooper Reservoir, South Carolina
Catfish, Shovelhead–70 lbs., Little Kanawha River, West Virginia
Char, Arctic–24 lbs., Tree River, Northwest Territory, Canada
Crappie, Black–5 lbs., Santee-Cooper Reservoir, South Carolina
Crappie, White–5 lbs. 3 oz., Enid Dam Reservoir, Mississippi
Gar, Alligator–279 lbs., Rio Grande, Texas
Gar, Longnose–50 lbs. 5 oz., Trinity River, Texas
Grayling, Arctic–5 lbs., Great Slave Lake, Northwest Territory, Canada
Muskellunge–69 lbs. 15 oz., St. Lawrence River, New York
Perch, Silver (White)–4 lbs. 12 oz., Messalonskee Lake, Maine
Perch, Yellow–4 lbs. 3 oz., Bordentown, New Jersey
Pickerel, Chain–9 lbs. 6 oz., Homerville, Georgia
Pike, Northern–46 lbs. 2 oz., Sacandaga Reservoir, New York
Pike, Walleye–25 lbs., Old Hickory Lake, Tennessee
Salmon, Atlantic–79 lbs. 2 oz., Tanaeiv, Norway
Salmon, Chinook or King–92 lbs., Skeena River, British Columbia, Canada
Salmon, Lake–22 lbs. 8 oz., Sebago Lake, Maine
Salmon, Silver–31 lbs., Cowichan Bay, British Columbia, Canada
Sauger–8 lbs. 5 oz., Niobrara River, Nebraska
Sturgeon, White–394 lbs., Snake River, Idaho
Sunfish, Bluegill–4 lbs. 12 oz., Ketona Lake, Alabama
Trout, Brook–14 lbs. 8 oz., Nipigon River, Ontario, Canada
Trout, Brown (Loch Leven)–39 lbs. 8 oz., Loch Awe, Scotland
Trout, Cutthroat–41 lbs., Pyramid Lake, Nevada
Trout, Dolly Varden–32 lbs., Lake Pend Oreille, Idaho
Trout, Forktail or Mackinaw–63 lbs. 2 oz., Lake Superior
Trout, Golden–11 lbs., Cook's Lake, Wyoming
Trout, Rainbow (Steelhead)–37 lbs., Lake Pend Oreille, Idaho
Trout, Sunapee–11 lbs. 8 oz., Lake Sunapee, New Hampshire (regarded
as Arctic Char by the American Fisheries Society)

* Source: International Game Fish Association and other authorities.

NOT TAKEN BY ROD AND REEL

MUSKELLUNGE–102 lbs., Minoqua Lake, Wisconsin
SALMON, Chinook or King–126 lbs. 8 oz., Petersburg, Alaska
SALMON, Lake–35 lbs., Crooked River, Maine
TROUT, Rainbow (Steelhead)–42 lbs., Corbett, Oregon

Saltwater Fish

ABREGO. See ALBACORE, Longfinned.
AHI. See TUNA, Yellowfin.
AHI (Maguro). See TUNA, Bluefin.
AHI (Menpachi shibi). See TUNA, Bigeyed.
AHIPALAHA (Tonbo). See ALBACORE, Longfinned.
AHOLEHOLE (*Kuhlia sandvicensis*). Also called Mountain Bass in Hawaii. Food: crustaceans, fish. Habitat: rocky coast.
AKU. See BONITO, Oceanic.
AKULE (Aji). See SCAD, Bigeyed.
ALABATO. See HALIBUT, California.
ALBACORE. Food: fish, plankton, squid. Habitat: offshore waters. False —see TUNA, Little; Great—see TUNA, Bluefin, Yellowfin; Longfinned (*Thunnus alalunga*); Pacific (*Thunnus germo*).
AMAAMA. See MULLET, Striped.
AMBERFISH. See AMBERJACK.
AMBERJACK. Food: fish. Habitat: offshore reefs, deep coastal waters. Greater (*Seriola lalandi*); Hawaiian, or Horseeye (*Seriola dumerilii*); Pacific (*Seriola colburni*); Yellowtail—see YELLOWTAIL.
ALLMOUTH or ANGLERFISH. See GOOSEFISH.
A'U. See SWORDFISH.
A'U LEPE. See SAILFISH, Hawaiian.
AWAAWA. See TEN POUNDER, Hawaiian.
A'U (Kajiki). See MARLIN, Pacific Blue.
A'U (Naraiga). See MARLIN, Striped.
AWA. See MILKFISH.
BANANAFISH. See BONEFISH.
BARRACUDA. Food: fish. Habitat: coastal waters and offshore reefs. California or Pacific (*Sphyraena argentea*); Great (*Sphyraena barracuda*); Guaguanche (*Sphyraena guachancho*); Northern (*Sphyraena borealis*); Ocean—see WAHOO.
BASS. Food: crustaceans, fish, mollusks. Habitat: rocky and sandy bottom coastal waters, offshore reefs. Bank Sea (*Centropristes ocyurus*); Blackear (*Paracentropristes pomospilus*); Black Sea (*Centropristes striatus*); California Sea, Giant Sea, or Giant Black Sea (*Stereolepis gigas*); California White Sea or White (*Cynoscion nobilis*); Channel—see DRUM, Red; Crimson (*Anthias asperilinguis*); Dumb—

453

see ROCKFISH, Kelp; Giant—see JEWFISH, Spotted; Kelp (*Paralabrax clathratus*); Lantern (*Prionodes baldwini*); Longtail (*Hemanthias leptus*); Marine—see TRIPLETAIL; Orangeback (*Prionodes annularis*); Reef (*Pseudogrammus brederi*); Rock Sea (*Centropristes philadelphicus*); Rough Tongue (*Ocyanthias martinicensis*); Sand (*Paralabrax nebulifer*); Shortfin Sea—see CORVINA, Shortfin; Silver (*Roccus americanus*); Southern Sea (*Centropristes melanus*); Splittail (*Hemanthias peruanus*); Spotted Rock or Spotted Sand (*Paralabrax maculatofasciatus*); Striped (*Roccus saxatilis*).

BLACKSMITH (*Chromis punctipinnis*). Food: crustacean. Habitat: Pacific coastal waters in marine vegetation.

BLANKETFISH. See RAY.

BLOATER. See BONITO.

BLACKFISH. See TAUTOG.

BLACK ROCKFISH. See GROUPER, Black; ROCKFISH, Black.

BLUEFIN. See TUNA.

BLUEFISH (*Pomatomus saltatrix*). Food: fish, squid. Habitat: Gulf of Mexico and warm Atlantic coastal and offshore waters.

BLUNTNOSE. See MOONFISH.

BOCACCIO (*Sebastodes paucispinis*). Food: fish, crab, squid. Habitat: deep offshore waters.

BONEFISH (*Albula vulpes*). Food: bottom feeder, mollusks. Habitat: coastal waters of East, especially Florida Keys.

BONEHEAD. See BONITO, California.

BONEJACK. See BONITO, Atlantic.

BONITO. Food: fish. Habitat: open seas. Arctic or Oceanic—see TUNA, Skipjack; Atlantic, Blue, or Common (*Sarda sarda*); Black—see COBIA; California or Pacific (*Sarda chiliensis*); Spotted—see TUNA, Little; Striped (*Sarda orientalis*).

BORRACHO. See ROCKFISH, Vermilion.

BOSTON BLUEFISH. See POLLOCK.

BREAM (*Archosargus rhomboidalis*). Food: crustaceans, fish, mollusks. Habitat: shallow Atlantic Ocean and Gulf of Mexico waters.

BROADBILL. See SWORDFISH.

BROOMTAIL. See GROUPER, Broomtail.

BUGARA. See SURFPERCH, Rainbow.

BULLHEAD. See CABEZON; IRISH LORD; SCULPIN, Pacific Staghorn.

BUTTERFISH (*Poronotus triacanthus*). Food: crustaceans, fish, plankton. Habitat: sandy coastal waters of Pacific Ocean.

CABEZON (*Scorpaenichthys marmoratus*). Food: crabs, mollusks, fish. Habitat: rocky bottom from tidepools to deep waters. The bluegreen flesh turns white when cooked and has a mild flavor. The flesh is safe to eat, but the roe is poisonous.

CABIO. See COBIA.

CABRILLA. See BASS, Kelp; HIND, Calico.

CALIFORNIA JEWFISH. See BASS, California Sea.

CALIFORNIA KINGFISH. See CROAKER, Tommy.

CALIFORNIA REDFISH. See SHEEPHEAD, California.

CALIFORNIA YELLOWTAIL. See YELLOWTAIL.

CATFISH. Food: fish, crabs, sea grasses. Habitat: coastal waters. Gafftopsail (*Bagre marinus*); Sea (*Galeichthys felis*).

CAVALLA. See CERO.

CAVALLE JACK. See JACK.

CERO (*Scomberomorus regalis*). Food: fish, squid. Habitat: Gulf Stream. Also called King Mackerel.

CHANNEL BASS. See DRUM, Red.

CHENFISH. See CROAKER, King.

CHERNA. See ROCKFISH, Black.

CHERNA CRIOLLA. See GROUPER, Nassau.

CHICKEN OF THE SEA. See ALBACORE, Longfinned.

CHILIPEPPER (*Sebastodes goodei*). Food: crustaceans, mollusks. Habitat: rocky coastal waters.

CHIRO. See TEN POUNDER.

CHOPA and CHUB. See RUDDERFISH.

CHUCKLEHEAD. See ROCKFISH, Greenspotted.

CIGARFISH. See SCAD, Bigeyed.

COBIA (*Rachycentron canadum*). Food: crab, fish. Habitat: Atlantic coastal waters.

COBBLER. See POMPANO, Carolina.

COD. Food: crustaceans, fish, mollusks. Habitat: offshore waters. Alaska, Gray, or Pacific (*Gadus macrocephalus*); Atlantic or Rock (*Gadus callarias*); Black—see SABLEFISH; Blue or Bull—see CABEZON; Buffalo, Cultus, Leopard, Ling, or Pacific Cultus (*Ophiodon elongatus*); Green—see LINGCOD; POLLOCK; Johnny—see ROCKFISH; CHILIPEPPER.

CODALARGER. See ROCKFISH, Canary.

CONVICT FISH. See SHEEPSHEAD, Atlantic; GREENLING, Painted.

CORBINA (*Menticirrhus undulatus*). Food: crustaceans, mollusks. Habitat: shallow Pacific coastal waters.

CORSAIR. See ROCKFISH, Rosy.

CORVINA. Food: crustaceans, fish. Habitat: coastal waters. Orangemouth (*Cynoscion xanthulus*); Shortfin (*Cynoscion parvipinnis*).

COWFISH. See TRUNKFISH, Horned.

CRABEATER or CRABFISH. See COBIA.

CREVALLE, CREVALLE JACK, CREVALLY. See JACK.

CROAKER. Food: crustaceans, fish. Habitat: in schools in shallow water.

Atlantic or Hardheaded (*Micropogon undulatus*); Banded (*Larimus fasciatus*); Black or Chinese (*Cheilotrema saturnum*); Blue (*Vacuoqua sialis*); Golden or Spotfin (*Roncador stearnsii*); King, Tommy, or White (*Genyonemus lineatus*); Reef (*Odontoscion dentex*); Yellowfin (*Umbrina roncador*), also called Catalina.

CULTUS. See **LINGCOD.**

CUNNER (*Tautogolabrus adspersus*). Food: crustaceans, fish, mollusks. Habitat: offshore rocky bottoms.

CUSK (*Brosme brosme*). Food: bottom feeders, crustaceans, mollusks. Habitat: offshore Atlantic waters.

CUTLASS FISH. Food: fish. Habitat: warm surface waters. Atlantic (*Trichiurus lepturus*); Pacific (*Trichiurus nitens*).

DAB. Food: bottom feeders. Habitat: sandy coastal waters. Longhead (*Limanda proboscidea*); Mottled—see **SANDDAB**, Pacific; Rough—see **PLAICE**, American; Rusty—see **FLOUNDER**, Yellowtail.

DEVILFISH. See **RAY**, Manta.

DOGFISH. Food: crustaceans, fish, seaworms. Habitat: offshore eaters. Smooth (*Mustelus canis*); Spiny (*Squalus acanthias*).

DOLLARFISH. See **BUTTERFISH; MOONFISH.**

DOLPHIN. Food: fish. Habitat: warm offshore waters. Common (*Coryphaena hippurus*); Pompano (*Coryphaena equisetis*).

DORADO. See **DOLPHIN.**

DRUM. Food: crustaceans, fish. Habitat: sandy coastal waters. Banded (*Larimus fasciatus*); Black (*Pogonias cromis*); Red (*Sciaenops ocellata*); Sand (*Umbrina coroides*); Spotted (*Equetus punctatus*); Star (*Stellifer lanceolatus*); Striped (*Equetus pulcher*).

EEL. Food: crustaceans, fish, worms. Habitat: coastal waters. American Conger (*Conger oceanicus*); Monkeyface (*Cebidichthys violaceus*); Moray or Blackedge Moray (*Gymnothorax nigromarginatus*); Rock —see **GUNNEL**; Sand (*Ammodytes americanus*); Wolf (*Anarrhichthys ocellatus*).

EELPOUT (*Macrozoarces americanus*). Food: crustaceans, mollusks. Habitat: offshore shallow to deep waters.

FANTAIL. See **ROCKFISH**, Canary.

FATHEAD. See **SHEEPHEAD.**

FILE FISH. Food: marine vegetation. Habitat: coastal waters. Common (*Stephanolepis hispida*); Orange (*Alutera schoepfi*).

FLORIDA KINGFISH. See **CERO.**

FLOUNDER. Food: crustaceans, fish, mollusks. Habitat: inshore and offshore waters. Arrowtooth or Longjaw (*Atheresthes stomias*); Broad (*Paralichthys squamilentus*); Broadfin—see **SOLE**, Rock; Channel (*Syacium micrurum*); Deepwater (*Monolene sessilicauda*); Diamond see TURBOT; Fourspot (*Paralichthys oblongus*), also called Fourspot Fluke; Great or Starry (*Platichthys stellatus*); Gulf or Sand (*Paralichthys albiguttus*); Hornyhead—see TURBOT; Longfin—see SOLE, Rex; Sand or Spotted (*Lophopsetta maculata*); Smooth or Smoothback (*Liopsetta putnami*); Southern (*Paralichthys lethostigmus*); Summer (*Paralichthys dentatus*); Winter (*Pseudopleuronectes americanus*); Witch (*Glyptocephalus cynoglossus*); Yellowtail (*Limanda ferruginea*).

FLUKE. See FLOUNDER.

FOOLFISH. See FLOUNDER, Smooth.

FROSTFISH. See TOMCOD, Atlantic.

GAFFTOPSAIL. See CATFISH.

GAG (*Mycteroperca microlepis*). Food: crustaceans, fish. Habitat: offshore reefs.

GARFISH. See SAURY.

GARUPPER. See GROUPER.

GIALOTA. See ROCKFISH, Yellowtail.

GOOSEFISH (*Lophius piscatorius*). Food: crustaceans, fish, mollusks. Habitat: Atlantic offshore waters.

GOPHER. See ROCKFISH, Kelp.

GREENBACK or **GREENJACK.** See MACKEREL, Pacific.

GREENFISH. See OPALEYE.

GREENLING. Food: crustaceans, fish. Habitat: Pacific Ocean kelp beds and rocky bottoms. Kelp (*Hexagrammos decagrammus*); Masked (*Hexagrammos octogrammus*); Painted (*Oxylebius pictus*); Red or Rock (*Hexagrammos superciliosus*); Whitespotted (*Hexagrammos stelleri*).

GRENADIER. See MARLIN SPIKE.

GROUPER. Food: crustaceans, fish. Habitat: Gulf of Mexico and offshore reefs. Black or Gray (*Mycteroperca bonaci*); Broomtail (*Mycteroperca xenarcha*); Marbled (*Dermatolepis inermis*); Misty (*Epinephelus mystacinus*); Nassau or White (*Epinephelus striatus*); Red (*Epinephelus morio*); Rock or Spotted (*Mycteroperca venenosa apua*); Salmon—see BOCACCIO; Tiger (*Mycteroperca tigris*); Warsaw (*Epinephelus nigritus*); Yellow or Yellowfin (*Mycteroperca venenosa venenosa*); Yellowedge (*Epinephelus flavolimbatus*); Yellowmouth (*Mycteroperca interstitialis*).

GRUNION (*Leuresthes tenuis*). Food: algae. Habitat: coastal waters of southern California.

GRUNT. Food: algae, crustaceans, fish, mollusks. Habitat: Gulf of Mexico and Atlantic reefs, rocky and sandy shores. Bastard Margaret or Ronco—see SAILORS CHOICE; Blue-striped, Bear, Humpback, or Yellow (*Haemulon sciurus*); Black (*Haemulon bonariense*); French or Open Mouth (*Haemulon flavolineatum*); Gray or Spanish (*Haemulon macrostomum*); White (*Haemulon plumieri*).

GUAHU. See WAHOO.

GUITARFISH. Food: crustaceans, mollusks. Habitat: shallow coastal muddy or sandy bottoms. Atlantic (*Rhinobatos lentiginosus*); California or Shovelnose (*Rhinobatos productus*).

GULF KINGFISH. See WHITING.

GUNNEL (*Pholis gunnellus*). Food: bottom feeders, crustaceans, mollusks. Habitat: coastal waters.

HADDOCK (*Melanogrammus aeglefinus*). Food: fish, mollusks, squid. Habitat: offshore waters.

HAIRTAIL. See CUTLASS FISH.

HAKE. Food: bottom feeders, crustaceans, fish, squid. Habitat: offshore school. Boston, Ling, Mud, or White (*Urophycis tenuis*); Carolina (*Urophycis earlli*); Longfin (*Phycis chesteri*); New England, or Silver (*Merluccius bilinearis*), also called Whiting; Pacific or Silver (*Merluccius productus*); Southern (*Urophycis floridanus*); Squirrel (*Urophycis chuss*).

HALFBEAK. Food: algae. Habitat: offshore waters. California (*Hyporhamphus rosae*); Common (*Hyporhamphus unifasciatus*).

HALFMOON (*Medialuna californiensis*). Food: crustaceans, algae. Habitat: kelp beds, rocky coastal waters. Also called Black or Blue Perch.

HALIBUT. Food: fish. Habitat: offshore waters. Arrowtooth—see FLOUN-DER, Arrowtooth; Atlantic (*Hippoglossus hippoglossus*); California, Chicken, or Southern (*Paralichthys californicus*); Northern or Pacific (*Hippoglossus stenolepis*).

HAMMERHEAD. See SHARK.

HAPUUPUU. See BASS, Black Sea.

HARDHEAD. See CROAKER, Atlantic.

HARDTAIL. See RUNNER, Blue.

HAULLULI. See MACKEREL, Snake.

HERRING. Food: plankton. Habitat: coastal and offshore waters. Atlantic or Sea (*Clupea harengus harengus*); Big, Bigeye—see TEN POUNDER; Blueback (*Alosa aestivalis*); Pacific (*Clupea harengus pallasii*); Round (*Etrumeus sadina*); Skipjack (*Alosa chrysochloris*).

HIND. Food: crustaceans, fish. Habitat: Atlantic offshore reefs. Calico or Red (*Epinephelus guttatus*); Rock (*Epinephelus adscensionis*); Speckled (*Epinephelus drummondhayi*).

HOGFISH (*Lachnolaimus maximus*). Food: crustaceans, mollusks. Habitat: Key West waters of Florida.

HORSE CREVALLE. See JACK.

HORSE MACKEREL. See BONITO, Atlantic; MACKEREL, California Horse or Jack; TUNA, Bluefin.

HORSEFISH. See **MOONFISH**.

HUMPBACK. See **SALMON** (under Freshwater Fish)

INDIAN RIVER PERMIT. See **POMPANO**, Atlantic, Great.

IRISHLORD. Food: crustaceans, fish. Habitat: Pacific coastal waters. Brown (*Hemilepidotus spinosus*); Redhead (*Hemilepidotus hemilepidotus*).

JACK. Food: crustaceans, fish. Habitat: coastal and offshore waters. Bar (*Caranx ruber*); Blue (*Caranx melampygus*); Common or Crevalle (*Caranx hippos*); Goggle-eye or Horse-eye (*Caranx latus*); Green (*Caranx caballus*); Hardtail—see **RUNNER**, Blue; Yellow (*Caranx bartholomaei*).

JACKSMELT (*Atherinopsis californiensis*). Food: crustaceans, plankton. Habitat: shallow coastal waters. Also called Blue, California, and Horse Smelt.

JEWFISH. Food: fish. Habitat: rocky coastal waters. Black—see **GROUPER**, Warsaw; Florida, Southern, or Spotted (*Epinephelus itajara*).

JOCU. See **SNAPPER**, Dog.

JUNEFISH. See **JEWFISH**, Florida.

JUREL. See **JACK**, Goggle-eye, Green.

KAHALA. See **AMBERJACK**, Hawaiian.

KAKU. See **BARRACUDA**, Great.

KAMANU. See **RUNNER**, Rainbow.

KELPFISH (*Heterostichus rostratus*). Food: crustaceans, fish. Habitat: Pacific coastal waters. See also **GREENLING**; **ROCKFISH**, Kelp.

KEY WEST PERMIT. *See* **POMPANO**, Great.

KINGFISH. See **CALIFORNIA KINGFISH**; **CERO**; **MACKEREL**; **WHITING**.

LADYFISH. See **TEN POUNDER**, Atlantic.

LAMPREY, SEA (*Petromyzon marinus*). Food: sucks blood of living fishes. Habitat: ocean waters; rivers and lakes; introduced by man into the Great Lakes above Niagara Falls.

LAWYER. See **SNAPPER**, Mangrove.

LEATHER JACKET (*Oligoplites saurus*). Food: fish. Habitat: coastal waters.

LING. See **COBIA**; **HAKE**; **LINGCOD**.

LINGCOD (*Ophiodon elongatus*). Food: crustaceans, fish. Habitat: California offshore waters, rocky bottoms, help beds. Flesh may be greenish (all trace of color disappears with cooking) and is not harmful to eat.

LOOKDOWN (*Selene vomer*). Food: crustaceans. Habitat: Florida and warm coastal waters.

LUMPFISH. See **TRIPLETAIL**.

MACABI. See **BONEFISH**.

MACHETE. See **TEN POUNDER**, Pacific.

MACKEREL. Food: crustaceans, fish, mollusks. Habitat: coastal and offshore waters. Atka (*Pleurogrammus monopterygius*); Atlantic or

Boston (*Scomber scombrus*); California Horse, Jack, or Pacific Jack (*Trachurus symmetricus*); Chub, Bullseye, Thimble-eye (*Scomber colias*); Florida—see CERO; Frigate (*Auxis thazard*); King or Spotted (*Scomberomorus cavalla*); Monterey Spanish (*Scomberomorus concolor*); Pacific (*Scomber japonicus*); Painted—see CERO; Snapping— see TAILOR; Spanish (*Scomberomorus maculatus*); Snake (*Gempylus serpens*); Yellow—see JACK.

MAHIMAHI. See DOLPHIN.

MAIDEN or FAIR MAIDEN. See SCUP.

MAIKO. See SURGEON FISH.

MAKO. See SHARK.

MANO KIHIKIHI. See SHARK, Hammerhead.

MANTA. See RAY, Giant Devil.

MARGATE (*Haemulon album*). Food: bottom feeder, crustaceans. Habitat: sandy and coastal waters.

MARLIN. Food: fish. Habitat: offshore waters. Black (*Makaira marlina*); Atlantic Blue (*Makaira ampla*); Pacific Blue (*Makaira mazara*); Striped (*Makaira audax*); White (*Makaira albida*).

MARLIN SPIKE (*Nezumia bairdi*). Food: fish. Habitat: Atlantic coastal waters.

MENHADEN (*Brevoortia tyrannus*). Food: plankton. Habitat: offshore waters.

MERO. See JEWFISH.

MEXICAN SKIPJACK. See MACKEREL, Frigate.

MIDSHIPMAN. Food: crustaceans, fish, squid. Habitat: Atlantic coastal waters. Atlantic (*Porichthys porosissimus*); Northern (*Porichthys notatus*); Slim (*Porichthys myriaster*).

MILKFISH (*Chanos chanos*). Food: plankton. Habitat: Hawaiian waters.

MINKFISH. See CALIFORNIA KINGFISH; CERO; MACKEREL; WHITING.

MOONFISH (*Vomer setapinnis*). Food: fish. Habitat: Gulf stream.

MOSSBUNKER. See MENHADEN.

MULLET. Food: bottom feeder, crustaceans, plankton. Habitat: inshore waters. Black or Striped (*Mugil cephalus*); Blueback or White (*Mugil curema*); Fantail (*Mugil trichodon*); Redeye (*Mugil gaimardiana*); Sea—see WHITING, King.

MUMMICHOG (*Fundulus heteroclitus*). Food: insects, plankton. Habitat: Gulf of Mexico and Atlantic waters.

MUSKELLUNGE. See BARRACUDA.

MUTTONFISH. See SNAPPER, Green.

NEEDLEFISH (*Strongylura marina*). Food: fish. Habitat: coastal waters.

NENUE. See RUDDERFISH, Pacific.

NERO. See ROCKFISH, Black.

NIGHTFISH. See GRUNION; SMELT; WHITEBAIT.

OCEAN WHITEFISH. See WHITEFISH.

OCEANIC SKIPJACK. See SKIPJACK; TUNA, Skipjack.

OIO. See BONEFISH.

ONO. See WAHOO.

OPALEYE (*Girella nigricans*). Food: aquatic vegetation. Habitat: coastal waters.

OPELU. See SCAD, Mackerel.

OYSTERFISH. See TAUTOG.

PACIFIC KINGFISH. See WAHOO.

PALOMETA. See POMPANO.

PAUU (*Caranx ignobilis*). Food: fish. Habitat: Hawaiian waters.

PERCH. Food: fish. Habitat: coastal waters. Barred, Rainbow, Silver, Striped, or Surf—see SURFPERCH; Black, Bluenose, Chinafin, Gray, Sea, or White (*Roccus americanus*); Blue—see CROAKER, Black; HALFMOON; ROCKFISH; Catalina or Green—see OPALEYE; Kelp (*Brachyistius frenatus*); Sand (*Diplectrum formosum*); see also SURFPERCH; TRIPLETAIL.

PERMIT (*Trachinotus falcatus*). Food: crustaceans. Habitat: shallow, sandy coastal waters.

PETO. See WAHOO.

PICIATA. See TOMCOD, Pacific.

PIGFISH (*Orthopristis chrysopterus*). Food: crustaceans, fish. Habitat: shoals in Gulf of Mexico and Atlantic waters.

PINFISH (*Lagodon rhomboides*). Food: crustaceans, fish, mollusks. Habitat: shallow Atlantic and Gulf of Mexico waters.

PINTADO. See MACKEREL.

PIPEFISH (*Syngnathus fuscus*). Food: plants and crustaceans in seaweed. Habitat: coastal waters.

PLAICE. Food: bottom feeders, marine invertebrates. Habitat: offshore waters. Alaska (*Pleuronectes quadrituberculatus*); American (*Hippoglossoides platessoides*).

POGY. See MENHADEN; SURFPERCH, Redtail.

POLKA DOT. See HIND.

POLLACK or POLLOCK. Food: fish. Habitat: offshore waters. Atlantic (*Pollachius virens*); Pacific or Walleye (*Theragra chalcogrammus*).

POMPANO. Food: fish. Habitat: outer reefs and coastal waters. Atlantic or Carolina (*Trachinotus carolinus*); California or Pacific (*Palometa simillima*); Gafftopsail (*Trachinotus rhodopus*); Great (*Trachinotus goodei*), also called Atlantic Permit; Longfin (*Trachinotus glaucus*); Paloma (*Trachinotus paitensis*); Round—see PERMIT.

POMPOM (*Anisotremus surinamensis*). Food: crustaceans, minnows. Habitat: Atlantic rocky shoals.

PORCUPINE (*Diodon hystrix*). Food: crustaceans. Habitat: coastal waters.

PORGY or PAUGY. Food: bottom feeders, crustaceans, fish, mollusks. Habitat: offshore schoolfish. Grass (*Calamus arctifrons*); Hawaiian (*Monotaxis grandoculis*); Jolthead (*Calamus bajonado*); Little Head (*Calamus proridens*); Northern (*Stenotomus versicolor*); Saucereye (*Calamus calamus*); Southern (*Stenotomus aculeatus*).

PORKFISH (*Anisotremus virginicus*). Food: crustaceans, fish, mollusks. Habitat: Key West shoals and deep waters.

POTBELLY. See ROCKFISH, Tambor.

PRIESTFISH. See ROCKFISH, Black, Blue.

PRINCESS ROCKFISH. See GROUPER, Yellow.

PUFFER (*Spheroides maculatus*). Food: crustaceans, mollusks. Habitat: coastal waters.

PUHI. See EEL.

PUMPKINSEED. See BUTTERFISH.

QUEENFISH (*Seriphus politus*). Food: fish. Habitat: coastal waters. See also CROAKER, White; HERRING, Pacific; WAHOO.

RAY. Food: bottom feeder, crustaceans, mollusks. Habitat: coastal and offshore waters. Atlantic Manta or Giant Devil (*Manta birostris*); Bullnose, Bullnose Eagle, or Whip (*Myliobatis freminvillei*); Cownose (*Rhinoptera bonasus*); Devil (*Mobula hypostoma*); Electric, Atlantic Torpedo (*Torpedo nobiliana*); Pacific Electric (*Torpedo californica*); Round—see STINGRAY, Yellow; Smooth or Lesser Smooth Butterfly (*Gymnura micrura*); Spiny or Giant Butterfly (*Gymnura altavela*); Spotted Eagle (*Aetobatus narinari*).

REDFISH. See ROSEFISH; SHEEPHEAD, California.

ROBALO. See SNOOK.

ROCKFISH. Food: crustaceans, fish. Habitat: coastal and offshore waters. Bass or Olive (*Sebastodes serranoides*); Black (*Sebastodes melanops*); Blue, Blue Perch (*Sebastodes mystinus*); Brown (*Sebastodes auriculatus*); Canary or Orange (*Sebastodes pinniger*); Copper (*Sebastodes caurinus*); Grass (*Sebastodes rastrelliger*); Greenspotted (*Sebastodes chlorostictus*); Kelp (*Sebastodes atrovirens*); Quillback, Brown, Orange-spotted, or Speckled (*Sebastodes maliger*); Rosy (*Sebastodes rosaceus*); Tambor or Turkey (*Sebastodes ruberrimus*); Tiger (*Sebastodes nigrocinctus*); Widow (*Sebastodes entomelas*); Yellowtail (*Sebastodes flavidus*).

RONCADOR. See CROAKER, Golden.

RONCO. See SAILORS CHOICE.

ROOSTERFISH (*Nematistius pectoralis*). Food: fish. Habitat: coastal and offshore waters.

ROSEFISH (*Sebastes marinus*). Food: crustaceans, fish. Habitat: offshore waters.

RUDDERFISH. Food: algae, fish. Habitat: schoolfish that follow ships offshore into coastal waters. Atlantic (*Kyphosus sectatrix*); Pacific (*Kyphosus cinerascens*).

RUNNER. Food: crustaceans, fish. Habitat: coastal waters. Blue (*Caranx crysos*); Rainbow (*Elegatis bipinnulatus*).

SABLEFISH (*Anoplopoma fimbria*). Food: crustaceans, fish. Habitat: Pacific offshore waters.

SAILFISH. Food: fish, squid. Habitat: offshore waters. Atlantic or Florida (*Istiophorus albicans*); Hawaiian (*Istiophorus orientalis*); Pacific (*Istiophorus greyi*); see also MARLIN.

SAILORS CHOICE (*Haemulon parra*). Food: crustaceans, fish, mollusks. Habitat: shallow Gulf of Mexico and Atlantic waters.

SALMON. Food: crustaceans, fish. Habitat: coastal and offshore waters. Black—see COBIA; Hawaiian—see RUNNER, Rainbow; Santa Catalina —see BASS, California; White—see AMBERJACK, Pacific; see FRESH-WATER FISH—SALMON.

SANDDAB. Food: crustaceans, squid, small fish. Habitat: sandy bottoms in offshore waters. Catalina or Longfin (*Citharichthys xanthostigma*); Mottled or Pacific (*Citharichthys sordidus*).

SANDFISH (*Diplectrum formosum*). Food: crustaceans, fish. Habitat: deep inshore waters. Also called Sand Perch.

SANDUCHA. See BONEFISH.

SAUREL. See MACKEREL, California Horse, Jack.

SAURY. Food: fish. Habitat: coastal and offshore waters. Atlantic (*Scomberesox saurus*); Pacific (*Cololabis saira*).

SAWFISH (*Pristis pectinatus*). Food: fish. Habitat: Gulf of Mexico and Atlantic sandy shores.

SCABBARDFISH (*Lepidopus xantusi*). Food: fish. Habitat: Pacific offshore waters.

SCAD. Food: fish. Habitat: offshore waters. Bigeye or Goggle-eye (*Trachurops crumenophthalmus*); Mackerel (*Decapterus macarellus*); Rough (*Trachurus lathami*); Round (*Decapterus punctatus*).

SCHOOLMASTER. See SNAPPER, Black.

SCOOT or SCOOTER. See BARRACUDA, California.

SCORPIONFISH. Food: crustaceans, fish. Habitat: rocky coastal and offshore waters. California (*Scorpaena guttata*); Hunchback (*Scorpaena dispar*); Red (*Scorpaena atlantica*); Spotted (*Scorpaena plumieri*).

SCROD. See COD, Atlantic; HADDOCK.

SCULPIN. Food: bottom feeder, crustaceans. Habitat: coastal waters. Arctic (*Myoxocephalus scorpiodes*); Buffalo (*Enophrys bison*); Calico (*Clinocottus embryum*); California—see SCORPIONFISH; Daddy or Shorthorn (*Myoxocephalus scorpius*); Deepwater or Fourhorn (*Myoxocephalus quadricornis*); Giant Marbled—see

CABEZON; Great (*Myoxocephalus polyacanthocephalus*); Longhorn (*Myoxocephalus octodecemspinosus*); Mailed (*Triglops ommatistius*); Pacific, Staghorn, or Smooth (*Leptocottus armatus*).

SCUP (*Stenotomus chrysops*). Food: crustaceans, fish. Habitat: coastal and offshore waters.

SCUPPAUG. See PORGY.

SEA BASS. See BASS.

SEA BREAM. See BREAM.

SEA PERCH. See SURFPERCH.

SEA RAVEN (*Hemitripterus americanus*). Food: marine invertebrates, fish. Habitat: coastal and offshore waters.

SEA ROBIN (*Prionotus carolinus*). Food: small crustaceans, fish, squid. Habitat: shallow coastal waters.

SEA SQUAB. See PUFFER.

SEATROUT. Food: crustaceans, fish. Habitat: coastal waters. Sand (*Cynoscion arenarius*); Silver (*Cynoscion nothus*); Spotted (*Cynoscion nebulosus*); see also GREENLING; LINGCOD.

SERGEANT FISH. See COBIA; SNOOK.

SHARK PILOT. See AMBERJACK.

SHARK. Food: crustaceans, fish, squid, some of the larger sharks eat sea turtles). Habitat: coastal and offshore waters. Angel (*Squatina dumerili*); Basking (*Cetorhinus maximus*); Blue or Great Blue (*Prionace glauca*); Bonito (*Isurus glaucus*); Brown (*Carcharhinus milberti*); Bull or Ground (*Carcharhinus leucas*); Cat or Leopard (*Triakis semifasciata*); Dusky (*Carcharhinus obscurus*); Fox, Swiveltail, or Thresher (*Alopias vulpinus*); Great White or Maneater (*Carcharodon carcharias*); Hammerhead (*Sphyrna zygaena*); Large Blacktip or Spinner (*Carcharinus maculipinnis*); Leopard or or Tiger (*Galeocerdo cuvier*); Mackerel or Porbeagle (*Lamna nasus*); Mako (*Isurus oxyrinchus*); Nurse (*Ginglymostoma cirratum*); Salmon (*Lamna ditropis*); Sand (*Carcharias taurus*); Soupfin (*Galeorhinus zyopterus*).

SHEEPHEAD (*Pimelometopon pulchrum*). Food: crustaceans, fish. Habitat: kelp and mussel beds in Pacific rocky coastal waters.

SHEEPSHEAD (*Archosargus probatocephalus*). Food: crustaceans, fish. Habitat: tidal Atlantic coastal waters.

SHINER. See BREAM; BUTTERFISH; MOONFISH; SURFPERCH.

SIERRA. See CERO.

SILVER KING. See TARPON.

SILVER SHUTTLE. See BONEFISH.

SKATE. Food: bottom feeders, crustaceans. Habitat: sandy, shallow, waters. Often mistaken for RAY. Barndoor (*Raja laevis*); Big (*Raja ocellata*); Brier or Clearnose (*Raja eglanteria*); Little (*Raja erinacea*); Thorny (*Rajaradiata*).

SKIPJACK. Food: fish. Habitat: offshore waters. Black (*Euthynnus lineatus*); Waveyback (*Euthynnus yaito*); see also TUNA, Skipjack; BONITO, Arctic; HERRING, Skipjack; RUNNER, Rainbow.

SKIPPER. See SAURY.

SNAPPER. Food: crustaceans, fish. Habitat: Gulf of Mexico and Atlantic inshore and offshore reefs. Bastard, Chubhead, Night, or Vermilion (*Rhomboplites aurorubens*); Black (*Apsilus dentatus*); Brown or Red—see GROUPER, Red; Dog (*Lutjanus jocu*); Gray (*Lutjanus griseus*); Green or Mutton (*Lutjanus analis*); Lane, Redtailed, or Spotted (*Lutjanus synagris*); Mangrove (*Lutjanus griseus*); Pensacola Red or Red (*Lutjanus blackfordii*); Schoolmaster (*Lutjanus apodus*); Yellowtail (*Ocyurus chrysurus*).

SNOOK (*Centropomus undecimalis*). Food: crustaceans, fish. Habitat: mudflats and sandy shore waters, river mouths.

SOLE. Food: crustaceans, fish. Habitat: coastal waters. Arrowtoothed—see FLOUNDER, Arrowtoothed; Butter or Scalyfin (*Isopsetta isolepis*); Deepsea (*Embassichthys bathybius*); Dover, Slime, or Slippery (*Microstomus pacificus*); English, Lemon, or Pointed Nose (*Parophrys vetulus*); Fantail (*Xystreurys liolepis*); Longfinned or Rex (*Glyptocephalus zachirus*); Petrale or Round-nosed (*Eopsetta jordani*); Rock or Roughback (*Lepidopsetta bilineata*); Sand (*Psettichthys melanostictus*); Yellowfin (*Limanda aspera*).

SOURBELLY OT SOURFISH. See SAURY.

SPEARFISH. Food: fish. Habitat: offshore waters. Longbill (*Tetrapturus belone*); Shortbill (*Tetrapturus angustirostris*).

SPOT (*Leiostomus xanthurus*). Food: fish. Habitat: coastal waters.

SQUAB. See PUFFER.

SQUAWFISH. See ROCKFISH, Blue.

SQUETEAGUE, GRAY. (*Cynoscion regalis*). Food: crustaceans, fish. Habitat: Gulf of Mexico and Atlantic coastal waters. Also called Seatrout and Gray Weakfish.

SQUID HOUND. See BASS, Striped.

SQUIRRELFISH. See GRUNT, Gray, White.

STINGRAY. Food: bottom feeders, crustaceans, mollusks. Habitat: coastal waters. Atlantic (*Dasyatis sabina*); Bat (*Myliobatis californica*); Diamond or Southern (*Dasyatis dipterurus*); Round (*Urolophus halleri*); Yellow (*Urolophus jamaicensis*).

STRIPER. See BASS, Striped.

STURGEON. See FRESHWATER FISH.

SURFPERCH. Food: crustaceans, fish. Habitat: coastal waters. Barred

(*Amphistichus argenteus*); Black (*Embiotoca jacksoni*); Calico (*Holconotus koelzi*); Kelp (*Brachyistius frenatus*); Pile (*Damalichthys vacca*); Rainbow (*Hypsurus caryi*); Redtail (*Holoconotus rhodoterus*); Rubberlip (*Rhachochilus toxotes*); Shiner or Silver (*Cymatogaster aggregata*); Spotfin (*Hyperprosopon anale*); Striped (*Taeniotoca lateralis*); Walleye (*Hyperprosopon argenteum*); White (*Phanerodon furcatus*).

SUGARFISH. See ROCKFISH, Bass.

SURGEON FISH. Food: algae. Habitat: offshore waters. Gulf (*Acanthurus randalli*); Hawaiian (*Acanthurus nigroris*).

SWORDFISH, BROADBILL (*Xiphias gladius*). Food: fish, squid. Habitat: offshore waters.

TAILOR. See BLUEFISH.

TALLY WAG. See BASS, Black Sea.

TARPON. Food: crabs, fish. Habitat: offshore waters. Atlantic (*Tarpon atlanticus*); Tourist—see JACK, Common or Crevalle.

TAUTOG (*Tautoga onitis*). Food: crustaceans, mollusks, fish. Habitat: offshore Atlantic waters.

TEN POUNDER. Food: crustaceans, fish. Habitat: coastal waters. Atlantic (*Elops saurus*); Hawaiian (*Elops hawaiensis*); Pacific (*Elops affinis*).

TILEFISH (*Lopholatilus chamaeleonticeps*). Food: crustaceans, fish, squid. Habitat: Continental Shelf and coastal waters.

TOADFISH (*Opsanus tau*). Food: crustaceans, fish. Habitat: shallow coastal waters.

TOMCOD. Food: fish, invertebrates. Habitat: offshore waters. Atlantic (*Microgadus tomcod*); Pacific (*Microgadus proximus*).

TRIPLETAIL (*Lobotes surinamensis*). Food: crustaceans, fish. Habitat: Atlantic offshore waters.

TROUT. See GREENLING, Kelp; SEATROUT; SQUETEAGUE.

TRUMPETFISH (*Fistularia tabacaria*). Food: fish. Habitat: warm offshore waters.

TRUNKFISH. Food: fish. Habitat: offshore waters. Common (*Lactophrys trigonus*); Horned (*Acanthostracion quadricornis*).

TUNA. Food: fish. Habitat: offshore waters. Albacore or Longfinned—see ALBACORE; Bigeye (*Thunnus obesus*); Blackfin (*Thunnus atlanticus*); Bluefin or Great Bluefin (*Thunnus thynnus*); Little (*Euthynnus alletteratus*); Skipjack (*Euthynnus pelamis*); Yellowfin (*Thunnus albacares*), also called Allison.

TURBOT. Food: crustaceans, fish, squid. Habitat: coastal waters. C-O or Mottled (*Pleuronichthys coenosus*); Curlfin (*Pleuronichthys decurrens*); Diamond (*Hypsopsetta guttulata*); Hornyhead (*Pleuronichthys verticalis*); Spotted (*Pleuronichthys ritteri*).

VICTORFISH. See BONITO, Oceanic.

Uku. See Snapper, Gray, Mangrove.

Ulua, White (*Carangoides ajax*). Food: fish. Habitat: Hawaiian waters.

Wahoo (*Acanthocybium solandri*) Food: fish. Habitat: offshore reefs.

Warsaw. See Grouper, Warsaw.

Weakfish. Food: crustaceans, fish. Habitat: Atlantic coastal waters. Gray (*Cynoscion regalis*), also called Squeteague; Sand, Silver, Spotted—see Seatrout; see also Bass, White Sea; Corvina.

Whitebait. Food: shrimp-type crustaceans. Habitat: coastal waters. Day or Surf (*Hypomesus pretiosus*) also called Surf Smelt; Night (*Spirinchus starksi*), also called Night Smelt; term Whitebait also applied to the true Smelt family (Osmeridae), Jacksmelt, Herring, and Silversides.

Whitefish (*Caulolatilus princeps*). Food: fish. Habitat: offshore waters.

Whiting. Food: crustaceans, fish, mollusks. Habitat: coastal waters. Gulf King (*Menticirrhus littoralis*); King or Northern (*Menticirrhus saxatilis*); Sand, Silver, Southern, or Surf (*Menticirrhus americanus*).

Widowfish. See Rockfish, Widow.

Wolffish. Food: crustaceans, mollusks. Habitat: offshore waters. Atlantic (*Anarhichas lupus*); Bering (*Anarhichas orientalis*); Northern (*Anarhichas denticulatus*); Spotted (*Anarhichas minor*).

Wrasse. Food: crustaceans, fish. Habitat: coastal waters. Blackear (*Halichoeres poeyi*); California or Rock (*Halichoeres semicinctus*) Clown (*Halichoeres maculipinna*); Creole (*Halichoeres parrai*); Yellowhead (*Halichoeres garnoti*) see also Cunner; Sheephead; Tautog.

Wrymouth (*Cryptacanthodes maculatus*). Food: crustaceans, fish, mollusks. Habitat: coastal waters, muddy bottoms.

Yellow caranx. See Jack, Crevalle.

Yellowtail (*Seriola dorsalis*). Food: fish, squid. Habitat: offshore California waters. See also Rockfish, Yellowtail; Runner, Rainbow.

Yellowfin. See Tuna.

RECORDS OF SALTWATER FISH*

TAKEN BY ROD AND REEL

Albacore–69 lbs. 1 oz., Hudson Canyon, New Jersey
Amberjack–120 lbs. 8 oz., Kona Coast, Island of Hawaii
Barracuda, Great–103 lbs. 4 oz., West End, British West Indies
Bass, California Black Sea–557 lbs. 3 oz., Santa Catalina Island, California.
Bass, California White Sea–83 lbs. 12 oz., San Felipe, Mexico

---
* Source: International Game Fish Association and other authorities.

BASS, Channel–see **DRUM,** Red
BASS, Giant Sea–in Atlantic waters, see **JEWFISH**
BASS, Striped–73 lbs., Vineyard Sound, Massachusetts
BLUEFISH–24 lbs. 3 oz., São Miguel, Azores (Atlantic Ocean)
BONEFISH–19 lbs., Zululand, South Africa
BONITO, Oceanic–see **TUNA,** Skipjack
COBIA–102 lbs., Cape Charles, Virginia
COD–74 lbs. 4 oz., Boothbay Harbor, Maine
DOLPHIN–76 lbs., Acapulco, Mexico
DRUM, Black–94 lbs. 4 oz., Cape Charles, Virginia
DRUM, Red–83 lbs., Cape Charles, Virginia
JACK, Crevalle–45 lbs. 12 oz., Indian River, Florida
FLOUNDER, Summer–20 lbs. 7 oz., Long Island, New York
JEWFISH–680 lbs., Fernandina Beach, Florida
MARLIN, Atlantic Blue–810 lbs., Cape Hatteras, North Carolina
MARLIN, Black–1,560 lbs., Cape Blanco, Peru
MARLIN, Pacific Blue–1,003 lbs. 12 oz., Kona Coast, Island of Hawaii
MARLIN, Striped–692 lbs., Balboa, California
MARLIN, White–161 lbs., Miami Beach, Florida
PERMIT–47 lbs. 12 oz., Boca Grande Pass, Florida
POLLACK–42 lbs., Scituate, Massachusetts
ROOSTERFISH–114 lbs., La Paz, Mexico
RUNNER, Rainbow–23 lbs., Island of Oahu, Hawaii
SAILFISH, Atlantic–141 lbs. 1 oz., Ivory Coast, Africa
SAILFISH, Pacific–221 lbs., Santa Cruz Island, Galapagos Islands
SAWFISH–890 lbs. 8 oz., Fort Amador, Canal Zone
SEATROUT, Spotted–15 lbs. 3 oz., Fort Pierce, Florida
SHARK, Great Blue–410 lbs., Rockport, Massachusetts
SHARK, Great White (Maneater)–2,664 lbs., Ceduna, South Australia
SHARK, Porbeagle–390 lbs. 8 oz., Fire Island, New York
SHARK, Thresher–922 lbs., Bay of Islands, New Zealand
SHARK, Tiger–1,422 lbs., Cape Moreton, Australia
SNOOK–52 lbs. 6 oz., LaPaz, Baja California, Mexico
SWORDFISH–1,182 lbs., Iquique, Chile
TARPON–283 lbs., Lake Maracaibo, Venezuela (Caribbean Sea)
TAUTOG–21 lbs. 6 oz., Cape May, New Jersey
TUNA, Bigeye (Atlantic)–295 lbs., São Miguel, Azores
TUNA, Bigeye (Pacific)–435 lbs., Cabo Blanco, Peru
TUNA, Blue fin–977 lbs., St. Ann Bay, Nova Scotia
TUNA, Skipjack–39 lbs. 15 oz., Walker Cay, British West Indies
TUNA, Yellowfin–269 lbs. 8 oz., Island of Kauai, Hawaii
WAHOO–149 lbs., Cat Cay, British West Indies
WEAKFISH–19 lbs. 8 oz., Trinidad, West Indies

NOT TAKEN BY ROD AND REEL

BASS, California Sea–800 lbs., Avalon, Santa Catalina Island, California
BASS, Striped–125 lbs., Edenton, North Carolina
BLUEFISH–27 lbs., Nantucket, Massachusetts
DRUM, Black–146 lbs., St. Augustine, Florida
FLOUNDER, Summer–26 lbs., Noank, Connecticut
SAWFISH–1,500 lbs., Aransas Pass, Texas
TARPON–350 lbs., Hillsboro, Florida

OVER 100 POUNDS TAKEN BY WOMEN WITH ROD AND REEL *

AMBERJACK–106 lbs. 8 oz., Pinas Bay, Panama (Helen Robinson)
BASS, California Black Sea–452 lbs., Coronado Island, California (Lorene Wheeler)
JEWFISH–204 lbs., Bahia Honde, Florida (Mrs. Phyllis Carson)
MARLIN, Black–1,525 lbs., Cabo Blanco, Peru (K. Wiss)
MARLIN, Blue–730 lbs., Cat Cay, British West Indies (Mrs. Henry Sears)
MARLIN, Striped–430 lbs., Mayor Island, New Zealand (Mrs. H. J. Carkeet)
MARLIN, White–152 lbs., Bimini, British West Indies (Mrs. Marion Stevens)
SAILFISH, Atlantic–104 lbs. 8 oz., Miami Beach, Florida (R. E. Pope)
SAILFISH, Pacific–796 lbs., Acapulco, Mexico (F. Bart)
SHARK, Mako–858 lbs., Whangaroa, New Zealand (Mrs. Rita Beaver)
SHARK, White–1,052 lbs., Cape Moreton, Australia (R. Dyer)
SHARK, Thresher–729 lbs., Mayor Island, New Zealand (Mrs. V. Brown)
SHARK, Tiger–1,314 lbs., Cape Moreton, Australia (R. Dyer)
SWORDFISH–772 lbs., Iquique, Chile (Mrs. L. Marron)
TARPON–203 lbs., Marathon, Florida (June Jordan)
TUNA, Bluefin–882 lbs., Wedgeport, Nova Scotia (Mrs. B. D. Crowninshield)
TUNA, Yellowfin–254 lbs., Kona, Island of Hawaii (J. Carlisle)
WAHOO–110 lbs., Walker Cay, British West Indies (Mrs. B. D. Crowninshield)

* SOURCE: International Game Fish Association.

Amphibians

HELLBENDER (*Cryptobranchus alleganiensis*). Food: insects and their larvae. Habitat: freshwater streams, behind rocks or other objects on river bottoms. Description: grayish or reddish blotched and wrinkled-skin creature with a flattened body and tail, 4 short thick limbs (4 stubby toes on front feet, 5 on hind feet); bites with sharp teeth while angler tries to throw it back; small lidless eyes; and may grow to 25 inches in length.

MUDPUPPY (*Necturus maculosus*). Food: bottom feeder, small invertebrates. Habitat: bayous, canals, streams. Description: 4 short stocky legs; red ear-like gills; a flat head, small eyes, large mouth; spotted grayish-brown body with a yellow line bordering a dark back; may grow to 15 inches in length. Also called a Dogfish, Hellbender, Water Dog.

FROGS

Alligator or Greenback (*Rana heckscheri*)
American Bullfrog, Jug-O-Rum, or Jumbo (*Rana catesbeiana*)
Cold Swamp, Leopard, Pickerel, Spring, or Tiger (*Rana palustris*)
Common, Green, Pond, or Yellow-throated (*Rana clamitans*)
Crawfish (*Rana aerolata*)
Gopher (*Rana capito*)
Grass, Herring Hopper, Meadow, Peeping, Shad, or Spotted Green (*Rana pipiens*)
Hoosier, Mink, Northern, or Rocky Mountain (*Rana septentrionalis*)
Lake, Pig, Southern, or Swamp Bullfrog (*Rana grylio*)
Pacific or Western (*Rana pretiosa*)
Redlegged (*Rana aurora*)
Wood (*Rana sylvatica*)

The above frogs are usually used for food rather than as bait, and the American Bullfrog's legs are considered choice. Food: crayfish, insects, mollusks, mice, fish, turtles. Habitat: swamps, lakes, ponds, reservoirs with brush or wooded shores.

PART IV

Federal Regulations for
Migratory Birds

Birds crossing state and national borders are protected by the Migratory Bird Treaty Act and international agreements between Canada, Mexico, and the United States. Regulations are adopted annually and administered by the Fish and Wildlife Service of the U.S. Department of the Interior. All persons 16 or more years of age must obtain a migratory bird hunting stamp (also known as the "Duck" stamp) to take birds designated as game under the Migratory Bird Treaty Act. Violation of any Federal regulation is punishable by a fine of not more than $500 and/or imprisonment for not more than 6 months. The Migratory Bird Treaty Act provides for fines of not more than $2,000 and/or imprisonment for not more than 2 years for anyone convicted of taking migratory birds with intent to sell, offer to sell, barter, or offer to barter them. No permit is required to possess and transport for personal use the plumage and skins of lawfully taken game birds. Any person without a permit may possess, dispose of, and transport feathers of lawfully taken wild ducks and geese for the making of fishing flies, bed pillows, mattresses, and similar commercial uses, but not for millinery or ornamental use. State regulations may be more restrictive, but are within the framework of, or identical with, those adopted by the Secretary of the U.S. Department of the Interior.

MIGRATORY BIRDS

Game: Avocets, Brants, Coots, Cranes, Curlews, Doves, Dowitchers, Ducks, Gallinules, Geese, Godwits, Knots, Oystercatchers, Phalaropes, Wild Pigeons, Plovers, Rails, Sandpipers, Snipes, Soras, Surfbirds, Swans, Turnstones, Willets, Woodcocks, and Yellowlegs.

Nongame: Auklets, Auks, Bitterns, Fulmars, Gannets, Grebes, Guillemots, Gulls, Herons, Jaegers, Loons, Murres, Petrels, Puffins, Shearwaters, and Terns.

Insectivorous: Blackbirds, Bobolinks, Buntings, Bushtits, Cardinals, Catbirds, Chickadees, Chuck-will's-widows, Brown Creepers, Cowbirds, Cuckoos, Finches, Flickers, Flycatchers, Gnatcatchers, Crackles, Grosbeaks, Hummingbirds, Kingbirds, Kinglets, Horned Larks, Meadow Larks, Martins, Mockingbirds, Nighthawks, Nuthatches, Orioles, Phainopeplas, Phoebes, Pipits, Roadrunners, Robins, Shrikes, Sparrows, Swallows, Swifts, Tanagers, Thrashers, Thrushes, Titmice, Towhees, Verdins, Vireos, Warblers, Waxings, Whip-poor-wills, Woodpeckers, and Wrens.

LEGAL HUNTING

Migratory game birds may be taken by the following methods unless they are specifically prohibited by State regulations:

1. By the aid of dogs, artificial decoys, manually or mouth-operated bird calls; with longbow and arrow, or with shotgun (not larger than No. 10 gauge and incapable of holding more than 3 shells) fired from the shoulder;

2. In the open, or from a blind or other place of concealment (except a sinkbox) on land or water;

3. From any floating craft (except a sink box), and excluding any boat or other craft having a motor attached, or any sailboat unless such water crafts are anchored, beached, or tied alongside of any type of fixed hunting blind. Exceptions: Rails may be taken from a motor-powered craft if the source of power has been completely shut off and the boat is immobile, or is being propelled only by oars, paddles, or poles. Motorboats, sailboats, or other such craft may be used only for picking up injured or dead birds.

4. On or over standing crops (including aquatics), flooded standing crops, flooded harvested crop lands, grain crops properly shocked on the field where grown, or grains scattered solely as a result of normal agricultural planting or harvesting.

PROHIBITED HUNTING

Migratory game birds may NOT be taken by the following methods:

1. With a net, snare, trap, crossbow and arrow, pistol, rifle, swivel gun, or machine gun;

2. With a shotgun, of any description, originally capable of holding more than 3 shells unless the capacity of the gun is reduced to not more than 3 shells in the magazine and chamber combined;

3. From, or by use of, aircraft, motor-powered vehicles, sailboat, and sink box. Such craft must be anchored, moored, tied to a hunting blind (except sink box), or beached. Motor-powered vehicles may be used only to pick up dead or injured birds.

4. By the use or aid of live birds as decoys, of recorded bird calls or sounds, recorded or electrically amplified imitations of bird calls or sounds;

5. By the use or aid of livestock as a blind or means of concealment;

6. By means or aid of any motor-driven land, water, or air con-

veyance or any sailboat used for the purpose of, or resulting in, the concentrating, driving, rallying, or stirring up of waterfowl, coots, or cranes;

7. By the aid of baiting on or over any baiting area such as the placing, exposing, depositing, distributing, or scattering of shelled, shucked, or unshucked corn, wheat or other grains, salt or other feed so as to constitute for such birds a lure, attraction, or enticement to, or over any area where hunters are attempting to take them. Birds may be taken over standing crops, flooded standing crops (including aquatics), flooded harvested crop lands, grain crops properly shocked on the field where grown, or grains scattered solely as the result of normal agricultural planting or harvesting.

POSSESSION LIMITS

No person on the opening day of the season may possess any freshly killed migratory game birds in excess of the daily bag limit or aggregate daily bag limit. Freshly killed migratory game birds may not be possessed during closed seasons.

No migratory birds may be taken at any time, by any means, from, on, or across any highway, road, trail, or other right of way, whether public or private, within the exterior boundaries of any established national wildlife refuge.

No person shall kill or cripple any migratory game bird without making a reasonable effort to retrieve the bird and include it in his daily bag limit. Every wounded bird should be killed at once.

No person may receive or have in custody any migratory game birds belonging to another person unless such birds are properly tagged.

No hunter who legally takes and possesses migratory game birds shall place or leave such birds in the custody of any other person for cleaning, picking, processing, shipping, transportation, or storage unless a tag is attached and signed by the hunter stating his address, the total number and kinds of birds, and the date they were killed.

TRANSPORTATION

Legal possession of migratory game birds taken by a hunter is deemed to have ceased after they have been delivered to another person as a gift, or delivered to a post office, a common carrier, a commercial cold storage or locker plant for transportation by the postal service or a common carrier to some person other than the hunter. Such birds transported in any vehicle as personal baggage of the possessor are not considered to be in storage.

No permit is necessary to transport lawfully killed and possessed migratory game birds into, within, or out of any state, or export such birds to a foreign country during and after the open seasons in the state where taken, subject to the following conditions:

1. If such birds are dressed, one fully feathered wing must remain attached so as to permit identification of their species while being transported between the place where taken and the personal abode of the possessor, or between the place where taken and a commercial preservation facility.

2. Any such birds transported from any state not later than 48 hours following the close of the open season therein may continue in transit for such additional time as may be needed immediately after shipment, but not to exceed 5 days for delivery to their destination.

3. The name and address of the shipper and of the consignee and an accurate statement of the numbers and kinds of birds must be clearly and conspicuously marked on the outside of the container or package.

IMPORTATION

Migratory game birds lawfully taken and possessed in and exported from a foreign country may be entered and transported in any state without a permit, subject to the following conditions:

1. Migratory game birds may be imported from Canada with one fully feathered wing, but shipments of such birds must be accompanied by tags or permits if required by dominion or provincial laws.

2. Shipments from Mexico must be accompanied by a Mexican export permit. Birds must be dressed, drawn, and have head and feet removed if imported from Mexico or any other foreign country except Canada. One fully feathered wing must remain attached so as to permit species identification.

3. Such birds must be transported from a foreign country not later than 5 days following the close of the open season where taken, and may continue in transit for not more than 5 additional days for delivery to their destination.

4. The name and address of the shipper and of the consignee and an accurate statement of the numbers and kinds of birds must be clearly and conspicuously marked on the outside of the container or package.

5. No migratory game birds (or parts thereof) may be transported from, to, or through any state or foreign country contrary to the laws of such places.

QUOTAS

The following migratory game birds may be imported and transported by one person, either in a single shipment or by multiple shipments, from foreign countries or their subdivisions (figures indicate total number per calendar week*): Brant, 6; Coot, 25; Cranes, 5; Doves, 25 singly or in the aggregate of all species; Ducks, 10 from Province of Ontario, 10 from any foreign countries except Canada, 12 from all other Canadian provinces except Alberta, British Columbia, Manitoba, Saskatechewan; Geese, 5 from foreign countries except Canada, 10 from Canadian provinces except Alberta, British Columbia, Manitoba, and Saskatchewan; Wild Pigeons, 10 of each species; Rails, 30 singly or aggregate of all species; Sora, 25; Wilson's Snipe, 8; Woodcock, 16.

Not more than 16 Ducks and 10 Geese per season may be transported from the province of British Columbia in Canada; and only 10 Ducks and 10 Geese per season from the provinces of Alberta, Manitoba, and Saskatchewan in Canada.

MIGRATORY BIRD REFUGES

The U.S. Fish and Wildlife Service (Department of the Interior) is responsible for the conservation of migratory bird resources. A national system of strategically located wildlife lands serve as sanctuaries for migratory birds, and studies are made of the relative abundance of species, their distribution, diseases, and habits. The service insures not only conservation of sport fish, wild birds, and mammals for their recreational and economic value, but makes it possible for anglers, hunters, and others to enjoy and use the fish and wildlife resources.

Alaska. Aleutian Islands (2,720,235 acres); Bering Sea (41,113 acres); Bogoslof (390 acres); Chamisso (641 acres); Curry (8,960 acres); Forrester Island (2,832 acres); Hazy Islands (42 acres); Pribilof Islands (173 acres); Saint Lazaria (65 acres); Semidi (8,422 acres); Tuxedni (6,439 acres).

California. Faralon (91 acres).

Florida. Anclote (208.4 acres); Brevard (12.4 acres); Cedar Keys (378.6 acres); Great White Heron (835.5 acres); Island Bay (20.2 acres); Key West (2,019.2 acres); Passage Key (36.4 acres); Pelican Island (3 acres); Pinellas (278 acres).

Georgia. Okefenoke (330,973.4 acres); Tybee (100 acres).

Hawaii. Hawaiian Islands (1,765 acres).

Louisiana. Breton (7,512 acres); East Timbalier Island (337 acres); Shell Keys (8 acres).

Michigan. Huron (147 acres); Michigan Islands (11.9 acres).

Minnesota. Mille Lacs (0.6 acre).

Montana. Fort Peck (575,589 acres).

Nevada. Anaho Island (247.7 acres).

North Dakota. Stump Lake (27.4 acres).

* A calendar week starts on Sunday.

Ohio. West Sister Island (82 acres).

Oregon. Cape Meares (138.5 acres); Oregon Islands (21 acres); Three Arch Rocks (17 acres).

Texas. Santa Ana (1,980.5 acres).

Washington. Copalis (5 acres); Flattery Rocks (125 acres); Jones Island (179.1 acres); Matia Island (145 acres); Quillayute Needles (117 acres).

Wisconsin. Gravel Island (27 acres); Green Bay (2 acres).

WATERFOWL REFUGES

Alabama. Wheeler (34,988 acres).

Alaska. Hazen Bay (6,800 acres).

Arizona. Havasu Lake (26,656.5 acres), see California; Imperial (28,711.2 acres), see California; Salt River (21,060.9 acres).

Arkansas. Big Lake (9,890.8 acres); Holla Bend (4,068 acres); White River (116,301.9 acres).

California. Clear Lake (33,559.6 acres); Colusa (4,039.7 acres); Havasu Lake (19,104.9 acres), see Arizona; Imperial (18,080.2 acres), see Arizona; Lower Klamath (21,459.6 acres), see Oregon; Merced (2,-561.5 acres); Pixley (4,243.7 acres); Sacramento (10,775.6 acres); Salton Sea (37,326.7 acres); Sutter (2,590.9 acres); Tule Lake (37,336.6 acres).

Delaware. Bombay Hook (13,810.3 acres); Killcohook (580 acres), see New Jersey.

Florida. Chassahowitzka (28,617.1 acres); Loxahatchee (145,478.4 acres); St. Marks (65.046 acres); Sanibel (2,821.4 acres).

Georgia. Blackbeard Island (5,617.6 acres); Piedmont (32,074.9 acres); Savannah (5413.6 acres), see South Carolina; Wolf Island (538 acres).

Idaho. Camas (10,535 acres); Deer Flat (10,795.2 acres); Minidoka* (25,629.8 acres); Snake River (376.4 acres).

Illinois. Chautauqua (4,470.3 acres); Crab Orchard (43,003.3 acres); Mark Twain (12,459 acres), see Iowa, Missouri; Mississippi River (20,120 acres), see Minnesota, Wisconsin; Upper Mississippi River (3,140.8 acres), see Minnesota, Wisconsin.

Iowa. DeSoto (1,855.4 acres); Mark Twain (10,328 acres), see Illinois; Mississippi River (30,316 acres), see Minnesota, Wisconsin; Union Slough (2,077.4 acres); Upper Mississippi (20,391.2 acres), see Minnesota, Wisconsin.

Kansas. Kirwin (10,864 acres); Quivira (6,416.5 acres).

Kentucky. Kentucky Woodlands (65,759 acres); Reelfoot (809.1 acres), see Tennessee.

---

* Also known as Sawtooth Forest State Bird Sanctuary.

Louisiana. Catahoula (5,308.5 acres); Delta (48,833.7 acres); Lacassine (31,124.5 acres); Sabine (142,716.5 acres).

Maine. Moosehorn (22,565.9 acres).

Maryland. Blackwater (11,216.3 acres); Chincoteague (417.8 acres), see Virginia; Martin (3,874.8 acres); Susquehanna (3.7 acres).

Massachusetts. Great Meadows (216.2 acres); Monomoy (2,695.8 acres); Parker River (6,403.2 acres).

Michigan. Lake St. Clair (5 acres); Seney (95,531 acres); Shiawassee (4,406.4 acres).

Minnesota. Mississippi River (221.3 acres); Mississippi River (15,-420.8 acres), see Illinois, Iowa, Wisconsin; Mud Lake (60,772.6 acres); Rice Lake (15,893.9 acres); Tamarac (34, 229.1 acres); Upper Mississippi (17,564.4 acres), see Illinois, Iowa, Wisconsin.

Mississippi. Horn Island (2,484.2 acres); Noxubee (44,764.6 acres); Petit Bois (748.7 acres); Yazoo (2,448.2 acres).

Missouri. Mark Twain (232 acres), see Illinois, Iowa; Mingo (21,645.8 acres); Squaw Creek (6,809.1 acres); Swan Lake (10,678.9 acres).

Montana. Benton Lake (12,382.5 acres); Black Coulee (1,480 acres); Bowdoin (15,436.6 acres); Creedman Coulee (2,728 acres); Hailstone (2,240 acres); Halfbreed Lake (3,096.8 acres); Hewitt Lake (1,680.9 acres); Lake Mason (18,883 acres); Lake Thibadeau (3,508.5 acres); Lamesteer (800 acres); Medicine Lake (31,457.4 acres); Nine-Pipe (2,022 acres); Pablo (2,542 acres); Pishkum (8,194.8 acres); Red Rock Lakes (39,943.4 acres); Wild Horse (3,200 acres); Willow Creek (3,118.9 acres).

Nebraska. Crescent Lake (46,534.3 acres); DeSoto (4,229.9 acres), see Iowa; North Platte (5,107 acres); Valentine (71,515.6 acres).

Nevada. Fallon (17,901.9 acres); Ruby Lake (35,697.7 acres); Stillwater (24,203.4 acres); Winnemucca (9,805.8 acres).

New Jersey. Brigantine (12,854.5 acres); Killcohook (906.5 acres), see Delaware; Troy Meadows (1,089 acres).

New Mexico. Bitter Lake (24,083.7 acres); Bosque del Apache (57,191.1 acres).

New York. Elizabeth Alexander Morton (187 acres); Montezuma (6,776.7 acres); Oak Orchard (3,144 acres); Wertheim (11.2 acres).

North Carolina. Mattamuskeet (50,177.3 acres); Pea Island (5,880.1 acres); Swanquarter (15,500.8 acres).

North Dakota. Appert Lake (1,160.7 acres); Ardoch (2,676.6 acres); Arrowwood (15,934.4 acres); Billings Lake (760 acres); Bone Hill (640 acres); Brumba (1,977.5 acres); Buffalo Lake (2,096.4 acres); Camp Lake (1,224.7 acres); Canfield Lake (453.1 acres); Chase Lake (1,921.7 acres); Cottonwood Lake (1,013.5 acres); Dakota Lake (2,756 acres); Des Lacs

(18,881 acres); Flickertail (640 acres); Florence Lake (668.9 acres); Halfway Lake (160 acres); Hiddenwood (568.4 acres); Hobart Lake (1,840.7 acres); Hutchinson Lake (478.9 acres); Johnson Lake (2,007.9 acres); Kellys Slough (1,620 acres); Lac Aux Mortes (5,881.8 acres); Lake Elsie (634.7 acres); Lake George (3,118.8 acres); Lake Ilo (3,963.6 acres); Lake Nettle (1,800 acres); Lake Zahl (3,856.8 acres); Lambs Lake (1,286.7 acres); Little Goose (359 acres); Long Lake (22,310.2 acres); Lords Lake (1,915.3 acres); Lost Lake (960.3 acres); Lostwood (26,747.5 acres); Lower Souris (58,693.5 acres); Maple River (1,120 acres); McLean (680 acres); Pleasant Lake (1,001 acres); Pretty Rock (800 acres); Rabb Lake (260.8 acres); Rock Lake (5,506.6 acres); Rose Lake (872.1 acres); School Section Lake (679.7 acres); Shell Lake (1,835.1 acres); Sheyenne Lake (797.3 acres); Sibley Lake (1,077.4 acres); Silver Lake (3,347.6 acres); Slade (3,000.2 acres); Snake Creek (13,498 acres); Snyder Lake (1,550.2 acres); Springwater (640 acres); Stewart Lake (2,230.4 acres); Stoney Slough (1,908 acres); Storm Lake (685 acres); Sunburst Lake (495 acres); Tewaukon (5,585.2 acres); Tomahawk (440 acres); White Lake (1,040 acres); Upper Souris (32,085.2 acres); Wild Rice Lake (778.8 acres); Willow Lake (2,847.7 acres); Wintering River (399.1 acres); Wood Lake (280 acres).

Oklahoma. Salt Plains (32,431.1 acres); Tishomingo (16,619 acres).

Oregon. Cold Springs (3,116.8 acres); Hart Mountain (731.1 acres); Klamath Forest (584.9 acres); Lower Klamath (1,340 acres), see California; Malheur (184,871.8 acres); McKay Creek (1,836.5 acres); Upper Klamath (12,532.8 acres).

Pennsylvania. Erie (1,558.8 acres).

South Carolina. Cape Romain (34,716 acres); Carolina Sandhills (44,927.4 acres); Santee (73,953.2 acres); Savannah (7,229.7 acres), see Georgia.

South Dakota. Bear Butte (436 acres); Belle Fourche (13,680 acres); Lacreek (9,442 acres); Lake Andes (442.7 acres); Sand Lake (21,450.9 acres); Waubay (4,649.7 acres).

Tennessee. Lake Isom (1,849.9 acres); Reelfoot (9,092.3 acres), see Kentucky; Tennessee (50,819 acres).

Texas. Aransas (47,261.2 acres); Buffalo Lake (7,663.9 acres); Hagerman (11,319.8 acres); Laguna Atascosa (41,767.5 acres); Muleshoe (5,809.1 acres).

Utah. Bear River (64,899.6 acres); Fish Springs (17,872.2 acres); Locomotive Springs (1,031 acres); Strawberry Valley (14,070.1 acres).

Vermont. Missisquoi (3,556.5 acres).

Virginia. Back Bay (4,588.8 acres); Chincoteague (9,029.9 acres), see Maryland; Presquile (1,328.9 acres).

Washington. Columbia (27,693.3 acres); Dungeness (556.5 acres);

Little Pend Oreille (2,251.3 acres); McNary (2,849.1 acres); Smith Island (65 acres); Turnbull (17,171.2 acres); Willapa (7,680.4 acres). *Wisconsin*. Horicon (20,795.9 acres); Long Tail Point (103.1 acres); Mississippi River (40,521 acres) see Illinois, Iowa, Minnesota; Necedah (39,607 acres); Trempealeau (706.9 acres); Upper Mississippi (47,465 acres), see Illinois, Iowa, Minnesota.

Wyoming. Bamforth (1,166 acres); Hutton Lake (1,968.3 acres); Pathfinder (46,341 acres).

Big Game Refuges

Alaska. Kenai (2,057,197 acres); Kodiak (1,815,000 acres); Nunivak (1,109,384.4 acres); Simenof (10,442 acres).

Florida. National Key Deer (6,730 acres).

Montana. Montana National Bison (18,540.7 acres).

Nebraska. Fort Niobrara (19,122.3 acres).

Nevada. Charles Sheldon (23,372.6 acres); Desert Game (328.1 acres); Sheldon Antelope (34,131.3 acres).

New Mexico. San Andres (57,215.5 acres).

North Dakota. Sully's Hill (1,991.4 acres).

Oklahoma. Wichita Mountains (59,019.6 acres).

Oregon. Charles Sheldon (627.5 acres) see Nevada; Hart Mountain (239,933 acres).

Washington. Little Pend Oreille (41,707.6 acres).

Wyoming. National Elk (23,790 acres).

Sportsman's Organizations

National Field Archery Association of the United States, Inc. This association is a nonprofit combination of bow hunters and field archers with 50 chartered state associations and over 1,500 affiliated clubs in the United States and abroad. There are more than 15,000 individual members in the N.F.A.A.; and from 500 to 1,000 archers compete for awards in the annual National Field Archery Championship Tournament. The Art Young Big Game Award, the Prize Buck Award, and the Art Young Small Game Award are given to successful hunters who belong to the organization. Big game is defined for the purpose of award as Antelope, Bear (Alaska Brown, Black, Grizzly, Polar), Caribou, Cougar, Deer, Elk, Rocky Mountain Goat, Jaguar, Moose, and Sheep (Bighorn, Dall, Desert, Stone). Small game is defined as (a) any animal or bird generally recognized as small game, whether protected or not; (b) any small animal, bird, fish, or poisonous reptile generaly recognized as a nuisance or harmful. The official publication *Archery Magazine* is 35 cents a copy, or $3 per year in the United States. Address: Box 967, Palm Desert, California 92262. Membership in the N.F.A.A.: $2.75 annually; junior membership (under 18), $1.00; Combination membership and magazine, $5.50 per year. Information may be obtained from headquarters: Route 2, Box 514, Redlands, California 92373.

National Rifle Association of America. Founded in 1871, it is a nonprofit organization with over 600,000 members who are hunters, target shooters, gun collectors, "plinkers," amateur or professional gunsmiths, and others who are interested in guns and shooting. The NRA conducts courses, for adults and juveniles, in the safe handling of firearms, and maintains a Legislative Service to inform members of national and state firearms legislation. The NRA was designated in 1950 by New York State as the agency to provide instruction in safe gun handling, and issue certificates of competence in hunter safety required by law of juveniles applying for a first license. In all states today, there are NRA-trained instructors conducting programs in gun safety sponsored either by legislation, rod and gun clubs, or shooting organizations.

"The NRA is the parent organization of rifle, pistol and shotgun shooting clubs and police and military marksmanship units; the custodian of the national classification system for rifle and pistol shooters; the source of awards for proficiency in rifle, pistol and shotgun shooting; and the certifying agency for firearms instructors, referees and training counselors."

More than 7,000 civilian and military marksmen compete with rifle and pistol in the annual National Matches sponsored by the NRA and the National Board for the Promotion of Rifle Practice, which are held at Camp Perry, near Toledo, Ohio. Annual NRA hunting awards are given to members who hunt the following big game: Pronghorn Antelope, Deer (Black-tailed, Mule, White-tailed), Elk, Bighorn Sheep taken legally during a prescribed open season. The Antelope must be a buck with a horn at least 12 inches in length, measured on the outside curve. The Deer (any species) must be a buck with at least 4 points on one side. Elk antlers should have a total of 10 points; and the shorter main beam, a minimum length of 48 inches. The Bighorn Sheep must have one horn showing three-quarters of a curl. The NRA encourages the use of game targets such as the silhouette of a Crow, Deer, Turkey, etc., instead of bullseye targets to practice shooting.

Handbooks, manual, leaflets, and the monthly *American Rifleman* are published by the National Rifle Association. Adult membership, including a subscription to the *American Rifleman* magazine, is $5 a year. Junior membership (under 18) is $3 a year. Address: National Rifle Association, 1600 Rhode Island Avenue, N.W., Washington 6, D.C.

International Game Fish Association. It is affiliated with the American Museum of Natural History, and membership consists entirely of fishing clubs throughout the world, and various scientific institutions interested in ichthyology. Requirements for membership in the IGFA include writing on your club letterhead that your organization is not comprised solely of charterboat or commercial fishermen, and that members have read and agreed to abide by rules and regulations of the IGFA. Inquiries should be addressed to the President, International Game Fish Association, Alfred I. DuPont Building, Miami, Florida 33131.

Camping Information*

Connecticut. State Park and Forest Commission, State Office Building, Hartford 15.

Delaware. State Development Department, 45 The Green, Dover.

Maine. Chamber of Commerce, Jackman; Department of Economic Development, State House, Augusta.

Maryland. Department of Economic Development, State House, Annapolis; Department of Forests and Parks, State Office Building, Annapolis.

Massachusetts. Department of Natural Resources, 15 Ashburton Place, Boston 8; Cape Cod Chamber of Commerce, Hyannis 59.

New Hampshire. State Planning and Development Commission, Concord.

New Jersey. Department of Conservation, 520 East State Street, Trenton 25.

New York. State Department of Commerce, 112 State Street, Albany 1; Bureau of Camps and Trails, Conservation Department, State of New York, Albany 1; New York Department of Commerce, Box 64-C, Mount Vernon 10.

Ohio. Department of Natural Resources, 1500 Dublin Road, Columbus 12.

Pennsylvania. Department of Commerce, Main Capitol Building, Harrisburg; Department of Forests and Waters, Harrisburg.

Rhode Island. Information Division, Development Council, State House, Providence 3; Department of Public Works, Division of Parks and Recreation, State Office Building, Providence 3.

Vermont. Vermont Development Commission, Montpelier; Fish and Game Service, State Office Building, Montpelier.

West Virginia. Conservation Commission, Room 663, State Office Building, Charleston; Forest Supervisor, P.O. Box 1231, Elkins.

SOUTH

Alabama. Alabama Department of Conservation, Division of Parks, Montgomery 4; U.S. Forest Service, Post Office Building, Montgomery.

---

* See also National Forests.

485

Florida. Development Commission, State of Florida, Carlton Building, East Wing, Tallahassee; Florida Park Service, 201 Park Avenue, Tallahassee.

Georgia. Division of Parks, 418 State Capitol, Atlanta; Georgia State Fish and Game Commission, 401 State Capitol Building, Atlanta 3; Secretary of State Parks, 214 State Capitol, Atlanta.

Kentucky. Department of Public Relations, Frankfort; Kentucky Department of Fish and Wild Life Resources, Frankfort; Division of Parks, Capitol Annex Building, Frankfort.

Louisiana. Department of Commerce and Industry, Tourist Bureau, P.O. Box 4291, Baton Rouge; Parks and Recreation Commission, P.O. Box 2541, Baton Rouge.

Mississippi. Biloxi Port Commission, P.O. Box 429, Biloxi; Mississippi State Parks, P.O. Box 649, Jackson.

North Carolina. Department of Conservation and Development, Room L-5, State Travel Bureau, Raleigh.

South Carolina. State Commission of Forestry, P.O. Box 357, Columbia.

Tennessee. Division of State Information, 236 Cordell Hull Building, Nashville 3: State Parks, Department of Conservation and Commerce, 203 Cordell Hull Building, Nashville 3.

Virginia. Virginia Department of Conservation and Development, SA-149, State Office Building, Richmond 19.

MIDDLE WEST

Arkansas. Publicity and Parks Commission, Dept. 549, State Capitol, Little Rock; Lake Norfolk Recreational Association, Box F, Mountain Home.

Illinois. Department of Conservation, 100 State Office Building, Springfield.

Indiana. Department of Conservation, Division of Publicity, 311 West Washington Street, Indianapolis 9.

Iowa. State Conservation Commission, Seventh and Court Streets, Des Moines 9.

Kansas. State Fish and Game Department, Box 581, Pratt.

Michigan. Michigan Tourist Council, Room 26, Mason Building, Lansing 26; Department of Conservation, Lansing 26.

Minnesota. Department of Conservation, State Office Building, St. Paul 1; Heart of Lakes Association, Richeville.

Missouri. Missouri Division of Resources and Development, Dept. D-952, Jefferson City; State Park Board, P.O. Box 176, Jefferson City.

Nebraska. I & E Division, Game Commission, Lincoln 9; Division of Nebraska Resources, State Capitol Building, Lincoln.

North Dakota. Greater North Dakota Association, Fargo; State Highway Department, Fourth Floor, Capitol Building, Bismarck.

Oklahoma. Planning and Resources Board, State Capitol, Oklahoma City 5; Department of Conservation, State Capitol Building, Oklahoma City 5.

South Dakota. South Dakota Department of Highways, Publicity Director, Pierre 19.

Texas. State Parks Board, Drawer E, Capitol Station, Austin.

Wisconsin. Conservation Department, 830 State Office Building, Madison 1; Chamber of Commerce, Menominee; Crystal Cave, Spring Valley; Better Resorts Association, Rhinelander 4; Hayward Lake Resorts Association, Box 101, Hayward,

WEST

Arizona. Arizona Development Board, 1521 West Jefferson Street, Phoenix.

California. All Year Tourist Information Center, Department R-4, 628 West Sixth Street, Los Angeles 17; Division of Beaches and Parks, Department of Natural Resources, P.O. Box 2390, Sacramento 11.

Colorado. Forest Service, United States Department of Agriculture, Denver; Department of Game and Fish, 1530 Sherman Street, Denver 3; Rocky Mountain Tours, 120 King Street, Denver 19; Sportsmen's Hospitality Committee, 216 State Capitol, Denver 2.

Idaho. Department of Commerce and Development, Room 434, Capitol Building, Boise.

Montana. I & E Division, State Fish and Game Department, Helena; Advertising Department, State Highway Commission, Helena.

Nevada. State Park Commission, Carson City; State Fish and Game Commission, Box 678, Reno.

New Mexico. State Tourist Bureau, State Capitol, Santa Fe; Department of Conservation, State Capitol, Santa Fe.

Oregon. Travel Information Bureau, Room 289, State Highway Department, Salem.

Utah. Tourist and Publicity Council, 327 State Capitol Building, Salt Lake City.

Washington. Washington State Department of Commerce, General Administration Building, Olympia; State Resort Association, 2101 Fifth Avenue, Seattle; Parks and Recreation Commission, General Administration Building, Olympia.

Wyoming. Wyoming Travel Commission, Room 60, Capitol Building, Cheyenne.

Sportsman's Readings

BOOKS

ATHERTON, MAXINE. *Every Sportsman's Cookbook*. N. Y.: The Macmillan Co., 1962.

BRELAND, O. P. *Animal Life and Lore*. N. Y.: Harper & Row, Publishers, 1963.

BROOKS, JOE. *The Complete Illustrated Guide to Casting*. N. Y.: Double-Day & Co., 1963.

BROWER, D. R., EDITOR. *Going Light—With Backpack or Burro*. San Francisco, Cal.: Sierra Club, 1958.

————. *Manual of Ski Mountaineering*. San Francisco, Cal.: Sierra Club, 1960.

CANNON, RAYMOND. *How to Fish the Pacific Coast*. Menlo Park, Cal.: Lane Publishing Company, 1953.

COFIELD, T. R. *Training the Hunting Retriever*. Princeton, N.J.: D. Van Nostrand Co., 1959.

COLLINS, JR., H. H. *Complete Field Guide to American Wildlife; East, Central, and North*. N.Y.: Harper & Row, Publishers, 1959.

CONANT, ROGER. *A Field Guide to Reptiles and Amphibians*. Boston, Mass.: Houghton Mifflin Company, 1958.

COYKENDALL, RALF. *Duck Decoys*. N.Y.: Henry Holt & Co., 1953.

EVANOFF, VLAD. *Natural Baits for Fishermen*. N.Y.: A. D. Barnes, 1959.

FARB, PETER. *Face of North America*. N.Y.: Harper & Row, Publishers, 1963.

HEILNER, V. C. *Salt Water Fishing*. N.Y.: A. A. Knopf, 1953.

HOLLAND, D. J. *Upland Game Hunter's Bible*. Garden City, N.Y.: Double-day & Co., 1961.

JANSEN, JERRY. *Successful Surf Fishing*. N.Y.: E. P. Dutton & Co., 1959.

JENNINGS, M. C. *Instinct Shooting*. N.Y.: Dodd, Mead & Co., 1959.

MIRACLE, LEONARD, AND DECKER, MAURICE. *Complete Book of Camping*. N.Y.: Harper & Row, Publishers, 1962.

MURIE, O. J. A. *A Field Guide to Animal Tracks*. Boston, Mass.: Houghton Mifflin Co., 1954.

O'CONNOR, JACK. *Complete Book of Rifles and Shotguns*. N.Y.: Harper & Row, Publishers, 1961.

O'CONNOR, JACK, AND GOODWIN, GEORGE. *Big Game Animals of North America*. N.Y.: E. P. Dutton & Co., 1961.

ORMOND, C. O. *Complete Book of Hunting*. N.Y.: Harper & Row, Publishers, 1962.

PARSONS, P. A. *Complete Book of Fresh Water Fishing*. N.Y.: Harper & Row, Publishers, 1963.

PETERSON, R. T. *A Field Guide to the Birds*. Boston, Mass.: Houghton Mifflin Company, 1947.

————. *A Field Guide to Western Birds*. Boston, Mass.: Houghton Mifflin Company, 1961.

PETTINGILL, JR., O. S. *A Guide to Bird Finding West of the Mississippi*. N.Y.: Oxford University Press, 1953.

SCHARFF, ROBERT. *Complete Duck Shooter's Handbook*. N.Y.: G. P. Putnam's Sons, 1957.

SPRUNT, JR., ALEXANDER. *North American Birds of Prey*. N.Y.: Harper & Row, Publishers, 1955.

WALDEN, HOWARD. *Familiar Freshwater Fishes of America*. N.Y.: Harper & Row, Publishers, 1964.

PERIODICALS

The *Ad-i-ron-dac* (bimonthly)—Adirondack Mountain Club, Albany, N.Y.; *American Forests* (monthly)—American Forestry Association, Washington, D.C.: *Appalachian Trailway News* (quarterly)—Appalachian Trail Conference, Inc., Washington, D.C.; *Audubon Magazine* (bimonthly)—National Audubon Society, New York, N.Y.: *Everglades Natural History* (quarterly)—Everglades Natural History Association, Homestead, Florida. *Hawaiian Trail and Mountain Club Bulletin* (monthly)—Honolulu, Hawaii. *The Living Wilderness* (quarterly)—Wilderness Society, Washington, D.C. *Long Trail News* (quarterly)—Green Mountain Club, Inc., Middlebury, Vermont. *National Parks Bulletin* (quarterly)—National Parks Association, Washington, D.C. *Natural History* (monthly)—American Museum of Natural History, New York, N.Y. *Pacific Discovery* (bimonthly)—California Academy of Sciences, Golden Gate Park, San Francisco, Cal. *Trail Blazer* (monthly)—Trails Club, Portland, Oregon.

Glossary

AUTOLOADING FIREARM. A self-loading gun with the trigger pulled separately for each shot.

AUTOMATIC FIREARMS. A gun which continues to fire if trigger is held.

BAG LIMIT. The maximum number of designated mammal, bird, or fish to be taken by one person during a specific period of time.

BAIT FISH. Chubs, Minnows, Shiners, Suckers, and other small fish used to bait hooks. Regulations usually prohibit the use of any part of a game fish for bait. Some states designate areas where no fish, fish eggs, liver, or meat may be used for bait.

BAITING. To distribute, deliberately place, or scatter shelled grain, food, salt, or other bait to entice game into an area.

BLIND. A hunter's hiding place to ambush game. It may be a camouflaged raft, rowboat, or other device constructed and used on land or water.

BOBBING. Fishing with a bunch of worms or other bait attached to a hookless line held in the hand or a line attached to a rod held in the hand.

BOUNDARY WATERS. Special agreements may permit fishing on the entire water area except the shore of another state, or to midchannel in a stream or boundary line of a state.

BOW AND ARROW FISHING TACKLE. Either the shaft or point of an arrow (or both) is attached to the bow or fishing reel by a line.

BROADHEAD. On an arrow has a steel head with wide sharp edges capable of cutting blood vessels in big game. Blades may vary in size from three-fourths to 1½ inches in width if used for taking Deer.

CALIBER. Diameter of a projectile or the bore size of gun barrel.

CARTRIDGES. Contain a primer, gun powder, bullet, shot, or slug. A blank cartridge contains only powder without a projectile and is used in training dogs to hunt. A centerfire cartridge has the explosive primer in the center of the shell, and a rimfire cartridge has explosive priming on the rim or flange around the base of the shell.

CHUMMING. Placing fish, or other bait in the water for the purpose of enticing game fish into an area.

CLOSED SEASON. A period of time during which it is unlawful to take specific mammals, birds, or fish.

COASTAL WATERS. All waters within the rise and fall of tides and within the marine limits of a state.

CLOSURES. Land or water areas closed to hunting and fishing. The closure of a stream may not include tributaries unless they are specifically mentioned.

CREEL LIMITS. Maximum number of fish, or pounds of fish, to be taken by a fisherman; called "bag" limits in some states.

CROSSBOW. A bow set crosswise on a stock; arrows are discharged by releasing a trigger.

FLY. A fish hook camouflaged by feathers, silk, thread, or tinsel arranged so as to imitate a natural fly or insect and entice a fish to grab it (fly fishing).

FLYWAYS. Routes of migratory game birds. Waterfowl follow four major routes annually, and the U.S. Fish and Wildlife Service studies their migrations and establishes annual restrictions on the number of birds to be taken in designated regions. *Atlantic Flyway*: Connecticut, Delaware, Florida, Georgia, Maine, Maryland, Massachusetts, New Hampshire, New Jersey, New York, North and South Carolina, Pennsylvania, Rhode Island, Vermont, West Virginia, and Puerto Rico. *Mississippi River Flyway*: Alabama, Arkansas, Illinois, Indiana, Iowa, Kentucky, Louisiana, Michigan, Minnesota, Mississippi, Missouri, Ohio, Tennessee and Wisconsin. *Central Flyway*: Colorado (east of Continental Divide), Kansas, Montana, Nebraska, New Mexico, North and South Dakota, Texas and Wyoming. *Pacific Flyway*: Alaska, Arizona, California, Colorado (west of Continental Divide), Idaho, Nevada, Oregon, Utah, Washington.

FYKE. A fish trap consisting of several successive conical nets with wide-stretched mouths.

GIGGING. Four barbless hooks fastened back to back and attached to a hand line which is dragged through water to catch hold of any part of a fish.

GILL NETS. Are held in position by anchors or stakes, and the gills of fish are caught in the mesh.

GOGGLE FISHING. Taking fish by means of a harpoon, spear, dart, arrow, or any missile held and propelled by hand while the fisherman is completely submerged in water.

HAND GUNS. Pistols and revolvers.

HAND-PROPELLED CRAFT. A canoe, boat, or other watercraft entirely propelled by paddling, poling, rowing, or sculling.

LAKES AND STREAMS. In fishing regulations, the dividing line usually refers to the mouth of a tributary stream at the existing level of a lake surface.

LONGBOW. A bow with a cord to bend and connect both ends of a strip of wood or other material so that an arrow can be propelled when drawn and released by the hand of an archer. The pull of a bow is the strength measured in pounds.

MINIMUM LENGTH OF FISH. Measure as the longest straight line from the tip of the head to tip of tail.

MINIMUM SIZE. May refer to the length or weight of a fish.

NONTIDAL WATERS. Lakes, ponds, reservoirs, and streams beyond the point at which the tide ebbs and flows.

OPEN SEASON. A period of time during which game may be taken legally. Dates usually include the first and last days of a season.

POSSESSION LIMIT. Maximum number of game permitted to be held by a person at one time, regardless of daily bag limits.

PRESERVE SHOOTING. Hunting on areas where game is bred, raised, and released during periods usually longer than state open seasons. Hunters pay fees to shoot within boundaries of game preserves. Individuals, clubs, or associations maintain such preserves, which are licensed by state conservation or game departments.

PRIVATE WATERS. Are entirely on property owned or leased by an individual, club, firm, or corporation.

PUBLIC WATERS. Natural bodies of water such as bayous, bays, brooks, creeks, lagoons, lakes, and streams; canals and reservoirs impounded by construction of dams or locks and controlled or operated by municipal, state, or federal agencies.

RECIPROCAL LICENSES. The cost to nonresidents is based on the fees charged by their home states to nonresidents from other states. Boundary waters reciprocal agreements may permit a person holding a valid license issued by one state to fish in waters jointly owned with another state without the necessity of purchasing a nonresident license.

ROUGH FISH. Destructive or undesirable fish such as Bowfin, Buffalo, Burbot, Carp, Drum, Gar, Suckers.

SAILBOAT. Regulations refer to a watercraft propelled entirely by one or more sails.

SCOOP NET. A hand net usually not over 36 inches in diameter.

SEINE. An encircling fish net held upright in the water by floats along the top and weights at the bottom. It can be hauled to a boat or landing place with fish in the net.

SET LINE. A line with many baited hooks attached at one end to a stationary or floating object which does not need the immediate control or constant attendance of a fisherman.

SHAKEOUT SEASON. A period between a dog training season and lawful hunting season when game may be hunted but not taken by a hunter.

SINK BOX. A raft or other floating device with a depression in which a hunter can hide below the surface of the water to ambush wildfowl before they can fly high.

SNAG HOOKS. With or without handles; are used to take fish in such a manner that the hook is not voluntarily taken in the mouth but is hooked into the body.

SNARE. A device to entrap animals and birds. It often consists of ropes or wires formed into a noose that drops around any game snatching at the bait.

SNATCH HOOKS. One or more single or treble hooks which are manipulated or jerked through the water (snatching) in order to impale or hook some part of the body of a fish.

STILL HUNTING. Without dogs, and stealthly tracking game until within shooting range.

STREAM. A bayou, canal, creek, river, or other watercourse.

TAKE. To catch, hunt, kill, or possess, or attempt in any manner to pursue, capture, trap, kill, or possess birds, fish, and mammals.

THROW LINE. A hook and line held by hand, and not attached to a pole (or rod) or anchored to a stationary object.

TIDAL WATERS. The regular ebb and flow of tides along a seacoast, and often penetrating many miles into freshwater streams.

TIP-UP. A metal spring device with a small flag and a reel attached to a pole which can be set in ice or snow. Any pull on the line by a fish releases the spring, and the flag signals a catch.

TROLLING. Dragging a hook and line with or without bait near the surface of the water behind a boat.

TROTLINE. Several baited hooks on a line anchored at one end, and overhauled at certain intervals to remove fish.

UNDRESSED. Animals—entrails removed, leaving body intact; birds—entrails removed, with head and feet left intact; fish—entrails removed, leaving head, tails, fins, and skin intact.